Chinese Communist Society:
The Family and The Village

C. K. YANG

Chinese Communist Society: The Family and The Village

containing

The Chinese Family in the Communist Revolution

and

A Chinese Village in Early Communist Transition

THE M.I.T. PRESS
Massachusetts Institute of Technology
Cambridge, Massachusetts, and London, England

The Chinese Family in the Communist Revolution

Library of Congress Catalog Card Number 59–14897

A Chinese Village in Early Communist Transition

Library of Congress Catalog Card Number 59–11517

both titles

First M.I.T. Press Paperback Edition, January 1965
Second Paperback Printing, May 1966
Third Paperback Printing, February 1968
Fourth Paperback Printing, October 1969
Fifth Paperback Printing, April 1972

ISBN 0 262 74001 X (paperback)
Printed in the United States of America

Prefatory Note

This is a reprint of two separate volumes, *The Chinese Family in the Communist Revolution* and *A Chinese Village in Early Communist Transition,* both originally published in 1959 by the present publishers. Save for the deletion of some passages on the commune, no revision or rewriting was undertaken, so that the two volumes will stand as work done in the earlier years of the Communist revolution; any thorough revision belongs properly to another task. Among phenomena that would adequately characterize traditional Chinese society were the family system and the peasant village, and any significant alteration of the Chinese society would involve change of these two components. Hence, the two separate volumes represent parts of a single effort to understand the drastic transformation of Chinese society under the Communist revolution, and there is sound ground for reprinting these two works in a one-volume edition.

Since the original completion of the two works, such momentous events as the "big leap forward" and the establishment of the communes have transpired, and Chinese society under Communism has experienced further alterations. Here, the question arises as to the continued usefulness of the two works in the light of the rapid changes. Re-examination of the two books suggests that they remain valid sociological studies of Chinese society and its transformation under the early phase of Communism as it involved the change of the family institution and the village community, because analysis of the pre-Communist setting stands generally sound, and events transpired in the post-publication years confirm the basic trends and significant forces as revealed in the two studies.

Thus, post-publication information from Communist literature supports these findings of the *Family* volume: (1) The Communist revolution has broadened the change of the family system from the upper and middle to the lower strata of the urban population and from the urban centers to the vast countryside. (2) This accelerated diffusion of family change resulted from a congeries of forces: the new marriage law and its individualizing values, the removal of economic production as major function of the family through collectivization of agriculture and nationalization of business, the rising status of women and the younger generation, the increased competition of extra-familial ties for the individual's loyalty, the secularizing influence which was stripping the family of its sacred character. (3) The extended joint family, so characteristic of the traditional upper strata, could no longer exist with the means of production removed from it, and its system of authority and status seriously undermined. (4) Interviews with refugees who came to Hong Kong after 1962 showed that the family institution was fast losing its core position in the network of social relations, particularly in the urban communities. In general, events in post-publication years indicated waxing and waning of these and other trends and forces, but brought no change to their basic orientation.

The *Village* volume is composed of two sections: one is a field study of Nanching village in its pre-Communist setting (1948–49) and its early Communist transition up through the land reform (1949–51), and the other is a documentary analysis of national collectivization of agriculture from the mutual-aid team campaign to the full establishment of higher agricultural producers co-operative (1952–58). During the latter part of 1958, a few months before publication of the volume, the nation's collectives were suddenly merged into huge communes. A hasty "Postscript" on the commune was appended to the volume. Now from hindsight this was clearly a premature attempt, for the few months were far too short for adequate assessment of the ill-fated gigantic adventure. Hence, in the present edition, we deleted the "Postcript" and other references to the commune, so that the volume can maintain its validity as a study of a peasant village, its early revolutionary change, and the wider national setting of agricultural collectivization which followed. On the other hand, the survival of the commune in its vastly modified form should not devaluate the book. On the eve of the commune, the general practice was to establish one higher agricultural producers co-operative for one village, though there were regional variations to this rule. After 1962, when the commune survived in a much simplified form, the village was restored as the basic unit of collective farming and rural community organization in general under the form of "production brigade." Hence our hope for continued usefulness of our village study in spite of the survival of the commune.

So far, the post-publication years have brought forth no evidence to invalidate our analysis of the pre-Communist village situation which built up pressure for a revolutionary change, and at the same time provided a base line for gauging information on developments under Communist rule including income and production figures. The Communist revolution (or some other form of drastic change) appeared inevitable when we examined the failure of Nanching's socio-economic structure to provide minimum subsistence and security to one-half of the village population. Thus, there was the peasant economy of microscopic family farms made up of tiny and widely scattered plots, worked with backward techniques, burdened with a crippling tenancy structure and rapacious rent rates which, together, condemned a significant portion of the villagers to semi-starvation, discouraged production reinvestment, and restricted cultivation to only the good land when inferior or even marginal areas should also have been developed to alleviate the desperate land shortage. At the base of this economy was a kinship system with all the conservative and restraining features against any drastic change. The relative political autonomy and economic self-sufficiency of the village restrengthened the conservative and particularistic forces. When the Communists capitalized on the situation and attained power, they decisively replaced the kinship dominance of the community structure with the Communist socio-political apparatus, turned the village into one big collective farm, and forcefully integrated it into the national economic and political structure. The process of this transformation, the meaningfulness it had for the villagers' life, and the problems plaguing the merger of large numbers of small peasant family farms into big collectives, as analyzed in this volume, remain critical information for understanding the development of Chinese Communist society. Communist statistics, whose reliability has often been disputed, were used with caution everywhere in the volume, checking them against available evidence including pre-Communist statistics.

Finally, both works in this volume have been written with a sociological frame of reference so as to facilitate comparative study on the family institution and the peasant village, their structural-functional characteristics, and the process of their change under the conscious direction of violent revolutions. It is hoped that in these two studies, the analysis of such universal elements as the sex, age, and marriage factors in the family institution, the earthbound characteristics and the kinship dominance of the peasant village community, and their reaction to revolutionary forces will continue to serve the interest of comparative sociologists in spite of elapsing years.

Social Science Research Institute   C. K. YANG
University of Hawaii
November 25, 1964

The Chinese Family
    in the
Communist Revolution

C. K. YANG

The Chinese Family
in the
Communist Revolution

with a Foreword by Talcott Parsons

Foreword

It is a pleasure to have the opportunity to say a word about this study of the Chinese family under the Communist regime. In my opinion Dr. Yang has with unusual success accomplished a dual purpose: he has made an important contribution to the general sociology of the family, and has also contributed to our understanding of the background of momentous events in the Far East which have such an important bearing on our own political responsibilities and destiny. Though probably a larger proportion of readers will be more interested in the latter contribution than in the former, I would like to emphasize their intimate connection: unless he had done an excellent piece of sociological analysis, Dr. Yang could not have produced a document of such practical significance.

For a generation in the sociological literature China has provided the stock example of a "familistic" society, one in which the family, and the kinship system ramifying from it, had an unusually strategic place in the total society, and, it has often been held, the family itself was unusually stable. The first of these generalizations has undoubtedly been true of the "classical" Chinese social system. But insufficient attention has been paid to defining the conditions under which the second held true. Dr. Yang shows us very convincingly that the old system generated very considerable tensions, both in the relation between the generations and that between the sexes.* As long as the old family system was reinforced by the old ideological, political, and class systems and certain features of a predominantly agricultural economy, the consequences of this strain could be successfully counteracted and the system as a whole remain substantially unchanged.

---

* Dr. Yang's most important predecessor in this line of analysis of the Chinese family is probably Marion J. Levy. See his *The Family Revolution in Modern China*, Cambridge, 1949.

The stability of these conditions has, however, broken down in the long series of social changes which have occurred since the revolution of 1911. The impact of the West, through missions, trade, education, medicine, and political intervention has upset the old equilibrium. In these circumstances there has been a strong pressure of the "disadvantaged" groups, the younger people and women, to be relieved of the handicaps to which they were subjected in the old family system, the subordination of the young to the authority and interests of the older generation, and of women to men. For understandable reasons the spearhead of these movements has been found in the cities, and in the intellectually and culturally more "emancipated" sections of the population; but they have by now spread far and wide.

Dr. Yang's essential thesis in this respect is that the Communists did not originate this fundamental process of change in the family, but that its roots go very deep into the constitution of the older society and the much more general process of change to which it has been subjected. Much of it was well under way before the Communist movement became very prominent. What the latter has done is to exploit and help along a process of change which is rooted in forces much bigger than itself. But it was given its opportunity by the tendency of the Kuomintang in its later phases to form an alliance with the older conservative elements which, in this as in several other respects, tended not only to try to check the process of change but even actually to turn the clock back.

In its more specifically sociological aspect, then, Dr. Yang's study takes the step beyond the more "static" view of the Chinese family as a structural type to a dynamic analysis of the conditions of its equilibrium, both internally and in relation to the other structures of the society. In its more political aspect the study brings forcibly and effectively to the reader's attention the fact that what has been happening in China is not the consequence of mere machinations of a conspiratorial cabal, but constitutes a fundamental process of change in the structure of a society, something that surely more Americans need to realize than the public discussion would seem to indicate is yet the case. Unfortunately the literature on which a sound appraisal of this process can be based has been seriously limited both in amount and in quality, and this book is hence a particularly welcome addition.

It cannot but strike the American reader that, on the background of the old system, the *direction* of change sponsored by the Communists, but only very partially brought about by them, has been precisely to make Chinese family conditions far more like our own than they were in the old system. What American now contests the right of young people to marry the persons of their own choice, or of married women to hold property in their own right? Yet these are typical of the things which the Communists have been promoting. Perhaps this makes a little more intelligible why intelligent people in China can favor the Communist movement.

What of the prospects for the future? The type of family organization with which we are familiar has never been typical of peasant societies, particularly those with a very high density of population. I strongly suspect that the success of the Communist movement in making its family reforms "stick" depends, more than on any other factor, on the success of its industrialization program in its *social* rather than economic consequences. This will not be primarily a question of the internal organization of families, but of their relation to the rest of the society in which they exist. But furthermore, it is highly questionable whether an industrial society, once fully developed and stabilized, can remain a "communist" society. So far the Communist movement has been a conspicuously successful agent of social change in the direction of industrialization of previously agrarian societies. How well it can survive success remains to be seen. It is not impossible that the type of family organization which has so far been developing under Communist auspices in China (as substantially also in the Soviet Union) will in the long run prove to be one of the most important foci of a shift from a Communist to something more like a "democratic" organization of society.

Talcott Parsons

Harvard University

Acknowledgments

In the preparation of this volume I am deeply indebted to the following: Dr. John K. Fairbank for helping to initiate my research and for the encouragement given by him and his wife, Mrs. Wilma Fairbank, in reading and criticizing the manuscript; Dr. Talcott Parsons for his stimulating ideas, valued suggestions, and generosity in writing the Foreword; Dr. and Mrs. Robert Redfield for reading the manuscript and contributing much to its improvement. The generous financial support from the Center for International Studies of Massachusetts Institute of Technology, the Trustees of Lingnan University, the Rockefeller Foundation, and the Social Science Research Council made possible the fruition of this work and is deeply appreciated. Special acknowledgment is due the University of Pittsburgh for partial relief from teaching duties during revision of the manuscript. I wish especially to thank Mr. Richard W. Hatch of the Center for International Studies, Massachusetts Institute of Technology, for carefully editing the entire text and Mr. Howard Linton of Columbia University Library for his kindness and generosity in providing library resources. Last but not the least, my wife, Louise Chin Yang, unselfishly contributed long hours improving the manuscript and sharing the ordeal of its preparation.

C. K. Yang

University of Pittsburgh
March 1958

Contents

The Chinese Family
in the
Communist Revolution

CHAPTER I

The Communist Revolution and the Change of Chinese Social Institutions

Wʜᴇɴ ᴛʜᴇ famed Communist general Ch'en I led his victorious troops into conquered Shanghai in the early spring of 1949, he told the apprehensive citizens of that city that China was going to see the "first real change" in two thousand years. Epitomizing the principles and programs of the Communist regime in China, his statement marked the distinction between the present Communist revolution and the political changes of the past.

In the past two thousand years of recurring dynastic cycles, of alternations of order and chaos, there had been a general continuity and consistent development of the institutional framework of Chinese society. There had been changes and innovations from time to time in Chinese history, to be sure, but they were generally limited in institutional scope and spaced at rather long intervals which allowed them to be gradually assimilated by the traditional institutional system. When any sudden change took on too drastic and extensive a character, it usually soon succumbed to the forces of tradition. Hence the frequent assertion that, for some two millennia, no major social revolution had successfully introduced extensive alterations in the basic pattern of Chinese society.

In the modern scene, the immediate vital effect of the Republican revolution of 1911 was limited mainly to the disintegration of the traditional system of central political control; there was no sweeping introduction of any new pattern of society. The subsequent four decades of the Republican period brought a gradual disintegration of China's traditional institutions and a rather chaotic beginning of a new social pattern, but these came largely by the spontaneous process of social change and not by the coordinated and conscious planning of an organized political power.

It is obvious that the domestic aim of the Chinese Communist regime is not limited to gaining political rule over the country. The declared purpose of the regime is the remaking of the total structure of China's political, economic, and social life. During the first ten years (1949–1959) of the regime its policies and action have encompassed wide grounds of institutional revision of Chinese society, including the imposition of a new national orthodoxy by relentless "thought reform;" the recasting of the economic institution through land reform, collectivization of agriculture, nationalization of industry and commerce, large-scale industrialization, liquidation of landlords and remolding of the urban business class; the introduction of a political institution based on the power of a large, formally organized elite; the enforcement of an educational system different from the old in its universality and its literary and technical content; the organized development of new forms of recreation carefully geared to the cultivation of the new ideological orientation; the concerted attack on the religious institution; and, as the focus of our special interest, the reform of the traditional family. Thus in the brief period of ten years there have been simultaneous attempts to alter the basic character of the entire institutional framework of Chinese society.

The importance which is attached by the Communist leadership to the remaking of the Chinese family institution is shown in the numerous directives issued by the major Communist agencies such as the Chinese Communist Party, the New Democratic Youth League, the Democratic Women's League, the Political Department of the People's Revolutionary Military Committee, and many other vital organizations ordering the effective implementation of the new Marriage Law.[1] There is little question about the earnest intention of the Communists to introduce basic changes in the Chinese family institution by concerted application of political, economic, and social pressure.

But the Communist regime is still new, and its effort to alter the family institution on a national scale did not formally begin until the promulgation of the new Marriage Law in May 1950. Within the limited time, it is hardly possible to see a nationwide change in such an ancient, deeply rooted institution as the traditional family. Nevertheless, events pointing to a broadening change of the family have been occurring in all parts of China under Communist rule. It is the purpose of the present study to analyze developments in Communist China which may disclose consistent trends in the change of the family institution, for, although such trends are now visible only in certain segments of the population, with the consolidation of Communist political power and the continued implementation of its policies, they are spreading to increasing portions of the population.

The Chinese Family in Traditional Society

Communist consideration of the remaking of the family as one of the basic measures in the transformation of traditional Chinese society shows that the Communist leadership has a full realization of the vital role of the family and the broader kinship system in the traditional social structure. Economically, the family has been the most important unit of organization in production, for not only has agriculture been almost exclusively a family undertaking but also in industry and commerce the family has been the most numerous organizational unit in investment and operation. There is hardly one major aspect of traditional social life that is not touched by the ties and influence of the family. It is somewhat difficult for an upper- or middle-class urban Chinese in his twenties today to visualize how dominant a part the family once played in public and private life during the earlier part of his father's generation.

In the early years of the twentieth century many of society's economic, educational, religious, recreational, and even political functions were intimately tied to the family institution. From cradle to grave the individual was under the uninterrupted influence of the family regarding his physical and moral upbringing, the formation of his sentiments and attitudes, his educational training, his public career, his social associations, his emotional and material security. In the Chinese community, particularly in the rural areas, there have been only a few social organizations or associations outside the family to serve the individual's social needs. Consequently, throughout his life the individual constantly struggled with problems concerned with the relations of parents and children, husband and wife, elder and younger brothers, the "in-laws," uncles, cousins, nephews, grandparents and grandchildren, and other members in the complex kinship circle.

Beyond the kinship circle the individual might have to deal with government officials, with his teacher or craft master, his colleagues, his employer or employees, and his neighbors and friends. But many of these social relations came through direct or indirect kinship contacts, and they were often patterned after the family system in structure and in values. Hence government officials were often referred to as "parent-officials" (*fu mu kuan*) and the people as "children people" (*tzu min*). The relationship between master and apprentice, or between teacher and student, operated on a simulated father-and-son basis. A solemn ceremony of a sacred character was used to introduce a new student to his teacher and an apprentice to his master, in order to establish the pseudo-kinship bond. And the devotion and reverence expected of a student or apprentice by the teacher or master was of the same type expected from a son by his father. Stores, handicraft shops, and farms employed mainly relatives, and the kinship bond was pervasive in the system of basic economic relations. Friends and neighbors addressed each other in fraternal or other kinship terms. Conversations between friends were punctuated with appellations like "elder brother" and "younger brother" and "uncle," even though the parties were not related as such.

Various forms of fraternal and sororal organizations stood out prominently among the few organized associations which existed beyond the kinship ties. The membership of most traditional social associations, from fraternities, sororities, and literary societies of the gentry to the business and craft guilds of the urban centers, was structured according to age and generation factors. The secret societies regarded their founders as "ancestors" and treated them with ancestor-worship rites. Their organization was patterned closely after the kinship structure, and authority was exercised through a hierarchy of generational status and age levels. The initiation of a new member was frequently done by drinking a few drops of each other's blood so as to establish the "blood tie" and to impart a measure of realism to the simulated kinship bond. Secret societies have played an important part in the life of certain segments of the traditional society, particularly among traveling entertainers, patent-medicine venders, and urban transportation workers, who had to operate outside the home territory where the kinship system was based, and among the poor peasants whose kinship ties were insufficient to meet their social and economic needs.

Under a social situation so thoroughly permeated with actual or simulated kinship ties it is to be expected that many of the kinship values should have general validity for society as a whole, and that the family should perform the function of being the training ground for general citizenship for society and for the state. An example is the so-called Five Cardinal Relations (*wu lun*, meaning the five basic norms of social order), which constituted the foundations of traditional social values. Mencius states that in "the relations of humanity — between father and son there should be solidarity and affection; between sovereign and minister, righteousness; between husband and wife, attention to their separate functions; between old and young, a proper order; and between friends, fidelity." [2] It is to be noted that heading the Five Cardinal Relations of humanity is the relation between father and son, and that of the five relations three belong to the kinship realm. The two non-kinship relations, those between ruler and officials and between friends, also rely partly for their actual operation on the moral strength of loyalty and status concepts required of the three kinship relations. In this sense, the mores of non-kinship relations may be regarded as an extension of the mores of kinship relations.

These Five Cardinal Relations, centering upon kinship ties, formed the core of social and moral training for the individual almost from the beginning of his consciousness of social existence until he became so conditioned to it that his standard of satisfaction and deprivation was based upon it, and the complex and extensive web of kinship ties created a feeling of a closed universe from which there seemed to be no escape, except perhaps death. The large number of suicides resulting from the strain of family relations among women (see chapters IV and VI) is a reflection of this situation. Here, for the unfortunate few, social pressure from the family institution appeared weightier than life itself, and the pain of death was considered lighter than the torture of living in a society which provided little outlet and security for a deviant from the traditional ideal of the family institution.

Such was the place of the traditional Chinese family and the broader kinship system in the general picture of social life about half a century ago. At present this situation still exists widely in rural communities and to a lesser extent among certain sections of the urban population. This is particularly so in mountainous sections of the country where confinement of the population in valleys discourages migration and accentuates the earthbound character and the kinship orientation of the peasant communities.

Organization of the Traditional Family

As an institution that has come to perform a multiplicity of functions and to play a vital role in the general organization of social life, the average Chinese traditional family seems surprisingly simple and small. If a family is taken to mean a biologically related group belonging to a single household sharing property and income together, the average Chinese family ranges in membership from four persons to six persons. From more recent statistical information we have the censuses of nine counties in Szechwan Province in 1942–43 giving an average range of 4.4 to 5.3 persons per family and a government report on twenty-three provinces presenting an average range from 4.1 persons in Jehol Province to 5.9 persons in Anhwei Province per family. The frontier province of Kirin in Manchuria had an unusual average of 6.9 persons per family,[3] which is reminiscent of the large frontier family in early American history.

To assume a multiplicity of functions and a vital social role in the fairly complex organization of traditional Chinese society, such a small membership appears inadequate — hence the expansion of the effective family relations beyond the confines of the household and the importance of the greater kinship circle to the life of the common man. Such a circle centers upon the nucleus of the parents-children relation and extends along the paternal lineage for generally three generations. The possible separation of married sons into independent households among the poor class weakens the parental control somewhat, but the parents-children relation is still intimate, and filial obligations remain strong. Under the leadership of and dominance by the parents, the married sons and their children, though in separate households, continue to operate as an effective organization performing many common functions.

In traditional social life there is the term *liu ch'in,* or "six kinship relations," which suggests a delimitation for the larger kinship circle as a functioning unit. Interpretations vary as to what constitutes the "six kinship relations," but a commonly accepted version is that they are the relations (1) between husband and wife, (2) between parents and children, (3) between brothers, (4) between the children of brothers, (5) between brothers' grandchildren, and (6) between brothers' great grandchildren.[4] In actual social life, however, the first four categories of relations are comparatively more intimate, and the last two types belong more to the organization of the clan than to the intimate kinship circle of the extended family. Nevertheless, kinship obligations of some degree are effectively present in all six categories of relations. The number of persons in an organizational unit of this type exceeds considerably that of the average household. In addition, the kinship relations of the fourth and fifth generations, as well as those of the immediate household of the maternal side (mainly those of the mother's and wife's), also involve a certain amount of mutual obligations, thus further expanding the effective unit of kinship organization for the common people whose households are usually small. It is the greater collective strength of the kinship circle, not the household alone, that accounts for the prominence of the family in the traditional pattern of social organization, although the household always remains the fundamental nucleus of the kinship structure.

A significant and well-known aspect of the Chinese traditional family is the integration of the extended kinship circle, normally within three generations along the paternal lineage, into a single household whenever economic conditions permitted. The Chinese family in this sense was like a balloon, ever ready to expand whenever there was wealth to inflate it. As soon as there was enough land or other forms of production to employ the married sons, they would remain in the father's household, with property and income managed in common under the leadership and authority of the parents, and the process of expansion of the small household into a "big family" began. Should wealth increase, the membership of the family would expand further by adding concubines and their children. The longer life span of the well-to-do also augmented the size of the expanding family. Sufficient economic means being a necessary ingredient, the "big family" was more common among large landowners and well-to-do merchants than among the average peasants and workers.

With the advantage of education, coupled with the more favorable operation of the law of chance in a large family (as compared with a small family), it was fairly inevitable that within three generations one or more of the sons would, in the days of monarchical government before 1911, pass one of the official examinations, become the holder of an imperial academic degree, and possibly enter officialdom. With this accomplishment, the family entered the ranks of the gentry. Even in the Republican period the advantage of education, particularly modern higher education, for the young sons brought the family into the group of local political leadership, which functioned somewhat like the old gentry. Hence the frequent association between the big family and the gentry group.

In comparison with the smaller family and the limited kinship circle of the common man, the big family presented a close, effective integration of a large number of members which stood as a source of social and economic strength. It is significant that this form of family organization was intimately associated with the classes having social, economic, and political dominance. Another significance of the big family was its function of serving as an exemplary model of traditional family organization for the common people, thus encouraging them to maintain a strong tie with members of the near-kinship circle in an effort to simulate the advantages of the big family which traditionally brought prestige and success. In this sense, the big family played an important role in the functioning of the traditional kinship system.

The major principle of structure, from the big family of the well-to-do to the smaller family of workers and peasants, is the already noted Confucian canon of kinship relations: "between father and son there should be solidarity and affection; . . . between husband and wife, attention to their separate functions; between old and young, a proper order." One may make the following annotation to this canon from its implicit meaning as well as from the ways it worked out in traditional family life. The relation between parents and children in general and between father and son in particular should be the closest, closer than any other type of kinship relation, including the relation between husband and wife, for this is the nucleus of all family relations and the seat of authority in the power structure of the family; the expansibility of the traditional family is made possible by the use of this relation as the controlling factor in family life. Second in importance is the relation between husband and wife, and here "attention to separate functions" implies a division of labor as well as a stratification of status of all family members in both sexes on the basis of age and generational levels.

This structural principle of dominance by the parents and stratification of status and distribution of functions by sex and age is applicable to the organization of kinship units of all sizes, from the small family of the common people to the big family of the well-to-do, even to the clan with hundreds or thousands of members. Whatever the size of the unit, any individual member can readily find his or her specific place in this organizational scheme. This proved to be a workable principle for the majority of the families, in spite of occasional deviation such as the presence of a dominant wife or the situation in which a man's youngest son was younger than his oldest grandchild should he take on concubines at a late age after his sons have been married for some time. The general applicability of this organizational scheme is particularly adaptable to the expansible character of the traditional family and to the distribution of functions in the kinship system.

The "Family Revolution"

This form of family organization, centering upon parental control of married sons and structuring the membership rigidly according to sex and age, produced in the past a stable family and contributed substantially to the long stability of the traditional culture. In the traditional society dominated by the kinship factor it seems to have served social needs well with its multiplicity of functions.

But the impact of Western ideas and industrial influences since the closing quarter of the last century increasingly altered the picture. In the traditional family a strong authoritarian character is inherent in the rigid parental control and the stratification according to sex and age. Pressure and tension bore down heavily upon the women and the young. The introduction of the Western idea of individual liberty and rights inspired the women and the young to review and to reject their traditional roles of submission in the family.

In the past the traditional family could function rather smoothly in spite of the many innate dissatisfactions of the women or the young with its authoritarian character, chiefly because of the dominance of the kinship factor in the old social pattern. In such a pattern the family and the larger kinship group formed a relatively warm atmosphere in which the individual found not merely economic security but also the satisfaction of most of his social needs. Beyond this warm atmosphere lay what the traditional individual considered the cold and harsh world wherein his treatment and fate became unpredictable. Consequently, the women and the young accepted their traditional status as dictated by the way social life was traditionally organized.

But this pattern of social organization became increasingly incompatible with the new needs that arose with China's gradual integration into the modern industrial and nationalistic world. The past three-quarters of a century of floundering efforts at transferring the family and kinship relations to modern economic and political undertakings produced endless contradictions between the particularistic and the universalistic patterns of social life.[5] From such contradictions developed the accelerating trend of change in the traditional family and its old role in the organization of social life, a change that proceeded by popular demand from the educated young for a "family revolution" from the second decade of the present century. There was little success in overcoming the incongruity between the kinship tie as an organizational requirement in the traditional order and the need for objective qualifications for individuals as components of modern economic and political structures. Moreover, the particularistic nature in the kinship-oriented pattern of social organization divided the population into numerous small, self-confined, and loosely interrelated kinship units, while the mass organization of modern industrial society and the national state demanded intimate integration between the social and economic organs based on universal standards for the individuals.

This incompatibility seems to have been in the awareness of China's modern leading reformers whose ideological movements aimed at guiding China into a modern industrial state. K'ang Yu-wei, who led China's first organized modern reform in 1898, pointed out that the "abolition" of the traditional family was a condition for proper performance of modern public duties.[6] But his reform movement proved abortive. Save for his unwitting pioneering influence in weakening the Confucian orthodoxy by inspiring a change of attitude, he and his reform movement had little direct effect on the traditional kinship system. Sun Yat-sen, the leading revolutionist to rise on the heels of K'ang's failure, sensed the same incompatibility when he urged the expansion of "familism and clannism" into nationalism. Although he advanced no specific steps for such transformation, the Republican revolution of 1911 which he fathered did have serious effects on the subsequent change of the traditional family institution.

Some students underestimate this revolution as merely a change of political formality from monarchy to a nominal republic, devoid of any serious social significance. Actually, it started the trend toward destroying the theoretical applicability of Confucian kinship ethics to the operation of the state, thus undermining the traditional dominance of the family in social and political life. Furthermore, the collapse of the monarchy brought the abolition of the old imperial laws which compelled conformity to the traditional family institution based on Confucian orthodoxy. Subsequent laws on kinship relations promulgated by various governments under the Republic increasingly veered away from the traditional pattern. This had at least the negative significance of undermining the strength of the traditional family institution by reducing that part of its compulsory character which was founded upon formal political control. Also gone with the monarchy was the encouragement given by the government to such acts of devotion to the ideals of the traditional family as erecting memorial arches for unusually chaste widows or temples for outstanding filial sons. The effective symbolistic value of such old objects erected before the Republic steadily wore thin with the passing years. Finally, the revolution of 1911 attracted into its ranks many women whose demand for a new feminine role in a different family institution was no less strong than their demand for a new political order. These women, though few in number, planted the seed for the many subsequent popular movements that were to seriously affect the continued operation of the traditional family institution.

These influences continued to brew in the political chaos of the young Republic while the problem of social and cultural reform claimed increasing public attention. A great ideological upheaval, the New Culture Movement or Renaissance, which started in 1917, broke out in full force in the May 4th Movement of 1919. In this movement of multiple significance the term "family revolution" was introduced

into the consciousness of the public. It was used by leaders and pro-
tagonists of the movement as a slogan, and by the conservative old
generation as a reprimand to rebellious youngsters who struggled to
deviate from the traditional family institution. It became current parlance in the rising cry of the times for a change in the way of life as
the political revolution gradually unfolded into its social and cultural
phases.

There was no organized platform for this popular movement called
the "family revolution," but its main objectives were clearly suggested
in its slogans, catch-words, and the increasing volume of its literature.
It demanded a new role for women in the family as well as in society
in general terms of sex equality; it advocated freedom of social association between opposite sexes; it demanded marriage by free choice
and love, not by parental arrangement; it called for greater freedom
for the young; it vaguely urged a new family institution similar to the
Western pattern.

Ill-defined and poorly coordinated as some of these objectives were,
they did form a sufficiently coherent group of new ideas that served
to focus the public's attention upon the problem of remaking the
traditional family and of gathering sympathetic forces for group action.
The roots of Western inspiration were unmistakable in this movement.
From the May 4th Movement to the late 1920's, Ibsen's plays on
women's status and the family gained wide circulation in Chinese, became successful stage productions in large cities, and brought forth
spirited discussions. But the main preoccupation of the movement
then was still with the traditional family institution. Books, pamphlets,
and articles on the family problem appeared in growing numbers, firing broadsides at the ancient institution as being destructive of human
rights, decadent in moral character, and as discouraging the spirit of
independence and progress. The institution that had withstood some
two millennia of dynastic changes and foreign invasions and all their
political and economic devastations now came to be viewed as symbolizing all of China's sins and weaknesses. The new demands and the
proffered solutions, however untried and incoherent in some respects,
were pictured as the road to happiness and strength. Nationalistic
sentiments which began to surge forth with increasing force in the
decade following World War I in China as well as elsewhere helped
to impress these arguments on the minds of the public.

Aside from the rising nationalistic sentiments, many other forces
stimulated by the May 4th Movement added strength to the family
revolution. One was a concentrated attack on the absolutism of the

Confucian orthodoxy and the social institutions modeled after it. Keynotes of the attack were: "skepticism toward all ancient teachings," "down with *Confucius and Company*" (the latter term meaning the traditional schoolroom and its Confucian classical teachings) and the "man-devouring doctrine of ritualism." This branch of the New Culture Movement called for a complete re-evaluation of traditional learning and institutions and for a new cultural orientation in the light of modern science and democracy.

As the "new current of thought" won widening acceptance in a decade of raging polemics following World War I, Confucian orthodoxy together with its kinship values and the family institution molded after it were no longer a matter of "sacred" character enjoying deep reverence and unquestioned conformity from the people and supported by compulsory political power. They became subjects for secular discussions and popular attacks from the educated young — so much so, in fact, that it was fashionable for modern Chinese intellectuals to criticize Confucianism. The result was a serious loss of prestige and strength by the Confucian orthodoxy. As the family institution was deeply enmeshed in the matrix of Confucian ideology and its institutions, it could not help but be weakened by this development.

The call for skepticism toward the old cultural heritage and a new orientation for the future found the most attentive listeners among modern educated young men and women, who felt the most strain from the rigid sex and age stratifications in the traditional family and society. The rise of the youth movement and the women's movement, as phases of the May 4th Movement, lent important support to the family revolution and in fact became inseparable parts of it. In a sense, the family revolution developed as a rebellion of the educated young of both sexes against the traditional social order.

Such a rebellion, breaking out within the family circle, was naturally viewed with alarm and even terror by the older generation, who found the process increasingly difficult to stop. Under the driving and infectious demand for freedom and equality, and in the growing destruction of unquestioned conformity to traditional institutions in general, many traditional families, mainly among the urban upper and upper-middle classes, were forced to undergo certain fundamental changes by the mid-1920's; and the family problem was pushed into the fore of the nation's attention along with other vital political, social, and economic issues of the day.

By this time another great upheaval was rapidly sweeping across China, bringing the stress of a political storm to bear increasingly upon the old social institutions. This was the so-called Second Revolution, which began with the early years of the second decade of the present century and culminated in Chiang Kai-shek's Northern Expedition of 1926 and in the establishment of the Nationalist government in Nanking a year later. The decade from 1927 to the full-scale Japanese invasion of China in 1937 saw the development of the Chinese Communist Party as a military and political power in the "red areas" that studded many parts of the country.

In this turbulent decade social and political forces served to accelerate the pace of the family revolution — although the term was by this time losing its impact of novelty and was less frequently heard. A vital feature of the period was the youthfulness and the Western educational background of the men who came into power, whether in the Nationalist or in the Communist camp. When Chiang Kai-shek led his expeditionary forces northward from Canton in 1926, he was but a young man of forty, and Mao Tse-tung, present head of the Chinese Communist Party, was only thirty-three. Young and modern educated men came to fill an increasing proportion of government offices at all levels.

Although the Republican revolution of 1911 had abolished the imperial laws which supported the traditional family institutions, old officials who manned the government in the early Republican years still exercised their political power largely in the Confucian mode in which they had been raised and trained, and the Republican laws, when enforced at all, were more frequently than not given a Confucian interpretation. But by the late 1920's the gap was fast widening between the Confucian mentality and the attitudes of the young political leadership, and consequently not only the *de jure* but also the *de facto* political control of the traditional family institution dwindled rapidly, particularly in the cities. So overwhelming was the ideological swing away from the Confucian orthodoxy and the social institutions molded by it that repeated restorationist efforts in the 1930's, such as local government orders to reinstate Confucian classics into the school curriculum and the Confucian tenet of the New Life Movement of the Nationalist regime, were unable to turn the tide. Although the scene of ideological struggle was enacted mainly in the cities, the new influence spread to an ever-increasing proportion of the population, especially among those who could afford a modern education.

Against this ideological background, the family revolution persisted on its course set by the previous period. Literature on the subject continued to pour forth from the growing number of mechanical presses.

Increasing social contacts between the young of opposite sexes, growing numbers of marriages resulting from romantic love, and "small families" on the Western model were among the visible results wrought by this process of change. These were living examples of a cause that had come to be embraced by an entire generation of the modern educated young. The youth movement and the women's movement continued to expand and to exert influence upon the development of the family situation. Anti-Communist measures frequently caused setbacks to these movements by hitting many of their organizations as Communist fronts, but this did not affect the spreading struggle among the young against the traditional family and their persistent clamor for its reform.

The Law of Kinship Relations promulgated by the Nationalist government in 1930 incorporated many of the ideological objectives of the family revolution, although many of the basic principles of the traditional family institution were retained.[7] Aside from the question of logical coherence and the lack of effective general enforcement, this compromise law stood as a crystallization of the persistent trend of change in the traditional family, a change which had been brewing for a quarter of a century.

It was true that this trend mainly affected the modern intelligentsia, the majority of whom stemmed from the upper and upper-middle classes in the cities. The importance of this group could not be measured entirely by its small numerical size because of its strategic function in giving direction to the social change and its dominant position in such mechanisms of social control as the government. But the influence of the family revolution in this period was definitely spreading, though slowly, to the urban middle class and a small portion of the city workers. The younger generation of the well-to-do landowners in the countryside also became increasingly affected by the new ideological trends as they went to the cities for a modern education, but, as they soon became identified with the urban intelligentsia and no longer remained members of rural communities, the countryside was not much affected by modern ideological movements.

It is obvious that the gradual change of the traditional family was not the result of ideological agitation alone without the operation of other supporting social and economic factors. The confinement of the family revolution and its related ideological movements mainly to the cities was due precisely to the presence of collaborating social and economic forces in the urban areas and the weakness or absence of such forces in the rural communities.

There was, for example, the concentration of modern educational facilities and the modern press in the cities, which operated as disseminating agents for new ideas about the family and other social institutions which were being challenged by the "new currents of thought." The rapid development of women's education and coeducation since the New Culture Movement was a particularly important influence. Similarly significant was the growth of urban occupational opportunities for women, which provided the economic ground for women's claims for a higher status in the family and in society. The city, with its greater social and economic mobility, offered more fertile ground than the rural community for the dissemination of modern democratic ideas incompatible with the authoritarian characteristics of the traditional family. The growing specialization of social and economic functions, including the commercialization of recreation, undermined the traditional self-sufficiency of the family by reducing many of its functions and thus lessening the individual's dependence upon it. Above all, the accelerating development of modern industry and the emergence of an urban economy geared to its needs after World War I worked to destroy the particularism of the old kinship-oriented social pattern, and compelled some kind of change in the mode of family life.

Growing population mobility, with frequent prolonged physical separation of some members from the family, affected the continued operation of the traditional family organization, which required constant, close contact among the members. Increased population mobility stemmed from a number of social situations, notably the steady deterioration of the handicraft and agricultural economy, the expansion of urbanization, and the high frequency of famines and wars. In the eight years of war against the Japanese invasion (1937–1945), there was no new ideological wave on the reform of the family, but the pouring of millions of modern-minded coastal refugees into the hitherto isolated Southwest undoubtedly aided the disintegration of many traditional families and the formation of new ones on the model promoted by the family revolution. When the curtain of enemy occupation was lifted by the Japanese surrender of 1945, the cities revealed a scene of family life marked by physical separation of members and deviation from the traditional standards, departing further from the Confucian pattern than in any preceding period.

The Communist Revolution and the Chinese Family

In 1949, four years after the Japanese surrender, when the Chinese Communists took over the reins of national political power, China entered upon a period in which drastic political revolution was but one phase of a comprehensive movement aimed at recasting the entire traditional social order by coordinated plans and compulsory measures. The reform of the Chinese family, along with the remaking of other major social institutions, became a part of an over-all drastic social change.

This crisis for the family institution contained no new substance. As already shown, this institution had been changing under constant stress and strain for the preceding three decades; and the Communist crisis, so far as the family was concerned, represented but a more drastic development of the same process, which was now being urged on under a different leadership and in a different manner.

Neither was the effort at altering the family institution anything new with the Communists. Long before the establishment of the Communist regime in 1949, members of the Communist movement had been playing a vital part, along with other reformers and intellectuals, in developing the family revolution and its supporting ideological movements. Ch'en Tu-hsiu, one of the founders of the Chinese Communist Party, ranked with Hu Shih in the New Culture Movement and in the relentless assault against the ideological and institutional citadel of Confucian orthodoxy. Particularly vital was Ch'en's place in initiating and developing the youth movement and the women's movement. Communists in general had been strategic in the agitating and organizing efforts of these movements. The Chinese Communist Party was co-author with the Kuomintang of the Second Revolution, which had serious effects on the development of the family revolution. (Present Communist interpretation of modern Chinese history claims Communist Party leadership in the May 4th Movement and the Second Revolution.) The actual development of the family situation in the "red areas" that came into existence after 1928 has remained largely unrecorded, but scattered information has indicated uncompromising Communist endeavor in changing both the traditional family institution and the kinship-oriented pattern of social organization in those areas.

Many sources of popular information in China for the past thirty years have pictured the Communists as iconoclasts toward the family as a social institution. Ch'en Tu-hsiu was charged by his political enemies with advocating the practice of "communal property and communal wives;" and the charge of practicing "communal wives" was directed against the "red areas" in the early 1930's.[8] There was a disquieting rumor of "forced assignment of wives" by the Communists in 1948 and 1949, a rumor so persistent and widespread that it caused a marriage boom in localities in the paths of the advancing Communist columns in their southward conquest because parents were hurriedly marrying off their daughters in an effort to save them from becoming "assigned wives."

It is probably true that relatively light restrictions were placed upon marriage and divorce in the "red areas" before 1949. This can be seen in such available documents of the period as the Marriage Regulations of the Chinese Soviet Republic and the Temporary Marriage Regulations, both promulgated in 1931 by the Chinese Soviet Republic, and the Marriage Regulations of the Border Area of Shansi, Chahar, and Hopei provinces. But there seems to be no substantiation to the charge of either the practice of "communal wives" or the discarding of the family as a social institution.

Facts as observed in Communist China after 1949 indicate no evidence for any of these allegations. The promulgation of the new Marriage Law on May 1, 1950, and the nationwide efforts at its enforcement by the Communist government through the network of organizations under its command seem clear indications of a Communist policy toward the family which insisted upon drastic reform of the traditional family but fully retained the family as a basic social institution. Even under the people's commune, the family remains the basic social unit, though vastly reduced in its functions. An unmistakable sign of Communist policy was seen in the complex responsibilities involved in divorce by the new Marriage Law, responsibilities that weigh particularly heavy on the husband. (See the English translation of the Marriage Law in the Appendix at the end of this work; see also Chapter IV.) Hence the drastic reform of the traditional family demanded by the Communists should not be taken as an iconoclastic view of the family as a social institution.

The reason for the Communist policy of reshaping the traditional family seems plain. The Communist regime is bent on building an industrial society on the socialistic pattern, and it is fully aware of the incompatibility between such a society and the kinship-oriented structure. Also important for the political purpose of the regime is the incompatibility between the individual's traditional loyalty to the family and the new requirements of his loyalty to the state and to the Communist Party.

Up to the Communist accession to power, the family revolution had proceeded largely as a part of a process of spontaneous social change in modern China. The inauguration of the Communist regime, particularly after the promulgation of the new Marriage Law, brought a different development. Change of the traditional family is no longer left to a spontaneous process but is subjected to the compulsory power of law and the pressure of a powerful, well-organized mass movement; and it is coordinated with other aspects of the Communist social, economic, and political revolution.

Traditional Chinese society was composed of numerous semi-autonomous local units, each of which was structured around the kinship system as its core, and each was only loosely related to the others. As a national social system, these units were integrated not so much by extensive functional interdependence and centralized control as by a fairly uniform institutional framework which enabled Chinese people everywhere to act together as a group on the basis of a common system of basic values. At the center of this decentralized system was the kinship structure with its sizable membership, its generational continuity, its rigid organization, and its multiplicity of socio-economic functions. In the structural strength and functional effectiveness of this kinship system lay much of the stability of the traditional social order and the long continuity of Chinese culture.

Now, under the strain of modern socio-economic influences in general, and of the family revolution in particular, the structural and functional integrity of the kinship system is sagging notably, and a new mold of family relationship has been developing to take its place. With its structural system weakened and its functional importance reduced, the kinship organization no longer serves as the strategic core of the social order. Nor is the emerging social order able to function with a dominant kinship system, for the rapidly developing social pattern is no longer composed of a loose conglomeration of compartmentalized local societies in which a strong kinship system is a stabilizing asset, but is based on a national system of functional interdependence of the local units and centralized control, a system in which a strong and dominant kinship organization would have a disruptive influence. In this sense, the change of the Chinese family and its extended kinship system forms a part of the broad transformation of Chinese society in the modern age.

As this study is focused on the disorganization of the traditional family and the development of a new family system, it must stress the inadequacies of the structural system of the old institution which caused its progressive disintegration under the pressure of modern socio-economic influences. Thus, the subsequent pages will disclose mainly the harsh and tyrannical features of the traditional family and its internal tensions and conflicts. This does not mean that noble qualities are lacking in the traditional Chinese family. The Chinese family has been an object of sentimental praise and even idealization by many Western writers who were generously and kindly disposed toward Chinese culture. And, objectively, the Chinese family has functioned stably and effectively in meeting the multifarious needs of its members and the broad requirements of the traditional social order for a thousand years. The Chinese family must have possessed many attributes of humanitarianism, moral strength, and social wisdom, in order to have been maintained by the people over such a long period of time. Anyone intimately familiar with old Chinese culture can readily reproduce many pictures of family life characterized by affection, mutual sacrifice, orderliness, moral dedication, and a long list of other features that make people feel nostalgic as they face the modern revolutionary scene of violence, chaos, and uncertainty.

But moral evaluation of the Chinese family institution is not the purpose of this study, and presentation of the merits of the old institution has little place in an effort to see why the traditional family is crumbling under the pressure of modern social values and socio-economic influences, or to explain the development of a different family system to better fit into the modern social order. If the reader finds in the subsequent chapters mostly tensions, conflicts, and injustices in the Chinese family, it is because these are the factors most closely associated with the modern change of that ancient institution.

CHAPTER II

Freedom of Marriage

MARRIAGE BEING the first step in the creation of a family, any change in the basic concept of marriage and in the procedure by which it is consummated affects the whole character of the family institution. Inevitably, therefore, the attack on the marriage system shook the foundations of the traditional Chinese family; and, theoretically as well as empirically, the marriage problem is of primary interest in the present analysis.

Marriage in traditional China had been under stifling ritualistic restrictions for a thousand years. In the half century of development of the family revolution the issue of freedom of marriage saw its most dramatic growth and formed the point for the most heated conflict between the younger generation and the traditional family. Inspiring the young was the Western idea of individual freedom and romantic love. Urging the old to reject this demand was the conscious fear of disrupting the long-established order of the family. The clash between generations resulted in untold numbers of tragedies — unreconciled family conflicts, runaway children, broken family ties, and moving stories of suicide. Sentiments and episodes in this clash provided leading themes for modern Chinese fiction and poetry. And the conflict continues in the present period under the Communist regime, spreading from the midst of the modern urban intelligentsia to the multitudes of workers and peasants.

Arranged Marriage and the Traditional Family Institution

To members of the older generation, particularly to the parents, the demand of the modern educated young for freedom of marriage violated the traditional family institution and threatened grave consequences. Fully aware that the form of marriage had a profound effect upon the arrangement of status of the family members, they were not in a mood to relax their traditional control over that critical event. It is therefore necessary to analyze the treatment of marriage by the traditional family in order to see the significance of the demand for freedom in the context of the traditional family institution.

For the traditional Chinese family marriage was not so much an affair of the matured children as an affair of the parents and of the family, with its chief purpose not so much the romantic happiness of the marrying children but fulfilling the sacred duty of producing male heirs for the perpetuation of the ancestors' lineage, the acquiring of a daughter-in-law for the service and comfort of the parents, and the begetting of sons for the security of the parents' old age. Marriage was not a crisis in which a family unit might be reduced and split by the departure of the married son; rather, it was an event not only to expand the family but also to provide additional protection and security to the family unit. To fulfill this purpose, marriage could not be allowed to transfer the center of affection, loyalty, and authority from the parents to the new couple. Hence the traditional discouragement of open affection between husband and wife, particularly when they were newly wed. In every way marriage and its ensuing relationships remained subordinated to the welfare and happiness of the parents and the continuity of the family organization. Such a consideration applied not only to the marriage of a son; the marriage of a daughter was subjected to the same consideration by the husband's family.

To put such traditional principles of marriage into practice was not an easy task. As the children, particularly the sons, were growing up, a centrifugal tendency was already developing away from the family and from parental ties. When marriage took place, the nucleus of an independent unit of family life already had its beginnings. To mitigate the centrifugal tendency, to subject the fresh nucleus to parental control, to force the ways of a grown-up woman, the daughter-in-law, into the mold of intimate family life as dictated by the parents, was very difficult. To achieve this, all the institutional devices of the Chinese family were brought to bear.

In this sense, marriage must of necessity be arranged by the parents. It must come by "orders of the parents and words of the go-between," and not by free choice of the partners. When the marriage had been dictated and arranged by the parents, the son was made to feel that the affair was seriously related to the parents, even though he might not be entirely convinced that his own role in it was totally unimportant. Especially critical was the parents' authority over the choice

of a daughter-in-law. This not merely affirmed the dominance of the
parents' role and the subordination of the son in the affair of marriage; it also strengthened the control of the parents over the daughter-
in-law by making her recognize that she came into the family by their
order and choice, not by her personal love for the son. The "words of
the go-between" had similar significance. The go-between was an indispensable substitute for open social life between the young of opposite sexes and for romantic love as the medium of marriage.*

Marriage born of romantic love has all the opposite effects of an
arranged marriage. The husband-wife relationship is the core, over-
shadowing the role of the parents, and the intimacy and affection in
such a marriage would seriously threaten the dominance of parental
affection, loyalty, and authority, if not replace it altogether. If the
daughter-in-law should come into the family of her own volition and
through affection for her husband, it would be difficult for her to subordinate her role to the will of the parents-in-law.

Thus one device to maintain parental control over the married son
and his wife was to deny to the young the ecstatic experience of
romantic love and to seek to divert it by other institutional means,
such as concubinage and tacit approval of prostitution, while trying
to keep the latter from becoming too disruptive an influence to the
family organization. For centuries the Chinese school child was made
to memorize Mencius' moral exhortation: "If the young people, without waiting for the orders of their parents and the arrangements of
the go-between, shall bore holes to steal a sight of each other, or get
over the wall to be with each other, then their parents and all other
people will despise them." [1] Mencius' explanation for this advice was
deeply imbedded in traditionally minded people. "The desire of the
child is towards his father and mother. When he becomes conscious
of the attraction of beauty, his desire is towards young and beautiful
women. When he comes to have a wife and children his desire is
towards them. . . . But the man of great filial piety, to the end of his
life, has his desire towards his parents." [2] For centuries the traditional
thought on marriage took this single track, stifling all romantic dreams.

In addition, there was an economic aspect to parental control over
the son's marriage. Normally the parents shouldered the financial
responsibility of the marriage and the starting of the new life of the

---

* The go-between was a diabolical character who specialized in fancy sales
talk. It was an important occupation for women in the traditional society, and
the practice continued among the majority of the population in recent years,
although its place under the Communist regime is in doubt.

couple. To be able to afford their children's marriage was the anxious hope of all parents, and the failure to do so was to have failed in the duty of parenthood and was considered a great misfortune in life. The parents' paying for the expenses of the marriage and letting the son use the family property to start his married life reaffirmed both to the son and to the daughter-in-law who was boss and who was subordinate.

The high cost of the traditional marriage is a well-known story. It was common to see parents sell or mortgage their property to pay for the marriage of their sons, and some of them sank so deeply into debt for this that they could hardly get out of it for the rest of their lives. In the villages in the vicinity of Canton in 1949 it took an average of thirty five piculs of rice for a peasant's son to get married, the equivalent of the net income of a little over a year for a poor peasant. Whatever other significance such sumptuous marriage ceremonies might have, the effect on the minds of the young couple could not be ignored, for it visibly demonstrated to them the dominant role of the parents and the family in their marriage. The more costly the marriage, and, for that matter, the more deeply the parents went into debt, the greater indebtedness the young couple felt toward the parents. When the parents strained their final savings and their last bit of credit in order to give the son a wedding feast, which would be attended by scores of relatives and friends in the cities and hundreds of people in the entire clan in the villages in some parts of the South as required by custom, the couple could not escape the pressure of the claim that their marriage was an affair of the family caused by the parents instead of an affair of the couple themselves motivated by love or personal attraction.

Besides the feast and other ceremonial expenses, a leading item in the cost of the traditional marriage was the amount to be paid the girl's family in kind or in cash or both. Such payment bore a variety of labels, such as the gift of betrothal, or ritual wealth, or body price, depending upon the social class and locality. Whatever the name, such payment was either symbolically or realistically a price for the person of the daughter-in-law, and it compelled the daughter-in-law to reckon with the authority and superiority of the parents-in-law who had paid the price for her.

The elaborate wedding ceremonies served the same general purpose, whatever additional functions they might have. Of foremost importance to the old tradition in a wedding ceremony was the performance of homage and sacrifice to the husband's ancestors. The rite of homage to the parents-in-law carried the same significance. These elaborate ritualistic performances by the new couple inspired in them the feeling that their marriage was only a part of the complex family institution, dramatized for them the importance of the ancestors and the family, dwarfed their own roles as individuals, and demonstrated to them the idea that marriage was a link in the cycle of critical events of the family. The gathering of a large crowd of kinsmen for the ceremony and the feasts also helped to magnify the importance of the family and the kinship group. It is interesting to note here that the bride's family and relatives were not invited to participate in the ceremony and celebration — clearly a means of preventing interference by the bride's family in the exercise of authority over the new daughter-in-law. There was no part of the traditional marriage procedure in which the two families gathered together for any kind of common celebration.

Families that could not afford an elaborate wedding as required by custom commonly resorted to the practice of taking a "child bride." A very young girl, sometimes even an infant, was purchased by a poor family which would raise her along with the young son. When they both reached marriageable age, they were married with a simple ceremony. While the ritualistic function was not outstanding in such a situation, the economic bondage of the couple to the parents was strong, for the parents had not merely raised the son but also the girl. The subordination of the child bride was even greater than that of brides normally married into the family, for she owed directly to the parents-in-law the efforts and expense of bringing her up. Consequently, the parents-in-law's treatment of a child bride was frequently more tyrannical than normally. It is obvious that in such circumstances the son or the wife could not consider their marriage as an affair that they themselves had sponsored or entertain the moral possibility of leaving the parents' household and setting up an independent family unit by themselves.

Taking a child bride as a form of marriage was still common in many rural sections throughout China proper in the early years of Communist rule.[3] While more will be said about this subject later, the following case serves to indicate the current character of this practice. In the immediate vicinity of the county seat of Yi-shi county, Shansi Province, Kao Chuan-wah, was taken as a child bride at the age of twelve. On the day of her betrothal, when the bridal chair was already at her door, she was still playing with other childern on the street, blissfully ignorant of what was taking place. At last, crying and kicking, she was dragged into the bridal chair by her parents and carried away "to suffer inhuman treatment under the cruel hands of the parents-in-law." [4]

Similarly, weird but rare forms of marriage, such as "marrying the spirit" and taking a "daughter-in-law-in-anticipation," which were occasionally practiced in some parts of China, particularly in the South, were products of the same situation. When a woman was betrothed to a man and the man died before the marriage, "marrying the spirit" in full wedding ceremony was sometimes arranged with the consent of the parents of both families, and the bride went through all the ceremonies next to a wooden tablet with the dead man's name and dates of birth and death written on it. Taking a "daughter-in-law-in-anticipation" was a practice in which a couple, having no son as yet, took in a bride in anticipation of the birth of a son. When the right of divorce was emphatically asserted by the Communist Marriage Law in 1950, a twenty-eight-year-old woman in Hupeh Province brought her eight-year-old husband in her arms to the court for a divorce. She had been a "daughter-in-law-in-anticipation." [5] While the economic factor played a part in these practices, they were primarily a product of an institution which considered marriage an affair of the family and dictated by the parents for the purpose of perpetuating and operating the traditional family organization. They illustrate the extreme to which marriage could be carried, even without a male spouse in actual existence, all for the purpose of completing this link in the cycle of events in the family in order that the organization of the family could at least symbolically approach the traditional ideal form.

Another factor contributing to the consolidation of the family organization and assertion of parental authority was the traditional practice of marrying the son as young as possible if the parents' economic means allowed. It was considered glorious to have grandchildren at an early age; and there is the folk tale of a well-known man who, at the age of thirty-six, was displaying his grandchild with pride. There is no systematic quantitative data to show how far this ideal was realized in the traditional society. As a general urban practice some three decades ago, it was common for sons to be married between sixteen and eighteen; for a daughter, marriage at nineteen was considered rather late. This practice is still current in rural districts today, as substantiated by sample population studies in rural areas. For instance, in the rural district of Cheng Kung in Yunnan Province, during the period 1940–1944, the age of first marriage for males was concentrated in the range of sixteen to twenty-one with the median at nineteen; for females the range was between fifteen and twenty, with the median at seventeen.[6]

A young boy of sixteen to eighteen was obviously unable to afford the expenditure of a traditional marriage and the support of a new family, especially in the traditional society in which employment opportunity outside of the family was limited and the struggle for existence was hard. Hence, the younger a son was married, the more dominant was the role of the parents in the marriage and in his married life. The daughter-in-law was subjected to the same influence owing to the dependency of the husband. In addition, marriage at an early age made it easier for her to conform to subordination to the mother-in-law than if she were married at a later, less pliable age.

To strengthen the effectiveness of these institutional devices and practices and to guard against their possible failure in meeting individual situations, the supernatural influence of religion was invoked to play a part in the traditional institution of marriage. After the go-between had brought two prospective partners together, the parents of both families would take the next step of consulting the oracles to see if the dates of birth of the boy and the girl were in harmony or in conflict with each other. Should they harmonize, the marriage had the approval of the spiritual world, and it was fate that had brought the two matrimonial partners together. The god in the moon had tied their legs together with a red ribbon, as the folk tale goes. The lengthy and elaborate wedding ceremony was permeated with religious acts of paying homage and sacrifice to the ancestors and the gods, all to impress the young couple with the irresistibility of fate and the sanction of institutional ideals and practices by the spiritual powers. After this, if the individuals still found the married state unsatisfactory, they would be advised to submit to fate, which would punish them for their individual failures.

Traditional marriage made possible the expansion of the conjugal family into the patriarchal "big family" to include married brothers and their wives who were organizationally integrated under the dominant role of the parents. At the death of the parents, if the big family was not to break up but to continue, as frequently was the case, the eldest son acted as the head of the family after the parents had set up the organization and laid down the pattern. Obviously, should marriage be considered primarily an affair of the young couple, initiated by themselves in the Western style of romantic love, it would be difficult to organize the married brothers and their wives into a tightly knit and delicately balanced unit. Without the dominant and coordinating role of the parents as expressed in the traditional marriage and in other ways, it would be difficult to settle the numerous family disputes between brothers and between their wives who occupied relatively equal status.

The system of arranged marriage and all of its institutional devices helped to assure the parents of the continued discharge of filial duties by their children after marriage. The preservation of the parents' dominant role after the children's marriage also strengthened the age and generational structuring of the family membership, for control over an individual by age and generational factors tended to weaken as he grew older, and marriage was a distinct mark and reminder of the advancement of age. Similarly strengthened by the institution of arranged marriage was intra-class selection of mates. When a marriage was arranged by the parents, the choice of a mate was less influenced by emotion and more by conventional considerations such as expressed by the proverbial admonition of "matching a bamboo door with a bamboo door, and a wooden door with a wooden door." * Organizationally, intra-class marriage tended to facilitate the assimilation of the daughter-in-law by the new family due to the greater similarity of ways of life between the two families. In short, the ramifying influences of the system of arranged marriage made it an inseparable part of the traditional family organization.

Weakening of Arranged Marriage under the Republic

Institutional devices succeeded in severing the connection between romantic love and formal marriage but not in completely suppressing the emotional appeal of romantic love, which cropped up in concubinage and such forms of extramarital relations as prostitution, and burst out in lamenting poetry and fiction. The strong desire for romance by the young constantly posed a serious potential threat to arranged marriage and frequently acted as a disruptive influence to the traditional family by behavior such as squandering money on other women at the expense of family necessities or taking in a nonconforming prostitute as a concubine. For the woman, since arranged marriage required her to enter abruptly into intimate relations with a man with whom she had had no previous contact, the secret desire for marriage through love had a strong appeal. Thus, a structural strain in the traditional family provided the wedge for the entry of a new and highly disruptive influence.

* The word "door" in the Chinese context carries the meaning of the prestige and status of a family.

When the cry for freedom of marriage through love was raised with the swelling tide of revolution soon after the turn of the century, the effect on the educated young was infectious, and acceptance of the new idea was ready and eager. While the revolution of 1911 was mainly a political event, it nevertheless signified the general call for a new order of life, leading many young men and women to hope for marriage through love and to make attempts which often resulted in tragedy. In 1912 a woman teacher in a Shanghai primary school openly made friends with a male colleague, fell in love with him, and the two secretly decided to be married. When the affair became known to others there was gossip accusing the two of promiscuity. The woman was especially attacked as one of immoral character. Under the crushing attack of public opinion and stern warnings from parents of both parties, the man weakened and told the woman he could not marry her. She now found society turned against her, and after leaving the man a heart-rending letter, she committed suicide. In some cases both the man and the woman were driven to suicide by group pressure in the form of social ostracism and public gossip.[7]

Although the stone wall of traditional mores stood firm in the first two decades of the present century, the movement for freedom of marriage continued to spread, mainly among the modern intelligentsia. The forceful impact of each subsequent revolutionary wave, such as the May 4th Movement of 1919 and the Second Revolution in the mid-1920's, gave the movement added impetus, and it became increasingly difficult for parents and social institutions to enforce the concept that marriage was primarily not a couple's own business but the business of the family and the parents. Other social and economic changes, wars, and political disturbances, resulting in identification of the individual with new group interests and in physical separation of family members, converged to loosen parental control over the young and increased the difficulty of retaining the arranged marriage system.

When the Nationalist government was established in Nanking in 1927, large numbers of modern young intellectuals came to occupy responsible positions in it, bringing with them the concepts of the family institution developed in the family revolution during the previous three decades. The consequence was the promulgation of a new kinship law which permitted marriage by free choice of partners conditioned upon parental approval. While this Nationalist law did not prohibit marriage by compulsory parental arrangement, it nonetheless provided for the first time legal recognition of marriage which realized the importance of the young couple's own interest. A major limitation of this legal act was the lack of active enforcement among the common people, who largely remained ignorant of its existence.

The years toward the mid-century found most parents of the urban intelligentsia facing the formerly bitterly contested issue with a spirit of resignation. The movement spread rather slowly to other segments of the population not benefited by modern education, the workers and the peasants, and the conflict between the generations over the form of marriage continued on a steadily increasing scale. When the Communists took over the country in 1949, the great change lay not in the introduction of a totally new concept of marriage but in steadily extending the new marriage movement to the workers and peasants whose family life so far had remained little touched by the new ideal.

Freedom of Marriage under the Communist Regime

The struggle for freedom of marriage based on love has always been stressed by the Communist movement, and this freedom had been written into laws and regulations on marriage in the "red areas" for two decades previous to Communist accession to national power in 1949.[8] The new Marriage Law, promulgated in May 1950, was one of the first major laws ensuing from the new regime. This law abolishes the "arbitrary and compulsory" form of marriage and establishes the "New Democratic" form of marriage.[9] Interference of parents in their children's marriage is ruled illegal.[10] The practice of paying a price for the bride, whether in the form of money or goods or articles, whether under the name of "body price" or "ritual gift of wealth," is prohibited.[11] To get married, the couple have only to register in person with the local government, and the marriage becomes legal if it is found to be in conformity with the provisions of the marriage law. Should the marriage be found contrary to the legal provisions, it is given no legal recognition.[12] Such legal provisions consist of the "complete willingness of the two parties"[13] and the prohibition of the following: the use of compulsion or the interference by third parties including parents,[14] the committing of polygamy by taking concubines or other polygamous behavior, child brides, interference with the remarriage of widows, the exaction of money or gifts,[15] violation of minimum age requirements for marriage,[16] and marriage between close kin, by the sexually impotent, or by those afflicted with loathsome diseases.[17] There is no requirement such as the ceremonial celebrations provided in the traditional marriage and in the marriage law of the Nationalist government.

The basic points of the Marriage Law had been developed in the family revolution in the pre-Communist period, and many of them, such as the prohibition of concubinage and other forms of polygamy, are found in the Nationalist marriage law. Instead of breaking any new ground, the Communist marriage law represents the continued advancement of the family revolution in two major respects, the extension of the new marriage concept to a larger proportion of the population and the use of political power to achieve institutionalization of the new marriage system. It is obvious that the form of marriage defined by the new law is unacceptable to the traditional mind. In the urban upper and upper-middle classes, from which the intelligentsia mostly stem, the long process of family revolution has broken down much of the resistance of the older generation, but resistance to the new form of marriage remains strong among the working class and the peasantry, where the voice for freedom of marriage has not been widely raised. It is in the latter segment of the population that the greatest change is being brought about by Communist propaganda, indoctrination, and enforcement of the new Marriage Law (see Chapter XII on propaganda). Political power, with many forms of social and economic pressure at its command, is thrown directly into the conflict on the side of the new marriage system against the old one. The development of the new family institution, hitherto mainly part of a spontaneous process of social change, is now being aided by the leverage of political power and law.

One means of using political and legal power to gain popular acceptance of the new form of marriage, especially among the multitudes of workers and peasants, is the new legal requirement of the registration of all new marriages. Couples intending to get married come before the Communist official in charge of marriage registration for the locality. He asks the couple whether the intended marriage is taking place with the consent of both parties, whether duress from any third party has been exerted, whether polygamy or concubinage is involved. If the answers agree with the legal provisions, and if the results of an investigation check with the answers, a marriage certificate is issued and the couple is legally married. In the cities, medical examination is required in addition to the above procedure.[18]

Although marriage registration is stipulated in the Marriage Law as promulgated in 1950, the Communist government issued a supplementary Rules for Marriage Registration in 1955 [19] to insure universal enforcement. This legal document introduces two new features. The first is the addition of marriage registration as one of the functions of the large number of lower-level government agencies such as the neighborhood offices in the cities and the People's Committees of village districts and towns in the rural areas, thus vastly increasing the accessibility of the registration facilities to the common people. Secondly, the registering officials are required to explain to the registrants the stipulations of the marriage law so as to acquaint them with their own legal rights and obligations before proceeding with interrogations and examination of the case for approval or disapproval of the registration. The measure has the merit of informing the common people of the contents of the new law as a vital step in its effective enforcement, which is in contrast to the conditions under the Nationalist government, when the majority of the population were ignorant of the existence of a new marriage law.

There is no systematic quantitative data on the extent of the success of these means in establishing the new form of marriage. Fragmentary figures in reports from various parts of the country show that a beginning of the new system is being made in rural communities which had not been generally influenced by the family revolution in the pre-Communist period. In 178 villages of Huailai county of Chahar Province, in the period of ten months following the promulgation of the Marriage Law on May 1, 1950, there were altogether some 400 marriages, of which some 300 were based on the free will of the contracted parties "plus the agreement of the parents on both sides." [20] In other words, about 75 per cent of all the marriages in the stated period followed the new form, although the expression of agreement of the parents on such marriages shows that some influence of the old tradition still exists among these new marriages. Again, in two rural subdistricts of Hailien county of Shantung Province, in an unspecified period of 1951, there were 290 traditional "selling-and-buying" marriages as against 227 marriages based on the free choice of partners and love.[21] There are fragmentary figures which do not provide any comparison with the number of traditional marriages in the same locality in the same period. Thus, it is stated that in the rural county of Yaoyang in Hopei Province 120 couples were married according to the provisions of the new law.[22] In the rural town of Pochen of Shantung Province, within the period of a year following the promulgation of the Marriage Law, 488 young men and women married of their own free will and for love, and many of them won parental consent only after a "bitter struggle." [23] All these localities are a part of North China. Statistics on other regions are available only in a few instances. A report covering seven counties in Chiahsing Special District of

Chekiang Province, four counties of the Hsuanch'eng Special District in the southern part of Anhwei Province, and Jukao county in the northern part of Kiangsu, a total of twelve counties, shows that "34 per cent of all women who were married [time unspecified] did so of their free will." [24] Such is the reported picture of the East China Region. In the Central-South Region "according to incomplete statistics, during the period from January to April, 1951, 23,600 new couples registered their marriage with the government." [25]

There are questions of accuracy and comparability regarding the above figures, particularly the percentages in the twelve rural counties of the East China Region. Nevertheless, they indicate that the idea of the new form of marriage is being widely disseminated among the conservative rural population. The new marriages in the hitherto isolated countryside, although few in number, are becoming fermenting agents, causing local youth to react against the repressive traditional family and to challenge its authority.

In terms of individual situations, these statistical figures represent an increasing number of cases of struggle by young peasants and workers for the freedom of marriage. Typical among the peasants is the case of Li Ta-kuei, a peasant girl in Hsiawan village of Luchiang county, Anhwei Province. She was betrothed to a maternal cousin against her wish. The engagement was so unpleasant to her that she once attempted suicide as a means of forcing its cancellation. When the propaganda corps of the Marriage Law came to the village to explain the new legal stipulations on marriage, she became emboldened. After some struggle with the family, she went to the subdistrict government and obtained a legal cancellation of the betrothal. Finally she married a young peasant with whom she had fallen in love.[26]

Among the urban workers the enforcement of the new Marriage Law yields similar cases of struggle between the young and the older generation. Typical is the experience of Yen Ts'ai-nü, a nineteen-year-old girl who worked in a Shanghai cotton mill. Her father and grandmother, in accordance with the old custom, betrothed her to a worker in a grocery store. Her first knowledge of the betrothal came when relatives arrived for the ceremonial feast. She was very angry and demanded that the betrothal be nullified. Her father and grandmother beat her for protesting. When she could not stand the mistreatment any longer, she went to the family of her deceased mother for support and appealed to the Association of Family Women (an affiliated organization of the Democratic Women's League) requesting assistance in the cancellation of the betrothal. The father and grandmother heard of this and rushed to the maternal relatives to raise trouble. The ensuing quarrel stirred up the whole neighborhood, and the case was taken to the people's court. The court ruled that the betrothal should be canceled.[27]

There are, however, less tortuous circumstances by which new marriage has come to the workers. Tai Yu-lan (woman) and Chao Ch'uan-yung were both workers in Cotton Mill Number 1 in Tientsin. They had been in love with each other for some time, but owing to the traditional stigma placed upon free choice of partners and love, had not dared talk about getting married. After they learned of the new Marriage Law in May 1950, they became engaged, and in March of 1951 they were married by the legal formality of registering with the local government.[28]

The preceding cases illustrate the re-enactment of social conflicts centering upon the marriage problem, a familiar scene among the modern urban intellectuals in the pre-Communist period, now being extended to the peasants and workers. But such cases may not represent a universal picture of the marriages reported as being in conformity with the new law. Thus, in the 178 villages in Chahar Province all the 300 new marriages were reported to be based on the free will of the partners as well as the consent of their parents, but it is hard to judge the relative weight between free will and parental consent. The latter in some instances might mean actual parental arrangement and verbal profession of free will by the boy and girl before the local official, an act of formality under previous instruction from the parents. On the other hand, there were many instances even in the pre-Communist period when a couple were married on the basis of love but, after going through the new simple form of marriage, again went through the full ceremony of the traditional marriage in order to appease the family and to gain institutional recognition from the local community.

At least, it is an established fact that the idea of the new form of marriage is being spread by propaganda and other means among the workers and peasants, and that those who wish to fight for the new privilege have the help of the law in places where local officials are sufficiently indoctrinated in the Marriage Law and are willing to enforce it. In such places members of the older generation no longer possess the coercive power that they held in the pre-Communist period in maintaining the traditional institution of marriage. The increasing accessibility of legal assistance to the people, as suggested from the fragmentary figures, points to the accelerating trend of the new form of marriage and to the rapid undermining of the authority and solidarity of the traditional family institution.

Resistance by Tradition against the New Marriage Ideas

A recurrent problem in an age of revolution is the relative effectiveness of law as a means of uprooting old institutions which have passed their days of usefulness. A new law imposed by a progressive minority upon a conservative public naturally meets popular opposition motivated by the still strong values and structure of the traditional institutions; and the conservative force of the opposing majority slows down the operation of a new law despite the vigor and absolutism of a fresh revolutionary political power. This problem is particularly pertinent to a country like China where the maintenance of the traditional social order has relied much more heavily on the operation of social institutions than on the functioning of formal government and law.

Thus there has been opposition to the new Marriage Law among local Communist officials, even though enforcement of the new law is a part of their functions. Indications point to the possibility that a large number of them neither understand nor accept the new legal principles of marriage. In October of 1951, almost a year and a half after the promulgation of the new Marriage Law, the Department of Interior of the Communist central government stated in a directive urging local political leaders to study the law carefully: "A very common phenomenon is . . . the adopting of antagonistic attitudes toward the Marriage Law by some subdistrict and village cadres . . . . Some even use imprisonment and torturing to handle marriage cases [in an effort to enforce the traditional institution]." [29] Similar directives and statements have been issued by other official and semi-official organizations.

It is significant that resistance against the new Marriage Law by the cadres is a reflection of the popular attitude among the local population. The requirement of marriage registration is strange to the common people whose social life, especially marriage, has been regulated hitherto mainly by tradition rather than by law. Traditionally, government and law enter into the picture only on the occasion of a grave violation of institutional practices. Even in the modernized city of Shanghai, where the people are more legal-minded than in the countryside, when a factory girl who was to be married was advised by a woman member of the labor union, "Don't forget to register with the government," two other women workers standing on the side asked, "Even marriage has to be registered?" Some other workers chimed in: "From ancient times to the present day, whoever has heard of having to register a marriage with the government, and what is the new fashion for?" [30] This attitude is especially common among many local officials in rural areas. The Preparatory Committee of the Democratic Women's League of the Central-South Region stated in October 1951: "Some cadres consider that the marriage problem is a private matter which the government and the court should not interfere with." [31]

If the requirement of marriage registration astonished the people, freedom of marriage and the new principle of marriage by love raised roars of objection. People charged that marriage by free choice of partners was to make marriage "a loose affair." Others said that "this will make a mess of the relationship between men and women." Still others were certain that "freedom of marriage will lead the world into general promiscuity." [32] The relaxation of the sex mores and the consequent fear of a general moral degeneration have been familiar charges from the opposition in family-reform movements in other lands in modern times, and its recurrence in China is but a part of a typical picture long known to students of sociology of the family.

Like registration, the practice of free choice in marriage met opposition not only from the common people but also from an appreciable proportion of party leaders and local government officials. In Shiht'ang village of the third subdistrict, Yungch'un county of Kwangsi Province, during the period from May 30 to June 6, 1951, the village head ordered the militia to arrest and cruelly torture ten women, forced them to parade in the streets, and made them the object of "struggle" in mass "struggle meetings." The charge was that these women manifested bad behavior. The case was later discovered by the people's court, and the village head was sentenced to four months' imprisonment,[33] for the women's "bad behavior" was their attempt to make love to men or to marry for love. Similarly, in P'uk'ou village of Chinhua county, Chekiang Province, when a peasant girl fell in love with the secretary of the village Youth Corps, soldiers and some of the members of the Youth Corps raised a "struggle" against the couple, accusing them of promiscuity because they had been seen once together in the same room. A "public trial" was held, and the two were told to confess to having been promiscuous.[34] In a suburban village of Hankow, when a young peasant couple fell in love, they were immediately made the object of "struggle" by the village women's association, in which the local militia and the village leaders participated. Deeply shamed, the woman unsuccessfully attempted suicide by hanging. Later, when the "corps of examination of the enforcement of the Marriage Law" arrived in the village, help was given the couple, enabling them to be legally married according to the new law.[35] In a village near the town of Shaohsing in Chekiang Province a village schoolteacher, Ch'ang Jui-p'eng, a member of the Youth Corps, fell in love with a "progressive" girl who was also a member of the Corps. When they became engaged and asked for consent from parents on both sides, they met objection from both families and from the villagers. Even the Youth Corps called a membership meeting to launch a "struggle" against them, saying that "our Corps is morally pure, but the relationship of these two is not pure." A decision was made to dismiss the two from Corps membership. Group pressure closed in on them. The man attempted suicide but failed. The girl became mentally ill. Later, the case was brought to the attention of the people's court, which straightened out their trouble, and they were married.[36]

These cases cited from official Communist reports, which show the new political leaders acting together with the local population in a common attempt to protect the traditional institution of marriage against the new principle of marriage based on free choice of partners and romantic love, indicate clearly the limitation of the power of law alone as a means of changing an age-old social institution. The high Communist leadership appears to be aware of this. Hsieh Chueh-tsai, Minister of the Department of Interior, has stated:

> The Marriage Law, once promulgated . . . cannot be expected to see unobstructed enforcement. China is a very ancient society, with many remnants of bad customs of feudalism . . . still existing strongly in not a few places. Therefore, the enforcement of the Marriage Law should not be regarded as a matter for the government alone, but should be a common object of study and propaganda for the cadres and the people before it can be thoroughly realized as a correct legal standard in the problem of marriage.[37]

Pursuing this theme, the Communist authorities emphasize "study" (indoctrination) of the new Marriage Law, especially for local leaders, and the acceleration of propaganda campaigns by both government agencies and public organizations such as the youth and women's organizations.

It is claimed that an intensive indoctrination campaign in 1953 yielded some 3,500,000 lower-echelon leaders trained in the understanding and interpretation of the new Marriage Law. They were distributed over 1,118 counties and 111 cities throughout the country to directly administer the new law among the people.[38] In view of the widespread ignorance of the new law among local Communist officials, many of whom were recruited from the hardly literate peasantry when the Communists came into power, such training of the local leaders was a logical first step in any attempt to effectively enforce the new marriage principles. In some localities, indoctrination and propaganda campaigns have produced to a certain degree a change of attitude among the leaders and people (see Chapter XII).

The New Marriage Law and the Traditional Family Organization

Granting a measure of success in the dissemination of the new marriage concept through indoctrination and propaganda, the introduction and stabilization of the new family institution still depends not only on the enforcement of the new law but also on a number of socio-economic factors that affect the functions and structure of the family.

Marriage now becomes an affair of the marrying couples themselves, intended for their own common life,[39] and no longer an affair intended for the perpetuation of the ancestral lineage. The prohibition of polygamy, even to assure the birth of a son, and the new right of a wife to have custody of her children in a divorce show that begetting male descendants is no longer a guiding principle of marriage, a change by which the sacred character of the traditional family is seriously undermined. The strong traditional bond between parents and the married son is obviously weakened under the new arrangement since free choice of a partner greatly reduces the parents' role in their children's marital affairs, a change with grave consequences for the traditional family which relied upon parental authority over the children's marriage as a leading integrating factor. The economic aspect of the parents' role is likewise affected. Parents continue to contribute to the marriage expenses of the children, particularly sons, but these expenses tend to decline; and there is a consequent decline in the importance of parental economic control over the children's marriage and the children's moral obligation to the parents.

One part of the traditional marriage expenditure, the often ruinously heavy purchase price of the bride, is now forbidden by law and is no longer in practice where marriage is conducted in the modern form. As will be seen later, the husband's attempt to recover the purchase price of the bride, if she should subsequently insist upon a divorce, is rejected by the people's court on the ground that paying a price for a bride is neither legal nor in harmony with the moral standard of the "new democracy."[40] Should this verdict be universally held, as the result of the accelerating indoctrination of the judicial workers to the new standard, even traditionally minded ones will hesitate to pay a heavy price for a bride, particularly in view of the idea of freedom of divorce now being introduced by the new ideology and guaranteed by the new law. No doubt, gifts may still be exchanged by the two families involved, but such gifts do not approach the amount of the traditional bridal price.

In the new marriages the girl's family now receives prepared food and some chickens or ducks, or even some grain, but these are given freely and not as the result of any bargaining. Frequently the girl's family receives nothing at all (see Chapter VI on the status of women). This particularly affects the traditional relation between the mother-in-law and daughter-in-law, for now the stigma of the latter's bondage and subordination, as symbolized by the traditional bridal price, is removed.

Another taxing burden in the traditional marriage expenditure, the ceremonial expenses which included the heavy item for feasts, is now also sharply reduced. The simplification of marriage ceremonies has been a pre-Communist trend since the early 1920's, culminating in the "group ceremony of marriage" in the 1930's developed under the Nationalist regime for the purpose of saving marriage expenses. Such group ceremonies involved scores or even a hundred couples at a time, and a local government official such as the head of the municipal bureau of social welfare or the mayor of a city officiated. More popular in the pre-Communist period than the "group ceremony" was the "civilized marriage ceremony" patterned closely after the Western style, with the presence of the parents of both families, a "witness," and a circle of relatives and friends. In either case, the ceremony was less elaborate and expensive than the traditional type. Under Communist rule, sumptuous weddings are not only condemned by the new ideology, which emphasizes utilitarian practicality, but are also discouraged by the general fear that any conspicuous display of wealth such as elaborate ceremonies and feasts is dangerous. Thus the pre-Communist trend toward ceremonial simplification has been accelerated by political pressure; and in practice most modern marriages under the Communists have been consummated by registering with the government followed by a simple "tea party" of light refreshments instead of the former lavish feasts, and attended only by a small group of close relatives and friends. Young couples now insist upon this type of wedding as a part of the fashion of the times, however much it may be against the parents' sense of values.

The simplified wedding ceremony has two implications for the traditional family. First, it reduces the expense of marriage and thus decreases the importance of the parents' role in the marriage of their children. Second, the attendance at such weddings by only a few close relatives instead of by the large extended family circle or clan mitigates the importance and the social pressure of the general kinship system on the matrimonial affairs of the young. Hence, the simplification of the wedding ceremony has the effect of dramatizing the role of the marrying couple and dwarfs the importance of both the parents and the kinship system since it focuses public attention on the marrying individuals and not on the kinship group.

The new ceremony differs from the old in still other aspects. While the bride and groom often put on special wedding clothes, such garments do not compare with the heavy elaborateness of the traditional costumes. In addition, others attending the occasion are no longer decked in gorgeous ceremonial clothing as in the traditional form. These changes make the wedding appear more secular than the deeply impressive affair of the family as emphasized by the elaborately costumed circle of relatives who attend the ceremony. Above all, the various religious acts such as offering sacrifices and bowing to the ancestors are now expunged from the ceremonies in a large number of the new marriages upon the insistence of the young couples. This secularization of the new marriages reduces the sacred character of both the family and the marriage and consequently weakens the dominance of the parents and the family over the married son and the daughter-in-law, a dominance which was strengthened by sacred sentiment in the traditional ceremonies. Most couples who are married under the new system no longer perform such religious acts as consulting oracles on the compatibility of the fates of the two persons intending to get married and ignore the tale about the god in the moon who predetermines matrimonial partnership, even though such superstitions may still persist among the uneducated common people.

Change in the marriage age is another important feature of the new marriage situation. Among the upper and middle classes for some three decades there has been a tendency toward later marriage. Previously for the man, the breadwinner of the family, marriage was common before the age of twenty; now the general practice is marriage after the age of twenty. It is very common now for a girl to be married between the ages of eighteen and the early twenties, whereas previously marriage after eighteen was considered late and it was difficult to find a suitable man for a girl over twenty. Among workers and peasants the man's marriage age has generally been two or three years later than for the upper and middle classes, and dislocation of the traditional economy in the past half century has had the effect of postponing it even later. The Communist Marriage Law now sets the minimum legal age of marriage as twenty for men and eighteen for women, instead of eighteen for men and sixteen for women as provided in the Nationalist law.

The effect of later marriage on the relation of the married son and daughter-in-law to the parents and the family can be plainly seen. The man is usually economically more independent after the age of twenty. He can better afford not only the expenses of marriage, now much lighter than before, but the support of a new family as well — or, if he works on the parents' farm or in their shop, he can at least make a greater contribution toward the support of the new family. His greater economic value significantly reduces the importance of the role of the parents and the family in marriage and consequently undermines the authority of the latter over his married life. An older daughter-in-law is also a less malleable person to be molded into her traditional position in a complex family situation. Her husband's greater economic value at marriage strengthens her attitude of independence toward the parents-in-law and other members of the family. Above all, an independent income brought in by the daughter-in-law in a rapidly collectivizing economy elevates her family status (see Chapter VIII). All these have serious effects on the role structure of the traditional family.

If marriage as arranged by parents is a significant factor in maintaining intra-class marriage, free choice of partners contributes somewhat to the weakening of class demarcation in matrimonial affairs. Present facts show no sign of inter-class marriage becoming a general phenomenon even among the ideologically progressive young men and women. Class factors still have a strong influence on the choice of mates. But when the class distance between a couple is not too great, the traditional barrier against their marriage seems to break down in the case of modern marriages.

The inter-class marriage of Lin Yi-k'ai, daughter of a small landowner in Shunteh county, Kwangtung Province, to Lo Jen-ch'eng, her father's farmhand, is an illustration. The two fell in love after Lo had been working on Lin's farm for three years. In 1951 the girl summoned enough courage to ask her parents for permission to marry Lo. The father was horrified; he thought the boy, only a farmhand, too poor and that the marriage would be one of "inviting the husband into the wife's house," a humiliation to the family of Lin. Clansmen in the village also raised objections to the marriage as a violation of the clan's tradition. The girl eloped with Lo to his village, intending to be married there. The peasants' association and women's association of the girl's village learned about the case, and representative members of the two organizations visited the girl's father to carry out a "struggle by reasoning," demanding that the couple be permitted to return to the village and be married. The old man became remorseful, for he was too old to farm and could not afford to lose these two young laborers from the family, and he acceded to the demand. The subdistrict government was quick to capitalize on the propaganda value of the event by turning the wedding into a public affair for the whole village, attended by four hundred people.[41]

Marriages of an upper-class son and a poorer middle-class girl or vice versa have been common among the intelligentsia in recent decades, but among the peasantry similar cases were rare until the Communists took power and promulgated the Marriage Law. The entrance of a daughter-in-law into the family from another class status adds obstacles to the assimilation of the new member and makes it harder to maintain the complex and delicate family organization of the traditional form. In a broader perspective, the situation accelerates the reshuffling of the population into a new class alignment under Communist rule.

When a couple initiate and control their own marriage, there is, of course, no longer ground for the continuation of abnormal forms of traditional marriage such as the taking of a child bride, "marrying the spirit," or taking a "daughter-in-law-in-anticipation." The new Marriage Law [42] and the interpretation given it by Communist judicial authorities [43] vehemently attack the practice of taking child brides because of its widespread existence and the acute suffering of the little girls.

It can be readily seen that the many changes of the marriage institution from traditional principles and practices to the new form affect the role of the parents in relation to the married son and the daughter-in-law so seriously that it has become difficult for the family organization to continue to operate as formerly. The shift of the center of marriage control from the parents to the young couple, the change in marriage procedures, together with other new social and economic factors, necessitate a new balance of roles involving the relation of the parents to their married sons and daughters-in-law and the relation between the wife and husband. The setting up by the married son of an independent household, thus ending the expansibility of a small family into a big one, a basic feature of the traditional family system, occurs increasingly as families come under the new influence.

While the new form of marriage based on free choice of partners has an obviously disintegrating effect on the structure of the traditional family, it is not yet clear what new form of family will emerge. In the urban centers, where the socio-economic functions of the family are being drastically reduced by the emerging socialistic economy, there is a strong tendency toward the development of a conjugal family of the Western type. But even here, whether the aging parents will become members of a married son's family is still a serious problem prior to the development of an effective collective program to meet the social and economic needs of the aged. In the rural communities, where kinship relations have always been a supreme social factor, the development of a conjugal, two-generation family to replace the old institution meets even more problems than in the urban areas. During 1949–1958, neither the land reform nor the subsequent collectivization movement produced any effective socio-economic pattern capable of systematically replacing the economic structure of the traditional family. J

Associated Problems of Marriage

THE PREVIOUS chapter analyzed arranged marriage as a structural factor in the traditional family and the rise of marriage by free choice of partners as an influence destructive to the old kinship system but also conducive to the development of a new one. Associated with the traditional form of marriage are several secondary problems concerning the stability of the family, namely, the remarriage of widows, the practice of polygamy, and the related issue of prostitution. The traditional restrictions against the remarriage of widows was an important device in enforcing the solidarity of the family group; the institutional recognition of polygamy was partly a means to insure the continuity of the family organization; and polygamy together with the tacit approval of prostitution had the function of mitigating men's tension under arranged marriage and retaining their loyalty toward the old family institution. Thus, recent institutional alterations regarding the remarriage of widows, polygamy, and prostitution have obvious effects on the ability of the family to continue functioning in the traditional form and on the trend toward a different kinship system.

Remarriage of Widows under the Traditional System

We have noted that the traditional form of marriage was characterized by its rigid subordination of the marrying individuals to the consideration of the husband's family headed by his parents. The question arises as to how such a marriage, reinforced by the religious idea of fate, dealt with a serious situation such as the death of a spouse, which affects both the continuation of the family organization and the status and welfare of the surviving spouse as an individual.

If the wife died, there was little institutional problem involved. Tradition allowed the widowed husband to take another wife or a concubine, whichever he desired. The membership vacancy in the family was thus filled, the weakened organization was restrengthened, and the process of family assimilation of the new member began all over again. In localities for which statistical information on this point is available widowed men were from 7 per cent to 10 per cent of all married men.[1] Their failure to remarry was usually due to poverty or old age and not institutional restriction. An outstanding institutional problem involved in the remarriage of widowed men was the frequent mistreatment of the deceased wife's children by the new wife or concubine, which was a disruptive factor to the family organization. Under the traditional system the paternal grandparents attempted to prevent such mistreatment, but, if the grandparents died while the children of the deceased wife were still very young, the only protective force for the unfortunate children except their father would be close relatives sensitive to such situations in an intimately integrated kinship system. In fact, a devoted father who had serious concern for his children's welfare often refrained from remarriage.

But it was entirely different for the widowed woman. Institutional restriction against the remarriage of widows is strongly reflected in fragmentary statistical sources which show a high ratio of widows among married women. Sample census figures of nine counties in Szechwan Province of Southwest China in 1947 show a ratio of one widow to every 3.15 married women.[2] Sample studies of nine localities in northern, eastern, and southwestern regions show a range of one widow for every 3.02 to 4.15 married women fifteen years of age and over.[3] Compared with one widow for every 5.55 married women of fifteen years of age and over in the United States,[4] these ratios of widows in China are much higher. Only in India, where there is one widow to every 3.14 married women, can the situation in China find a counterpart.[5]

The general traditional situation was that a widow seldom remarried as long as the husband's family could support her. A certain number of widows in poor families did remarry on account of economic pressure, in which case the husband's family usually exacted a price as a condition of her remarriage. The higher frequency of the remarriage of widows among the poor indicates a weaker family organization in the lower than in the middle and upper classes; but even among poor families it was common to find that after the death of the husband the widow became the only adult in the family with income-earning capacity, the parents-in-law, if living, being too old to work. In such cases the widow frequently remained in the family in order to support the parents-in-law as well as her own children.

The institutional interpretation of the restriction against the re-marriage of widows is fairly obvious. The mores of chastity required a woman to be married to only one man to the end of her life. The strength and universality of this custom are expressed in the ubiquitous stone memorial arches that stud the landscape of China in memory of chaste widows. Since the traditional marriage cemented a wife not only to her husband but also to the husband's parents and family, morally the death of the husband did not dissolve the bond of marriage or change the widow's status and obligations as a daughter-in-law. The function of these mores was plainly to preserve the integrity and solidarity of the family by preventing the widow from leaving it, regardless of her personal interest or sacrifice.

Besides the moral assumption of a lifetime bond, a widow who wanted to remarry faced many other institutional obstacles. The husband's family had invested heavily in the marriage through the price for her person. Hence the family's claim to the right of preventing her remarriage and the right to exact a price in case permission for remarriage was granted.

The children posed a difficult problem. Even if the husband's family granted the widow remarriage, she was not permitted to take the children, particularly her sons, who belonged to the family, not to her. The children were liable to be mistreated after her departure, and their rightful share of the family property was frequently encroached upon by predatory relatives, especially if the children were too young to defend their own rights. In some cases, such as the death of the paternal grandparents, or if the widow should be living in a city or at some distance from the deceased husband's family where his parents could not exercise effective control over her, the widow might be able to take her children into a new marriage. But even in such cases the general discrimination and mistreatment of them by her new husband and his family still posed a thorny problem. Even the local community discriminated against children brought along by a remarried widow, and the new husband's clan would not take them into clan membership, a serious matter in rural communities, especially in the southern part of the country where the influence of the clan is strong.

There were still other considerations which helped to discourage the remarriage of widows. If she left a family to remarry, she was not permitted to take any family property except her own belongings of jewelry and clothing, and at times not even these, owing to the traditional concept of communal ownership of property. Her chance of finding a husband with a comfortable livelihood was generally poor.

Because of social discrimination against marrying a widow ("taking a second-hand article") motivated partly by the value of chastity, a man earning a comfortable livelihood would prefer to marry a virgin. Merry widows were few in traditional China, and those few seldom enjoyed any merry ending.

The operation of institutional restrictions against the remarriage of widows can be seen in local situations in various parts of the country, especially in connection with clan regulations. The Preparatory Committee of the Honan Provincial Women's Association under the Communist regime reported in 1949 that in the northern part of Honan, the current rule of the clans was that a widow could not remarry. Should she remarry against the objection of the family, the whole clan had the right to interfere, even the right to kill her. If she should persist, the family of the widow's own parents and the family of the deceased husband had the right to sell her to another man as wife. The following incident in 1949 in Honan Province is testimony to the effectiveness of this rule:

> A woman whose family name was Ch'en was married to a man named Hsu. The husband died eight years after the marriage, and both the woman's and the husband's families did not permit her to remarry. In 1949 the widow took the matter into her own hands and married the head of a neighboring village. Two months after this, the woman's uncle, a local bully, and her own brother, ordered her to hang herself. She begged for mercy from her own brother, saying, "Brother, I have worked for you for years, won't you have mercy on me as my brother?" and she turned to her uncle saying, "Uncle, won't you do some talking for me?" Both turned a deaf ear to her pleas. She then requested to see her children and to put on her good clothes before dying, but this was also denied. She adamantly refused to hang herself; so her own brother strangled her to death, then hung her body up below the roof.[6]

At times a local bully might sell a widow without the knowledge of the widow or her families. The buyer and his helpers would arrive and take her away by force. Such cases have been reported fairly recently in many rural areas.[7]

The Wang clan in Shiyiao village in Linch'uen county of Kiangsi Province had a rule that widows might not remarry and that a widow committing fornication would be tortured to death by the clansmen. In 1950 a widow in that village wanted to marry the cousin of her deceased husband. Being afraid of the clan's punishment, they had secret sexual relations, and she became pregnant. This fact terrified her into fleeing the village and hiding in her mother's home in another village, but when the baby was born her brother wished to evict her from the house, accusing her of shaming the family. Her mother intervened and succeeded in having her live in the farm tool shed. The brother attempted to kill the baby. A Communist Party worker heard the commotion, prevented the killing, took the case to the subdistrict government, and had the widow and the man legally married.[8] In T'anghsia village in Chuchih county of Chekiang Province there was a clan rule prohibiting the remarriage of widows. A widow fell in love with a widower in the same village and they had sexual relations. When the situation was discovered by the clansmen the man was beaten up and chased out of the village, the woman was subjected to public humiliation, and her house and all her other property were taken over by the clansmen.[9]

Remarriage of Widows in the Pre-Communist Period

It is obvious that preventing the remarriage of widows was an institutional device to strengthen the family organization at the expense of the widow's interest. In this sense, a widow's lack of freedom to remarry constituted a point of potentially disruptive tension in the general stability of the traditional family institution. In the traditional social setting this tension was kept under control by institutional pressure bearing directly upon a widow's remarriage and by general social and economic pressure against the widow who contemplated remarriage. But such tension was bound to erupt in an age when the individual's interest becomes a criterion of social values, and when an individual's role receives dominant consideration in the matter of marriage. Abolition of the traditional restriction in the remarriage of widows thus became a logical part of the Chinese family revolution. Sacrifice of widows' interests by the once-commanding value of chastity, the threat against their security, and the actual mistreatment they were subjected to — all contributed to the turbulence of the family-reform movement and to the violence which has characterized the movement in certain areas under the Communist regime.

In the pre-Communist period the remarriage of widows was not an active issue. While there was general agitation against the traditional value of chastity and condemnation of the institutional restrictions on widows' remarriage, the problem received no independent emphasis either in the family revolution or in the marriage law under the Nationalist government. The remarriage of widows as an issue thus gained only implicit recognition in the family-reform movement.

The reason for the relative lack of independent agitation on the issue lies in the fact that the main force of the family revolution had been unmarried young urban intellectuals whose focus of attention was on freedom for the first marriage. Widows were not numerically important in the movement. True, in the course of the past three or four decades' development of the movement many educated young women who were married in the modern fashion became widows. For them the problem was simple. They fully assumed the freedom to remarry should they choose to, for they entered the husband's family as "free" women on an entirely different basis from the traditional marriage, and the family could not effectively prevent them from leaving. When the individual's interest as expressed in the free choice of partners became the basis of marriage, death of a spouse which dissolved that marriage also theoretically ended the obligatory bond between the widow and the deceased husband's family. This represents the attitude of the modern-minded widow.

Economically, since such women were almost invariably from the upper or upper-middle class, the problem of financial difficulty weighed less. The traditional concept of family property remained strong as a last bulwark for a weakened institution, and the modern widow who chose remarriage still could not take along a part of her deceased husband's family property into her new marriage. But her own parents' family would support her should she wish to leave the husband's family and wait for the development of a new marriage. Among young male intellectuals the discrimination against marrying a widow became much weaker than before, owing to the gradual devaluation of the old concept of chastity. So it became possible for a modern widow to find a suitable mate who could afford a comfortable livelihood. Such cases were not rare among modern urban intellectuals. The problem of children still remained a serious one, though the modern widow occasionally succeeded in taking her children into the new marriage. Thus in the pre-Communist period the problem of widows' remarriage arising among urban intellectual women was individually treated on the basis of new concepts introduced by the family revolution. But as a family issue it enjoyed no independent prominence in the movement, and its modern solution was not clearly defined in the Nationalist kinship law. As to workers and peasants, remarriages proceeded along traditional arrangements, and the modern issue of marital freedom was scarcely raised. The integrity of the traditional family institution among the lower class was not affected by this change as was the case with middle and upper-class families having modern educated women as daughters-in-law.

Change in Widows' Remarriage under Communist Rule

When the Communists rose to power in 1949, the issue of widows' remarriage assumed a different status under the general acceleration of the family revolution. The scope of marriage reform was broadened from first marriage to other aspects of the marriage institution, including remarriage of widows. The issue thus became an independent subject in the family revolution and gained formal clarification in the Communist Marriage Law. In the general prohibition of interference on the freedom of marriage by any third party the law specifically forbids interference in the freedom of a widow's remarriage (Marriage Law, Articles 2 and 3). The stipulation on the prohibition of "exaction of money or gifts in connection with marriage" (Article 2) explicitly includes the forbidding of the sale of widows or the exaction of a price for their remarriage.[10]

Furthermore, when the main motivating force of the family revolution shifted from intellectual agitation in the pre-Communist period to enforcement of the new Marriage Law under Communist rule, an inevitable effect was the spread of the movement from urban intellectuals to other segments of the population owing to universal application of the law. Widows among workers and peasants, who previously were little affected by the movement, now awakened to the new privilege of remarriage. In North China "some widows long repressed by feudalistic public opinion have now chosen their partners and have been married on the basis of free choice." [11] It is reported that in the six months following the promulgation of the Marriage Law, 469 widows were married of their own free choice in thirty-four rural subdistricts in the Chengchow Special District of the province of Honan.[12] Fragmentary figures and reports such as these appear widely in published statements and discussions on the marriage question in various parts of the country. The anti-Communist press in Hong Kong printed frequent reports of large numbers of widows in the villages of Kwangtung Province being forced by Communist political workers to remarry. While the report of the use of force in such cases appears to be obvious anti-Communist opinion, Communist statistics indicate the rapid weakening of the rigid traditional restriction on the remarriage of widows under the encouragement of the propaganda drives of the new Marriage Law and the enforcement of it in cities as well as in villages.

Widows' freedom to remarry has also been facilitated by new views regarding the problems of children and property. On the question of a widow's children Communist law completely rejects the traditional view of treating children primarily as a means of carrying on the family lineage. Under the new law raising children is considered a responsibility of parenthood, and the custody of the children in case of the remarriage of a widow is based on the interests of the children and the widow, not the interests of the deceased husband's family.[13] Thus runs a legal interpretation by the Communist court:

> Can a widow take her own children into the new marriage? This question should be clarified. This question is particularly relevant in case the grandparents possess the economic means of raising the children and are gravely concerned over the possible extinction of the family lineage should the children be taken away to a new marriage. . . . The solution of the question depends on the wish of the widow. If the widow agrees, the children can be left with the grandparents to raise. But if the widow does not agree, the grandparents have no right to stop her from taking her own children. In the common traditional pattern, if there is a child still in the nursing period, a widow may take her child along to another marriage. But when the child grows up, the grandparents usually insist upon taking the child back, thinking that the child must return to and acknowledge the ancestors, and that the child of the Chang family cannot possibly be allowed to adopt the surname of the Li family. People also generally call the children brought along by a widow to a new marriage "taking along a calf," and regard this as an extremely disreputable thing. Actually, all this is feudalistic thought, incompatible with the idea of protecting the children's interests. For between the mother and the children, there exists a blood-and-flesh relation and a natural emotional tie; the mother is more devoted to and more concerned over the raising and the education of her children than anybody else. For the children, the mother sacrifices everything. Therefore, when a widow remarries, it is at once natural and to the interest of the children that she should take them along to the new marriage, and nobody should have the right to interfere.[14]

On the problem of a widow's property at the time of her remarriage, the Communist legal view is given as follows:

> When a widow remarries, she may take along the part of the property that is her proper share, for men and women have equal rights in the new society. In land distribution [of the land reform], a widow in the villages is given her share of land, so it is her right to take along her own property. If she cannot manage her own land or house and other property when she goes away to a new marriage, and cannot find someone to manage it for her, she can convert it into cash or commodities and take it along. . . . In short, a widow has the independent and free right toward the disposal of her own property, and no one has the right to interfere. Any interference is illegal. For example, in Milaweitzu village . . . the widow Meng

Li-shih was taking along some things to her new marriage. The head of the village, Yu Chin-sheng, came out to prevent her from taking these things. The widow said to him, "All these are my personal belongings, and moreover, old man Meng and the family agreed that I take these along." But he said, "Hurry up and leave these things, if you talk any more, I'll tear the clothes off your body." Unreasonable interference such as this is an offense against the law according to the stipulation of the Marriage Law.[15]

Instances of widows remarrying in accordance with this new principle have been reported from widely different parts of the country. The following report, while obviously tinged with propaganda, presents such an event:

Hsieh Hou-hai is a widow who used to live in the village of Yang-an in the rural county of Li-shih of Shansi Province. Her husband died, leaving a son, now eleven years old. Poverty-stricken, hungry most of the time, and short of even tattered clothes, her life as a widow was an extremely difficult one. The husband's mother and two married brothers discriminated against her in every way. She thought of remarrying, but did not dare to for fear of reprisals by feudalistic influences. When land reform took place, her husband's family received land, and her own share was clearly written in her own name. Under the encouragement of propaganda mass meetings on the Marriage Law, she decided to remarry. A friend recommended a peasant to her, Lo Chun-mao, in the neighboring village of Hung-lo-kou. She arranged to meet him in person, and found him likable and satisfactory. They were soon married. At the time of her marriage, she took both her son and her share of the land into the new family. The deceased husband's family objected, but the objection was overruled by the subdistrict government. Later, she said in gratitude at meetings of the village women's association: "Women suffered all the misfortunes in the old society, and widows were not treated as human beings. . . . Now I can remarry, and furthermore, I can take my son and my property with me. Under the new principles, we women have really risen up." [16]

After the land reform, the collectivization of land and other means of production under the agricultural producers' cooperatives and later the people's communes further reduced property as a restriction against widows' remarriage. A similar trend is found among urban workers as illustrated by the following case in Shanghai. Describing the rebellion against traditional widowhood by family authority and the religious idea of fate, it is written in the style of propaganda literature, but the event itself is probably factual.

Ah Hsiang is a woman worker in the Yungta Cotton Mill. She had been a widow for nearly seven years. During the previous year [1949] she became acquainted with Chia Lung-ch'ang, a mechanic for her unit, and the two fell in love. Chia wanted to marry her, and she was willing, but both the mother-in-law and her own mother were very feudalistic. The mother-in-law said to her frequently, "Your widowhood is your fate. Quiet down and burn more incense for the good of your next life." And her own mother said to her, "Don't have so many ideas. You are a member of the Wang family when alive, and a ghost of the Wang family when dead." Hence, she did not accept Chia's proposal. Yuan, her big sister, was a woman committee member of the labor union. She knew about Ah Hsiang's troubles, and went to talk to the mother-in-law and the mother. But the trips were in vain, and Yuan was scolded by the two old women who just could not understand. Yuan let the heat cool down a bit, then told Ah Hsiang to move into the factory dormitory. She also told Chia to prepare a house and buy some furniture and utensils. When things were ready, Yuan took the two to court, and served as witness to their legal marriage.[17]

Although there is no quantitative data on how much the traditional restriction of the remarriage of widows has given ground, such cases indicate a spreading of the new trend among both urban workers and conservative peasants in rural communities.

Polygamy and Prostitution

In the traditional system polygamy had the formal function of insuring the perpetuation of the family lineage as well as the informal function of providing for men the romantic experience that was suppressed in arranged marriage. The informal function of providing romantic experience was also related to the traditional existence of open prostitution.

Traditionally, polygamy was practiced by the upper-middle- and upper-class minority, but the family among the poorer majority was usually monogamous. This class difference was caused solely by the economic ability of the well-to-do to support more than one wife and the resulting larger number of children, for, institutionally, there was no class restriction on polygamy in recent centuries. Polygamy therefore was the luxury of the rich minority.

One form of polygamy was the taking on of a "parallel wife" (*p'ing ch'i*) by a married man with the full wedding ceremony, which admitted the second wife to equal status with the first wife. A similar form was taking a "secondary wife" (*p'ien fang*) whose status was beneath the first wife but above that of the concubines. These forms were not commonly practiced even in the traditional social order, for they generally aroused violent objections from the first wife and her own family, at times leading to litigation against the husband's family. But the traditional family institution recognized these two forms of polygamy when they were practiced on socially approved grounds such as the first wife being found to have lost her virginity before marriage, her commission of an unusually offensive act against the husband or the parents-in-law, or, above all, her failure to bear a son for the perpetuation of the ancestral lineage.[18]

It is to be noted again that an underlying principle for the approval of such practice was the institutional consideration of the family as the dominant factor in marriage, not the married couple themselves, much less so the wife. Another underlying principle was the dominance of the male in the traditional family.

A much more common form of polygamy was concubinage, a concubine being an informal wife taken into the house with no formal wedding ceremony and thus with no ritualistic recognition or institutional guarantee for her security or the permanency of her position in the family. The same institutional principles underlying approval of the preceding forms of polygamy applied to the social recognition of concubinage. To obtain sons for the family's lineage was a common traditional reason for men to engage in this practice. The idea of "letting one trunk support two branches" is a clear illustration of this. Should an uncle have no son, he might pay the expenses for a married nephew to take a concubine (sometimes a "secondary wife"), and the son born of this concubine would be considered the uncle's adopted son. This son would perform the rites of ancestor worship for the spirit of the uncle when he died, and he would thus be acting as the perpetuator of the uncle's branch of the family.

The fact that a man's wealth and prestige were frequently measured by the number of concubines he possessed might also be considered a motivating factor in concubinage. An additional motivation was the economic value of a big family, for concubines could bring more children, especially sons, as economic assets. But the deeply rooted human factor was the desire for more variegated sex experience and romance, and the complete dominance of the male role in the traditional family facilitated the practice of concubinage for this purpose.

Thus, although the traditional institution of marriage minimized the importance of the individual, it did not completely ignore the personal desires of men, who held the dominant role. Should the formal marriage fail to satisfy a man's desires, he had institutional approval for seeking satisfaction in less formal ways. In the formal marriage he conformed to the requirements of the family organization, leaving the choice of his wife to parental authority and accepting such practical social considerations as the class status of the wife's family; but in taking a concubine such considerations for the family and for the parents were institutionally exempt, and a man could base his choice almost completely on personal desire.

Should a son object to the choice of a mate made by the parents for family reasons, such as to cement a connection with a wealthy family, the parents might tell the boy that he could take a concubine later. Again, a son might have illicit relations with a female servant with the tacit knowledge of the parents, and if he sincerely liked her, she could be made a concubine after the boy's formal marriage. A female servant could not meet the traditional family requirements for a wife, but for a concubine, since almost any choice would do so long as it pleased the man, he might take a servant girl, a singsong girl, or even a prostitute. In fact, taking prostitutes as concubines was by no means uncommon. Should the choice prove too much against the wish of the parents or too disruptive to the family organization, the son could set up a separate household for her; and there was no limit to the number of choices except his financial ability to support the concubines and their children.

Because of the lack of family and parental supervision over the taking of concubines, and because of the general inferiority of the concubines in class origin (they were usually bought from poor families), concubines were neither dignified by formal marriage ceremonies nor accorded full membership status in the family. They held inferior positions, performed unpleasant household tasks, and did not enjoy any recognized share of the family income as did the wife — although they could win favorite consideration from the husband and received private gifts from him. Their children, including sons, did not have ceremonial status and family opportunities equal to those of sons born of the wife; they could not claim an equal share of inheritance with the latter, except when the wife had no son. The role differentiation between the wife and the concubines and between the wife's sons and the concubines' sons was a means of maintaining the sanctity of family authority over formal marriage, a device to carefully stratify the members of a family in order to facilitate the exercise of hierarchical authority in the administration of a fairly complex domestic situation, and to prevent the taking over of the control of the household by female members generally originating from an inferior social class, particularly in view of their greater romantic influence over a husband who was frequently the head of the family.

Such was the institutional device to remedy the suppression of romantic love by arranged marriage, a device to prevent the man's romantic disappointment from becoming a disruptive factor to the institution of arranged marriage from which the stability of the traditional family drew much of its strength. The same principle furnished grounds for institutional approval of cohabitation with a woman on the side, and for frequenting prostitutes — except when carried to the point of financially ruining the family.

Although always classified as a vice, prostitution was tacitly approved of by traditional society. Traditional merchants as well as government officials transacted much of their business, and traditional scholars wrote some of their best lines of poetry, in whorehouses.* Prostitutes were considered sources of romance since love had been ruled out in formal marriage. If prostitution was ill-regarded by traditional mores, the basic reason was the frequent economic ruin of the wayward son and not any intrinsic moral abhorrence. A recent well-known Chinese writer who used to entertain his father in houses of prostitution in Peking was praised by friends as a filial son who catered to his father's desires. In a society where women's interests were consistently sacrificed for the welfare of the family and men's pleasure, there was little question of the moral degradation of a human being in "trading skin and flesh as a livelihood." The use of houses of prostitution as a center of social entertainment continued until the Communist government seriously tried to stamp out open prostitution.

Like many other aspects of the traditional family, old concepts of polygamy and prostitution were shaken by the impact of modern values emphasizing the intrinsic dignity and rights of the individual. From its beginning the family revolution and the women's movement which became its strong motivating force made polygamy a major target of attack, holding it to be a gross infringement of the dignity and rights of womanhood and a factor in the Chinese family institution that must speedily be removed as incompatible with the spirit of the modern age. The consecration of the monogamous marriage by Christian mis-

---

* The romantic school of the branch of Chinese poetry known as *Tz'u* drew much of its motif from love affairs with prostitutes. For example, the famous line by Ch'in Kuan of the eleventh century, "The willow-lined river bank, the dawn-breeze, and the night-worn moon," is in fact depicting the pre-dawn scene in which the poet himself was emerging from one of the houses of prostitution that used to line the banks of the Ts'in Huai River in Nanking.

sionaries encouraged this movement. By the 1930's monogamy had established itself as the dominant moral standard among the urban intelligentsia; Nationalist law adopted it as the legal form of marriage; and polygamy in its traditional forms was no longer practiced by the "new youth," the modern educated young of the well-to-do urban families who came under the influence of the family revolution. But the reform was limited to urban modern intellectuals, and its propelling force was informal group pressure generated by the modern social movements, the legal recognition of monogamy by the Nationalists remaining largely on paper. Polygamy continued to flourish among the financially well-to-do; and merchants in the cities, landlords in the villages, warlords, and unregenerated officials in the government continued to take concubines or practice polygamy in its various forms to the end of the Nationalist days on the Chinese mainland.

When the Communist government promulgated the new Marriage Law in 1950 the long-demanded abolition of concubinage and polygamy was once more written into the statute (Marriage Law, Article 2), and monogamy became the only legal form of marriage (Article 1). The Communist Marriage Law went further than the Nationalist reform by giving the children of concubines (previously taken) full and equal status with those born of the first wife, thus disregarding the organizational principle of the traditional family.

In the new concept of marriage as an affair of the marrying couple for their own interest and not primarily an affair of the family for the perpetuation of the ancestral lineage and for the welfare of the husband's parents, polygamy obviously cannot be justified as a means of assuring sons to carry on ancestral sacrifice or to provide security for the couple's old age. And since marriage is the outcome of free choice and love instead of parental authority, a man's need for romantic experience is supposedly satisfied, thus theoretically invalidating polygamy as a compromise measure to arranged marriage. Furthermore, even in the traditional family the wife was usually in opposition to the taking of concubines, and now the wife's objection becomes important, for she comes as a free person, owes much less socially and economically to her husband and his family, and is no longer bound by many of the traditional requirements of the family institution such as having to bear a son.

The new attitude toward polygamy, fully developed in the pre-Communist family reform movement among the urban intelligentsia, is now crystallized into legal interpretations under the Communist regime. In ruling against the practice of "letting one trunk support two branches" and of polygamy in general, the Communist Judicial Department of the Northeast Regional Government rendered the following typical opinion:

> In the old society, the feudalistic ruling class treated women as a tool for enjoyment, and openly practiced polygamy. Many things were utilized as excuses for taking concubines, including the wife's inability to bear a son. . . . Today, in our new society, both sexes enjoy equality, and women are no longer men's tools for enjoyment. . . . Should men take on additional wives on the excuse of begetting sons, they not merely violate the principle of sex equality, but also breach the rule of monogamy. The law can never permit this.
>
> All people like children and wish to have them, but ways of having them should be found in a reasonable direction, and the problem should not be solved in violation of the principles of sex equality and monogamy. First, it should be understood that a woman's inability to bear children may be due to physiological defects of either the man or the woman, and some care in medical examination before marriage will help solve this part of the difficulty. If the defect is discovered after marriage, and there is no way of inducing fertility, then the contracted parties must content themselves with the situation, for the bearing of children is not the only purpose of marriage.
>
> Some people cannot break away from the old thought that without offspring, the ancestors will be without religious sacrifice, and they consider it a tragedy of the first magnitude to see the "sacrifice of incense" discontinued. Actually, what good will it do the dead ancestors to continue the sacrifice of incense, and what harm will it do them to have it discontinued? This is nonsensical superstition, and it is incorrect.
>
> Some others think that without sons in their old age, they will be helpless and without support. Actually, this worry is rather unnecessary. If we labor actively and put effort into the development of production, when the reconstruction of the state is completed, the state will aid the aged who cannot labor and have no means of support, such as shown in the case of the Soviet Union. But, if you must worry about this point, you may adopt children. This will help the children who are without parents, meanwhile it will satisfy your desire for children.[19]

Statistical information is not available on the extent to which this legal principle has been put into practice in stamping out polygamy, but case histories and circumstantial evidence indicate trends regarding the practice of polygamy both in new marriages since the Communist Marriage Law went into effect in 1950 and in old marriages consummated before that date.

With repeated propaganda campaigns from 1951 to 1953 on the new

Marriage Law and continued discussion of this subject since then in various group meetings, particularly in women's organizations, it would seem that the common people in urban and rural communities have learned directly or indirectly that polygamy is no longer approved by law and that monogamy is the only legal form of marriage. With the obviously serious effort to enforce the new Marriage Law and with large numbers of local officials having received special training for this task, it is likely that the new legal requirement of marriage registration and investigation has succeeded in checking polygamy in most of the new marriages. Even if the process of registration and investigation should fail to reveal or prevent a polygamous marriage, later events may bring legal interference. A new concubine or "secondary wife" cannot be hidden from the neighbors for long. Even if the majority of the neighbors remain traditional-minded and regard the event with approval, the young people who are indoctrinated in the new Marriage Law would soon report the case to the local authorities. Furthermore, domestic jealousy and conflict between the wife and the concubine would probably soon lead either or both of them to appeal to the law, now that most women have heard of the new prohibition on polygamy. In addition, supporting more than one wife requires larger financial means than most people have under Communist rule. It is therefore reasonable to assume that among new marriages there is little polygamy practiced as a fully institutionalized affair where a man openly takes more than one wife with public acknowledgment and approval.

There must remain many cases of non-institutionalized polygamy among marriages of the "new youth" who grew up in the family revolution. In the Republican period many educated young men who were married under parental authority and were disappointed in the culturally backward wife later married a girl of their own choice and went off to live in another locality. The new wife might or might not be aware of the husband's previous marriage, which remained socially and legally effective; the husband considered the previous marriage unjust and void insofar as he was concerned, and refused to acknowledge the polygamous nature of the situation. With all its domestic and legal complications, this type of polygamy is of a transitional nature in the sense that it involves modern educated men being caught between the traditional parental authority and a new age of marriage by romantic love. Since under Communist rule legal approval and registration cannot be obtained for a new marriage by a man who already has a wife at home, if that fact is known to the registration official, the only way for a man to enter into a new marriage is to keep his still effective first marriage a secret. Such cases of "surreptitious polygamy" cannot last long without institutional approval or legal recognition.

Communist literature has dealt at length with this particular form of polygamy. One instance involved a twenty-nine-year-old Communist Party member, K'ung Hsien-sun, who married a peasant girl, Chao Ming-fen, also a party member, in 1947 while he was working for the Communist revolution in the rural areas of Shantung Province. With an urban intellectual background, K'ung soon tired of his peasant wife, and in 1947 he left her for advanced training in Manchuria, where two years later he secretly married another woman whom he tried to take to Tientsin when he was assigned there in 1954. When the first wife learned of his transfer to Tientsin and did not receive any call for her to come, she became suspicious and hurried to Tientsin to stay with him. She continued to live with him for over a year, at which time she intercepted a letter from the second wife and uncovered the truth. By this time she had a five-month-old baby girl. She took her case to the party cell and eventually to court. As a consequence, the Communist Party dismissed K'ung from membership, the court sentenced him to one year's imprisonment for polygamy, and he was ordered to contribute to the support of the baby girl after the completion of his prison term.[20]

The large number of existing traditional polygamous marriages constitutes a problem for the Communists. Communist law does not force the dissolution of a polygamous marriage already in existence if no suit is brought to court; if suit is brought, it is settled according to the new Marriage Law. The following instance occurred in the rural district in the northern province of Shantung in 1951:

Ch'en Shou-tuan, 61 years old, lived in Ch'enshuang-lou village in Feng county of Shantung. In 1943 he bought a concubine, Chu Nien, 18 years of age, for the price of about 160 pounds of wheat. The concubine gave birth to a daughter but had no son. Both Ch'en and his wife mistreated the concubine. Unable to stand the cruelty, the concubine ran away to a neighboring village and lived with a village Communist cadre there. This was soon discovered, and Ch'en brought the case to the county people's court. The court ruled that the case was one of fornication by the concubine, reprimanded her, and ruled that the baby girl should be given back to Ch'en for custody. This decision was along the line of the traditional principle in the institutional approval of concubinage. The case was later appealed to the superior people's court in T'eng county, which reversed the decision and ruled that the daughter should be in the custody of the mother, that the buying of a concubine has no legal effect, and that full legal recognition should be given to the marriage between the concubine and the village cadre.[21]

Thus, although Communist policy seems to be not to disturb existing polygamous marriages until they are challenged, cases such as this serve to undermine existing polygamous bonds. The mistreatment and grievances of concubines are generally known, as is the buying of young concubines by much older men, and many concubines would run away if the law would guarantee them safety and they could find a livelihood. Now, in a sense, they are encouraged to do so.

Following the pre-Communist tenet of the family revolution, Communist ideology attacks prostitution as the product of sex inequality, the treatment of women as merchandise, and the outcome of traditional suppression of inter-sex social life and romantic love. When such factors are removed and replaced by the socialistic economic and social order, it is held, prostitution will disappear. Disregarding the question of validity of this claim for the moment, one may note the fact that the new moral standard no longer lends even tacit approval to prostitution. The drastic suppression of the some two hundred brothels in Peking in 1950, and the re-education of the prostitutes for respectable occupations and a new form of life, first dramatized the new moral standard. Similar measures of government suppression of open prostitution have been carried out in Shanghai and other cities. Strict Communist police supervision of hotels serves to check covert prostitution. It is true that in published reports of the Three-Anti movement in the first part of 1952 many officials in the Communist government were charged with visiting prostitutes; [22] and the anti-Communist press in Hong Kong has continued to report stories of prostitution as a result of economic hardship in Canton and other cities. Nevertheless, the government drive has the significance of actively using political power to set up a new marriage institution which no longer condones prostitution.

Aside from prostitution, there has been a certain amount of extra-marital relations among the Communists, especially during the years of struggle for power which sent them marching and wandering all over the country. But Communist Party principles have regarded such behavior as a deviation, not as a moral norm. Chu Teh, the old chief of the Communist Army, once lectured the young party workers in Yenan, "I have heard of people dying of hunger, but not of people dying of the sexual urge." The Marriage Law gives illegitimate children a legal kinship status with the father, who is required to support them (Article 25), thus discouraging licentious behavior. The stabilization of normal married life among the party members after their accession to national power also tends to reduce such deviational conduct.

CHAPTER IV

Freedom of Divorce

TRADITIONALLY THERE was rigid institutional restriction on divorce so as to enforce family solidarity. Although the chief significance of the changes in the marriage system lies in the development of a new family institution among the young generation, leaving the existing traditional marriages undisturbed, the new freedom of divorce may affect all marriages, new as well as old. As an overwhelming majority of existing families in China are still based upon traditional marriage, any widespread application of the new freedom of divorce may shake the foundations of large numbers of families and affect the stability of the social order in general.

In the Republican period the voice for freedom of divorce had already been raised, but obtaining a divorce, though permitted under Nationalist law, was held in abeyance by the influence of traditional institutions. Under Communist rule the situation has changed appreciably. Communist policy professes not to disintegrate by decree the existing traditional marriages,[1] but the Communist Marriage Law unequivocably provides for freedom of divorce as a means of dissolving any marriage, new or old.[2] Ch'en Shao-yü, a leading Communist who took an active part in drafting the Marriage Law, stated explicitly:

> In the New Democratic society the legal protection for freedom of divorce, just as the legal protection for freedom of marriage, serves as a necessary means to oppose and to abolish the old feudalistic marriage institution. It will give physical and mental emancipation to men and women who have been forced to suffer under the old marriage institution to insist upon divorce.[3]

The operation of Communist law as guided by this pronouncement not only affects the integrity of a large number of Chinese families but also has significance for the stability of the social order under Communist rule.

Divorce in Traditional Marriage

To analyze the effect of the new freedom of divorce on the family in modern China, particularly under Communist influence, it is necessary to consider the institutional control over divorce under the traditional system. Traditional matrimony was an event by which the husband's family acquired a daughter-in-law (*ch'ü hsi fu*), and for the woman it was an event by which she found a home. The Chinese character for marrying off a daughter, *chia*, is composed of two radicals, one meaning woman and the other meaning home. In common traditional usage the term marriage was seldom employed; the event was usually mentioned as *ch'ü hsi fu* or *ch'u chia* (finding a home elsewhere).

So far as the woman was concerned the bond to a new home was meant for life, not to be broken even upon the death of the husband. Hence there was no institutional ground upon which a woman could obtain a divorce. Should she become dissatisfied with the marriage, even on justifiable grounds such as extremely cruel treatment, she was advised to tolerate the situation and preserve family unity by exercising forbearance and self-sacrifice and by resignation to fate. The folk adage, "When you marry a chicken, stick with the chicken; when you marry a dog, stick with the dog," was a constant reminder to her in her moments of depression or despair. Should she forget, others in the family would remind her by similar adages such as, "Obey Heaven and follow Fate." And the idea of fate as a reinforcing factor for the institutional bond was instilled in her through every step of the elaborate and religiously colored ceremony of her marriage. Should she still attempt to leave her husband against institutional sanction, she would face the charge against her from the family and the community as an "immoral character," as a wife who "does not observe the womanly ways." This would ruin her chance of remarriage and her respectable status in the community. If she did not stop at such discouragement, authority and even physical punishment might be brought upon her by the family, the clan, or even the government.

A wife traditionally came into a family with a price paid for her person and a heavy family investment in her wedding. She was reminded of this should she threaten to leave. Even in the modern city of Shanghai in 1950 there was the case of a traditional wife who had been married into a family as a child bride at the age of nine. Both the mother-in-law and the husband had given her repeated beatings and scoldings in her ten years of married life. After the Communist Marriage Law was promulgated, she heard of the possibility of divorce but was discouraged by the traditional requirement of paying back the price of her person. A labor union officer in the factory where she worked told her that such a refund was no longer necessary under the new law. Bolstered by this information, she went to court and won her divorce free of charge.[4] Such traditional demands on a wife who wished to get a divorce were universal except among the well-to-do minority where money was a secondary matter and the restraint was mainly one of a moral and social character.

In addition, the difficulties of children and property were as strong obstacles against divorce by a woman as against a widow's remarriage. If divorced she was not permitted to take her children out of the family, particularly sons, and, since she had no share in the family property, she could not take anything with her. A divorce would mean the difficulty of a livelihood if her own parents were not wealthy or willing to support her, and opportunity for women's employment in traditional society, especially in the rural community, was very limited. As in the case of widows, the possibility of a divorced woman getting married again into a comfortable family was slim because of social discrimination. And if the husband's family continued to object to the divorce, although the wife might have actually departed from that family, they might forcibly prevent her remarriage by abducting her or by making trouble with her parents and her new husband's family.

In extremely unbearable situations a traditional wife might leave her husband's family and go back to her parents' family, particularly if she had no children; but this was regarded as deviant conduct and as a separation, not as a divorce in the institutional sense. The husband and his family would continue to try to get her to come back. Economic difficulties and concern for her children, or the husband's threat to take another wife might well persuade her to return; and it was not infrequent to see such separations occur repeatedly in a single marriage.

At times, under excessively unbearable situations, suicide was the way out; and the large number of women who took their own lives on account of domestic difficulties is vivid testimony to the lack of any traditional institutional formula for readjustment of a wife's matrimonial relationship in case of absolute failure to achieve harmony between the wife and her husband or other family members, especially the mother-in-law. The following Communist report furnishes some idea of the rigidity of the old marital bond.

In sixteen counties in southern Shansi, from July to September of 1949, there were twenty-five women who died of inhuman treatment by their husbands or their fathers- or mothers-in-law. In Hotsin and Wanchuan counties of the same province, in the second half of 1949, twenty-nine women committed or attempted suicide by hanging themselves or jumping into the well for the same reason. In the months of July to September in Wenshui county and in November in Taiku county there were twenty-four legal cases involving the loss of human lives; among these fourteen were women who met death for the same reason. In Pingyao county the wife of Chao Ping-sheng demanded a divorce and Chao killed her. In Lingchuen county Li Shao-hai, a young married woman, committed suicide on account of mistreatment by her husband and mother-in-law.[5]

Such rigidity of the marital bond, of course, did not apply to men in a male-dominated institution. Tradition allowed a husband to return a wife to her own family on a large number of grounds. But even such a return did not constitute divorce in the modern sense of the word, for a wife who was returned to her own family still retained many claims against the husband and his family. Actually, the return of a wife occurred only rarely. In a poor family the husband and his parents could ill afford to lose a wife, not merely because her service as a housewife would be lost but also because it would be difficult to find the financial means to take another wife. Should a wife prove unsatisfactory, the husband and the parents-in-law could try to force her into submission. Should this fail, the husband and the family would have to be content with a dominant wife, and wife-dominated families were not uncommon even in traditional China, as attested by the numerous hen-pecked-husband jokes. In a well-to-do family a wife could be put aside and ignored and a concubine or "parallel wife" could be taken to fill her position.

It is natural, then, that one seldom heard of divorce in traditional families. In a sample population study of nine localities distributed in various parts of China in the pre-Communist period, five localities reported no divorce for women and four reported no divorce for men. In the three localities reporting divorce among women, the rates of divorced women were 0.02 per cent, 0.115 per cent, and 0.885 per cent of all married women. In the four localities reporting divorces for men the rates of divorced men among all married men were 0.034 per cent, 0.273 per cent, and 0.510 per cent.[6] In a sample census of nine rural counties in Szechwan Province in Southwest China, the rate of divorced women in 1947 was 0.126 per cent of all married women and that of divorced men 0.57 per cent of all married men.[7] These figures may err, but in a general way they reflect the negligible proportion of divorces as a general phenomenon among traditional families in the pre-Communist period.

These figures attest to the proverbial stability of the Chinese family, but, if modern divorce rates in the West are an indication of typical high tension in family relationships, the very low divorce rates in Chinese traditional communities do not signify a low degree of family tension. In fact, since divorce was not given institutional approval by the Chinese family, any tension remained unrelieved and bore especially heavily on the wife; and the Chinese family stability implied by the figures above was achieved at the price of personal sacrifice made largely by the women.

Freedom of Divorce in the Communist Law

A strong demand for the right of divorce formed an important part of the family revolution. After half a century of agitation and struggle, the right of divorce for both men and women had gained acceptance at least among the new intelligentsia in the Republican period. To the newly educated generation the demand was altogether reasonable since the basic premise of marriage itself had already shifted and marriage was no longer considered a bond tying a woman to a family for life but the result of love between two individuals. If the two individuals could not get along together, the new generation saw no reason for the continuation of their suffering. Gone from the young minds was the once dominant consideration of marriage as a means for the perpetuation of the family, and ancestral lineage was no longer a matter of grave concern.

By 1930 the Nationalist government had translated the demands of the young into law permitting divorce. Although the new law retained many favorable considerations for the perpetuation of the ancestral lineage, and no effort was made by the Nationalist government to acquaint the common people with their new legal right, for the educated young who knew about the new law a legal instrument was available to facilitate a divorce should they choose to go to court. New urban developments meanwhile had opened increasing fields of employment for women, which reduced the economic difficulties of a divorce. Divorce and remarriage of divorcees became fairly common among the new intelligentsia in the cities, but the new conception of divorce, while threatening the organization of a small number of urban families in the upper and middle classes, left the families of the peasantry and the urban working class almost untouched. Such was the picture under Republican China.

When the Communists came to power in 1949, they inherited this development, and the new concept of divorce was fully written into Communist law. In fact, the subject of divorce received more elaborate attention than any other subject in the Marriage Law, taking up nine out of a total of twenty-five articles. These nine articles set forth the right of divorce for either of the matrimonial parties and seek to guard the economic interests of the divorced wife and the children, but the husband's parents and the family in general are excluded from any legal attention. As it was consideration for the solidarity of the patriarchal family as the dominant factor in traditional marriages which had formerly ruled out divorce, so it is consideration for the married individuals as the dominant factor in new marriages that now justifies divorce. Hence: "Divorce should be granted when husband and wife both desire it. In the event of either the husband or the wife insisting upon divorce, it may be granted only when mediation by the people's subdistrict government and the subdistrict judicial organ has failed to bring about a reconciliation" (Marriage Law, Article 17).

Divorce is facilitated for the wife by the new legal stipulations concerning the custody of and responsibility for the children, the settlement of family property, and support for the divorced wife. Custody of the children shall be decided "in accordance with the interests of the children" (Marriage Law, Article 20), which in the actual operation of the law means most frequently the granting of custody to the wife; and "after divorce, if the mother is given custody of a child, the father shall be responsible for the whole or part of the necessary cost of the maintenance and education of the child" (Article 21). The father's responsibility may be discharged by payment "made in cash, in kind, or by tilling the land allocated to the child" (Article 21). "In case of divorce, the wife shall retain such property as belonged to her prior to her marriage. The disposal of other family properties shall be subject to agreement between the two parties. In the case where an agreement cannot be reached, the people's court shall render a decision after taking into consideration the actual state of the family property, the interests of the wife and the child or children, and the principle of benefiting production" (Article 23). It may be mentioned here that since Communist land reform the wife's share of the family property may be written in her own name and may even be registered in a separate deed, thus assuring her a fair share in case of a divorce.

"After divorce, if one party has not remarried and has difficulties in maintenance, the other party should render assistance" (Article 25). The "other party" which has to render assistance means the husband in most cases. Later, the socialization of urban business and collectivization of agricultural land minimized the importance of property settlement in divorce.

The Consequence of Increased Family Instability

With political support for the assertion of individual rights against family "oppression," and with propaganda on the new concept of marriage and divorce penetrating into the working class and the peasantry, the influence of the family revolution has spread from a minority of the urban intelligentsia to a much larger segment of the population. There are visible signs that the stability of a large number of families has begun to waver and that divorces are on the increase. The Minister of Justice of the Communist Central Government, Shih Liang, a woman, reviewed the situation seventeen months after the promulgation of the Marriage Law in May 1950:

> Statistics from different localities show that after the promulgation of the Marriage Law the number of matrimonial suits received by judicial organs of different levels increased appreciably. In twenty-one large and medium-size cities, including Peking, the number of matrimonial suits received was 9,300 for the months from January to April 1950, and it was 17,763 for the months from May to August of the same year. In other words, there was an increase of 91 per cent in the four months following the promulgation of the Marriage Law in comparison with the preceding four months. In ten county-seat towns in Hopei, P'ingyuan, and other provinces the number of matrimonial suits received was 986 for the months from January to April 1950, and it was 1,982 for the months from May to August of the same year. The increase here has been 101 per cent. In Hupei Province the average number of matrimonial suits dealt with by each people's court was 13.7 for February of 1951, and it was 23.9 for July of the same year, showing a considerable increase.[8]

Some two years later, in March 1953, the municipal court of Canton handled about eight hundred matrimonial cases as compared to one thousand-odd cases of labor-capital conflict. Domestic disharmony came to rank with labor-capital struggle as the two numerically largest items of litigation during the early Communist rule.[9] Such was the situation in the major urban centers.

It is noteworthy that the rural communities, which remained so long in the tight grip of traditional conservatism, are also sharing in

the increase in matrimonial suits which reflect growing family instability. The beginning of serious rural reaction to the new concept of
divorce is shown in Ch'en Shao-yü's statement made in April 1950,
just before the promulgation of the Marriage Law: "According to
statistics from the eight cities of Peking, Shanghai, Tientsin, Harbin,
Sian, Kalgan, Shichiachuang, and Paoting, from 71 rural counties in
the old liberated areas of North China, from some places in the old
Shensi-Kansu-Ninghsia border area, and from eight rural counties of
Shansi Province 17.4 to 46.9 per cent of all urban civil litigation cases
are matrimonial cases, and 33.3 to 99.0 per cent of all rural litigation
cases are matrimonial cases." [10] "In the Central-South Region the
32,881 matrimonial cases constitute over 60 per cent of all civil suits
received by the People's Courts during the months from January to
May 1951." [11] Matrimonial cases accounted for 90 per cent of the 700
civil cases handled during the months from January to the end of
August 1952 by the People's Court of the rural county of Laipin,
Kwangsi Province of the Central-South Region.[12]

While these reports do not present the contents or nature of the
matrimonial suits, they do give a general indication of growing family ·
instability as the new agitation of the family revolution has made it
increasingly difficult for the traditional family institution to maintain
role harmony among members who have become exposed to the idea
of individual liberty as against family restriction. This is particularly
true of the role of the wife, as a very high proportion of the matrimonial cases are brought to court by women (see the discussion on
women's status in Chapter VI). Where the traditional family institution is operating effectively, family conflicts are very seldom brought
to court for settlement, sometimes not even when human life is involved.

Among the increasing number of matrimonial cases, divorce suits
constitute a high percentage. Of the 32,881 matrimonial cases of the
Central-South Region in 1950, 29,972, or 90 per cent, were divorce
suits. A year later "divorce suits constituted from 46.44 to 84.32 per
cent of all urban matrimonial cases, and from 54.1 to over 90 per cent
of all rural matrimonial cases according to statistics from the four
cities of Peking, Shanghai, Tientsin, and Harbin, from seventy-one
counties in the old liberated areas of North China, and from some
places in the old Shensi-Kansu-Ninghsia border area." [13]

The trend of the high proportion of divorce cases apparently persisted at least until 1953. In the month of March in that year 80 per
cent of all cases received by the municipal court of Canton were divorce

suits, and the percentage may have been higher in the subsequent months owing to the launching of the "enlarged propaganda campaign on the Marriage Law" to acquaint more people with their new rights in marriage and divorce.[14] The Communist authorities have published little further statistical information on marriage and divorce since 1953, possibly because of fear of the socially disturbing nature of the figures; but a hint of the general continuation of this trend is seen in the report made in July 1957 by Tung Pi-wei, Communist judicial leader, that domestic conflicts still constituted an increasing and prominent proportion among all cases handled by Communist courts throughout the nation.

Only a few facts are mentioned in the official reports regarding the contents of the divorce figures. First, there is the almost overwhelming proportion of divorce suits brought by women as compared to those brought by men, especially in the rural communities, where conservatism is strong and the suffering of women under the traditional institution has been deep. For example, in 1950 in the cities of Shanghai, Peking, and Tientsin, 546 of the 800 divorce suits, or about 68 per cent, were brought by women, 176, or about 22 per cent, by men, and 78, or about 10 per cent, by both husband and wife.[15] In the provincial town of Nanchang, in Kiangsi, from January to October 1951 it was stated that 84.3 per cent of all divorce cases received by the municipal people's court were brought by women.[16] Of the 21,433 divorce cases in 32 cities and 34 rural county-seat towns mentioned in the *Jen-min Jih-pao* (People's Daily) of September 29, 1951, 76.6 per cent were brought by women. The 1951 edition of the *Hun-yin Fa Chi Ch'i Yu-kuan Wen-chien* (The Marriage Law and Its Related Documents, p. 72) listed 763 divorce cases in three rural counties in Shansi Province; of this total, 705 cases, or 92.4 per cent, were initiated by women. Among 29,972 divorce cases in 1951 in the Central-South Region, including both urban and rural areas, "The vast majority of them were brought by women who have suffered the severest oppression from the unreasonable institution of traditional marriage." [17]

Without specifying time or locality, Ch'en Shao-yü, who led the drafting of the Marriage Law, gave an analysis of the age composition of the parties involved in divorce suits. According to him, "About 50 per cent of them were between the ages of 25 and 45, about 40 per cent youths under 25, and about 10 per cent were very young people married before their maturity and old couples." [18] Teng Yung-ch'ao, wife of Premier Chou En-lai and a leading figure in the Democratic Women's League, which was vitally concerned with the drafting and enforcement of the Marriage Law, surveyed the statistical information possessed by the government on marital conditions and stated that the "vast majority of those demanding divorce were young and middle-aged laboring people." [19]

Not much is said about the causes of divorce. Obsessed with attacking the "feudalistic" marriage institution, Communist leaders take for granted that the evils of the traditional institution form the fundamental cause of the present divorces, something too obvious to need any statistical proof. Thus,

the first major cause of divorce is the lack of harmonious relationship between husband and wife resulting from the marriage institution of the old society based on compulsory arrangement and male dominance over the female. This constitutes the ground for divorce in the vast majority of the divorce cases received by the people's courts. From this it can be seen that under the present conditions in China freedom of divorce, like freedom of marriage, is an expression of the revolutionary struggle against the remnants of feudalism. The second cause of divorce is the result of particular conditions of the minority, such as prolonged parting between husband and wife, one party committing a crime, one party sexually impotent on account of physiological defects, one party having a loathsome and incurable disease, or one party being progressive while the other is backward in ideology.[20]

There is a little more detail in the official figures for the city of Canton.

From May 1, 1950, to February 23, 1951, the People's Court of Canton dealt with 534 marital suits which may be classified into four types: (1) cancellation of engagements, 18 cases; (2) divorces, 319 cases; (3) cancellation of cohabitation relationship, 131 cases; (4) non-support of children, 66 cases. Among all the cases divorce suits constituted 59.7 per cent, cancellation of cohabitation relationship 24.5 per cent. Of these two types of cases, those brought by women constituted 78 per cent of the total and those by men 22 per cent. The causes of divorce may be listed as (1) dictated marriage, (2) polygamy, (3) mistreatment, (4) abandonment [majority of cases brought by women], (5) disharmony, (6) extramarital love affairs, (7) physiological defects, (8) spouse leading a decadent and corrupt life [including refusal to labor and unwillingness to stand poverty], (9) uncertainty of spouse being alive or dead.[21]

The large number of cancellations of cohabitation relationships, resulting chiefly from family separations during the anti-Japanese war, shows a weakening of the traditional concept of marriage and family in the cities. Under the traditional social order such a relationship was disapproved of as a threat against the orthodoxy of the family institution and was a clandestine affair. It was never an open relationship having semilegal status. Its widespread practice during World War II and the pre-Communist postwar period can be seen in the fact that almost one-fourth of all the matrimonial suits were cohabitation cases. The Communist Marriage Law extends no recognition to cohabitation except the possibly related provision holding the parents, especially the father, responsible for any children born out of legal wedlock. There is no information on the extent of such practice under Communist rule, but general observation suggests that it is not very common.

These fragmentary divorce figures are given in such a form that they cannot be compared to figures for periods preceding the Communist regime; therefore there is no statistical evidence whether or not this is a new phenomenon created by Communist rule. In the Nationalist period divorces were notably on the increase, especially after 1930, but they were largely limited to the big cities where the sanctity of the traditional marriage institution had been seriously undermined. The traditional kinship system, including the institution of marriage, had been strongly maintained in the countryside, and divorce in the modern sense was still repulsive to the peasantry. The sharp resistance to the injection of the divorce idea into rural communities even under Communist rule, to be considered later, attests to the newness of the divorce factor in the rural social situation. Hence, while it is not known how many urban divorces mentioned above represent a consequence of Communist reform, it may be taken with some degree of certainty that rural divorces constitute a new phenomenon in the hitherto vast redoubt of the traditional institutions.

Even in cities considerable legal expense was entailed under the Nationalist government to obtain a legal divorce, something only the upper and middle classes could afford, and only an educated few were acquainted with the law. But the use of lawyers is no longer part of the Communist legal system, and the people's court has abolished court fees. The propaganda campaigns on the Marriage Law are introducing legal knowledge to the common people. Hence the poor and even the illiterate can use the court to settle matrimonial disputes and to obtain divorces. The many cases of legal divorce among the urban working class [22] is a new phenomenon, then, and some increase in urban legal divorces since the establishment of the Communist regime seems quite possible.

Economic Support, Property, and Children in a Divorce

The possibility of a marked increase of divorces under the Communist regime draws support from other factors. Aside from the encouragement given by vast propaganda efforts and the increased accessibility of legal aid, divorce is facilitated by women's new legal privilege of being able to take along their share of property, to receive maintenance assistance, and to have custody of the children. The Nationalist marriage law gave some consideration to the woman's share of property but ruled that the husband's family should have the custody·of the children, evidently out of respect for the traditional importance of perpetuating the ancestral lineage and because children were a security asset of the family. The Communist Marriage Law favors the interests of the divorced woman and the children.

There is some information on the actual operation of the Communist law in assisting women in a divorce to obtain economic support and property compensation. In a report entitled "Examples of Legal Decisions on Matrimonial Cases Rendered by the People's Court of Tientsin," [23] published in 1951, there is the case of a college graduate who married an illiterate girl by parental arrangement. When the incongruity of cultural levels between them led to divorce, the court ordered the husband to support the wife until her remarriage and to buy her a sewing machine to help make her self-supporting. In granting the divorce the Communist court advised: "The suffering (between the couple) is a product of the old society and a gift from the institution of arranged marriage . . . . Each day that the matrimonial relationship lasts will give the defendant an additional day of suffering and will reduce the wife's chance of remarriage. For the long term interest of the wife, a divorce should be granted . . . . She should actively take part in production and become self-supporting. She should choose a good companion in the process of her work, and this will give her a happy future." The report listed another case involving a working couple married by parental arrangement. While both husband and wife had agreed to a divorce, the husband refused to pay back the wages the wife had earned in a cotton mill for several years which had been handed over to the parents-in-law as a traditional practice. The court in granting the divorce ordered the husband's family to return the accumulated wages.

Another Communist document recounts a court decision in Shanghai granting a divorce to the owner of a photographic shop and his wife. The court ordered the husband to contribute to the support of the divorced wife from the income of the shop and to give her one half the proceeds should the shop be liquidated.[24] This legal decision was made in 1951 when private business was still in operation. Since the spring of 1956 the majority of businesses have been turned into joint ownership between private parties and the state. Presumably, under the new circumstances the economic interest of a divorced woman would have to be taken care of by the wage income of the husband.

Such court decisions, although totally contrary to tradition, would not necessarily seem strange to the urban population, which has lived in the midst of change. In the countryside, where the old family institution has been relatively insulated from modern influences, the implementation of the new economic benefits and property rights for the woman seeking a divorce has been more difficult, as reflected in the following Communist statement:

> Those still possessed of the old legal views often take the stand that "officials do not attend to cases which are not contested by the parties involved." As a consequence, they sacrifice the legal interests of the divorced women and the children and act against the official policy. Some women are still not acquainted with the Marriage Law, and they did not take the initiative to bring up property demands in connection with their divorce procedure. The property question of such cases has been completely ignored on the ground of "no court action without legal contention." But there have been cases of no court action even if legal contention of property rights was made. In such cases, the women were frequently told, "You already got a bargain by receiving a divorce, and you still want property on top of that?" or, "The other party already feels terrible about the divorce, and you still want to grab some property in addition?" In Ch'ien county of Shensi Province in 1951, ninety-three cases of divorce were handled by the court, and women were given property by the court in only thirteen of these cases. In the past two years [1951 and 1952] the court in Wuhsiang county of Shansi Province handled over two thousand divorce cases, among which over 33 per cent obtained no solution to the problem of women's property.[25]

The increasing number of divorce cases granting economic support and property rights to women serve as an important influence, one which has been reinforced by the successive campaigns from 1951 to 1955 to indoctrinate the political leaders and to acquaint the people with the new Marriage Law.

With regard to another major traditional obstacle against divorce, the custody of children, Communist courts have given dominant consideration to the interests of the children as individuals. Thus, in granting a divorce to a couple in Tientsin in 1951 the municipal court awarded the custody of a thirteen-year-old boy to the mother in addition to ordering the husband to give the wife a lump-sum financial settlement and contribute to the support and education of the child until he reached the age of eighteen. The court opinion clearly expressed the new principle in settling the problem of the custody of children:

> Because the marriage was an arranged one, there has always been domestic friction. The wife once attempted suicide by swallowing gold, and the situation also became unbearable for the husband, who is now asking for a divorce but insisting on the custody of the child. . . . This insistence upon keeping the child is motivated by the feudalistic thought of perpetuating the ancestral lineage, and not by sincere consideration for the welfare of the child. When the wife keeps the child, it does not prevent the husband from doing his duty for the child's upbringing and education.[26]

In awarding the custody of a five-year-old son to a wife who had been married as a child bride and suffered cruelty from the husband's family the Tientsin court struck a recurrent note: "The wife is a woman worker with a dependable income, and she has a mother to help care for the child. The husband shuns labor and only hawks black beans on the street, and his income is uncertain . . . . Comparing the situation on both sides, it is better to let the wife keep and raise the child. The husband should not be motivated by the feudalistic thought of perpetuating the ancestral lineage and ignore the interests of the child." [27]

The granting of economic benefits and the custody of children to women may discourage men from seeking divorce as a settlement of domestic discord, and it may serve to curb the traditional mistreatment of the wife in the family, thus altering the role relationship between husband and wife. In this sense, the new legal standard may to a certain extent have a stabilizing influence on the family while at the same time improving the status of the wife. This influence is, of course, much weaker than the traditional restrictions against divorce. Meanwhile, as large numbers of existing traditional marriages have irreconcilable tensions and conflicts, the dominant effect of the operation of this new legal principle has so far been to facilitate divorce and to increase the divorce rates.

Indiscriminate Granting of Divorce

That divorce is being established as a new factor in family relationships in Communist China and becoming an "important weapon in abolishing the feudalistic institution of marriage and in liberating the long oppressed women from their yoke" is further interestingly substantiated by charges that many local government organs have been indiscriminate in granting divorces. Such charges have been made not only by people unsympathetic to the Communist regime or its new Marriage Law but also by Communist government leaders. Thus Shih Liang, the woman Minister of Justice, charged some political workers with irresponsibly spreading the word that "divorce may be granted even when the spouse is not pleasing to the eye." [28] In Hang county of the southern province of Chekiang "some subdistrict political workers have been very thoughtless in their disposal of matrimonial cases. Less than half an hour was spent on each case, whether it was one of divorce or marriage registration. In some places the general attitude toward divorce cases is 'no wish will be denied.' Some couples just happened to quarrel and want a divorce, and the government would actually grant it to them, only to see them return soon, asking to restore the husband-wife relationship." [29]

Hsü Teh-hsing, a member of the Committee of Laws and Institutions, made the following statement:

In some places local cadres have adopted an irresponsible and sloppy style of work. In propaganda they lay one-sided emphasis on the "freedom of divorce," and in legal procedure they unrestrictedly favor the party demanding divorce, consequently creating a situation of indiscriminate divorce in which everyone's wish [for divorce] is granted. For instance, the Special Office of Yungchow in Fukien Province followed the one-sided demand of those cadres who came down South to work and granted divorces to twenty-one couples without having given a hearing to the other party's story. It was said that this was done for the morale of the cadres. In Nank'ang (a rural county in Kiangsi Province) Hsiao Shih-hsiu and his wife had been a happy couple. Once they had a quarrel and decided to get a divorce, and the court actually granted it. In Sheh county of Hunan Province Kuo Ch'ou-nü and her husband divorced and reunited as often as three times in a single year.

When divorces are granted as lightly as this, the result is bound to be an increase of abnormal phenomena such as getting a divorce one day and asking to be reunited the next, Some of the reasons presented by men for divorce even include "spouse not having a pretty face," "spouse having coarse skin," "spouse too small in stature," "spouse illiterate." Some women have demanded a divorce on the grounds of "husband too poor, livelihood not comfortable," or "husband unemployed." . . . All these leave the masses with a very bad impression regarding the "court as an office of divorce" or the "Marriage Law as a divorce law." [30]

It is notable that most of such occurrences were reported south of the Yangtze River where, in the early years of Communist rule, both the quality and quantity of local political workers were below the level of those in the northern provinces. In the northern part of the country, where political workers were more experienced and better trained and the new order better established, the divorce problem seems to have been handled more carefully, particularly in the cities. Thus the Department of Justice of the Northeast Regional Government explained that "the People's Government is not promoting divorce, and the Marriage Law is not a divorce law. Those who take 'freedom of divorce' for 'divorce at will' are committing a grave error." [31] It gave examples of court rejections of divorce requests based on flimsy grounds. In the northern city of Tientsin many requests for divorce on weak grounds have been rejected by the court. Among such cases was a wife who wanted a divorce since she did not wish to go back to the village to farm with her unemployed leather-worker husband, and another concerned a man who wanted to get rid of his wife to make room for another romance.[32] If a divorce involves a Communist Party member serving in the revolutionary armed forces, or if it involves a situation where a divorce would affect production, the chance of obtaining a court grant is limited,[33] as the interests of the armed forces and of production claim priority in the attention of the Communist state.

One explanation for some of the cases involving reunion soon after divorce is the possible ignorance of the serious meaning of the term divorce among the common people. It may well have been mistaken by some people for the same situation as when the wife decided to go back to her parents' home as a consequence of a quarrel and then would return to the husband when the heat of the moment had passed. Divorce as a permanent legal separation in the modern sense remains unfamiliar to most of the people.

Social Resistance against Divorce

It is important to note that even under communism strong social resistance against divorce survives, particularly in rural communities, which not only precludes the possibility of rapid spreading of indiscriminate divorce but also limits legitimate divorces.

To the many people who feared that marriage by free choice of partner and romantic love would lead to promiscuity, the idea of freedom of divorce and political support for it was an even more unthinkable evil. Local sentiment in many places ran strongly against the Marriage Law for its sponsoring freedom of divorce and regarded it as a step that would "plunge the family and social relations into general chaos," that would "break up the family," that would "wipe out moral obligations." [34] In East China "the people regarded freedom of divorce as a step that would lead men to 'lose both person [wife] and wealth,' and regarded the right of 'child brides' to cancel their marriage contracts as being against moral conscience." [35]

Such attitudes survived among Communist party workers also, who, ironically enough, used their new revolutionary power to enforce traditional moral standards. This situation is best summarized by the following significant statement by a Communist writer in 1951:

> Remnants of the feudalistic marriage institution are still persisting in serious proportions in the vast countryside. . . . Many cadres of subdistricts and villages are still deeply imbued with feudalistic ideology and are following a bad style of work, thus directly and indirectly protecting remnants of the feudalistic marriage institution and hindering thorough enforcement of the Marriage Law.
>
> The feudalistic ideology of the subdistrict and village cadres is based mainly on the following points:
>
> They fear that the Marriage Law will lead the world into chaos. After the promulgation of the Marriage Law, in the provinces of Liaotung and Heilungchiang of the Northeast, in the provinces of Hopei and Pingyuan in North China, in the provinces of Shantung and Chekiang in East China, and in many other places, subdistrict and village cadres are generally afraid to disseminate knowledge of the Marriage Law. In Pingyuan Province, some village cadres locked up the Marriage Law in their desk after receiving it. One village cadre in Chekiang Province even said, "Whoever makes propaganda on the Marriage Law in my village, I'll break his leg!" This gives law-breaking landlords and certain bad elements a chance to attack the Marriage Law as a divorce law, and to accuse the government of mobilizing the masses for divorce. This arouses fear among a part of the masses regarding the Marriage Law in some places. When propaganda meetings are held for the Marriage Law, younger women are often not allowed to take part lest they become emboldened to demand divorce.
>
> Many subdistrict and village cadres are straightforward, fearless fighters in the struggle against the feudalistic land system, in the sharp class struggle between the peasants and the landlords. But when it comes to the struggle against the old marriage institution, it is different. It is a strug-

gle between backward thought and progressive thought within the peasant himself. They realize that, if the Marriage Law is thoroughly enforced, the relationship between the sexes will radically change, the old family institution will gradually alter. But they are accustomed to the feudalistic institution and the old relationship between the sexes. Therefore, they are unwilling to accept the Marriage Law; they even resist it. . . .

Another factor is the policy of the "supremacy of men" in handling divorce cases. They [rural cadres] regard divorce as putting men in a disadvantageous position, costing them both "person [wife] and wealth." Hence, they set up a variety of conditions for divorce by women, or even make open, unreasonable interference. In Liuchia village of Hsienyang county, Hupei Province, when Su Chin-chun demanded a divorce from her husband, her husband colluded with the village cadres, locked her up in a room, tortured her, and forced her to accept four conditions. (1) She was not to get a divorce, and for three years she was not to visit her own parents' home. (2) She must report to and obtain permission from the parents-in-law every time she went to the toilet. (3) She was not to talk to anyone from her parents' village. (4) She must report to the village council of women if she travelled away from the village. Many subdistrict and village cadres, and even the cadres of some county people's courts, hold that in a divorce, the woman should take as little property along as possible, and that it is best not to let her take any property at all. The people's government in several subdistricts of Yutz'u county in Shansi Province even illegally set up a rule governing the settlement of property in a divorce: "When the woman initiates the divorce, she cannot take any property; when a man initiates a divorce, the woman may take along property." As a result, after a divorce, many a woman is forced by hunger to seek reunion with her husband, thus returning to a life of torture.

Still another factor is the use of old moral concepts in the settlement of divorce troubles. Divorce is taken as an "immoral affair," as a "loss of face," as "breaking up the family." Hence, many subdistrict and village cadres in handling divorce cases always attempt reconciliation and do not permit divorce as a solution.[36]

In another Communist official report some subdistrict and village cadres were pictured as adopting a policy of open suppression against divorce demands by women. Women demanding divorce were imprisoned for "forced reconciliation." They were treated with "reform by education." They were locked up in granary buildings as a measure of suppression. In Mienyang county of Hupei Province a woman was removed from her position as delegate to the people's representatives council because she demanded a divorce. In Chun county the secretary of propaganda of the Chaotien subdistrict government encouraged his uncle to beat the aunt who had succeeded in obtaining a divorce, and forced her to kowtow to apologize for her mistake and to restore the husband-wife relationship. Such local leaders regarded divorce as spreading an "unfavorable influence" and as a "disreputable affair." [37]

In Yihsing county in the southern part of Kiangsu Province a peasant woman, Yang Mei-hua, twenty-one years old, could not bear the cruelty of her husband and mother-in-law. She ran away in the traditional style and wished to marry another man. She was caught by the village workers and given a severe beating. In the end she hanged herself.[38] In the Central-South Region "many women said, 'To get a divorce, there are three obstacles to overcome: the obstacle of the husband, the obstacle of the mother-in-law, and the obstacle of the cadres. The obstacle of the cadres is the hardest to overcome.' " [39] The large number of resulting tragedies is partly recounted in the following report:

> Those of the old legal view make freedom of divorce a target of attack. They think: "Good women should hang themselves (as a result of family discord), only bad women seek divorce." They either reject women's demands for divorce by misinterpreting the new law regarding the requirements of reconciliation, or they lay one-sided emphasis upon the wifely obligation toward the family and reject women's demands for divorce regardless of mistreatment suffered by the women. In Ninghsia county of Kansu Province a woman named Li could no longer bear the mistreatment of her husband and repeatedly demanded a divorce. In her last attempt she pleaded with the court: "If my request for divorce is rejected, my only alternative is to die." But the judge named Tien, who was retained from the Kuomintang government, replied: "You may die if you wish, but you cannot have a divorce." Li returned home and hanged herself. The number of women who have committed suicide or have been killed in various parts of the country has reached alarming proportions recently. The vast majority of these deaths were results of the lack of legal support for their struggle for freedom of divorce because of unreasonable matrimony and domestic mistreatment. In eight special districts in Shantung Province 504 women committed suicide or were killed during the period from January to June of 1952. In eight counties in the southern part of Szechuen Province 116 women met similar deaths in the first half of 1952. In Liaoch'eng, a special district of P'ingyuan Province, 56 women met similar deaths in the months from January to April of 1952.[40]

It is interesting to note that peasant leaders who have been able to fight hard to overthrow the traditional institution of property ownership cling to the traditional institution of family and marriage although changes in the system of property ownership eventually bring about a change in the family system. They exemplify the difficulty of attempting to change a social institution by decree without the necessary political leaders who understand and accept the new idea. Many modern laws attempting to introduce new institutions in the Nationalist period died on paper because of the same situation. The Communists are trying to meet the situation created by the Marriage Law not only with extensive propaganda and indoctrination of the local leaders but also by coordinating these efforts with the change of other social, economic, and political institutions.

The suppressive action of the local leaders and the bitter struggle in numerous divorce cases show that the idea of divorce is spreading extensively; and the terror with which local leaders have regarded the idea, as well as some of the ruthless measures they have used to combat it, suggest the potential strength of the development of the divorce factor. Hence, while the actual number of divorces in China may still be few when viewed by Western standards, the function of these cases as living examples of a new idea of improving personal welfare cannot be ignored, particularly when the idea is supported by a revolutionary political power and dramatized by women's new privileges of taking children and property along in a divorce. When bold women lead off and break the thick ice of ancient tradition against divorce, others are likely to follow their example. In the village of Tunghua in Lushan county of Honan Province a child bride, Li Hsiu-yuan, demanded a divorce, but the local officials were against it, and for three months, the case hung fire. Seeing this trouble, other women who wanted divorces did not dare to bring their demands to court. However, after the "democratic reform campaign" was concluded in the village Li Hsiu-yuan was granted her divorce, and immediately following this, seventeen women obtained divorces or annulments of betrothal contracts. Simultaneously, there was an increase in marriages based upon free choice of partners in the village.[41]

Significance of Freedom of Marriage and Divorce

Since freedom of marriage and divorce may be viewed as the most significant factors in the disorganization of the traditional Chinese family system and the development of a new one to supersede it, it seems worthwhile to summarize their effects.

First, the generational composition of the family has been affected. With marriage focused on the couple to the exclusion of interference by parental and family authority, the husband-wife relationship becomes the center of the new family, and the married son's parents occupy only a peripheral position. The traditional arrangement of the parents-children relationship taking precedent over the husband-wife relation is now reversed. In the husband-wife-centered family the married son's parents are no longer *ipso facto* members holding a controlling position. Should conflict arise between the parents and the daughter-in-law, the parents' position is no longer protected by institutional authority or law, and they may have to leave the son's family. Even in the 1920's, when freedom of marriage first became a strong demand by the young urban intellectuals, modern women had already raised the question of setting up separate households from the parents-in-law, and many of them succeeded in doing so. In such cases a two-generation family replaces the traditional three-generation system.

Even if the parents continue to live with the married son's family, they no longer enjoy a controlling position in the family. Should they have several married sons, they no longer possess the authority to hold them together in a closely organized unit or integrate them into a single household. They can live only with one of the married sons at a time. Thus their continued living with the married sons no longer has the same significance as before, for the traditional primary importance of the parents in the family is now being superseded by the primacy of the husband-wife relation. The parents in the new family are an adjunct, not a controlling authority; their continued presence depends a great deal on the pleasure of the daughter-in-law. This new situation nullifies the ability of the traditional family to expand into a large, multi-generational structure.

Second, the size of the family has been affected. While the average of four to six persons per family for the majority of the population will remain unless altered by a change in birth rates, the size of the middle and upper classes will be reduced, for the old large family composed of parents and married sons, so common in the wealthier classes, is no longer possible when marriage is no longer an affair designed for family expansion. As the generational composition of the family changes, there is a corresponding reduction in size.

Third, the solidarity of the family organization has been affected in various ways. The relation between parents and married sons and daughters-in-law is weakened by the modern affirmation of the husband-wife relation as the closest tie. The solidarity of the traditional family, based on the primacy of the parents-children relation, is thus diminished. The new conjugal family gains solidarity by a closer husband-wife relation not morally subjected to alienation by parental inter-ference, but this new solidarity has the effect of restricting the strong family tie to the small circle of the married couple and their unmarried children.

The new right of remarriage for widows, with the related privilege of taking children and property to their new home, has obvious dis-organizing effects on the solidarity of the traditional family, which treated a widow as a member permanently related to the family as a whole and not to the husband alone. The new marriage would be similarly centered on the husband-wife relation and not on her relation to the new parents-in-law.

The new trend against institutionalized polygamy affects various aspects of the family differently. The discontinuation of polygamy means the loss of its formal function in helping to insure continuity to the ancestral lineage and a large membership to the traditional family. On the other hand, the informal function of providing men with romantic experience or additional sexual pleasure has always been a disruptive influence on domestic harmony. Thus the abandon-ment of polygamy would increase the solidarity of the family organiza-tion. The suppression of open prostitution as institutionally condoned behavior has a similar effect.

Fourth, by emphasizing the couple's mutual interest, modern mar-riage by free choice of partners assigns no importance to the continua-tion of the family lineage. Belief in the necessity of continuing the family lineage made marriage a religious act in ancestor worship which, among other functions, served to expand the membership of the kinship system and to generate solidarity among them by translating biological relatedness from common descent into a social bond. The longer the family lineage continued, the larger the number of de-scendants. But a large number of descendants from a distant ancestor would not know each other or recognize any social ties and obligations among themselves if ancestor worship did not translate biological relatedness into a living social bond. The traditional identification of marriage with the sacred function of perpetuating the ancestral lineage had the purpose of insuring both size and solidarity for the kinship organization. Now that the main purpose of modern marriage is to fulfill only the romantic or other requirements of the couple, the result is the weakening of the relationship between the couple and other kinship members, especially collateral relatives, thus reducing the organized kinship circle to a small group of lineal male descendants and their wives.

The reduction in size and solidarity of the family and its extended kinship organization is of major significance. A small family without support from a large kinship organization cannot perform the multiplicity of socio-economic functions and retain its traditional position as the core of the Chinese social system.

Crumbling of the Age Hierarchy

THE STRUGGLE for freedom of marriage and divorce represented a rebellion of the young against parental authority over the
arrangement of the children's marriage and their married life, but the
ascendance of the young and the retreat of the old resulting from this
rebellion concerned more than parental authority over children's marriage. These influences undermined the structure of traditional family
authority in general. If the change in the form of marriage mainly
affected the roles of the married sons in relation to the roles of the
parents and other family members, the undermining of family authority
by the rise of the young affected the general structure of the entire
traditional family organization, for it altered the role of practically
every member in the family and changed the mode of family integration. There is hardly a more significant aspect of the Communist revolution than the attempt to shift the foci of power from the old to the
young in the family as well as in society in general.

The Traditional Age Hierarchy and the System of Family Status and Authority

In the traditional structure of family status and authority age was
a leading factor. The Five Cardinal Relations, the basic principles of
family organization, taught that family members should be arranged
into "proper order by their age." The importance of age was clearly
pointed out by Mencius' statement: "In the Kingdom there are three
things that command universal respect. Nobility is one of them; age
is one of them; virtue is one of them. In courts nobility is first of the
three; in local communities age is first; but for helping one's generation and presiding over the people the other two are not equal to
virtue." [1] The organization of the local community was centered upon
the kinship group, hence the supremacy of age. Elsewhere in Confucian

teachings, upon which generations of Chinese down through the centuries have been reared, the importance of age as a factor in family status and authority was elaborated and emphasized with tireless repetition. A modern middle-aged Chinese today still retains vivid childhood memories of being ceaselessly reprimanded for not having observed the age line and for showing disrespect to those senior to him. Such reprimands were so much a part of an individual's upbringing that he finds it difficult later in life to address even older friends and senior colleagues by their first name, preferring to call them by their surnames with the prefix of *sen sheng* (the English equivalent of mister), literally meaning "born earlier," or *hsiung*, meaning elder brother.

This "proper order by age" formed the foundation for the hierarchy of status and authority in the traditional Chinese family. In its kinship connotation age implied two factors, generation and chronological age. The generational structuring of Chinese kinship members has been analyzed by H. Y. Feng in his *Chinese Kinship System*. He says, "The architectonic structure of the Chinese kinship system is based upon two principles: lineal and collateral differentiation, and generation stratification. The former is a vertical and the latter a horizontal segmentation. Through the interlocking of these two principles every relative is rigidly fixed in the structure of the whole system." [2]

The status and authority of family members were defined first by the stratified successive generational layers as shown in Feng's chart, reproduced below, and, second, by chronological age. Thus all members in a senior generation enjoyed higher status and authority than those in a junior generation, and, among members in each differentiated group of relatives of the same generational level (as represented by each square in the chart), older members took precedence over younger ones. A third factor in the situation was the proximity of biological relatedness or kinship. This was what Feng calls vertical segmentation based on lineal and collateral differentiation. Feng's chart shows that Ego was under heavier pressure from the status and authority of members closer to him in kinship and senior to him in both generation and physical age than with members of the same generational and age seniority but more distant to him in kinship. Ego's status and authority over members junior to him in generation and chronological age was also graduated by the proximity or distance of kinship. Thus Ego's relation to lineal relatives was closer than to collateral relatives, and the closeness of Ego's relation to collaterals was in inverse proportion to the number of collateral degrees. Ego's relation to a patrilineal relative was closer than to a corresponding matrilineal relative. It was an

The Chinese Kinship System

4th Collateral	3rd Collateral	2nd Collateral	1st Collateral	LINEAL	1st Collateral	2nd Collateral	3rd Collateral	4th Co
				Kao tsu fu, Kao tsu mu,				I
			Tsèng tsu ku fu, Tsèng tsu ku mu,	Tsèng tsu fu, Tsèng tsu mu,	Tsèng po tsu fu, Tsèng shu tsu mu,			I
		Piao tsu fu, Piao tsu mu,	Ku tsu fu, Ku tsu mu,	Tsu fu, Tsu mu,	Po tsu fu, Po tsu mu, Shu tsu fu, Shu tsu mu,	T'ang po tsu fu, T'ang shu tsu fu, T'ang ku tsu mu,		
	T'ang piao po fu, T'ang piao shu fu, T'ang piao ku mu,	Piao po fu, Piao shu fu, Piao ku mu,	Ku fu, Ku mu,	Fu, Mu,	Po fu, Po mu, Shu fu, Shu mu,	T'ang po fu, T'ang shu fu, T'ang ku mu,	Tsai ts'ung po fu, Tsai ts'ung shu fu, Tsai ts'ung ku mu,	
Tsai ts'ung piao hsiung, ti, *Tsai ts'ung piao tzŭ, mei,*	T'ang piao hsiung, ti, *T'ang piao tzŭ, mei,*	Piao hsiung, Piao ti, *Piao tzŭ, Piao mei,*	Tzŭ, Tzŭ fu, Mei, Mei fu,	EGO	Hsiung, Sao, Ti, Ti fu,	T'ang hsiung, T'ang ti, *T'ang tzŭ, T'ang mei,*	Tsai ts'ung hsiung, ti, *Tsai ts'ung tzŭ, mei,*	Tsu h... T... *T... T...*
	T'ang piao chih, *T'ang piao chih nü,*	Piao chih, *Piao chih nü*	Wai shêng, *Wai shêng nü,*	Tzŭ, *Nü,*	Chih, *Chih nü,*	T'ang chih, *T'ang chih nü,*	Tsai ts'ung chih, *Tsai ts'ung chih nü,*	
		Piao chih sun,	Wai shêng sun,	Sun, *Sun nü*	Chih sun, *Chih sun nü,*	T'ang chih sun, *T'ang chih sun nü,*		
			Wai shêng tsêng sun,	Tsêng sun, *Tsêng sun nü,*	Tsêng chih sun, *Tsêng chih sun nü,*			
				Hsüan sun, *Hsüan sun nü,*				

The heavy squares represent the nuclear group of relatives. Those in italics, indicate their descendants not been carried over into the next generation, e. g., the children of *nü* are *wai sun* and *wai sun nü* but not in the following square. The Roman numerals represent ascending and descending generations.

important part of a child's education to learn to recognize and distinguish the degree of *ch'in* (closeness) and *su* (distance) in his contacts with his kinsmen as a basis for the proper amount of deference or obedience to be shown to them. In this respect, kinship relations take on the form of a series of concentric circles with Ego as the center — hence the foremost place for parents-children and sibling relationships in the Confucian system of family ethics.

The interlocking operation of these three factors, generation, age, and proximity of kinship, resulted in a system of status and authority that assigned to every person in the kinship group a fixed position identified by a complex nomenclature system.[3] The identification of status for distant relatives was facilitated by giving the same middle name to all sons born into the same generational level so that the kinship position of a person could be readily identified by the generational name whenever distant members met. An important feature of this system was that it could fit a kinship group of any size, from a small conjugal family to a vastly extended family like a clan with ten thousand or more members, thus giving the small family a ready organizational framework for expansion whenever economic conditions permitted.

This hierarchy of status and authority imposed strong compulsion on the individual to observe his own place in the group through, among other factors, the operation of the mores of filial piety and veneration of age. Filial piety demanded absolute obedience and complete devotion to the parents, thus establishing the generational subordination of the children. In traditional society an individual from childhood to the end of his life was completely immersed in an atmosphere which compelled the observation of filial piety. The lesson of filial piety was carried in nursery stories, in daily exhortations and reprimands, in tales and novels, in textbooks from the first primer to the most profound philosophical discourse, in the numerous "temples of filial sons and chaste women" (*chieh hsiao tz'u*) which studded the land, in dramatized living examples of extremely filial children.

The requirement of obedience to parents, fully supported by formal law in the Ching dynasty before 1912,[4] is still supported by the informal coercive instrument of clan regulations in the rural communities and even by "unregenerated" local officials in the Communist government, whose judgment of civil cases is frequently based more on social institution than on the already changed formal law. Under traditional social order it took exceptional courage and imagination to be an unfilial son.

To be sure, coercion was not the only means by which filial piety was instilled into the individual's mind. Equally important was the emphasis upon parental affection, parent-children interdependence, the children's moral obligation to repay parental care and affection by observing filial piety. Parental affection and feelings of gratitude were very active factors, for Chinese parental affection toward the children is traditionally both genuine and strong. In the old family institution the parents depended upon the children for their old-age security; hence their deep devotion to the care and upbringing of the children. Where the parents belonged to a humble station, they pinned their hopes of social and economic advancement on the future development of the children, particularly the son, another basis for the strong traditional affection toward children. Consequently, the old family structure and ethics did not permit a son to leave his parents in a humble social position when he himself had gained social and economic advancement, the basis for the automatic granting of honorific titles by the imperial government to parents of sons who had won social distinction by passing the traditional civil service examinations.

Dependence upon the children, especially the sons, was particularly strong with the mother. Since her status in the family depended upon the bearing of male heirs, it was not uncommon in traditional society for a mother to sacrifice her health, at times even her life, for the benefit of the children, especially the sons. The writer was told in his boyhood that an aunt contracted tuberculosis and finally died from it on account of her sacrifice for and worry over her son. It matters little whether that was the real cause of her illness and death; what is important was the significance the story had for inducing a feeling of filial piety among the young. The poor family selling property and undergoing extreme sacrifice to give the son an education reflected the same principle.

In recent decades, the once strong parent-children interdependence has been steadily diminished by the increasingly individualistic development of children, the elevation of the social and economic status of the young, the separation of married sons from the parental household through the new form of marriage, the decreasing significance of the family as a basic unit of economic production, and the gradual shifting of the individual's center of loyalty away from the family. These factors, which have an adverse effect on the value of children as an asset to the parents, plainly tend to dilute traditional parental devotion. In addition, the rise of democratic and individualistic trends in the Republican period resulted in widespread resentment against the oppressive features of filial piety which required absolute obedience, devotion, and sacrifice on the part of children. Thus filial piety, once the most emphatically stressed value in the traditional social order for over two thousand years, was subjected to open challenge in the 1920's, gradually lost its sacred and binding character among the modern intellectuals by the 1930's, and, by the time the Communists became the ruling power, was publicly discredited by them as feudalistic, designed for the exploitation of the young.

While the functioning of filial piety was limited to relationships between parents and children, the veneration of age was traditionally a means of inspiring respect and obedience by the young toward all the other senior members of the family and society as a whole. To demonstrate the glory and prestige of age, an individual's sixtieth birthday and every subsequent tenth birthday were celebrated with a feast and ceremony as elaborate and impressive as the family and close relatives could possibly afford. This ritualistic glorification symbolized increased respect for the person's status and authority and implied a greater consideration of his personal needs by others.[5] In vital matters of the family and community his advice was heeded, although he might no longer have the heavy family responsibilities or the actual compelling power of his younger days. The old grandfather and, to a lesser degree, the old grandmother were frequently the only ones in the family who could restrain a despotic or wayward father, relying upon the support of the mores and law for their authority. The seat of honor on family and community occasions was for the old man. Not only did the family try to give him the best material benefits in food and clothing; the clan also accorded him honor. In the southern provinces of Kwangtung and Kwangsi, where the distribution of pork to male clan members was a token of clan membership and status, he was given a double share. He was at the pinnacle of the age hierarchy.

The social logic for this practice was the consideration of old people as a symbol of wisdom. In a society of empirical knowledge and predominant illiteracy the old person had the advantage of experience. He had traversed the greater part of a life cycle and so had seen the operation of major crises in life from routine matters of birth, marriage, and death to other happenings such as major clashes between family members, devastation of wars, visits of natural calamities such as flood and droughts, or the appearance of a portentous star in the skies. When younger people were stunned by a happening, an older person remained calm and knew what to do. He knew the procedure for handling the birth of a baby, the marriage of the young, the burial of the dead, the settlement of a dispute in accordance with the traditional sense of justice, and the safe direction in which to flee when calamity struck. His stock of common sense even included the administration of medicine to the sick. An "old man of worldly affairs" was the guiding hand of the family and the community. His "I have lived longer than you" was the ready and effective reminder to the occasionally disrespectful young.

Where empiricism and illiteracy prevailed, age was also an asset in technical fields. In every traditional craft, the "old master" was most respected, not the brilliant and vigorous young worker. In agriculture his experience was similarly valued by the community. In 1949 the writer tried to introduce into a village an improved weeder which worked much more effectively than hand weeding or hoeing. The younger peasants tried it and liked it very much, but a few days later nobody wanted to use the new instrument because "the old people concluded that it will hurt the root system of the plant." The writer challenged the younger peasants to experiment with the instrument by offering to pay for any damage resulting from it, but to no avail. Confucius' advice of learning to farm from an "old farmer" still stood firm.[6] From handicraft to farming, the "old master" was the model of skill and knowledge. There were few books and no school of technical training in traditional society. The old master taught and advised and laid down rules for the young to follow. He led the family and the community in economic matters.

Thus old people in traditional society were far from being decrepit seniles living off the kindness of society on empty prestige, for age had very practical significance for both the family and the community. The veneration of age not only compelled respect for the aged but also lent prestige to all senior members in the hierarchy of age.

Functioning through the strength of filial piety and veneration of age, the hierarchy of age served to provide a status system for the operation of family authority, to firmly initiate the young into the institution of family life until they reached full maturity, to establish security for the old, and to impress upon the individual the dominance of the family as a corporate body. The long stability of the traditional family institution was due in no small measure to the successful operation of this factor.

But such stability was achieved at the price of strenuous repression of the young and was weakened when it came under fire from modern ideologies and social movements that advocated equality and freedom, particularly freedom for the young. Under the weight of the age hierarchy, the status of the young was indeed low, at times helpless. The authority of parents over the child was absolute. Infanticide, approved by the community, was an expression of it; and even as the child grew older, the parents' threat against his life was by no means completely eliminated. The proverb "The son must die if so demanded by the father" was a means of compelling obedience from the young in traditional China, especially in rural communities, although the carrying out of the threat was extremely rare. A childhood that passed without frequent physical punishment was an exception rather than the rule. When a child reached his mid-teens, his increased physical strength and his ability to run away bolstered his security, but the requirement of filial piety kept a tight rein on him. The necessity of observing this moral code was not merely impressed upon him in the operation of the family institution and group pressure of the community; it was also enforced by formal law. In the Ch'ing period sons were flogged or banished by the court merely on the charge of disobedience brought by the father.[7]

In the Republican period few such cases came to public attention, but the rigid enforcement of filial piety by the clans was not much relaxed in places where the clan organization was strong, such as in rural communities in the Central-South provinces. It is interesting to note that P'eng Teh-huai, a prominent Communist general, was once close to being condemned to death by his clan on the charge of being unfilial to his stepmother.[8] In the writer's own boyhood in the 1920's there was still the frequent verbal threat of being taken back to the ancestral village "to be drowned in a pig's cage by the clan elders" in case of gross disobedience to the parents — although he lived in the city, where the clan wielded no direct influence. Such legal and social pressures drove fear and a feeling of rigid subordination deep into the mind of the young individual.

Although less absolute and rigid than parental dominance over the children, the pressure of status and authority of senior members over junior members in the age hierarchy was by no means light. This was especially so with members of one's own superior generation having a close degree of kinship tie, such as one's grandparents and older uncles. Before them one behaved only with great respect, and one did not argue with or talk back to them. In material rights and privileges their share undisputably came first. On ceremonial occasions one stood or sat in an inferior position to them. They were the "respected elders" even though some of them might not actually be chronologically older. They were held up to the young as models of good conduct, as masters of arts and skills. Before a person reached the age of thirty his words had little weight; his conduct and his work were under constant criticism by senior kinsmen around him. Not until the fourth decade in one's life would one begin to gain serious consideration from senior members in the age hierarchy.

Rise of the Young under the Republic

The practical value of age as a major basis for the great respect of the age hierarchy began to be challenged with the impact of revolutionary currents early in this century. The dominant note of the modern times has been the acquisition of Western knowledge and technological skills and the development of new institutions to implement Western-inspired ideas in an effort to save China in the struggle for national existence; and these could not be acquired simply by experience in the traditional social environment. The only means of acquiring them were through learning and training in schools and through new sources of information; and the required method of developing them, in China as elsewhere, was through science, not empiricism enriched by age.

In the acquisition of new knowledge, new skills, and new ideas the young (those from families capable of affording a modern education) had a distinct advantage over the old. The young had plasticity of mind, eagerness for the new and the adventurous, fewer obstacles in the consciousness of vested interests and entrenched traditional social relationships. Above all, rigid repression of the young by the hierarchy of age gave them an eagerness to alter their old status by acquiring new knowledge and skills and by promoting the adoption of new institutions. Hence, the modern educated young Chinese formed a nucleus from which new influences germinated and gradually developed into leading forces in political, economic, and social trends. The young were no longer bowing to the old at every turn, and age was no longer always a mark of personal prestige and social authority.

Over the past half century every political revolution and social development has acted as a new force in expanding the number and influence of the modern educated young. In the course of its limited success in encouraging revolutionary ideas championed by the young the Republican revolution of 1911 put a larger number of young elements into prominent political positions than there ever had been under the old imperial government. In the turbulent years of 1917 to 1919 the young were presented to the nation as a distinctive age group under the term "new youth" by the rising crescendo of the youth movement, culminating in the May 4th Movement of 1919, which placed the educated young in a position of new importance in political and cultural fields. Led by the historic periodical, *Hsin Ch'ing-nien* (The New Youth), tons of literature in the form of magazines, press articles, and pamphlets poured forth on the subject of the new youth and its problems, forcing the new age group to the nation's attention. Political and economic crises of the period, the necessity of new means for their solution, together with the impotent traditionalism of the old and the general illiteracy of the common people, created a new role for the modern educated youth and led them to demand revision of the subordinate status of the young. For the first time a powerful social and political movement put up a young group in opposition to the old and the institutions the latter stood for.

When the Second Revolution swept the country in the mid-1920's, the exaltation of the young was carried to new heights. The revolutionary regime based in Canton was marked by the youthfulness of the personnel that staffed it. Every branch of the new political machine that baffled and at times frustrated the old was led and manned mainly by young men and colored by the outlook of youth. The occasional presence of an old man over sixty in their midst was a spectacle, for here was "an old dog that had learned new tricks." When the seat of political power, the center of formal social control, was captured by the young, the sanctity of the age hierarchy could not be expected to remain intact.

In the cultural field the "Renaissance" of the May 4th Movement was a product of the young, and by the mid-1920's it had made deep inroads into the educational system of the country, particularly in the storm center of the South. The quantity of "New Culture" publications in all fields had by that time distinctly pushed Confucian classical works to the side, at least in the cities. The new literature, particularly in works of fiction, clearly steered away from the traditional motif of fairy tales and from Confucian themes and drew its inspiration from Western ideas that concerned the special problems of the young. Its undisputed literary dominance together with its modern theme of romantic love led the educated young and indirectly the younger generation in general, toward an outlook of life and love which retained little respect for the age hierarchy and frequently held little consideration at all for the old.

In the economic field accelerated industrial development after World War I gave increasingly responsible positions to the young, who alone commanded modern technical qualifications. Technical dreams of the young set the blueprints for the nation's economic development. The "old master's" prestige declined with the diminishing importance of the traditional crafts under the crushing superiority of modern technology. The old master still held sway in the vast pre-industrial sector of the country's economic structure, but his technical competence no longer commanded the moral respect of the educated young, and his outmoded technical role could no longer support the age hierarchy in that modernized segment of the population which was leading the trend of economic development. The social and economic plight of the growing army of unemployed old craft masters was hardly conducive to the effective maintenance of age as a criterion of technical competence.

The older generation watched in bewilderment the making and unmaking of governments, the waging of the unending civil wars, the ever-rising prestige of new commodities and new economic organizations, the unfamiliar events that occupied increasing space in the newspapers and in the people's daily conversations, the untraditional ways of training and educating the young — all these changes staged by a group that had hitherto been in an inferior position in the age hierarchy forced society to grant more consideration to the young. In the family, if the young still paid a measure of respect to parents and senior members in the age hierarchy, it was done with a tinge of begrudging formality and seldom with the spontaneous sincerity and voluntary devotion formerly developed by filial piety and veneration of age.

The vital change of attitude toward age was limited largely to the modern educated young, the new youth, but the new youth were an articulate group playing a strategic role in the shaping of social trends. The facilities of modern education were rapidly expanding, with its middle and primary levels steadily extending to members of the lower middle class, and the mass education movement which started after the May 4th Movement of 1919 served as another vehicle for the diffusion of the new attitude into a small part of the working class and the peasantry. Largely centered in urban areas, the change affected also the young elements of the richer portion of the rural population as they took to the cities for better educational facilities, where their attitude toward the traditional age hierarchy was altered by absorbing new ideas and by insulation from the immediate pressure of parents and senior kinsmen at home.

When the great upheaval of the 1920's settled down to a divided course in the 1930's, with the Kuomintang dominating the nation and the Communist Party setting up red areas in the South, the traditional Chinese attitude toward the age hierarchy had already been substantially diluted. The two decades that followed saw the continued extension of the new influence to growing numbers of the young, aided by the increased absence of the young of all social classes from home in a period of increasing population mobility, which freed the younger generation from the immediate pressure of the age hierarchy in the kinship system. In the early 1930's such mobility was mainly a consequence of the accelerated development of urbanism, which set many of the young on the move away from home for jobs or educational opportunities. After 1937 the Japanese invasion drove millions far from their local communities, and the young were left free to develop the new attitude toward age with a minimum of immediate interference from older kinsmen. Thus, long before 1949 the ground had been prepared for the developments under communism.

Status of the Young under the Communist Regime

The triumph of the Communist revolution carried the exaltation of the young to a new height. If youth furnished the vital force of China's previous revolutions, it certainly did so even more emphatically with the Communist revolution. Its radical ideological departure from tradition first found acceptance only in the more plastic young minds, and the Communists possessed great skill in organizing the young for the service of the revolution.

The elevation of the status of the young under the Communist regime has been, first of all, a highly organized movement, not a spontaneous development. Secondly, that movement has spread from the hitherto confined circle of upper- and middle-class young intelligentsia to the numerically large group of young workers and peasants. For some three decades before Communist accession to power youth organizations had had a steady growth, but they were comparatively small in membership and poorly integrated. Under the Communist regime youth organizations have been vastly expanded in membership, centrally directed, and well-disciplined.

The New Democratic Youth League is an example. According to statistics of September 1951, its national membership had reached 5,180,000 — twenty-seven times the membership figure of 190,000 of April 1949. There were 24,200 branches in various parts of the country. Classification of the membership was as follows: workers, 33.88 per cent; peasants, 51.18 per cent; students, 11.44 per cent; others, 2.5 per cent. Females accounted for about 30 per cent of the total. By 1957 the

League membership had leaped to 23,000,000, "accounting for 19.17 per cent of the total number of young people in China." [9]

It is notable that students who monopolized the youth movement in the pre-Communist period now comprise only a little over one-tenth of the membership of the most important organization of the young under the Communist regime. In this respect, the Democratic Women's League, with its vast network of affiliated organizations, also has a fast expanding membership, the majority of whom are now women peasants and workers, not intellectuals. Above all, the Chinese Communist Party itself, which has experienced a phenomenal growth in membership since 1949, is dominated numerically by the young, who are drawn mainly from the peasantry and the workers, only a minority coming from the urban intelligentsia.

Youth organizations and other organizations containing a majority of young members serve a variety of purposes, among which is the conscious and unconscious function of advancing the power and status of the young. In this sense, these organizations have the significance of representing a formally organized struggle, aided by political power, to alter the status of the young in the traditional age hierarchy.

Organized struggle for status by the young is actively advanced by the publication of literature on the subject of youth in unprecedented quantity. Let us consider the publishing activities of the New Democratic Youth League in 1951 alone: "For the purpose of propaganda and education, the Youth League publishes 61 newspapers and periodicals for its general membership throughout the nation. The Youth Publication Company under the Central Committee of the Youth League, which was established in 1950, has published 14 categories and 260 kinds of book series and periodicals, which total 8,800,000 copies. *Chung-kuo Ch'ing-nien pao* (Chinese Youth), the daily newspaper serving as the official organ of the Central Committee of the Youth League, will be published on April 27 of this year [1951]. (*Chung-kuo Ch'ing-nien Shuang-chou-k'an* (Chinese Youth Biweekly), also an organ of the Youth League's Central Committee, is among the most widely circulated periodicals in the country." [10]

If the youthfulness of the personnel of the Southern revolutionary regime in the mid-1920's had the effect of elevating the status of the young, the same is even more true of the present Communist regime. Although the top leaders of this regime are generally older than their counterparts in the mid-1920's, Mao Tse-tung and the majority of the leading party figures started their political career in close connection with youth organizations.[11] The three decades of struggle for power advanced their age, but it did not lessen their identification with the cause of youth.

As for the middle- and lower-ranking party members who form the lower echelon of the Communist regime, the average age level is lower than that of corresponding personnel in any previous Chinese government. A government announcement on the recruitment of young men and women for training to be junior officers in police work listed an age limit of eighteen to twenty-three.[12] Similar age limits for other types of political work can be seen in other recruiting announcements. Young men in their twenties and thirties head local government departments that concern the vital interests of tens of thousands of people. In urban neighborhood and village indoctrination and propaganda meetings it is the young leaders who do the talking and lay down the line, and it is the older people who have to do the listening and following. In enforcing policies, be it a bond sales campaign, suppression of counterrevolutionaries, mass trial of landlords and local bullies and the redistribution of land, the Five-Anti movement against businessmen committing bribery, evasion of taxes, theft of state property, cheating on state contracts and theft of confidential state economic information, or a score of other major and minor movements that have disorganized the traditional pattern of life under Communist rule, it is the young leaders, ranging in age from the teens to the thirties, who have been running the show.

The amount of political power and responsibility vested in the hands of young local leaders is certainly without precedent in China's history; and it is shared by young men and women belonging to public organizations which are regularly mobilized to participate in current movements and to help enforce government policies. Members of the Youth League, the Democratic Women's League, the student union, and many other organizations work side by side with party officers in carrying out major government policies.

The young have come to possess not only coercive power but also social prestige under the new standards set up by the regime. To the young go the large proportion of awards for "model workers," "model farmers," winners in production emulations; they are the recipients of many other honors symbolizing new values [13] that are foreign to the old generation. The leading "model workers" held up as examples of production efficiency for the rest of the workers, from Ma Heng-chang in mining to Nan Chien-hsiu in the textile industry, the counterparts of Stakhanovites in the Soviet Union, are young men and women, most of them in their twenties. The influence of youth begins to invade even the old empirical field of agriculture wherever improvements of agricultural methods are being vigorously introduced:

> In the patriotic production movement in the villages, members of the Youth League are vigorous shock brigades. They not only participate in agricultural production but also actively propagandize the agricultural policy of the People's Government among the people. They lead in organizing mutual-aid teams, in popularizing new agricultural methods. For example, Kuo Yu-lan in Heilungkiang Province and Wang Ching-mei in Hopei Province, both female members of the Youth League, have won the title of model agricultural workers. They both have popularized seed-selection, the soaking of seeds before sowing, and other new agricultural methods in their own communities, and the yields from their fields are higher than the average of other farmers. In the irrigation project of controlling the Huai River, members of the Youth League inhabiting the banks of the river mobilized large numbers of young people to participate in the work. Last winter [1951], in the northern part of Anhwei Province alone, one-third of the 600,000 labor conscripts were young people. Among these young workers were 16,000 members of the Youth League who formed the leading force of the labor conscripts. In the county of Pu-yang, Youth League members accounted for 30 per cent of the model irrigation workers.[14]

If it was the young technical men of the modern bourgeois intelligentsia who dimmed the prestige of the traditional "old craft masters" in the pre-Communist period, now the progressive young workers and peasants are doing the same thing on a more extensive scale. In traditional days a brilliant and successful young man might be held up as an example for members of his own generation, but never for his senior members in the age hierarchy or the old masters of the trade, who might regard him with benign approval but always considered him immature, with more to learn from older people. Now in every factory, every neighborhood, and in the villages young models of production and revolutionary conduct are glorified with fanfare and honored with material rewards. Ended is the sanctity of the time-honored rule that the old teach and the young learn, the old lead and the young follow. A student leader told his professor in 1951: "You and your generation are too beset with considerations and worries for decisive action, so we young ones should lead in changing the nation's way of life."

Change of Status of the Old in the Family

It is clear that the traditional older generation with its conservatism is regarded as an obstacle to progress. Even though there is no substantiation to rumors of summary gross mistreatment of all old people as an age group, such rumors reflect the general decline in status and power of the older generation. This change has inevitable effects on the status of the older generation within the family organization.

The political struggle in which the young are playing a leading part is carried into the family. From the time the Communists took control of the nation, and through the successive crises of the suppression of counter-revolutionaries, the Five-Anti and the Three-Anti movements, and the "thought reform" of the intellectuals, every progressive young person has been increasingly under group pressure to disregard kinship ties and the prestige of age and ferret out dissenters and recalcitrants for correction and, at times, even for elimination.* Since parents and uncles and elder brothers have been openly accused or secretly reported by junior members in the age hierarchy for offenses leading to police surveillance, fines, labor correction, imprisonment, or even death, the progressive young person is as much feared at home as in public. It is common to find older people suddenly stop talking about public matters, particularly political affairs, as soon as a progressive young family member comes home, especially if he comes home from school, where ideological indoctrination has been vigorously carried on. While the exact proportion of progressives among the young will remain unknown for some time, there is little doubt of the widespread effect of the new ideology on young minds and the rapid extension of this effect from the bourgeois intelligentsia to the much wider circle of young workers and peasants, as seen in the membership growth of the Youth League. Sharp is the contrast between this situation and the traditional order when family mores were in complete harmony with the nation's political ideology, when a successful and prominent son paid homage to his socially humble parents and other senior kinsmen.

Communist law and political principles no longer provide any support for the superiority and rights of an individual over another based on age. On the contrary, they tend to limit traditional authority and the rights of the old over the young. The prohibition of mistreatment of children limits what the parents can do with the young.[15] Elaborate legal stipulations on the protection of children's interests in the family have the same effect.[16] The single legal requirement of children is that they must support the parents and must not mistreat or abandon

* The Five-Anti movement, aimed at the business class, has been explained before. The Three-Anti movement is aimed at correcting corruption, wastefulness, and bureaucratism among government officials and employees.

them.[17] In stipulations of the Marriage Law responsibilities of parents are much heavier than their rights over children — a reversal of the requirements of traditional filial piety which compelled almost one-sided devotion by the children.

There are no stipulations in Communist law governing the relationship of the older generation to the young aside from that of parents to children. However, since the parent-child relationship is stronger than the relationship between other members in the age hierarchy, when the parents' position is greatly weakened the position of other senior members in the family over the young deteriorates more rapidly. For a young progressive the traditional authority of an uncle or an aunt carries little weight, and that of more distant seniors in the age hierarchy means even less. Published documents show more political accusations by the young against other relatives than against parents.[18]

If the older generation finds no protection for their traditional status from politics and law in the revolution, it finds the safeguards also weak in other directions. Wherever modern economic development prevails, older people are finding it difficult to retain positions of leadership in family production. The replacement of numerous family businesses in trade and industry by state enterprises and the development of collectivized agriculture have had serious effects in this respect. The tendency of increasing economic qualifications and rights of the younger family member and the growing system of free education lessen the dependence of the young and reduce the economic authority of the older generation as a factor in maintaining its traditional status in the age hierarchy.

The development of centers of activity outside the home for the young adds another difficulty to the maintenance of the age hierarchy as a system of family status and authority, both because of the lack of time to teach the traditional ideas to the young at home and because of the conflicting ideology being instilled into the minds of the young in outside centers of activity. The development of modern schools during the past half century and the rapid growth of membership of youth organizations under the Communist regime are examples of this development. Under the Communists young men and women are recruited in large numbers as paid workers or volunteers for a great variety of public activities which take them away from home part time or full time at an age from the early teens to the twenties, an age in which they would have remained very close to home in the traditional system. The following is illustrative of the increasing separation of the young from family influence.

> In Feng Ch'i village near the city of Canton over forty young men and women, led by some twenty Youth League members, cultivated an acre of "tabooed" land [land that the villagers would not till for superstitious fear of bringing misfortune]. They sold the rice yielded from it, bought lumber with the money, built a house, and called it "The Home of Youth." They used the house for ideological classes, meetings, and activities. It has become the youth center in the village.[19]

The establishment of a center of organized activities exclusively for the young as an age group in the rural community is a new phenomenon, for all activity of the young except school was traditionally centered in the home. It is interesting to note the name of the center, "The Home of Youth," still using the word "home" which has a connotation of strong social affinity for the Chinese. At this "home" the older generation can no longer exercise discipline and control over the young. With the superiority of age being seriously undermined, with the young tending to move out of the range of family education and discipline, with the legal support of filial piety gone, with the basic concept of the marriage of the children being changed, the welfare and security of the old becomes a weighty consideration in this transitional period. True, Communist law requires children to support their parents. In Shanghai, for example, an old woman abandoned by her son obtained support from him by order of the "people's court." [20] But the law does not prosecute such cases unless brought to court. In spite of increased accessibility to the law, there is a question whether every neglected or abandoned parent will bring the case to court in a situation where rule by law is still unfamiliar to common people. There is little doubt that such legal support is incomparably weaker than the guarantee provided by the traditional family for the welfare and security of the old.

The spectacular rise of the young and the decline of the old in power and prestige are plainly products of that stage of revolution which needs plastic young minds to accept the novel ideology, to practice the new standards, and to effect a drastic break with the traditional past. As the revolutionary situation settles down to an established order, with its new institutions and tradition sufficiently developed, age as a factor affecting the status and authority of individuals will undoubtedly resume some degree of importance, and accumulated knowledge and experience through age will again bear weight in the social evaluation of an individual. But it is doubtful whether age will ever resume the former traditional importance which summarily subjected the young to an inferior position in disregard of his other qualifications. The development of industrialization, which emphasizes technical competence, not age, and the popularization of science, which discounts empiricism, are both major goals of the present Communist revolution. Should the revolution successfully set up its institutions and traditions, these two factors among others will preclude a full return to the former Chinese consideration for age.

CHAPTER VI

The Ascendancy of the Status of Women in the Family

DIFFERENCE IN SEX, as in age, was a factor in the stratification of status and allocation of authority, which in traditional China meant the subordination of women in the dichotomy of family membership based on sex difference. This was partly a result of the patrilineal and patrilocal nature of the Chinese family structure, in which the definition of membership of the patrilineal kinship system and the distribution of rights and duties in it called for a male-dominant system of status and authority so as to prevent interference and disruption from maternal kinship ties. Subordination of female members, like subordination of the young, in the traditional family always constituted a point of tension which was kept under control by various authoritarian features of the old family institution.

In the modern period the liberal humanistic values and socio-economic developments of industrial urbanism seriously weakened the features which forced women into a subordinate position, and there was a general movement toward the emancipation of women. The alteration of women's status both in the family and in society became a major theme of the family revolution. Since the Communist revolution from its beginning advocated equality between the sexes even more emphatically than other social movements, it was inevitable that a change in the role of women should become an ever important factor in the reshaping of the family institution under Communist rule.

The Status of Women in the Traditional Family

The traditional status of women may not have been so low in China as in some of the contemporary cultures, the Islamic and the Japanese for example. The status of a Chinese woman improved with age and the bearing of children, and she could become the head of a household. Socially, women achieved distinction in various fields of endeavor, including art and scholarship, and they occasionally occupied the throne, as exemplified by the powerful nineteenth-century Empress Dowager. Among the common people, especially in the South, women's active part in economic production bolstered their position in the family and mitigated the general social discrimination against them. Nevertheless, the low status of Chinese women whether in the family or in society is proverbial. In traditional Chinese fiction the female character was frequently introduced by the line "unfortunately [she] was born a woman." K'ang Yu-wei, the precursor of modern reformers at the end of the last century, listed being born a woman as one of the calamities of life.[1]

The status of the female in the traditional Chinese family changed in different stages of her life. Her status in childhood and girlhood was not particularly low compared to that of her brothers or male cousins in the same household. In spite of her low evaluation as a family asset, she enjoyed a fair share of parental affection and material family benefits. The first serious discrimination came in the matter of educational opportunity, which went first to the son even when the idea of education for women had started to be accepted in modern cities, for educational investment in a girl was considered irrecoverable owing to her eventual departure from the family. Her most trying period began with her marriage into another family.[2] She was a stranger in a new family, under relentless intimate surveillance and discipline from the parents-in-law, unprotected by the supposedly intimate husband, and left to fate by custom and law. Before she gave birth to a son, she was considered only a half-qualified member of the family. With the birth of a son, she fulfilled her duty in perpetuating the ancestral lineage and found protection and security in the future of the son. Motherhood of a male descendant always lessened family discrimination against her and from then on, her lot improved as the children grew older. When she became a grandmother, she was usually the supreme woman in the household, ranking in status next to her husband should he still be living.

In each stage of her life she held an inferior position to the male members of the family of the same generational level in vital matters, and to those in the generation above hers in all matters. This inferiority of status, mitigated by parental and general family affection while she was still at home, explains the harsh situation of the bride trying to adjust to the intimate ways of the superiors who were strangers to her, including the husband whom she had married by parental arrangement and not by personal choice. With marriage began the most personally humiliating and emotionally disturbing stage of a woman's life, generally covering the age from sixteen or eighteen to the thirties, after which the mother-in-law would either have died or retired and the children would be grown. In this stage one saw the raw subjugation of an individual, for the most relentless measures were sometimes taken by the family against the young female who tended to reject subordination.

The young wife was subordinated not only to the males of the family but also to the mother-in-law and, to a lesser degree, to other females in the superior generation. It could be argued that the mother-in-law, in order to exercise discipline upon the daughter-in-law, must enlist the approval and cooperation of her own husband and her married son, and that her authority was delegated by the male. This seems to be only academic. What really mattered was that only the young wife's submission made it possible for the traditional family to assimilate a new female member into its intimate life and thus prevented the breaking off by the young wife and her husband into an independent family.

Loss of Women's Lives in the Traditional Family

The process of subordination and adjustment of the wife was so painful, and the traditional family institution, recognizing no right of divorce, left so little possibility of escape, that it sometimes resulted in the loss of her life by suicide or by murder. The long history of family conflicts ending in the death of the wife was echoed in the slogan of the May 4th Movement: "Down with the human-devouring ritualistic tradition."

In 1935, when statistics were grossly incomplete, 1,353 suicides were reported in 244 counties and in 22 provinces. Of this total, 351, or 26.0 per cent, were caused by domestic discord or matrimonial difficulties, which constituted the largest single item among all causes of suicide in China (economic difficulties caused 341 cases, or 25.2 per cent, of all suicides). Among the 351 cases of suicide caused by family conflict 253, or 72 per cent, were women.[3]

In the Communist period a greater amount of information on this subject is published, although figures are still fragmentary in character. The following are excerpts from reports in the Communist press:

According to incomplete statistics, women who committed suicide or who were killed on account of . . . family mistreatment numbered over

10,000 in the Central-South Region, and 1,245 in Shantung Province, both in the past year [1950], and 119 in the nine counties of the Huaiyin Special District in the northern part of Kiangsu Province during the months of May to August, 1950.[4]

In the special district of Changsha, Hunan Province, during the period from May to August 1950 incomplete statistics show that 99 women lost their lives on account of family mistreatment, and among them 68 were forced to commit suicide, and 31 were killed or died from inflicted injuries. In the county of Huangan of Hupei Province during the two months of July and August 1950, 14 women died from the same cause. In Shangshui county of Honan Province during a period of three months in 1950, 90 women were driven to death by family mistreatment. In Ningyuan county of Hunan Province in the period of two months 17 women committed suicide for the same reason.[5]

In Tsuiyang county of Honan Province during the period of not quite a year in 1950, 212 women were killed or committed suicide. In Shangch'iu county of the same province during the months from January to April 1951 over 30 women committed suicide on account of matrimonial problems . . . . In Tsang-hsien Special District during the first half of 1951, 47 women were forced into suicide or killed by family situations. [Among these cases] in the village of Chaohsiamatou in Chiaoho county, the woman Han Kuo-chen was axed to death by her husband when she threatened to get a divorce.[6]

During the past year [1950] among the 936 cases involving the loss of human lives handled by the people's courts of various levels in the province of Shansi somewhat over 600 cases, or about 66 per cent, were women who were either tortured to death or forced into suicide.[7]

Available Communist literature published after 1952 contains no further statistical information on the subject, possibly because of the socially disturbing nature of such figures at a time when the Communists wanted to consolidate their political power by stabilizing the social order. The significant point is that these statistics do not represent the entire number of women who lost their lives but only those incidents which came to the attention of the authorities. In T'eng-hsien Special District of Shantung Province it was only as a consequence of the court making an issue out of the case of P'an Shi, a wife who was tortured to death by her husband and mother-in-law, that 103 other cases of women who had been killed or committed suicide in that district came to the attention of the authorities.[8]

The lack of basic population data for the territories for which the above fragmentary statistics are given makes it impossible to compute rates. One can get an idea of the situation in the following statement by a woman leader made in 1951: "My mother was so mistreated by my father that she hanged herself. My father sent me into the Wang family as a child bride when I was only nine. I know well the suffering of women. Later, in the struggle against local bullies, I joined the Communist Party. The people elected me chairman of the peasants association of the Shawangtien subdistrict [of Mingchuan county in Honan Province]. . . . Since the promulgation of the Marriage Law, women have become organized, and people do not dare to oppress women as before. Some mothers-in-law and husbands still try to mistreat wives. This problem has to be solved, otherwise a small incident can develop into a big tragedy. We are trying hard on this point. . . . And in this subdistrict, which comprises twelve villages with a total population over 2,200, not one woman has been forced into suicide or beaten to death since the Liberation [the fall of 1949]." [9] It is significant that this woman leader was proud that no women's lives had been lost in a small community of 2,200 people inside of two years. It suggests the possibility that in a community of some 2,200 people over a period of two years, people would expect one or more cases of the killing or suicide of women.

Lacking comparable statistics on deaths of women from domestic discord in the pre-Communist period, it is not known to what extent such deaths in the foregoing figures are a part of the traditional situation and to what extent they are a result of new conflict arising from the introduction of the family revolution into rural communities hitherto isolated from modern influences. Commenting on the rise of such deaths in all parts of the country during 1951 and 1952, a Communist writer, Ch'en Yu-tung, stated that those women who met death "were mostly progressive in thought, militant in spirit, strong in their capacity for work, and young in age," enthusiastic about the new rights of marriage and divorce, and active in the struggle against the old family institution.[10] From this characterization, these women were so-called activists in the Communist movement.

This statement from a writer who had access to Communist official data suggests that the alarming figures of suicides and killing were not so much a part of the pre-Communist situation as a result of the increase and sharpening of domestic conflict stimulated by extension of the women's emancipation movement and the family revolution into the rural countryside, the stronghold of traditional conservatism. Moreover, the years covered by these statistical figures, 1950–1952, were years when the new Communist regime carried its revolutionary fury into rural communities to liquidate the landlord class and to uproot the "feudalistic system." Executions, tortures, and other forms of physical punishment were liberally used in this struggle; and in the general flare of violence men employed their new political power to defend their traditional authority over rebellious women, as we have noted in Chapter IV. In such a situation it is fully possible that the number of suicides and the killing of women would increase noticeably. But even if the figures do not represent the normal traditional situation, they reveal the rigidity of the old family institutions, its intolerance toward deviation, and the lack of any channel of personal readjustment for women who might dare to violate the ancient mores by raising new demands and showing rebelliousness.

Factors in the Traditional Subordination of Women

To hold women in general, and young and middle-aged wives in particular, to an inferior status where mistreatment abounded and even death lurked, the authority of the family was supported by all the repressive features of the traditional institution of arranged marriage. We have noted that this institution minimized the roles of the marrying couple, reducing the significance of the bride as an individual. The practice of the husband's family in paying a symbolic or realistic price for her, the "buying and selling marriage" as it is called by modern youth, was a particularly influential factor in giving her a subordinate status. That it continued to exist widely as late as 1951 and 1952, the early years of Communist rule, is shown in the following reports:

> In Ts'ang county of Hopei Province the "buying and selling marriage" is still the rule. There is a common saying in that locality, "In a betrothal, when a daughter goes out, an ox comes in." The meaning of this saying is that the money obtained from selling the daughter is sufficient to buy an ox. In Yinch'iu county of the same province the man's family has to pay the girl's family one hundred feet of cloth, and some even pay a thousand catties of grain.[11]
>
> In Yungnien county of Hopei Province when a girl is betrothed the man's family has to pay the girl's family a certain amount of cotton or the equivalent in cash. The girl's family will not give up the girl in case the promised amount is not fully paid. In Szu village in P'inglo county of Ninghsia Province the village head, May Yu, for the marriage of his son paid the girl's family forty silver dollars, thirty-eight feet of cloth, and 800 catties of wheat. To pay this, Ma Yu sold seventeen mow of his land and some other property. After the marriage the entire family suffered from hunger, for the family was financially bankrupt.[12]
>
> In the rural district of Shaohsing county in Chekiang Province the

common practice of figuring the price for a bride is by her age, paying one picul [133 pounds] of rice for each year. In Kiashan county of Chekiang Province the ritual cash for a bride is from twenty to thirty-piculs of rice, aside from the price for the go-between.[13]

And the consequence of this practice? In Changnan village, in Kiashan county of Chekiang Province, Ch'en Chin-lao beat his wife. When a leader of the land reform program came up to stop him, Ch'en snapped back: "I bought her for 1,200 catties of rice. What does it matter if I give her a little beating?"[14] And wife beating was not limited to the peasantry. Thus ran a Communist report from the modern city of Shanghai in 1950: "Among the most serious problems brought forth by women workers is the common practice of beating and mistreating wives. Some husbands beat their wives until they bleed from their wounds. Even the chairman of a labor union beats up his wife."[15]

We have also noted that in traditional marriage the woman be-longed to the husband's family for life. The traditional wedding ceremony was attended only by the relatives of the husband's family, the girl's family held its own celebration separately without partici-pation from members of the husband's family, and there was no oc-casion during the whole process of the wedding when the two families met together. This had the effect of serving notice on the girl's family not to meddle in the affairs of the husband's family concerning the treatment of the bride. And since, except on ceremonial occasions, frequent visits by the wife to her own parents' home were discouraged, the wife was deprived of her own family's support in case of mistreat-ment.

In addition to concubinage, which posed a constant threat against the wife, and the absence of freedom of divorce, which served to block the wife from a peaceful means of escape from an unpleasant situation, there were three other traditional limitations which applied not only in marriage but to the general status of women in Chinese society: loss of her name, seclusion, and lack of education.

After marriage a woman discarded her own given name and was known to the community only by her surname prefixed with the sur-name of her husband's family. In the home she was addressed by a kinship term denoting her position in the family organization which omitted both her surname and given name. In effect, her individual existence in society was effaced.

Women were generally secluded. They were not only prevented

from contact with men outside the family, thus forestalling romantic love as a basis for marriage, but also, after marriage, cut off from opportunities for independence in political, economic, and social activities. Even in the early years of Communist rule traditional Chinese still insisted on this practice of secluding women, especially when such seclusion was being threatened:

> Restricting and interfering with women's participation in social activities is a form of mistreatment. After the victory of the Chinese people's revolution, due to the growth of political awakening, the broad masses of women have begun to participate in social activities, but they face a great deal of resistance. Some women who participated in the women's association, in literacy classes, or in newspaper-reading groups, have come home to confront the long faces of a husband and mother-in-law. Some women have returned from a meeting and the family would not give them food to eat, and some have even been locked out of the house. Some husbands and mothers-in-law summarily forbid women from participating in any social activity. Still other women are beaten up or even tortured to death by their husbands and mothers-in-law because of participation in social activities. Such conditions occur not only among peasants and workers, but also among urban bourgeoisie, and even among the intelligentsia.[16]

Lastly, women were not only generally denied the benefits of formal education but also discouraged from developing any ability or talent useful for a career outside the home. "A woman's lack of talent is in itself a virtue" was a frequently used proverb to check any worldly ambitions of a woman, especially in recent decades when a daughter demanded to go to school like her brothers. The result was the general lack of professional skills among women and the incomparably higher percentage of illiteracy among women than among men. In a village in South China surveyed in 1950, 65 per cent of the men but only 8 per cent of the women of ten years of age and over were literate. In the sample census of nine counties in Szechwan Province in 1942 and 1943, 48 per cent of the men but only 19 per cent of the women were literate.[17]

Forced seclusion and imposed ignorance, lack of occupational opportunities, general discrimination against working women, and repressive marriage customs inevitably resulted also in women's economic dependency in traditional society. And, since that dependency was accompanied by the lack of family property rights for women, the simple threat of hunger forced them to submit to the inferior status assigned them by the male-dominant family institution.

Change in the Subordination Factors Under the Communist Regime

The foregoing factors have been among the most responsible influences in shaping the traditional status of women, particularly that of the young and middle-aged wife. In the past half century of family revolution such influences have been progressively weakened, at least among the bourgeois intelligentsia, by the reformation of the marriage institution, the development of modern urban economy giving rise to more occupational opportunities for women, the development of women's education, and the general social movement for equality. This trend toward elevating the status of women was well marked prior to the rise of Communist power; it has been accelerated since the Communists took over national control. Much of this aspect of change in the family has been discussed previously, but some leading points will be reviewed here.

The principle of sex equality as one of the causes espoused by the Communist revolution is clearly written in the regime's Marriage Law (Article 1). In a legal opinion rendered by the municipal court of Tientsin on the case of mistreatment of a wife, we find the following statement: "The attitude of belittling women still widely exists among a part of the people in the city of Tientsin. Some say, 'Women cannot possibly be the equal of men in any way'; 'If women do not listen to men in the family, to whom should they listen?' and 'Beating her is to discipline and teach her for her own good.' Such attitudes must be seriously corrected." [18] The Communist government and party organizations have encouraged people to bring in cases of mistreatment of women for public correction by law or by group pressure. In Hsiangt'an county of Hunan Province during the month of June 1950 there were 180 cases of mistreatment of women, but only 40 cases were brought into the court by the parties involved. "We must make ceaseless efforts to bring such cases to public attention," [19] exhorted Hsü Teh-hsing, a member of the Committee on Laws and Institutions in the central Communist government. In the province of Shantung, after the court in T'eng Hsien Special District had made a big case out of the murder of P'an Shi by using it as an example, 119 cases of mistreatment of women were brought to court by the people in the neighboring Linyi Special District.[20]

It may be noted that no similar efforts to execute the principle of sex equality had been made by previous governments in modern China, and that up to the time of Communist accession to power the cause had been carried forward only by the slow and spontaneous process of social movement.

Cases of murder and suicide of women resulting from family conflict, once they come to the attention of superior Communist authorities, bring drastic punishment, and such cases are used widely as examples for propaganda and indoctrination purposes. The murder of P'an Shi in Shantung Province and the killing of Kao Ch'uen-wa in Shansi Province are examples. Nevertheless, it seems that for some time to come the persistence of traditional social attitudes and the old family institution among a considerable proportion of local junior party leaders will prevent legal action in large numbers of similar cases by concealing them from superior authorities who have more understanding and firmer convictions on the new concept of women's status.

Plainly, the alteration in the form of marriage under communism, the effort to prohibit "buying-and-selling" marriages, and the serious attempt to prohibit polygamy by the Communist Marriage Law all operate to elevate woman's status. Moreover, the traditional mode of appellation for a woman after marriage is also being changed.

Echoing the call of the Western feminine movement, this issue was raised during the early years of the Republic. As the women's movement developed, and as a small number of women trained in modern education came out to take up independent occupations in the cities, married women began using their own surnames and given names, usually with the husband's surname prefixed to the maiden surname, thus showing her marital status by a double surname. As the young generation of modern intellectuals advanced in age and moved into positions of responsibility and as the old generation receded into social and economic positions of lesser importance, the new manner of appellation increased steadily until it became a part of the normal order of urban social life. The Nationalist law, reflecting the factual development, stipulated that a married woman might use her own surname and given name, but prefixed with the husband's surname to show her marital status, and that for a man marrying into a woman's family (which occurs only very rarely) the man's given name should be headed by the wife's surname so as to show equality of treatment.

The Communist Marriage Law stipulates that "husband and wife each have the right to use his or her own surname and given name." [21] This does not prevent husband or wife from prefixing the spouse's surname in front of his or her own surname, making a double surname, which is the current practice with middle and upper-class educated women. Neither does it prevent the continued use of Mrs. for the women. After the Communist assumption of power a large number of maiden names appeared in newspapers and publications, belonging to women holding important political positions. Reading them, one did not know whether their owners were married, or, if married, to whom they were married, and sometimes one was surprised to learn that so-and-so was the wife of an important official.

The individualization of appellation for married women, besides reflecting their greater independence, naturally weakens the social significance of the family as an organized unit of common action, symbolized by presenting the wife to the public by the prefix of the husband's surname; and it tends to reduce the importance of the patriarchal lineage as the backbone of the family organization.

Of particular interest is the vigorous Communist campaign on literacy and technical education for women, a nation-wide movement covering not merely cities but also penetrating into rural areas, extending a pre-Communist trend from the upper and middle classes into the large numerical base of workers and peasants. Under the Communist regime every city is buzzing with literacy classes for women as well as for men. In 1950 in the Shanghai textile factories alone, where women employees form the majority of the working force, there were 170 literacy groups organized into classes, with the total membership of 9,000.[22] That number in proportion to the total of illiterate women workers in the textile industry may not have been great, but it signified the beginning of a growing phenomenon. In 1951 in the cities of "Darien and Port Arthur, of the 9,115 illiterate women workers, 8,640, or about 94.5 per cent, participated in a literacy program." [23] Technical training classes for the improvement of workers' skills and evening trade classes in the cities were opened to women students. In July 1952 in the northern city of Tientsin there were 7,247 literacy classes with about 300,000 students, among whom more than 100,000 were women. Attached to these literacy classes were 81 nursery stations where mothers attending classes could leave their children.[24] In one district in Peking women accounted for 85 per cent of the members of literacy classes.[25]

The literacy campaign is also waged actively in rural communities. Thus, "in six counties including Hsingning and Mei in the eastern part of Kwangtung Province there are 3,000 evening schools, and women account for over 60 per cent of the students." [26] "In the coastal counties of Shantung Province, there were 597 literacy classes for women in 1949, but these increased to 1,687 classes by the spring of 1950, with a total enrollment of 40,000 women. In Chunan county alone in 1950 there were 450 classes, with 14,300 women students. In the rural town of Huiming, 15 of the 16 street neighborhoods set up literacy classes. . . . In the village of Houku in Poshan county, Shantung Province, a literacy class for women was established in March 1949, with an initial enrollment of 22. One year later the enrollment had grown to 74." [27]

Since 1952 Communist publications have been comparatively silent about the family problem, and they no longer single out women as a special object for literacy and universal education campaigns. Presumably, since the principle of equality between the sexes has been fully established and illiteracy is widespread for both sexes in China, any present educational campaign aims equally at men and women. On this assumption, women are reaping their share of benefit from the ever-quickening pace of Communist efforts in mass education. If the southern city of Canton was representative, 80 per cent of all school-age children in 1956 were in schools, and the Communist authorities planned to have the entire school-age population in schools in another year.[28] As to adults, the Communist plan in 1956 was to completely "sweep away" illiteracy in cities as well as in the rural areas within seven years.[29]

The accelerating development of education for women, which will be reflected in the social and economic status of women and in turn further the alteration of the Chinese family organization, has been powerful indeed. A discussion of the comprehensive influence of the women's movement over the course of the past half century and its acquisition of political power under the Communist regime is now in order.

CHAPTER VII

The Ascendancy of Women's Status Through the Women's Movement

THE CHINESE women's movement, like its counterpart in the West, has been an organized collective effort to attain status equality with men in all major sectors of social life, including the family. Although much of this massive drama is enacted outside the home, women's role in the family is but a structural segment of their general status in the entire institutional system of society, especially in the economic and political institutions. In this sense, the development of the women's movement forms an integral part of the process by which the traditional family institution is transformed.

The Pre-Communist Setting

The history of the Chinese women's movement is as long as that of China's modern revolutions. The participation of a large number of armed women in the Taiping Rebellion in the early 1850's still remains an intriguing historical riddle. One ramification of the abortive 100-day Reform of 1898 was the advocacy of giving women a modern education and the unbinding of their feet. Subsequent revolutionary activities to overthrow the monarchy attracted many women. An example was Chiu Chin, who published the first "Women's Journal," organized the "Restoration Army" in Shaohsing of Chekiang Province, and was finally executed in 1907, a martyr of the revolution. Battalions of women were organized in many parts of China in the Republican revolution of 1911, a revolution which promoted women's rights to education, "to make friends," to marry by free choice of partners, and to participate in government. A Republican parliament in 1913 was stormed by a mob of women demanding implementation of women's suffrage as fulfillment of the revolution's promise. Police dispersed the mob, and the men parliamentarians laughed off the episode.

Like China's revolutions, the women's movement ran a course of ebb and flow. After the disillusionment of 1913 the movement settled back to a more staid course, mainly promoting modern education for women, unbinding of the feet, and modern training in order to become a "virtuous mother and good wife." Then came the thunderous New Culture Movement of 1917 and the May 4th Movement of 1919, which injected renewed social and political consciousness into the women's movement. All the social, political, and economic demands which modern womanhood had made in the Western world became their inspiration and guidance. Publications on the subject of modern womanhood were vastly expanded in volume and were eagerly read by the increasing number of literate women in the middle and upper classes in the cities. Women's organizations began to appear in large cities under a variety of labels, such as *Fu-nü Hsieh-chin Hui* (Association for Collective Advancement of Women) and *Fu-nü Chiao-yü Ch'u-chin Hui* (Association for the Promotion of Women's Education). What had been mainly a rising tide of opinion and individual action was now being crystallized into an organized collective movement.

The Second Revolution in the mid-1920's carried the women's movement to new heights. The political character of the movement was greatly sharpened by the tenet that feminist rebellion against traditional restrictions could not be successful without women's full participation in political power; and many women donned uniforms and became political workers in the Kuomintang and the Communist Party as members of the propaganda corps, as organizers, even as soldiers in the Northern Expedition of 1926. The 1924 declaration of the first plenary session of the Kuomintang Party recognized sex equality in law, in economic matters, in education, and in society. "Women's emancipation" associations sprang up in the path of the Northern Expedition. A few women sat in the high councils in the early coalition regime of the Kuomintang and Communist Party. Women's occupations developed steadily in urban areas during this period.

The split between the two parties led to divergent courses in the development of the women's movement in the Kuomintang area and in the "red areas" after the late 1920's. In the red areas the women's movement continued to develop as a part of the Communist political movement, as will be discussed later, but in the Kuomintang area the political aspect of the movement was checked whenever the leadership turned too much to the left. Otherwise the women's movement in general continued almost unhindered; from the late 1920's on, at least the principle of sex equality was generally accepted by the urban intelligentsia, and the voicing of this principle was widely heard by the urban population as a whole, particularly by those in the middle and upper classes. There was an accelerated pace in the development of women's educational and economic opportunities in the cities, and women's appearance on the social scene was fast becoming an accepted fact.

While these developments continued during the period of the war against the Japanese invasion (1937–1945), there was also a resurgence of the political aspect of the women's movement in the Kuomintang area. Women's extensive participation in the war effort provided the motivation for a reawakened political interest among feminist leaders. The ravages of war and the growing unsatisfactory conditions of the Kuomintang regime, coupled with the strong propaganda and organizing efforts of the Communists, increasingly drove a number of feminists towards the left, many of whom became directly or indirectly affiliated with Communist efforts in the political scene. The Kuomintang's rein over the political energies of the women's movement was weak; for, in spite of party control of the leadership of many major women's organizations, members in these organizations as well as women in general had not been organized to participate actively in political work. Meanwhile, the Communists emphasized political action as the leading instrument for attaining the goals of the women's movement.

Predominance of the Political Character of the Women's Movement Under Communist Leadership

In Chinese traditional society, despite the occasional rise of women rulers such as Empress Wu Tse-tien in the T'ang dynasty and the Empress Dowager in the Ch'ing period, women occupied no recognized routine position in the political world, and political activity was neither encouraged nor approved of by the traditional code of conduct for women. Infringement of social and political restrictions in the Ch'ing period was punishable by law. Hence the feminist leaders' enthusiastic participation in China's revolutions, and the fact that, despite the many recessions of political interest in the women's movement during its half century of development, this interest always swept up to new heights in every resurging wave of modern Chinese revolutions.

The Communists from the beginning recognized the potential political strength of the women's movement, and during the thirty years of their struggle for power consistently nursed its development to augment their political force. Taken under Communist wings, the women's movement became a branch of the Communist political movement, the influence of the Communist Party being evident as early as Women's Day of March 8, 1924, when a rally was held under Communist leadership in the First Park of Canton. Above the din of the city rose the shouted slogans of a small band of women, mostly students and workers: "Down with imperialism," "Down with warlords," "Same work, same pay," "Protection for child labor and pregnant mothers," "Equal education," "Abolish child brides and polygamy," "Prohibit the buying of slave girls and the taking of concubines," "Formulate a child protection law." A demonstration parade followed the rally. Thus began a new page in the women's movement, and for a quarter of a century thereafter these slogans continued to echo throughout the nation, and women were increasingly pitched into the political battle that eventually led to the triumph of Communist power.

Communist decisions in 1926 on the women's movement perhaps marked the beginning of a major Chinese party making a political arm out of the women's movement by working out systematic tactics for recruiting and organizing its members and by expanding the movement from the modern urban intelligentsia to women workers and peasants.* In "red areas" during the late 1920's and early 1930's political mobilization of women peasants, and to a lesser extent women workers, was an important feature of the nascent Communist political power. The setting up of a large number of representatives' conferences of women peasants and workers in this period was an expression of this. Another expression of Communist policy on the women's movement was the promulgation in 1931 of Marriage Regulations which

* In the third enlarged meeting of the central committee of the Chinese Communist Party decisions on the women's movement contained the following points: 1. In party work among women emphasis must be laid on carrying the activities to the common people. 2. Though women workers constitute the backbone of the women's movement, women students are also important, for they are the bridge between the party and women workers, and they are an important influence in breaking up the thought and habits of the traditional familistic society. 3. Peasant women occupy a very important position in the Chinese women's movement, and it is necessary to train leaders for this branch of work. 4. Women's publications must be in simple and popular style, emphasizing the intimate experience of women's own suffering and practical needs. 5. Efforts must be made to increase women party members and to develop leaders for the women's movement. (Lo Ch'iung, "The Principles of Development of the Chinese Women's Movement," *Hsin Chung-kuo Fu-nü* (New Chinese Women), January 1953, pp. 29–30.)

placed only light restrictions on marriage and divorce. In the subsequent two decades, through the period of the Japanese invasion, mobilization of women for political and military struggle remained the main theme of Communist leadership in the women's movement as well as a major instrument in the attainment of the movement's goal of sex equality in social, economic, and political status. From 1930 on, many professionally prominent women, especially writers, became active Communist leaders, and women constituted an important component in the Communist political force.

On Women's Day of March 8, 1951, a little over a year after inauguration of the Communist government, an editorial in the official New China News Agency acclaimed the contributions of the women's movement: "In the anti-Japanese war, in the people's liberation war, under the leadership of the Communist Party, large groups of women workers and revolutionary intellectual women joined the great struggle for the liberation of the nation. They actively participated in military mobilization and in the work in the rear. They took part in the land reform movement and the production movement. China's women have formed a powerful, integral part of the people's revolutionary ranks, and have made great contributions to the victory of the national revolution."

The first charter of the Communist regime, the Common Program, stated: "The People's Republic abolishes the feudalistic institutions which hold women in bondage. In political, economic, cultural, educational, and social aspects of life women possess equal rights and privileges with men. Freedom of marriage is adopted for both men and women." The new Marriage Law was formulated in accordance with this principle. When the Communist constitution replaced the Common Program as the basic law, the same principle was reaffirmed.[1] On Women's Day of March 8, 1951, when Communist participation in the Korean War and land reform were raging simultaneously, women were being exhorted by the New China News Agency editorial: "The duty of Chinese women is to join the people of the nation to develop the 'Resist America, Aid Korea' patriotic movement, support Korea's People's Army and China's Volunteer Army, oppose America's rearmament of Japan, enforce land reform, struggle for a good harvest this year, develop the patriotic emulation of production, suppress counterrevolutionary elements, strengthen the learning of patriotism, and let the 'Resist America, Aid Korea' patriotic movement pervade the daily activities in production work, political study [indoctrination], and general living."

These editorial exhortations set the pattern for local activities of the women's movement throughout Communist China. Thus, in the district consisting of sixteen counties in the northern part of Kwang-tung Province, party cadres issued a directive on Women's Day of March 8, 1951, outlining the work of the women's movement:

> Review the strength and line up the organizations of women in the locality; use action to set the masses of village women in motion; lead them to join in the work of mopping up bandits, fighting local despots, reducing land rent, and refunding land rent deposit; strengthen the suppression of counterrevolutionary elements; develop various types of [class] struggles in the land reform movement; answer the government's call to help in repairing highways and bridges, in building up the people's militia, and in developing water control work. For the cities, the missions of women are to join the patriotic emulation of production, improve the quality of production, save raw materials, reduce the cost and increase the quantity of production.[2]

To put the Communist political program into practice, women go through rigid indoctrination. In schools, women students, like men students, must take full part in the process of political study through the "big class" and the "small unit" discussions, the endless political and propaganda gatherings, group study of newspapers and discussions of current events, and, on special occasions, participate in demonstrations, in speechmaking and in posting slogans, in group visits to government propaganda exhibitions, such as the exhibition on the reconstruction of the U.S.S.R. or the exhibition of criminal evidences of counterrevolutionists. Women students must take leaves of absence from school from time to time to participate in land reform work, to copy documents for the government, and to launch special political campaigns when the government is short-handed. Recreation such as dancing, singing, movies, plays, and parties are thoroughly permeated with political implications; newspapers and radios blare out political tunes continuously. Throughout the waking hours, the plastic young individual is imbued with the new political atmosphere.

Mothers watched in amazement as their daughters went through the political mill during the earlier days of the Communist regime. Now they have found themselves forced to go through a similar program. Street and neighborhood meetings lay claim to their time and energy. Care of children and household duties must be put off so that they may attend meetings from one to three times a week. They are told:

> We must remold ourselves in order that we may survive in and not

be washed away by the current of this great age. To meet the demands of the social situation, we must learn to make progress and overcome our own weaknesses. . . . Most of us do not have interest or confidence in political study; we even let household duties prevent us from thinking and learning, confining our views only to our husbands and children to the exclusion of everything else. We must have determination to overcome such weaknesses.[3]

At one neighborhood indoctrination meeting held in Canton in the summer of 1951 in a small, hot room crowded with over one hundred people, mostly women, the bawling of a baby rose above the voice of a speaker who was yelling himself hoarse on the "Resist America, Aid Korea" movement. The speaker stopped, inquired, found that a mother had brought her two young children to the meeting for lack of someone to care for them at home, ordered the mother to lock up the two children in another room for the duration of the lengthy meeting, and went on with the lecture.

Women may not close their minds and just sit through the meetings. Many such classes have quizzes besides compulsory attendance (at least one person from each house, frequently the wife), and the lecturer, usually a young student in the late teens or early twenties, asks questions. One woman in Canton, the wife of a medicine store owner, was asked to repeat the reasons why America was China's enemy. She stood up and talked irrelevantly. Punishment for her was compulsory attendance at ten extra meetings, one every night for ten consecutive nights. Women who have failed in such tests and who can read and write have been made to copy a hundred times some political articles from indoctrination pamphlets so that "they will remember."

We can be sure that many women have resented such forced indoctrination but it is impossible to ignore such evidence as the following propaganda story.

In the northern part of Shanghai city lives Mrs. Ts'ao, a woman of fifty-eight. She lives with only a young granddaughter, and her life has been a lonely one.

She started to work in a Shanghai silk factory at the age of nine. But she worked only half a day, and the other half of the day was devoted to schooling; so she was able to read and write. When she grew up, she continued to work in the same silk factory until 1932, when the Japanese invasion destroyed it. . . .

Ten years ago Mrs. Ts'ao felt that, after working so hard, all that she had was loneliness and bitterness. She became a pessimist and took to Buddhism as a solace. She refitted her living room into a shrine chamber and put an idol of the Goddess of Mercy on the altar, hoping that in so doing she would be spared further suffering. Old ladies in the neighborhood came to join her in burning incense, praying, and chanting. Seven or eight years of pious worship seemed to do little good, for the Japanese invasion and the worst part of the Nationalist rule came in succession. The painted surface of a whole side of the sounding-box for chanting had been knocked off by rhythmic beating and yet the good days in her dream were still nowhere near.

Then the Communists came to Shanghai. What she saw and heard gave her the impression that the world was very different. After the campaign to suppress the counterrevolutionists started, many characters long known to be bad men in the neighborhood had been arrested, and this pleased Mrs. Ts'ao very much.

Soon the neighborhood set up a local committee for the purge of counterrevolutionists and took over her shrine chamber for an office. Later the neighborhood's Inhabitants Committee and the Family Women's League [a subsidiary of the Democratic Women's League] also set up office in her shrine chamber. From then on, great changes began to take place in her mind.

The Family Women's League held frequent meetings in her place. At first, during a meeting, she hid behind the door, peeping out in curiosity. As time went on, sister Li in the League said to her, "Old lady, why don't you join in and listen?" She was happy at the invitation. From then on, at every meeting, she would sit down and listen. Gradually the terms "liberation," "changing place" [changing one's social status by revolution], and "Resist America, Aid Korea movement" began to make sense to her. She said to sister Li of the League, "Meetings make more sense than worshipping Buddha, for the meetings have helped me to understand a number of things I didn't understand before. From now on, when the old ladies in the neighborhood come again to burn incense and worship Buddha, I am going to ask them to worship chairman Mao and give the incense money to the government to buy airplanes and artillery. This includes myself." She severed her relationship with Buddha. . . .

When the Family Women's League moved its office to new quarters, she was sorry to see the League people go. She took out a piece of red silk which she had kept for years and gave it to sister Li and said, "There must be a picture of chairman Mao in your new office. Please drape this over the picture. Should there be any material left, please make a big bunting out of it and put it in front of the picture."

Sister Li asked her to invite some of her old ladies who used to worship Buddha with her to a meeting. At the first meeting over twenty old ladies came, and sister Li helped her to chair the meeting. At the meetings, they talked about family affairs, the Communist Party, and the world situation, and they agreed to visit twice a month families of soldiers and those who had died for the revolution. . . .

At a mass rally at the railway station to welcome the Korean delegation, people pushed her to the platform to make a speech. She said, "In the past, I only knew that the Goddess of Mercy saved people from suffering, but now I realize that the one who really saves people from suffering is chairman Mao."

She is now doubling her efforts at "learning" and is reading pamphlets all the time. She is getting ready to help the old ladies use their spare time to make match boxes and do bookbinding in order to contribute the proceeds to the purchase of airplanes and artillery.[4]

Pressure from the general political atmosphere and the influence of the group is clearly marked in the case of this old woman, especially in view of her loneliness and the consequent desire for company. If her case represents a relatively uneducated woman, the following is that of a young woman student told in an article of self-confession:

In the past the goal of my life was to please my future husband and raise my future children, to manage a household, to serve as a model for a "kind mother and a good wife." Mother taught me the "three obediences and four virtues" and other ethical rules of good womanhood. I was a good girl of the traditional type who never ventured out the door. I remember at the age of ten I still had to have the maid dress me, and at twelve I still had to have the maid accompany me to school. I was such a weak, helpless, temperamental burden on others.

At seventeen I stepped out of the family to go to school and began to take my first breath of freedom. Throughout my middle school period, though I was able to get out of the control of the feudalistic family authority, my life was so decadent. I fell into the abyss of love. I pursued happiness. Hypnotized in the clutch of love, I was wasting my youth away.

The gongs and drums of the "liberation" woke me up like thunder in spring, and I began to crawl out of the dirt. In September of 1950, still with dirt on my body, I entered the university [not named]. The school was like a big family of revolutionists, making me feel strange at every turn. I was groping about and made some trials. I wished to wipe the dirt off my clothes, but my hands were so weak and tired.

One after another, the high tides of social and political movements passed before my eyes, marching columns paraded beside me, and the soaring notes of group singing rang in my ears. I felt alone, I felt the pressure of solitude. I was perplexed, sometimes so terribly perplexed. Sometimes I sat alone on the lawn and cried, and sometimes I cried under the covers in bed. When schoolmates asked me why my eyes were so red, I failed to answer.

As the days flew by, the "old" and the "new" were battling in my mind. In that battle, time and again, the "new" fell down and the "old" stood up with renewed arrogance. I was spiritually tortured. In such days suffering wore down my spirit and the "old" things corroded my soul.

I will eternally remember my roommate, little Wei. She was younger than I and called me Big Sister. I was very grateful for her help, but she also put me to shame. She could take hardship and was a person of action. She was very progressive, good at revolutionary doctrine, and lived very actively and happily. When she did things, she was as systematic as a mature adult. I often laughed at her for resembling a boy, and she always answered proudly, "In the age of Mao Tse-tung women will never trail behind men." She surely had a deep effect on me. She was a member of the Young Communist League. Her every act and her work made me so ashamed of myself and made me feel like a weakling.

Last November [1950] I began to change. I made a resolution not to imagine things and not to linger with the "old" any longer. I started out to catch up with little Wei, retracing her past footsteps. I took action. I came to hate my bird-nest-like coiffure [permanent] and I cut it off. Now my short and straight hair looks as beautiful as that of Wei. I tore up my once-fashionable cowboy pants [dungarees]; humans do not wear dog's clothing. Now I wear the cotton clothes and cotton shoes of the laboring people, and when I walk side by side with Wei people say, "You two look like sisters, so thrifty and solid." This pleases me so.

That was my first victory in the new direction.

Then came the movement to join the armed forces under the "Resist America, Aid Korea" movement. I pushed aside my mother's objections. I wanted to offer my life to the fatherland, to the people. Big red paper flowers were pinned on me. They symbolized the redness of my heart. I felt so honored and proud. When the students threw me up into the air, I was so very happy. That was the second victory in my battle of thought.

Now I have gone one step further and joined the New Democratic Youth League. Through education by the League I have come to recognize clearly the two divergent roads. One leads to decadence and decline, filled with lifeless atmosphere, darkness, and death. The other leads to happiness, activity, hope, light, and new life. . . .

I anticipate Women's Day this year with enthusiasm. I have prepared my uniform. I am going to throw myself into the human current and follow the flag and march forward bravely. I want to shout with millions of sisters and let the shouting become a strong current.

We want to be masters of the new society. We are the nurses of mankind. We bear the mission of mankind's prosperity. We have to break the chains on our hands and create the garden of happiness for humanity.[5]

This story of the making of a young convert as a result of group pressure, youth, and idealism is typical of numerous confessions made by young students at political meetings. It has been estimated that from 10 to 30 per cent of all girl students in colleges and universities were members of the Youth League by the end of 1951, and there seems to have been continuous increase in League membership. These are the girls who become leaders for women's organizations and who help push the vast multitudes of common women into the political line.

Although we do not find such detailed stories about peasant women, short reports show substantially the same emphasis on political action in the women's movement in the countryside under Communist rule. The Communist press stated that during the battle for Hainan Island [1950] in the southern part of Kwangtung Province numerous women were organized into carrier, food transportation, and service corps, helping tens of thousands of troops passing through that part of the country. In two villages in Suich'i county (Kwangtung Province) alone, over twenty thousand mosquito nets were laundered for the army, not counting the innumerable clothes washed. When the Communist army was in urgent need of food, one peasant woman carried over a thousand catties of rice in one night to the fighting men. Many wives were said to have encouraged their fisherman husbands to join the battle of crossing the sea, and many women directly participated in the crossing.[6]

According to reports, in other rural areas of Kwangtung Province political activities by women claimed attention from a public that had not seen women playing a similar role before. In Shihsing county a peasant woman with only a kitchen knife in hand captured alive a counterrevolutionary "bandit." In Shunteh county peasant women organized an espionage corps and captured a counterrevolutionary leader and a long-hidden Japanese spy. In another village in Shunteh county peasant woman Chang Shu-fen, a production and anti-bandit heroine, helped local troops to wipe out over ten counterrevolutionary "bandits" and capture many pieces of fire arms.[7]

Since 1953 there has been a noticeable tendency to tone down the political mission of women and increase the emphasis on their devotion to economic production and family duties, the Communist government having turned to the task of consolidating its power through stabilizing the economic and social order, but the political responsibility of women is by no means overlooked. In 1955 a woman in the northern city of Tientsin was commended for her discovery of a "spy" among her neighbors, leading to his arrest and eventual execution,[8] and similar reports continue to appear in the Communist press.

The Organization of Women

In pre-Communist days activities of the women's movement consisted mainly of publishing promotional literature, shouting slogans, and, on occasion, of women students speaking to street crowds, group meetings for charity, and agitating for women's welfare legislation. An occasional woman intellectual broke away from home or committed suicide to dramatize the demand for freedom of marriage; a woman intellectual might create a social sensation by insisting upon being addressed as Mr. instead of Miss or Mrs.; and, with expanding literacy and education among women, a few women leaders reached high political and social positions in either the Kuomintang or the Communist Party. But women's activities were mostly unorganized, and such organized activities as women's participation in politics were rather sporadic except among women Communists. Moreover, they were almost entirely limited to urban educated women, who belonged mostly to the middle and upper classes; the working class and peasant women remained little touched by the movement.

Assumption of power by the Communist Party changed this picture. Organizational efforts became persistent, systematic, and extensive, affecting an increasing proportion of the female population. For the celebration of Women's Day of March 8, 1951, for example, Communist leaders in Shanghai started their organizational work early. The Family Women's Leagues in various parts of the city organized mobilization units, visiting from house to house in each neighborhood, asking women to sign up for the demonstration parade. The mobilization units also held "accusation meetings" in every neighborhood for the women to recall their experiences of rape or insults under Japanese rule so as to arouse the anger of the women and draw them out to the demonstration. As a result, 300,000 women of Shanghai turned out on that day's demonstration.[9] No doubt a majority of the 300,000 were not voluntary or willing participants but acted under direct or indirect pressure. Nevertheless, the mobilization of a third of a million women for an occasion was unprecedented in China even in a large city like Shanghai.

The women's movement is no longer confined to the educated elements of the urban middle and upper classes. The objective of broadening the Communist women's movement to embrace the entire female population of the country is clearly set forth in the "General Principles for the Organization of the Council of Women Representatives" passed in September of 1950 by the third meeting of the executive committee

of the All-China Democratic Women's League, which is the highest
directing body of the women's movement. According to the resolution,
the Council of Women's Representatives is to be the chief instrument
by which the Democratic Women's League directs the "broad masses
of women" of the country, and any woman with citizenship rights who
supports the principles of the Democratic Women's League has the
privilege to elect or be elected to the Council. The goal is to expand
the "women's organization to the masses." Hence, every province,
county, subdistrict, city, town, and village has a Council; so has every
profession and occupation, every large scale enterprise employing
women, every organization and every school with women members.[10]
The Communist system of organization permeates every territory and
occupational unit in the country primarily to serve political purposes,
namely, to help transmit and execute government orders and policies,
and to bring women's demands and opinions to the attention of the
government.[11]

To insure that the organizational system does not serve any other
purpose and is not controlled by dissenting elements, leaders of the
Democratic Women's League are given a prominent position in the
Council at every level and in every occupation.[12] Again, to insure the
desired political orientation, the Democratic Women's Leagues in
many localities specify that the core of the branch organizations must
be founded upon the proletarian section of the population. "In cities
women laborers should be the core around which all patriotic and
democratic women will be united; in the villages poor peasant women
and hired women farm laborers should be the core around which
the women of middle peasants will be united." [13]

The extent to which women are becoming politically organized has
been indicated in numerous official reports. In 1951, in the four administrative regions of Central-South, East, Southwest, and Northwest,
women already accounted for about 30 per cent of the 88,000,000 members of the peasants' associations, and in places where the organizational work had been well done women accounted for as high as 50
per cent of such membership. Women occupied from 10 to 15 per cent
of the positions of committee members, chairmen, or vice-chairmen
of the peasants' associations; and large numbers of them had been
mobilized to take part in the village defense corps, and to cooperate
with the local militia in the surveillance of "law-breaking landlords"
and local bullies. It was stated that the number of organized women
doubled after land reform and in some places increased four- or five-
fold; that in Kwangsi Province organized women numbered about

490,000 before land reform but increased to 1,300,000 after land reform, and that in Tsinkiang Special District of Fukien Province the number of organized women grew from 48,000 before land reform to 220,000 after land reform.[14]

A large number of local reports show that peasant women everywhere in the country are coming under an organizational network dominated by the peasants' association and the Democratic Women's League. There are no figures for a nation-wide urban picture, but reports on individual cities show the same trend, women taking to organizations outside the home on an increasing scale. For example, in Shanghai:

> The number of organized women in 1951 was 301,412. Among them were 162,563 women workers in various occupations, 70,000 peasant women in suburban villages, 32,030 women students, 8,240 women teachers, 4,266 women employees in the government, 20,578 family women, and 3,753 members of different democratic women's groups. It is estimated that there are about 1,500,000 adult women in Shanghai, and 22 per cent of them are now organized. It can be observed from these figures that women workers form the mainstay of the organized women in Shanghai. Among all the organized women workers, over 2,000 of them have joined the All-Shanghai Labor Union and have participated in the leadership of the basic labor union organizations.[15]

Women's Political Power

We have noted that occasional political power for women on a very high level is not new in China, and that there have been women members both in the Kuomintang high councils, such as the party's central committee and other government organs, and in the Communist Party and in its government. But such women, besides belonging exclusively to the modern educated upper-class, were exceptions in a man-dominated system of power. That common women such as laborers and peasants now hold responsible positions as a regular part of the political system is striking evidence of the new situation brought about by the changed social status of women under Communist rule.

Identification and selection of activists from among the general population is an important step in the Communist effort to build a new local leadership for the revolutionary regime, and women supply a considerable number of such activists. In thirteen rural counties and one city of Hunan Province 16,507 activists were selected and trained from the beginning of 1950 to the end of 1952, of whom 2,907, or about 17.6 per cent, were women.[16]

In localities where the people's representative councils have been set up there are considerable numbers of women representatives. In twenty-three counties of Heilungchiang Province of the Northeast, 12,000 women representatives were sent in 1951 to the people's representative councils, accounting for twenty per cent of all representatives sitting in such councils.[17] In the village and subdistrict councils of peasant representatives in Hsingning and Mei counties, Kwangtung Province, women accounted for 30 to 40 per cent of all the representatives. In the county councils of peasant representatives in Hsingning, Pingyuan, Chaoling, and Mei counties there were 204 women representatives in 1951, accounting for 28 per cent of all the representatives. In the First Kwangtung Provincial Council of People's Representatives in 1951 women representatives accounted for about 13 per cent of the total number of representatives.[18] By 1952 it was officially reported that women constituted an average of 15 per cent of all representatives in such conferences throughout China,[19] representing an increase of 5 per cent over 1950. In the city of Peking 48 per cent of the representatives were women, scoring a gain of 26 per cent over 1950.[20] The main actual function of such representative councils is only to transmit government policies and to discuss ways and means of implementing them, since only the Communist Party makes policy decisions. Nevertheless, since a position as representative carries political prestige and influence in the home community, the membership of women in such councils may be regarded as a sign of women's new political power and influence.

A more direct expression of women's new political importance is their position in village governments and in peasant associations, which are the center of influence in local politics under the Communist regime. In Hsingning county women members in peasant association committees numbered 3,827 in 1951, comprising a majority of the committee membership. In Ta Pu county, Hsiao Siu-ying became the head of her village and was regarded by the party officials as a model village head. In Mei county there were three women heads of peasant associations, in Chaoling county there was one, and in Pingyuan county, there were two.[21] Both village heads and peasant association chiefs wield considerable power, especially over certain people such as landlords and those accused as local despots.

Social class origin constitutes an important factor in qualifying for local political power in the Communist regime, particularly in rural areas. No member of the landlord or rich peasant class may hold political positions. Hence, those women newly become important in the rural power structure are almost all poor peasant women. In Shantung Province a university professor interviewed a woman village head who was of poor peasant class origin and formerly illiterate. After being the village head for over a year, she had learned to read and write, and she kept a diary of her executive work. In that diary, statements such as "This proposal has the fault of levelism" revealed a fairly complex and firmly indoctrinated mind. Another example is found in a woman representative in the village government council of Nanpu village of Panyü county, Kwangtung Province:

> In a visit to my home village after a prolonged absence the most un-imaginable thing I found is how progressive the women folk have become in this old, culturally a-century-behind place. When I first arrived I heard the woman representative for the village was none other than the female sorcerer, the "spirit-worshiping Ti." Immediately, an ugly, laughable, and contemptible face appeared in my memory of things ten years ago. In the past this poverty-stricken female feigned the incarnation of gods and spirits, talked of mysticism to the ignorant women in the village. She threatened, she bluffed, she swindled, she aroused excitement. She used every trick to gain money. I thought, "It couldn't be a fact!" If such a person could become the village's woman representative, the appointment of public officers would be too indiscriminate. But she was no longer the picture in my memory; she has become a vanguard of the new age. When she spoke before the women audience of the village, she talked fluently and systematically on the new political line.[22]

Female sorcery was an occupation for the poverty stricken when there was no other alternative to make a living. Here again, in con-formity with Communist stated policy, the poor are being brought in as the core of the new local government. In this case, the skill in human relations and facility of speech so necessary in her former trade became invaluable assets for this woman in her present position of power. New local leaders are uncovered and promoted usually through the process of "visiting the poor and questioning the victims of suf-fering," which has been a preliminary step to conducting local Com-munist programs. The ability of the prospective leader is tested through his or her performance in the class struggle when a program such as land reform unfolds. The new leader is confirmed or approved if he or she shows courage, organizing ability, and an uncompromising spirit toward the landowning class and "feudalistic" influences.

Another component of the power structure in local government is the militia, now called "people's soldiers." In pre-Communist days the militia was a bone of contention between conflicting factions in local politics. Under Communist rule it has been made into the armed support for the new political leadership against any possible counter-revolution from old vested interests, particularly from uprooted land-lords. Hence the presence of women in the local militia is a new factor of possible significance, for the participation of women in local militia is not a fortuitous fact but a regular phenomenon in many localities under the new regime.

In Chungshan county, Kwangtung Province, when 648 local militia were mobilized in 1950 to fight anti-Communist guerillas in the mountains, 440 of them were women, constituting the majority.[23] After land reform, in 1951, Hsingning county of eastern Kwangtung Province had 8,136 women militia under arms. Before land reform the village of Ningsiu in the same county had four women militia, but after land reform the number increased to 204, almost half of the total of 421 militia members of the village.[24] Participation of women in the militia in rural communities is found not only in the province of Kwangtung but also in other parts of the country, particularly in the South and Southwest regions, where women are robust and used to outdoor work. The participation of women in the Korean war and in the training programs for military cadres is also a notable fact.

To summarize, after fifty years, during which it advanced and retreated alternately, the major scenes of battle being the cities and the main engaging force the bourgeois intelligentsia, the Chinese women's movement now embraces the urban working class and the peasants in the countryside; and the engaging force, besides growing immeasurably, is increasingly better organized for a systematic attack on the traditional status of women in the family as well as in society. Whether the gains already made can be consolidated and exploited further depends, among other factors, on the development of industrialization, which can give occupational opportunities to women to sustain their new independent status, and on the success of agricultural collectivization which recasts women's role in production and redefines their share of income.

Stages of Development in the Women's Movement

In reviewing the Chinese women's movement, several stages of development are discernible. The initial stage, lasting from the last decade of the nineteenth century to the Republican revolution of 1911, consisted of the early introduction of Western ideas on equality between the sexes and on human rights and freedom and the resulting individual action by a few pioneering women and sporadic, short-lived organized adventures. Occurring at a time when the subordination of women was a part of the institutional framework of society firmly enforced by mores and law, such early actions were of spectacular excitement to the public; but there was little change in social institutions which might have given the required coordinated support to these actions. Many of the pioneers died as martyrs, and group activities had no sustained organized existence. Nevertheless, this initial development performed the function of presenting the first open challenge against the age-old institutionalized subordination of women, which had previously been held as a principle of social life as unalterable as heaven and earth. Doubt regarding an established tradition had been planted in the public mind.

The second stage covered the first half-dozen years of the Republic, during which there was a general retrenchment of the women's movement. The excitement of early action had cooled down considerably. But the movement made a steady gain in women's education, which trained leaders for the continued development of the movement and disseminated its basic ideas to an ever-increasing number of women students. Alongside this was the development of a literature as a medium to propagate the movement and to expand its following among both men and women. The course was staid and unspectacular, but the advance was steady.

The third stage began with the New Culture Movement of 1917 and the May 4th Movement of 1919 and lasted until the early part of the Second Revolution, 1921–1924. In this period the movement was no longer a current isolated from changes in other social institutions but received its support from the two momentous movements that marked the beginning of this stage, movements that supplied the major ideological orientation for subsequent social and political developments. Women's occupational opportunities began to develop, though slowly, providing a livelihood for women who were inspired by the movement to leave their traditional dependent status. This was an important step forward, for previously such women were mostly forced back to traditional subordination by economic necessity. Above all, by this time a new generation of feminine leaders had arisen from the increasing number of women's and co-educational schools, and an ever-growing following for the movement was created by the literature of the movement. Growth in leadership and in following resulted in the crystallization of the movement into local and national organizations, and in its organized form it became an important influence in the rapidly changing social setting of the times. The family revolution, already a powerful force, was a result of and at the same time an assistance to the women's movement.

The movement was marked by increasing identification with revolutionary political movements in the fourth stage, which began when the Second Revolution was in full swing in the mid-1920's and ended with Communist conquest of the China mainland in 1949. Coordinated support now came from changes in the political as well as the educational, economic, and family institutions. There developed an interdependence between the women's movement and the revolutionary political movement. On the one hand, the women's movement could expand its following and materialize its demands through the universal and coercive nature of a political power which professed full sympathy for the women's cause and encouraged the development of the women's movement in order to win its following as a part of the working force for the revolution. In this stage the women's movement began to extend beyond the urban intellectuals to include peasants and workers, a process developed most effectively under Communist leadership.

The fifth stage of development came with the success of the Communist political movement, its installation as the national ruling power, and incorporation of the basic objectives of the women's movement into law. The principles of the women's movement are now in harmony with the ideology of the new governing power. Through the universal and compulsory force of law, women's new status, long demanded by the movement, is being extended to an ever-increasing number of women in both urban and rural communities in all sections of the country.

We would point out that the present stage does not signify the complete and universal triumph of the movement's objectives throughout China. In a country with such a huge population, vast area, widespread illiteracy, and backward communications, it will take much longer than a half-dozen years to turn the new law into a universally effective standard and to translate the movement's principles into a stabilized institution.

Moreover, the status of women is most intimately related to the structure of the family, and the family still has basic significance for economic production in spite of the rapid nationalization and collectivization of production by the Communist government. As the majority of families stemming from traditional marriages continue to operate on traditional principles in most respects, the sudden change in women's status, which has disruptive influences on family unity and harmony and therefore adverse effects on economic production, is a development which could pose a serious threat to the economic programs of the Communist government.

Now in the stage of consolidating its new power, Communist leadership feels the need for general social harmony in order to make its plans materialize, and a rebellious women's movement operating on its previous militant pattern would be a disruptive influence. In the latter part of 1955 there appeared a new Communist line stressing the "building of a democratic and harmonious new family, united for production and devoted to the cause of socialist reconstruction" as the main responsibility of women. The new line significantly states: "The new Constitution has guaranteed women's equality with men in political, economic, cultural, social, and family interests, and the state has come to protect women's rights in marriage, in the family, in motherhood, and in the welfare of children. Henceforth, women no longer need to initiate a militant struggle for such things." [25] While previously the Communists had made great efforts in mobilizing "bourgeois women" to participate actively in social and political struggles under the women's movement, in 1956 they were told that their responsibility lay in homemaking and encouraging their husbands and relatives to accept the socialization of commercial and industrial enterprises.[26] But with the development of people's communes in 1958, the policy is again the mobilization of women for production. Under strict Communist direction, the women's movement is no longer an independent militant movement battling exclusively for the interests of women; it has become mainly a tool of the general Communist cause.

The degree of human dignity and the share of material benefits that women will gain from the new social order as compared with the old is a matter that concerns the nature of the authoritarian structure of the new social order and its relationship to the intrinsic interests of the individual regardless of sex. The question has been raised whether women emancipated from one form of social bondage are not falling into another. What is discernible from present observable facts is that the tendency toward greater sex equality in the social, political, and economic status for women is definitely destructive to the traditional family institution and tends to help develop a new family system more in harmony with the changed social status of women.

CHAPTER VIII

Changing Family Economic Structure

MODERN CHANGE in the family owing to economic influence theoretically begins with the alteration of the economic institution, as would be true with Western society, where the modern economic order was originally developed. But in China, where a new economic pattern was being introduced from the West, it was the ideological promotion of a modern economy that formed the first step; and changes in some of the economic aspects of the family system stemmed from ideological agitation rather than from the immediate pressure of a new economic environment. Thus economic relations among the family members concerning property rights and women's participation in traditional occupations started to change before the actual development of an industrial economic order. But ideological agitation and new economic development were not mutually exclusive influences on the family; the two forces were operating side by side, with sometimes one and sometimes the other playing the leading role. And when a drastic change in the general economic institution finally came, socio-economic environmental pressure became the major factor in altering the basic economic position of the family and in forcing a change in the family economic structure. This historical sequence provides the framework for analyzing change in the economic aspects of the family.

Economic Position and Structure of the Traditional Family

Related to the present discussion are several well-known characteristics of the economic structure of the traditional Chinese family, the most outstanding of them being the predominance of the family as a unit of production: a unit of organization of labor, capital, and land for the acquisition of goods and services to meet the needs of the members of the household. This condition more than any other compelled the individual to center his loyalty in the family and placed the family in the central position in the traditional pattern of social organization.

In agriculture, partnerships and other forms of organization were numerically negligible in comparison with the vast majority of China's traditional family farms. In commerce and industry the family as a unit of organization was equally dominant. When a boy reached working age, he worked in the family business. Should the family business be too small to employ him, he would be apprenticed if possible to a firm owned by relatives. Should a village boy wish to make a living in the city, he would be given an apprenticeship or a job in a relative's firm. City stores and handicraft shops were mostly family businesses in which the working force consisted mostly of kinsmen, and the kinship system was the most important network of employment. In the southern city of Canton a Communist survey in 1950 showed that, of the 20,000-odd industrial and commercial enterprises large and small, about 94 per cent were family businesses.

The dominance of the family as an organizational unit of production led to the development of another prominent characteristic of the Chinese family, namely, the provision of collective security for its immediate members and the extension of economic aid to more distant kinsmen. It was the function of the traditional family not only to care for the aged within its financial means but also to support the sick, the disabled, and the unemployed. Even a distant relative meeting economic misfortune had a moral claim on the family for assistance. (Hence the often-mentioned absence of Chinese relief cases in the United States during the great depression.) Such functions were basic factors in the strength of the traditional family organization and the extended kinship ties.

A high degree of economic self-sufficiency was another vital characteristic of the traditional family. Only those necessities that could not be fashioned at home or grown from the soil were purchased from outside. In agriculture the degree of family self-sufficiency is indicated by the fact that some 80 per cent of the family's needs were supplied by the family itself.[1] Although city families were much less self-sufficient, family labor was utilized to the maximum to process materials purchased from outside to supply the needs of the family members. Economic self-sufficiency, together with the family as the leading organizational unit of production and economic security, gave the family overwhelming dominance over the individual, exacting from him undivided loyalty and forcing him to submit to the authority of the family.

Internally, the economic organization of the traditional family was structured with reference to age and sex differentiation. The acquisition of goods and income was predominantly the responsibility and right of the male, and the processing of materials for consumption at home was mainly the duty of the female members. This division of labor was enforced by many institutional devices, such as superstitious taboos against employment of women in many types of work and social customs and guild rules that would admit only males into certain occupations. J. L. Buck's survey showed that women supplied only 16.4 per cent of all the farming labor,[2] mostly in the form of helping with the harvest during busy seasons, weeding, and other secondary chores. With some local exceptions, only in home industry did women generally occupy a significant place in income-acquiring activities. For instance, women in the northern part of China participated less in main production work than women in the South, where women were more accepted in both agricultural and urban occupations.

Age as a structuring factor in production was uniform throughout the country. The average family started training a child for production by the age of from eight to ten, having him perform minor tasks and acquainting him with the scene of labor. From early teen age a child began to take a fairly active part in production if the family was financially unable to send him to school. Children supplied 10.9 per cent of the agricultural labor on a traditional Chinese farm.[3] By fifteen or sixteen a boy was considered a full-fledged worker in agriculture and in many other fields of production, and he assumed his full share of labor or contributed his share of income to the family if he worked outside. In family production he worked under the direction of his father, who remained the leading organizer and income provider for the family. The father's age signified both prestige and technical competence, and he gradually retired into the position of advisor and supervisor as he neared the age of sixty, performing a decreasing amount of physical labor, the amount of which was determined by the economic circumstances of the family. From twenty to thirty years of age, the son's position in the economic organization grew in importance in proportion to the aging of the father until he took full leadership upon his father's death or upon the father's retirement into a supervisory capacity. For a woman a full share of labor in the household economy began at fourteen or fifteen, and her share was particularly heavy immediately following her marriage into the husband's family, where she worked under the direction of the mother-in-law, who was the chief organizer of the household and who would surrender her leadership only upon her retirement into a supervisory capacity or at her death.

In the scale of values, only the labor of acquisition of goods and services or income from primary production was rated high. Household labor, whether in processing food or clothing for consumption, in sanitary activities like washing and cleaning, or in child care, was rated so low that no man would perform it without feeling some sense of inferiority. The difference of value assigned to various types of labor contributed toward the stratification of status and authority of the members of the family.

Property ownership and management of income as a factor in the economic structure of the family was again based on sex and age differentiation. The right of property management belonged to the leader of the family's economic organization, the head of the household; when the head of the house died, it passed down the line of male inheritance.* On this ground, the head of the house also dictated the disposal of income brought into the family by various members should they work outside; minor members in the status system, the young and the women, did not have complete control over the disposal of their own income.

Although management was dominated by the head of the household, family property was collectively owned, with other family members retaining their share. Under the collective principle family property was often legally registered in a form of corporate ownership known as t'ang (hall) under the direction and management of the head of the house and could not be disposed of without common consent of all the male members, each of whom held a share. A son might not have his share without the father's consent or until the death of the father. Female descendants had no claim on family property. A woman might own family property on the death of her husband, but she could not dispose of it without consent of the son if she had male children. As already pointed out, no divorced woman was permitted to take any part of the husband's family property into a new marriage or back to her own parents' family. Even without further details on the complex subject of family property ownership, it can be seen that it gen-

---

* Should there be no male heir after the death of both husband and wife, an unmarried daughter might have some claim to the family property, but she could not take the property into her husband's family upon her marriage should there be claims on it by male collateral descendants of the extended family. In the absence of both male and female descendants, male collateral descendants would claim the property.

erally discriminated against the female and junior members of the family.

The Chinese system of collective ownership of family property was largely a result of the earthbound peasant economy, which required the organized labor of the entire family to till a plot of land; and the traditional distribution of property rights within the family was developed mainly from the male-dominated structure of the family as a unit of economic production. The strong organization of the family proved itself equally effective for traditional commercial and handicraft production, the vast majority of which was on a small scale as it was limited in its development by a confining localized economy.*

Change in the Right of Ownership of Family Property

Objection to the discriminatory features in the traditional system of family property ownership has long been a feature of the Chinese family revolution, especially from modern educated women; and when equality was accepted as a general principle by the educated young, sex equality in property ownership rights became a logical demand. When the Kuomintang government promulgated its marriage and kinship law, considerable concession was made to women, giving conditional equality of inheritance to sons and daughters.[4] When the Communists wrote their new Marriage Law, the matter of property rights was redefined more unequivocally to the advantage of women and children. Article 10 of the Communist Marriage Law stipulates that "husband and wife have equal rights of ownership and disposal of family property," and the following interpretation of that Article was given by the Communist government:

Family property falls into the following three categories:
1. Property belonging to husband and wife before their marriage.
2. Property acquired by husband and wife during their common living. This again may be subdivided into three types:
    a. Property acquired by the common labor of husband and wife. The wife's labor in housekeeping and raising children should be regarded as having the same value as the husband's labor in earning a livelihood. Hence, property acquired by the husband's labor should be regarded as acquired by the common labor of husband and wife.
    b. Property inherited by either or both parties while married.
    c. Gifts received by either or both parties while married.

* When the unit of organization grew large in certain commercial and industrial enterprises, the family organization often proved inadequate and the partnership organization came into operation.

3. Property of children who have not reached maturity, such as land and other kinds of property acquired by children in the process of land reform.

With the principles of equal rights between men and women and equal status between husband and wife in the family established, husband and wife have equal rights of ownership and disposal of family property in the first and second categories, and equal rights of administration of the family property in the third category. On the other hand, with the same principles as a base, husband and wife may make mutual voluntary agreements regarding ownership, disposal, and administration of any kind of family property.[5]

Under land reform, which was completed in all the major regions of China by 1953, both women and children have a clear share of the land distributed to the family by the government. Separate deeds could be issued to the wife and each of the children on request.[6]

On the matter of inheritance the Marriage Law stipulates that "both husband and wife have the right to inherit each other's property" (Article 12), and that "parents and children have the right to inherit one another's property" (Article 14). In the latter, the word "children" in the Chinese text is actually "sons and daughters."

The new system of family ownership of property under Communist law is thus radically different from the traditional practice. How far this new arrangement is being accepted by the people is not known, but several facts should be considered. Since equality in family property rights was long a part of pre-Communist agitation in the family revolution, it may be assumed that the new arrangement gains ready acceptance among the modern educated generation of urban upper and middle classes. As for the working class and the peasantry, propaganda and indoctrination of the Marriage Law and the efforts of the women's movement no doubt popularize the new idea; and in an age of revolution in which an individual is alerted to review his own interest in a different light the chance of its acceptance is high. That legal decisions support the new system can be seen in a large number of cases published in the Communist press during the early years of the regime. One such case in 1951 concerned a woman, Ma Ts'ui-yü, in Shanghai. Ma married into a "big family" where her husband and his married brothers lived together under the authority of the mother-in-law. In 1950 Ma's husband died, and soon afterward his brothers proceeded to dissolve the big family by dividing up the family property. The mother-in-law and the brothers decided not to give Ma her deceased husband's share of the property on the traditional ground that she had born no son. When Ma brought the case to the Communist court it upheld her claim for the deceased husband's share, citing the law that "husband and wife have the right to inherit each other's property." Another typical case involved the property rights of a peasant girl in Lulung county of Hopei Province. The girl, stimulated by the propaganda of the Communist Marriage Law, fell in love with a young Communist Party member and wanted to marry him, but her parents regarded the untraditional love affair as a humiliation to the family and forbade her to leave the house. In 1951 she brought the case to court, which not only recognized her freedom to marry but also permitted her to take her share of land from her parents' family to her new family.[7] Thus she not merely brought no "ritual wealth" or "body price" into the family when she married, but actually took away property that traditionally belonged to her parents.

A last and interesting point for consideration is the recognition of household services as a part of productive labor contributing to the acquisition of family property. Under Communist law such services furnish legal ground for women's claim to family property, but apparently this new valuation of household labor is far from gaining popular acceptance despite a vigorous propaganda campaign to popularize it.

In this connection it must be noted that the weight of private property rights as a factor in elevating the status of women and young family members is being drastically reduced by the socialization of the Chinese economy. By 1957 China's farms had been collectivized into the agricultural producers' cooperatives, and urban private businesses had been socialized into joint state-private concerns controlled by the state. By the end of 1958, the more thoroughly collectivized people's communes replaced the agricultural producers' cooperatives as the national form of rural production. The individual or the family no longer owns land, business enterprise, or any other significant means of production, and private property is reduced mainly to personal articles, with private ownership of houses in serious doubt.

It is obvious that as private property ceases to be a major factor in status stratification, redistribution of property rights can serve only in a limited way in the alteration of the status of the family members. It is the equalizing right to work outside the family, not property rights, that will serve that function. The reduction of family property to an insignificant position has another important meaning, namely the removal of the means of production (in the form of land or business enterprises) from family control, thereby depriving the family of the hitherto most basic factor in integrating its members into a strongly organized group.

Women's Participation in Production

An important factor which is changing the economic status of women in the family as well as in society is the increasing participation of women in production and the development of occupational opportunities for women. This is a new and disruptive factor in the economic structure of the traditional family.

The relation between traditional women's status and their formerly limited role in production is vividly illustrated in the case of Chou Po-lin in Yenchi county of Kirin Province. Chou was a farmer tilling four mow of land. After promulgation of the new Marriage Law, when Chou's wife claimed sex equality during a family squabble, Chou said to his wife: "Now that men and women are equal, let us also be equal in labor." Subsequently Chou tilled only two mow of land, leaving the other two mow for his wife to till. As a consequence, the other two mow of land were left to waste, since his wife could not farm.[8] Chou knew that she could not farm that two mow of land! There was no possibility that she could, as tradition had kept women from participating in productive labor, particularly in the northern section of China.

In the traditional social order it was an informal taboo for upper- and middle-class women to work at income-earning jobs if the family could support them, as it would seriously damage the social dignity of the family. With poor families in which the husband's earnings could not keep the family going, such as with peddlers, laborers, and poor peasants, it was common to find, particularly in the South, women taking up an occupation or working alongside the husband in a small business or in the fields, all in addition to heavy household duties. But all traditional occupations admitting women as independent workers were poorly paid and offered no prospect of a woman's becoming prosperous or gaining social respect. As soon as a husband could support the family, the wife followed the upper- and middle-class practice and ceased to work. Even the idea of women receiving an education to prepare for a profession or occupation met strong resistance from upper-class families.

During the Republican period the increasing influence of modern education, the agitation of the women's movement, and the development of a modern urban economy gradually broke down the disapproval of working women. In a sense, from the day when women were emancipated from their crippling bound feet, which had been a heated issue in the earlier part of the century, the course was set for women to walk with "liberated" feet to the outside world and to work. Within two decades the idea of women participating in income-earning work as a normal part of life and not merely because of dire economic necessity gained general acceptance among the urban intelligentsia. Urban occupational fields with better social and economic prospects opened up for women: factory work, sales work, many kinds of personal services such as those provided by barbers and waitresses, medicine, teaching, scientific research, stage arts, clerical positions, government jobs, and even a few high-level political posts. But in rural communities, particularly in the North, the traditional restriction stood firm in the pre-Communist period.

When the Communists assumed national power, the right of women to participate in productive labor was written into the statute: "Both husband and wife shall have the right of free choice of occupation and free participation in work and in social activities" (Marriage Law, Article 9). Promotional efforts have been made to put this legal stipulation into practice, and the mobilization of women into production has become a leading policy of the government in order to meet the labor requirement of the Communist program of increasing agricultural and industrial production in the modernization of China's economy.

Thus, in 1950 elaborate propaganda fanfare heralded the first group of women tractor drivers and locomotive engineers in the Northeast. All-women-operated railroad trains in Tientsin and Shanghai in 1951 were Communist showpieces demonstrating sex equality of work.[9] In the same year in the Northeast, the bastion of modern Chinese industrial development, a substantial number of women were engaged in a variety of technical and skilled occupations as a result of Communist encouragement. In the cities of Darien and Port Arthur 1,196 women were in 35 kinds of technical and skilled jobs in heavy industry including operating lathes, repairing ships, and metal casting; and 6,183 women were in 14 kinds of light industry jobs. Among these women workers were one factory manager, seven technical assistants, 81 foremen, and 1,178 sub-foremen. In 1950 in Mukden 1,100 women workers were promoted to positions of factory administration and leaders in labor unions. In the field of mining, 814 women were found in 39 kinds of skilled jobs in the Fushun Coal Mining Company.[10]

Since then there has been steady increase in the variety of skilled and unskilled occupations open to women as the tempo of Chinese economic development has quickened. In 1954 a woman worker made news by mastering high-temperature welding at perilous heights on construction projects. From 1949 to 1954 the number of women employed in industrial, commercial, and political jobs increased from 420,000 to 1,900,000 throughout the country.[11] By the end of 1955 women accounted for 14 per cent of workers and staff members in all state enterprises, including 2,500 in administrative positions and 16,000 technicians. In professional fields during the same year there were 65,000 women medical and public health workers and 33,000 women educators, including 7,500 teaching in higher educational institutions.[12] There has also been a steady increase in the number of women in political and military services in the government. Ts'ai Ch'iang, a prominent Communist feminist leader, declared that there were 500,000 women officers in 1951 as compared to 764,000 in 1955, an increase from 8 per cent of all officers to 14.5 per cent.[13] It is now normal to find women mingling with men officers in Communist government offices. In the early years of Communist rule in 1950 and 1951 women police were a common sight in many cities, and they eyed in a prejudiced way bourgeois members of their sex who did not work, led a "parasitic" life, and had a low degree of political consciousness.

While the foregoing data leave many statistical problems unanswered, they nevertheless serve to indicate the trend away from the days when the only occupations for women were low-paying jobs such as embroidery and needle work, domestic service, and hard labor like carrying dirt or crushing rocks for construction projects — jobs which reinforced women's servitude. No doubt sizeable numbers of women under the Communist regime are still engaged in such jobs, but the new situation differs from the old in that, in addition to these jobs, women are now being admitted to a large variety of occupational fields offering possibilities of status advancement, fields that had been traditionally closed to their sex.

Since the widening of occupational opportunities for women had been going on for more than three decades previous to the inauguration of Communist power, Communist figures on the employment of women in some fields contain contributions from pre-Communist development. An example is the Communist figure of 70 per cent of all textile industry workers in the country being women.[14] The fact is that women were numerically important in the textile industry even in pre-Communist days. The proportion of women workers has also always been high in many light industries such as the manufacturing of matches.

However, even after taking previous developments into consideration, the situation of women's employment under the Communists still presents two new features. One is the opening of administrative and supervisory positions to women in places where members of both sexes work together, which means that men may be taking orders from a woman superior, something unusual if not intolerable in traditional public life. Secondly, a whole class of women formerly sheltered by a favored economic position from having to work are now being compelled by new circumstances to join society's working force. These are the upper- and middle-class women whose husbands belong mainly to two groups, businessmen and intellectuals who include educational, technical, and government workers. Since, except for some high-ranking technicians and officials, salaries for intellectuals are generally insufficient to support a family, a large number of wives from this group have had to seek work if possible. In fact, it has been a general rule that when the Communist authorities assign work for a man, they also try to find a placement for the wife. To the Communists, the non-working wife is almost as unthinkable as the traditional bound feet; and the low salary arrangement for men serves the function of obtaining a maximum working force from the population by compelling women to work. Having the same effect was the widespread unemployment of intellectuals during the first half-dozen years of Communist rule, a situation that forced women to look for work whenever possible. In spite of the rosy picture the Communists painted of the economic growth of the country, over 6,800 intellectuals alone registered for employment in Shanghai in September 1956.[15] As to women belonging to businessmen's families, the Communists' steady liquidation of private business through a variety of means has made it necessary for women to leave their sheltered position and seek employment.

Thus, ideological promotion, financial pressure from the collapse of an old economic institution, and increasing employment opportunities in a new economic order jointly bring into the nation's working force large numbers of women who never had to work before. From this it appears that growing female participation in production outside the family is inevitable.

This new situation is largely confined to urban occupations, except for isolated cases such as tractor driving. In the agricultural sector of the economy the development of new occupational opportunities differs according to geographical regions. In the northern section of the country, where women were traditionally kept from main agricultural production tasks and confined to minor jobs such as weeding and processing grain, a new field of economic activity is opened through Communist ideological promotion and pressure from the collectivization of agricultural production. Realizing the predominant importance of agriculture to the country's economy at the present stage, the Communist government from its very start has put efforts into promoting women's labor in farming. As early as 1950, when land reform was being carried out in the Northeast and North China, women who received their own share of land for the first time were stated to have participated increasingly in major agricultural tasks such as plowing, sowing, and harvesting. In many localities in these two regions women taking part in such tasks accounted for 50 to 75 per cent of all able-bodied women.[16] In the Northeast, where the Communists had established their power earlier than in many other regions, it was stated that in Kirin Province women participating in year-round agricultural production numbered over 857,000 in 1951, constituting about 83 per cent of all adult women; and in Jehol Province over 400,000 women were said to have taken part in major farming jobs.[17] Another report stated that in 1951, in the three Northeastern provinces of Jehol, Heilungkiang, and Kirin, 40 to 50 per cent of all adult women participated in spring planting, 70 to 80 per cent in summer cultivation, and over 90 per cent in autumn harvesting.[18]

In South China there has been a similar drive for women to participate in all aspects of agricultural production. In Ch'ao-an county of Kwangtung Province, for example, it was claimed that in 1951, 3,000 peasant women cleared 3,000 mow (about 460 acres) of new land, and that elsewhere in the same province women were active in major agricultural work.[19] Even if the relative reliability of these statements is taken for granted the extent of women's contribution to agricultural production as a result of Communist efforts is not clear, for women in South China have always taken part in most aspects of agricultural work, at times including plowing. This is especially true with districts like Ch'ao-an and the "four counties" of Kwangtung, where wholesale emigration of men to foreign lands had left women the responsibility for tilling the soil.

But even in South China women were traditionally kept from certain types of agricultural work. For instance, for women to labor on dike work was a religious taboo, as it was believed the presence of women on a dike might cause it to collapse. It is significant, then, that in many instances during 1951 Communist cadres mobilized whole villages, including women, for emergency repair work on dikes that were being threatened by rising rivers. In the southern province of Kwangtung, in Chungshan county, it was a group of peasant women who led the emergency repair of a dike breakage, rescuing some 32,000 mow of paddy fields from flood. In Panyü county women supplied two-fifths of the workers in a major job of repairing a 38,000-foot dike. An age-old superstition has thus been broken, and peasant women have entered into another aspect of agricultural work which had traditionally been closed to them.[20]

A standard Communist technique in stimulating enthusiasm for production is the use of emulation contests to glorify and reward "model workers," a technique applied to encourage agricultural as well as industrial production. Women in agricultural production have produced a large number of "model workers." In 29 counties of Liaotung Province in the Northeast 3,096 women were made model agricultural workers, and in six counties of the Chuangho district in the same province women supplied 17.9 per cent of the 835 model agricultural workers during 1951.[21] In the southern province of Kwangsi in 1953, 53 or 15.6 per cent of 339 model agricultural workers were women.[22]

The most effective pressure to increase the participation of women in agricultural work in the North as well as in the South, has been exerted by the collectivization of the farm economy, which will be discussed later. Here we would note that women supplied one-third of all the work-days in the agricultural producers' cooperatives throughout the country in 1954,[23] and that in 1955, in Ch'angteh district of Hunan Province in the South, women accounted for 1,100,000 of the 2,500,000 labor units used in accumulating fertilizer.[24]

Development of Child Care for Working Mothers

The Department of Women's Labor of the All-Shanghai Labor Union noted in one of its early reports:

> State Cotton Mill of Shanghai No. 1 employs a large number of women. Almost 80 per cent of these women workers are married and 70 per cent of the married women workers have children. These mothers, even those returning home from night shift, have to cook, care for the children, wash clothes, and can sleep only three or four hours a day. This is the average picture of the female textile worker in other places. Some of them even have to wait on their husbands and parents-in-law when they go home from work and suffer from beating and malnutrition.[25]

The northern city of Tientsin presented a similar picture. A survey of two industrial districts there in 1952 showed that 1,104 out of 4,310 working women were married, and that there was an average of one child to every two working married women. Household chores and child care were causing low efficiency among these women and compelling many of them to leave work.[26] Other reports indicate that such conditions were typical for city factories in the country as a whole.

The problem of working mothers, not entirely a new product of Communist rule, was generally ignored in pre-Communist days. A working mother added the burden of work to her regular domestic duties, still retaining her traditional role in the family. In the traditional three-generation or multi-generation family grand- or great-grandparents too old to work could care for the child while the mother worked, but in the cities a large proportion of families were conjugal families with no aged grandparents — due to economic reasons and the relatively short life-span. Thus the working mother was an exception, since she generally had to place her children outside the family. The Communist regime, having chosen to mobilize women, including mothers, for production, has met the problem of working mothers by setting up nurseries in both urban and rural communities — an institutional innovation with obvious potential effects on the structure of the family.

The development of nurseries in urban centers had an early start. By the end of 1951, a little over two years after the inauguration of the Communist regime, "there were over 15,700 nurseries, kindergartens, and other types of child-care agencies in different cities, caring for some 520,000 children, the number of such agencies representing a nine-fold increase over the pre-Liberation period." [27] Most of them were nursery stations or rooms attached to large manufacturing and mining enterprises, schools, and public offices where large numbers of mothers worked.[28] Of neighborhood nurseries open to the public, there were 4,300 in all cities in the country in 1952.[29]

Such early reports seemed impressive but the development of nurseries has apparently fallen far short of meeting the needs of a society in which it is official policy to promote women's labor. "In Peking there were only eleven nurseries before the Liberation, and these have increased to sixty-five [February 1951], forty-seven of which have been attached to public offices. Recently four nursing rooms have been added. But in Peking there are over four hundred government offices, over eight hundred schools, and over thirty comparatively large factories. Because of the absence of nurseries and nursing rooms in the vast majority of the government offices, women cadres cannot work with ease of mind, and some of them have even stopped working. Some unmarried women comrades, seeing the burden of motherhood, are unwilling to get married, and those already married resort to contraception." [30]

Lack of finances and shortage of trained personnel have proved serious obstacles to expansion. Obviously, a large proportion of the early nurseries were temporary affairs hastily set up without adequate organization, equipment, personnel, or operating expenditures. Unofficial reports disclosed high sickness and death rates among children entrusted to such agencies, which undoubtedly deterred many working mothers from using them. By 1955 there were only 4,000 nurseries among manufacturing and mining enterprises throughout the country, caring for 127,000 children, and 687 public neighborhood nurseries in 60 cities caring for some 38,000 children.[31] Those figures registered a decrease from 1951–1952. By the fall of 1956 only 6,000 nurseries were reported for industrial and commercial enterprises and government and educational institutions.[32]

Other difficulties developed to impede the transference of women from the home to urban occupational fields. By 1956 many reports noted a tendency among Communist administrators to discriminate against employing women in a large variety of jobs even though they had adequate qualifications. The reasons given were the "trouble involved" in employing women; that nurseries had to be set up; and that pregnant mothers had to be granted leave with pay, thus increasing the operating cost of the enterprise or office. The Department of Agriculture and Forestry of the Kwangtung provincial government refused to employ a twenty-year-old girl graduate from a school of accounting on the ground that she had a fiance and would soon be married and have children, thus bringing "all incidental troubles" to the department.[33] Such reports agree with statements from Communist leaders. Ts'ai Ch'iang, a feminist leader, raised objections at the Eighth Communist Party Congress to the discrimination against employing women by the Communist government.[34] Yang Chih-hua attacked the unfavorable attitude which regarded the employment of women as "being uneconomical and presenting too many problems." [35] Recent complaints by Communist leaders about early marriages of industrial workers, especially women, are related to the question of young working mothers being hampered by children.[36]

These difficulties, however, caused only temporary interruptions in the long-term growth of employment of urban women outside the home. The leap-forward campaign in 1958 brought a renewed increase of the country's women industrial and office workers to seven and a half million from about three million in 1957.[37] In Shanghai 460,000 women worked at industrial jobs in 1958 as compared with 190,000 in 1949.[38] In Peking women workers in industrial, commercial, and cultural fields numbered 210,000, a gain of 50 per cent over 1957, and the Peking Tramcar Company in 1958 hired three times as many female employees as in the previous eight years.[39] Even the interior city of Sian saw a gain of 23 per cent of women industrial workers in 1958 as compared with 1957, and 80 per cent of the city's commercial service occupations were said to be staffed by women.[40]

The mobilization of peasant women for agricultural production also brought active efforts to set up nurseries in rural communities when mutual-aid teams were started as the first step toward collectivization. "Many villages have begun to establish seasonal nursery units during busy seasons for mutual-aid teams. There are over 10,000 such organizations throughout the country [1951]. In rural communities where the problem of child care is solved, much of women's labor that used to be buried in the home begins to emerge in production activities. For instance, in Honan Province during the busy farm season 3,582 child-care teams and 76 nurseries have been organized for the mutual-aid teams in agricultural production. This makes it possible for 27,359 mothers to participate in agricultural production." [41] Another local example was the village of Hsushichen in Chienyang county of Fukien Province. "The mutual-aid team for farming in that village mobilized 8 old women to take care of 12 children so that the younger able-bodied women could work." [42]

The campaign of organizing seasonal nursery units among women agricultural workers apparently made progress in 1952, for it was claimed that the number of temporary nursery teams during busy farming seasons increased that year to 148,000, caring for about 800,000 children throughout the country. In six "special districts" of Anhwei Province 30,696 mutual-aid child-care units were organized in the spring and summer of 1952, caring for 157,575 children. In the southern part of the same province establishment of nursery organizations relieved 141,969 women for agricultural production, including "many women who previously did very little labor or did not know how to labor." Such nursery organizations were mostly staffed by women too old for active agricultural labor but glad to earn some "labor points." An old woman caring for four children earned from

3 to 4.55 labor points a day, depending on the number and ages of the children being cared for, as compared with the average of 10 labor points earned by a regular agricultural worker per day. These "labor points" were paid for by the agricultural mutual-aid teams of which the working mothers were members, the cost of child care becoming a part of the cost of agricultural production in such cases.[43]

Acceptance of the cost of nursery organizations as part of the cost of mutual-aid teams and later of agricultural producers' cooperatives and the utilization of otherwise idle old people for public child care were among the reasons for the early success of nursery work in some localities, but, as has been the case with the urban nursery movement, there seems to have been little progress after 1953. No further statistical figures on rural nursery work are seen in the available Communist press or literature after that year. On the other hand, reports continue regarding the conflict between the new burden of labor production and the old duties of child care and household chores for peasant women. During 1954 and 1955 there were many reports of children being injured or drowned in ponds and rivers owing to the absence of the mothers who were working in the fields.[44] In the pre-Communist period, there were occasional injuries or deaths of children caused by the absence of mothers who were working during busy farming seasons, but such cases "increased precipitously after the rapid growth in the number of agricultural producers' cooperatives" in 1955.[45]

In 1956 the problem of child care and domestic duties continued to plague Communist staff members who tried to mobilize peasant women for full agricultural production work. The head of an agricultural producers' cooperative in Chien-shih county of Hupei Province lectured his peasant wife: "To gain emancipation, women must do production work just like men." But the wife had to care for the children, cook, gather firewood, carry water, make shoes, sew and mend, collect feed for the pigs, and tend the vegetable garden, with the result that she earned only a small number of "labor points." The husband scolded her for not going out to work more often, for "living on the exploitation of men," and the wife in turn accused him of not helping out with the domestic work. In T'ung-shan county of Kiangsu Province an agricultural producers' cooperative set down a regulation that in order to receive a full worker's remuneration a woman had to work 270 workdays of the year. But a survey showed that a peasant mother spends a total of 131 days a year in child care and domestic

chores, and that, at the maximum, she can work only 170 full workdays and 60 half workdays. A quota of 270 full workdays is obviously
impractical.[46]

Whereas in urban occupations the employment of women, particularly mothers, seems to be slowing down somewhat because of difficulties in providing nurseries and childbirth benefits, there has been
little letup in the drive for getting peasant women to take part in full
agricultural production duties. In 1955 Communist propaganda still
stressed woman's participation in collective agriculture as the only
road to emancipation from man's domination and family oppression.
The Communist press publicized many stories of peasant women who
had previously suffered mistreatment from husbands and parents-in-
law but were now respected by the latter because they brought income
home by working on the cooperative farms.[47]

The sweeping transformation of the cooperatives into people's communes throughout China in the latter part of 1958 brought a systematic effort at resolving the contradiction between the burden of
domestic chores and the Communist policy of the full mobilization
of women for agricultural production. On International Women's
Day, March 8, 1959, the *Jen-min jih-pao* (People's Daily) claimed that
the drive of "socializing household work" has set up in China 3,600,000
public mess halls and 4,980,000 nurseries and kindergartens staffed by
some 7,000,000 women child-care workers. Thus freed from cooking,
child care, and many other domestic chores now collectively performed,
nearly "100 per cent" of all rural women have joined productive labor
in the communes. But since the commune system as a socio-economic
order is still in the experimental stage, its eventual success or failure
will determine whether this drastic alteration of women's position in
the role structure of the family can become institutionalized, or if it
is just another transitional phenomenon in a revolutionary process.

Transformation of the Economic Institution

Functionally the most potent development affecting the family system has been the transformation of the general economic institution,
a transformation which operates to replace the family as the dominant
organizational unit of production. In the pre-Communist period the
rise of large commercial and industrial enterprises in the limited
modernization of the urban economy had disorganizing effects on the
traditional family, but that influence was not extensive, as attested
by the fact that 94 per cent of all commercial and industrial firms in
the city of Canton were still family enterprises in 1950. Above all, the

agricultural sector of the economy that employed over 80 per cent of the population remained in the firm grip of the family organization. Extensive change of the general economic institution came only after the Communists had started to enforce their socialist economic program at a rapid pace. Leading aspects of this change are the socialization of commerce and industry, the collectivization of agriculture, and the program of industrialization.

The economic importance of the family was founded upon private ownership of the means of production and free enterprise. When the Communists took power in 1949, they declared toleration of private business in a "relatively long transitional period of new democracy" during which a mixed economy of private and state enterprises was to be maintained. But this period of mixed economy proved to be quite short. Less than a year after the inauguration of the Communist government a warning was issued to the effect that the development of private business would not be allowed to "pursue its own natural course" but must be guided by state plans so as not to delay the coming of the socialist economy.[48]

From the day the Communists became the nation's governing power an atmosphere of doom descended upon private business. The high-living upper and upper-middle class either fled Communist rule or faced impending bankruptcy, thus depriving urban business of the bulk of its luxury consumers. The year 1950 saw a nation-wide decline of private businesses in all cities. A slight recovery in 1951 was followed by the scorching Five-Anti movement (against tax evasion, theft of state economic information, bribery of officials, cheating on government contracts, and theft of state property), which imposed ruinous fines on a large proportion of urban businessmen in 1952. At the same time, constant financial drain from taxes, forced subscriptions to a variety of bonds and loans, increased wages, and benefits to workers that were not based on a rise in productivity drove private businesses into insolvency. But a financially insolvent business was not permitted to close down without government permission, which was generally not granted. As large numbers of financially bankrupt businesses were compelled to stay open (so as to avert sudden widespread unemployment and economic chaos), businessmen had no alternative but to turn to the Communist government bank for loans to continue operation. In most cases the loan became the government's share in the business, and the firm was turned into a joint state-private enterprise, with the state's representative dictating its operation.

State enterprises and their ramifying system of control over private business developed rapidly after 1952. In 1949, 36.7 per cent of the nation's industrial products in terms of value were turned out by state enterprises, cooperatives, and state-private firms, and 63.3 per cent came from private enterprises. In 1952 the respective figures were 61.0 and 39.0 per cent.[49] From 1952 to 1955 state ownership took over almost all heavy industries, a substantial percentage of light industries, almost all of the wholesale, and a considerable proportion of the retail trade. Businesses remaining in private hands had come to operate as subsidiaries to the system of state enterprises which also effectively controlled the rapidly extending system of cooperatives.[50] Private industries relied mainly on orders or processing contracts from government agencies and state enterprises, and depended on state organizations for the supply of raw materials. Private trade similarly depended on state-owned wholesale agencies for the distribution of goods, and faced increasing competition from state stores and marketing and consumers' cooperatives in addition to the difficulties of a shrunken urban market. In spite of a moderate revival of private retail trade in 1954, it became clear that the days of independent operators were gone.

In 1955, the movement for socialist transformation of business enterprise was accelerated, and in January of 1956 it was announced that all of the remaining private enterprises in industry and commerce in the nation's leading cities, (Shanghai, Peking, Tientsin, Sian, Mukden, Nanking, Canton, and Chungking) had become private-state operations.[51] Later, Communist premier Chou En-lai stated: "By the end of June 1956, 99 per cent of capitalist industrial enterprises in terms of output value and 98 per cent in terms of number of workers and employees have come under joint state-private operation. Of the private commercial and catering establishments, 68 per cent in terms of the number of shops and 74 per cent in number of personnel have been transformed into joint state-private shops, cooperative shops, or cooperative groups. The conversion of capitalist industry and commerce into joint state-private enterprises trade by trade and the carrying out of the fixed interest system in these enterprises have prepared the way for nationalization of capitalist means of production." [52] The last part of the statement referred to the fact that, under joint state-private operation, the private share of capital was being given a flat 5 per cent interest rate regardless of the profit or loss of the business, but that in the future the private share would be turned over to the state. In view of the rapid conversion of private businesses into the state-private system, the day of complete nationalization is not distant — possibly during the period of the second five-year plan (1957–1962).

The above data omit the multitudes of handicraftsmen, small traders, and peddlers. Although there are no statistics on the total number of handicraftsmen in the country, it was announced that by September 1956, 4.7 million of them had been organized into producer cooperatives, and that only a small number of them were still working on a private basis.[53] In Peking all of the city's 53,000 craftsmen had been "cooperativized" in January of the same year. The organization of small traders and peddlers into cooperative stores has also developed steadily in the cities and towns,[54] but recent Communist policy has been to permit the continued existence of some small craftsmen, service establishments, traders, and peddlers instead of forcing them all into state-directed organizations such as cooperatives.[55]

In spite of reservations in the new policy about small handicraftsmen and traders, it is obvious that the family has been displaced as a unit of production and employment. No longer are the members of the family the basic components of the organization of production; nor do individuals look toward the family as the most important center of economic support or economic opportunities. Instead, state enterprises operating outside of the kinship system have become the basic unit of industrial and commercial organization, and individuals must look toward them for employment and economic opportunities.

The nationalization of an industrial and commercial system that contains close to ten million small businesses and individual operators will require huge numbers of technically trained personnel and solutions to a complex of problems. As Communist leadership is as yet unable to meet either of these two conditions, it is inevitable that mismanagement and dislocation will occur in both the industrial and the distributional system, as has been admitted in Communist reports.[56]

In the agricultural sector of the economy the family has also lost its significance as the dominant organizational unit in production. The first Communist measure for changing the agrarian economic system was the land reform completed in 1952, which redistributed land to landless peasants and those having insufficient land.* But

* See Liao Lu-yen, "The Great Victory of Three Years of Land Reform Movement," *Hua Ch'iao jih-pao*, New York, October 22–24, 1952. The percentages of land redistributed and peasants benefited in the land reform are revealed in sample investigations conducted by the Communist government. In the Central-South Region about 40 per cent of all the land had been confiscated and redistributed to about 60 per cent of all the peasants, with each landless or poor peasant gaining 1/6 to 1/3 of an acre. The corresponding figures for the East China Region are close to those for the Central-South Region. In the Southwest Region, where land ownership was more concen-

new land for the poor peasants did not remain in their private possession for long. Even in the pre-Communist period, efforts to modernize Chinese agriculture had found almost insurmountable obstacles in the "small farm economy" consisting of, among other things, diminutive farm units and widely scattered tiny plots of land belonging to the same farm. For the Communist regime, which is dedicated to large-scale mechanized production techniques and follows the Leninist line of changing farms into "agricultural factories" with mechanization and rationalized management as a means of elevating the peasants to economic parity with industrial workers, the collectivization of agriculture is as inevitable as the nationalization of business enterprise. And hastening the collectivization drive is the pressing need for capital for the industrialization program, capital which can be obtained more easily from 750,000 government-controlled collective farms or 26,000 communes than from some 120,000,000 independent peasant farms.

The Communist program of collectivization is divided into four stages: the development of (1) mutual-aid teams, (2) the elementary type of agricultural producers' cooperatives, (3) the advanced type of agricultural producers' cooperatives, and (4) the people's communes.

Mutual-aid teams are groups consisting of half a dozen to twenty or thirty peasant families who pool their labor and equipment to work on the land possessed by the families. Essentially it is a labor pool. The individual worker, not the family, is the basic unit of the organization, and remuneration is based on the number of "labor points" earned by each worker, the average for a full-time worker being 10 points per day. Land ownership, work animals, and farm implements used by the team receive separate compensation. By the end of 1952, 60 to 80 per cent of all peasant households in the Northeast and the "old liberated areas" of North China had been organized into mutual-aid teams, and in the southern part of the country 25 to 40 per cent of peasant households belonged to a total of some six million teams.[57] While continued increase in the number of mutual-aid teams has been reported after 1952, national statistical figures have not been available. Even at this elementary step of collectivization, the peasant family retains a certain degree of economic significance chiefly in the ownership

---

trated than other regions, 60 per cent of all the land had been redistributed to over 70 per cent of all the peasants. In the Kuanchung area of the Northwest Region, where land ownership was rather dispersed, 20.3 per cent of all the land had been distributed to about 30 per cent of the peasants. See also *Shih-chieh Nien-chien* (World Year Book), Peking, 1952, pp. 336–339.

of land and not as a dominant organizational unit of agricultural production.

The so-called elementary type of agricultural producers' cooperative is essentially a land pool, with certain heavy farm implements and work animals also thrown into common use. The remuneration system is basically the same as in mutual-aid teams, but the difference lies in the development of a unified management concerning the type of crops to be planted, capital investment, distribution and organization of the labor force, marketing of farm products and distribution of earnings. In the advanced type of agricultural producers' cooperatives land ownership is no longer recognized as a factor for remuneration, it being taken for granted that after the land reform average peasants own a relatively equal amount of land. Work animal and heavy implements are taken into common ownership by the cooperative with compensation. With the peasant becoming chiefly a wage earner, the advanced cooperative has all the fundamental features of the collective farm in the Soviet Union.[58]

The development of agricultural producers' cooperatives made slow progress in the first few years of the Communist regime. There were 300 agricultural producers' cooperatives (types unspecified) throughout China in 1951, about 4,000 in 1952, 14,000 in 1953, 670,000 in 1954. There was some increase in 1955, but during the year many small cooperatives were combined into larger ones, reducing the actual number of cooperatives to 650,000 but with 16,900,000 peasant households as members, accounting for about 15 per cent of China's 120,-000,000 peasant households.[59] Toward the end of 1955 the drive for "cooperativization" was greatly accelerated, and in the fall of 1956, Chou En-lai announced with satisfaction to the Chinese Communist Party Congress: "By the end of June 1956 a total of 992,000 agricultural producers' cooperatives had been organized throughout the country. Their members make up 91.7 per cent of the country's peasant households; those joining cooperatives of the advanced type constitute 62.6 per cent of all peasant households." [60] Liao Lu-yen, Minister of Agriculture, significantly declared in the light of this development: "The small peasant economy has been changed throughout the country." [61] By the early part of 1958 the merging of smaller cooperatives reduced the national total number of cooperatives to about 750,000, each having an average of 170 households, some 300 laborers, and 2,000 mow (approximately 300 acres) of land.[62]

The attempt to collectivize a peasant economy of microscopic family farms and intensive cultivation gives rise to serious organizational problems in inculcating an impersonalized collective role conception in the peasants' minds, in developing a businesslike attitude, in creating a technically and administratively qualified leadership for the vastly expanded operational unit, in coping with interference on collective labor by such remaining private undertakings as home industries and raising vegetables on the family plot, and in satisfactorily dividing the collective income between capital accumulation, needs of the state, and remuneration for the members. Reports in Communist literature indicate that a significant number of the cooperatives failed in surmounting these difficulties, and that only some of them worked well. On the other hand, cooperatives command the general advantages of a greatly expanded pool of labor, land and resources, and a unified administrative authority. These advantages brought about the rapid extension of irrigated areas through numerous hydraulic projects, and increased adoption of improved techniques of cultivation, resulting in the Communist claim of an increase in national agricultural output since collectivization.

The experience of some successful cooperatives and certain general technical advantages of collectivism encourage the Communist leadership into believing in the universal practicability of collectivization by imposing military discipline to overcome the organizational difficulties that have plagued the poorly operated cooperatives. This is among the major considerations that have motivated the drastic merging of the country's 750,000 cooperatives into 26,500 people's communes in the last four months of 1958. As a unit of production an average commune contains some 5,000 households, 10,000 laborers and 6,000 mow (about 900 acres) of land.[63] This huge organization completely obliterates the family as a unit of production by collectivizing even the private plots previously reserved for family use under the cooperative system and by setting up communal industries to replace home industries and to diversify economic operations in rural communities.

In 1955 Mao Tse-tung declared in a speech that one of the urgent reasons behind the hastening of the collectivization program was the need to accumulate capital for industrialization.[64] The same need for industrial capital contributed to the establishment of the commune system which appears more effective than the cooperatives in extracting income from the peasantry. Aspirations for the status of an industrialized nation have been firing the imaginations of the Chinese people for a century, and Communist leadership in China, like its counterpart in the Soviet Union, dedicates itself to the realization of this popular dream. This dedication serves to mitigate some of the harsh features of the Communist power and retain the support of some of the intellectuals for it. It is obvious that industrialization on an extensive scale will have profound effects on the Chinese family system, as demonstrated by the experience of Western industrial society and the Soviet Union.

The present scale of industrial development appears small compared to that of leading Western powers, but it represents a vast acceleration when compared with progress in the pre-Communist period. The heart of the initial development is the first five-year plan (1953–1957). In the first two years of the plan, many industries failed to reach their targets owing to the initial shortage of capital, technical knowledge, organizational and administrative skill, despite limited Soviet assistance.[65] But by the third year, 1955, the program picked up momentum as increasing numbers of industries fulfilled their assigned quota.[66] The vigorous steel-making campaign by both modern and native methods in 1958 further accelerated the development of related industries and stimulated the people's awareness of the industrialization movement. The progress is shown in the following figures for four basic industries during 1952–1958.

Commodity	1952	1954	1955	1957	1958
Steel (million metric tons)	1.4	2.2	2.8	5.35	11.08
Coal (million metric tons)	63.5	80.0	93.0	130.00	270.00
Cement (million metric tons)	2.9	4.6	4.5	6.86	9.30
Electricity (billion kilowatt hours)	7.3	10.9	12.3	19.30	27.50

(Sources: State Statistical Bureau figures released by the New China News Agency, June 14, 1956, and April 14, 1959.)

At the conclusion of the first five-year plan in 1957, the country's total industrial production increased by 132.5 per cent in value over 1952.[67] The feverish leap-forward campaign in 1958 further raised the industrial output in that year by 65.0 per cent over 1957.[68]

Influence on the Family of Industrialization, Nationalization of Business, and Collectivization of Agriculture

We may summarize the significant changes in the economic position and structure of the family which are implied in the Communist nationalization of commerce and industry, acceleration of industrialization, and collectivization of agriculture.

First and foremost is the general replacement of the family as a dominant and independent unit of production in all sectors of economic production, chiefly by removing the means of production from family ownership. Second is the abolition of the head of the family as the leader and chief organizer in production activities, his traditional role being taken over by the new staff members in the state-monopolized economy.

Third, the economic status of women, and to a lesser extent that of the young, tends to be raised by the nationalized and collectivized economy since under such a system the unit for remuneration for work is not the family but the individual worker regardless of sex, age, or family position. The operation of the wage system in industry and commerce in this respect is self-evident. The remuneration system in the cooperative farm is illustrated in the following case:

> A cooperative society of agricultural production has been successfully organized in the village of Sanliushu of Kuangjao county, Shantung Province. The system of remuneration is based upon the number of labor points earned by an individual: (1) A man working a full day receives ten labor points. (2) Labor performed by women is counted in two ways: (a) Those who work in the field performing the same tasks as those performed by men get the same remuneration as men: each working day by one woman counts ten labor points. (b) Women working on special jobs such as picking cotton or preparing animal feed are remunerated according to piece rates expressed in labor points. The roasting of ten catties of animal feed is reckoned as one labor point, and the picking of fifteen catties of cotton is counted as eight labor points. (3) Remuneration for labor performed by children of both sexes is according to the same system. In the cooperative organization of auxiliary industry, such as cutting reeds from marshes, catching fish and shrimp from streams, and making sauces, individuals work and share the fruits of labor collectively according to the same system of remuneration based on labor points.[69]

Now women and children are able to see concretely how much they contribute economically to the family, as measured by wages or labor points they receive, compared to those received by the head of the family or to the total income of the family. Later, under the commune system, the children are fed and cared for by the commune, and each person receives his remuneration in kind and in wages directly from the commune administrators, no longer through the head of the family as previously done under the cooperatives. This effectively invalidates the traditional reprimands used by husbands and parents: "I feed you and you must listen to me"; "I have fed you and raised you and you must obey me." The subversive effect of this change on the structure of family status and authority based on age and sex differentiation cannot be ignored.

Here we would repeat that a deep-rooted tradition does not suddenly lose its force. One Communist report has stated:

> But, at the present, among the mutual-aid and cooperative organizations of agricultural production there is a widespread practice of giving women unequal pay for equal work with men. In a few mutual-aid organizations no labor points at all are entered into the record for women. In a large number of mutual-aid organizations the remuneration for women's labor is arbitrarily fixed as one-half that of a man's labor, regardless of the actual labor efficiency of the women. Some organizations nominally base the remuneration for women's labor upon record of work done and evaluation of labor points, but the number of labor points received by women are always somewhat below the actual labor efficiency of the women. . . .
>
> In Ch'eh Fang village of Yi county in Liaohsi Province some of the people were contemptuous of women's participation in production, regarding them as the "little worker," the "half-size worker," or remarking that "two of them cannot do the work of one [man]." As a consequence, few women participated in production. This year [1952], when the agricultural producers' cooperative was established, when women raised the question of equal pay for equal work at a meeting, many male cadres said: "Women may fool around with cooking, but they are no good for production work," or "If a man earns ten labor points in a day, a woman should earn less." At that meeting someone made the proposal that the recording of work done and the evaluation of the number of labor points should be based on actual results of labor regardless of sex, as, for example, the pulling of weeds by women and the cultivating work by men are about equal in the amount of energy exerted and in the actual result, so both cases should be rewarded with eight labor points each. Some male cadres refused to accept this argument. Failing to arrive at an agreement, both men and women went to work as an experiment. As a result, the male cadres were convinced and said, "Women's work in weeding is not any lighter than men's cultivating, and the two types of work should be rewarded with the same number of labor points." From then on, the principle of sex equality and the same pay for the same work has been implemented in that cooperative. Women in the village became enthusiastic in production, and mothers would say to the women's cadres, "Hurry up and solve the nursery problem so that I can enter into production." [70]

Similarly, there have been a large number of cases of discrimination against giving equal consideration to labor performed by children.[71] The people's commune in its present form may alter this discriminatory tradition by the egalitarian nature of its remuneration system of "free supplies" of food and other necessities of life, but this system is far from having been stabilized.

Fourth, the mobilization of women and children into collective agricultural production reduces the self-sufficiency of the family economy. This is shown concretely in the case of a mutual-aid team in the village of Wangnankou in Laiyang county of Shantung Province. This team was composed of 16 farm families which together possessed 311 mow of land (roughly 50 acres). There was a shortage of labor and 16 women were mobilized to work. "Since the women brought back material benefits in the form of labor points on an equal footing with men, the parents-in-law became pleased and began treating them with a greater measure of equality. The parents-in-law are now willing to see the home spinning and weaving stopped, and to buy cloth for the daughters-in-law the same as for other members of the family." [72]

Under guidance from the state, collectivized agriculture increasingly emphasizes the planting of high-yielding marketable crops best suited to a certain area, thus departing from the tradition of stressing home-consumption, self-sufficiency crops. For instance, a cooperative in Shansi Province reduced the varieties of crops from nineteen to eleven, devoting a large proportion of its land to corn, a high-yielding marketable item.[73] As the family no longer harvests the varieties of crops needed to sustain itself but must rely increasingly on the market, it ceases to be a self-contained unit of economic production and consumption. Family solidarity based on the economic factor is consequently reduced.

Fifth, the general character of collectivized agriculture and state-controlled enterprises is different from that of the family organization. These new organizations are not the products of biological relatedness, for membership is acquired only by the criteria of work capacity and is structured according to the need for work, not according to sex and age.[74] Hence the new pattern of economic organization not only tends to break down the traditional dominance of the family as a fundamental unit of production and its high degree of self-sufficiency, it also undermines the particularistic influence of the family.[75]

Industrialization has an additional disorganizing influence on the traditional family by providing employment and hence economic assistance for the women and the young to escape pressure from the family system of status and authority. Although in the pre-Communist period, modern factories in big cities supported young men and rebellious females deserting the old-style household, many young men and women and dissatisfied wives who left home at the beckoning of the new idealism of freedom and equality were forced to return home by the failure to find a livelihood. Industrialization developed at a slow pace, job opportunities were few, and most of the connections that might lead to jobs were in the hands of relatives who would almost invariably lead them not to a job in a factory but back home where they came from. The accelerated development of modern industries under the Communist regime makes a major difference in this respect in comparison to the pre-Communist period.

CHAPTER IX

The Shifting Center of Loyalty

The Family as the Center of Loyalty in Traditional Society

THE TRADITIONAL Chinese family organization structured on the principle of the Five Cardinal Relations, with its emphasis on the status system of age and sex differentiation, naturally lay heavy stress on loyalty between members of the family and to the family as a group. The central feature of traditional Chinese society as a whole was that the individual's loyalty toward the family transcended all his other social obligations and that the family was the determining factor in the total pattern of social organization.

The ties of affection as a basic factor of loyalty among members of the traditional family were so strongly developed that they dictated the values and outlook of social life for the individual. Thus, Liang Shu-ming wrote from the viewpoint of a traditional scholar:

The life of a single individual is an incomplete life. A single man or a single woman can be counted only as half of a human being. There must be sexual relationship before a complete life starts. Following this come parents and children, elder brother, and younger brother. This is the so-called family. Beyond the family, social relationships bring about the tie between ruler and subjects, between friend and friend. Life exists in these relationships, and the family is the most fundamental of them by nature. The so-called Cardinal Relations center upon the relations of family which are natural relationships, for man holds closest to him what is closest by nature. Man normally rejoices over what is joyful to his loved ones, and grieves over what is grievous to them. Loved ones echo to each other physically, understand each other mentally, establish between themselves a sympathetic consonance and a mental and physical interdependence. This is affection. A beautiful and satisfying life is no other but the fulfillment of these relationships. On the contrary, the greatest misfortune of life is the lack of these relations. The widower, the widow, the orphan, the aged without children — these suffer the greatest misfortunes of a normal life, and they are [traditionally] called the "inarticulates." They are so called because they have no loved ones to whom they can tell their stories of sickness, hardship, poverty, and misfortune. How different this is from the Western style which makes orphans out of children and makes lonely old people out of parents by having the children live apart from their parents; how different this is from the Western style which values not companionship but separation, and condones an unstable relationship of marriage.

For the Chinese, the family is the fountainhead of his life and the place which he regards as his final repose. It is extremely difficult to stabilize life except by the tie of the family. Life usually brings more grief than joy, but the family provides the sentiments of joy. To the Chinese people, the family provides consolation and encouragement, and practically performs the function of religion.[1]

Moreover, the principle of Cardinal Relations fixed the degree and depth of affection between family members according to an established scale based on the proximity of kinship. Thus the strongest affection was fostered between parents and children, and the next strongest between husband and wife; then came that between brothers, between brothers and sisters. Descending in the scale were affection between cousins, between uncles, nephews and nieces, between oneself and uncles' wives, between one's own wife and the wives of brothers, uncles, and other collaterals.

By this code, the strongest affection, that between parents and children, husband and wife, and brothers and sisters, embraced a circle that constituted the basic membership of the average family; one's affection for the more distant relatives such as grandparents, uncles, aunts, and cousins, and for the even more distantly related clansmen, was greater than one's affection for other members of society; and beyond the fringe of the kinship group lay people who were regarded with some degree of distrust and inimical interest. The family, the circle of relatives, and the clan constituted the irreplaceable warm spot of life in a harsh world. "Thinking of home" by sojourners in distant places was one of the most popular and moving themes in Chinese poetry for two thousand years. Perhaps only those who have experienced the traditional Chinese family life can fully appreciate the feeling in such well-known poetic lines as "A cup of dull liquor with home ten thousand *li* away." And perhaps only a traditional Chinese can be really overcome with joy when he meets a relative or a clansman in a distant place.

This is not to say that the traditional Chinese family made a picture of undiluted affection. We have seen that there were numerous sources of family conflict and tension. But loyalty to the family was nevertheless preserved by the dominance of the family in the individual's social and economic interest and by the classical requirement of self-sacrifice and forbearance for the interest of the group. As Liang wrote on this point:

> The principle of Cardinal Relations demands union and not separation among family members. But sometimes when it is not possible to unite, nor is it possible to separate, then each conflicting party exercises forbearance for the preservation of the group and lets the unresolved problem remain unresolved. In the actual situation, few can take the decisive step of separation [by leaving the family], and equally few can really practice the principles required for union, and eight or nine out of ten cases are those in which the family members just bear each other [in order to preserve the family as a group].[2]

The formula of compromise and self-sacrifice, not the definition or protection of the rights of the individual, traditionally preserved loyalty in the Chinese family in spite of disruptive factors. The standard line of the mediator of a family conflict was, "After all, we are all family members," and to a person threatening to take a conflict outside the family for settlement the popular exhortation was, "Family dirt should not be aired outside." The Confucian adage, "Brothers may fight within the house, but will join hands to resist insults from without," remained a valid description of the situation when the traditional family was strong.

Most important in the present context, the successful maintenance of the family as the center of the individual's loyalty requires the continued dominance of the family as an economic structure and as a unit of social interest — in other words, the continued operation of the traditional family which subordinates the role of the individual to the interest of the group; and we have seen that for the past half century the structural strength of the traditional family has been progressively weakened.

Increased Outside Contacts of the Young

In turning to loyalty as a basic element in the Chinese family we are shifting our focus essentially to a factor of family solidarity directly related to the conditioning of the young. From the preceding discussion we have seen that the converging forces of the family revolution increasingly broke down the traditional seclusion of the family members and confinement of their work and interest to family concerns, a practice which once served to exclude the development of competing centers of loyalty outside the family. It goes without saying that an inevitable result of the family revolution and its accompanying social changes was the steady increase of opportunity for youth to have contacts outside the family and therefore to be exposed to new influences which conflicted with traditional family loyalties.

In terms of factors already discussed we need only mention here the economic developments, the modernizing of education, and the increasing population mobility of the Republican period. All of these had profound effects on the attitudes of youth and acted to awaken the interest of the young in affairs and modes of thinking which diminished the traditional strength of family ties. Their effect was heightened by the dislocation of the war period, which forced millions of Chinese, the greater proportion of whom were young people, onto the roads and to distant parts of the country far from the centers of established family influence.

Another pre-Communist factor in the weakening of family loyalty was the growth of social and economic associations that absorbed an increasing proportion of the time and interest of the young. The traditional social order had few organizations for the young, especially women. Whereas the traditional fraternities and sororities were small in membership and did not steer the course of life away from the center of the family, the organizations for the young, ranging from clubs and societies to organizations of an economic and political nature, which developed in the modern period, imbued their members with an idealism inimical to the traditional order besides increasing their physical separation from family contact.

Here again, as we have seen, Communist accession to power gave added impetus to developments already under way. Large-scale Communist programs mobilizing the young for political, economic, and social activities have brought millions of young men and women, and even older children, into contact with new centers of ideology and interest that contradict the moral and organizational principles of the traditional family; and the nationalization and collectivization of economic life has progressively weakened traditional economic reliance upon the family as a factor in generating family loyalty.

More specifically, the development of modern education, which under Communism is a powerful factor undermining family loyalty, has been dramatically accelerated by the present government. The enrollment of students in higher education throughout the country under Communist rule showed a marked increase from the pre-Communist years; and under the policy of "opening school doors to workers and peasants" and the vigorous campaign to wipe out illiteracy, the enrollment of primary and middle schools, especially the former, has increased even more rapidly (see the accompanying table). Leisure-time and evening classes have appeared in growing numbers. Moreover, and of special importance, this kind of influence is now exerted on the very young as a result of women's participation in production and the accompanying development of nurseries. The weaning of the young child away from uninterrupted family care, supervision, and education at the most formative period deal a heavy blow to the traditional conception of the family as the center of one's life and one's loyalty. Under present conditions, when both parents work outside the home all day, the children are placed in nurseries and learn to become independent at the early age of five or six. For the wives there is the choice of giving up work and taking care of the children or continuing to work and letting outside contacts claim the loyalty of the children, and economic and political pressure dictate the latter.

The organization of the young for political, social, and economic activities is far more extensive under the Communist regime than ever before. Some idea of the organization of youth has been noted before. Organizational efforts are also being vigorously pushed in the age group below youth. The Young Pioneers, which organizes children 9 to 14 years of age, claimed a national membership of 5,200,000 in 1952 and 10,000,000 in 1956. Together with the 5,000,000 members in 1952 and 20,000,000 in 1956 of the New Democratic Youth League, which organizes young men and women 15 to 25, the total membership of the organized young reached 10,200,000 in 1952 and 30,000,000 in 1956. Youth of the urban business class form only a minority of the membership, as students constituted only 11 per cent of the total membership of the New Democratic Youth League in 1952.[3] Although no data on the class composition of Youth League membership is available after 1952, the continued expansion of the League among workers and peasants indicates a probable increase of their percentage in League membership since then. Every youth organization serves to dilute the traditional loyalty toward the family.

The Development of Individualism

Extensive outside contacts are, of course, not necessarily destructive to family loyalty unless accompanied by the inculcation into the individual's mind of the acceptance of a new pattern of social life that does

TABLE 1

Number of Students Enrolled in Modern Schools in Continental China, 1946–1956

Types of educational institutions	1946	1949	1950	1951	1952	1954	1956
Universities, colleges, normal colleges, other institutions of higher learning	129,366	130,058	143,267	175,284	219,750	......a	400,000
Middle schools and institutions of similar standing	1,878,523	1,271,342	1,576,377	2,007,781	3,078,826	3,580,000	5,000,000 (estimate)
Elementary schools and institutions of similar standing	23,683,492	24,391,033	28,923,988	43,173,540	49,034,081	51,190,000	57,000,000 (estimate)
TOTAL	25,691,351	25,792,433	30,643,632	45,356,605	52,332,657	......a	62,400,000

Source: *Jen-min Chiao-yü Yüeh-k'an* (People's Education Monthly), October 1952, p. 6; *Jen-min jih-pao* (People's Daily), July 23, 1955, p. 3; New China News Agency, August 31, 1956.
a Figures not available.

not rely upon the family as a central factor. Chinese immigrants in the United States have enjoyed extensive contacts with another culture and have lived far apart from their families for protracted periods, but the members of the first generation still preserve strong family loyalty, for they cling to the ideology of the traditional social pattern. The youth of changing modern China, by contrast, have been increasingly susceptible to a new ideology incompatible with the organizational principle and value standard of the traditional family.

An outstanding element in the new ideology is the Western concept of individualism, which runs directly counter to the spirit of the traditional Chinese family and is incompatible with the traditional loyalty devoted to it. Traditional Chinese moral standards demanded not merely self-sacrifice from the individual but also that he take responsibility for self-cultivation according to Confucian ethics and try to find the solution for all domestic disharmonies in his own efforts at self-perfection. Self-cultivation, the basic theme of Confucian ethics traditionally inculcated in the child's mind from an early age, did not seek a solution to social conflict in defining, limiting, and guaranteeing the rights and interests of the individual or in the balance of power and interests between individuals. It sought the solution from the self-sacrifice of the individual for the preservation of the group. And this responsibility of self-sacrifice fell heavily on the young and on the women. The requirements of *hsiao, ti,* and *ching-chieh* (filial submission of the children, fraternal subordination of the younger brother, and chastity of the women) formed a much greater proportion of traditional moral teachings than the obligations placed upon the head of the family, the older generation, and the men.

Western individualism as a social ideal therefore did not have much attraction for the traditional Chinese mind. Individualism as a philosophy has been a subject of protracted polemics from the days of the New Culture Movement of 1917 down to the present; and it is now the object of renewed condemnation from Communist ideology as a legacy of bourgeois culture. But there is little doubt that the greater recognition of individual rights and interests under the slogan of freedom and equality has had strong appeal for the long oppressed young men and women and has acted as a fermenting agent for China's modern revolutions, particularly the family revolution. Increased extra-familial contacts, reduced control of the family over the individual, and the development of new organizations and new centers of interest based upon the defined share of the individual's rights and privileges have all contributed to the spreading influence of the concept of individualism as a guiding principle for one's social life during the past half century.

That the majority of Chinese probably still find Western individualism a violation of their sense of moral responsibility is suggested by the number of rural Communist leaders who have resisted the idea of divorce and the claim of property rights by divorced women. But there is little doubt that the Western concept of individualism has made deep inroads on the minds of the modern intelligentsia who have been leaders in the movement towards social change. One of the many situations reflecting this has been the popular condemnation of "familism and clannism" over the past three or four decades.

Grounds for that condemnation have been many. One was that the full development of an individual's abilities and initiative was obstructed by the system of "familism and clannism." A further argument was that the individual's interests and rights must find full development in some other organizational context than the old familially oriented pattern. Spurred by the influence of nationalism and idealism for a "new society," the individual increasingly identifies his interests and rights with that of the state and the mass society, no longer solely with that of the family and clan. It is characteristic of an age of revolution that, when the established institutional framework of society fails to hold its ground against antagonistic influences, the individual is inclined to review his own position in reference groups in accordance with new ideological orientations. It was in the midst of such a revolutionary situation that individualism rapidly expanded its influence in modern China.

Control of the nation by Communist leadership has inevitably brought strong condemnation of individualism as "undisciplined liberalism" and a product of "decadent capitalism." But the present urge toward state collectivism calls upon the individual to sacrifice for a group far different from the family; and, whatever its ultimate fate under the Communist regime, individualism has already performed the function of alienating the individual from family loyalty.

The State as the New Center of Loyalty

In China's modern scene, aside from individualism based on the ideas of individual freedom and equality, there has been probably no more powerful ideological factor subversive to family loyalty than the call of nationalism. Under its pressure all modern Chinese reformers have tried to shift the center of loyalty from the family to the state.

K'ang Yu-wei in his *Ta T'ung Shu* (The Great Commonwealth) pointed out the incompatibility between family loyalty and national interest. Sun Yat-sen in his *San-min Chu-i* (Three People's Principles) exhorted his countrymen to broaden familism to nationalism by widening the center of loyalty from the family to the nation. The defeats China had suffered from foreign powers made the adoption of nationalism and patriotism a matter of urgent necessity. The Japanese invasion and the ensuing eight years of devastating war extended the influence of nationalism from the intelligentsia to other classes of the population.

The state as a morally higher center of loyalty had been an established factor in the modern trend of social, economic, and political events prior to the rise of the Communist regime, but in no previous period has the interest of the state and its machinery been more sharply defined and loyalty to it more drastically demanded than under the Communist rule. By propaganda, indoctrination, and pressure from the law the requirement of loyalty to the state and "the people" above everything else is being systematically forced into the consciousness of the population.

The effort to focus loyalty upon the state and its machinery is seen in many of the propaganda documents, giving evidence of benefits reaped by individuals who have chosen the state and its policies as the object of personal devotion. Thus, when a humble worker is elevated to a prominent position, when a brutally treated laborer sees his boss arrested, when a landless peasant gets free land, when an oppressed widow is able to remarry through enforcement of the new Marriage Law, when a slave-girl gains freedom from her purchaser, when a mistreated underdog sees the vindication of justice, the recitation inevitably ends with the uniform statement from the hero of the story: "How grateful I am to the Communist Party!" or "I have Chairman Mao to thank for this!" or " I wouldn't have this day if it were not for the Communist Party!" Whether such remarks are actually uttered by the individual or are attributed to him by the Communist script writer seems immaterial. Two things are clear. One is that the individual benefiting by the action of the regime is naturally grateful to the benefactor, and the other is that it is the intention of official propaganda to encourage the feeling of gratitude, and therefore loyalty, to the state.

Significant is the new moral value being set up by the political movement requiring individuals specifically to put the state above the family as an object of loyalty. Should any member of the family commit an offense against the state, it is one's new duty to expose that member to the government. Failing to do so is to commit the error of "sentimentalism," or "inability to break through personal feelings and face-saving," and this may bring punishment by law on the ground of knowingly harboring criminals. In the first decade of Communist administration of the country successive popular campaigns and movements have brought sharply to the people's attention this new requirement of regarding the state as the supreme object of loyalty. In the movement of punishing landlords and local bullies, in the movement of suppressing counterrevolutionaries, in the Three-Anti and the Five-Anti campaigns * against corrupt officials and "law-breaking" businessmen, high tension was created and emotional pressure exerted to compel individuals to expose any family member who had broken the Communist law and to discourage any effort to shield such a member.

To effect such a change in the object of personal loyalty and affection is of course difficult. To accomplish it, communism employs mass meetings and propaganda campaigns of great emotional tension, highlighted by the confessions of individuals. The individual and the group are thrown into tortuous emotional convulsions in the process of "thought struggle" and "thought remoulding."

During the Five-Anti movement in 1952 in Shanghai over 600 members of the New Democratic Youth League in Futan University were pressured into going home to persuade family members to confess their crimes. Many of the young men and women in the League pledged: "I am going to persuade my father to confess. Should he refuse, I will expose him to the government." As a result of their exemplary actions and campaigning, 1,146 other men and women students in that university also went home to do persuasion work.[4] The Communists alleged that the vast majority of businessmen in Shanghai and other cities had committed some degree of offense against the state — bribing officials, evasion of taxes, theft of public property, theft of state economic secrets, or cheating on government contracts. To extract confessions from such a large number of alleged lawbreakers the party enlisted young people, and while this movement was going on mobilization meetings were held in practically every school, every factory, and every organized group in the large cities throughout the country. The violence done Chinese family

---

* The Three-Anti campaign was against bureaucratism, receiving bribes, and wasting public funds. The Five-Anti campaign was against evasion of taxes, theft of state economic information, bribery, cheating on state contracts, and theft of state property.

traditions by communism is dramatically illustrated by reports in the official press.

One recalls that when Confucius was asked, "Should the son serve as witness against the father who has stolen a sheep?" the Master's reply was, "The son shields the father, and the father shields the son." [5] Chinese history records examples of sons pardoned for killing their parents' murderer because they were practicing filial piety, and even in the modern period the murderer of the Shantung warlord, Chang Chung-ch'ang, was pardoned by the Kuomintang government because he was avenging his father's death. It is in such a context of loyalty to parents which was held above loyalty to the law of the state that one must put the conflict inspired by Communist ideology which is typified in the case of a college student, Li Kuo-hsin, who wrote:

> My father was a bigwig in the feudalistic secret societies. Due to support from the secret societies and due to his shrewdness, he was for nine years the head of Hochiang subdistrict. In March 1950 he participated in a rebellion and fled from home. At first I blamed the government for lack of understanding: my father had been forced into action by bandits, and the government was unjustly accusing him of being the leader of rebellious bandits. After repeated "study" (indoctrination) I finally came to see many things wrong with father. Still I did not recognize his serious crimes and the reasons for his rebellion.
>
> I joined the New Democratic Youth League. The education I received from the League helped me to take a big step forward in the improvement of my thought. I was deeply moved by the example of a comrade who correctly dealt with the problem of his reactionary father. With this inspiration, I began to analyze my father's rebellion. After a long search I found out the reasons for his rebellion. First, he had embezzled several thousand catties of government rice, and he was afraid of prosecution. Second, he had ignored three summonses from the local government. Thus I came to recognize that his rebellion was not the result of force by bandits but a systematic and premeditated action against the revolution and against the people.
>
> After that my attitude towards my father began to change from sympathy to hatred. In discussion meetings of the cell I brought up my father's counterrevolutionary activities, his embezzlement of the people's wealth, his taking of a concubine in Chengtu. I thoroughly exposed these facts, decidedly and unemotionally criticized them, thus further deepening my hatred for him.
>
> I was told that the government demanded that the family look for my father. I firmly decided to take up the duty of locating him. I first contacted the responsible comrades in the local armed forces and planned the

work together with them. I went to my relatives for information, but to no avail. I returned home with the armed comrades and tried to get information from mother. My mother told me that a relative had seen my father in Siaopeichieh in Kwanghan county. I started out to find him. When I finally arrived it was six o'clock, but because of the urgency of the matter I did not stop to rest. Searching inside and outside the town, I finally found him in a small teahouse.

He was sitting alone. His shrunken and pale appearance almost made me fail to recognize him. But he recognized me. I was so happy. Was not that my father? My heart started to beat fast, but I calmed myself. With tears in his eyes my father told me, "Since I parted from your brothers and sister, I have had to depend entirely on practicing medicine for a living. Before September, business was not bad, but after that there was hardly any business. Hunger, cold, and sickness almost took my life. Fortunately, the owner of a medicine store next door gave me a pot of charcoal fire and some money. The owner is willing to recomend me to the union of Chinese doctors in Kwanghan. If I join the union, I'll have a practicing certificate, and I can practice anywhere without restriction."

My father and I talked till late at night. We entered the city and had dinner together. Before parting, he told me, "When you get home, be sure to bring me some money."

When I returned to the hotel I fell into a heart-rending state. I ran a high fever, my body trembled; I turned and tossed in bed but could not sleep. New and old thoughts were struggling within me. I pitied my father. All alone here, he had suddenly met his own child, and how eagerly he was pinning his hopes on me. How could I have him taken back to be shot? On the other hand, still without repentance, he continued to be an enemy of the people. He was entirely selfish, only emphasizing his own suffering, disregarding the suffering of others. . . .

Though he was hateable, he was my own father. I could not be severe and cold, severing myself from sentiment. Wouldn't it be all right if I went home and told people that I had gone to Kwanghan and had failed to find my father?

That would not do. I would save my father, a local bully, a landlord, but indirectly I would become a counterrevolutionist. I thought of getting some poison and forcing him to take it. But this wouldn't do either. I was sympathizing with him. I was forgetting that I was a youth of new China, a member of the League.

After a night of conflict I finally shattered my incorrect thoughts and I consolidated myself on the principle of "no compromise in revolution, and no sentimentalism in struggle." I reaffirmed my stand.

I went to the police bureau and informed the responsible comrade. Then I went to my father and demanded that he recant his past and reform. He said, "How could you do this to me?" and tried to escape by saying that he was going to eat. By that time the armed comrades were already at the door. My father had no choice but to pretend to be willing to reform, and gave himself up.

He was taken to the county government of Kwanghan. I waited until he wrote out his repentance and confession before starting back to Chengtu. He was imprisoned in Kwanghan and later was sent back to Hwayang county by armed guards. My duty was at last done. I felt light-hearted; I was happy, for I had rid the people of a dangerous character.[6]

Cases like this one show that a new answer has been given to the old Confucian paradox. If loyalty in the parent-child relationship, so strongly guarded by filial piety and by law for centuries past, can be swept aside by the violent storm of Communist revolution, loyalty toward other family members is even more surely threatened. Although the traditional relationship between Chinese husband and wife was not so strong as that in Western culture, it was, nevertheless, a significant force in a system where women's occupations were undeveloped and where women enjoyed few property rights. In the traditional Chinese family organization the position of the husband, the only one from whom a wife could expect affection, and the strongly enforced mores of chastity conditioned her to put loyalty to her husband above everything else. There is a long tradition of Chinese wives who committed suicide when the husband died, as a demonstration of perfect loyalty and the conviction that it was better for a wife to go to heaven with her husband than go on living alone on earth. There is deep signficance, then, in this story from a Communist report:

Ou Hsiu-mei was a peasant woman in a village in Lien county in the northern part of Kwaungtung Province. She was married very young through a matchmaker to Liang Wen-chiu. Liang was a local political boss, having been the chief of a *chia* unit [a local administrative unit of one or more villages] under the Kuomintang regime, and he extorted the villagers through conscription, bribery, and other channels. Ou did not like this, but her thought was conditioned by the traditional advice to "follow a chicken when married to a chicken and follow a dog when married to a dog." After the establishment of the Communist regime, Liang went into the hills as a subleader in anti-Communist armed activities. After that, villagers ceased to communicate with her. Suffering from isolation and seeing that others whose husbands served in the Communist army had the help of neighbors in working the fields, she began to envy others and feel ashamed of herself. Meanwhile, a few party cadres, seeing that she originated from a poor family, tried to indoctrinate her.

Liang sometimes returned home from the hills secretly. Ou used the opportunity to talk to him: "What future do you have by working in the anti-Communist forces? There is still time for you to turn back, and the people's government will let you redeem your crime by making contributions to the revolution." But Liang replied, "Chiang Kai-shek will soon come back and better days will not be far off. If you tell the villagers that, it will help." She had doubts about this, but fear made her keep silent.

Women members among the village cadres and leaders of the peasants' association came to talk to her. "If millions of Chiang Kai-shek's troops have been wiped out, what chance will your husband have? One day he will be caught and shot, and then you will be a bandit's widow." Again they said to her, "You were a poor child by origin, and the victims of your husband are all poverty-stricken peasants like yourself. If you will help catch your husband, ridding the people of a dangerous character, you will win great merit, and both the people and the government will respect you and love you, and you will gain a new life. Do you want to come on the side of the people, or do you wish to follow the road to death with your husband?"

She could not sleep at night, those words turning over and over in her mind. Close to the Chinese New Year's Eve she made up her mind and went to the peasants' association to promise that she would catch her husband inside of one month.

She thought of a plot whereby she could trick her husband into being captured. When Liang came home on New Year's eve, she told him, "The present situation is tense, sentinels are posted all over the place, searching all suspected homes. Return on the second night of the New Year and hide at the foot of the hill. I will bring you some food and liquor." After he left she hastened to the peasants' association and informed them of her plan.

At the appointed time she took a basket of food and went to the foot of the hill. Liang was waiting and started to gorge himself. But he was already in the midst of soldiers who were closing in from all directions in the dark. One soldier carelessly flashed his flashlight. Liang immediately knew something was up. He threw down his chopsticks and bowl and started to run. Ou wrapped her arms around him but Liang pushed her and kicked her. The soldiers closed in with torches, lighting up the whole hillside. Liang jumped into a quagmire pond, hid himself under the surface, leaving only his nose out to breathe. After a tiresome search, one soldier pushed a stick into the mire and by chance poked him in the head. Involuntarily he screamed in pain, and was caught.

At the mass trial Ou accused Liang of his crime. She said she did not want to be the wife of a bandit any longer. She demanded that the government shoot him, and said she would eternally follow the Communist Party. Her name soon spread to the whole county. On March 30, 1951, at the county meeting of peasants' representatives, and at the meeting of the evaluation of merits in anti-bandit campaigns, she was elected anti-bandit hero, special class.[7]

When the Three-Anti and the Five-Anti movements swung into high gear in the cities throughout the country in 1952, there were widespread campaigns in urban areas to mobilize wives to persuade their husbands to confess their crimes and to expose these crimes to the government should the husbands remain unregenerated. In the coal-mining area of Mentoukou, west of Peking, where the Committee on Wives actively led the workers' wives to participate in the Three-Anti movement, according to statistical information in February 1952, twenty-three wives had succeeded in persuading their husbands to confess their crimes, and over three hundred cases of corruption were uncovered through the grapevine of the workers' wives.[8] The psychological process in such a transference of loyalty is illustrated in the case of Chiang Shu-k'un, a woman worker in a tobacco factory, who pushed her husband into confession.

> The case took place in the interior town of Paoting of Hopei Province in North China. Chiang's husband, Ho, was an accountant in the printing plant of the provincial Bureau of Revenue of Hopei which printed tax stamps. Ho stole a large amount of newly printed tax stamps and hid them under the bed for over a year, waiting to dispose of them. The theft of the stamps aroused a sensation in the printing plant, but the thief was not discovered.
>
> Chiang discovered the stamps when the Three-Anti movement was sweeping the country in 1952. She recalled her unhappy childhood and marriage and how the State Tobacco Factory where she worked was now like a second home. Cadres and workers in the factory had helped her in learning new skills. She worked hard in literacy class. She was a model worker, a member of the New Democratic Youth League, and a member of the Communist Party.
>
> Now she knew that Ho was no longer her husband but a thief who stole state property. If she spared him, she would be ungrateful to the state and to the party. She reported him, and he was arrested on Chinese New Year's Day. This made Chiang very happy and did not spoil her New Year's holiday. The news of Chiang's exposing her husband served as encouragement to all the women workers in the factory, and at the mobilization meeting of the Three-Anti movement, a flower of honor was pinned on her.[9]

Since we have selected our illustrations on the basis of the loyalty demanded in the most important categories of traditional kinship relations, we must touch upon the loyalty between brothers and between brothers and sisters. The traditional social order placed heavy requirements of fraternal loyalty on the individual, especially on the younger brother, and the popular Chinese phrase "cooperation between hands and feet in worries and in difficulties" is a realistic reference to the traditional concept of fraternal relationship. Two cases given emphasis in the Communist press illustrate the present mood.

Hun Yi-ch'un, head of the *Chieh-fang Jih-pao* publishing company in Shanghai, became concerned when his elder sister was being "struggled" against by the peasants' association in her town as a landlord and a local bully. Hun utilized his important status as the head of an official regional newspaper to write to various official organs concerned with the case, saying that his sister was a good person, a widow who relied on the land for livelihood and not for exploitation, and that the struggle against her was unjust. After investigation, superior party organs, rejecting his protest, stated: "Hun in the land reform failed to make a demarcation between friend and foe, lost his proper stand, and protected the landlord." [10]

Yu Ch'uan-ming was a Communist Party member, a professor of Western languages in Peking University, and the chief of the executive office of the Peking Municipal Committee of the All-China Union of Educational Workers. He had an elder brother who was being "struggled" against as a landlord, local bully, and secret agent for the Kuomintang, allegedly having killed seventy to eighty Communist political workers. Yu tried to protect his elder brother by advising him to hide his property and by writing to local government organizations for help. As a result, Yu was removed from party membership in order to "preserve the purity of the party ranks." The party's charge against Yu included denunciation of him as a "disloyal element to the proletarian class who stole his way into the party." In Yu's own open statement of self-criticism, he said, "My failure to recognize my own error is due entirely to. . . my inability to sever thoroughly the feudalistic fraternal sentiments and come over to the stand of the party." [11]

One may well ask whether the drastic shift in the center of loyalty away from the family, a shift which is being motivated by terror and emotional tension generated in a succession of high-pressure political movements, can possibly be permanent. As the Communist regime consolidates its power and begins to settle down to an established political and social order, it may relax some of its pressures. Moreover, a complete breakdown of family solidarity would hardly be conducive to the social and economic order the Communists are trying to establish; and, in fact, few cases such as presented here have been reported in the Communist press since 1953. We would judge that in the long run the degree of the transfer away from the family to the state and to extra-familial organizations will be determined not by campaigns and exhortation but by the success or failure of communism in actual practice in assuming many of the social and economic functions of the traditional Chinese family.

CHAPTER X

Secularization of the Family Institution

Up to this point we have considered elements in Chinese family structure and relationships which in the main have their counterparts in varying degrees of strength in Western society. The unique, and possibly most basic, feature of the traditional Chinese family was its sacred character. In a variety of forms, the religious element was elaborately and inseparably woven into the fabric of the family institution; and it helps to explain why the disruptive factors, such as the excessive exercise of authority by the male and senior family members, failed in the past to shake the foundation of the family. When under strain from the authoritarian family structure and buffeted by frequent domestic conflicts, the individual tended to drift away from the family, and interdependence of utilitarian interests and the exigency of a realistic situation were not sufficient to tie him firmly to the family, the sacred concepts and symbols of the unity of the family lifted his interest and feelings above himself and focused them on the group. Thus also, especially in the traditional concept of marriage based on the perpetuation of the ancestral lineage, the ancestors religiously symbolized the collective existence of the family group, a psychological process which explains why many an unjustly treated mother in the traditional family who contemplated leaving her husband's home stopped short of action at the sight of her son playing in front of the ancestral altar.

One reason for the weakening of the traditional Chinese family has been the rise of skepticism toward that institution. Discussing and doubting the fundamental soundness of an institution as the means of meeting the problems and needs of social life is the beginning of the operation of a highly subversive influence, for in skeptical discussion there lurks an alternative that may threaten to replace the existing institution.

In the traditional Chinese social order, the sacred character of the family institution imposed a deterministic view toward it, admitted no discussion of its soundness as an institution, and tolerated no suggestion of alternatives. As in other social institutions, it enforced a dogma. A wife might blame her unhappiness on her husband's or mother-in-law's wickedness, and perhaps lament her own ill fate, but she never thought to blame the institutional arrangement of traditional family life as the cause of her sorrows. If extremely mistreated, she might commit suicide, but in so doing she would still be following the path marked out for her by the institution without questioning the theoretical soundness of traditional family relationships. Members of a community witnessing or discussing the occasional brutal treatment of a daughter-in-law tended to view the case from the standpoint of personality deviation, not from the soundness of the family institution itself.

The impact of Western science on China, which inevitably inspired skepticism, with its implication of alternatives for ancient learning and ancient institutions, has steadily increased since the 1920's. From the beginning of the modern period the young educated generation has been encouraged to penetrate through the once awesome, sacred character of the traditional family in an effort to assess its fitness and adequacy in meeting modern needs. Guiding their course of skeptical criticism has been the logic and methodology of modern science, which are hardly reconcilable with the religious factors lending a sacred character to the family institution. The modern mood has, if anything, been even more encouraged under communism.

The primary factor in lending a sacred character to the traditional family was the cult of ancestor worship, vividly demonstrated in traditional residential homes in South China. There the ancestral altar in the main hall, the general dimness of the place, and the rows of golden ancestor tablets, darkened by incense smoke and reflecting the eerie light from the flickering sacrificial lamp, created a sacred atmosphere in the family dwelling, inspiring awe in the children. The constant reminder of the relationship between the living and the dead, between the existing family and the spirits of its creators, constituted a major function of ancestor worship which imposed a sense of sacredness on the family as an institution. The principles, inspired sentiments, symbols, and rituals of ancestor worship assured a religious veneration for the departed ones.

Sharing the sacred veneration for the dead, in a sense, were the old people in the family, who resembled the ancestors in having performed the sacred function of creating and perpetuating the family lineage. Thus an elderly head of the family was sometimes addressed as *lao tsu-chung* (the old ancestor) as a form of flattery (the matriarch in "The Dream of the Red Chamber," for example, was thus addressed), and the prestige and authority of the elders possessed a sacred character. The one insult the traditional Chinese would not tolerate was any slighting reference to parents or ancestors; and the destruction of the graves of other people's ancestors was punishable by traditional Chinese law. In this connection it is significant that Communist law gives no special protection to graves. Presumably, with traditional concepts still existing in the minds of a large number of local cadres, offenders against the old law might be punished, but the formal legal ground for such punishment would be violation of private property, not sacrilege against a social institution, which is contrary to the atheistic view of Communist ideology.

For two or three decades now the strength of ancestor worship has been waning rapidly among Chinese urban intellectuals, for Western values, dominated by science and materialism, repudiate ancestor worship as a part of popular superstition. A large number of the modern educated elements no longer regularly performed the ancestor worship rituals, and those who still did regarded the ceremony as a formalistic act without the traditional attitude of sincere veneration. In the Communist movement the note of anti-superstition is even more uncompromising than it has been in other social movements, and ancestor worship is unequivocally regarded as a superstitious act. On the traditional duty to have children as a part of ancestor worship, the opinion of a Communist court was expressed thus: "Some people just do not understand this. They regard it as an extremely grave matter to be without offspring to continue the sacrifice and the burning of incense for the ancestors. Actually, what good will it do the dead ancestors to have incense burning continued, and what does it matter to them if incense burning is discontinued? This is a kind of nonsensical, superstitious thought, and it is incorrect." [1] This is not only the attitude of the Communist court, but it also reflects the pre-Communist attitude of the agnostic younger generation of urban intelligentsia who came under the influence of modern science and materialism in modern schools. The difference is that in the pre-Communist period this attitude was not so sharply defined, not so much a conscious guide for action, and was seldom expressed in such undisguised terms by a court as a criterion for the settlement of problems of kinship relations. It would be incongruous to see a Communist stemming from the urban intelligentsia performing traditional rituals before an ancestral shrine.

The institutional framework of traditional Chinese society was characterized by the prominence of *li*, which we may translate as ritualism, denoting a *system of semi-formal norms of behavior* in all basic situations of social life. Although the family institution relied no less on *li* as an operational factor than on other institutions, *li* as a strategic component of traditional Chinese culture has remained scientifically unexplored. Here we would only point out the sacred character of ritualism so far as it concerns the family institution, and its change in the modern period.

Ritualism as the acting out according to prescribed procedures of what was considered the ideal pattern of social relations served to focus the individual's attention toward an external situation and therefore performed an important function in the integration of the family. While rituals were present in almost every aspect of the traditional family, they were particularly prominent in the critical events of birth, marriage, and death of family members. The religious element was present in the ritualistic performances for all such critical events that marked the stages in the life cycle for both the family and the individual members. The sacred character thus injected into such events inspired awe and respect for the family institution.

The sacred nature and the feeling of fatefulness in the traditional marriage ceremony has been noted previously. The religious element permeated the rituals attending the birth of a new family member, especially the first son, when rites were performed to thank the ancestral spirits and the gods for the blessed event. The exact time of the birth, the year, month, day, and hour of the arrival, was carefully noted down and interpreted in the light of the magical belief that the time of birth foretold the future luck or misfortune not merely of the child but also of those related to him. Ceremonial feasts were given and religious rites performed when the baby reached the age of one month and one year, celebrating the child's survival and thanking the gods and spirits for their auspicious influence. Thus the earthly event of birth was turned into a sacred occasion in an effort to generate a serious attitude among the family members toward adding a new member to the group by expressing hope for his future and his relation to the group and publicly demonstrating this attitude to the wider kinship circle.

Death was intimately related to the development of mysticism and religious beliefs from earliest times. More than any other ritual, mortuary rites served to impart a sacred nature to the family institution, for they were rigidly prescribed and most elaborate, lest any abbreviation or error bring anger and retaliation from the spirit of the dead. Their psychological effect can be judged from the experience of an American girl who had married a Chinese and who, when she went to her husband's interior village upon her father-in-law's death, was completely mystified and exhausted after going through rites which lasted forty-nine days — as required by tradition for a well-to-do family. A traditional Chinese going through the same experience would inevitably have been filled with awe for the supernatural significance of critical events connected with family life. Moreover, such rituals were also performed on the death anniversary of a family member as a part of the cult of ancestor worship to perpetuate that feeling and reinforce the impression of the family as an organization of the living under the blessing, guidance, and surveillance of the spirits of the dead.

For the modern educated Chinese, knowledge of and respect for the ritualistic aspect of the family has been drastically reduced for the past three decades. The New Culture Movement that started in 1917 and subsequent social movements regarded ritualism as the leading source of the harsh features, misery, and backwardness of traditional Chinese society; and the anti-superstition movement directed against ancestor worship attacked all traditional religious rituals. The modern Chinese intellectuals who still continue to perform the rituals do so to please or appease insistent parents or other members of the older generation, and not from personal acceptance of the doctrine of ritualism. It seems certain that, so far as the Chinese intellectual is concerned, there were sufficiently powerful influences some years before the advent of communism to assure that sacred rituals would disappear from family life with the dying of the older generation.

Under Communist rule the trend toward secularization is spreading slowly from the modern urban intelligentsia to other segments of the population. The Communists are making no systematic effort to suppress the performance of old rituals, but they identify traditional ritualism as a vestige of the "feudalistic culture," and the social atmosphere being created discriminates against traditional ritualism in general. The Communist anti-superstition movement adds strength to this development owing to the presence of the religious element in a large number of the old rituals.

Thus the already marked trend toward simplifying rituals concerned with critical events in family life is accelerated by the Communists; and the new marriage ceremony has dropped the religious rites, including the consultation of the oracle which gave the traditional marriage a sacred, predetermined character. Under Communist rule there is strong discouragement of elaborate funerals, discouragement which cannot remove the mysticism and religious sentiment about death but does reduce the sacred nature of death as a public event, which once had the function of confirming the unity of the family weakened by a member's death. The birth of a baby and the birthdates of old family members are likewise being increasingly treated as common secular events stripped of the ritualism and religious content which traditionally served to accentuate the significance of such events for the integration of the family group.

In view of the official Communist hostility toward private wealth and the drive against superstition it seems plain that few would now dare to continue the performance of old rituals with any degree of elaborateness on the occasions of birth, marriage, or death; and one can imagine the effect of present secularizing influences concerning the family institution on the minds of the some thirty million members of the Young Pioneers and the New Democratic Youth League who will mature into leadership in the next adult generation.

Another of the significant Chinese institutions associated with the family are the traditional festivals, which before the extensive development of urban commercialized recreation during the past half century were the major form of family recreation. Their importance lay not only in the fact that the entire family participated, thus emphasizing the family as a center of life and confirming its solidarity through periodically reconvening all the members, but also in their sacred character; for most of the traditional festivals were organized around a supernatural idea, a saint, a god, a spirit, or a supernatural legend, and they were celebrated with religious rites.

The Ch'ing Ming on the third day of the third month (for cleaning and repairing the ancestors' graves), the Dragon Boat Racing Festival on the fifth day of the fifth month, the Girls' Festival on the seventh day of the seventh month (for anticipating a happy marriage), and the Moon Festival on the fifteenth day of the eighth month (celebrating the autumn harvest) are examples of such events organized around supernatural ideas. The Chinese New Year holiday, although based on the calendar, was traditionally replete with religious rites. All such festivals were used as occasions for family reunion, and members of the family working or living away felt obligated to come home and celebrate with the family if it was humanly possible; for, whatever the nature of recreation and pleasure involved, the supernatural connotation and rituals that characterized these events inspired in the individual a sacred feeling toward the family institution.

Again, the change in this aspect of Chinese family life was started by the urban intellectuals, for whom festivals came to have less and less sacred meaning. In the modern period there has been a steady increase in the number of families who no longer celebrate many of the traditional festivals; and modern educated girls have ignored the Girls' Festival as they have come to believe in romantic love and not in predestined wedlock. But for the common people the traditional festivals have continued to be important — despite the development of commercialized recreation which offers keen competition and the development of the new system of memorial days based upon personalities and events of modern political and social significance which, claiming increasing public attention and interest, are totally devoid of any sacred significance to the family institution.

Under the Communist regime, no direct effort has been made to discourage the continued celebration of traditional festivals, except some of the highly superstitious ones like the community celebration of the birthday of a certain god. But the rapid development of new forms of group recreation, like singing, folk dancing, and community stage plays, together with mass mobilization for the celebration of a new set of memorial days of secular, social, and political character, tend to reduce the importance of traditional festivals.

It can be readily seen even from the foregoing brief discussion that the secularizing influence of the whole modern period has inevitably affected the traditionally strong Chinese allegiance to the family and the strength of the old system of family status and authority. The family as an institution for effective integration and control over individuals is being replaced by a less stable family organization, governed by the legal mechanism of the state and the secular forces of social and economic life.

However, even under Communist pressure, the trend toward secularization is developing only gradually. A part of the concept in ancestor worship is the belief that the soul of the dead must return to the home district to enjoy sacrifices offered by the offspring in order to avoid the tragedy of causing the soul to wander homelessly, a belief which led the traditional Chinese to live near home and to die at home if possible. In spite of the anti-superstition movement the Communists had difficulty in 1955 in mobilizing peasants in Shantung Province to migrate to the Amur Region partly because of the popular fear that, once migrated to that far-off territory, the soul of the dead would be prevented from returning to the old homeland by the mountain barrier of Shan Hai Kuan which divides China proper from Manchuria. It was only after vigorous persuasion that a substantial number of peasants changed their minds and migrated.[2] Religious attitudes and beliefs, unlike the economic and political structure, cannot be forcibly changed in a short time by a revolution.

CHAPTER XI

Disorganization of the Clan

THE DOMINANCE of the clan organization in Chinese village life has been noted by many observers. Composed of several hundred to upward of ten thousand members living mostly in the same community, the clan has traditionally provided the numerical base for a variety of collective social and economic functions for its members, impossible for relatively small individual families to perform. It may be said that the Chinese family derived much of its traditional social and economic importance from its membership in the numerically large clan organization.

As to the extent of the clan's influence, one needs only to note that in North China a large proportion of the villages bear clan surnames. Names like Wangchiats'un (the village of the Wang family) or Lichiats'un (the village of the Li family) represents the stereotype for the names of Chinese villages. In South China, even in villages not bearing a clan's surname, it was generally difficult for an individual or family not belonging to the local clan to live there. And it is well known that down to comparatively recent times Chinese governments relied upon the strength of the clan for the maintenance of local peace and order.

While a systematic treatment of the clan lies beyond the scope of this study, we would point out some of the main forces at work under the Communist regime concerning features of the clan organization which have been of basic importance to the family. There were no extensive changes introduced into rural clans during the Republican era; and the data in this discussion concern mainly conditions in the southern provinces where the organization of the agnate clan (or the sib) is stronger and its influence greater than in other parts of China.

It is notable that the Communist regime is the first Chinese government that has not relied upon or made use of the clan for the maintenance of local peace and order or for the consolidation of its political power. Although pre-Communist governments and political leaders expressed dissatisfaction with "familism and clannism" as a hindrance to modern developments, they made no systematic attack against the clan organization, and there is no Communist law that prohibits the clan as a legitimate form of organization; but vital forces are at work that have a disintegrating effect on it.

Change of the Age Hierarchy and Kinship Relations

The organizational framework of the clan relied heavily upon the age hierarchy and the proximity of kinship, as explained in Chapter IV,[1] since it was through these two principles, especially that of the age hierarchy, that the large membership of a clan could be structured in an orderly way and each of the individuals living in it could identify his status. Age hierarchy and proximity of kinship constituted the foundation both for the formal organization of authority in the clan and for the performance of many of its functions.

Obviously, therefore, the rise in status of the young and the women, marriage by free choice, the weakening of the family as a unit of production and as a center of loyalty — all such factors which have affected the system of status and authority of the traditional family have similarly affected the organization of the clan; for the traditional family was the basic cell of the clan organization, and whatever has weakened the family has inevitably also weakened the larger structure of the clan.

Furthermore, the fury of the class struggle in the Communist land reform had a disorganizing influence on the clan structure since the economic stratification of the clan membership became an explicit object of revolutionary destruction. Clannish authority and status based upon age hierarchy and proximity of kinship inevitably lose their effectiveness in the process of any violent class struggle; for, when a person is accused of being a local bully, a bad landlord, or a usurer, no amount of seniority of generation or age, often not even the proximity of kinship, can protect him from an outraged victim or an angry revolutionary mob. Certainly this has been dramatically demonstrated in Communist China. Reports of "accusation meetings" and public trials in the land reform show that, although kinsmen, especially the young and the women, had difficulty at first in speaking up against a relative if the latter was an older person high in status and authority based on age hierarchy and proximity of kinship, when one or two "victims" who had been carefully coached beforehand spoke up, the ice was broken, and under the pressure of emotional tension and the contagion of mass excitement others soon followed suit in pouring out anger and rage against the accused, and a long respected old aunt or uncle would be publicly beaten up, clapped into jail, or shot, depending on the seriousness of the alleged crime.

In the "struggle meeting" in Tzuchien village in Yukan county of Kiangsi Province for instance: "Liu Ch'i-sen was an old local bully and landlord. He had victimized many persons in the same clan, and some in the same fang (a sub-unit of the clan consisting of members of close relationship from common descent). During the first stage of the land reform, he had escaped punishment. But during the re-examination of the land reform, poor peasants and farm laborers of the same clan and the same fang finally arose to mete out justice to him." [2] In a village in Kwangtung Province over five hundred women formed a crowd and went to their landlord relatives to demand refunds of rent reductions and "to square off" past economic injustices. At mass meetings the same women "broke through clannish attitudes and kinship sentiments" to accuse landlord relatives in the same clan — for "what are we afraid of when we have the Communist Party as our support?" [3]

Change in the Agencies of Clan Authority

Formal control of the clan rested mainly on two agencies. One was the elders' council, vested with the formal authority of making policies and decisions. The other was a form of executive organ, a council of administrators that bore different names in different localities, for carrying out decisions made by the elders and administering the property and business of the clan. In the informal aspect of the power structure, landlords and leaders of organized armed groups and other elements whose political influence and connections usually extended beyond the village generally controlled both of these agencies either by personal participation or by putting in their own people.

That system of authority has suffered mortal blows from revolutionary activities in the land reform and subsequent reconstitution of village organization under Communist rule. There has been no formal attack by the Communists against the elders' council as an organization, but its influential members have been stripped of property and status by land reform. Members of the council of administration of clan property and business have been singled out for accusations of embezzlement of public funds by other clansmen, especially by poor peasants and farm laborers who had been consistently kept out of power in the clan organization, and being accused of such crimes brings ruinous fines, public beatings, imprisonment, and at times death. Consequently, since no one dares to serve in them now, clan agencies have either automatically disbanded or are at a standstill with many of their members classified as criminals.

Replacing the elders' council and the administrative agencies are authoritarian Communist organizations deriving their power from the peasants' associations controlled by the policy of "relying upon poor peasants and farm laborers, making alliances with the middle peasants, and overthrowing the landlords." The village Women's Association in some localities has come to share some of the power.[4] Youth organizations such as the New Democratic Youth League are also instrumental in the new village authority. These new agencies may still be subjected to the influence of kinship relations to some extent, but their basic principles of organization exclude kinship ties.

Finally, the traditional clan possessed its own armed forces in the form of local militia, especially in the southern provinces, forces which were wholly under the control of the landlords and other elements of power in the clan. Under communism the old militia is replaced by "people's soldiers," who are still local militia in fact but under control of the Communist government and no longer a part of the clan organization. Disarming the old militia and squeezing out hidden arms from the villages constituted a violent phase in the early period of the Communist conquest.

Change in the Economic Functions of the Clan

The clan, at least in the southern part of the country, owned common property and performed many important economic functions, and clan properties were often quite extensive.[5] Income from clan property was used to finance the village school, the maintenance of the ancestral temples, ancestral sacrifices and related functions, public works such as construction and repair of roads and bridges, military defense of the village, and at times relief for the poor. Up to the Communist accession to power in 1949 many clans in the vicinity of Canton apportioned land to poor members at nominal rent. A very important economic function of the clan was the collective undertaking of the irrigational and water control projects which formed the foundation of China's irrigational agriculture and accounted for much of the peasants' reliance upon the clan in the past. In a village in Kwangtung Province in 1936 the clan built a long dike to reclaim a large tract of tideland which added almost one-third more cultivated land to the village, and the distribution of irrigational water on this land continued to be under the clan's control until the Communists took over.

This picture has been drastically changed under Communist rule. Land reform regulations require the confiscation of clan property for redistribution to the poor and landless peasants, thus leaving the clan without funds to carry on its functions. Vital economic functions such as irrigation, water control, and local road construction and maintenance now belong to the Communist government, with assistance from new local organizations such as peasant associations. From 1955 to 1958, when agricultural producers' cooperatives became the national pattern of agricultural organization, those economic functions which the government did not take over from the clan passed on to the cooperatives, which collaborate with the government in the performance of such functions. The cooperatives have increased in size generally with one cooperative embracing an entire village, performing, aside from collective farming, a wide range of economic functions such as the reclamation of wasteland, irrigational projects, and the collective struggle against flood and drought that once were under the leadership of the clan.[6]

Changes in Social Functions of the Clan

As previously indicated, it had been a clan function to finance schools and at times to give free education to poor but worthy sons. Although the land reform regulations permit retention of part of the clan property for education, the control of this property has been transferred from the clan to the new village government and the peasant association.[7] Besides, the Communist government is directly subsidizing rural education on a large scale.

Administering ancestral sacrifices and maintaining ancestral temples was a major function of the clan, and the spring and autumn sacrifices to the ancestors once were leading events in the social life of the villages. Gathering hundreds and at times thousands of members in the ancestral temple for the solemn ceremony under the guidance of the elders, such sacrifices periodically demonstrated the tangible existence of the clan as well as the collective strength of the group, inspired strength and morale in the individual members, and stimulated loyalty to and pride in the kinship organization. Reinforcing these psychological effects were the mystical symbols of the ancestors' tablets, the incense and candles, the impressive religious rites, and the many honorific articles and inscribed exhortations left behind by worthy members of preceding generations for posterity to remember, admire, and follow. The joyous feasting which concluded this event served to heighten the spirit of solidarity and to evoke allegiance to the clan.

Now, with clan property confiscated, to find money for discharging ceremonial functions becomes a major difficulty. In many villages in Kwangtung in 1951 the clan failed to provide even for the spring and autumn sacrifices, and a few older members undertook the sacrificial ceremony from private funds, but the ceremony was far from the grand affair it used to be. Most of the ancestral temples have been taken over by peasants' associations and other new organizations as headquarters and as classrooms, and the buildings have come to serve functions unconnected with the maintenance of the sacred character of the clan and family organization. In many of the ancestral temples objects of an honorific nature, such as carved wooden plaques bearing the names and honors of worthy sons of the clans, some over a century old and given to the clan by great officials and even by the Ch'ing emperors, have been removed and burned by peasants' associations in order to eradicate the last trace of "feudalism."

Another function of the clan was to sponsor public recreation such as the celebration of traditional festivals with presentations of stage operas. This function was continued by the clan in a few places in the first two years of the Communist rule, but it is no longer common practice since the clan has no source of income to finance such undertakings. Increasingly, the peasants' associations, the village Youth Corps and the Women's Association have come to undertake the function of providing public recreation — of a very different nature and social orientation.

Organizationally and functionally crippled by land reform and agricultural collectivization, the clan no longer retains its traditional dominance as the core of rural community life. Finally the people's commune provides a systematic replacement for the clan's structural-functional position in the rural community, for the commune system combines local political, military, economic, educational, recreational, and welfare service functions into a unified organization.

In urban communities the clan has long been weakened by population mobility and by the non-kinship nature of the economy. In the pre-Communist period it still retained a partial existence in the form of surname associations which owned income-yielding properties or collected dues from members, held annual membership meetings, and performed the function of consolidating kinship ties as a basis for mutual assistance, and such associations are still active in non-Communist Hong Kong.[8] In Communist China even this diluted form of the clan, the surname association, has passed out of existence under the vigorous attack on "familism and clannism."

Ideology and Propaganda in the Change of the Family

CONSTRUCTIVE REVOLUTIONARY change in the institutional framework of a society proceeds both from disruptive influences which cripple the structure and functions of established institutions and from the creative influences of a new ideology which offers an ideal picture of a different set of institutions to be constructed on the foundations of the old.

That disruptive forces alone, without an accompanying creative concept, will not lead to the rapid development of new institutions is demonstrated by the limitation of the function of modern industrial development as an influence on the traditional Chinese family institution. Modern industrial employment in China provided an avenue of escape from traditional family control and thus disrupted the traditional pattern of family life, but it did not produce any immediate change in the traditional family or set in motion any conscious movement toward the development of a new family institution. It was a notable characteristic of the Chinese who emigrated to Southeast Asia to work in modern mines and factories that, although they remained away from home for protracted periods of time, they adhered ideologically to the traditional family and remained faithful to it. It was the second generation Chinese, educated in modern schools where the ideal of the Western family pattern was impressed upon them, who first made the shift away from the traditional mode of family life.

An interesting case history is provided by the silk workers in Kwangtung Province in South China, where in the early 1900's modern silk factories were established in and around Shunteh district which almost exclusively employed female workers on the mechanized jobs, in raising silkworms and preparing the worms' food from the leaves of mulberry trees — in short, where women were the main workers and gained economic independence in an industry outside of the home. Since the factories were in a rural area quite isolated from contacts with modern ideas, these women became deviant types of individuals, particularly the unmarried girls who developed a cult of collective spinsterhood, leading a pseudo-family life in highly organized sororities. Some of them who had been forced into marriage either by their parents' authority or by the superstition that a woman must be married in order to obtain a home for one's spirit after death used their wages to reimburse the husband's family for the marriage expense, told the husband to take another wife or a concubine, and left the husband's family to continue with their independent livelihood. Some of them turned to homosexuality. As a group they developed an attitude of disdain and contempt toward women who married, lived with the husband's family, and accepted the low status traditionally assigned to a wife and a daughter-in-law. Similar conditions also prevailed among professional female servants in southern cities.

Thus, without the influences from any new ideology, the economic independence of these women workers resulted in mock marriage, in their refusal to live with their husbands, in actual spinsterhood, in pseudo-family life through sorority organization, in homosexuality — all destructive to the traditional family; but their rebellious and independent spirit created no new family institution to replace the old one, and their deviating behavior could hardly be said to constitute a part of the constructive influence in the modern family revolution.

The true significance of modern economic development lies not in its providing economic independence to oppressed members of the family but in the convergence of such new economic independence with the intellectual and emotional drive of a new social idealism that promises a better social order, including a new form of family. Only in the building of a different family institution in accordance with the new ideological pattern does the new economic independence become a positive influence. Hence the importance of the ideological aspect of the Chinese family revolution and of the mass communication of a new ideology.

In the pre-Communist period new idealism in a loosely organized form was derived from the feminist movement and the family pattern in modern Europe and the United States. By 1930 it was partly formulated into a legal statute, the law of marriage and kinship, under the Nationalist government; but throughout the pre-Communist period the primary means of popularizing the ideas of the family revolution and in familiarizing the people with the new legal standards was not political action but the written language — hence the confinement of the family revolution largely to the urban intelligentsia who could read. Personal discussions, motion pictures of modern love and marriage, and living examples of modern marriages and incidents of rebellion against the family all served as lesser means of communication in carrying certain aspects of the new idealism to the illiterate segment of the population who remained impervious to the huge volume of modern literature on the family revolution. But their influence was limited and did not travel far beyond the metropolitan areas. The family revolution was thus confined to the urban centers, leaving the vast countryside in the tight grip of the traditional family institution.

Under the Communist regime, the new Marriage Law emerges as a more systematic embodiment of the new idealism concerning marriage and the family. With the Marriage Law as the ideological base, the storm of the family revolution has spread from the urban intelligentsia to members of the working class, from the urban areas to the broad countryside, as shown by the foregoing facts of increasing family instability, mounting figures of divorce, and the growing number of new marriages in the larger section of the population beyond the restricted circle of the former urban upper and middle classes. The significant feature of this development has been neither the requirement of the registration of all new marriages nor the many legal decisions settling family conflicts according to new legal stipulations which are in harmony with the revolutionary idealism but the extensive use of mass propaganda by the Communist regime.

Literature, the chief means of spreading the family revolution in the pre-Communist period, remains a major instrument under communism. Articles in newspapers and magazines, pamphlets, and books continue to incite rebellion against the old family and to invite acceptance of the new ideal, but much of the substance of such literature, particularly works of fiction, has changed. Marriage and the family life of the worker, peasant, and the lower-middle class have become substitutes for those of the upper and upper-middle class as leading subjects for discussion and fictionalization. If the illiterate masses still cannot read these reflections of themselves, at least the attention of those who can read is being turned to the family problems among the broader segment of the population. So far as the literate segment of the population still constitutes the main carrier of the new influence and the basic group from which the elite are recruited for the enforcement of Communist policies, this change of content in the literature is instrumental in spreading the family revolution from the urban intelligentsia to the other classes.

A major difference from pre-Communist literature on the family problem has been the far greater use made by the Communists of folk literature and printed materials simple enough for the common people to understand. Folk stories based on themes of the new marriage and the new family are turned out in large quantity by organizations such as the Democratic Women's League, not only for reading by people with a low level of literacy, but also for storytellers in the market places to recite to illiterates. Folk ballads on the family problem have also been a new form of literature aimed not at the intelligentsia but at the "broad masses." "Newspaper-reading groups," where a literate leader reads to an illiterate group, have been another means by which the message of the family revolution is travelling in wider circles.

Distinctly new and effective on the Chinese scene as an instrument of propaganda for the common people are the serial pictorial pamphlets in the style of American comic books. Serial drawings depicting traditional stories had come into wide circulation among the common people in the last two pre-Communist decades, but they are now being utilized for changing the family institution and are published in daily newspapers such as the *Chieh-fang Jih-pao* in Shanghai and the *Su-nan Jih-pao* circulating in the southern part of Kiangsu Province. A large number of propaganda leaflets and handbooks on the subject of the problems of marriage and the family are written in the simple, daily language of the common people.[1] "The family revolution expressed in literature has definitely shed its bourgeois frivolousness and has gone to the people."[2]

The wide use of "blackboard newspapers" and "wall newspapers," which are bulletins written on blackboards and on papers posted on walls, is another cheap and effective means of utilizing the medium of the written language in propaganda for the Marriage Law. As both these forms are hand-written, they need not rely on the printing press, which remains scarce in rural areas, and are easily adaptable to rural settings.

In the pre-Communist period motion pictures on the family problem seen by the common people, literate or illiterate, were confined to the urban areas, and stage plays were mostly for the intelligentsia, the modern stage play emphasizing dialogue and unaccompanied by music being a new form introduced from the West. Communist scripts for stage plays are written against the background of the common people and deal with specific points of the new Marriage Law. Such typical pieces as "The Thousand-Year-Old Glacier Begins to Thaw," "The Little Son-in-Law," "The Marriage of Little Dark No. 2," "New Ways for a New Event," and "New Conditions" present concrete problems and solutions along lines laid down by the Marriage Law. Moreover, theater audiences are no longer limited to the modern urban intelligentsia; nor are the performances limited to those given by theatrical groups of students from modern schools. Commercial theatrical companies and large numbers of skilled theatrical groups of the government's Recreation and Culture Corps, are now producing such plays in rural towns for the first time.[3] The modern stage play has thus been popularized by the Communists and utilized as a form of propaganda which reaches all classes of people.

The Communists' skillful use of the theater arts for propaganda purposes is clearly revealed in the rise of theatrical groups in all parts of the country, particularly in rural communities, almost from the beginning of the Communist regime. In 1951 it was officially reported that there were 1,500 amateur theatrical groups in Laiotung Province alone. In Lushan county of Honan Province, there were 240 amateur theatrical groups in 1952. During the years 1951 and 1952, "25 per cent of all the plays put on by the 240 theatrical groups dealt with the theme of the Marriage Law."[4]

Besides creating their own version of modern stage drama, the Communists are attempting to reduce the influence of the traditional operas which have so long been a popular means of enforcing the traditional values of the family institution. "The government is planning to outlaw the continued performance of traditional operas that emphasize the virtue of chastity, praise polygamy, and teach sex inequality."[5] Municipal governments in Hankow, Nanking, and other cities have suppressed many "feudalistic" operas. Where specific legal action has not been taken in this respect, indoctrination of the actors and actresses in all parts of the country and the censorship of the theater is bringing about similar effects. In addition, a large number of playwrights are assigned the task of revising the old operas in order to eliminate the "feudalistic values" and to fit the stories into the revolutionary setting, and by 1956 the vast majority of the popular old operas had been thus revised.

An outstanding accomplishment of the Communist regime in propagandizing the Communist concept of the new family is the utilization of the extensive organizational system of the young and the women, the two groups most dissatisfied with their treatment under the traditional system of family status and authority. The Communist organizations of the young, which comprised a national membership of some 30,000,000 in 1956, reach into every class and every part of the country. Organization of the women appears to be even more extensive, for as early as the fall of 1950 it was reported that 30,000,000 women had become affiliated directly or indirectly with the All-China Democratic Women's League in 31 provinces, 83 cities, and 1,287 counties,[6] and membership is certain to have increased since then. Members of such extensive organizations are among the first to "learn" the new Marriage Law and to be baptized by its idealism.[7]

Ideas of the new Marriage Law travel not only through the youth and women's organizations but also through the channels of other organizations with staggering figures of membership, such as the Communist Party, the labor union system, and the armed forces, members of all such organizations being required to participate in organized sessions to "study" the Marriage Law.[8]

Then there is what is called the "propaganda network," organized by volunteers (generally members of the Communist Party or the New Democratic Youth League) to publicize all official policies and ideas, including the new Marriage Law, to co-workers in offices, shops, factories, urban neighborhoods, and villages. It was officially claimed that there were in excess of five million of these volunteers in 1952. That they are instrumental in spreading the new ideas of marriage and the family among the common people, particularly in the hitherto isolated villages, is illustrated in the case of Lushan county of Honan Province in Central China, where in 1952 there were over three thousand members in the county's propaganda network who tried to acquaint the masses in every village with the Marriage Law through "broadcasting platforms, labor recruiting units, newspaper-reading units, blackboard newspapers, and in market places and teahouses." [9]

Members of the various organizations such as the Youth Corps, the Democratic Women's League, and the Communist Party act not only as propaganda agents in many ways, but are also active in counseling on marriage and family problems in factories, shops, and in villages.[10] Sessions are organized to acquaint the public with the Marriage Law. In the East China region fifteen million peasants heard lectures on the Marriage Law when it was made the central subject of study by government order for the winter literacy classes for peasants in that region.[11]

Whatever the reaction from a traditional people to lectures and other forms of propaganda, the striking fact is that a vast number of them have now heard about an arrangement of family life at sharp odds with all they were taught and accustomed to in the past. Even if a part of the peasant public do not accept such strange ideas, they have come to feel that a major change of family life is impending. The present vast organized effort to acquaint the public with the new ideas on the family institution is a situation never before encountered in China.

A totally new propaganda device is the "exhibition of marriage problems," a Communist invention. Such exhibitions, first organized in large numbers from 1951 to 1953, display pictures and drawings to dramatize the "unreasonableness" and tragedies of the old institution of family and marriage and to show the happiness brought to couples married in accordance with the Marriage Law. Speakers talk to the crowd as they file past the exhibits, and they give counsel to individuals in a separate room.

In an exhibition in Shaohsing, a rural town in Chekiang Province, a converted traditional woman was used as a living sample; she poured out her tale of misfortune to the visitors. She was a woman who with her little daughter had been chased out of the family by the mother-in-law. She took her daughter and went into a Buddhist convent for eight years. After the Communist government promulgated the Marriage Law, she heard about it and appealed her case in court. The court punished the mother-in-law and gave the complainant a job in a tea factory. According to the official report, "She is now a happy woman, full of gratitude to the Communist government and deep conviction for the principles of the Marriage Law as well as the wickedness of the traditional family institution. Whenever a crowd of visitors gathers in front of her, she gives her talk and wipes away her tears as she tells her heart-rending story of mistreatment by the mother-in-law and husband, and her listeners are deeply moved." [12] Undoubtedly, such living examples of suffering from the traditional family are effective in arousing resentment against the age-old institution and in gaining converts to the new ideas as displayed in the highly dramatized pictures and drawings. This exhibition drew over 10,000 visitors in five days. An exhibition of the same kind in Shanghai, sponsored by the local Democratic Women's League, lasted for ten days in October of 1951 and drew 160,000 visitors.

In the rural communities of Shantung Province a more modest version of the city exhibitions, the "exhibition sheds for the propaganda of the Marriage Law," has been used with visible effect. In such sheds there are the same types of pictures and drawings and the same setup of speakers and counselors. It is estimated that the majority of the visitors to the sheds are young people of both sexes, but there are also middle-aged and old people. In Laiwu county of that province it was officially reported that about half of all the adult population of the county had visited the exhibition shed. Several young women demanded divorces after visiting the shed, and some parents after being exposed to the new ideas also permitted their children to obtain divorces.[13] In Wenteng county of the same province, when an agricultural fair was held in May 1951, an exhibition shed for the marriage problem attracted fifteen thousand visitors in six days. An old man went into the shed to look at the pictures and drawings depicting incidents of the "wickedness of the feudalistic marriage and family" and the "happy new marriages." He returned with his family to look at the pictures again. After that, he brought a group of neighbors to view the same thing. After looking at the drawings and listening to the lectures, many young men and women sought counsel from the counselors and asked about the new procedures of marriage or divorce, "fully ready to carry their new-gained ideas into action." [14]

Lastly, the Communists have shown effective skill in "setting the masses in motion," in focusing public attention on an objective, and in employing group pressure to induce individuals to march toward that objective. While this is a process deserving fuller analysis, the only intention here is to point out that the mass meeting is the beginning of a collective process of implanting in the public mind a new motivation for group behavior and that it constitutes a cornerstone of the Communist mass propaganda technique.

A mass meeting may serve any ulterior purpose, such as popularizing the idea in the Marriage Law by utilizing the striking effect of an "unusual" issue or incident, for instance, the tragic death of a person on account of family conflict; for any unusual issue switches the attention of the audience from their routinized daily behavior and thought and focuses it on the issue which is magnified and dramatized for emotional effect. In the mass meeting the emotions of an unruly crowd are unleashed to throw the routinized thought and behavior further out of balance, to release institutionally inhibited feelings, to heighten the sense of popular justice by circular reaction induced by slogan-shouting, yelling, and repetitive speeches and stories, and finally to pass an unconventional resolution to settle an "unusual" issue. Immediately after passing the resolution as a "popular demand" comes the moralization of the lesson, which is the real aim of the whole show. Still reeling from the high emotional tension generated, the audience is induced to accept not only the solution to the issue but also the moral lesson as interpreted by the masters of the show, the chairman, and the directors of the mass meeting. Thus a new rule is set up to govern an aspect of social life that used to be governed by a very different rule, and the formerly inviolate traditional pattern is broken.

This generalized process of mass meetings, which has served to destroy age-old patterns of behavior, is being applied explicitly to change the institution of the family and marriage. The following is the summary of a concrete case:

> In Ts'angshan county of Shantung Province a young peasant woman, P'an Shi, was tortured to death by her mother-in-law, Ch'i Sung Shi, and the latter's common-law husband, Kuo Yu-shan. The torturing was extremely cruel, but no one dared to protest publicly, for Kuo was the village head and a Communist Party cadre. After all, torturing a daughter-in-law to death had happened before.
>
> The case was discovered by superior government authorities of the T'eng county Special District. In view of the cruelty of the case and in view of the current policy of enforcing the Marriage Law, the higher authorities decided to make an issue out of the case as an example to the local population and unregenerated cadres.
>
> The two murderers were arrested and were made to confess the full details of their crime. The second step was to call a meeting of "representatives" of the local population in the several surrounding counties. Among the several hundred gathered representatives were village and subdistrict cadres, such as village heads and other local officials, local progressive elements, and some die-hard, ancient-minded mothers-in-law and older people. At the meeting the carefully prepared case was reported with full dramatic details to the audience. The story acquired real life and emotional character by bringing in the prisoners to rehearse the confession. The audience was horrified and moved by the story. What should be done in this case to vindicate justice? It was "decided by the meeting" to take the next step: calling a "public trial" mass meeting to be attended by local people. Meanwhile, the full moral of the story, the wickedness of the ancient institution of family and marriage and the necessity for introducing a new pattern as delineated by the Marriage Law and motivated by the spirit of personal freedom on the basis of sex equality, was fully elucidated. After the meeting of representatives Wang Hung-yi, a party cadre representing the second subdistrict of Ts'angshan county, related the effect of the meeting on his own thinking:
>
> "In the past, I felt that the freedom of divorce stipulated in the Marriage Law was looking for unnecessary trouble, shattering people's pre-destined matrimonial ties. I did not recognize that the Marriage Law aims at the harmony of family life and the development of production. Now, after listening to the explanations on the Marriage Law, I am beginning to recognize the error of my past thought.

"I am a newly liberated peasant. I have a daughter. When she was very young, I found a husband for her. The husband's family was a feudalistic one and would not give her enough to eat and to wear, but constantly scolded and beat her. My daughter could not stand it and in 1949 tried to obtain a divorce from the subdistrict government. The subdistrict government refused her request. At that time I said to my wife, 'She is married into the family, how could she think of a divorce?' In this situation, not only was the divorce attempt a failure, but the husband's family also increased the cruelty of treatment toward her and said that 'it would matter very little even if she were beaten to death.' Finally, through struggle, my daughter obtained a divorce, found someone to love, remarried, and now she is quite happy. Right along, I felt that this was a disreputable event. Now I know that, as a subdistrict cadre, if I do not first dig out my own feudalistic thoughts, I cannot thoroughly enforce the Marriage Law for the government."

Besides Wang Hung-yi, other representatives also spoke up along the same vein. Altogether, the representatives uncovered in the meeting 119 cases of mistreated child brides and 91 cases of mistreated wives. "Thus, all the participating representatives and cadres gained a good education."

Then at a great mass meeting came the "public trial" of the murderers. As "planned," upward of ten thousand people came. After inflaming speeches and personal confessions by the murderers, the chairman asked for opinions regarding the sentence from the audience. "Mass emotions swelled to a high tide, there was a deafening roar in unison for 'Drastic punishment for the brutal murderers!' The people's court accepted the demand of the masses and announced the death penalty for the brutal murderers, Kuo Yu-shan and Ch'i Sung Shi." . . .

When the mass trial and the shooting were over, both the representatives and the participants of the mass meeting returned to their respective villages to set off the secondary effect of the exciting event. For three or four days individual village mass meetings were held to hear the reports of the event from those who had participated and to discuss the problems of the Marriage Law in the light of the event. "There was a general recognition of the injustice of the institution that the people were accustomed to." The happy ending to cases of freedom of divorce and freedom of marriage served as models of the new way in the discussions. As a consequence of the village mass meetings and discussions, "many brutal characters who were used to mistreating women lost their courage and became humbled, and many oppressed women were emboldened, starting legal procedure to get a divorce." [15]

This is but one of a large number of similarly significant cases illustrating the part played by mass meetings as a means towards changing the popular attitude toward the traditional family institution. There was a similar case in Pishan county in the neighborhood of the scene of the foregoing case. After the mass meeting and the shooting of the murderer, a leader said, "In my village there are many brutal mothers-in-law. Previously, the oppressed women just took the mistreatment and did not dare to protest. After having the experience of this mass meeting, I now know how to tell them to rebel." [16] In Kwangtung Province there have been many such cases. Particularly significant is a case in which the technique of the mass meeting was used to overcome the public anger of a whole village in Fukien Province against the enforcement of the Marriage Law on a divorce case, driving a wedge into the solid opposition of the village leaders and the village population and gaining popular acceptance for the principles of the new law.[17]

In analyzing such cases of public exhibitions and mass meetings, the change of attitudes among some of the older people and local leaders seems significant, but perhaps even more important is the beckoning of a new idealism and new means to realize it as dramatized to the young. For it is the young men and women who, once converted, are the members of a new family institution which is acquiring real life in the developing Chinese social order, as the institutional authority once vested in the older group is now being replaced by the formal political authority of a regime that no longer operates on the principles of the institutional framework of traditional society. The conservatism of the older people can slow down but cannot prevent the development of a new family institution once the new concept has claimed the young minds.

The propaganda activities we have cited took place between 1950 and 1953, since which time there has been a cooling off of agitation to introduce drastic and speedy change in the family system. Certain propaganda work, such as the elimination of "feudalistic" family values from traditional operas, is still carried on. But other types of propaganda such as public exhibitions, mass meetings, and even general publicity work for the family revolution have noticeably slowed down and in some places stopped altogether since 1953. Since that year, the "high tide" of the family revolution has been retreating — but only, as will be discussed later, because the urgency of the problem of economic development has relegated family reform to a secondary place.

CHAPTER XIII

Recession of the "High Tide" and Long Term Trends

AN EFFORT has been made in the previous chapters to an-
alyse the major aspects of the traditional Chinese family system which
have undergone change in the past half century, especially under Communist leadership. We have noted that during the years from 1950 to
1953, the early years of Communist rule, the tempo of the family revolution was especially rapid, affecting a larger section of the population
than in any previous period. In its broad sweep of recasting the institutional framework of Chinese society, the fury of a newly successful
revolution bore down hard on the family as on other aspects of traditional social life. We have noted also that since 1953 the organized
mass campaign to change the family system has noticeably slowed
down in its pace, and Communist leadership has directed its full
strength to other issues deemed more immediately urgent for the
construction of the socialist state, namely, the first five-year plan of
economic development, the collectivization of agriculture, and the
nationalization of industry and commerce. Although the family revolution is being presently eclipsed, we should not assume that the traditional family system is to be spared from further change. In conclusion,
therefore, it seems relevant first to review the current situation and
then to make a summary with implications for the future.

Modern changes in the Chinese family system have been the result
of both ideological motivation and environmental pressure from new
socio-economic developments. As an ideological movement, the family
revolution has developed in the form of a pulsative process, waxing
and waning with the greater movement of the socio-political revolution of which it is a part. Each pulsation in the process has consisted
of an initial upsurge, a steady rise of the movement to a "high tide,"
in the Communist terminology, and a recession in which some mem-

bers of the movement fell back in disillusionment but others re-formed their ranks in preparation for another assault, with a repetition of the cycle until a new institutional order succeeded in replacing the old one. During each high tide the social atmosphere was charged with tense emotions and revolutionary acts carried to a level which could not be sustained over a long period because of the lack of coordinated support from revolutionary developments in other related aspects of social life.

The general operation of this process has been suggested in the body of this study. The first wave of the family revolution began with the initial upsurge in the last decade of the nineteenth century, rose to a high tide in the Republican revolution of 1911, but retreated soon afterwards into a period of placid advocation and moderate reforms. A resurgence of the movement came with the New Culture Movement of 1917 and the May 4th Movement of 1919, reaching its crescendo in the Second Revolution during the mid-1920's. A recession of the movement followed the Kuomintang-Communist split, and the restorationist counter-current temporarily drowned out the battle cry of the family revolution. The confusion and disappointment of the revolutionists were vividly portrayed in the works of modern fiction of the late 1920's and early 1930's. A good example of such fiction is Mao T'un's *Disillusionment*, which depicts the demoralization and decadence of the frustrated revolutionary youth. The resuscitation of the Communist movement during the great national crisis of the Japanese invasion in 1937 brought renewed strength to the smoldering family revolution as an organized radical drive for the remaking of the family institution. The movement advanced and spread as a part of the Communist revolution, and its development from 1950 to 1953 undoubtedly represents another of its high tides, especially the large-scale campaign for enforcement of the new Marriage Law in 1953. After that year the movement once more entered into a recession which has continued to 1958 when the communes were set up.

The Communist period clearly demonstrates that a major reason for recession is the lack of coordinated support from other related aspects of the social revolution. Preoccupied with the building of the socialist economic order, Communist leadership has been unable to give sustained attention to the family revolution on a mass-organized scale. The lack of coordinated support is seen in the shortage of nurseries to facilitate employment and economic independence for women both in the cities and in the countryside, in the loud condemnations by feminist leaders of discrimination against employing female workers in Com-

munist state enterprises due to the added expense in providing assistance for childbirth and child care, and in the Communists' inability
to provide enough jobs for the women newly emancipated from the confines of the "feudalistic family."

Whereas women were told before 1953 that their only road to liberation was to "participate in productive labor," in 1955 they were advised to wait for the call by the state to take part in production, and
that meanwhile they should recognize the social value of being a
"family woman." As unemployment spread in the urban areas in the
spring of 1957, there was even the proposal of sending some of the
employed women back to the family in order that unemployed men
could have jobs; and the new propaganda line in urban areas was:
"If women who stay at home can encourage their husbands and children to take part in socialist reconstruction, and educate their children
to become members for the next shift in the work of socialist reconstruction, then their domestic service already contains revolutionary
and social value, and the salaries and income of their husbands and
other family members already contain their own labor." [1] In the countryside, emancipation of women from "feudalistic family oppression"
has lost its priority to the dominant national drive toward complete
collectivization of agriculture, and the most important advice for
women is to participate in the collectivization movement.[2] The Democratic Women's League in a rural coastal town reported in 1955 that
it had great difficulty in trying to distribute to the public four hundred
copies of the *Hun-yin Fa T'u-chieh* (Popular Pictorial Edition of the
Marriage Law) for not even the popular organizations were willing
to accept them.[3] This is certainly in sharp contrast to the widespread
enthusiasm with which documents relating to the Marriage Law were
handled before 1953.

Since 1953, the Communist press has published little factual information about the problems of marriage and the family, and it has not
been clear how the new trend is expressed in the actual marriage and
family situation in the country as a whole, but a report on the interior
province of Shensi in 1956 exemplifies the recession of the last high
tide.[4] According to this report, which came out of a field survey, the
wide publicity of the Marriage Law in 1953 produced many new marriages based on free choice, but since then there has been a general
revival of the arranged marriage in the province, especially in the
rural communities where it is practiced on a cash-and-carry basis as
in the old rural tradition, in two rural counties more than 90 per cent
of the marriages being consummated in this traditional manner. The

report quotes many cases, the character of which appears humorous to modern eyes but serious to the traditional-minded peasants. Here are a few of them, all from localities in Shensi Province:

> Cases wherein marriageable girls are handled like a commodity by their parents and sold to the highest bidder have been known. . . . In one village in Chi-shan county . . . the village chief bought his son a wife with money be got by selling a cow and two huts. . . . In another village [in the same county] a girl was offered for sale twice. The last price was 240 yuan [about a hundred dollars]. When the buyer came up with something like 100 yuan, he was shouted out of the house. . . . In a village of Shang county a boy and a girl were much in love. The girl's parents demanded a wedding gift of 150 yuan. All the boy could produce was 100 yuan. This amount was rejected, and the girl was forcibly sold to an older man who was better off. An old villager in Fu-p'ing county sold his divorced daughter for 1,200 yuan plus a good coffin. The deal, however, was called off when the coffin ordered was found to be of inferior quality. In another village in Yen-yang county a man had already sold two of his three daughters. The third, who happened to be an activist, objected to the cash deal and wanted love her own way. She was locked up in the house by her father.

Since such cash deals, long an institutionalized practice in poor rural areas, are ruled out by the Communist Marriage Law, they "have gone underground under various disguised names and procedures," according to the Shensi report; and the people charge that, since the Marriage Law has come into operation, they have had to pay more than previous prices in undercover deals. The report further states that since 1953 the Women's Association, the Youth League, the courts, and the Communist Party branches and People's Councils have not bothered much about the Marriage Law unless homicide cases are involved in family conflicts, and that those who resist the cash-down, arranged marriage eventually lose courage for lack of public support. People have referred to the vigorous publicity of the Marriage Law in 1953 as "a light breeze that leaves no traces at all."

There is some degree of authenticity in this report, for it was made by a correspondent for an official Communist newspaper which would be eager to publicize the success of the Marriage Law if there had been such success. The unresolved question it raises is how far does the condition in Shensi Province represent the situation in other parts of the country? Since cash-down, arranged marriage has been most common in poverty-stricken rural areas, and Shensi is one of the poorest provinces in China proper, the high percentage of return to traditional marriage in Shensi may be exceptional. We would judge that what is happening in Shensi is in harmony with the general national picture, in which the noticeable slow down in organized mass campaigns to change the system of marriage and the family permits reassertion of the traditional pattern; and that, therefore, the Shensi report hints at what may be happening in other parts of the country although the degree of revival of the traditional system of marriage may differ from place to place.

This is not to say that the revival of traditional marriage indicates a tendency toward reconsolidation of the old family system so that it will constitute a component of the socialist society that the Communists are trying to build. Although there may not be another series of mass campaigns to disorganize the traditional family and to bring about a new one, ideological and environmental factors in operation converge toward continued and steady weakening of the traditional system and the development of a new institution of marriage and family organization.

As our study has shown, the process of family change in China, including the new family idealism encouraged by structural alteration of the political, economic, and social factors, has gathered too much momentum to be halted. We have seen that this spreading process began in the closing years of the last century with the lone voices of a few non-conforming young men and women and grew in the subsequent four decades to engulf the whole modern educated segment of the urban population, the segment which held a dominant position in modern China, and that Communism has augmented its strength by extending support for it to the urban working class and to the peasants. There is still in motion, then, a long term process which will survive temporary setbacks and which works inevitably toward three principal ends: the breakdown of the traditional family system, the development of a new family institution, and the decline of the family as the core of Chinese social organization. It is in such a context of continuing change that we would summarize our study.

In the past half century there has been a growing loss of stability and organizational integrity of the traditional Chinese family system caused by such converging factors as the extending influence of romantic love, the changing procedure of marriage, the freedom of divorce, the rebellion of the women and the young against the traditional stratification of family status and authority, the shrinking family function in economic production, the rising competition of extra-familial centers of loyalty, the secularizing influences that quietly strip the family of its sacred character and remove its belief in group perpetuation, and the contagious spirit of a new family idealism being disseminated by modern education and propaganda in the midst of a violent social revolution.

The sphere of these influences is steadily widening. Even in the period of recession marked by the report we have cited on Shensi Province in 1956 the Communist courts in that province handled 8,163 cases involving marital discord during the period from January to June, and 4,980 of these cases, or 61 per cent, ended in divorce.[5] Such a recession as the temporary continuation of a past in which the parents obtain compensation for the economic investment in raising a daughter who is to be married out of the family is sure to be reversed if the Communists can achieve economic betterment of the peasantry, including nation-wide development of an old-age pension system; and it is already countered by the spreading influence of romantic love, the continued protest and rebellion of the young, and the declining authority of the parents over the children's marriages due to interference from the Marriage Law and to the general weakening of the authority of the elders.

With a firm Communist policy of the collectivization of agriculture and nationalization of commerce and industry, the individual's economic dependence upon the family, so dominant a factor in the structure and solidarity of the traditional family, is being increasingly replaced by the economic organization of the state. Save for those too young yet to earn an independent livelihood, the individual's economic security no longer weighs as heavily as before in compelling the preservation of family unity in the face of domestic conflict or in upholding the family as the supreme center of loyalty in one's social existence; and it is difficult to see how the traditional family economic system can retain its functional and structural integrity. The older generation may retain the traditional concept of the family, together with its system of authority and status as shaped by the past economic order, but the young generation is growing up in a collectivized and nationalized economy.

As the inevitable disorganization of the traditional family system continues, there is still uncertainty as to the new form of family institution which would be developed to replace the old one, especially in agrarian communities. The new family idealism distinctly calls for two renovations, namely, alteration of the traditional system of family authority and status, and the establishment of a monogamous marriage based on free choice of partners. But marriage is only a part of the family institution, and what form the alteration of the authority and status structure will take has not been clearly indicated. Neither the Communist law nor the vaguely presented new family ideology gives any clear definition as to the function and structure of the new family to be set up.

Whereas the traditional family had a clearly defined functional orientation, that is, to perpetuate the ancestral lineage, to raise the young, and to support the old, and its pattern of authority and status was carefully geared to that orientation, no such clarity of function-structure definition is found in the new ideology of the family system. Since 1952 the Communist slogan has called for the building of a "democratic, harmonious, and united new family for production," but it is obvious that the family is no longer an organizational unit of production under the collectivized and nationalized economy, and that the role structure among the members cannot be geared to the needs of a function that the family no longer performs as an organized unit. There is also the difficult problem of developing practicable means to achieve the "democratic, harmonious, and united" features for the new family under a socio-economic milieu that favors the detachment of the individual from family ties.

The lack of a specifically defined idealistic form of family as conscious guidance leaves the development of a new family institution to the shaping influence of a spontaneous process resulting from the interplay between ideological values and the new socio-economic structure. In the urban environment which is conducive to the development of an universalistic economy, this process has already resulted in a large number of two-generation conjugal families in which the married son and his family set up an independent household away from his parents where the parents may come to visit but not as permanent members exercising authority and control in the new family. In the countryside it has been common in the past to find an arrangement similar to the French *famille souche*, "in which one of the sons marries and continues to live with the parents while the other sons and daughters marry and go out of the family unit," [6] and which worked successfully chiefly because of the institutionalized authority and status of the parents over the married son and his family. The present Communist policy tends to try to preserve this type of family while at the same time seeking to promote "democratic harmony" by curbing the parents' authority on the one hand and urging the young couple to respect the parents on the other, the object being to avoid disruption of economic production resulting from mass development of family conflicts. The Communist press has publicized many cases in which the son and his wife live "democratically and harmoniously" with the parents on the basis of "mutual affection and mutual respect." [7]

It seems doubtful that the *famille souche* on a "democratic and harmonious" basis can become generally successful at the same time that the "feudalistic" system of family authority and status is brought under vigorous attack, and the individuals, particularly the daughters-in-law, are finding economic independence outside of the family. An economically independent daughter-in-law would be unwilling to use her own earnings to help support the traditionally despotic parents-in-law, especially the mother-in-law. A common result is the breakup of the three-generation family, as shown in the following which occurred in 1953.[8]

In Toukan village in Shaho county of Hopei Province K'ang Ch'ing-ho was a peasant with a petty business on the side. He took a wife, and they got along well at first. Then the mother-in-law started to abuse the wife and told the son to beat her; later the mother-in-law joined in the beating. Finally, the daughter-in-law took her child and ran away. K'ang was unhappy both over his personal loss and the difficulty of finding money to get another wife. Then came the Communist regime, and K'ang became progressive and joined the Communist Party. Later, he fell in love with a female party member and married her. The same conflict arose between the new daughter-in-law and the mother-in-law. This time, the Communist wife, who was a full-fledged agricultural worker, asked for a divorce in the subdistrict government after being beaten up by the husband. The officials in the subdistrict government tried to reconcile the couple by lecturing both parties. K'ang remembered the misfortune of his first marriage and was willing to compromise, but the wife was insistent upon separation from the mother-in-law. The mother-in-law was furious, reminding her son of the traditional filial obligations. However, separation was effected, with the mother-in-law given her own portion of the family land and a separate house around the same courtyard. The son still helped her do the heavy farm work necessary for her support. Later, the daughter-in-law and the mother-in-law became fairly amicable to each other.

There is ample evidence from urban experience that separation from the parents-in-law and the setting up of an independent household, which reduces the traditional extended family to a conjugal form, is encouraged by the social atmosphere developed under Communist rule. There are families in which the parents-in-law live successfully with the married son and his wife, but the controlling position in the family has passed from the parents to the young couple, with the parents as adjuncts and not masters. Such families may retain the three-generation membership, but its internal structure departs radically from the traditional pattern. There now seems to be a trend toward the conjugal family and a weakened form of the three-generation family even in the rural areas if the above story is at all representative.

With the traditional family institution being progressively weakened, and with the present trend, so far as it can be discerned, toward the two-generation family or a weakened form of the three-generation family, there is a plainly visible decline in the vital position of the kinship system which, as we have pointed out, is a central factor in the traditional Chinese social order. We have seen that just as Western society is characterized by an industrial pattern, traditional Chinese society is marked by a familial pattern of social relations. The "blood and flesh" bond took precedence over all other social ties, and the identity of surname between individuals generated a spontaneous feeling of kinship and imposed a compelling sense of mutual obligation. In this sense, then, the changes in the family and the clan not only affect the structure of the kinship system itself but also cripple its functional position in Chinese society, and the present process of change alters the basic pattern of Chinese society.

Our analysis has shown that the kinship system owed its former importance in the web of social relations to many of its functions which are being reduced or removed by Communist socio-economic developments. We have seen that the larger kinship system was an extensive group for mutual aid. An especially important economic aspect of the traditional family was the fitting of its structural features to the function of giving material care and security to the individual throughout his entire life cycle — raising him from infancy, providing him with the means or channels of livelihood in his adult years, and supporting him in old age — functions which made the family the very root of his social life and which have been progressively reduced by the rise of modern urban economy in the pre-Communist period, the steady subversion of the whole system of family authority and status over the past half century, and now by the collectivization of farms and nationalization of businesses by the Communists.

It has also become clear that the former family and extended kinship system as an informal but basic political unit in the sense that it was indispensable for the maintenance of peace and order has little or no meaning in the Communist political system, which extends its direct control down to the level of the individual, and under which, in fact, the systematic destruction of the political function of the kinship system has been a major measure taken to clear the way for the development of a new social order.

Lastly, we have seen that the accelerated development of modern schools, first under the Republic and now in the Communist state, has increasingly replaced the family as the basic educational center for learning occupational skills and for moral and citizenship training at the same time that the trend towards secularization is making deep inroads into ancestor worship, the family religion and the most universal cult in China, which contributed not merely stability to the family institution but also an attitude of piety in the religious life of the Chinese people.

In considering implications for the future we would note that the reduction of functions results not only in the decrease of dominance of the family and the clan in the organizational scheme of Chinese society as a whole but also in the diminishing size, solidarity, and stability of the family itself.

Although the membership of the two-generation or the weakened three-generation family does not appear to be much smaller than that in the former common people's average household, each of such individual families now must stand on its own limited numerical strength, as the rapidly disintegrating extended kinship system is unable to give it the former strong collective support. And a new factor having possible effect on the size of the family is the increasingly vigorous birth control movement since 1956. In March of 1957 editorials and articles in the Communist press, including the leading official organ, *Jen-min Jih-pao* (People's Daily) in Peking, openly put aside the anti-Malthusian tradition of Marxism and expressed alarm at the prospect of further increase at the annual rate of 2 to 3 per cent of the already excessive population of six hundred million. While the idea of birth control had already been accepted by the urban intelligentsia for several decades, Communist leadership now finds it urgent to develop a birth control movement among the workers and peasants who have not heard of it before. Should the propaganda drive and available medical facilities eventually succeed in making birth control effective among the common people, there would be possible reduction in the size of the family. As reduction in membership would decrease the collective strength of the family in the performance of many of its social and economic functions, the birth control movement portends a further weakening of the functional position of the family system.

That the reduction of family functions weakens the interdependence among family members, with the consequent decrease in solidarity in the family group, is clearly indicated in the high divorce rate among the new marriages under Communist rule. When romantic interest shifts from the spouse to a third party, there is now no strong socio-economic bond to hold the couple together, as emphasized by accounts in the Communist press.[9]

Most important in the long run, in addition to the functional and structural features of the Chinese family institution emerging under communism, is the incompatibility between the social dominance of the kinship system and the basic features of a modern industrial society under authoritarian socialism. The contrast between the particularistic and the universalistic pattern of social organization has been pointed out by Talcott Parsons. When kinship relations as a particularistic factor play a dominant role in social life, they result in a national society which is subdivided into numerous small, semi-autonomous, and mutually exclusive kinship cells. This localized, uncoordinated subdivision of the social structure is contradictory to the nature of a sensitively integrated mass society with a highly centralized control which intimately coordinates all the component parts down to the level of the single individual. The dynamic nature, the functional diversity, and the high degree of integration of such a mass society impose on the individual the requirement of specialization and universalism, the development of which would be hampered should the particularistic kinship relations retain the dominant position in the web of social relations. Thus, when Communist authorities assign specialized jobs to each college graduate throughout China as they have done every year since 1951, the individual's kinship ties play no part in the decision of job assignments. In some cases, husband and wife are assigned jobs in different localities in knowing disregard of the family relationship in order to meet the requirement of the state. Sharp indeed is the contrast between this system and the traditional situation in which nepotism based on kinship ties was condoned and even socially obligatory.

Modern Chinese intellectuals and the Communists are aware of the fact that a society subdivided into numerous self-containing kinship groups is neither conducive to centralized control nor favorable to the development of an industrial social order. The attack for half a century against familism and clannism, the numerous cases of political accusations against one's own kin with Communist encouragement, and the cultivation of a large number of extra-familial socio-economic ties are aspects of a conscious or unconscious social effort at detaching individuals from the firmest of traditional Chinese social ties, the kinship tie, in order to refit them into the mesh of new social relations based on the requirements of an industrial economy and a centralized political state.

When we examine this fundamental change, with its obviously profound meaning for the future, we see that it is taking place at various tempos in different types of communities and among different groups of the population. It is being materialized rapidly in the urban environment, the cities having been the staging center of the family revolution for half a century. In the country, in spite of Communist ideological encouragement and pressure from agricultural collectivization, change of the kinship system among the peasants faces the counterforces of the immobility of the agrarian population and the lack of diversity of the agricultural economy; as family members stay together and the bulk of the peasantry remain earthbound to the same village as kinship groups, the old kinship relations have many occasions to reassert themselves whenever the untested socio-economic pattern fails to meet the infinitely varied needs of the individual. Even in an agricultural producers' cooperative, with its obliteration of private ownership of land and heavy farm equipment, there are still many aspects of social and economic life in which the individual must turn to other fellowmen for assistance not provided for by the cooperative organization or other non-kinship bodies; and traditional experience will influence a person to turn to close kin in such circumstances. Under pressure from Communist ideology and adverse socio-economic factors, the rural kinship system will weaken, but it may not disintegrate to the same degree as in the urban community with its mobile population and its diversified economy, which continuously detaches individuals from their kinship groups and reshuffles them into widely separate compartments in the social and economic structure.

The acceptance of fundamental social change is faster among the younger than the older generation. Those who were under the age of twenty when the Communists took over the country in 1949 accept the new family pattern and become adjusted to non-kinship organizations more readily than those over this age. In terms of educational levels, those with higher education yield to the influence of modern trends more rapidly than the uneducated or the poorly educated because of the difference in opportunity in absorbing the new family idealism. In terms of economic gradations, change develops more readily among higher than among lower income groups, as the spreading of the family revolution from upper and middle classes to the workers and peasants has shown. The higher economic groups not only enjoy more contacts with new ideas through education, but they can also better afford the risk of experimenting with a new arrangement of life as there is a greater margin of economic security to cushion the shock from possible failure. A wealthy family can better afford than a poor one to let a son or a daughter enter marriage without insisting upon obtaining a return for the economic investment in raising her.

Taken as a whole, the general materialization of the long-term trends depends on the eventual success of the new socio-economic order in adequately assuming many of the vital functions which formerly were performed by the traditional family and its extended kinship system. Before the new social system has thoroughly proved its worth and dependability, the people, especially the older people, will not lightly risk giving up their time-tested system of social relations, which not merely has demonstrated its material benefits to them but is also deeply woven into their emotional disposition. The system of arranged marriage being driven underground by the enforcement of the Communist Marriage Law is a case in point. As the gigantic experiment of the Communist revolution gropes along its uncharted path, the course of development of these trends will be marked with cycles of advance, halt, and reversal, as it has in the past turbulent half century. Should these trends eventually come to take root among the larger proportion of the Chinese population, Chinese society will by then have permanently shifted from the age-old organizational pattern centered upon the kinship system as the core, the pattern which so long characterized Chinese civilization.

The Marriage Law of the People's Republic of China

Promulgated by the Central People's Government on May 1, 1950

Chapter One: General Principles

Article 1.

The arbitrary and compulsory feudal marriage system, which is based on the superiority of man over woman and which ignores the children's interests, is abolished.

The New Democratic marriage system, which is based on free choice of partners, on monogamy, on equal rights for both sexes, and on protection of the lawful interests of women and children, shall be put into effect.

Article 2.

Polygamy, concubinage, child betrothal, interference with the remarriage of widows and the exaction of money or gifts in connection with marriage shall be prohibited.

Chapter Two: Contracting of Marriage

Article 3.

Marriage shall be based upon the complete willingness of the two parties. Neither party shall use compulsion and no third party shall be allowed to interfere.

Article 4.

A marriage can be contracted only after the man has reached twenty years of age and the woman has reached eighteen years of age.

Article 5.

No man or woman in any of the following instances shall be allowed to marry:

(a) Where the man and woman are lineal relatives by blood or where the man and woman are brother and sister born of the same parents or where the man and woman are half-brother and half-sister. The question of prohibiting marriage between collateral relatives by blood within the fifth degree of relationship is to be determined by custom.

(b) When one party, because of certain physical defects, is sexually impotent.

(c) Where one party is suffering from venereal disease, mental disorder, leprosy, or any other disease which is regarded by medical science as rendering the person unfit for marriage.

Article 6.

In order to contract a marriage, both the man and the woman shall register in person with the people's government of the subdistrict or village in which they reside. If the marriage is found to be in conformity with the provisions of this law, the local people's government shall, without delay, issue a marriage certificate.

If the marriage is found to be incompatible with the provisions of this law, no registration shall be granted.

Chapter Three: Rights and Duties of Husband and Wife

Article 7.

Husband and wife are companions living together and shall enjoy equal status in the home.

Article 8.

Husband and wife are in duty bound to love, respect, assist, and look after each other, to live in harmony, to engage in production, to care for the children, and to strive jointly for the welfare of the family and for the building up of a new society.

Article 9.

Both husband and wife shall have the right to free choice of occupations and free participation in work or in social activities.

Article 10.

Both husband and wife shall have equal rights in the possession and management of family property.

Article 11.

Both husband and wife shall have the right to use his or her own family name.

Article 12.

Both husband and wife shall have the right to inherit each other's property.

Chapter Four: Relations between Parents and Children

Article 13.

Parents have the duty to rear and to educate their children; the children have the duty to look after and to assist their parents. Neither the parents nor the children shall maltreat or desert one another.

The foregoing provision also applies to stepparents and stepchildren. Infanticide by drowning and similar criminal acts are strictly prohibited.

Article 14.

Parents and children shall have the right to inherit one another's property.

Article 15.

Children born out of wedlock shall enjoy the same rights as children born in lawful wedlock. No person shall be allowed to harm or to discriminate against children born out of wedlock.

Where the paternity of a child born out of wedlock is legally established by the mother of the child, by other witnesses, or by other material evidence, the identified father must bear the whole or part of the cost of maintenance and education of the child until it has attained the age of eighteen.

With the consent of the natural mother, the natural father may have custody of the child.

With regard to the maintenance of a child whose natural mother marries, the provisions of Article 22 shall apply.

Article 16.

A husband or wife shall not maltreat or discriminate against a child born of a previous marriage.

Chapter Five: Divorce

Article 17.

Divorce shall be granted when husband and wife both desire it. In the event of either the husband or the wife insisting upon divorce, it may be granted only when mediation by the subdistrict people's government and the subdistrict judicial organ has failed to bring about a reconciliation.

In the case where divorce is desired by both the husband and wife, both parties shall register with the subdistrict people's government in order to obtain a certificate of divorce. The subdistrict government, after establishing that divorce is desired by both parties and that appropriate measures have been taken for the care of children and property, shall issue the certificate of divorce without delay.

When only one party insists on divorce, the subdistrict people's government may try to effect a reconciliation. If such mediation fails, it should, without delay, refer the case to the district or city people's court for decision. The subdistrict people's government shall not attempt to prevent or to obstruct either party from appealing to the district or city people's court.

In dealing with a divorce case, the district or city people's court must, in the first instance, try to bring about a reconciliation between the parties. In case such mediation fails, the court shall render a verdict without delay.

In the case where, after divorce, both husband and wife desire the resumption of matrimonial relations, they should apply to the subdistrict people's government for a registration of remarriage. The subdistrict people's government should accept such a registration and issue a certificate of remarriage.

Article 18.

The husband shall not apply for a divorce when his wife is with child. He may apply for divorce only one year after the birth of the child. In the case of a woman applying for divorce, this restriction does not apply.

Article 19.

The spouse of a member of the revolutionary army on active service who maintains correspondence with his (or her) family must first obtain his (or her) consent before he (or she) can ask for a divorce.

As from the date of the promulgation of this law, divorce may be granted to the spouse of a member of the revolutionary army who does not correspond with his (or her) family for a subsequent period of two years. Divorce may also be granted to the spouse of a member of the revolutionary army who has not maintained correspondence with his (or her) family for over two years prior to the promulgation of this law and who fails to correspond with his (or her) family for a further period of one year subsequent to the promulgation of the present law.

Chapter Six: Support and Education of Children after Divorce

Article 20.

The blood ties between parents and children do not end with the divorce of the parents. No matter whether the father or the mother acts as guardian of the child or children, they still remain the children of both parties.

After divorce, both parents still have the duty to support and educate their children.

After divorce, the guiding principle is to allow the mother to have custody of a baby still being breast-fed. After the weaning of the child, if a dispute arises between the two parties over the guardianship and an agreement cannot be reached, the people's court shall render a decision in accordance with the best interests of the child.

Article 21.

After divorce, if the mother is given custody of a child, the father shall be responsible for the whole or part of the necessary cost of the maintenance and education of the child. Both parties shall reach an agreement regarding the amount of the cost and the duration of such maintenance and education. In the case where the two parties fail to reach an agreement, the people's court shall render a decision.

Payment must be made in cash, in kind, or by tilling the land allocated to the child.

Such an agreement reached between the parents or decision rendered by the people's court in connection with the maintenance and educational expenses for a child shall not prevent the child from requesting either parent to increase the amount above that fixed by agreement or by judicial decision.

Article 22.

In the case where a divorced woman remarries and her husband is willing to pay the whole or part of the cost of maintenance and education for the child or children by·her former husband, the father of the child or children is entitled to have such cost of maintenance and education reduced or is entitled to be exempt from bearing such cost in accordance with the circumstances.

Chapter Seven: Property and Maintenance after Divorce

Article 23.

In case of divorce, the wife shall retain such property as belonged to her prior to her marriage. The disposal of other household properties shall be subject to agreement between the two parties. In the case where an agreement cannot be reached, the people's court shall render a decision after taking into consideration the actual state of the family property, the interests of the wife and the child or children, and the principle of benefiting the development of production.

In the case where the property allocated to the wife and her child or children is sufficient for the maintenance and education of the child or children, the husband may be exempt from bearing further maintenance and education costs.

Article 24.

After divorce, debts incurred during the period of marriage shall be paid out of the property acquired by husband and wife during this period. In the case where no such property has been acquired or in the case where such property is insufficient to pay off such debts, the husband shall be held responsible for paying these debts. Debts incurred separately by the husband or wife shall be paid off by the party responsible.

Article 25.

After divorce, if one party has not remarried and has difficulties in maintenance, the other party should render assistance. Both parties shall work out an agreement with regard to the method and duration of such assistance; in case an agreement cannot be reached, the people's court shall render a decision.

Chapter Eight: Bylaws

Article 26.

Persons violating this law shall be punished in accordance with law. In the case where interference with the freedom of marriage has caused death or injury, the person guilty of such interference shall bear criminal responsibility before the law.

Article 27.

This law shall come into force from the date of its promulgation. In regions inhabited by national minorities, the Military and Political Council of the Administrative Area of the provincial people's government may enact certain modifications of supplementary articles in conformity with the actual conditions prevailing among national minorities in regard to marriage. But such measures must be submitted to the Government Administration Council for ratification before enforcement.

Reference Notes

Chapter I. The Communist Revolution and the Change of Chinese Social Institutions

1. *Hun-yin fa chih ch'i yu-kuan wen-chien* (The Marriage Law and Related Documents), Peking, 1950, pp. 1–21.

2. *The Works of Mencius* (tr. James Legge), Shanghai, 1949, Book III, Part I, ch. 4.

3. *Chung-hua min-kuo t'ung-chih t'i-yao* (Statistical Abstract of the Republic of China), Nanking; 1947 ed., p. 4, 1935 ed., p. 219.

4. *Chia tzu hsin-shu* (New Book on Chia Tzu), quoted in *Tz'u yuan* (Source of Phrases), Shanghai, 1949, p. 173.

5. See Talcott Parsons, *The Social System*, Glencoe, Illinois, 1951, pp. 85–87.

6. K'ang Yu-wei, *Ta t'ung shu* (The Great Commonwealth), Shanghai, 1923, Part I.

7. *The Civil Code of the Republic of China* (tr. Hsia Tsin-lin), Shanghai, 1931, pp. 249–291.

8. See, for example, "Absolute Proof of the Communists' Practice in Communal Wives," in *Kuang-ming chih-lu* (The Road of Light), Nanking, vol. I, no. 7–8, June 1931, pp. 1–7.

Chapter II. Freedom of Marriage

1. *Works of Mencius* (tr. Legge), Book III, Part II, ch. 4, p. 268.

2. *Ibid.*, Book V, Part I, ch. 1, p. 345.

3. *Hun-yin fa hsuan-ch'uan shou-ts'e* (Propaganda Handbook of the Marriage Law), Peking, 1951, pp. 9–11.

4. *Jen-min jih-pao* (People's Daily), Peking, March 9, 1950, p. 3.

5. *Hun-yin fa chih ch'i yu-kuan wen-chien* (The Marriage Law and Related Documents), Peking, 1950, p. 89.

6. Ta Chen, *Population in Modern China*, Chicago, 1946, p. 114.

7. Hsü Chen, *Chung-kuo fu-nü yün-tung shih* (The History of the Chinese Women's Movement), Shanghai, 1930, pp. 34–60.

8. See, for example, the "Hsiu-cheng shen-kan-ning pien-ch'ü chan-hsing t'iao-li" (Revised Temporary Marriage Regulations in the Border Region of Shensi, Kansu, and Ninghsia Provinces), *Shen-kan-ning pien-ch'ü cheng-ts'eh*

t'iao li lei-chih (Collection of Policies and Regulations of the Border Region of Shensi, Kansu, and Ninghsia Provinces), 1944.

9. Marriage Law, Article 1 (see Appendix).

10. *Ibid.*, Article 3.

11. *Ibid.*, Article 2.

12. *Ibid.*, Article 6.

13. *Ibid.*, Article 3.

14. *Ibid.*, Article 3.

15. *Ibid.*, Article 2.

16. *Ibid.*, Article 4.

17. *Ibid.*, Article 5.

18. *Shing-tao jih-pao*, Hong Kong, December 11, 1951, p. 4.

19. *Jen-min jih-pao*, Peking, June 3, 1955, p. 2.

20. *Ibid.*, March 29, 1951, p. 2.

21. *Ibid.*, August 9, 1951, p. 2.

22. *Ibid.*, March 29, 1951, p. 2.

23. *Ibid.*, September 29, 1951, p. 3.

24. Liu Mien-chih, "The Policy of Simultaneous Mobilization of Men and Women Peasants and of Effective Protection for Women's Legitimate Rights Must be Thoroughly Enforced in the Land Reform," *Hsin Chung-kuo fu-nü* (New Chinese Women), no. 25–26, December 1951, p. 16.

25. *Jen-min jih-pao*, September 29, 1951, p. 3.

26. *Chieh-fang jih-pao*, February 11, 1952, p. 5.

27. *Hun-yin fa hsin-hua* (New Talks on the Marriage Law), Shanghai, 1950, pp. 9–10.

28. *Hun-yin wen-t'i shou-ts'e* (Handbook on the Marriage Problem), Peking, 1951, p. 24.

29. *Hsin Chung-kuo yueh-k'an* (New China Monthly), no. 24, October 1951, pp. 1245–1246.

30. *Hun-yin fa hsin-hua*, p. 19.

31. *Hsin Chung-kuo yueh-k'an*, vol. 4, no. 5, October 1951, p. 1249.

32. Propaganda Handbook of the Marriage Law, 1951, pp. 13–16.

33. *Ch'ang-chiang jih-pao*, Hankow, January 8, 1952, p. 2.

34. *Jen-min jih-pao*, October 9, 1951, p. 3.

35. *Ch'ang-chiang jih-pao*, January 8, 1952, p. 2.

36. Yen Yung-chieh, "A Good Way of Making Propaganda on the Marriage Law," *Hsin Chung-kuo fu-nü* no. 25–26, December 1951, p. 44.

37. "Studying the Marriage Law and Enforcing It," *Hsin Chung-kuo fu-nü*, no. 12, July 1950, p. 4.

38. *Jen-min jih-pao*, May 13, 1953, p. 3.

39. Marriage Law, Articles 6 and 7.

40. Some local courts in the rural areas still rule in favor of returning the price of the bride in case the divorce is initiated by the wife, but such courts are manned by "unregenerated" cadres who are the object of criticism by the Ministry of Justice of the Central Government of the Communist regime. See "Judicial Workers Ignoring Women's Interests and Being Irresponsible toward Matrimonial Cases," *Jen-min jih-pao*, November 10, 1951, p. 3.

41. *Wah-kiu yat-po*, Hong Kong, May 9, 1951, p. 4.

42. Marriage Law, Article 2.

43. See statement by Shih Liang, Minister of Justice, in *Hun-yin fa chih ch'i yu-kuan wen-chien*, p. 16.

Chapter III. Associated Problems of Marriage

1. Ta Chen, *Population in Modern China*, Chicago, 1946, pp. 112–113; *Chung-hua min-kuo t'ung-chih t'i-yao* (Statistical Abstract of the Republic of China), Nanking, 1947, p. 244.

2. *Chung-hua min-kuo t'ung-chih t'i-yao*, p. 9.

3. Ratios computed from Table 43, Ta Chen, p. 112.

4. Fifteenth census, vol. IV, Part I, p. 11. In this comparison, there is also the age factor at the time when the women became widowed. In the United States, the median age at which women become widowed is 51 (Statistical Bulletin, vol. 33, no. 8, August 1952, published by the Metropolitan Life Insurance Company). This means that widowhood in the United States is largely dictated by late age and not imposed by institutional restriction. Unfortunately no comparable data is available on the age of Chinese widows.

5. P. K. Wattol, *Population Problem in India*, p. 36, quoted in Ta Chen, p. 112.

6. "Report on Widow Ch'en's Case by the Huai-yang County Court," *Hun-yin fa chih ch'i yu-kuan wen-chien* (The Marriage Law and Related Documents), Peking, 1950, p. 52.

7. *Ibid.*; also, "A Directive from the Central-South Regional Military and Political Committee," *Shing-tao jih-pao*, Hong Kong, September 4, 1951, p. 2.

8. *Ch'ang-chiang jih-pao*, Hankow, January 12, 1952, p. 2.

9. *Chieh-fang jih-pao* (Liberation Daily), Shanghai, January 9, 1952, p. 3.

10. *Hun-yin fa chih ch'i yu-kuan wen-chien*, pp. 29 ff.

11. "Marriage Law Being thoroughly Enforced in Various Parts of North China," *Jen-min jih-pao*, March 9, 1951, p. 2.

12. *Jen-min jih-pao*, September 29, 1951, p. 3.

13. Marriage Law, articles 13, 15, 16, 22; also, *Hun-yin fa hsin-hua* (New Talks on the Marriage Law), Shanghai, 1950, p. 51.

14. *Hun-yin fa hsuan-ch'uan shou-ts'e* (Propaganda Handbook of the Marriage Law), Peking, 1951, pp. 7–8.

15. *Ibid.*, pp. 6–7.

16. "Change of the Marriage Institution in Rural Communities in Shansi and Suiyuan Provinces through Land Reform," *Hun-yin wen-t'i tso-t'an* (Symposium on the Marriage Problem), Canton, 1951, pp. 49–51.

17. *Hun-yin fa hsin-hua*, Shanghai, 1950, p. 5.

18. Florence Ayscough, *Chinese Women Yesterday and Today*, Boston, 1937, pp. 57–61.

19. *Hun-yin fa hsuan-ch'uan shou-ts'e*, pp. 24–26.

20. *Hun-yin wen-t'i shou-ts'e* (Handbook on the Marriage Problem), Peking, 1951, pp. 41–42.

21. *Jen-min jih-pao*, October 15, 1951, p. 3.

22. See major Chinese newspapers such as the *Jen-min jih-pao* of Peking, *Ch'ang-chiang jih-pao* of Hankow, and *Chieh-fang jih-pao* of Shanghai, issues from January to June, 1952.

Chapter IV. Freedom of Divorce

1. *Hun-yin fa hsuan-ch'uan shou-ts'e* (Propaganda Handbook of the Marriage Law), Peking, 1951, pp. 60–62.

2. "Questions and Answers on the Enforcement of the Marriage Law," by the Committee on Laws and Institutions, in the *Hun-yin fa chih ch'i yu-kuan wen-chien* (The Marriage Law and Related Documents), Peking, 1950, p. 27.

3. Ch'en Shao-yü, "Report on the Process and Reasons in the Drafting of the Marriage Law of the People's Republic of China," *Hun-yin fa chih ch'i yu-kuan wen-chien*, pp. 69–70.

4. *Hun-yin fa hsin-hua* (New Talks on the Marriage Law), Shanghai, 1950, pp. 3–4.

5. *Hun-yin chuang-k'uang mu-ch'ien fa-chan li-an* (Sample Cases on the Present Development of Marital Conditions), by the People's Court of Shansi Province, January, 1950.

6. Computed from Ta Chen, *Population in Modern China*, Chicago, 1946, Table 43, p. 112.

7. Computed from Table 3, census of nine counties in Szechwan Province, *Chung-hua min-kuo t'ung-chi t'i-yao* (Statistical Abstract of the Republic of China), Nanking, 1947, p. 9.

8. Shih Liang, "Seriously and Thoroughly Enforce the Marriage Law," *Jen-min jih-pao* (People's Daily), Peking, October 13, 1951, p. 3.

9. *Wah-kiu yat-po*, Hong Kong, April 17, 1953, p. 4.

10. Ch'en Shao-yü, cited note 3.

11. *Jen-min jih-pao*, September 29, 1951, p. 3.

12. *Wah-kiu yat-po*, Hong Kong, September 8, 1952, p. 4.

13. *Hun-yin fa chih ch'i yu-kuan wen-chien*, pp. 70–71.

14. *Wah-kiu yat-po*, April 20, 1953, p. 4.

15. *Hun-yin fa chih ch'i yu-kuan wen-chien*, p. 72.

16. *Jen-min jih-pao*, September 29, 1951, p. 3.

17. *Ibid.*

18. *Hun-yin fa chih ch'i yu-kuan wen-chien*, p. 74.

19. Teng Yung-ch'ao, "A Report on the Marriage Law of the People's Republic of China," *Hun-yin wen-t'i shou-ts'e* (Handbook on the Marriage Problem), Peking, 1951, pp. 7–8.

20. See note 13.

21. Report by Kuo Hsin-lan, woman judge in the People's Court of Canton, March 8, 1951, *Shing-tao jih-pao*, Hong Kong, March 10, 1951.

22. *Hun-yin wen-t'i shou-ts'e*, p. 34; *Hun-yin fa hsin-hua*, pp. 43–45.

23. *Hun-yin wen-t'i shou-ts'e*, pp. 37–39.

24. *Hun-yin fa hsin-hua*, p. 56.

25. Ch'en Yu-t'ung, "Liquidation of the Old Legal View as a Condition for Thorough Implementation of the Marriage Law," *Hsin Chung-kuo fu-nü* (New Chinese Women), no. 9, September, 1952, pp. 7–8.

26. *Hun-yin wen-t'i shou-ts'e*, pp. 38–39.

27. *Ibid.*, p. 40.

28. Shih Liang, cited note 8.

29. Li Cheng, "Strengthen the Learning of the Marriage Law Among Village and Subdistrict Cadres," *Jen-min jih-pao*, October 9, 1951, p. 3.

30. Hsü Teh-hsing, "Let Us Correctly Enforce the Marriage Law to Abolish the Feudalistic Marriage Institution," *Hsin Chung-kuo yueh-k'an* (New China Monthly), no. 19, May 1951, p. 34.

31. *Hun-yin fa hsuan-ch'uan shou-ts'e*, p. 60.

32. "Examples of Court Decisions on Matrimonial Cases," *Hun-yin wen-t'i shou-ts'e*, pp. 34–35.

33. *Ibid.*, p. 36; also, *Hun-yin fa hsin-hua*, pp. 46–48, and the Marriage Law, Article 19.

34. *Jen-min jih-pao*, October 13, 1951, p. 3.

35. *Chieh-fang jih-pao*, Shanghai, January 14, 1952, p. 3.

36. *Jen-min jih-pao*, October 9, 1951, p. 3.

37. Hsü Teh-hsing, cited note 30.

38. *Jen-min jih-pao*, September 30, 1951, p. 3.

39. "Statement by the Preparatory Committee of the Democratic Women's League," *Hsin Chung-kuo yueh-k'an*, October 1951, p. 1248.

40. Ch'en Yu-t'ung, cited note 25.

41. Tso Chung-fen, "Representatives' Conference of Model Laborers Implementing the Marriage Law in Lushan County," *Hsin Chung-kuo fu-nü*, no. 12, December 1952, pp. 10–12.

Chapter V. Crumbling of the Age Hierarchy

1. Meng Tzu, Book II, Part II, ch. 2. The quotation represents a slight alteration by the author from James Legge's translation, *The Works of Mencius*, pp. 213–214.

2. Han-yi Feng, "The Chinese Kinship System," *Harvard Journal of Asiatic Studies*, vol. 2, no. 2, July 1937, p. 160, reprinted separately in 1948. An explanation of the terms in the chart follows:

Lineal relatives:
Fu — Father
Mu — Mother
Tsu fu — grandfather
Tsu mu — grandmother
Tseng tsu fu — great grandfather
Tseng tsu mu — great grandmother
Kao tsu fu — great great grandfather
Kao tsu mu — great great grandmother
Tsu — son
Nü — daughter
Sun — grandson
Sun nü — granddaughter
Tseng sun — son of grandson
Tseng sun nü — daughter of grandson
Hsuan sun — son of "son of grandson"
Hsuan sun nü — daughter of "son of grandson"

First collaterals descended from males through males:
Hsiung — elder brother

Sao — wife of elder brother
Ti — younger brother
Ti fu — wife of younger brother
Po fu — elder brother of father
Po mu — wife of elder brother of father
Shu fu — younger brother of father
Shu mu — wife of younger brother of father
Po tsu fu — elder brother of grandfather
Po tsu mu — wife of elder brother of grandfather
Shu tsu fu — younger brother of grandfather
Shu tsu mu — wife of younger brother of grandfather
Tseng po tsu fu — elder brother of great grandfather
Tseng po tsu mu — wife of elder brother of great grandfather
Tseng shu tsu fu — younger brother of great grandfather
Tseng shu tsu mu — wife of younger brother of great grandfather
Chi — son of brother
Chi nü — daughter of brother
Chi sun — grandson of brother
Chi sun nü — granddaughter of brother
Tseng chi sun — great grandson of brother
Tseng chi sun nü — great granddaughter of brother

Second collaterals descended from males through males:
T'ang hsiung — son of father's brother, older than ego (wife — sao)
T'ang ti — son of father's brother, younger than ego (wife — t'ang ti fu)
T'ang tzu — daughter of father's brother, older than ego
T'ang mei — daughter of father's brother, younger than ego
T'ang po fu — son of grandfather's brother, older than father
T'ang shu fu — son of grandfather's brother, younger than father
T'ang ku mu — wife of son of grandfather's brother
T'ang po tsu fu — son of great grandfather's brother, older than grandfather
T'ang shu tsu fu — son of great grandfather's brother, younger than grandfather
T'ang ku tsu mu — wife of son of great grandfather's brother
T'ang chi — son of "son of father's brother"
T'ang chi nü — daughter of "son of father's brother"
T'ang chi sun — grandson of "son of father's brother"
T'ang chi sun nü — granddaughter of "son of father's brother"

Third collaterals descended from males through males:
Tsai ts'ung hsiung — grandson of grandfather's brother, older than ego
Tsai ts'ung ti — grandson of grandfather's brother, younger than ego
Tsai ts'ung tzu — granddaughter of grandfather's brother, older than ego
Tsai ts'ung mei — granddaughter of grandfather's brother, younger than ego
Tsai ts'ung po fu — grandson of great grandfather's brother, older than father
Tsai ts'ung shu fu — grandson of great grandfather's brother, younger than father
Tsai ts'ung ku mu — wife of grandson of great grandfather's brother
Tsai ts'ung chi — great grandson of grandfather's brother
Tsai ts'ung chi nü — great granddaughter of grandfather's brother

Fourth collaterals descended from males through males:
Tsu hsiung — great grandson of grandfather's brother, older than ego
Tsu ti — great grandson of grandfather's brother, younger than ego
Tsu tzu — great granddaughter of grandfather's brother, older than ego
Tsu mei — great granddaughter of grandfather's brother, younger than ego
    (The above four terms also apply to relatives of ego's generational level beyond
    the fourth collateral on the male side.)

First collaterals descended from females through males:
Tzu — elder sister
Tzu fu — husband of elder sister
Mei — younger sister
Mei fu — husband of younger sister
Ku mu — father's sister
Ku fu — husband of father's sister
Ku tsu mu — grandfather's sister
Ku tsu fu — husband of grandfather's sister
Tseng tsu ku mu — great grandfather's sister
Tseng tsu ku fu — husband of great grandfather's sister
Wai sheng — son of sister
Wai sheng nü — daughter of sister
Wai sheng sun — sister's grandson
Wai sheng tseng sun — sister's great grandson

Second collaterals descended from females through males:
Piao hsiung — son of father's sister, older than ego
Piao ti — son of father's sister, younger than ego
Piao tzu — daughter of father's sister, older than ego
Piao mei — daughter of father's sister, younger than ego
Piao ku mu — daughter of grandfather's sister
Piao po fu — husband of daughter of grandfather's sister, older than father
Piao shu fu — husband of daughter of grandfather's sister, younger than father
Piao tsu mu — daughter of great grandfather's sister
Piao tsu fu — husband of daughter of great grandfather's sister
Piao chih — son of father's sister's son
Piao chih nü — daughter of father's sister's son
Piao chih sun — grandson of father's sister's son

Third collaterals descended from females through males:
T'ang piao hsiung — son of daughter of grandfather's sister, older than ego
T'ang piao ti — son of daughter of grandfather's sister, younger than ego
T'ang piao tzu — daughter of daughter of grandfather's sister, older than ego
T'ang piao mei — daughter of daughter of grandfather's sister, younger than ego
T'ang paio ku mu — daughter of "daughter of great grandfather's sister"
T'ang piao po fu — husband of daughter of "daughter of great grandfather's sister," older than father
T'ang piao shu fu — husband of daughter of "daughter of great grandfather's sister," younger than father
T'ang piao chih — son of "son of daughter of grandfather's sister"
T'ang piao chih nü — daughter of "son of daughter of daughter of grandfather's sister"

Fourth collaterals descended from females through males:
Tsai ts'ung piao hsiung — son of "daughter of daughter of great grandfather's sister," older than ego
Tsai ts'ung piao ti — son of "daughter of daughter of great grandfather's sister," younger than ego
Tsai ts'ung piao tzu — daughter of "daughter of daughter of great grandfather's sister," older than ego
Tsai ts'ung piao mei — daughter of "daughter of daughter of great grandfather's sister," younger than ego

3. Feng's study gave 41 groups of relatives each with a distinct category of kinship terminology. *Ch'ing Wei Lu* (A Collection of Nomenclature) in volumes 1 to 8, gave 160 different kinship terms, with each term capable of further subdivision by the ranking of physical age. As Feng did not use the *Ch'ing Wei Lu* in his research, there may be some disagreement between his results and the listing in the *Ch'ing Wei Lu*. Nevertheless, both works show vast numbers of people that could be included in the traditional hierarchy of status and authority based primarily on the factors of generation, age, and proximity of kinship.

4. See Ch'ü T'ung-tsu, *Chung-kuo fa-lu yü Chung-kuo sheh-hui* (Law and Chinese Society), Kunming, 1944.

5. See the presentation of this point in Marion J. Levy, Jr.'s *The Family Revolution in Modern China*, Cambridge, 1949, pp. 127–133.

6. Fan Tz'u asked Confucius how to farm, and the reply was, "I do not know as much as an old farmer." See Confucius, *Analects*, Book XIII, ch. 4.

7. See *Ch'ing-ch'ao Hsü Wen-hsien T'ung-k'ao* (Compendium of Documents of the Ch'ing Dynasty), Shanghai, 1934, ch. 242, pp. 9861.

8. Edgar Snow, *Red Star Over China*, New York, 1944, p. 292.

9. Feng Wen-pin, "Present Conditions and Work of the Youth League," *Ch'ang-chiang Daily*, January 8, 1952, p. 4; New China News Agency, Peking, May 12, 1957.

10. Feng Min-pin, "The Chinese New Democratic Youth League as the Standard Bearer of the Tradition of Revolutionary Struggle of the Chinese Youth," *Hsin Chung-kuo yueh-k'an* (New China Monthly), no. 19, May 1951, p. 52.

11. *Hsin Chung-kuo jen-wu chih* (Who's Who in New China), 1950, Hong Kong, pp. 2–3.

12. *Nan-fang jih-pao*, Canton, April 19, 1950, p. 3.

13. Feng Wen-pin, in *Chang-chiang jih-pao*, January 8, 1952, p. 4.

14. *Hsin chung-kuo yueh-k'an*, no. 19, May 1951, p. 52.

15. Marriage Law, Article 13.

16. *Ibid.*, Articles 13, 14, 15, 16, 20, 21, 22.

17. *Ibid.*, Article 13.

18. Of the 73 cases in which young family members brought public accusation against relatives from March 1 to September 25, 1951, in the province of Kwangtung, 26 were against parents. See *Wah-kiu yat-po*, Hong Kong, September 25, 1951, p. 4.

19. *Jen-min jih-pao*, May 5, 1951, p. 6.

20. *Hun-yin fa hsin-hua* (New Talks on the Marriage Law), pp. 29–30.

Chapter VI. The Ascendancy of the Status of Women in the Family

1. K'ang Yu-wei, *Ta T'ung Shu* (The Great Commonwealth), Shanghai, 1923, Part I.

2. Marion Levy, *The Family Revolution in Modern China*, Cambridge, 1949, pp. 106–118.

3. *Chung-hua Min-kuo t'ung-chi t'i-yao* (Statistical Abstract of the Republic of China), Nanking, 1935, pp. 360–361.

4. Directive by the Council of Administration on the Conditions of Enforcement of the Marriage Law, *Hsin Chung-kuo yueh-k'an* (New China Monthly), no. 23, September 1951, p. 1244.

5. "A Preliminary Survey of the Enforcement of the Marriage Law in the Past Year and Opinion on its Further Thorough Enforcement," by the Preparatory Committee of the Democratic Women's League of the Central-South Region, *Hsin Chung-kuo yueh-k'an*, no. 24, October 1951, p. 1247.

6. *Jen-min jih-pao* (People's Daily), Peking, September 29, 1951, p. 3.

7. *Ibid.*, December 6, 1951, p. 6.

8. Li Ai-min, "Use Typical Cases to Educate the Cadres and the People," *Hsin Chung-kuo fu-nü* (New Chinese Women), no. 25–26, December 1951, p. 45.

9. *Jen-min jih-pao*, December 6, 1951, p. 3.

10. Ch'en Yu-t'ung, "Liquidation of the Old Legal View as a Condition for Thorough Implementation of the Marriage Law," *Hsin Chung-kuo fu-nü*, no. 9, September 1952, pp. 7–8.

11. *Jen-min jih-pao*, September 29, 1951, p. 3.

12. *Ibid.*, May 7, 1951, p. 2.

13. *Chieh-fang jih-pao*, Shanghai, January 9, 1952, p. 3.

14. *Ibid.*, September 1, 1951, p. 3.

15. *Hsien-tai fu-nü* (Modern Women), no. 9, August 1950, pp. 13–14.

16. Wu Ch'uen-heng, "Beating, Scolding and Mistreatment of Women Should Not be Allowed to Continue," *Hsin Chung-kuo fu-nü*, no. 25–26, December 1951, pp. 20–21.

17. *Chung-hua Min-kuo t'ung-chih t'i-yao* (Statistical Abstract of the Republic of China), Nanking, 1947, pp. 10–11.

18. "Samples of Court Decisions on Matrimonial Cases by the People's Court of Tientsin," *Hun-yin wen-t'i shou-ts'e* (Handbook on the Marriage Problem), Peking, 1951, pp. 31–32.

19. Hsü Teh-hsing, "Let Us Correctly Enforce the Marriage Law to Abolish the Feudalistic Marriage Institution," *Hsin Chung-kuo yueh-k'an*, no. 19, May 1951, p. 34.

20. Li Ai-min, cited note 8.

21. Marriage Law, Article 2.

22. Yang Chih-hua, "Work on Women Labor in the Past Year," *Hsin Chung-kuo fu-nü*, no. 15, October 1950, p. 22.

23. "New China's Lucky Women Workers," *Jen-min jih-pao*, March 6, 1951, p. 2.

24. "Women's Enthusiastic Participation in Literacy Short Courses in Tientsin," by the Tientsin Branch of Democratic Women's League, *Hsin Chung-kuo fu-nü*, no. 14, September 1950, p. 20.

25. Sun Chu-feng, "Experiences in Mobilizing Educated Family Women to Teach Literacy Short Courses," *Hsin Chung-kuo fu-nü*, no. 9, September 1952, p. 8.

26. *Wah-kiu yat-po*, Hong Kong, March 13, 1951, p. 4.

27. *Hsien-tai fu-nü*, no. 9, August 1950, p. 2.

28. *Ta Kung Pao*, Hong Kong, March 19, 1956, p. 1.

29. *Jen-min jih-pao*, March 31, 1956, p. 1.

Chapter VII. The Ascendancy of Women's Status
Through the Women's Movement

1. "How Should Family Women Better Serve Socialist Reconstruction," *Hsin Chung-kuo fu-nü* (New Chinese Women), no. 10, October 1955, pp. 18–19.

2. *Shing-tao jih-pao*, Hong Kong, March 8, 1951, p. 2.

3. *Ta Kung Pao*, Hong Kong, March 8, 1951, p. 3.

4. *Ibid.*, August 20, 1951, p. 3.

5. *Ibid.*, March 8, 1951, p. 3.

6. *Nan-fang jih-pao*, Canton, April 14, 1950, p. 2.

7. *Shing-tao jih-pao*, March 8, 1951, p. 2.

8. *Hsin Chung-kuo fu-nü*, no. 10, October 1955, p. 28.

9. *Shing-tao jih-pao*, March 15, 1951, p. 2.

10. *Fu-nü tai-piao ta-hui tsu-chi kang-ning* (Principles of Organization of Conference of Women Representatives), Peking, 1950, ch. 1, article 2.

11. *Ibid.*, ch. 2, article 3, sections a, b, c and d.

12. *Ibid.*, ch. 2, article 8, sections a and b.

13. *Shing-tao jih-pao*, March 7, 1951, p. 2.

14. Liu Mien-chi, "The Necessity of Simultaneous Mobilization of Peasant Men and Women in Land Reform and of Effective Protection of Women's Legal Rights," *Hsin Chung-kuo fu-nü*, no. 25–26, 1951, p. 16.

15. Chang Yün, "Women's Movement in Shanghai in the Past Year and its Mission from Now On," *Hsien-tai fu-nü* (Modern Women), no. 10, September 1950, p. 6.

16. "A Letter from the Preparatory Committee for the Democratic Women's League of Hunan," *Hsin Chung-kuo fu-nü*, no. 11, November 1952, p. 36.

17. *Ta Kung Pao*, Hong Kong, March 13, 1951.

18. *Wah-kiu yat-po*, Hong Kong, March 7, 1951, p. 2.

19. Lo Ch'iung, "The Principles of Development of the Chinese Women's Movement," *Hsin Chung-kuo fu-nü*, no. 1, January 1953, p. 31.

20. Teng Yung-ch'ao, "New China's Women Advance Again and Again," *Jen-min jih-pao* (People's Daily), September 24, 1952, p. 2.

21. *Nan-fang jih-pao*, May 2, 1951, p. 2.

22. *Shing-tao jih-pao*, April 18, 1951, p. 2.

23. *Ibid.*, August 20, 1951, p. 2.

24. *Ibid.*, June 17, 1951, p. 6.

25. "How Should Family Women Better Serve Socialist Reconstruction," *Hsin Chung-kuo fu-nü*, no. 10, October 1955, pp. 18–23.

26. *Jen-min jih-pao*, editorial, April 8, 1956, p. 1.

Chapter VIII. Changing Family Economic Structure

1. John L. Buck, *Land Utilization in China, Statistics*, Chicago, 1937, pp. 301–303.

2. *Ibid.*, p. 303.

3. *Ibid.*

4. *The Civil Code of the Republic of China* (tr. Hsia Tsin-lin), Shanghai, 1931, Article 1138.

5. *Chih-hsing hun-yin fa wen ta* (Questions and Answers on the Enforcement of the Marriage Law), Central People's Committee on Laws and Institutions, Peking, 1950, pp. 41–66.

6. *Hun-yin fa hsuan-ch'uan shou-ts'e* (Propaganda Handbook of the Marriage Law), 1951, pp. 31–32; *T'u-ti Kai-ke Chung-yao Wen-hsien Lei-chih* (Collection of Important Documents on Land Reform), Peking, 1951, p. 69.

7. *Hsin Chung-kuo fu-nü* (New Chinese Women), no. 25–26, December 1951, p. 28.

8. *Hun-yin fa hsuan-ch'uan shou-ts'e* see note 6, p. 39.

9. *Shing-tao jih-pao*, Hong Kong, March 18, 1951, p. 2.

10. *Jen-min jih-pao* (People's Daily), Peking, March 7, 1951, p. 2.

11. "How Should Family Women Better Serve Socialist Reconstruction" (A Conclusion from Discussions), *Hsin Chung-kuo fu-nü*, no. 10, October 1955, pp. 18–19.

12. *Hsin Chung-kuo fu-nü*, editorial, no. 3, March 1956, p. 4.

13. New China News Agency (hereafter referred to as NCNA), September 24, 1956.

14. Ts'ai Ch'iang, "Take a Further Step to Organize the Masses of Women under the Flag of Patriotism," *Hsin Chung-kuo yueh-k'an* (New China Monthly), no. 19, March 1951, pp. 1020–1021.

15. NCNA, September 13, 1956.

16. Fan Fu, "Peasant Women's Contribution to Land Reform," *Hsin Chung-kuo fu-nü*, no. 15, September 1950, pp. 12–13.

17. *Jen-min jih-pao*, March 5, 1951, p. 1.

18. *Ibid.*, March 7, 1951, p. 2.

19. *Shing-tao jih-pao*, Hong Kong, March 8, 1951, p. 2.

20. Fan Fu, cited note 16; also *Wah-kiu yat-po*, Hong Kong, March 13, 1951.

21. *Jen-min jih-pao*, March 5, 1951, p. 1.

22. *Ta Kung Pao*, Hong Kong, March 4, 1953, p. 2.

23. See note 11.

24. *Jen-min jih-pao*, May 16, 1956.

25. "Let Us Concentrate on the Home-Chore Problem of the Women Textile Workers," the Department of Woman Labor, All-China Labor Federation, *Hsin Chung-kuo fu-nü*, no. 25–26, December 1951, pp. 8–9.

26. "Various Means of Child Care for Working Mothers," Democratic Women's League of Tientsin, *Hsin Chung-kuo fu-nü*, no. 8, August 1952, p. 10.

27. *Jen-min jih-pao*, December 14, 1951, p. 4.

28. "For a General Development of Child Welfare Enterprises," Child Welfare Department, All-China Democratic Women's League, *Hsin Chung-kuo fu-nü*, no. 25–26, December 1951, pp. 12–13.

29. *Ta Kung Pao*, Hong Kong, April 29, 1953, p. 3.

30. Hsü Chuan, *Jen-min jih-pao*, letter from a reader, March 8, 1952, p. 2.

31. *Jen-min jih-pao*, August 5, 1955, p. 2.

32. NCNA, September 26, 1956.

33. *Kung-shang jih-pao*, June 25, 1956, p. 3.

34. NCNA, September 24, 1956.

35. *Ibid.*, September 26, 1956.

36. Huang Lien-hai, "A Survey of Early Marriages among Young Factory Workers," *Chung-kuo ch'ing-nien pao* (Chinese Youth), Peking, September 6, 1956.

37. NCNA, March 7, 1959.

38. *Ibid.*, March 5, 1959.

39. *Ibid.*, March 6, 1959.

40. *Ibid.*, March 7, 1959.

41. See note 28.

42. *Chieh-fang jih-pao*, Shanghai, March 14, 1951, p. 2.

43. "Popularize the Experience of the 30,000-odd Mutual-aid Child Care Units," the Democratic Women's League of Northern Anhwei, *Hsin Chung-kuo fu-nü*, no. 8, August 1952, pp. 12–13.

44. *Jen-min jih-pao*, May 29, 1955, p. 6.

45. *Jen-min jih-pao*, editorial, May 16, 1956, p. 1.

46. *Ibid.*

47. Yen Ling, "Cooperativization Is the Road to Thorough Emancipation for Rural Women," *Hsin Chung-kuo fu-nü*, no. 12, September 1955, pp. 3–4.

48. Lo Chin-fan, "Whither Private Enterprise?" *Nan-fang jih-pao*, Canton, August 6, 1950, p. 1.

49. "Graphic Presentation of the First Five-year Plan," *Jen-min jih-pao*, July 8, 1955, p. 2.

50. Li Fu-ch'un, "Report on the First Five-year Plan," *Jen-min jih-pao*, July 8, 1955, p. 2.

51. *Jen-min jih-pao*, January 22, 1956, p. 2.

52. Chou En-lai, "Report on the Second Five-year Plan," NCNA, September 20, 1956.

53. NCNA, September 10, 1956.

54. *Ta Kung Pao*, Hong Kong, April 28, 1956, p. 1.

55. Chou En-lai, see note 52; also, Chinese Communist Party Congress, "Proposals on the Second Five-year Plan for the Development of the National Economy," NCNA, September 28, 1956.

56. Chou En-lai, cited note 52; also, comments and reports on the second five-year plan, *Wah-kiu yat-po*, Hong Kong, October 13 and 15, 1955, p. 4.

57. Liao Lu-yen, "The Great Victory for Three Years of Land Reform Movement," *Hua-ch'iao jih-pao*, New York, October 22–24, 1952.

58. "Is There Any Difference between a Higher Agricultural Producers' Cooperative and a Collective Farm?" *Cheng-chih hsueh-hsi* (Political Study), no. 6, June 1956.

59. Wang Keng-chin, "The Great Accomplishments of New China's Agriculture in the Past Three Years," *Hsin Chung-kuo fu-nü*, no. 10, 1952, pp. 28–29; Mao Tse-tung, "On the Problem of Cooperativization of Agriculture," *ibid.*, no. 10, October 1955, pp. 2–8.

60. Chou En-lai, cited note 52.

61. Liao Lu-yen, "Explanations on the Model Regulations for the Advanced Type of Agricultural Producers' Cooperatives," *Jen-min jih-pao*, June 17, 1956, p. 2.

62. Liao Lu-yen, "The Task for 1959 on the Agricultural Front," *Hung Ch'i* (Red Flag), no. 1, January 1959.

63. *Ibid.*

64. Mao Tse-tung, "On the Problem of Cooperativization of Agriculture," cited note 59.

65. Ronald Hsia, *Economic Planning in Communist China*, Institute of Pacific Relations, New York, 1955, especially ch. 5.

66. NCNA, September 11, 13, October 3, 1956; also, Chou En-lai, cited note 52.

67. State Statistical Bureau figures released by NCNA, December 31, 1957.

68. *Ibid.*, April 17, 1959.

69. *Chieh-fang jih-pao*, Shanghai, March 25, 1952, p. 2.

70. "Agricultural Cooperatives and Mutual-aid Organizations Should Practice the Principle of Same Pay for Same Work," *Hsin Chung-kuo fu-nü*, no. 9, September 1952, p. 6.

71. *Nung-yeh sheng-ts'an Hu-tso-tsu Ts'an-k'ao Tzu-liao* (Source Book on Mutual-aid Teams of Agricultural Production), vol. 1, Ministry of Agriculture, Peking, 1952, p. 9.

72. *Chieh-fang jih-pao*, Shanghai, March 22, 1952, p. 2.

73. *Jen-min jih-pao*, May 15, 1955; also, May 20, 1956, p. 2.

74. "The Growth of Hanyin Mutual-aid Team," *Hsin kuan-ch'a* (New Observer), Peking, February 16, 1952, pp. 18–19.

75. Marion Levy, *Family Revolution in Modern China*, Cambridge, 1949, ch. 8.

Chapter IX. The Shifting Center of Loyalty

1. Liang Shu-ming, *Chung-kuo min-tsu tzu-chiu yün-tung chui-hou chi chüeh-wu* (The Final Awakening of the Chinese National Self-salvation Movement), Peking, 1932, pp. 67–68.

2. *Ibid.*, p. 70.

3. Li Wen, "The New Mission of Youth Organizations," *Nan-fang chou-k'an* (Nan-fang Weekly), Canton, no. 37, October 1, 1952, p. 6.

4. *Chieh-fang jih-pao* (Liberation Daily), Shanghai, April 28, 1952, p. 3.

5. *Lun Yü*, Book VIII, ch. 18.

6. Li Kuo-hsin, "How I Weathered my Family Crisis," *Ta Kung Pao*, Hong Kong, April 18, 1951, p. 2.

7. *Shing-tao jih-pao*, Hong Kong, April 15, 1951, p. 2.

8. Ch'en Yi-ching, "Some Experiences in Mobilizing Wives of Workers and Staff Members to Participate in the Struggle against Corruption," *Hsin Chung-kuo fu-nü* (New Chinese Women), no. 25–26, December 1951, p. 8.

9. Wen Ying, "He Is Not my Husband, but a Thief Stealing State Property," *ibid.*, p. 10.

10. *Chieh-fang jih-pao*, March 10, 1952, p. 1.

11. *Jen-min jih-pao* (People's Daily), Peking, December 1, 1951, p. 3.

Chapter X. Secularization of the Family Institution

1. *Hun-yin fa hsuan-ch'uan shou-ts'e* (Propaganda Handbook of the Marriage Law), Peking, 1951, p. 25.

2. *Jen-min jih-pao* (People's Daily), Peking, July 3, 1955, p. 2.

Chapter XI. Disorganization of the Clan

1. Hu Hsien-chin, *Common Descent Group in China and Its Functions,* New York, 1948, chs. 1 to 2.

2. "Ancestral Clannish Attitude and Feudalistic Influence Collapsed under the Reexamination of Land Reform in Tzu-chien Village of Yukan County, Kiangsi Province," *Ch'ang-chiang jih-pao,* Hankow, January 10, 1952, p. 2.

3. *Nan-fang chou-k'an* (Nan-fang Weekly), Canton, no. 9, March 3, pp. 14–15.

4. See ch. 4 for figures and cases of women rising to political power.

5. Hu Hsien-chin, cited note 1.

6. *Ta Kung Pao,* Hong Kong, April 23, 1956, p. 1.

7. *Ch'ang-chiang jih-pao,* January 12, 1952, p. 2.

8. *Wah-kiu yat-po,* Hong Kong, April 18, 1955, p. 4.

Chapter XII. Ideology and Propaganda in the Change of the Family

1. *Jen-min jih-pao* (People's Daily), Peking, October 28, 1951, p. 3.

2. T'ao Chih, *Hun-yin hsin kuan-tien* (New View of Marriage), Peking, 1951, p. 58.

3. *Ch'ang-chiang jih-pao,* Hankow, February 9, 1952, p. 4; "Commentaries on Cultural Life," *Jen-min jih-pao,* December 4, 1951, p. 3; "A Report on Hui-an County of Fukien Province," *Hsin Chung-kuo yueh-k'an* (New China Monthly), no. 24, October 1951, p. 1050.

4. Tso Chung-fen, "Representatives' Conference of Model Laborers Implementing the Marriage Law in Lushan County," *Hsin Chung-kuo fu-nü* (New Chinese Women), no. 12, December 1952, pp. 10–12.

5. *Jen-min jih-pao,* December 4, 1951, p. 3; New China News Agency, July 25, 1956.

6. Ts'ai Ch'iang, "The Work of the All-China Democratic Women's League during the Past Year and Its Main Missions for This Winter and the Coming Spring," *Hsin Chung-kuo fu-nü,* no. 15, October 1950, pp. 19–21.

7. See the directives issued to local branches and membership by the Youth Federation and the Democratic Women's League, *Hun-yin fa chih ch'i yu-kuan wen-chien* (The Marriage Law and Related Documents), Peking, 1950, pp. 14–18.

8. *Ibid.,* pp. 11–13, 19.

9. Tso Chung-fen (cited note 4), pp. 9–10.

10. There was the case of a female party member claiming to have changed the traditional attitude of a whole village towards the problem of family and marriage, reported in the *Chieh-fang jih-pao,* Shanghai, January 14, 1952, p. 2.

11. *Jen-min jih-pao,* October 28, 1951, p. 3.

12. *Ibid.*

13. *Chieh-fang jih-pao,* February 9, 1952, p. 3.

14. "The Propaganda Shed for the Marriage Law in Wenteng County of Shantung Province," *Hsin Chung-kuo fu-nü,* no. 24, October 1951, p. 1248.

15. *Jen-min jih-pao,* October 22, 1951, p. 3.

16. *Ibid.*

17. *Chieh-fang jih-pao,* August 9, 1951, p. 3.

Chapter XIII. Recession of the "High Tide" and Long Term Trends

1. "How Should Family Women Better Serve Socialist Reconstruction," *Hsin Chung-kuo fu-nü* (New Chinese Women), no. 10, October 1955, pp. 18–19.

2. Yen Ling, " 'Cooperativization' Is the Road to Thorough Emancipation for Rural Women," *Hsin Chung-kuo fu-nü*, no. 12, 1955, pp. 3–4.

3. Hsia Kuang, "The Vicissitudes of the *Popular Pictorial Edition of the Marriage Law*," *Hsin Chung-kuo fu-nü*, no. 10, October 1955, p. 22.

4. *Chung-kuo ch'ing-nien pao* (Chinese Youth), Peking, August 30, 1956.

5. *Ibid.*

6. F. Le Play, *Les Ouvriers Européens*, Tours, 1879, I, 457, quoted in Marion Levy, *Family Revolution in Modern China*, Cambridge, 1949, pp. 55–56.

7. Lin Chen, "Husband-wife Harmony and Harmony in the Whole Family," *Ch'ang-chiang jih-pao*, Hankow, February 4, 1952, p. 2; *Hun-yin fa hsuan-ch'uan shou-ts'e* (Propaganda Handbook of the Marriage Law), Peking, 1951, p. 62; Hsieh Chuio-tsai, "Let Us All Take Part in the Campaign to Implement the Marriage Law," *Hsin Chung-kuo fu-nü*, no. 10, October 1955, p. 19.

8. *Jen-min jih-pao* (People's Daily), Peking, June 13, 1953, p. 2.

9. Liu Lo-ch'ün, "Why Did Our Husband-wife Relationship Break Up?" *Hsin Chung-kuo fu-nü*, no. 11, November 1955, pp. 6–7.

Index

A Chinese Village
in Early
Communist Transition

C. K. YANG

A Chinese Village
in Early
Communist Transition

Preface and Acknowledgments

In China today some 80 per cent, or 500,000,000 of the country's 600,000,000 people, still make their living from agriculture, and most of these teeming millions of tillers of the soil are grouped into some 1,000,000 peasant villages. A compact group of houses hugging some winding streets, a population from a few scores to several thousand, and a broad enveloping belt of open fields — these are the physical components of the peasant village, in which flows a life of simplicity, hardship, and stability, but in which also brew forces that have toppled dynasties when miseries in agrarian life became humanly unbearable and uncontrollably widespread. It is now well recognized that it was the strength of such forces that carried the Communist revolution to its initial victory. What goes on within these seemingly simple peasant communities is likely to remain a vital factor affecting the social transformation of this ancient land.

It is the purpose of this volume to try to understand the problems of one of the innumerable Chinese peasant villages by analyzing its pre-Communist pattern of life and studying the changes that the Communist revolution has wrought. The emphasis here is on an analytical presentation of the major aspects of village life and recent changes in them, not on the formulation of a body of abstract principles governing the structure and functions of the present village.

In this study the village community is conceived of as an aggregate of peasant population nucleated in a compact settlement and integrated into functional groups by a system of institutions. Our focus is on the system of institutions and the related configuration of social groups in the village, particular emphasis being placed on the functional interdependence between different aspects of life which gives rise to the complex interrelationship among the institutions. Such interrelationship is seen in the overlapping membership of such social groups as the peasant farm organization, the family, and the local power groups. Through this network of institutional interdependence the individuals and groups operate together as a consistent system and the village community develops a functional unity.

While the functional unity of the institutions and the social groups makes the village a distinct entity, it does not isolate the village from social and cultural ties with the regional and national community.

Being a part of a complex civilization and a component of a state, as Robert Redfield points out (*Peasant Society and Culture,* Chicago, 1956, chapters i and ii), the peasant village receives influence from and reacts to developments in the greater communities of the surrounding region and the nation. Cognizance of the interrelationship between the village and the greater community is vital to the understanding of both the village's traditional pattern of life and its recent upheavals. Without the national influences the peasantry would not have developed and maintained the highly sophisticated Confucian ideology so vital to the operation of the village social order; the Communist revolution was not automatically generated within the peasant villages.

Our analysis of one village located in the suburban area of a southern city has its obvious limitations as a reflection of the broad problems of rural China in both the pre-Communist and the Communist periods. As a vast and geographically variegated country with only a primitive system of transportation and communication in the past centuries, China has long bred profound localism and regionalism in different sections of the country. The representative character of one village is severely restricted by prominent local differences. But the significance of sample studies is by no means diminished. A necessary step in understanding a country divided by localism is to establish the local types; and adequate study of each divergent part is an obvious requisite for proper understanding of the whole. Hence there is typological significance in the present study of a representative of southern suburban villages.

A suburban village is characterized by its proximity to the city market and its susceptibility to urban social and political influences. With the rapid development of modern means of transportation and communication, especially under the organized efforts of the Communists, urban economic, social, and political influences are being brought nearer to an increasing number of outlying villages, a condition which tends to extend some of the characteristics of the suburban village to the interior rural communities and to increase the representative significance of the recent changes pictured in our sample. Furthermore, we cannot ignore the national components of the village culture and organization which impart universal significance to many aspects of our sample. Examples of such components include the gentry leadership and the Confucian ideology in the pre-Communist period and the national uniformity of a large proportion of the Communist devices being instituted into the village life.

Nevertheless, the presence of local characteristics is kept in view in the analysis of our village. Effort is made in this volume to point out whether, so far as we can observe, certain aspects of life in the village are unique to the locality or common to other parts of China. Whenever data are available, conditions in this village are compared with those in other localities in order to increase the usefulness of this particular sample in the interpretation of China's national problems.

This study originated in 1948 as a field-work device to acquaint students in sociology courses with social reality. Sending the students to study various aspects of life in a village small enough to be manageable within limited research resources served as a live demonstration of sociological concepts from characteristics of population aggregates to the functioning of the institutional framework of a community. Our field work lasted from 1948 to 1951. When the Communists took over the territory in October 1949, we had covered one year of the village under Nationalist rule. After the Communists' arrival, field investigation became increasingly hazardous and difficult. Since we had reported the project to the subdistrict government ruling that village, we were permitted to continue our work, although with reduced intensity. Since 1951 our information has been gleaned from the Communist and non-Communist press. The Chinese press in Hong Kong contains considerable information about the general locality in which our village is located; and, although such press reports do not concern our particular village directly, they reveal conditions in many neighboring communities which serve as a close reflection of possible developments in our village. Also, since our field work terminated in 1951, we turned to the Communist and non-Communist press for national and regional information concerning the important subject of collectivization in order to present the general picture of a drastic change of which our village is a part.

Although Communist regulations compelled us to leave the entire written record of the field investigation in Communist China, the field information in this volume was reproduced from memory in 1952, when impressions of the three years of continuous contacts with the village life were still fresh. The writer is confident that important events and significant situations as presented here are faithful to reality. There are, however, certain limitations on the accuracy of statistical data. The over-all figures, such as the total acreage of land and the total number of persons and families in the village, are well remembered, but subdivisions of these figures and other statistical details are retained in memory only in terms of general proportions. Where such quantitative data are needed for tracing out a statistical pattern, our findings are stated in approximate proportions or percentages, and actual figures are deduced from them. These figures have been checked against comparable figures available for neighboring villages and the surrounding districts, and against regional and national averages found in the Communist and non-Communist press. The names of the persons and the village are fictitious, but the general location of the site and the social situations and concrete events are factual.

The handling of Chinese units of weights and measures and value presents some difficulties. In measurement, one acre is equivalent to 6.6 mow. In weight, the local unit is the traditional catty (*ssu ma chin*), which is equivalent to 1.33 pounds. Whenever convenient, the English equivalent is given in the text. The matter of monetary unit before 1954 offers an almost insurmountable difficulty owing to the unbridled inflation in the postwar period. In the rural districts, and even in the cities, the people had become inflation-wise in those years and used the weight of unhusked rice as the standard of commodity values in preference to the astronomical and daily fluctuating figures of the paper currency. Thus the price for a day's farm labor or for a boatload of fertilizer was quoted in so many catties of unhusked rice. From the fall of 1950 on, the Communist government succeeded in harnessing the inflation and effected stability in its currency, but the astronomical figures were inconvenient to use in this study. The new Communist yuan after 1954 returned the monetary unit to the small denominations comparable to the prewar currency. In 1957 one United States dollar was exchanged for about 2.60 yuan in the Hong Kong market, and this rate of exchange is used in this study.

In preparing this volume for publication, I wish to express my indebtedness to the Trustees of Lingnan University, to the Center for International Studies of the Massachusetts Institute of Technology, to the Rockefeller Foundation, and to the Social Science Research Council for their generous financial support of the research and writing, and to the University of Pittsburgh for partial relief from teaching duties during the revision of the manuscript. I am deeply grateful to Dr. and Mrs. Robert Redfield for their encouragement, their reading of the manuscript, and their valuable suggestions for its improvement. I am particularly indebted to Mr. Richard W. Hatch of the Massachusetts Institute of Technology for his careful editing of the entire manuscript and for his advice in strengthening the organization of the materials. I also wish to thank Mr. Howard Linton of Columbia Uni-

Preface and Acknowledgments

versity Library for his kindness in providing library resources. An expression of deep gratitude must be extended to my wife, Louise Chin Yang, for her constant encouragement and untiring assistance in improving and preparing the work for publication. To my family, special mention is made for their patience in enduring the difficulties of family living that writing books involves.

C. K. YANG

University of Pittsburgh
March 1958

Contents

PART I

The Pre-Communist Village

CHAPTER I

The Village of Nanching

T HE SITE of our study, Nanching (literally, the Scene of the South), is located in the vicinity of Canton, the capital city of Kwangtung Province, near the northern edge of the rich Pearl River Delta. The natural and human environment of this village partake of the characteristics of its broader regional setting.

Climatically, Kwangtung Province is a part of tropical China, and the village is a little over twenty miles south of the Tropic of Cancer. Here "the year may be divided into three seasons. There is a long wet summer with excessive humidity and considerable heat from the middle of April to the middle of October, then a relatively dry, cool winter with pleasant days to the middle of February, followed by two months of transition with foggy and muggy weather." [1] In the vicinity of Canton, the average temperature during the coolest months of December, January, and February rests in the upper fifties (degrees Fahrenheit), and it rises to the upper eighties and lower nineties during the hot months of June, July, and August. Although the average summer temperature is not too high, the excessive humidity makes the heat extremely uncomfortable. The winter is so mild that killing frost is uncommon, and snow is unknown to the inhabitants of Nanching.[2]

Precipitation is derived from the monsoon and occasional typhoons from the ocean to the south. The province is one of the wettest in China, and the total annual rainfall in the vicinity of Nanching is about 66 inches. Therefore the growing season for Nanching extends throughout the year, permitting the maturation of many crops. Abundance of precipitation makes it suitable for the planting of rice as the main crop, putting the village community into the rice region of China.

Topographically, Kwangtung is a mountainous province of the South China coast where, according to the Liangkwang Geological

Survey, less than a third of the land is cultivable and less than one sixth of the area is under cultivation. That survey would set the cultivated area of the province at 17.7 per cent, which is the average for China's rice region,[3] as against 19.6 per cent for China as a whole. A report of the Ministry of Agriculture and Commerce put the cultivated land of this region as low as 8 per cent of the total area.[4] The population of the province in 1951 was estimated to be 26,000,000,[5] giving an average density of 285 persons per square mile for the province as a whole and 3,494 persons per square mile of crop area.[6] The heavy pressure of the man-land ratio upon the livelihood of the people in this region is obvious.

Our Nanching village is located in the Pearl River Delta, where flat cultivable land is more abundant than anywhere else in the entire province. The delta is an alluvial plain of 2,890 square miles, of which about three-fourths are arable. The general population density for this delta land reaches "the amazing concentration of 3,100 people for every square mile."[7] The delta is made up of numerous low hills of red sandstone enveloped by podzolized red earth, which is a red acid soil of low native fertility with strongly expressed horizons of eluviation and illuviation of clays.[8] Nevertheless, because of the hot climate and heavy rain, and because of the intensive fertilization, the soil is made to provide a multi-crop agricultural economy for the support of its population.

In spite of the heavy population pressure, the province as a whole and the Pearl River Delta in particular have escaped the catastrophic famines which periodically befall many localities of North China. The abundance of precipitation and the year-round growing season have at least provided subsistence for the majority of the local population, and the local history of Panyü county, in which the village of Nanching is located, discloses no record of famine for the past two hundred and fifty years.[9] There have been individual cases of starvation due to crop failure, and peasant riots caused by food shortages have occurred; but on the whole, human catastrophes such as destruction from war and exploitation by economic classes, rather than natural calamities such as drought or floods, have been the historic causes of widespread misery and death. Compared to many other parts of China, it must be said that the regional setting of Nanching is "generously endowed by Heaven."

Economically, the province is characterized by a high degree of urbanization. In addition to Canton with its population of about 1,250,000 in 1948 and 1,789,000 in 1957, as announced by the Office of

Population Investigation of the Canton Municipal People's Council on November 5, 1957, there are at least twelve towns with over 100,000 population, and a large number of smaller ones. The fact that the nonfarming population is about 33 per cent of the province's total population, compared to about 27 per cent for China as a whole,[10] reflects the high development of commerce and native industry in the province. In its agricultural economy, Kwangtung historically ranked among the highest in tenancy, with over 40 per cent of its peasants belonging to the tenant class, compared to 20 per cent for North China.[11] Access to the ocean, the greater development of commerce and industry, and the high percentage of tenancy were correlated factors that affected the life of the people.

Cultural and political isolation has long been a characteristic ascribed to this province by students of Chinese history and geography. True, the province is fenced off by a barrier of mountains in the north and the Pacific Ocean to the south. Historically, it was the southern frontier set apart from the other provinces of China. Politically, the central authority of Peking was thinned to a negligible degree when it reached down here by way of the extended lines of primitive transportation through difficult mountain passes. It was a popular ground to which exiles were banished from the imperial court, and it was frequently a haven for political refugees escaping from wars and dynastic purges of the northern centers of power struggle. Political integration of the territory with the central government was not effectively tightened until the seventeenth or even the eighteenth century.

Even in modern times the political autonomy of the territory, particularly in the mountainous countryside, has always been stronger than in many other parts of China. All of the major modern revolutions have originated here. The Taiping Rebellion and the Hundred-Days Reform of the nineteenth century, the Republican revolution of 1911, the Second Revolution that led to the establishment of the Nationalist government, the Canton Commune, and the first "red area" of Haifeng and Lufeng in southern Kwangtung Province in the 1920's, which pioneered the present Communist revolution — all can be traced back to this general territory. It is true that once the revolutionary movements marched off to the main stage in the North, as they all inevitably did, Kwangtung Province would become the backwash of the revolutionary tide; but its comparative quietness and relative isolation from the main stage of power struggle would give it a chance to nurse another revolution so long as restive forces continued to operate.

Among the prominent factors in this situation are the mountains, which blocked political authority from the north, and access to the ocean to the south, which made possible contact with revolutionary ideas from foreign lands at the same time that it stimulated commerce and industry. The same factors helped to mold many other cultural and social phenomena more or less peculiar to this territory. The people in this province speak dialects different from Mandarin, the major vernacular of China, although they use the universal system of Chinese written language. They have cultivated many local folkways and mores not common in other sections of the country. Their clannish kinship system is stronger than that in most sections of China. They have sent millions of their sons to the "South Seas" (Southeast Asia), to America, Australia, and Europe, making Kwangtung the leading emigrant province.

But these items of local color should not obscure the fact that the political and economic life of the province has always flowed in the general bloodstream that circulates inside China as a whole, and that its local institutions rest upon the foundation of a national culture, including a national historical tradition, common to all parts of the country where the Chinese people dominate. Local restive forces, such as the peasants' problem of land ownership and the issue of modernizing traditional political and social institutions, have been parts of the national current; and the revolutions hatched locally eventually merged into the national scene, making local autonomy perform an incubating function for nationwide developments. The commercial and industrial developments in this province, and the remittances from its emigrants, have played a part in China's domestic economy and in the balance of her international trade. The divergent dialects that the people speak represent only different ways of pronouncing the same words commonly used in other parts of the country. The exceptionally strong development of the clan organization has operated on the kinship principles of Confucianism, nationally accepted for the guidance of kinship relations. The relatively marked development of a progressive and individualistic outlook, a characteristic commonly ascribed to the people of this province, has been subject to the control of the integrative values of the kinship system and social stratification, both of which followed the common pattern of China as a whole.

These characteristics of the national culture and the local variations are all ingrained in the life of the village community of Nanching.

Nanching is about five miles from the city of Canton, the political capital and the economic center of the province. Before 1936 the village was connected to the city only by dirt paths and short stretches of paths paved with large stone slabs. These paths, still in use in 1951, were generally less than five and sometimes only about two feet wide. All were too narrow for vehicle transportation; for, since animals of burden were not used in Nanching, probably due to the lack of pasture land to feed them, all land transportation was by human carriers using the carrying pole. The village is about a mile from the Pearl River, on the other side of which lies Canton city. A small stream connects the village with the Pearl River, but since the stream winds in a loop of about three and a half miles before reaching the river, direct water transportation from the village to the city was seldom used except for bulky cargo like fertilizer. Studies made elsewhere in China have shown that among all native modes of transportation the most expensive is the human carrier and the least expensive is water transportation, and that short-distance transportation to local markets using human carriers costs more per unit-distance than long-distance transportation to primary markets using animal and water conveyances.[12]

The short distance to the city, to which a round trip could be made by foot in half a day, has always subjected Nanching to many urban influences, such as the commercialization of agriculture, but over a long period the costliness of using human carriers limited the full operation of these influences and prevented the complete incorporation of the village's economy into the city economy. Consequently, the village was able to preserve its own identity as an agricultural community with a significant degree of self-sufficiency from the soil. This was especially so some decades ago. When the writer visited the village several times during the years 1924–1926, the life of the community appeared to be completely rural in character, with very little visible trace of urban influence.

But the influence of the city crept in steadily. In the late 1920's the commercial and industrial development of Canton was accelerated, and the use of mechanical transportation steadily increased. A motor road built through the edge of the village now connects it with the city and the surrounding territory, and in 1951 a regular bus service operated, with a station just outside the village gate, charging a fare low enough for the villagers to pay. During harvesting seasons trucks came to the village at regular intervals to transport locally grown produce to the city for individual peasants who paid by every 100 catties of weight, the peasant riding free. In addition, motor launches had come into operation between the city and a village on the bank of the Pearl River, and villagers from Nanching and the surrounding communities rode on them and used them to transport produce to the city. Both passenger and cargo traffic were facilitated by the greater speed and lower costs, but the use of human carriers was still common in 1951, for the profit from agriculture was so low that the peasants frequently could not afford even the lowered cost of mechanical transportation or any other form of transportation which took money out of their meager earnings.

Once in the city, the Nanching peasant and his produce had access to transportation and communication to the other provinces of China as well as to the outside world. To the north of the city the Canton – Hankow Railroad in 1937 tunneled through the mountain passes where human carriers used to struggle over the narrow paths on precipitous slopes of towering peaks, and this line linked the city with railway systems in other parts of China. One could go to Shanghai in three and a half days and to Peking in five. At high tide coastal steamers under 3,000 tons connected the city directly with all coastal cities of China. Some eighty miles to the south lies the great commercial center of Hong Kong, connected with Canton by both railroad and steamer, and from Hong Kong modern transportation and communication were available to all parts of the world. Villagers from Nanching could go to Hong Kong well within a day; and goods could be transported almost as fast. Through these arteries of transportation and communication flowed economic and social influences from the outside world into the village life of Nanching.

About half a mile east of Nanching is the little market town of Pingan Chen with approximately 2,500 population in 1950. It had a town market that met every five days where the surrounding villagers came to buy and sell. There were about forty stores selling such daily necessities as groceries, dry goods, cotton, baskets, and bamboo articles. A small group of industries included two machine mills milling rice for the peasants, three or four small handweaving factories turning out cloth of a coarse grade, three masonry and carpentry shops doing construction and repair work for the surrounding villages, and two bamboo shops weaving bamboo strips into baskets and other articles. The town also had one large and two small tea houses which sold food to the marketing people, and more important, served as social centers for the more prosperous villagers within a radius of about two miles. The town was also a little local political center, for located here was the office of the ch'ü, a subdistrict government of the Canton municipal authority, administering the public affairs of the surrounding villages, including Nanching.

This market town supplied the bulk of Nanching's immediate commercial needs. The rice stores and the rice mills also bought a sizable proportion of Nanching's rice for shipment to Canton. Some of the pigs raised in the village were sold to the two meat stores in the town. The periodic market performed the functions of supplying the surrounding population with food and miscellaneous articles and providing the peasants with an opportunity to sell their produce, eggs, and poultry directly to consumers. Thus, economically, the town with its market provided a trading center for the local population and a transmitting point for the flow of goods and finances between Canton and Nanching, for from Canton the town bought its stock and to Canton it sent its goods collected from the countryside. So, indirectly, the economic influence of Canton was brought to the very door of Nanching.

Part of this influence was expressed in the high price of agricultural land in Nanching, in the heavy population the land supported, and in the high percentage of tenancy, as will be discussed later. Before Communism it was a nationwide characteristic of China that agricultural land in the vicinity of large cities commanded a premium price. Besides its proximity to the city, Nanching has a favorable location in the delta. Floods from heavy spring and summer rains pose a frequent threat in the Pearl River Delta, where most of the land is low and subjected to frequent inundation by the rising river. Many of the fields of the alluvial plain have been reclaimed from the shallow mud flats along the river bank by dikes, and in the past every year large numbers of weak dikes were broken by raging currents, causing extensive damage to the fields. But the land of Nanching and its vicinity is just high enough to escape flooding without being so high as to suffer from a lack of irrigation water. The alluvial soil is good, and with intensive fertilization, can be made to produce heavy crops with reliable harvests which enjoy a nearby market.

In terms of its principal characteristics and problems, Nanching at the time our study was made was typical of the villages near large southern cities in the pre-Communist period. That Nanching, despite its proximity to the city, retained its identity as an agricultural community deriving its livelihood primarily from the soil was fully evident from a panorama of the local scene. If the locality were visited in May or June, when the pouring rains had mitigated, one would see the surrounding countryside as a deep green carpet of thriving crops interspersed with trees and villages, villages that lay one or at most two miles apart. It was a thickly settled land in which stood the compact group of houses that was the village of Nanching in 1951.

There were about two hundred houses altogether, tightly grouped to form a well-defined outline roughly the shape of a T. Enveloping the houses was a broad belt of open land consisting of paddy fields and vegetable gardens, which were partitioned into numerous tiny patches by low banks of packed earth and crisscrossed by irrigation ditches flanked by dikes, also of packed earth. Along the dikes and some of the low partition banks tropical fruit trees such as lichee, guava, and peach had been planted. Amidst the low-lying fields there were occasional patches of higher land covered with more fruit trees, and nestled among the trees were one or two scattered farm houses. About thirty small ponds, some lying close to the edge of the village site, were scattered through the fields. These ponds, located on low ground where rain water collected, supplied the needs of the villagers in their daily life as well as part of the irrigation water for the fields. A more important source of water was the stream that ran along the southern and eastern boundary of the village's fields. One branch of this stream meandered through the fields into the village, and at high tide small boats and junks could be rowed into the heart of the village.

From the low land along the main stream the ground gradually rose toward the west and the north until it merged into the low hills of red earth that formed the western and northern boundaries of the village's fields. The rising land was terraced into fields, and where it was too high for water to reach, it was used for pasturing and as burial grounds. Studding the hillsides were numerous graves, some old and some new, some with elaborate tombs, but most of them indicated by simple stone markers. From this semicircle of hillside the spirits of the dead ancestors could watch their descendants living in the village where they once lived, working in the fields where they once worked, and struggling with the natural and human forces with which they too had contended for nearly a thousand years.

The village houses, the enveloping fields and vegetable gardens, the ponds and ditches and the streams, the interspersed fruit trees, and the graves on the hills wove out a picture that the Chinese for centuries have come to call "t'ien, yuan, lu, mo" (fields, gardens, houses, graves), a classical expression signifying "homeland" or the roots of life. These were the primary elements in which the deep and continuous roots of the community life of Nanching were anchored. With these elements the community became a place where people were born, struggled for sustenance, and died, leaving behind descendants to carry on the recurring cycle. And the village became the ku hsiang, "the old homeland" with which the traditional Chinese identified the material interest and sentimental attachment of his entire social existence. It is plain that such a community as Nanching was not the result of a sudden conglomeration of immigrants from many sources. Rather, it was the product of a centuries-old process of marriage and reproduction on the same plot of land, and the foundation of the community organization rested on the tightly knit kinship group.

Nanching was composed mainly of two large clans, the Wong clan and the Lee clan, which together claimed the overwhelming majority of the village population and dominated the affairs of the community. In addition, there were three minor clans, the Chen clan, the Chang clan, and the Ho clan, each of which was numerically small, all occupying the eastern periphery of the village. Although the minor clans had little or no voice in community affairs, they were recognized as established and integral parts of the village. Thus, characteristically, this was a multi-clan village. Aside from the members of the clans, Nanching had a few families and individuals of other surnames who were temporary residents of the village or agricultural laborers from outside, none of whom owned land or a house in the village, and all of whom were regarded by the villagers as "floating elements," "sojourners," or "guests" whose roots of life did not belong there. Above all, the basic groups that made up the village were biological in character, bound by common origin and marriage and defined by patrilineal surnames, and membership in them was not open to subscription. Hence, as a general rule, the village as a unit of permanent community life was closed to outsiders.

Between members of different clans there was a clear demarcation, expressed not only in the independent centers of life within each clan and the inter-clan rivalry which was alive in practically everyone's mind, but also, and visibly, in the separation of living quarters within the village grounds. The Wong clan occupied the western half of the village, the Lee clan occupied the eastern half, and the three minor clans built their houses on the eastern edge. There were gates on the village streets separating the territories of the Wong and the Lee clans. The Ho clan had a gate on the main village street demarcating its own quarters, and each of the other two minor clans lived on its own street but without a separating gate. Each branch within a clan also had its own street, not always marked off by a gate. Thus the physical plan of the village was blocked out into many individual cells on a kinship basis. It is important to note that there was no clear demarcation between the fields of the clans, although there was a general concentration in one place of land that belonged to members of one clan; and there was buying and renting of land between members of different clans.

There is no accurate account of how far back the biological root of

life in Nanching can be traced. There seems to have been an ecological
succession of clans in the community. Old villagers said that in the dim
past there was a Hua clan and a Fang clan who inhabited the northern
end of the present village site. Apparently both of them were crowded
out by the late comers, and there were no descendants of either clan in
the village. The Lees were the oldest of the living groups in 1951. The
ancestral tablets of the most recent dead in the Lee's ancestral hall
showed the inscription of the forty-second generation from the first
ancestor who came to settle in the village, and the Lee's genealogy
showed that the first ancestor made his home here in the year 1091.[13]
Since the most recent dead of the Wong clan were recorded as members
of the thirty-seventh generation from the first settler, and there was
no genealogical record available, it seemed possible that this clan came
about one hundred years after the Lee clan. The minor clans came
later.

Settlement of this village by the Wongs and the Lees took place at a
time when the Chinese dynasty of Sung was hard pressed by northern
invaders, particularly the Mongols, and large numbers of Chinese
sought refuge in the mountainous frontier of Kwangtung Province.
As the Lee's genealogy traced their original home to Chu Lu county of
the present Hopei Province of North China, it is fully possible that
their ancestors were among the refugees trekking south during the
tragic years of the Sung period. The Wongs came from the southern
part of Shensi Province of North China, according to the old members
of that clan, but no further details were known. Nevertheless, coming
from North China, here they settled, worked the land, and multiplied
for over eight centuries. As they multiplied, and as surrounding settle-
ments closed in, they built dikes and filled in the shallow and rapidly
silting river banks to create more land. In 1951 the southwestern section
of the village's fields was a solid piece of well-cultivated land where
once were piers where boats used to dock. The latest action in building
land from the river took place in 1936, carrying on the ceaseless struggle between multiplying man and niggardly nature.

There is little doubt that the early settlers once had to face the pressure of indigenous aboriginals, for as late as the fifteenth century one
of the ancestors of the Lee clan was decorated by the local government
for a successful fight against the Miao tribes in the neighborhood. But
this phase of the settlement had been deeply buried in the past, leaving
no visible effect on the current life of the community. Whatever alien
influence Nanching may have been subjected to in the past, its mode
of life and culture were Chinese in character, having been modified

only to adapt itself to the exigencies of local conditions. This could be seen in the prominence of the ancestral halls that dominated all other buildings of the village, in the annual routine of work and recreation guided by the nationally used almanac (*t'ung shu* or *li shu*), in the traditional system of national values that helped bring up the young and determined the life outlook of the old. These were the national as well as the local roots of the community life of Nanching.

Our study of this Chinese village focuses on a time when for over half a century Nanching had been subjected to the strains and stresses of a changing world, but its people were still imbued with faith in their ancient system of life.

In a public bus plying between Nanching and Canton there was a sign painted immediately above the windows: "In case of accident, each rests with his own fate." That bus, a product of modern science and industrialism, was operated not according to a compatible rationalism which included such things as accident insurance, adequate mechanical inspection, and safety rules, but in the spirit of the ancient Chinese trust in fate. In a sense, that bus symbolized the situation in Nanching. The villagers by and large still embraced "fate" as a guide to their mental outlook, particularly in life's main crises. Fate was the most common explanation for their birth as a male or female, for the prominence or lowliness of their social situation, for the life or death of their parents and siblings, for the state of their own marriage, for the success or failure of their enterprise, for the joy or sorrow of their personal circumstances, as well as for their encounter with the greater forces such as wars, banditry, or floods. A large proportion of the adults still consulted geomancers and fortune tellers for a glimpse of their veiled "fate."

While there is a whole range of interpretations of such mysticism, the old concept of fate may be viewed as faith in the framework of the traditional Chinese culture with its strength undergirded by supernatural beliefs. This concept cannot be divorced from the concrete content of the traditional culture.

Disregarding the supernatural part for the moment, the villagers' deep faith in fate disclosed that the community life of Nanching was still deeply rooted in the traditional culture at a time in modern history when that culture was about to be subjected to the full force of Communism — that is, to an unprecedented revolutionary impact. It is the basic fact of historical climax that underlies all that follows here in our examination of a typical southern suburban Chinese village in transition.

CHAPTER II

Population Composition

POPULATION AND land are primary factors affecting the mode of life and its course of development in an agrarian community. Since this was especially true in Nanching, where the people's existence rested almost completely on the extraction of a livelihood from the soil with hand labor, the factor of land will be the subject of treatment for several subsequent chapters. Here we shall consider the size and composition of the village's population, the family as the basic unit of population, and the population as a working force based on the family as a primary working team.

Size, Density, and General Characteristics of the Local Population

In 1948 the population of Nanching was about 1,100 persons, divided into about 230 households. By 1951 about twenty people had been added to the village population, but the majority of these were emigrants who had returned to the village because of current disturbances in the cities; it was doubtful whether they would stay in the village permanently, the custom being for a Chinese to return to his native village only as a temporary haven when deprived of his livelihood in the city. Therefore, the figures of 1,100 persons and 230 families were still representative of the general situation and are used throughout this study.

The total area of the village land, exclusive of the village site, was approximately 1,400 mow or 233 acres, of which about 1,200 mow or a little less than 200 acres were crop land. There was, then, a general density of 3,200 persons per square mile of land owned by the villagers and a specific density of 3,520 persons per square mile of crop land. Taking 1,100 as the basic population figure, there was 1.08 mow or about one-sixth of an acre of crop land per capita. This seems to be in harmony with the general regional setting, particularly that of the

Pearl River Delta, for it compares closely with the figures of 3,495 people per square mile of crop land, with an average of 1.1 mow per capita for the Liangkwang region, and 3,100 people per square mile for the entire area of the delta, as mentioned by Cressey.[1] The population pressure here is apparent. But it is important to bear in mind that the pressure of the man-land ratio upon the actual life of the village operated through social institutions, especially that governing the ownership and use of land.

In the village's population males somewhat outnumbered females in the approximate ratio of 110:100 for all ages. This ratio was fairly normal for the populations of villages near large cities in many other parts of China.[2] The lower number of females is explained primarily by the higher death rate for female babies due to the great value placed upon male babies by the Chinese kinship system.[3]

In Nanching one found the same high value placed upon male babies, which led to negligence in caring for female babies in their most vulnerable period of life in an environment where modern medicine and sanitation were not developed. Cases of infanticide of female or male babies were not found in the period of our observation. That the excess of males was not greater may have been due to several factors. One was the emigration of male workers to cities and distant lands, leaving the women in the village. Another was the institution of "old maid houses," the membership of which consisted of many spinsters as well as divorced women who chose to return to their own parents' village to live. There were four "old maid houses" in the village, with a total membership of about sixty women. Another contributing factor was the development of embroidery as a subsidiary industry in the village. This kept many women of landless families, who otherwise were likely to seek work in the cities, in the village.

The age composition for both sexes was roughly as follows: under fifteen years, 30 per cent or 330 persons; between fifteen and fifty-five years, 55 per cent or 605 persons; over fifty-five years, 15 per cent or 165 persons. Somewhat less than half of the first group seemed to be under five years of age. Insofar as these figures are only general percentages reproduced from memory, it would be unsound to compare them with figures for other localities in China. Nevertheless, there was a smaller percentage under fifteen years than in many other Chinese rural communities.[4] This may be a reflection of a lower birth rate resulting from the year-round and seasonal emigration of many of the males of working age.

There were a fair number of old people of both sexes beyond the age of sixty in the village, one reason being that, although the young people might tend to emigrate, it was customary for the émigrées to return to the village to spend their old age. Among the ten or so persons beyond the age of seventy, one spoke fluent English, having worked in Singapore most of his life. A very poor widower who lived a miserable life by himself died in 1950 at the age of seventy-three. Although there were no available data on life expectancy, general observation seemed to show that the high frequency of deaths under the age of ten and especially under five was a preponderant factor in evaluating the longevity of the village's population. The villagers said that if a child passed his tenth year safely he had a fair chance of living to the prime of life, and that if he passed his fortieth year safely his chances of living another fifteen or twenty years were good.

The Wong clan had a hand-written genealogical record in which the date of birth and death of every male member was carefully kept. A calculation was made of the average span of life of those born in the middle of the eighteenth century and of those born during the last decade of the nineteenth century. The average life span of males of the first group was in the lower forties and that of the second group in the upper thirties. No similar calculation was made of the Lee or other clans because of the inaccessibility of their records. If the Wong record was representative, the shortening by three or four years of the average life span is significant; for it might reflect many phenomena, including the possible lowering of the standard of living for a large number of the peasants during recent times resulting from political disturbances, civil wars, social instability, and growing concentration of land ownership in the hands of a minority group.

Regarding the complex problem of the balance of births and deaths, the crude birth rate in the year 1949 was about twenty-one and the crude death rate about eighteen, giving an annual rate of growth of about three per thousand population. This was considerably lower than the rate of five per thousand as estimated by Ta Chen for China as a whole.[5] The birth and death rates were also lower than those in most rural communities where sample studies have been made.[6] The lower birth rate might reflect, among many factors, the seasonal and year-round emigration of male workers in the reproductive age. The absence of any epidemics in the village in 1949 contributed toward the comparatively low death rate. The record for one year is not enough to produce a conclusive picture on the complex problem of the balance of births and deaths, which are subject to such fluctuating factors as economic conditions, marriages, and epidemics; but there is little doubt that the village's population had been experiencing a long-term slow growth. Old villagers over sixty concurred in the impression that the village was more populous than when they were young; and the continuous efforts at extending farm land into the river substantiated their observation.

Size of Family

The 1,100-odd villagers of Nanching lived in some 230 separate families. Household is probably a more accurate term for these basic kinship units, for married brothers might have separate units of living but maintain very close family relations, particularly if their parents were still living. Nevertheless, in conformity to common usage, the term family is used here with the above qualifications.

The average size of a family was about 4.8 persons, excluding the year-round emigrants who visited the village only occasionally. The average family with no emigrants generally consisted of parents, their children, and at times the father's living parent or parents. For the majority, if the parents had two or more married sons, the parents lived with one married son's family but frequently visited the other sons' families. In common with other parts of China, the "large family" where parents and all married sons maintained a common unit of living was in the minority in this village, occurring mainly among the wealthy.

The size of the family increased with the accumulation of wealth. Among the resident villagers, Wong Han was a wealthy landlord with considerable landholdings in the village and an import and export firm in the city of Canton. A man in his early sixties, he lived with his wife, two concubines, two married sons and their wives, one unmarried son and two unmarried daughters, and three grandchildren, all as one household with common property. Although the married sons and their wives spent most of their time in their common city residence, family unity was effectively maintained among the fourteen members. This was one case of a wealthy family still maintaining its residence in the village. Other wealthy families had moved to Canton or Hong Kong to enjoy the luxuries of city life and the opportunity for urban enterprises, usually leaving behind a concubine and her young children to watch over the house and the land in the village. An example was Wong Hung, who had become a wealthy merchant in Hong Kong and left his third concubine and his twelfth and thirteenth child in the village. Thus his village household had only three members in spite of the large size of the family maintained by all the normal kinship ties and supported by common, undivided property. Two other wealthy families were in a similiar situation.

Descending the economic scale, we find Wong Yu, a middle peasant in his mid-forties, who farmed about three and a half acres of land and maintained a fairly comfortable standard of living compared to the general level of the village. He had a younger married brother who lived in a separate household; his mother had died about ten years previously, but his father, then in his early seventies, was still living. He and his wife and their four children lived with his old father; the family consisted· of seven members. Another middle-peasant family farming about two and a half acres of land consisted of husband, wife, and two young children, with both of the husband's parents dead, and one married younger brother living apart in another household. This family had four members. Further down the economic scale there were many families with unmarried sons who had already passed the customary marriage age, thus limiting the size of the family. Wong Mi was a case in point. He was already twenty-three, with both of his parents in their mid-sixties; but since the family was able to rent only an acre of poor land and could not finance his marriage, he lived with the old parents, and the family consisted of three members. Wong Chun, a landless peasant in his forties, had been in the same position when he lived with his aged parents ten years before, and now, both parents having died, he lived alone. There were ten or fifteen families in the village with single unmarried sons.

Even if the poor peasants were able to marry, poverty was a serious restricting factor on the size of their families. The village in 1949 had a high infant-mortality rate of about 300 per thousand live births. Owing to poor nutrition and lack of medical care, the incident of death bore more heavily upon the infants of the poor than upon the well-to-do. One poor family in 1948 consisted of a young couple and a four-year-old daughter. In 1949 a son was born. Less than two weeks after birth the mother had to work in the fields a good part of the day, leaving the baby home with the little sister. Being a child herself, the little sister could not care adequately for the baby and the baby cried a great deal. Since the mother did not have much milk, because of poor nutrition and hard work, she started to feed the baby mashed sweet potatoes when he was only two weeks old. In less than six months the baby died. Such occurrences were not uncommon with the poor, who considered it fortunate if they were able to raise two children to maturity out of six or seven live births. The mother has to work so hard that miscarriage is also a limiting factor in the birth rate of the poor. One mother in her fifties had been pregnant nine times, four pregnancies ending in miscarriage and only two infants reaching maturity. Another woman in her late fifties had had thirteen pregnancies, seven of which ended in miscarriage, with only one son and one daughter who attained maturity.

Although infanticide was not found in this village during the period of field investigation, there were cases of abandonment of babies, another limiting factor in the size of the poor family. One family consisting of only a young couple had a baby girl. Inquiring about the happy incident, we found the baby gone. The mother told us that the baby had been given to "a very good orphanage" a week after its birth; but later she admitted that the baby had been left at the door of a prosperous looking house in the city in the early hours of the morning because she had to work and could not care for it properly. She was offered a supply of milk powder in the hope of recovering the baby, but when the father went to the house to inquire, no one knew where it was.

The Working Force

Although not everyone of working age among the 1,100-odd people worked, there was no marked division of the population into a group who worked and a group who did not, as was the case in many other village communities.[7] Except for the winter months when farming was slack, one saw few idlers on the village streets during the daytime, almost everyone being busy with some task in the village or in the field. Even old people were engaged in light jobs in spite of their slow pace. Those who did not work were the young children who frolicked on the streets and the very old who dozed or chatted in the doorways of the spacious ancestral halls.

The only sign of the gentry group, whose tradition was to shun labor by hand, was seen in one unemployed teacher of traditional learning. He had formerly taught in the village traditional school, but since the establishment of a modern elementary school in the village he had been out of a job. He owned slightly less than two acres (12 mow) of poor land from which he collected rent, and he depended entirely upon this rent for his living. Since the rent was small, he lived a very meager life, but he refused to till the soil himself to better his own living.

Large landlords did not work at physical labor or engage directly and actively in agricultural enterprises. The large landlords in Nanching lived in the city, with the exception of Wong Han and his two grown-up sons. But even Wong Han and his sons lived in the city for a part of the year, and when they returned to the village it was generally only to collect rent and to see that their land was being properly cared for by the tenants. Those who constituted the leisure class of the village were the few concubines left behind there with their children; and the children, when ready to enter the upper grades of elementary school or high school, would be taken to the city for further education to fit them for living in the city rather than in a rural community like Nanching. There were many such examples in the village. Wong Hung's fifth son remained in the village with his own mother and attended the village school for several years, after which he was taken by his father to Hong Kong to enter school where he could learn English and acquire modern knowledge that would prepare him for a commercial career. In 1949, when he was about eighteen years old, he returned to the village for a prolonged visit. A slickly dressed city boy, he was one who loafed and did no work. He may be viewed as a sample of many of the younger generation of the wealthy class who had drifted permanently from the village and should not be counted among the resident population.

Below this class, there were a dozen or so small landowners, including many widows, who were too old to work and depended upon the meager rent from their land for subsistence. But even these people were constantly trying to find light work in order to supplement their income.

Aside from the foregoing elements, everyone performed some sort of productive task. In the upper bracket of the middle peasants there were a few who did not perform physical labor but who nevertheless actively organized and supervised productive activities. Such a person was Lee Feng. He had received a high school education in the city of Canton, and was now in his forties. Since he possessed a knowledge of the domestic and international situation seldom found among villagers, he was active in local politics and could be regarded as a member of the "new gentry." But he actively managed a farm of about four acres and a fish pond, the physical work being done mainly by hired labor with his own occasional participation. He tended the fish pond himself. He once personally carried a hundred pounds of vegetables from his own fields to the railway station, and after arriving in Hong Kong, again personally transported it to the Hong Kong market in order to cut the middleman's profit in Canton. This was heavy physical labor. It was obvious that this fellow tried to avoid physical labor if he could, but he was willing to perform it if necessary. Not all of his time was devoted to farming and marketing, for he kept busy visiting people or going to meetings in the nearby town. Others of similar economic status but without similar educational background and political interest generally devoted all their time to organizing and supervising farming, with personal participation in the physical work. For the landless peasants and farm laborers, idling, of course, was not possible. The work day was long at busy seasons, beginning when dawn barely broke and continuing till it was too dark to see.

The working age for males began differently with families of different economic status. The period of school education lasted as long as family finances permitted, often extending beyond the late teens for the well-to-do. In the middle-peasant families, one to three years of schooling was generally given a child between eight and twelve; after that, he began to help in the field at light jobs such as weeding by hand and carrying light bunches of harvested crops from the field to the piles before they were carried home by the father. At fifteen or sixteen he was considered a full-fledged worker, learning to assume heavy duties such as plowing and carrying heavy loads on his shoulders and drawing water from the irrigation pond to the fields by the hand or foot pump. His active working age continued until he was about fifty-five, when his physical vigor began to decline and his physical labor tapered off to lighter tasks. Wong Yu's father, for example, still helped with weeding and harvesting vegetables in the field and acted as the weighing man in the local fruit market, although he was in his early seventies.

In the poor family the working age began earlier, for generally the poor child enjoyed no schooling and the family's need for all available labor was ever present. He began to help with light jobs in the fields at the age of eight or nine, or he might be hired to watch water buffaloes, a traditional occupation common to the rice region of South China for young boys beginning at the age of nine or ten. From then on, whether working at home or being hired out, his physical labor increased with age until maturity, and tapered off at a later age than for those who were economically better off.

With the exception of the members of the large landlord families, women in the village worked in the fields or at other employment in addition to their household duties. Working women were a common tradition in the province, and the bound feet which had crippled women for many types of work in other places were not seen at all in this village, not even among women over sixty. Except for heavy tasks such as using the plow, women were seen at practically all types of jobs that provided a living, particularly in busy farming seasons. The trans-planting of rice seedlings, weeding, harvesting, picking vegetables, selling the produce in the local market — should this be preferred to selling to the wholesale houses in Canton — were jobs in which women participated regularly. Their participation in production activities was less continuous than that of the men, and they appeared less ubiquitous than men in the fields, because the heavy burden of household duties kept them home a good part of the day. Judging from conversations with the village women, a peasant's wife who had young children probably spent one-third of her time helping to earn a living, and wives with grown-up children worked more than this proportion.

Generally given no school education even in the well-to-do families until after ten years of age, a girl began her working age earlier than a boy. At the age of about eight she started with light household duties such as watching the younger children and fetching light objects; she also worked along with her mother in the fields at light work. Her duties at home and in the fields increased until she was married off at sixteen or seventeen to another family, where her arduous domestic and production tasks continued until she reached her fifties, when they tapered off to lighter tasks. The woman's burden was so heavy that she generally looked older than her age.

From the foregoing description it is clear that, aside from the some-what fewer than 150 children under the age of five, almost everyone in the 1,100-odd population was a part of the working force that toiled to wrestle a living from the land and from subsidiary occupations. The few who did not work had gone to the city, save for a few of their women and young children left behind. There was no significant leisure class resident in the village.

CHAPTER III

The Land and Its Exploitation

THE BASIC importance of Nanching's agrarian economy was evident in the physical outlay of the settlement: a compact group of houses enveloped by a broad belt of open fields, presenting an ecological pattern in which the village site was spatially adjusted to the convenience of exploiting the land.

As for the 1,100-odd inhabitants, their labor in coaxing the land to yield a crop was the central theme around which all other individual and social activities were organized and toward which their outlook on life was oriented. Their success and failure and their sadness and joy in life were determined largely by whether there had been a "good year" or a "bad year." This was part of a national outlook as expressed in the universally popular couplet posted on doors everywhere on the Chinese New Year: "The winds harmonious and the rains timely; the state at peace and the people secure." And the requirements of an agrarian life, with successful agricultural production as a constant guiding objective, exerted a shaping influence on the village's socioeconomic structure, a structure which included the strong family unit and its extended kinship system, the self-sufficient and restrictive economy, a diffused pattern of social and economic life that restrained the development of specialization, the earthbound local political system that was only loosely integrated into the central political organization of the nation, the lack of a popular learned culture, and the worship of deities of the natural forces that served as a reassurance of agricultural success. Since the peasantry constituted over 80 per cent of the nation's population, it is fully understandable that agrarian well-being was of major consideration in the social and political principles in the Confucian orthodoxy which still dominated the thinking of those in this village who were over forty years of age. Thus the agrarian economy had bred and nurtured the characteristics that marked the life of Nanching as well as the Chinese national culture of which this village was a part. Of decisive importance to the agrarian economy were the land itself and the ways of its exploitation which bore the closest relationship to the existence of the community.

The Land and Its Types

The 1,400 mow or roughly 230 acres of land which represented the village's most valuable economic asset fell into three categories in terms of utilization: the heavily cropped low land, the partially planted hillsides, and the grass-grown highlands and hill tops where erosion from the torrential tropical rains had exposed protruding rocks. The cultivated land consisted of irrigated and unirrigated fields. On the basis of productivity, the fields could be further classified as fertile fields, medium fields, and poor fields. The unirrigated lands were usually the poor fields, while the medium and the fertile fields were found in the irrigated areas. Obviously, the accessibility to water made the distinction between different grades of land where rice culture constituted the backbone of the local economy, rice needing inundated fields in which to grow. Native fertility of the soil was important in this matter. An instance was the "new enclosure," a highly fertile patch of about fifteen acres recently enclosed from the river's mud flat, its native fertility being regarded as an outstanding point of its value. But most of the village land had been steadily farmed for many centuries. The humus content and other sources of fertility of the soil represented human efforts in improvement and maintenance more than native fertility, which was originally limited in the clayey soil. With accessibility to water the matter of fertility was remedied by the existing agricultural techniques.

Thus for most of the village land the availability of water was the chief determinant of its class and value. Good land must be relatively low land in order to be easily irrigated. For this purpose, enclosed fields (*wei t'ien*) were most valued among irrigated lands. They were so called because they were enclosed from the mud flat of the river bank by a dike that kept out the river water. At low tide the land was on the same level or slightly higher than the level of the river; at high tide the river was higher than the enclosed land, making damage from floods an ever present threat, as an ill-maintained dike might break or the river might rise above the normal high mark against which the height of the dike was calculated. At frequent intervals along the dike there were gates equipped with wooden doors that could be lifted or lowered to let in or keep out water. From these gates led a maze of irrigation ditches that crisscrossed the entire enclosed land. Throughout the spring and summer, when rice and other crops needed water and the river was high, water was let in to inundate the fields; and the entire low land of the village glimmered from the water as it showed through the thick green fields divided into numerous tiny patches by lines of earth embankment. In the late summer and fall, when the river was lower than the land level, excessive water in the field was drained out through the gates.

From the enclosed fields, the land rose gradually. Where ditch water no longer reached, the low terraced fields were irrigated by hand or foot pumps from the ditches, or at higher points, from ponds that were located at every low point to collect the rain water from surrounding higher surfaces. The pumps were narrow wooden troughs of varying lengths, usually from eight to twelve feet, inside each of which was a moving chain of little interconnected wooden compartments. One end of the trough was equipped with an iron crank hinged to the moving chain, and the other end was open to let in water. When in use, the trough was placed against the bank of the ditch or pond, with the lower end in the water, which flowed into the wooden compartments. The crank was operated either by hand or by foot with additional treading spokes on a wooden axle, and the moving chain of compartments drew the water up and emptied it into the field through the upper end. Even for the toil-hardened peasants it was a back-breaking job to operate the pump by hand; and even the thickened soles of their feet would become sore and blistered from the continuous treading on the turning wooden wheel.

If one's own field was not next to a ditch or pond, water was first pumped into the field next to the ditch or pond, then pumped again from this field to the next until it reached one's own field. Such fields were usually terraced on a slope, and the task was similar to drawing water up a ladder rung by rung. Where the land rose too high, and there were too many rungs for the water to travel, it was uneconomical to irrigate. Here began the dry, unirrigated land. Water was generally carried in buckets in limited quantities for the dry crops on such fields. Where land was so high that even the carrying of limited quantities of water became uneconomical, there began the waste spaces given to growing grass or used as burial grounds. This was a picture of the broader South China scene of terraced hillsides and the relatively unproductive higher land even where the slopes were gentle enough for cultivation but difficult to irrigate by manpower.

The intensive struggle for water and irrigated land was carried on collectively, the family and sometimes the clan being the basic organized unit. Terracing the rising land patch by patch and pumping water level by level were done by individuals under the leadership of the head of the family. But the enclosing of land from the river was beyond the ability of single families; to accomplish this task, the clan moved into action. An example was the building of the "new enclosure" in 1936.

Shock waves of the world depression emanating from the Western industrial economy finally reached this village, thousands of miles from the center of the economic storm. Beginning in 1933 and 1934, prices dropped, urban unemployment mounted, and the matter of making a living in the cities became increasingly difficult. Many who had emigrated from the village now returned, first living with close relatives and later trying to get back to farming. Even those who had never left the village began to feel the pinch of sinking farm prices and tried to farm more land to make ends meet. The need for more land was keenly felt by the entire village. Those were the years when the cry of "bankruptcy of the countryside" rang throughout China, and its mark was imprinted on many aspects of China's rural life wherever modern economic influences had penetrated. The sinking prices of silk, for example, delayed marriages in the silk-raising districts in Kiangsu Province.[1] And what happened in Nanching was another aspect of the effect of the great depression.

Here many families in the Wong clan owned sections of the mud flat of the river on the southern edge of the village land. The mud flat was submerged by water in spring and summer, particularly from late May through June, when the flood waters usually gushed down from the tributaries in the mountainous northern part of the province. By August the summer flood would recede below the level of the mud flat, and the planting of a rice crop on the flat for autumn harvest was normally possible. The mud flat was therefore a one-crop land, provided the flood water retreated early enough for planting. There had long been the suggestion of turning this area into multi-crop land by diking off the river, but the lack of co-operation between the families holding ownership to the flat land prevented action. Now that the need for more land had become urgent, the Wong clan finally decided to use its public funds and mobilize the manpower of the entire clan to build the dike, the land thus reclaimed to be rented at a nominal rate to each family in the clan on the basis of so much land per male for a period of fifteen years, after which the disposal of the land would revert to the full authority of the owners.

By 1936 the "new enclosure" was completed. There were two versions on the amount of land reclaimed. One was 72 mow or about 12 acres, and the other 90 mow or about 15 acres. Since the latter claim was more often encountered in conversation with the villagers, it is the figure adopted in this study, although no actual measurement was made to verify it. For present purposes, the significant point was the function of collective leadership of the clan in the villagers' struggle for land.

About one third of the village's cultivated land was of the enclosed type, reclaimed during varying periods in the past, as the stream, once a broad river, continued to silt up. Another third of the cultivated land was irrigated by pumps from ditches and ponds. The remaining one-third was unirrigated land. A part of the uncultivated highland could be added to this last type, if economical use of it could be found, for a good part of it was average soil free from rocks. The proportion of the unirrigated land was, therefore, a flexible one, as proven by past events.

Crops and Yields

The most productive land of the village was the some 800 mow or about 133 acres of irrigated fields, and from this the villagers derived the major part of their agricultural income. This irrigated land, the "water fields" in local terms, was devoted to rice and vegetables, rice being by far the leading crop. In 1948–49, about three-fourths of the irrigated land were rice fields and about one-fourth vegetable gardens. There was some reduction in vegetable acreage after the Communists came in.

Rice was planted in both "enclosed fields" and fields irrigated by pumping, since wherever sufficient water could be economically obtained, it was the standard crop. The yield per mow (slightly less than one sixth of an acre) differed on individual farms according to a variety of factors, such as existing fertility of the land, ease of water supply, strain of rice planted, and the investment of fertilizer and labor. Taking the average amount of investment of fertilizer and labor and the most common local strains of rice as norms, yields per mow varied from 200 to 450 catties,[2] or about 266 to 595 pounds, per crop, and from 400 to 900 catties, or 532 to 1,190 pounds, for the two crops per year. Yields under or above this range occurred in exceptional cases. The diked lands were high yielding fields, most producing between 350 and 400 catties per mow each crop and double that amount for the year. Most of the land irrigated by pumping yielded 300 to 350 catties per crop. Fields yielding from 200 to 300 catties per crop were usually the higher and less fertilized land, and it is estimated that less than one-tenth of the village's rice fields fell into this class. In our field canvass the most frequently encountered figure for the whole village was 350 catties per mow per crop, or 700 catties (931 pounds) of unhusked rice a year. This is used as the standard average yield for the village's rice land in this study.

The some 200 mow, or roughly thirty-three acres, of vegetable gardens were irrigated fields divided into patches of rectangular shape, each about six to eight feet wide and from thirty to one hundred feet in length, surrounded by ditches three to four feet deep constantly filled with water. A wooden dipper with a long handle was used to water the plants from the ditch. Various kinds of vegetables were planted on these water-surrounded patches — among them eggplant, cucumbers, several varieties of Chinese cabbage, and certain types of squash — but the most common and most valued vegetable crop in this village and the immediate vicinity was the leek. Probably half of the village's income from vegetable gardening was from leek cultivation, the vicinity being the leading supplier of leeks consumed in Canton and Hong Kong.

The yield from vegetable gardens is difficult to estimate for many reasons. The quantity of yield and the market value of each vegetable was different. Generally, several kinds of vegetables were simultaneously planted in the same patch. Also, the market value of vegetables fluctuated from time to time. One common Chinese cabbage, the *pai ts'ai*, for example, yielded six harvests in one season lasting from September to April. The leek, a biennial plant, was planted about March and grew until late winter of its second year. About sixteen harvests were reaped from the same plants in the two-year period, averaging eight harvests a year. In the first year, the leaves of the plants were often bleached by covering them with tubular tiles to keep out the sunlight. Bleached leeks commanded a high price. When the leaves grew to be from eight inches to a foot long they were cut off about an inch above the root and taken to market. When another set of leaves came up, they were harvested the same way. Toward the second half of the second year, the plant was allowed to bear flower buds, but before the buds bloomed they were cut off together with the long stem, and these were sold as leek flowers. After several cuttings, the plant's rate of growth slowed vastly, and the end of the plant's useful life was reached; in the final harvest, the whole plant was pulled up by the roots. Villagers who planted leeks said that in a year when the weather was right and the market demand high one mow of leeks might bring six times the gross income of a mow of rice, but in a poor year, if the market value of the vegetable should drop, there might be a loss on the investment. Averaging the fat years with the lean, and taking all kinds of vegetables together, one mow of vegetables generally brought in a gross income equivalent to about 1,500 catties or 1,995 pounds of unhusked rice, which was a little over twice the yield from one mow of rice.

Because of the high yield, vegetable gardens contributed heavily toward the support of the dense population on the village land. Why the area of vegetable crops was not increased beyond the existing general proportion may be explained by several factors. Vegetables were a cash crop, the income from which depended largely on the fluctuations of the market. An average peasant could not afford to invest all or even the greater part of his land in this risky venture, in spite of the possibility of attractive gains. It might mean starvation for the whole family should the vegetable market sharply decline, for the peasant lived from hand to mouth with little or no margin of savings. The market price of rice was usually more stable, and besides, the family could consume it as the staple food. A poor peasant, Wong Mi, put half of his six-mow (about one acre) farm into leek cultivation in 1949; the next spring the price of leeks dropped steeply, and he and his old parents were near starvation. The heavy investment in fertilizer, labor, and additional equipment, such as tiles for covering the leeks and bamboo sticks for supporting the vines of squash and beans, raised the cost of vegetable production above that of rice. Because the average peasant was short of capital, his ability to raise vegetables was restricted. A technical factor also entered into the matter. After a patch of land had been planted in vegetables for three years, it had to be turned into a paddy field and submerged under water in order to kill the insects and pests which multiply fast in the tropical climate. Flooding was a means of pest control. Moreover, the heavy fertilizer already gone into the vegetable patches made a good base for growing rice without much additional fertilizer during the first year. Since fertilizer must be progressively increased during the second and the third year of rice planting, in the fourth year, if the peasant could afford it, the field was returned to vegetable gardening. This system prevented the continuous use of the existing patches for vegetable raising and restricted any sudden transfer of certain rice land to vegetable gardens.

The higher, unirrigated land was devoted to dry crops such as sweet potatoes and taro, peanuts, and certain types of beans such as meng beans and red beans. Where the land was lower and water more accessible, squash and some types of green-leaf cabbage might be planted, but the area of such land was small in proportion to all the unirrigated land. Income from the unirrigated land was low, averaging the equivalent of about 200 catties of unhusked rice annually per mow, less than one-third of the average yield from rice fields. Because of the low income, much of the higher land that could be cultivated was not under cultivation.

The serious shortage of land was a topic of constant conversation among the villagers, and the fact that even the inclined walls of the irrigation ditches were frequently planted with rice or vegetables in order to utilize every inch of soil with water bore witness to their complaint. When asked why so much of the higher cultivable land was not utilized, the villagers usually answered that water was hard to lift to that height and that such land, being at the edge of the village, was difficult to watch against theft of the crop. The water problem was admittedly a difficulty, but there were fields just as far away from the village where rice and vegetables were planted. The real reason lay in many factors that made such higher land uneconomical to farm for the average peasant, and water was only one of them, though a vital one. While the yield was light, rent in proportion to the cost was high, as will be seen later. The use of laborious primitive hand methods of farming, including the carrying of water by pails up the slopes, strictly limited the number of mow a peasant family was capable of cultivating. Under such limitations the peasant family could afford to farm only the land which could yield a sufficiently large crop to justify the labor and capital investment. Hence the seeming paradox of neglecting cultivable dry land while population pressure on the land was heavy, a situation quite common with peasant agriculture having a low per capita productivity.

However, under certain circumstances when it became profitable to cultivate such unirrigated land, it was done. An example was the raising of jasmine flowers in the late 1920's and the early 1930's. At that time there was a foreign market for Chinese jasmine tea, and tea manufacturers paid a good price for the flower. According to the villagers, close to one hundred mow of the dry land was covered with the fragrant jasmine plants and almost every peasant family raised a few patches of jasmine. After 1933–34 the acreage dropped sharply because of the depression that cut the foreign market for Chinese tea. By the time of the Japanese invasion in 1937 there was no more jasmine cultivation.

Among the factors determining the choice of crops were marketing conditions and the availability of economical means of transportation to the markets, a situation apparently common to other parts of China where the process of commercialization of agriculture was seriously breaking down local self-sufficiency.[3] In Nanching the considerable acreage in vegetables that helped to sustain a high population density, and the episode of jasmine raising, resulted from the village's close proximity to Canton and the accessibility to cheap water transportation. The city of Canton was ringed by a belt about five or six miles wide where vegetable gardens densely dotted the rustic scene, and Nanching lay within that belt. Another factor in the development of truck farming in this territory was the accessibility to fertilizers, which vegetables needed more than other crops. Both human excreta and garbage were common fertilizers for truck farming here, and a major proportion of both came from the big city. At high tide in the spring and summer, when the little stream was navigable, one saw large wooden barges docked at the edge of the village unloading city garbage and night soil. Wooden barges loaded with the same contents were frequently seen slowly sailing on the Pearl River ten or twenty miles downstream, but the price of the cargo would be much higher there than in Nanching. An enveloping belt of vegetable farms around an urban center is an ecological pattern characteristic of Canton as well as other cities. Nanching's location within this belt served to tie the village to the economy of the city.

Fruit cultivation was comparatively unimportant to the total economy of the village. The major fruits raised were the tropical lichee and guava. Lichee is a fruit unique to this region and commanded a good market price, but guava is a cheap fruit. Both were subsidiary crops planted on spare grounds such as small patches of raised land among the diked fields and on both sides of the broad dikes. There were no orchards in the village. It was estimated that only about 2,000 catties (2,660 pounds) of lichee and about 6,000 catties (7,980 pounds) of guava were produced in 1949, which brought an income equivalent to approximately 2,000 catties of unhusked rice for the lichee and about 1,000 catties for the guava, totaling about 3,000 catties (3,990 pounds) of unhusked rice.

The Method of Farming

Some general observations on the method of farming are necessary here in order to understand the leading technical factors that governed the life of the villagers and placed certain limitations upon that life. The first of such factors were the major types of activities in the farm calendar. For rice culture, this factor has been presented in considerable detail in Fei's works on three Yunnan villages and on Kiang Ts'un village.[4] Although geographically in another region, the major features of rice culture were essentially similar in Nanching; therefore, only an outline of the local practice need be given.

In this double-crop region, rice was planted in March and August and harvested in late June or July and again in November. March to November was the major farming season, which was interspersed with slack periods. Early in March the earth was turned with an iron-tipped wooden plow pulled by a water buffalo. The very poor who could not afford a buffalo used a large iron-tipped wooden hoe for the same purpose. The tool was a thin hardwood plank of rectangular shape about one foot wide and two feet long, with a sharp iron edge clamped to the digging end and a long wooden handle on the other end. We have seen a woman in her late fifties and a young boy of twelve or thirteen each laboriously swinging such a hoe to turn the earth. The speed of this exhausting labor was of course much slower than plowing with a buffalo.

The plowed soil was raked smooth, fertilizer was applied, and water was let into the field, which was then ready for the transplanting of rice seedlings. Seedlings were raised in a seedbed, a tiny patch fenced off on the side or corner of the field. Some peasants bought seedlings from other peasants who raised more than they could use for themselves. Seedlings of an improved strain were sold in a neighboring agricultural experimental station, but only the wealthier peasants could afford to buy them. Here lay the differential disadvantage of the poor peasants.

Beginning from the middle of March, the transplanting of seedlings took place. The whole family production team was on the scene. The peasant, his wife, and older children each took the seedlings by the bunch, ten to fifteen plants, and pushed them into the soft inundated soil. The bunches were planted in rows, with about a foot between bunches and 1.2 feet between rows, a method which called for reform by modern agriculturists. For the first thirty or forty days the emerald green crop demanded little attention except keeping the water at the proper level. But after this period came the first weeding; the second weeding a month later. This was done by hand, and everyone in the peasant's family old enough for such work participated. With the second weeding went the job of adding fertilizer. Soon after the second weeding, the rice plants would begin to "draw stalk," the stalk bearing the rice grains. Swaying in the breeze under the baking tropical sun, the heavily laden plants turned the rice fields into a broad golden-yellow landscape that gladdened the hearts of the peasants. The grain was now allowed to stand to "draw starch" to fill the hull of the kernels.

Excessive rain or a storm at this time would flatten the heavily laden stalks to the wet ground, causing spoilage of the kernels. When the kernels had "drawn enough starch," water was let out of the field, and both the soil and the stalks were allowed to dry under the hot sun. The drying of the stalk made it easier to detach the kernel in the threshing process. Rain at this stage would cause the kernels to sprout on the stalks, resulting in spoilage.

Then came the harvest, when all the rice plants would be cut off a few inches above the ground with a sickle. Threshing was done on a threshing board constructed of a series of serrated crossbars supported underneath by a large wooden tub and surrounded on three sides by a bamboo mat to prevent the grain from flying off in all directions. The peasant, stripped to the waist, firmly grasped a bundle of the rice plants, and repeatedly whipped it hard against the threshing board until all the kernels were detached from the stalks and dropped into the catching tub underneath. Bundle by bundle the threshing was done until the whole crop was finished. Then the grain and the stalks and leaves would be taken home with a carrying pole on the peasant's shoulder. The plant was used as fuel at home.

The grain was dehydrated by spreading it out on the ground to sun. The spacious stone-paved yards in front of and inside the ancestral halls served as the main drying grounds. When the grain was sufficiently dried it was swept up from the floor and put in a wooden winnower to blow off the dirt before storing or selling. The winnower was a large wooden box equipped with a hand-cranked fan like a wheel made of thin wooden slats. The husking of the rice, formerly done by pounding in a stone mortar, was now done in the mills by modern machinery in Pingan Chen or other nearby points. A few stone mortars still existed in the village; in peasant houses they were occasionally used to pound flour from glutinous rice in small quantities mainly for home consumption.

The months of June, July, and August were the busiest farming season for the local peasants; for as soon as the exhausting harvest work was done, no time could be lost before starting the chores of plowing, fertilizing, pumping water into the fields, and transplanting seedlings for the second crop. Any time lost here might mean insufficient water for the plants, for precipitation tapered off after September. Not until the transplanting was done could the peasants enjoy any respite. The process of the second crop repeated that of the first. During the period of the two crops from March to November, the peasants had their slack seasons between transplanting and the first weeding, between the first weeding and the second, and between the second weeding and the harvest.

But this was a multi-crop territory. The slack season of the rice crop was generally taken up by chores required for the vegetables which demanded continuous attention, since practically every peasant family devoted a part of the farm to vegetable gardening. To begin with, the digging of the deep ditches to make a rectangular patch for vegetables and the banking of the walls of the patch with damp mud bricks was a hard and skilled job. This was frequently done by skilled farm laborers hired by the peasant, who might possess the skill but might not have the special tools which, besides the regular digging hoe, included a flat-tip iron digger that resembled a giant chisel attached to a wooden handle.

Generally, in any period throughout the year some vegetable crops were growing in the fields. In the hot and damp period of late spring and summer eggplant and several varieties of squash and beans were grown. Most of the green-leafed vegetables would become stunted in their development if planted in this period. The green-leafed vegetables such as the several kinds of Chinese cabbage and the regular cabbage familiar to the West thrived in the cooler and drier period of fall, winter, and early spring. Leeks, however, grew the year round and supplied one of the few green-leafed vegetables during the hot and humid season, a fact partly responsible for its high market value during the summer and its economic contribution to the villagers' livelihood.

When one crop of vegetables was harvested, the soil was turned and the clods broken up by a digging hoe and leveled with an iron rake. Fertilizer was applied, and seeds or seedlings of a new crop were planted. Hand weeding was a constant job; watering with the long-handled wooden dipper had to be done an average of three times a day, and in the very hot season when evaporation was rapid, as frequently as six times a day. The soil had to be cultivated with the hoe frequently as the heavy tropical rains packed the earth continuously. Instead of the two applications of fertilizer common with the rice crop, fertilizing was much more frequent for vegetables. Besides the heavy fertilizing of the soil at the beginning of a crop, usually with city garbage, additional fertilizing, usually with diluted urine or a mixture of diluted urine and excreta, was given every ten days or so with most vegetables. Although the peasant had to dispose of his rice only twice a year, he had to spend much time in marketing his vegetables. Each time he had enough ripened eggplant or cabbage ready for harvesting he must spend the greater part of a day cutting them and taking them to the wholesale houses in the city. Since the retail market in nearby Pingan Chen took only a small proportion of his produce, insignificant in relation to the total quantity he raised, the peasant often did not bother with retail selling in the market place because of the uneconomical consumption of time. Leeks required cutting every thirty to forty days during the vigorous growing period; and the cutting, washing, bundling, and marketing of the produce demanded much of the peasant's time.

Thus slack seasons between the rice crops did not leave the tropical farmers of Nanching completely free. Even during the winter months they were busy, since many vegetables thrived in the cool months when the rice fields lay fallow. The peasant's personal life was dictated by the schedule of farm chores, many of which, like planting and harvesting, could not be delayed too many days without causing economic loss. A peasant who combined rice crops with vegetable gardening, as was the general rule in this village, might have some days when he felt relatively free during the slack season of the rice crop, but he did not have any protracted period of complete leisure which he could devote to the development of other social, economic, or cultural interests.

His mental outlook was conditioned by the simple organic cycle of his crops. His economic ties with the urban centers and his occasional visits there did not change the basic conditioning factors relentlessly exerted upon him by the simple, cyclical, demanding, and poorly remunerative farm schedule. The rich and complex urban culture standing at close proximity to him failed to inculcate in him an urban way of life. So the peasants of Nanching, only five miles from a great city and economically related to it, remained bound to their agrarian tradition; and the novelties and fascinations of the city appeared to them totally incongruous to their compelling earthy scheme of existence, however socially and economically restrictive such a scheme might be.

Features of Farm Management

Some features of the local farm management may be presented as another set of technical factors governing the life and activities of the peasant. First comes the size of the farm. Nanching shared a common feature of the rice region of China, namely, the minute scale of farm operation. The majority of the farms were from five to ten mow (about 0.83 to 1.66 acres). Fairly common were farms over ten but under fifteen mow. Less common but still found in good numbers were farms above fifteen but under twenty mow. But farms over twenty mow were few. There was only one large farm, that of Wong Yung, who operated about seventy mow (somewhat less than twelve acres), in 1949. Large farms on diked land of 1,000 mow or more each, often found along the banks of the lower Pearl River, were not encountered in this vicinity or within the border of Nanching. At the other extremity of the scale, there were some farms of only two or three mow (less than half an acre), but these were also few, for such farms did not afford a family even minimum subsistence.

Associated with the size of the farm was the scattering of minutely divided plots of land, a common feature of China's farm economy in both the wheat and the rice regions which Nanching fully shared. Repeatedly we had to travel over the entire domain of the village land in order to see all the plots of land farmed by one peasant. Wong Yu, for example, farmed about twenty mow in the period 1948–1950, with the land divided into about thirty plots situated in five or six different locations, some of which were right at the edge of the village site, a highly desirable location, while others were far out on the periphery of the village land. It was about a mile from the village site to the farthest plot, and it took us about two hours to zigzag our way along the paths on the earth embankments in the fields to see all his plots varying from a fraction of a mow to one or two mow each. Plots larger than two mow were rare. Not less than a thousand plots were found among the some 800 mow of irrigated land in the village. In view of the obvious inefficiency of the system, consolidation of scattered plots within one farm had long been advocated as a necessary step in the improvement of China's agricultural production.

Martin Yang, in his study of the Tai Tou village, suggested the leading factors that went into the making of this system. First was the Chinese inheritance system, which was not based on primogeniture but divided the land among all male heirs, though not necessarily in equal shares. Here began the process of dividing a piece of land into separately owned plots which might be farmed by the owner or rented to others. To equalize the value of each share of land or to arrive at the approximate value of a certain share, pieces of poor land went with pieces of good land in different locations in the making of one share of land to an heir. The selling of land in small parcels, frequently a fraction of a mow, by peasants who were accustomed to selling only as little of their land as absolutely needed to meet financial exigencies was also an important factor in dividing the land into numerous small portions. As these processes of inheritance and buying and selling in small plots continued for centuries, few large plots of land remained intact. A possible exception was the land newly enclosed from the river, where owners possessed plots of five to thirty mow each. But this land was now divided into numerous plots for renting to the clansmen, as previously mentioned. At the end of the fifteen-year period, when the land was to revert to the owners, should an owner decide to farm his own land, some of the individual plots would be much larger than the average plots. But such plots would not be able to resist for long the process of subdivision under the traditional system of land ownership, inheritance, and trading. A rich landlord might own fairly large contiguous plots, but he generally subdivided them into small plots to rent out since he usually did not engage in farming directly.

An important factor in farm management was that of labor, for farming here was done almost exclusively by human toil. Using the slow hand methods, the average peasant family experienced a shortage of labor at peak seasons of farm work, especially during the period when one crop of rice was being harvested and another crop had to be planted. In such seasons all available hands in the family were mobilized into action. The village school was let out so that the children could help. It was a boom time for the hired labor market, and many migratory laborers came into the village. The size of the farm of the average peasant, who was limited in his ability to afford hired help, was conditioned by the amount of land the members of the family could farm. The general impression of a labor surplus in the Chinese countryside did not apply to those peasants who depended upon operating a farm as the main source of livelihood.

In conversations with the villagers we learned that the amount of land that a husband and a wife in their prime could farm was six mow, in the proportion of five mow of rice and one of vegetables. With the help of two or three older children under fifteen and possibly an old parent, this amount could be increased to about eight or nine mow by straining every hand that could be pressed into service during the busy days. But this took for granted that every workable person would not be ill when he was needed and that everything would go smoothly. Generally, for farming even this amount of land the average peasant needed a few work units (a unit being one man putting in an average working day of ten to twelve hours) of hired labor or exchange labor to tide him over the peak season. This labor situation was reflected most clearly in the large number of farms of five or six mow in the village.

The need for help besides home labor was shown in the figures produced by Chen Han-seng in his study of ten villages in the same county where Nanching is located. According to Chen, the average number of work units of day labor hired per mow was o.8 for poor peasants, 1.0 for middle peasants, and 3.9 for rich peasants.[5] This condition seemed to be common in other parts of China, particularly the rice region where farming was more intensive than in the wheat region. In the rice region of Eastern and Central China, for example, the percentage of hired labor to the total farm labor was 4.5 for small farms, 15.7 for middle-size farms, and 20.1 for large farms.[6] Sample studies of other localities produced a similar picture, which is applicable to Nanching. The low percentage of help hired by the poor peasant was not a result of his having little need for such help. It reflected, rather, his inability to afford much hired labor and hence his inability to operate a larger and more efficient farm. This situation explains why, although they constituted a majority in Nanching, the poor peasants did not cultivate an equivalent percentage of the total land.

Another situation associated with farm labor was the shortage of work animals, the water buffalo. In 1949 the village had about thirty-five water buffaloes altogether. For the spring rice crop, these met the total needs of the village adequately, for there was a longer period after the autumn harvest and before the spring transplanting over which the plowing work could be spread. But plowing for the second crop had to be done immediately after the harvest of the first crop, and there was little time over which the work could be spread. It was then that the shortage of buffaloes was keenly felt and animals had to be borrowed from other villages.

Because buffaloes were employed for plowing and only occasionally for pulling carts, the period of their usefulness in the year was limited. Also, a buffalo cost locally the equivalent of 1,000 to 1,500 catties of unhusked rice, a price few could afford. Consequently, most peasant families in the village possessed no buffalo but rented from others who had them. In fact, most of the buffaloes were owned by families who raised them for renting out after taking care of their own needs. Two families were keeping five buffaloes each and depended heavily upon renting them for income, as each family farmed only three or four mow of land. Since the rent per day for an animal without a laborer attached was about the equivalent of twice the wage for a unit of day labor, for the poor peasant, who could not afford hired labor, the hiring of a buffalo to plow the land was a heavy financial burden. Many tried to work for families with buffaloes in exchange for the service of the buffalo, but such arrangements could not always be made. Even Wong Yu, who farmed twenty mow of land, borrowed the buffalo of his brother-in-law from the next village in 1948–1950 and worked several days for him in return. Peasants who could not hire buffaloes hoed their fields by hand, a slow process in a situation where labor was already short, and one which did not turn the soil as evenly nor as deeply as plowing with a buffalo. Like the limitation on hiring help, the shortage of work animals was a factor in the smallness of the majority of the farms. This, again, was a feature of the farm economy common to other parts of China. The percentage of farms possessing no animals in Kiahsing of Chekiang Province in the rice region, for example, was 58.97 for small farms, 16.19 for middle farms, and 0.42 for large farms.[7]

The possessions of the average peasant in the village consisted mainly of the house he and his family lived in, what little land he might have, and the few simple farm tools he used. Since he had very little cash, he could not hire human labor or work animals, and frequently he could not afford to buy even enough fertilizer for a good yield and for proper maintenance of the fertility of his land. In 1950, although some better-off peasants in the village bought rice seedlings of an improved variety from a neighboring agricultural experimental station, the majority of the peasants could use only seeds saved from their own previous harvest of whatever variety they had planted. Asked what they felt was most needed, most villagers replied (from what little they knew of modern agriculture): an insecticide and applicators for their vegetable patches. Three well-to-do peasants in the village had recently acquired some imported insecticide and sprayers, and their effectiveness had been demonstrated. The majority of the peasants could only look on with envy, for they could not regularly afford even the cheaper native insecticides such as diluted lime solution or a solution made by soaking tobacco leaves in water. For them, the common method of combating pests was to remove them by hand, a job at which women and older children were frequently engaged. It is needless to say that, besides being slow, this method was useless when the pests were widespread.

The average peasant's lack of financial resources was further worsened by his poor position to command credit at reasonable rates. Credit facilities have always constituted a need in agricultural production because of the relatively long-term turnover as compared with many other types of business enterprises. This was particularly serious with the poor peasant in Nanching. When he contracted a loan it was usually for unproductive purposes connected with family crises like marriage or a funeral. It was the rich peasants and some middle peasants who had the credit standing to borrow money for improving production or expanding the farm.[8] The question of credit facilities will be discussed in Chapter V.

CHAPTER IV

Land Ownership and Tenancy

THE NANCHING peasant's relationship to the land was not represented only by the ways he exploited it. Between him and his cultivation of the soil stood the institutionalized system of Chinese land ownership and tenancy; and no less important than the ways in which the peasant exploited the land was his status in this system. It determined to a great extent the success or failure of his economic ambition, his social position in the community, the life he led, the fortune or hardship that faced his family, and the upbringing he could give his children. Although it was a permanent part of the complex national agrarian economy, and therefore Nanching's agrarian problems were a part of the situation that had given rise to the nationwide agrarian movement, the system of land ownership and tenancy had certain different features in each locality. In this chapter, then, we shall examine the system as it operated in Nanching during the two decades prior to the Communist take-over.

Stratification of Economic Status and Land Ownership

The ownership of land was usually considered the most important factor in determining a peasant's economic status, and the possession of a large holding obviously assured him a high place; but ownership was by no means the sole consideration in the shaping of a peasant's economic position. The owner of a small plot of land might have less income than the tenant farmer working a large rented farm. Looking at the stratification of economic status in Nanching, it seems practical to use the common classification of peasants into large landlords, rich peasants, middle peasants,, and poor peasants on the dual basis of land ownership and the size of the farm.

Measured against the local norm, those possessing over thirty mow (about five acres) constituted the landlord class. Those who possessed twenty to thirty mow or operated a farm of over thirty mow of owned or rented land were the rich peasants. The middle peasants possessed six to twenty mow or operated a farm of similar size. The poor peasants, the largest group, were those owning approximately five mow or less or operating a farm of similar size. These definitions must be interpreted against the size of the family. A large family of eight trying to live on the rent from ten mow of land or operating a farm of the same size would belong to the class of poor peasants, whereas a small family of two operating a rented farm of five mow and doing some farm work for others might live as well as a lower-middle peasant.

Field investigations during 1948–49 disclosed five families that owned over thirty mow of land each and about twenty-five families that might be described as rich peasants. Together, these thirty families constituted the upper class of the village. The general impression is that the middle peasant families accounted for somewhat less than one-third of the 230 families in the village, that is, about seventy families. There were about thirty families who had nonagricultural occupations or depended mainly on remittances from emigrants for a living. This left about one hundred families who were in the poor peasant class, a group that included the landless peasants. The situation is reconstructed in the accompanying tabulation.

	Approximate number of families	*Percentage*
Landlords and rich peasants	30	13.0
Middle peasants	70	30.5
Poor peasants	100	43.5
Nonagricultural	30	13.0

One can compare this approximate picture with Chen's study of 840 peasant families in ten villages in the same vicinity as Nanching. The study listed 64.3 per cent poor-peasant families, 23.0 per cent middle-peasant families, and 12.7 per cent rich-peasant families.[1] Since Chen did not explain the basis of his classification, close comparison is difficult.

Collective Land

Who owned how much land? First, it is necessary to recognize two types of land ownership, collective and private. The principal types of collectively owned land in this village were clan land, education land, and temple land. Clan land found in this village was largely confined to so-called sacrificial land, the income from which was used for sacrificial ceremonies to the ancestors, upkeep of the ancestral halls, and other activities connected with ancestor worship. The Wong clan, a poor clan, held only thirty mow of such land in this village. The clan land of the Lees was located in another county about eighty miles to the south, where the headquarters of the Lee clan were located, the clan in this village being only one of the branches. Every year the Lee clan of Nanching received over 10,000 catties of unhusked rice from the income of the headquarter's clan land. In addition, the subdivisions of the Lee clan did possess altogether about twenty mow of sacrificial land within Nanching.

Education land was also under the ownership and management of the clan, but it was set aside for educational purposes. In the imperial days, besides subsidizing the clan school, the income from this land also paid for the stipends of scholars who had passed the primary grade of civil service examinations and for travel subsidies for scholars to go to the provincial and national capitals to take higher examinations. In the Republican period it was used exclusively to support the village school. The Wong clan had somehow lost or sold its former education land. In the 1920's a wealthy merchant of the Lee clan contributed twenty mow of irrigated land for the support of a village school to educate the young of all clans within the village.

Temple land was owned by the temple, and the income from the land supported one priest and the temple. There was only one temple in this village, located immediately outside the northwestern corner of the village site. It had about ten mow of land under its ownership.

Altogether, there were about eighty mow of collectively owned land of various types, accounting for 6.2 per cent of the 1,200 mow of the village's cultivated land, leaving 93.8 per cent in the private ownership of individuals and families. This percentage of collectively owned land was low for a province where the clan and its economic functions were among the most highly developed in China. A village about two miles from Nanching had in 1948 about 70 per cent of its total cultivated area under clan ownership. Clan land averaged about 30 per cent of all the cultivated land in the whole Panyü County in which Nanching was located;[2] and clan land was the leading form of collective land ownership in the province. The bulk of the Lee's clan land lay elsewhere, as pointed out. The Wongs formerly had large clan possessions, according to the elders, but different crises befalling the clan during the past century had led to the sale of most of the land to defray emergency expenses. This explained the relatively small percentage of collectively owned land in Nanching, a situation which affected the livelihood of the villagers substantially, particularly the Wongs, among whom there was a higher percentage of tenancy than among the Lees.

Collective ownership of land affected the livelihood of the peasants differently in different cases. Collective land, especially that in possession of the clan, tended to remain in collective ownership over a long period of time. The institutionalized value attached to such land was high; and selling the clan's land not only weakened the clan's financial resources but also caused a serious loss of clan prestige, since it was considered an offense against the ancestors' good reputation — only unworthy descendants would sell instead of adding to the property built up by their predecessors. The selling of collective land was therefore infrequent, though it did occur at times, especially by clans of declining economic and organizational strength such as the Wongs.

With the land remaining in possession of the clan, individual peasants could work on it only as tenants. The terms for renting collective land in this village were the same as for private land, with the land going to the highest bidder. The renter of collective land was thus subjected to all the normal disadvantages of tenancy, although he reaped certain indirect benefits in the form of clan services supported by such rent. But the terms of rent might be different in some cases, having a different impact on the peasants' life. In the neighboring village mentioned above, clan land, which accounted for 70 per cent of all the cultivated area, was rented to male clan members at nominal rates. In such a case collective ownership of land by the clan had the obvious effect of equalizing the right of clan members to use the land and preventing concentration of land ownership in private hands, a situation particularly beneficial to the poor peasants possessing insufficient or no land. A common complaint against clan ownership of land was corrupt management in the form of embezzlement of rents and favoritism in renting good land to well-placed members. While there was apparently some truth in such charges, a representative factual picture of clan land management has yet to be given.

Private Land

Private ownership accounted for 93.8 per cent of the cultivated land in Nanching. There were five families, A, B, C, D, and E, who were large landowners by village standards though pitifully small by Western criteria. The land possession of these families in 1948–49 totaled 310 mow (about 51.7 acres) and was distributed as shown in the accompanying tabulation. These 310 mow constituted 25.8 per cent of

Family	Number of Mow Owned	Approximate Acreage
A	120	20.0
B	70	11.7
C	60	10.0
D	30	5.0
E	30	5.0

the village's total cultivated land, but the five families made up only 2.18 per cent of the village's 230 families, or 2.5 per cent of the 200 agricultural families, excluding the thirty families that derived their main income from nonagricultural sources. On the other hand, about twenty families, or 8.7 per cent, of the 230 families possessed absolutely no land. Between these two extremes land ownership seemed to be quite diffused. The rich peasant normally possessed five to ten mow of land, the middle peasant three or four mow, and the poor peasant a fraction of one mow up to two mow. Of the middle and poor peasants who constituted the overwhelming majority of the villagers, almost every family possessed a small amount of land but seldom enough to yield the minimum subsistence for an average family of 4.8 persons. Even the aged Wong Ho, who died in 1950 of insufficiency of food and malnutrition, had two mow of unirrigated land and one fish pond. But between him and Family A the difference in land possession was 60 times, and the difference was even greater between the large number who had only a fraction of one mow and Family A.

Petty owners who possessed a fraction of one mow to two or three mow were numerically a large group. Most of them were poor and middle peasants who farmed their own small plot of land augmented by as much land as it was financially feasible for them to rent. But many of them rented their tiny possessions out to others, supplementing the meager rent by other means when it was insufficient for family subsistence. Such was the case with widows, particularly old widows, who had neither grown sons to do the heavy farm chores nor the means to hire labor to operate a small farm. Similar conditions existed with families whose adult male workers had emigrated to cities and foreign lands. Such emigrants usually managed to send home some savings to buy a small piece of land; but, since rent from the tiny plot of land was insufficient to maintain the family in the village, the emigrants regularly remitted modest sums to supplement the rent. These petty landowners who did not work on the land numbered about thirty families in 1948–49. Landowners who did not work on the soil were technically speaking landlords, but they differed substantially from large landowners, most of whom did not work on the soil either.

Although no detailed account of the distribution of land ownership in this village is presently available, Chen's study of 923 families in ten villages in the same vicinity in 1933 might reflect upon the local picture; his data make up the accompanying tabulation.[3] From the

Peasant Classes	Number of Families	Mow Owned	Per Cent of Families	Per Cent of Mow Owned
Agricultural laborer	83	0	9.0	0
Poor	540	540.5	58.5	22.1
Middle	193	789.8	20.9	28.3
Rich	107	1,212.0	11.6	49.6
Total	923	2,442.3	100.0	100.0

writer's observations, Chen's percentage of land owned by rich peasants applied to Nanching in 1948–49, but his percentage of land owned by middle peasants seemed somewhat high and that owned by the poor peasants somewhat too low. It is to be noted that Chen's study was made in 1933. The protracted war against the Japanese invasion of 1937–45 and the inflationary postwar years wrought changes upon the distribution of land ownership throughout China. In some places the changes accentuated the concentration of land ownership, and in others tended to decentralize it to some degree. The latter applied to Nanching.

Traditionally, a considerable number of the Lee clan went off to cities and foreign lands to engage in business, while members of the Wong clan were more closely tied to the soil as tillers; hence there were more landowners among the former clan and more tenants among the latter. But the wartime disruption of urban production and the concomitant inflation boosted prices of foodstuffs and made agricultural production more profitable than before. Kwangtung Province was a rice-deficient area, and as war disrupted transportation by which rice was imported, the price of locally produced rice soared. Consequently, when many of the Lees returned from the war-torn cities financially bankrupt, the Wongs were in a good position to buy the much coveted land of the Lees' who needed money and were forced to sell. Thus some of the poor peasants in the village were able to acquire more land than they had owned before the war, even though most of the rich peasants seemed to be able to hold their possessions, possibly because they had a larger margin of savings than others to face the war emergency.

Although a wide gap existed in the matter of land ownership between the rich and the poor peasants in this village, the local picture did not tally with the generalization of the Chinese Communist Party that the landlords and the rich peasants who constituted 10 per cent of the rural population owned 70 to 80 per cent of the land, while the middle and poor peasants and the agricultural laborers who constituted 90 per cent of the rural population owed only 20 to 30 per cent of the land.

Tenancy

About 70 per cent of all the cultivated land in Nanching was rented, and about 30 per cent was tilled by the owners, making totals of about 840 mow of rented land and about 360 tilled by the owners. Aside from the few who lived on income from rent, we did not encounter a single peasant who did not rent some land from others. This was definitely not a community where the owner-farmer played an important part as was the case in many North China localities. A high percentage of tenancy was a characteristic of the rice region of China, particularly in the vicinity of big cities.

But tenancy was not necessarily a sign of poverty. The situation in this village might be represented by the accompanying rough estimates on the proportion of rented land in an average peasant's farm in the different classes. It was normal to find a poor peasant operating a

	Per cent of Land Owned by Tiller	Per cent of Land Rented from Others
Poor peasant's farm	20	80
Middle peasant's farm	30	70
Rich peasant's farm	40	60

five-mow farm of which he owned about one mow and rented the remaining four. Of course, he might own only a fraction of a mow or even none, but the number of tenants who owned no land was rather small. If the middle peasant generally farmed about ten mow, it was quite usual for him to own two to four mow of it, renting the rest from others. The rich peasant usually had enough land of his own to support a family at the average standard of living of the village, but the rich peasant usually had more working capital than the middle or poor peasant and used it to expand the size of his farm by renting in more land. This was especially so because the war and postwar period had made food production generally profitable; and Nanching was near a big city where fertilizer was relatively cheap and where a hungry market for food was right at hand. Family D, mentioned above, farmed about seventy mow of land in 1948–1950 but owned only about thirty mow, most of which represented recent acquisitions. In a village about five miles away one peasant operated a farm of 200 mow, all of which was rented land.

Although tenancy was general in Nanching, the burden of rent payment influenced differently the various classes of peasants. For the rich peasant who farmed twenty mow (3.3 acres) or more, the rented acreage in addition to his own land represented an increase in income even though the rent payment might take away a part of the fruits of his labor and investment. But for a peasant who farmed only five or six mow (less than an acre), the payment of rent required a sizable part of the minutely small income needed for his family's subsistence and for reinvestment in the next crop, thus hindering his ability to improve production. It is necessary at this point to consider the types of tenancy and rent in order to see the weight of this burden.

Types of Tenancy and Rent

While there were differences in nature between collective and private ownership of land, there was no practical difference in the type of tenancy and the amount of rent charged under either type of ownership. The situation had been somewhat different forty or fifty years previously, when the Wong clan possessed a sizable amount of clan land. At that time, the clan demanded no deposit from the tenants, the rent of the clan land was less than 10 per cent of the yield, and the right of renting the clan land was shared equally among all males of the clan. This system was still in effect in 1949 in Po Tsun, a neighboring village about four miles from Nanching. There, the collective land of the Wu clan comprised about one-half of that village's total cultivated area, and each male descendant was entitled to rent 1.5 mow of land from the clan at the nominal annual rent of 40 catties of unhusked rice per mow, the equivalent of about 7 per cent of the average yield of the irrigated fields there. The amount of land a male member could rent fluctuated with the increase or decrease of male clan members. In Nanching the "new enclosure" land mentioned previously brought an annual rent of only 15 catties per mow, less than 2 per cent of the average yield from that rich virgin soil, but this privilege was to run for only fifteen years from 1936, ending in 1951, the year of the Communist land reform. Whenever discussing the hard lot of their life, Nanching peasants inevitably complained about the insufficiency of land in the village, and they frequently pointed to the Wu clan in Po Tsun as an example of good fortune bestowed by the departed ancestors, while lamenting the poverty of their own clan as measured by the lack of low rent clan land. The some thirty mow still in the possession of the Wong clan was so small and the clan's financial needs so heavy that it was rented out in the usual manner as private land. Land belonging to the subdivisions of the Lee clan was treated in similar manner.

Practices of permanent tenure, frequently found elsewhere, did not exist in Nanching or in the vicinity. Land for rent was normally thrown open to bidding by prospective tenants every three years, and the highest bidder received the land for that period. At the end of three years, the bidding process was theoretically repeated, but in a majority of the cases the original tenant continued to keep the tenure since he had invested in the land by fertilizing it and a frequent change of tenants was undesirable for proper maintenance of the land. In practice, an owner usually kept the original tenant except in case of habitual rent default or in case of a much higher bid from a more desirable tenant.

The three-year period of tenure as current in the village was partly connected with the technical requirement of a three-year rotation between the vegetable and rice crops. A shorter period than this was not acceptable to the tenant, who had invested heavily in preparing the land for vegetables, including ditch digging and fertilizing, and expected the investment to cover a period of three years. In fact, at the end of a three-year period of vegetable planting, when the land was turned into a paddy field, the heavy fertilizing of the former vegetable patches made it unnecessary to add much fertilizer to the rice crop during the first year. If the tenure terminated at the end of three years, the tenant lost the remaining fertility of the land that had come from his investment. The tenant was therefore frequently forced to put up a higher bid to keep his tenure in the face of the constantly heavy demand for land under the pressure of the existing man-land ratio.

The three-year period of tenure was common with private as well as collective land; but the shorter the period of tenure and the more frequent the bidding, the greater was the opportunity for the owner to exact higher rent from the tenant. There were some private owners in the village who gave only one year's tenure, mostly with the higher land where only rice was planted and where the shortage of water during the dry months made it difficult to plant vegetables. The shorter tenure was an effort to push up the rent within the technical limits of the higher inferior land. This accounted for the higher rent occasionally charged for poorer land than for good land.

During the period of our investigation, rent was paid in kind, in terms of unhusked rice, because of the run-away inflation and the resulting extreme currency instability. Before the war, however, it was paid mainly in cash. It was a fixed rent, so much per mow, as share-cropping was not practiced here. One reason for fixed rents was that, in the general absence of drought or flood which could cause extensive crop damage, the harvest was fairly reliable and it was possible to figure out a constant amount of rent for the year. Another reason was the general lack of participation in capital investment and management of the farm by the owners of the land. The large landlords were mostly absentees who saw greater profit in investing their capital either in owning more land or in urban business than in participating in agricultural production with the tenant. The small landowners were short of capital themselves.

The amount of rent varied greatly with the quality of the land. Officially, land fell into high, medium, and low grades, and this classification was generally used by the villagers. In Nanching, high- and medium-grade lands were irrigated, while low-grade land was generally unirrigated. A mow of high-grade land planted to rice generally yielded between 350 to 400 catties of unhusked rice per crop, or between 700 to 800 catties per year, and the usual annual rent was between 300 to 400 catties, which was about 43 to 50 per cent of the yield. The medium-grade land yielded between 300 to 350 catties per crop per mow, or 600 to 700 catties per year, and the usual annual rent was 300 catties, which was about 43 per cent of the yield. Since the low-grade unirrigated land produced irregular amounts of yield, depending on the type of crop planted and the regularity of precipitation, there was variation in the rent charged. The most frequently encountered amount was 50 catties of unhusked rice, which was about 25 per cent of an annual yield of 200 catties of the same grain, a yield that was common with this grade of land. In all cases, rent was collected twice a year, right after each harvest, when the tenant had rice on hand to pay.

In spite of the better quality of high-grade land, the most common rent quoted for both the high and medium grades was 300 catties of unhusked rice, a figure that was generally mentioned by the villagers as the average rent for irrigated fields. Because of the relatively lower yield from medium-grade land, the rent in proportion to the yield was thus actually higher for medium- than for high-grade land. This put the highest rent rate in proportion to the yield on the medium-grade land, while the best land was rented relatively cheaper. This appeared to be part of a national pattern in China. T. H. Shen, in surveying the national situation, stated: "The rate of rent for the low-class irrigated land is the highest, and that for the high-class is lower." [4] Chen Hanseng, noting the same situation in his study of peasant economy in Kwangtung Province, in which Nanching is located, commented as follows:

> Perhaps the proportion of a share rent has some connection with fertility of land, as well as with the means of production. This may be illustrated by the share rent in Wung-yuen [county], where the landlord collects a rent in grain which is 40 per cent from the best land, 50 per cent from land of medium grade, and 20 per cent from the poorest land. The share rent does not, however, depend on the fertility of the soil alone but largely on the respective amount of labor power and fertilizer which the tenant puts into the land. In this particular district, the tenant of good land often supplies more means of production per mow than other tenants because such investment is certain to pay. Improving the soil, he is actually in a better position to bargain with the landlord who cannot afford to lease his good land to tenants who cannot or will not keep up the fertility of the soil. It is for this reason that the landlord gets less rent from the tenant of the best land, paradoxical as this may seem, than he gets from the tenant of medium-grade land.[5]

Chen's explanation applied well to conditions in Nanching, and it also largely explained why the rich and the upper-middle peasants farmed the best land while the rest had to farm medium- and low-grade land.

In addition to his ability to maintain and improve the land, his ability to pay rent regularly was another factor that affected a tenant's qualification to compete for good land. Although the village was generally free from major natural calamities of flood and drought, yet partial damage to the crop by storms, by irregularity of temperatures, or by excessive rains at the wrong time were frequent occurrences. Family and individual circumstances such as marriage, birth, illness, or death might press heavily upon the peasant's financial resources. All these affected the tenant's ability to pay rent regularly or in full amount; and, obviously, rich peasants, being in a better position than poor ones to weather crises, had the best opportunity to rent the best land.

A last feature of rent was the requirement of a "rent deposit" by the tenant at the beginning of his tenure as a guarantee against default.

The amount of deposit varied greatly with individual landlords, but a common figure was one-half of a year's rent. If there was a change of tenant after a short term such as three years, the deposit was usually returned to the departing tenant; in long-term tenure, the landlord frequently kept the deposit. This requirement also had the effect of limiting the ability of the average peasant to rent any sizable amount of land at one time to expand his farm, for the total amount of deposit required for a large acreage would be beyond his means.

The Landless and Agricultural Laborers

As previously mentioned, there were about twenty families in Nanching that had no land at all and constituted the bottom group in the village's pyramid of land ownership. A few of these families were tenant farmers, but the majority, since they could not finance even the buying of tools, fertilizer, and seeds, worked as "long-term" agricultural laborers on an annual basis. As such, they normally were paid about 1,000 catties of unhusked rice per year and board and room if they owned no home. This income might equal or even exceed what they might have wrested from a small rented farm, but it was not enough to support a family of average size without supplementary employment undertaken by other members of the family. For this reason, many of them never married, and the largest number of bachelors were to be found among landless peasants. Wong Tu-en, a landless peasant working for a rich peasant for nearly ten years, was still a "bare stick" (unmarried man) in his fifties; and there were others in the village like him. They were objects of ridicule and pity in the eyes of the villagers, whose life centered upon the family.

The limited number of landless peasants was not enough to supply all the hired labor required by the village during peak seasons of farm work. The deficiency was partly met by large numbers of migratory workers who streamed into the locality at rice-planting or harvest time. They were mainly the "boat people," a different ethnic group who lived on boats on the river, "a people of floating homes," a people who, according to one theory, were the aborigines of the land before the invading Chinese crowded them out on to the water centuries ago. Living and moving about on their boats, they utilized the slight climatic differences between the northern and southern ends of the Pearl River Delta and worked in different localities in succession, moving from south to north since planting and harvesting began earlier in the south.

When they entered the vicinity of Nanching, they did not live in

the village but would either live on their own boats or build temporary sheds from straw and bamboo on top of the dikes near the periphery of the village. In the past twenty years the supply of "boat
people" laborers had increased, giving competition to those in the
village who depended upon agricultural work entirely or partially for
an income. Up to the 1920's, the predominant occupation of the "boat
people" had been the transportation of goods and passengers, their
boats being at once homes and a means of production; but the boat
as a means of production was increasingly affected by modernization
of transportation after the 1920's. As steamboats and motor launches
mounted in number on the Pearl River, and the building of a steel
bridge spanning the river connecting the two parts of the city of
Canton took away a substantial part of the ferrying business, the boat
people looked increasingly for employment on the land which they
had previously shunned, and agricultural work became a major field
for them.

Aside from the landless peasants in the village and the migratory
boat people, a large number of poor peasants also did piece work for
other peasants for a small supplemental income. At peak seasons one
man working a normal day of ten to twelve hours received an average
of 15 catties of unhusked rice, and in slack seasons about 8 to 10
catties. A woman's wage was about two-thirds those amounts. Such
earning was a welcome addition to a poor peasant's family income.
The peasant could dovetail his own planting and harvesting, within
climatic limits, and work for others, or he could work for others because his own farm was too small to need all the family's labor. For
the landless and those short of land, farm labor was an important
source of supplementary income.

Thus there were in Nanching those who established permanent
right to the land through ownership, those who acquired temporary
right to it through tenancy, and those whose relationship to the land
was through employment under an owner or tenant. Whatever his
status, the life struggle of a Nanching peasant constantly revolved
around one single objective: to become the owner of land and more
land. The system of land ownership and tenancy had clearly taught
him that farming his own land would yield him the largest benefit,
and that owning a sufficient amount of it would enable him to live
exclusively on rent and free himself and his children from toil and the
attendant social and economic restrictions imposed on those who must
till the soil for a meager living. The few landlord families in the village reminded him constantly of the value of land ownership and all

the blessings of life that it bestowed. It was this proven worth that underlay the almost sacred attitude with which the peasant regarded the land in his possession, especially land inherited from the ancestors which might be augmented by new purchases but should not be whittled down by selling. An important derivative from the value of land ownership was the peasant's attachment to the soil and his consequent social and economic immobility.

Theoretically the same sense of value could be transferred to tenancy or farm employment if these two forms of indirect relationship to the land could be proven to yield a greater economic and social benefit than that which private ownership of land had brought in the past. In this theoretical assumption lies an interpretation of the possible success or failure of the Communist collectivization experiment, which aims at replacing private ownership of land by the collective farm in which the peasant's relationship to the land is established through the large collective organization, thus transforming the peasant into a new type of farm employee.

CHAPTER V

Production, Consumption, and Supplementary Income

The Village's Production and Consumption

THE AGRICULTURAL production of the village's 1,200 mow of cultivated land, rendered in terms of unhusked rice, was approximately as follows: 600 mow of rice produced 420,000 catties of unhusked rice, 200 mow of vegetables produced 280,000 catties of unhusked rice, and 400 mow of dry land produced 40,000 catties of unhusked rice, for a total production of 740,000 catties. After milling, each 100 catties of unhusked rice yielded an average of 65 catties of husked rice.[1] At this percentage of yield, the 740,000 catties of unhusked rice gave 481,000 catties, or 640,000 pounds, of husked rice ready for consumption. Was this amount of husked rice sufficient for the consumption of the village as a whole?

It is estimated that an adult male consumed about one catty (1.33 pounds) of rice a day, averaging heavy consumption during hard-working busy seasons against lighter consumption during slack periods. This included rice as the main staple plus whatever vegetables and, at times, meat that the consumer could afford. In a year, the food needs of an adult male were about 365 catties or 485 pounds. This compares closely with Fei's average of 470 pounds.[2] Averaging the differences between sex and age, each person was estimated to equal 0.75 of an adult male in his prime.[3] This ratio reduced the 1,100 persons in the village to about 825 adult male units. The total food consumption for 825 adult male units was about 301,125 catties or 311,062 pounds in a year, to which should be added about 30 per cent of this amount, or 90,337 catties, for minimum expenses of clothing, housing, and other absolute necessities. Thus a total of 391,462 catties, or 510,644 pounds, of husked rice was needed for minimum subsistence of the entire village, a level which made no allowance for special expenses resulting from marriage, birth, death, or unexpected medical care.

Comparing the total production of 481,000 catties and the total minimum needs of 391,462 catties of husked rice, there appears to be a surplus. But one must deduct the rent which was taken out of the village by absentee owners and not consumed within the village, as well as taxes and costs of production.

Although we do not know the exact amount of rice taken out of the village in the form of rent, the cases of the large landowners mentioned previously furnish a basis of estimate. Family A had 120 mow of land and maintained a large house in which five or six people lived constantly. This family would need rice from about 80 mow for consumption at a very high standard of living, leaving the rent from about 40 mow not consumed within the village. Family B owned about 70 mow and lived in the city; since their house was occupied by poor relatives, the rent from all this land was taken out of the village. Family C, with about 60 mow, was in the same situation. Family D, which owned about 30 mow, ranked with the rich peasants living in the village and operating a large farm; so the product from the land was retained within the community. Family E had about 30 mow and a fish pond; since the rent from this land and pond was consumed by the concubine and her two children plus one female servant all living in the village, none was taken out. Thus, among the five large landowners, there was a total of 170 mow of land the rent from which was taken out of the village. As all that land consisted of good irrigated fields, the rent from the 170 mow amounted to about 51,000 catties of unhusked rice or 33,150 catties of husked rice. Taxation probably took about 10 per cent of the total gross yield from the village, with the estimated factor of tax evasion taken into consideration. The tax then was equivalent to about 48,100 catties of husked rice. Since the total cost of production for the entire village was difficult to estimate because of the diversification of crops, no exact figure can be included here; but, excluding cost of labor, it should not have exceeded at a maximum the figure of taxation.

We find, then, that the village's net production available for its own use was approximately 362,000 catties of husked rice as against a minimum requirement of approximately 391,000 catties, leaving a deficiency to be made up as far as possible by nonagricultural earnings from outside the village, such as wages for embroidery work, remittances from emigrants, earnings from seasonal work in the city, and activities such as peddling.

Family Income and Consumption

To move from the over-all or village balance between agricultural production and consumption to the situation of individual families is a more complex procedure owing to the unequal distribution of village income; but the approximate situation can be derived by establishing the minimum needs of an average family and measuring them against the estimated income of the various classes of peasants in the village.

Using the previously applied standard of 0.75 adult male for each person regardless of age or sex,[4] the food consumption of an average family of 4.8 persons would be that of 3.6 adult males. Such a family would have an annual need of 1,314 catties of husked rice for food. Adding 30 per cent of this amount for other necessities, the total minimum need for an average family for a year would be about 2,141 catties or 2,848 pounds of husked rice. This figure was used as the norm against which we measured the probable income of the various classes of peasants in the village.

To estimate the income of a peasant family, it was necessary to estimate first the leading items of cost of agricultural production in the village. Since these varied with the grades of land and the kinds of crops planted on them, we took as a representative basis medium-grade land which was irrigated and planted in rice. This grade of land was the most common in the village, and the rice crop was quantitatively the basis crop. The year for the following estimates was 1948, the year before the Communists took over the government. Five items figured prominently in the cost of agricultural production: taxes, rent, fertilizer, seeds, and labor. Because of the wide variation in the amount of hired labor used on individual farms, it was excluded from consideration.

Only land tax paid directly by the peasant was considered. (There were heavy taxes on the sale and transportation of rice and produce, but they were paid only by the merchants.) In 1948 the main tax on medium-grade land was about 50 catties of unhusked rice per mow, or 7.1 per cent of the average yield of one mow of rice crop. The local subdistrict government levied a police fee of about 35 catties of unhusked rice per mow, or about 5 per cent of the yield. The two items totaled about 85 catties, or 12.1 per cent of the yield per mow. (This tax was paid by the landlord only, a common practice in most parts of China, although in some localities it was divided between the tenant and the landlord.) In addition, the owner of the crop paid five catties, or about 0.7 per cent of the yield, per mow for "crop protection" to a local armed band of racketeers. The three items together made a total of 90 catties, or roughly 13 per cent of the yield. (The burden of government taxes was frequently heavier than this for the small landowners. The tax collector was given a quota for the entire village; and, as the large landlords often used power and political influence to reduce the amount they should pay, the remaining sum was transferred to the small owners by arbitrarily raising the rates on their land. There were no data on the amount thus transferred, but it was known that this occurred practically every year.)

Rent for medium-grade land in Nanching averaged 300 catties of unhusked rice per mow, or about 43 per cent of the yield. The amount of fertilizer varied for individual plots of land, but the villagers considered it normal to apply either 20 catties of human excreta or 50 catties of soya bean cakes, which had the equivalent value of about 40 catties of unhusked rice in 1948, or about 5.7 per cent of the yield. The amount required for seeds per mow, which varied with the different germination rates of the seeds, averaged about ten catties, or 1.4 per cent of the yield. (For comparison, the major difference in the cost of production for vegetables, aside from the more intensive labor, was the much greater amount of fertilizer needed, which averaged the equivalent of about 200 catties of unhusked rice per mow, or five times higher than that for rice.)

Adding up the four items, the cost of production for one mow of rice land owned and farmed by the peasant himself was about 20 per cent of the yield, the peasant retaining about 80 per cent of the fruits of his own labor. For one mow of rice land rented from others but farmed by the peasant himself, the cost was about 51 per cent of the yield, the peasant retaining only 49 per cent of the crop. Although these figures are approximations, since items like labor and maintenance and replacement of farm tools have not been included, they give a sufficiently accurate view of the general family situation to enable us to determine the incidence of deficit or surplus among families of the different classes in the village.

It is obvious that the very large landlords had incomes which vastly exceeded what was needed for an average standard of living. Family A, for example, which owned 120 mow, had a large two-story house with spacious halls and foreign-style tile floors, a large stone-paved front yard, and a garden, all surrounded by a high brick wall with iron-bar gates.

Let us consider a family owning 30 mow of land and living on the rent from it. The rent income was about 9,000 catties of unhusked rice, which, after paying government taxes and local levies at a rate of 85 catties per mow, netted about 6,450 catties of unhusked or 4,192 catties of husked rice. This was three times the 2,141 catties needed for minimum consumption for an average family. Family E represented such a family. They had a pretentious brick house of eight rooms with a garden in the front, which had been built not from income from the land but from business earnings of the husband. It was understood that the income from the 30 mow and one fish pond was used entirely to support the concubine and her two young children and female servant living in the house. They were well dressed in native style and ate meat and vegetables with rice as the staple food. At one meal, for example, they were having one dish of egg pudding with chopped pork and green onion, one dish of fresh fish steamed with slices of salted fish, one dish of green Chinese cabbage, and turnip soup, all in addition to their main staple of rice. A check with the neighbors revealed that this was normal fare with the family. On the first and fifteenth days of every month, as well as on festival days, they would have chicken or duck and roast pork bought from the neighboring town.

Even for a small landlord of 20 mow, life was quite attractive. He collected a gross rent of 6,000 catties of unhusked rice, and, after paying government taxes and local levies, there remained a net income of 4,300 catties of unhusked or 2,795 catties of husked rice, which was 30 per cent above that needed for estimated minimum consumption.

Turning to those who operated farms instead of living on rent, we find that a rich peasant who operated a farm of, say, 30 mow, which was common with this class, could have a better life than a landlord living only on rent he received from the same amount of land. It was common for a rich peasant to own about 40 per cent of the land he farmed and to rent the other 60 per cent from others. On this basis, he owned 12 mow and rented 18 mow. The gross yield from his own 12 mow would be 8,400 catties of unhusked rice, and his net yield after deducting taxes and levies and fertilizer and seeds would be about 6,720 catties. The gross yield from the 18 rented mow would be 12,600 catties, and the net yield after deducting the cost of production and rent would be 6,174 catties. He therefore had a total net income of about 12,894 catties of unhusked or 8,381 catties of husked rice.

When we turn to the next class, the middle peasants, we find that most of them were able to meet the minimum expenses of the family. Consider a peasant operating a farm of 10 mow, for example. Since it was normal for a middle peasant in Nanching to own about 30 per cent of his land and rent the remaining 70 per cent from others, he would own three mow and rent seven mow. The three mow he owned gave him a gross yield of 2,100 catties of unhusked rice, and after paying taxes and other items of cost mentioned above, he had a net yield of 1,680 catties. His seven rented mow brought in a gross yield of 4,900 catties, and a net yield of 2,400 catties after deducting rent and production costs. Thus his farm altogether gave him a net yield of 4,080 catties of unhusked or 2,652 catties of husked rice. Compared with the 2,141 catties of husked rice needed for minimum consumption of the family, the middle peasant seemed on the surface to have a margin of savings to spare. However, since the middle peasant usually employed some hired help that had to be paid from this net income, and a part had to be put aside for reinvestment in next year's crops, his margin of safety even for normal living was precarious. If there should be expenditures for an unusual occasion like illness, marriage, or death, or if there should be too many mouths in the family to feed, or if he should suffer a partial loss of his crop from damage by storm or ill-timed rains, the middle peasant would have to go into debt or seek supplementary income outside of his own farm.

The middle peasant's position is illustrated by a family in the village which operated a farm of slightly over 11 mow. There were an old grandfather in his seventies, husband and wife both in their forties, and three children all under ten. The house had been inherited from the forefathers. The grandfather and three young children all slept in the front room, where there were three wooden-board beds; the back room was occupied by the couple and was used partly for storage of harvested grain, which was simply piled on the dirt floor in a corner. There was a half-story second floor covering the back part of the house which was used for storing grain and straw for fuel. The house had no windows and was dark and damp and disorderly inside, since it was impossible to keep the dirt floor clean. The grandfather watched the children while the mother helped in the field, so only a limited amount of field help had to be hired. The normal menu for the family was plain boiled rice with boiled fresh vegetables like cabbage or eggplant which came from their own land but was of an inferior quality that could not be sold on the market. A few times a month and on festival days they had a little meat. We often saw the children eat standing in front of the house, each holding a bowl of rice with a few pieces of eggplant or squash or a few strips of green vegetables piled on top. Both the adults' and the children's clothes were patched. The husband said that his nine mow of rice and two mow of vegetables in

1949 brought him a net income of about 3,500 catties of unhusked rice (roughly 2,300 catties of husked rice), and that they barely met family expenditures for that year and saved enough for fertilizer and seeds for the crops of the following year. The price of leeks, which they had planted, had fallen sharply; but, fortunately, no one had been seriously ill, the children were too young to incur the expense of marriage, and the grandfather was still chipper, holding death at arm's length in spite of his advanced age.

If the middle peasant was in a precarious position, the poor peasant's situation was generally very hard indeed. A peasant farming six mow would be a representative case — although some poor peasants in Nanching farmed more, and many farmed only two or three mow. Since for this class it was normal for the peasant to own only 20 per cent of his land, the peasant farming six mow would own 1.2 mow and rent 4.8 mow. With all his land in rice, he received a net income of 672 catties of unhusked rice from his own land and 1,646 catties from his rented land, making a total of 2,318 catties of unhusked or 1,507 catties of husked rice. Compared to the norm of 2,141 catties of husked rice for minimum needs, he was at best some 30 per cent short of sub-sistence requirements, even before he set aside any reinvestment capital for the crops of the following year. Any crop damage from weather or any unusual family needs put him in an inextricable position. It was easy to see why many poor peasants remained single for life or married very late, why so many of their children died in infancy, and why, when an adult died, the family had difficulty in finding a plot to bury him. Elaborate honorific funeral processions were for people like them to sigh over, reflecting the proverb "the poor are without a burial plot."

Wong Mi, previously mentioned, was a peasant of this class. He farmed six mow in 1948–49, of which one was his own. Three mow of his farm were in vegetables and three in rice. He said that he received a net income of about 3,000 catties of unhusked rice or 1,950 catties of husked rice in a period which saw a sharp decline in the price of green vegetables. This income had to feed his family of three, which comprised his father, mother, and himself, besides providing for in-vestment in fertilizer for the vegetable patches for the following year. Fortunately, vegetable crops, upon which he depended heavily, had short intervals between planting and harvests, thus enabling him to circulate his limited capital more easily than the long-term rice crop. The old father in his sixties still helped in the field, and they hired no help. Their small brick house, divided inside into three rooms, was in good condition; it had been inherited from the ancestors and was not a product of current income. They ate rice and green vegetables from the field, and meat was not tasted except for the Chinese New Year and certain other special events during the year. The old mother's clothes were full of patches; those of the father and son showed fewer patches.

Another family, farming only four mow of land, was in a worse condition. The land, one-half a mow owned and the rest rented, was all in rice because of the shortage of both labor and capital to develop a vegetable garden. Their house, which had a thatched roof and thin board walls, was a windowless dark hovel filled with smoke from the cooking stove; their furniture consisted of three wooden-board beds and a rough wooden square table. Piles of straw occupied much of the single room. The family consisted of one middle-aged couple and a sickly looking boy of seven or eight. The wife said that they collected medicinal herbs from among the weeds on the field embankments and hillside to sell in the city, and that both she and her husband worked on other farms to earn some supplementary income. Houses like this one were in the minority even among poor peasants, most of whom had inherited good brick houses. It was when the good houses were burned by the Japanese in the war, as had occurred with many houses in both the eastern and the western ends of the village, or when the peasant became so poor that he had to take down the house in order to sell the timber and bricks, that the houses built to replace them resembled the one described above.

Peasants in Nanching generally wore no shoes. Since the paddy fields were flooded most of the time and the vegetable patches were surrounded by flooded ditches, it was not practical to wear shoes for work; and the year-round warm weather made them unnecessary for protection except for a few weeks toward the end of winter. But there were numerous cases of infected foot wounds resulting from stepping on sharp objects such as broken glass and china, particularly when the main fertilizer used was city garbage in which such objects were mixed. A wounded foot frequently kept a peasant from work for days; and foot wounds constituted the vast majority of the cases treated in a first-aid station set up in the village in 1948–1950. The rich and many of the middle peasants wore wooden sandals for protection after they left the fields, and some of them wore cloth shoes during the cold period of the year; but few of the poor peasants wore even sandals, being unable to afford the small price for them.

We have seen that, of the some 200 families in the village who relied on the land for an income or livelihood, about 30 belonged to the rich-peasant class, about 70 to the middle-peasant class, and about 100 to the poor-peasant class. The foregoing income estimates indicate that a minority of the population lived quite comfortably, a considerable section lived on minimum subsistence with a precarious margin of safety, and the largest group could not make enough from the farm alone to provide even bare subsistence for the family. Stated in another way, yields from the soil alone, whether in the form of rent or production or a combination of the two, adequately supported only one-half of the 200 families. For the other half, operating a farm did not provide a minimum livelihood without some supplementary source of income, such as hiring oneself out as a farm laborer or taking up part-time nonagricultural occupations.

It should be noted here that an obvious defect in our estimate of the approximate income of the villagers is the use of the rice crop alone as the basis of calculation. Since most peasants devoted a part of their farm to truck gardening, which had a different rate of return from investment as compared with the rice crop, it is necessary to give some consideration to the economy of the vegetable crop to give a proper perspective to our estimates of income. As already stated, the general estimate of the gross yield of one mow of vegetables was about twice that of rice, i.e., 1,400 pounds of unhusked rice a year. The leading items in the cost of production were the same as for the rice crop, but there was a greater requirement of labor and fertilizer, the latter estimated to be the value of about 200 catties of unhusked rice per mow a year. Following the foregoing principle of calculation, the net income from one mow of vegetables worked by the peasant himself on his own land would be about 1,100 catties of unhusked or 715 catties of husked rice, and the net income from one mow of rented land would be about 880 catties of unhusked or 572 catties of husked rice, both appreciably higher than the income from one mow of rice crop.

The high yield and shorter turn-over of investment made vegetable crops popular with the poor peasants, and undoubtedly they helped substantially to ease their financial plight, as clearly shown in the case of Wong Mi. For the village as a whole, the higher yield of the vegetable acreage was equivalent to adding 200 mow of rice to the villagers' irrigated land if all irrigated land were planted with rice alone, which partly explains the ability of the existing cultivated land to support such a dense population.

Nonagricultural Sources of Supplementary Income

The Nanching peasants derived supplementary incomes both from subsidiary activities associated with agriculture and from nonagricultural sources, including some specialized occupations, the development of which was not related to the difficulty of making a living from agriculture. It is useful here to list the nonagricultural occupations in the village and the number of persons engaged in each:

Carpentry	1
Masonry	1
Grocery store operator	1
School teacher	2
Seeress	1
Catching frogs and snakes	1
Storytelling	1
Temple priest (Taoist)	1
Peddlers	7
Domestic service	4

The carpenter, the mason, the teachers, and the temple priest were not the direct result of pressure from the difficulty of pursuing an agricultural occupation; but the specialized occupations were not entirely separated from agriculture, for in the above list only the two teachers, four out of seven peddlers, and the four female servants did not own any land. All the others owned small amounts of land. Both the carpenter and the mason were buying small plots in the postwar years, when their business was better than usual. The little grocery store at the center of the village sold candies, cookies, fruit, dry grocery items like salted cabbage, and religious articles like candles and paper money for burning to the spirits. Since this business was very limited, the villagers doing much of their buying in the neighboring town or in the city of Canton, the family owning the store depended upon rent from some land for a part of their income. The seeress worked for a small fee as a spiritual medium, invoking the spirits to talk through her to the living, but she owned a little land; and it was certain that if she had had enough land to live on, she would not have taken up such activities for a living, as her occupation was regarded as degrading and was usually pursued only by the poor in all parts of China. The frog and snake catcher owned two mow of land himself, but he rented them out. Certainly he kept to his poorly paid occupation only because he did not have enough land to assure him a living. The priest had the temple land to support him aside from small donations from worshippers. All the seven peddlers engaged in their trade because of the difficulty of making a living from farming. Two peddled fish, one hawked meat, the others vegetables which they bought from the farmers. The first three peddled in the neighboring town of Pingan Chen on market days and in the surrounding villages on non-market days. They would leave early in the morning, two baskets hanging on the ends of a carrying bamboo pole balanced on their shoulders, trot under the tropical sun hawking their goods from door to door, and return to the village at night. When business was poor, they sought work as farm laborers.

Handicrafts were relatively undeveloped in Nanching. Basket weaving was a common home industry in other parts of China, and here there was excellent material, bamboo, available in abundance, but it was in Pingan Chen that basket weaving was done professionally. Spinning and cloth-weaving, another common home industry in Chinese villages, were done in shops in the southern part of Canton city and in the neighboring Pingan Chen, but not in Nanching. One result of the comparative lack of home industry in this village is worth noting. Whereas ruinous competition from machine-made goods from both Chinese and foreign sources had directly impoverished rural populations in parts of the country where home industry was well developed, its effect on Nanching was only an indirect one. The reduction of handicraft industries in Canton and the neighboring towns created unemployment, thus making it harder for the people from Nanching to find work in towns and cities when it became difficult to make a living at home.

The single home industry of some importance to the villagers was silk embroidery, done by women from late teen age until they were stopped by failing eyesight or old age. This industry was found in about thirty households, including all the "old maid houses" in the period 1949–1951, and the villagers said that there had been more families engaged in it before the Japanese invasion. It was highly skilled work that required long training. A good worker earned the equivalent of 10 to 15 catties of unhusked rice a day, and a less skilled worker earned one-half to two-thirds as much. For a difficult and elaborate piece of work the remuneration was even higher. Payment was by piece rate, and work was not always continuous, depending upon the market. Since it required extreme cleanliness, poor peasant women whose houses were not clean and who had to handle dirt in the fields could not engage in it.

The embroidery was done on a piece of silk, sometimes white and sometimes of other colors, depending on the choice of color for the background by the artist. An artist traced a design on the silk in outline form: flowers, birds, landscapes, historic moral scenes, each to fit the occasion for which the finished piece was intended. Colors to fill the outline were either indicated verbally by the artist or on a colored picture supplied for the embroiderer to follow. The silk with design and instructions was given by the embroidery stores to the embroiderer, who would take it home to work on. The embroiderer supplied her own silk threads of various colors, embroidering needles, and the wooden frame on which the work was mounted.

The finished pieces were used for pillow cases and as pictures to hang on walls, and small pieces were used for slippers, to mention the most common uses. They were bought as gifts for such occasions as weddings, births, a birthday of an important person, the opening of a new store or shop, or moving into a newly built house. Some of these products were marketed locally, but most were exported to Hong Kong and Southeast Asia, and some to the United States. There were half a dozen women in Nanching who turned out beautiful work, and we were amazed by the contrast between the primitive rustic environment, including the simplicity of the peasant women, and the artistic insight which guided their dextrous hands. Despite instructions from the stores, there was still the need for artistic discretion.

In addition to the specialized occupations and embroidery, an important supplementary source of income was the raising of poultry and pigs. Almost every family raised two or three to a dozen chickens. Those who raised only two or three did so mainly for eggs, which were generally sold to egg collectors who came to the village every few days. Only rich peasants could afford to eat the eggs. When the chickens were too old to lay eggs, they were sold at the market in Pingan Chen, and on special occasions like the Chinese New Year they were eaten at home. Those who raised more than a few chickens sold them in the market. Chicken prices had always been high in this area, and in 1948–1951 each catty of live chicken was worth 7.5 catties of unhusked rice. It took an average of three months to raise a chicken to marketable size. At harvest times, chickens picked up rice grains dropped in the fields and on the threshing and drying grounds; ordinarily, they scavenged in the streets and yards for ants and insects and garbage, getting some unhusked rice or rice scraps and chaff as a supplement. Wandering chickens were a part of the village street scene.

Ducks were raised only by a few families because of their special requirements. They were generally raised in large flocks of 100 to 200 and at times even 500. A bamboo shed was erected on the sloping bank of a stream or canal to house them at night. In the daytime they were let out into the stream, where they foraged for small fish and shrimps and floating duckweed, and where they roamed the mud flats and earth embankments for the midget land crabs which formed an important part of their diet. At times, when the midget crabs invaded the paddy fields and damaged young rice plants, a flock of ducks would be let into the field to eat them up. Ducks were sometimes also let into the fields to scavenge for left-over grain. Some supplementary feeding of rice chaff was given occasionally, but not daily. The major cost of duck raising lay not in the feed but in labor, since one person, sometimes a teen-age boy, had to watch the ducks both day and night, and in the erecting of a bamboo shed, renting the land, and buying ducklings from the city. Thus the investment for a flock of ducks was fairly heavy, but, since it normally took only sixty to seventy days to raise them from ducklings to weights of two or three catties for the market, the turnover of the investment was relatively short and the profit relatively attractive.

That only a few families were engaged in this business was partly a result of the restriction of the market. Ducks produced in this vicinity were consumed not only in Canton but were also shipped to Hong Kong and Macao. There had been over twenty families in Nanching raising ducks in the 1920's and the early 1930's, when business in Canton, Hong Kong, and Macao was good, and there was no major disturbance or war to disrupt transportation; groups of duck junks used to anchor on the Pearl River near the village to collect ducks from the vicinity for export. But now these junks were gone. In the postwar years up to 1951, urban buying power was reduced by economic dislocation and widespread unemployment, and transportation and trade with Hong Kong and Macao was disrupted by civil war and by government restrictions on import and export, thus sharply reducing the export of ducks and simultaneously reducing the village's sources of supplementary income. Indeed, the economic position of the Nanching peasants was sensitive to the pulse beat of the greater political and economic situation of the nation.

Like poultry raising, raising pigs was a common source of supplementary income in villages throughout China, and in Nanching about twenty or thirty families kept pigs. Although the pigs were scavengers, garbage in the village streets and rice chaff providing a substantial part of their feed, only one to three pigs were raised by a family, because the regular feed for a greater number would not be within the means of an average peasant. Pigs were generally raised from piglets bought from dealers in Pingan Chen or in Canton, and when they grew to 100 to 200 catties, they were sold to butchers in Pingan Chen or to pig collectors who occasionally came to the village. A sow was sometimes kept for bearing litters and the piglets were sold to other families. Since pork prices were high in this section of the province in 1948–1951, a catty of pork was worth about six catties of unhusked rice, and a live pig of 100 to 200 catties brought a substantial price and gave family finances a needed lift. But aside from the cost of piglets and feed, there was the constant risk of pig epidemics which might completely wipe out the investment. There had been talk about inoculation of pigs by the government against epidemics, but no such program had actually been introduced in this vicinity in the pre-Communist period except for a small-scale experiment carried out by a neighboring agricultural experimental station.

Fish farming was another auxiliary industry in Nanching. There were about ten ponds around the village site that had a good supply of water from the stream and a mud bottom with a cover of water plants. These were stocked early in the spring with fish "seedlings" bought from peddlers. The fish were fed chopped grass and in nine months to a year grew to a length of from eight inches to a foot long and were ready for marketing. Then the pond would be pumped dry and the leaping fish in the puddles caught by small nets or by hand. Most of the fish ponds belonged to the two leading clans, who rented them out to the highest bidder, bidding being held once a year. Because of the investment involved in rent, in the fish "seedlings," and in the labor of collecting good grass and cutting it up, only the middle and rich peasants could engage in this business. It was not an opportunity for the poor, though poor peasants occasionally worked in groups to dam up a section of the small stream in the dry winter and managed to catch some fish and shrimp.

Hard-pressed peasants could earn small sums in temporary occupations which required no capital. One of these was cutting grass from the hillside to sell for fuel; but since hilly land was limited in Nanching, and one could not cut grass that was within the boundaries of neighboring villages, the amount of grass that could be cut was relatively small. Another supplementary occupation was catching grasshoppers to sell in the city for feeding pet birds, but the price was low and the number that could be caught in a day was limited.

All the above auxiliary sources of income undoubtedly helped a large number of families through their financial straits. But many peasants had neither the capital nor the skill for most of these undertakings, and where neither skill nor capital were required, such as in grass-cutting and catching fish from the stream, the situation became one in which "the gruel was too limited for the large number of begging monks." Even the opportunity for farm labor was limited, for only rich peasants and a portion of the middle peasants could afford to hire any sizable amount of help. There was also the competition from the migratory boat people, who worked for lower wages than native laborers.

Credit Facilities

When a peasant was faced with insufficient income to meet absolute needs, when he lacked capital for farming or for an auxiliary enterprise, or·when neither supplementary work in the village nor employment in the city was within his reach, he resorted to borrowing. Credit facilities formed an important part of the agrarian economy in Nanching. Poor peasants were not the only group associated with indebtedness; a considerable number of middle and rich peasants also contracted loans. Chen's study of ten villages in the same county as Nanching showed that 51.4 per cent of all the families investigated were in debt, the distribution of indebted families being 48.6 per cent for rich peasants, 52.8 per cent for middle peasants, and 58.9 per cent for poor peasants. The percentage of indebted families was 5.7 for all landlords' families, and 22.9 for agricultural laborers' families.[5] These figures reflected to a great extent the situation in Nanching.

It is essential to keep in mind that the different classes had different reasons for contracting loans. Investigations in Nanching disclosed that the poor peasants generally borrowed to meet immediate pressing needs, such as paying rent and buying food and seeds or fertilizer to keep the family and the farm going. It was common for the poor and middle peasants to borrow to meet critical situations of family life, such as a marriage or a funeral, since the large sum required for such an occasion was beyond the margin of savings of many middle peasants and most poor peasants. In 1948–1950 it took the equivalent of about 3,000 catties of unhusked rice to get a son married, a sum close to the gross annual income of a middle-peasant family and exceeding that of a poor-peasant family. Among middle peasants in a better financial position and among rich peasants it was common to find borrowing for improvement of the farm and for auxiliary production. In 1949 Wong Yu borrowed 600 catties of unhusked rice to go into partnership with another peasant to bid for a fish pond. Borrowing for fertilizer to increase productivity was quite common.

The channels of borrowing varied with the size of the loan and the credit standing of the prospective debtor. For smaller sums, and for persons of good credit standing among friends and relatives, the most popular method was to organize a credit society. This was a national institution prevalent in all parts of China, and the mechanics of it have been excellently treated by Yang Hsi-meng in his book, *A Study of China's Credit Societies* (in Chinese). Fei gave a brief summary of it as follows:

> This society is a sort of savings system, into which each member pays a certain amount at certain intervals and from which he is paid a certain sum on a specified date. The size of the payment to be made by each participant and the time at which he will be paid are prearranged. Anyone in need of money may organize a society by enlisting ten other members. Each will pay a predetermined proportion of the $100 which the organizer receives . . . Thereafter the society meets every six months, usually in March and September, at which time one member receives $100 and the rest make their payments. Members other than the organizer pay sums directly proportionate to the order in which they are paid, so that, in effect, the first five are paying interest for loans they have received, while the last five are receiving interest for money they have deposited. The organizer, on the other hand, repays just $100 during the five-year life of the society and has thus secured a loan without interest. But he is obliged to offer a feast at each meeting and has the responsibility of collecting the money. Furthermore, in case of default by any of the subscribers, he is held accountable. The functioning of this system depends on the invariable discharge of their obligations by the subscribers, and this is secured only by existing ties of friendship and kinship.[6]

The chief advantage of the credit society was its ability to provide a loan at the normal rate of interest without subjecting the debtor to the extortion of private usurers. A person of good credit standing could sometimes organize or belong to several societies and obtain a sizable loan by combining the proceeds from the different societies. The normal rate of interest for a loan in 1948–1950 was about 20 per cent for six months, or about 40 per cent per annum. This was considerably lower than 30 to 100 per cent for six months quoted by Chen for many localities in this province.[7] One reason was the village's proximity to a big city where money was more available than in interior districts.

Borrowing from private lenders was another channel of credit. There were no professional money lenders in Nanching, but there were several in the neighboring town of Pingan Chen. In Nanching rich peasants and smaller landowners as well as those with a little savings to spare would lend money to needy friends or relatives at the normal rate of interest. They were generally not usurers. But lending money or grain to a friend or relative frequently resulted in quarrels and spoiled the social relationship in case of default or delay in repayment of capital or interest or both. Consequently, people with modest savings either kept the money at home or left it with a friend or relative engaged in a sound business for a rate of interest much lower than the normal rate for loans.

Some villagers obtained loans from merchants in Pingan Chen, and a rice mill there frequently made loans in grain to peasants in the vicinity. But making loans was not important with the town merchants, and the borrower had to have very good credit standing. It was not known to what extent the several usurers in town affected the poor peasants in Nanching. Since in our conversations with the villagers we did not hear any talk of usury, as the writer had heard it constantly in talking to villagers in North China, we assumed that this phase of the credit situation was unimportant in the over-all picture of the village.

For the poor peasant without a good credit standing the most common channels of credit were the pawn shop and effecting a temporary transference of his own land if he had any. In both cases, the loan was granted to a peasant not on his credit standing but on the tangible property he could put up as security. The proverbial description of a person absolutely at the end of his means was to say that he "has pawned every article in his possession." There was no pawn shop in Nanching nor was there any in Pingan Chen; but there was one in a village about two miles away which was owned by a big landlord there, and a person who wanted to use a pawn shop could always go to the city where there were plenty of them. Pawn shops' interest rates were high. The one in the nearby village charged in 1948–49 a rate of 20 per cent for every three months, or 80 per cent per annum, and this was comparatively low as against those in some interior districts.

A temporary transference of land to obtain a loan was called *dien t'ien*. The debtor transferred his land to the creditor for the period of the loan. Since the creditor could farm the land himself or could rent it out, no interest was charged. The deed remained in the hands of the debtor, who kept legal ownership of the land. Poor peasants with a small piece of land resorted to this means only when all other channels of credit were blocked, but there were many families in this village who had mortgaged their land this way.

The unfavorable credit standing of poor peasants was a major disadvantage in their efforts to improve their situation by borrowing. This difficulty was augmented by the tradition that "the son must pay his father's debt." In fact, a man was held responsible for unpaid debts contracted by persons within the same household, even though the original debtor had died within a generation's time, the Chinese family being a collective unit of production and consumption. The added weight of indebtedness for relatives reduced the poor peasants' chance of extrication from insolvency, for it was common to find that a poor peasant's father had died leaving unpaid debts. One means of freeing oneself from indebtedness was to work out the debt by performing farm labor for the creditor, a fairly common practice in Nanching for small loans when the creditor could use farm labor.

Channels of Emigration

When farming alone could not provide a livelihood for half of the villagers, when other occupations were not available in the village, and when credit facilities generally discriminated against the neediest of the peasants, agrarian life for the poorer half of the community was bleak and often impossible. While only one case of death from insufficiency of food and malnutrition was observed in the village during the period of investigation, the economic plight of a large number of the poor peasants constantly struggling along with half-filled stomachs and listening to the hunger cries of their children was a common story. For these peasants, the solution lay in going beyond the economically restrictive confines of the village borders.

If the agricultural community of Nanching offered few opportunities for employment, right at hand was the big city of Canton, a city of over a million population, where beckoned a great variety of occupations. Transportation lines led from Canton to Hong Kong, Macao, coastal cities like Shanghai, and yonder to foreign lands like Southeast Asia. And so for half a century after modern transportation came to this territory, the poor and the hard-pressed in Nanching had been going to Canton and to more distant destinations to seek a living. Before the great depression hit this part of the world in 1933 and 1934, there were about one hundred families having one or more members as long-term emigrants. When the cities were hard hit by the depression, the subsequent Japanese invasion, and the postwar inflation and political disturbances, many emigrants were driven back to the village. Now, in 1948–1951, there were only about forty or fifty families having such long-term emigrants.

Emigrants were of two types: seasonal and long-term. Seasonal emigrants were those who went to the city for a few months or shorter periods in a year, generally during slack periods at the farm, and returned to the village when busy farm work called or when city employment was no longer available. Long-term emigrants were those who were away for a longer period, visiting the family in the village from time to time, perhaps once or twice a year, or perhaps at even longer intervals, depending mainly upon the distance to be traveled and the financial means available. They generally returned to the village to spend their old age and to die where their ancestors were resting. Those who had moved out with their families were no longer counted as members of the community.

Seasonal emigrants generally went to Canton, from which they could easily come home to attend to farm work and be close to the family. Their predominant occupation was "selling hard labor" (*mai k'oo li,* hence the pidgeon English word "coolie"). They worked as porters on docks, in warehouses and wholesale houses that needed heavy moving done daily, at pulling rickshaws and carts, at carrying and digging dirt. When the city was being modernized and the streets widened and paved from the 1920's on, there was work in crushing rocks and carrying dirt for roads and building construction; when rickshaws were replaced by pedicabs after the Japanese invasion, rickshaw pullers became pedicab drivers. In this sense, the modernization of the city during the past quarter of a century opened opportunities of employment for many of the villagers who otherwise would have been at the end of their means.

Peddling vegetables in the city also engaged many of the villagers in their spare time. But to carry seventy or eighty pounds of goods on one's shoulders to the city and hawk it from door to door needed as much strength as many of the "hard labor" jobs, and many of the young poor peasants who had the strength to peddle shunned it because of the humiliation that was frequently involved. Wong Mi said, "I don't want the few cents when every time I have to curry the favor of a customer and take his insults with a smile in the process of bargaining. I am poor, but I would rather starve farming than to half-starve peddling." The dignity of this poverty-stricken young peasant was also found in many other poor peasants like him. In fact, there were more women than men who peddled in the city for supplementary income, the women being more accustomed to swallowing their pride.

Long-term emigrants, for the most part, went to Hong Kong. A few went to Southeast Asian points like Indo-China and Singapore, and occasionally a few went north to places like Shanghai. There the dominant occupations for them were peddling, small businesses, shop help, "hard labor," sailing, and, for a few, engaging in large businesses. Generally speaking, there were more Lees from this village who engaged in business and went to Southeast Asia where one could earn more money, and more Wongs who worked at "hard labor" jobs and were sailors. Lee Tou was a merchant dealing in wholesale groceries in Hong Kong, for example; and there were many Lees who became small business men in Canton or Hong Kong. Almost all those who went to work on ships were Wongs. This was chiefly due to the functioning of kinship relations in economic life. One who knew of an opportunity in one's own occupation usually recommended it to a kinsman. A Lee already engaged in business in Hong Kong would hire his own relatives as help or recommend them to fellow businessmen who might need help. A Wong in the "hard labor" business, an activity tightly controlled by secret societies, or in marine work, did the same for his own kinsmen.

There were exceptions to this general division, since an individual, once in the big cities, might get into any occupation on his own initiative or by chance. Wong Yu went to Hong Kong because the few mow of land his father had were not enough to support the family. In Hong Kong he set up a little stall in the market place, selling cooked food. There he even took a wife and lived in a rented shack and was able to send a little money home now and then to his aging father. The Japanese invasion of Hong Kong drove him home, and he had to take up farming, but his modest savings from the city enabled him to buy a little land to add to the family's limited possessions. Wong Hung, whose concubine lived in the village until 1950, was also a businessman, and a very successful one. His father had been a landless tenant peasant, and in his early teens Wong Hung had been taken by a relative to work on a ship. Shifting from ship to ship, he finally landed in Hanoi, Indo-China. There he got a job with a French exporter of jute and jute bags used for packing rice for shipment. He learned French and English and in time established his own business and prospered. One villager said that he was worth a quarter of a million Hong Kong dollars (about $40,000 United States currency at the exchange rate of 1951), and he was then in his mid-fifties. He bought land in the village to support his concubine and her children, and he built a foreign-style house surrounded by a Chinese garden to entertain foreign business colleagues who wished to see rural China.

Long-term emigrants generally sent money home to buy a little land and to keep the family going. No success has been achieved in trying to estimate the amount of such remittances for the entire village, but the effect of remittances on the economic life of the village was clearly visible. Since there were more Lees in business who earned more money than the Wongs, there were more large landowners among the Lees than among the Wongs until the Japanese invasion. Then the trend began to reverse itself, as explained previously. The investment in buying land was a demonstration of the substantial amount of remittances received by the village. But the majority of these landowners kept their families in the village; they were not absentee owners who drained wealth from the village.

There were many emigrants who had permanently drifted away from the village. Wong Ho, who died of malnutrition, had a son engaged in a small business in Shanghai. This son went to Shanghai with his father in the 1920's and took a wife in Shanghai, but unlike his father, he did not return. He did not even send money home to his aged father. There were large landlords who had migrated to Canton and Hong Kong permanently, using city earnings to buy land in the village and taking rent from the village to re-invest and spend in the cities, a process which worked to the impoverishment of the villagers. Families B and C belonged to this type, and Family A belonged more to this type than to the type of occupying owners. Young sons of large landowners and rich peasants tended to remain permanently in the cities where they received their education. The Japanese war forced two or three of these young educated men to return, and they took up farming. But this was clearly due to circumstances, and not their own choice. Lee Chan-piao, the son of a returned emigrant from Hong Kong, had a high school education in Canton and had worked in the city as a clerk in the municipal government for some years before the Japanese invasion. He had returned to operate his father's farm of about twenty mow and two fish ponds. His livelihood was above the average in the village, and he had married a city girl. But his constant desire was to return to the city as soon as there was an opportunity of employment, a desire that was encouraged by his city-bred wife. He was a typical product of the effects of migration and the widening gap between urban and rural life in China.

Surveying the broad picture of emigration, it is significant that it was the city and not another village which provided a destination for temporary or permanent exodus. The urban centers in this respect operated as a safety valve for the hard-pressed elements in the countryside and for the overstrained agrarian economy. On the other hand, when the urban economy was plagued by a depression or disrupted by political and military disturbances, the unemployed or otherwise economically dislocated persons could return to the village where their kinship roots lay and where the soil would provide subsistence until times became better again for them to return to the city. The urban and the village economies thus helped each other regain balance when either was struck by a crisis. This was possible partly because the commercialization of agriculture had not developed to the extent of destroying the substantial degree of self-sufficiency of the agrarian economy, a self-sufficiency that insulated the village life from being too deeply affected by spreading influences from the dislocation of economic life in the city.

The Question of Pre-Communist Change

Had the economic situation of the village always been like this, at least in the past half century? What changes had taken place in the economic life of the community in recent decades? And was the lot of the majority of the villagers better or worse compared to fifty years ago? While there is no statistical data on these questions, we can summarize some of the known facts in order to throw limited light on these questions.

Land, the basic means of livelihood, had been expanding very slowly by encroaching upon the river, but the limit of such expansion had been about reached under traditional agricultural techniques and organization. Methods of cultivation had remained the same as long as living villagers were able to recall. Contacts with improved methods had been extremely limited, and new ideas, such as the effort to introduce a new weeder that could raise the efficiency of weeding per person at least five fold, had been vigorously resisted because of the villagers' doubts of their value. The only new elements in agricultural technique found in Nanching were the occasional use of chemical fertilizer and modern insecticide applied with sprayers. But the villagers thought that the chemical fertilizer's fertility did not last as long as night soil, city garbage, and soya bean cakes; and modern insecticides were beyond the means of the common peasant. Consequently, the influence of these innovations on the village's economy had been negligible.

The basic system of land ownership had remained the same, and old villagers recalled no major change in the general rate of rent charged by owners. There might have been some change in the period of land tenure, for old villagers talked of five-to-ten-year periods which no longer existed; but it would seem that, if there had been a general shortening of tenure, frequent bidding would have pushed up the rent rate.

It has been mentioned that the clan land of the Wongs had been reduced, which might have meant a certain increase in economic difficulties with the Wongs, many of whom were tenant farmers; but we could not be certain about the trend in the distribution of owner-ship of private land over the past half century. Chen's study of ten villages in the same county indicated a tendency toward concentration of land ownership from 1928 to 1933. Although it was not possible to tell to what extent this was applicable to Nanching, it was a fact that the possessions of Families A, B, and C, the largest owners, represented acquisitions within the past half century. Before the rise of these families, there had been at least one large landlord family. In the 1860's, a prospering middle peasant, Lee Ch'ang, bought an increasing amount of land and sent two of his three sons to school. One of the sons passed the provincial grade of the imperial examinations, became an official, acquired wealth and expanded his family land to over 100 mow around 1890. But by the time of the Republican Revolution (1911), the entire family had moved away to the city where the grandchildren squandered the family fortune and became poor. In the 1930's, the last of the family land was liquidated. There were no records to show how many large landlords there had been in former times or the extent of their aggregate possessions of land as compared with the present situa-tion. Certainly the instances of decentralization of land ownership in recent years were wartime phenomena which did not represent a long-term trend in the past half century.

There had been one discernible change in land ownership in Nan-ching. The expansion of the city economy in the last fifty years had attracted large numbers of emigrants from this village and, in turn, increased the amount of land bought by their earnings. Although the majority of such purchases were small plots, their total effect would be to reduce the ownership of land by the tillers of the soil; and the process of increasing holdings by emigrants who acquired capital in the city explains to some extent the high percentage of tenancy in the village, the development of absentee ownership, and the removal from the village of rent to the equivalent of the total yield of some 170 mow of land, 14 per cent of the total cultivated area — a possible factor in the deteriorating economic position of many peasants in the village. All these were typical phenomena in a village so near a big city, phenomena that had long attracted the attention of students of rural problems of modern China.

There had been gradual changes traceable to the growth of com-merce in general in the past fifty years. There had been little change in the economic character of the rice crop, but the villagers thought that vegetable acreage was greater than forty or fifty years ago, an observation apparently substantiated both by the sizable amount of vegetables, particularly leeks, produced in the village and exported to Hong Kong and Macao and by the growth of population in Canton, which must have increased the local need for vegetables. The development of the Hong Kong market and the growth of Canton, both new facts in the past half century, had unquestionably influenced the whole economy of the village. The growing of jasmine before the depression, the raising of ducks, and handicraft embroidery were in part results of modern commercial developments that reduced the self-sufficient character of the village life and increasingly integrated it with the economy of the outside world. That integration was visible in the machine-made cloth that the villagers generally wore, in the shoes they bought, and in the kerosene they burned in their lamps instead of soya bean oil.

In any attempt to visualize the effects of pre-Communist change, it is essential to recall the political vicissitudes of the local and national situations over the past fifty turbulent years. Civil wars, particularly in the 1920's, when they came as regularly as the seasons, had meant the disruption of transportation and markets for agricultural products; they had meant the kidnapping of young peasants as carriers of military equipment and supplies for warlord soldiers even though the village escaped destruction. There had been many changes and depreciations of currencies accompanying the changes of government resulting from the civil strife. In the early 1920's, nickel coins were issued to take the place of the old ten-cent silver pieces; later the nickel coins were decreed void, and peasants who held them suffered a complete loss. The old twenty-cent silver coins were constantly cheapened by the reduction of their silver content. The steady depreciation of the copper coins, continuing from the early 1920's until the time of the Japanese invasion in 1937, and caused mainly by Japanese smuggling of counterfeits, caused a considerable long-term loss for the peasants, whose small transactions left them with sizable quantities of depreciated copper coins. The most severe losses in the 1920's were from repeated annulments of the many paper currencies issued by the ephemeral provincial regimes. Many peasants held such paper money as savings. There was a repetition of these tragic experiences in the wartime and postwar inflation of the CNC (Chinese National Currency) and the Gold Yuan of the Nationalist government. Since Nanching, being near a great city, had long been a part of the monetary economy, the monetary disorders of the past half century had repeatedly wiped out a part of the savings of its people. The peasants, slow at the shell game of the money market, many a time woke up to find their savings depreciated or totally worthless.

The villagers, who traditionally viewed the past as better than the present, all said that life was harder these days than in their forefathers' time. We had no accurate basis for a statistical comparison of the present village economy with that of former periods, but there were two features of the village which seemed to confirm the villagers' view.

The first was the houses. They were generally built of bricks, many with one- or two-foot stone foundations above the ground. Almost all were at least forty to fifty years old and although the brick and stone work of many of them still stood strong, within one often found rotting timber unrepaired and unreplaced. It was plain that they had lacked proper maintenance by the occupants for the past ten or twenty years. A sharp contrast was found in the flimsy quality of all except a very few of the newer houses. The houses of Families A and E, built within the last thirty years, matched the quality of the old houses; but the new houses in all other cases were inferior. One family of rich-peasant status had built a house in the early 1940's. Although it was a brick structure, the bricks were of poor quality, the brick laying was poorly done in irregular layers, and the timber was cheap local soft wood. It had no stone foundation; it looked shabby compared to any of the average old houses. At the eastern end of the village, where many old houses had been burned by Japanese troops, there rose from the ruins unsightly shacks of thin wood planks, with a few cheaply built brick houses scattered among them. Since houses in a Chinese village represented the savings of the villagers, the difference in the average quality of the old and the new houses in Nanching appeared to symbolize a decrease of savings and a general deterioration in the economic welfare of the village.

The second feature we noted was the appearance of the ancestral halls or temples. The main ancestral halls of both the Wong and the Lee clans, with their extensive stone foundations, their fine bricks, their elaborate ornaments of carved brick, wood, and plaster, the mural paintings, the great hard-wood timbers of the pillars and roof joists, the spacious stone-paved yards, and the massive effect of the whole structure, were still inspiring sights. But the villagers said that the building of such structures would be quite beyond the means of the present generation; and, in fact, the ancestral halls of the Chen and Chang clans, which had been burned by the Japanese, had not yet been rebuilt, despite the fact that being without an ancestral hall meant being without a collective symbol of the clan. The many small ancestral halls set up by the subdivisions of the clans of the Wongs and the Lees were in poor condition; the timber had been allowed to rot and the roofs left to leak without repairs. Such neglect was not because of the descendants' lack of interest but was brought about by the lack of means. Here again was another indication that the economic condition of the village as a whole had deteriorated compared to that of half a century ago.

CHAPTER VI

Kinship System

THE LIFE of a peasant community like Nanching was characterized not only by its agrarian economy but also by the prominent place of kinship relations in its social structure. Since the family functioned as an organizational unit in agricultural production, and in turn, occupation on the soil was uniquely conducive to the development of strong and stable kinship ties, agrarian life was in a large measure woven out of the social fabric of kinship relations; and the peasant was more kinship-minded in his dealing with the social world than any other section of the Chinese population.

Dominance of the Kinship System

The dominant position of the kinship system in this as in other village communities stemmed especially from the immobility of the agrarian population. As already pointed out, the population of Nanching was mainly the result of biological multiplication within several clans. Generation after generation of kinsmen had continued to live on the same spot and pursue the same occupation, agriculture, until their number had reached that of a sizable community. The lack of occupational diversification in the agricultural economy and the insulating character of subsistence farming fostered a uniform mode of life, enhanced intimate economic and social co-operation, restricted population mobility, and furthered the internal cohesion of the lineage group, the kinship organization.

The lack of diversified opportunities of employment, characteristic of an agrarian economy, forced sons to follow in their father's footsteps, a process which had gone on for over thirty generations for both the Wong and the Lee clans, until the population in the village had become firmly integrated into the form of kinship groups. From cradle to grave, one did not leave the rigid ties and intimate influence of one's own kinsmen. Traditional values had been fully developed to orient the individual's attitudes and sentiments ever toward the family and the clan and their economic foundation on agricultural livelihood. A son with wanderlust was told, "Pleasant are the thousand days at home, but difficult is even half a day spent on the road." "Li hsiang pei ching" (to leave one's home community and to turn away from the family well) was the classic lament of the traveler or of one who was forced to seek a living in the "cold and harsh outside world." In Nanching, kinship relations represented the paramount force tying the individual into a tightly-knit organization beyond which he contracted few direct and intimate social bonds. If familism and clannism characterized Chinese society in general, it was in this part of China that they were most fully developed and well maintained.

Familism and clannism were visibly built into the physical plan of the village. The houses were grouped by clans so that each clan occupied a distinct section of the village, and each section was separated from another by gates. Even families of each subdivision of a clan were generally concentrated on the same street or alley. Interclan rivalry was intense, sometimes flaring into open conflict. At such times, children of one clan did not dare to play in another clan's territory.

The kinship structure consisted of the clan, the clan subdivisions, and the individual families. The "Great Ancestor" (t'ai kung) or original male settler of the Lee clan had five sons; each married and propagated in this village. All male and unmarried female descendants of the Great Ancestor were constituents of the clan. The descendants of each of the five sons constituted the membership of a subdivision, a fang or house. The Lee clan had five subdivisions, and the Wong clan had four, all residing in the village. Under each subdivision were the individual families.[1] Due to the expansibility of the Chinese family system, there was in theory no rigid limitation on the size of the family. Classical principles prescribed intimate family relations among descendants from a common ancestor within five generations, as expressed in mourning and other ceremonial obligations, the participation in which served as important identification of family membership. Families consisting of members of five generations living under a common roof were by no means unknown in China, but in Nanching intimate family relations functioned among the members of three generations who held common property and carried on common consumption and production. In a poor family having several married sons, one of them would live with the parents while the rest set up separate households, thus creating a three-generation family and several two-generation conjugal families counting the married sons' children.

Within this web of kinship relations an individual was born, received his physical nourishment, mental development, initial social status, assistance in his career, aid in his unfortunate moments of unemployment and disability, support and comfort in his old age, and burial upon his death. Encouragement for his descendants to offer sacrifices to his spirit when he was gone was meant not so much to take care of him in the other world as to perpetuate the family tradition in this one. No stronger bond between man existed in his social consciousness. And many of the extra-familial social relations were projections of the family relations, symbolized, for example, by appellation between friends, which included a large number of kinship terms such as elder brother and sister, younger brother and sister, and "senior uncle" (elder brother of one's father). In our field investigations we used such terms to foster the good will and friendship of the villagers.

Functional Factors in the Family System

As a highly integrative system, the family organization functioned by devices that tended to identify the status, the interest, and the sentiments of the individual with the integrity of the organization. To prevent the development of individual interests from disrupting the solidarity of the family group, emphasis was laid upon the ascriptive aspect of the status of the members. Both the integrative and the ascriptive aspects were among the important structural factors that enabled the family system to function successfully.

Marriage and Divorce

Marriage, an event critically affecting the structural form of the family system, might mark the breaking of the younger generation into independent family units, thus reducing the size and ending the organizational continuity of the parental family, or it might add new members to the parental family, increasing its size and its ability to maintain an organized continuity through successive generations. Marriage in Nanching, as in other parts of China, was oriented toward the second objective, and the means to achieve it was the practice of arranged marriage which embodied strong integrative and ascriptive features.

In this practice, the parents chose mates for their children and made all important decisions concerning their marriage, which was taken as a family matter under the dictate of the head of the family and not as an event designed exclusively for the interests of the marrying individuals. The classical purpose was to perpetuate the patrilineal family, to beget male offspring who would perform the ancestral sacrifice, to continue the "smoke from the incense," to obtain a daughter-in-law to serve and help the parents, and to establish a growing family with earning power for the security of the parents' old age. Should a son balk at being married or at the parents' choice of a mate, he was reminded that this marriage was not his business but that of the parents and the family.

The procedure and ceremonies of traditional marriage were designed both to prevent the married son from breaking away into a new family unit with his wife and to integrate the bride, a stranger, into the intimate life of the husband's family, to whose authority she was subjected thereafter. The traditional idea of fate in wedlock, the paying of a ceremonial price for the bride, the dwarfing of the significance of the marrying individuals by the accentuated symbolism of the family and the broader kinship group in all the ceremonial acts and elaborate feasting, and the ever-present element of ancestor worship in every stage of the wedding procedure all impressed upon the marrying parties and others at the scene the importance of familial continuity as a basic purpose of the whole costly and elaborate event.

In Nanching and in other villages in this province, marriage ceremonies for a son consisted of two parts, one being performed within the immediate family and the other in the clan. In the second part the new couple offered sacrifice to the ancestors in the main and subdivision ancestral halls, and the family provided one to three feasts for all members of the clan. It was this part of the ceremony, along with the ceremonial price for the bride, that constituted the major expense in the marriage of a son, totaling about 3,000 catties of unhusked rice in Nanching and its vicinity in 1948, more than a year's income for a poor peasant. The whole expense was usually borne by the groom's parents. It was this sum that frequently sank the entire family of a poor peasant and many a middle peasant into financial insolvency; but the expense, huge when measured against the average family's wealth, was an important factor that bound the marrying individuals to the family and subjected them to family authority.

The traditional arranged marriage was still the dominant institution in Nanching in spite of its propinquity to Canton, where a family revolution against the ancient system had been raging for half a century. During the past decade there had been a few marriages through free individual choice of partners and romantic love, but without exception these were returning emigrants who brought their wives home from the cities; and even in these cases the traditional wedding ceremony was repeated in the immediate family as well as in the clan in order to gain recognition for the marriage from the community. In one such case, the wife, a city working girl, was very insistent that the traditional wedding ceremony should be performed in the village in spite of the husband's objection to the high cost of the feast for the clan. The original wedding in the city having been a simple private affair attended by only a few friends, the woman was plainly concerned about the lack of formality in her marriage; and in her mind it was the elaborate ceremony and the clan feast in the village that would give public witness, recognition, and security to her status as wife at a time when the marriage law of the government was hardly known to the common people.

The vast majority of the marriages in the village were monogamous. Polygamy was traditionally permitted on the formal ground of obtaining male heirs in case of failure by the wife to bear a son, but it was also a practice that permitted a man to make up for the loss of romantic experience in his arranged marriage. As polygamy required the husband's ability to support one or more additional women and the children they might bear, it was obviously beyond the economic means of the poor and middle peasants. The polygamous families were those of large landlords, except one which was that of a rich peasant who was also a local politician. Except for the concubine of one rich peasant, who had been a girl from the "boat people," in all the cases investigated the concubines had at one time been prostitutes bought from their owners in the cities. Wong Hung's concubine had originally lived with him in Hong Kong, but his wife had been jealous and mistreated her badly; so he brought her to the village to live, visiting her a few times a year. Since the concubines behaved properly in the village, observing the strict rules of sex segregation and refraining from associating with male villagers, they all enjoyed good status as members of rich families.

The practice of exogamy based on surnames deserves brief attention here. Men and women bearing the same surname might not marry, although marriage to maternal cousins was permissible. The national tradition of surname exogamy might have had some significance for the community life in Nanching aside from the eugenic nature of the problem as discussed by writers on other occasions. Under this exogamous practice, parents in this village usually had to go to neighboring clans within a radius of five to ten miles to get a bride for their marriageable son. The resulting marital bond had the effect of broadening the social ties of the villagers and creating contacts and relationships which constituted a part of the existence of the larger local community beyond the confines of a clan or a village. Without this, the high degree of economic self-sufficiency in the village as a unit and the strong and exclusive character of the clan organization might have resulted in the development of mutually isolated clannish communities, with frequent armed conflict between them.

Formal divorce was not known in this village. A wife mistreated by her husband or his family often returned to her own parents for varying periods of from a few months to many years, sometimes for life. But such action did not constitute a formal divorce in the modern sense of the term, for both sides still had claims against each other as husband and wife in spite of the physical separation. Aside from the lack of institutional recognition of the right of divorce, any permanent severance of a matrimonial tie was difficult for the wife because of the lack of women's property rights and means of self-support, social discrimination against remarriage of divorced women, lack of rights to take the children with them, and possible mistreatment of the children left with the husband's family. For men, the lack of the right of divorce in the old tradition had less serious implications than in the case of women. Men held superiority over women in formal social status, and they were the sole possessors of family property. Armed with these two major weapons, some men did mistreat their wives, beating them into submission if necessary. Wife beating was not common in this village, but it was by no means unknown. On the other hand, there were many hen-pecked husbands in this community. But they were deviants from the institutionalized pattern of roles within the family, as shown by the common feeling that there was something "unnatural" about hen-pecked husbands, who were always the subject of jokes.

The underlying principle governing divorce was that, just as marriage was not the result of individual wish and choice, so breaking a marriage was not a matter for the individual to decide. With supreme emphasis upon the integrity of the family, there could only be adjustment and sacrifice of individual interests for the benefit of the family; and the absence of divorce as a means of adjustment of individual interests even in cases of irreconcilable domestic conflict was especially marked in this village as compared to the city.

However, as just pointed out, there was the not uncommon practice of long-term separation when the wife returned to her parents' home to live; and there were several such returned wives in Nanching. As a rule, they belonged to the "old maid" houses, usually good, clean brick

houses with three or four rooms each, where the majority of members
spent their days chatting and doing some handicraft like embroidery
and returned to their own parents' homes to sleep. Only the homeless
slept there. Three types of women constituted the membership:
separated wives, widows, and a few unmarried women. Separated
wives and widows belonged there on the theory that once a woman
was married to another family, she belonged body and spirit to a family
other than the parents' and after her death her spirit could not return
to the parents' home. In case of alienation from her husband's home,
her spirit must have another home to attach itself to in order to avoid
the tragedy of becoming a homeless wandering soul. An "old maid"
house represented a home for the spirits of such women. Should death
draw near a member who was living in her own parents' home, she was
moved to the "old maid" house to die, so that her spirit would know
where to return. There was always a little altar in each house where
carved wooden tablets of deceased members were placed in rows. Religious sacrifices were offered on the death anniversary of each member
by those living. It was apparent that "old maid" houses were pseudo-
families intended to maintain the moral, spiritual, and material value
of the family for those who had broken loose from family ties.

Age and Generational Levels

In the integration of successive generations into an extended kinship
system, the status arrangement of a large number of members became
a structural matter of paramount importance. The kinship organization here as elsewhere in China operated mainly by a system of status
ascribed on the basis of age and generational levels which to some
degree transcended sex differences. A kinship member's form of behavior and allocation of material benefits in relation to those of another member were partly determined by age and generational factors.
Within the same generation, older members took precedence over
younger members; members of a senior generation took precedence over
those of a junior generation. Since every individual had a certain age
and belonged to a generation, this scheme offered a practical device for
clearly establishing the status of every member in a kinship group
whether it consisted of a small family or of a clan with 10,000 members.

The operation of the system was aided by the differentiation between
the lineal and the collateral relations, the rigidity of one's status regarding age and generational differences being greatest with close kin.
Based upon generational levels and upon the factor of lineal or collateral descent, the *Ta Ch'ing Lü Li* (Laws and Regulations of the

Ch'ing Dynasty) distinguished forty-one different groups of kinship members, each group designated by distinct kinship terms.[2] Within a group, each member was designated by an individual term based on sex and age, age being arranged numerically by the order of birth, such as "first elder sister" or "third elder brother." These terms were used by kinship members in addressing one another. Although older members and those in a senior generation usually addressed younger ones and those in a junior generation by individual names, proper kinship terms were used in mentioning junior members to a distant relative or to a stranger. As each of the forty-one groups of relatives might consist of one to over ten members, the total number of kinship terms that an individual must learn to recognize was very large. One American reader of the chart of kinship terms suitably remarked, "We don't even recognize the vast majority of these people in our culture, to say nothing of having a specific term of address for each one of them." Learning the complete system of kinship terms constituted an important part of a peasant's training to fit him for social life in a kinship-oriented community.

In Nanching it was the effective operation of this complicated system of kinship terms that enabled each individual in the kinship group to identify his own status, to assert his authority or to offer his obedience, to exercise his privilege or to fulfill his obligations with regard to the distribution of material and nonmaterial benefits. It was the ability to identify each individual's position which enabled the Wong and the Lee clans, each with over 400 members, to function as an orderly organization. In general, the Confucian canon of maintaining a "proper order by age" still guided the social relations in this village.

However, although the observation of filial piety and the reverence for age were lessons instilled in the minds of the villagers from early childhood by nursery stories, folklore, school texts, themes in novels and operas, and social pressure, the observation of "age hierarchy" as a tradition had not remained strictly intact during the recent decades. The village's proximity to the big city and the large number of emigrants returning periodically or permanently to the village had been channels of entry for the general spirit of the modern age characterized by the rising status of the young and their rebellion against "oppression" by the age hierarchy.

In the late 1930's there had been armed conflict in the village between a young group and an older group, with several elders from both the Wong and the Lee clans taking part. The fight was for the control of an organization connected with the right to collect crop-protection fees. The villagers were reluctant to talk about the details of that internal conflict. They consistently blamed it on the unruliness of the young, but they also expressed the opinion that, if the older generation had been able to retain the full respect of the younger members of the clans, it would not have occurred. Whether the villagers' opinion was right or wrong, the incident was indicative of the modern trend away from the established system of status and authority based on age and generational levels. To the young, the world was changing, and the scene of change in the city was near enough to influence them. Although the continuation of traditional life in the village still sustained a measure of respect for the old, the new forces which were dooming traditional life in the cities were beginning to be felt by more and more young people in the village.

The age hierarchy was still strong within the intimate families in the village, being supported by the function of the family as the basic production unit in an agricultural economy, the father's leadership in production activities, the maintenance of the parents' property rights, and in most families, the children's dependence upon the family economic organization. Among poor peasants, where family property was negligible, the family production unit too limited for even the subsistence of the entire family, and children had to shift for themselves at an early age, their economic self-reliance might diminish their filial respect. Whereas Wong Yu, whose family was a financially comfortable one, was filial toward his aged father, Wong Mi, the poor peasant, was known to have beaten his old mother and to have been rebellious toward his father. But even in the case of Wong Mi's family and others of the same class, the father still exercised a substantial amount of control over the son because of the traditional influence of filial piety and because of village group pressure directed against the rebellious son.

Filial piety, being limited to the parent-child relationship, contributed directly toward the effectiveness of the traditional family organization but not to that of the extended kinship system. Thus the general decline in respect for age and generational levels, even though it did not yet seriously threaten the family, caused a loss of organizational strength of the clan. It was indicated in Nanching in the increasing lack of control over the young by the older generation and by the fact that collective action by the clan was now more difficult than a generation ago. The diking of the "new enclosure" land had long been urged by the elders, but it was undertaken only when extreme need for land became obvious.

Women's Status

The stratification of status by sex was an important factor in the functioning of the traditional family and the larger kinship group. In a patrilineal and patrilocal kinship system, it was to be expected that there would be general dominance by men in all essential aspects of kinship functions, and that women would be placed in a subordinate role.

Woman's status in Nanching, as elsewhere in China, could be viewed in two stages, the premarital stage as daughter and the postmarital stage as wife and mother. A daughter's economic value to the family was lower than that of a son, since her economic tie with her parents' family was severed by marriage and her marriage required a dowry, which often exceeded the bride's ceremonial price paid by the husband's family. For the majority of the peasants who constantly struggled between hunger and a half-filled stomach, the lower economic value of a daughter cast a shadow over her status in the family and accounted much for the general attitude of discrimination against the female infant. However, there was little discrimination in treatment between a girl and her male siblings during childhood. One saw little girls eating the same food, wearing clothes of the same quality, and playing happily with their male siblings and other boys in the neighborhood. They enjoyed the usual superior status over younger brothers on the basis of age seniority. It was fairly common Chinese practice when financial tragedy befell a poor peasant's family when the daughter was about ten or twelve years old for the parents to sell her into indentured slavery as a "slave girl" and spare the boy in the family, such a girl not regaining her freedom until she was married; but during the period of our investigations we did not find any families in Nanching who had sold their daughters.

Under normal circumstances, a young daughter enjoyed a respected status and a warm life in the family, but in the clan she was not treated as a full-fledged member. She was not given a portion of pork from the pigs used in the annual sacrifice to the Great Ancestor, which was the symbol of full-fledged clan membership; nor was she entitled to a share of clan land, which was available for rent only to each male member, as previously described.

When a girl was married, the husband's family was careful to see that she severed all economic ties with her parents' family, particularly if she came from a poorer family. She entered the husband's family as a stranger and remained more or less in that status until she became a mother, especially the mother of a son. Since until then her husband was discouraged from showing her any strong affection and from taking her side in case of conflict between her and the parents-in-law, even her husband was somewhat of a stranger to her in her initial period as a wife, and the dominance of the parents-in-law was often absolute. After the birth of a son, she was accepted as a full-fledged member of her husband's family, and her security increased. As the son grew up she relied upon him as an ally, often more so than upon her husband, for the protection of her rights and privileges. When her parents-in-law died or retired into inactivity, she became domestic master of the household, although her decisions were always subject to the veto of her husband who, with the mature son, had economic control of the family.

The pre-motherhood stage as a wife was normally the most difficult period in a woman's life. The husband's family had the institutional right to send her back to her own parents' family on many traditional grounds, including alleged loss of virginity before marriage and the failure to bear a son. Although such action was infrequent, and no instance of it was discovered in this village during the course of our investigation, the threat was ever present. She enjoyed no rights to her husband's family property; and her own personal possessions, such as individual savings, clothes, or ornamental jewelry, were usually of insignificant value. Whatever her feelings, the fact that she could not get a divorce and the occupational limitation within the visible confines of the small village community were compelling reasons for remaining with her husband's family despite unpleasant treatment.

The wife had one appreciable form of protection against mistreatment from her husband and his family — her own parents' family and clan. Since marriage was the joint affair of the two families, domestic quarrels between husband and wife might develop into a conflict between the two families. A wife's parents might visit the husband and his family members to demand that they cease the mistreatment or to seek redress for a wrong. If the wife's family was poorer or weaker than the husband's and such action would be ineffective, and the wife's cause was an obviously just one, the wife's clan might intercede and the issue would become a point of contention between the two clans. In the Wong's printed copy of their clan genealogy there was a rule forbidding male clan members from marrying any girl of a Chen clan in a village about three miles away, the result of a conflict between the two clans caused by the mistreatment of a Wong girl married into the Chen clan.

Close as Nanching was to the city, a center of law and government, legal protection for the individual was not well developed here; and it was only the matching force of related kinship groups that helped to assert and maintain the legitimate status of an oppressed family member.

Economic Structure

We are interested here only in those salient features in the economic structure of the family which directly affected the organization of the family as a basic unit of social relations in Nanching.

Farms were without exception family enterprises. The grocery store, the masonry shop, and the carpentry shop in the village were all family enterprises. Consequently, an individual's livelihood depended almost solely upon his membership in the family, particularly for minors and women. Even emigration of a mature son to the city would not entirely free him from economic control by the family as a unit of production, unless he severed all his family ties or became so successful in his urban adventure that he established another family unit of production in the city. The majority of emigrants eventually returned to the family fold in the village and resumed their place in the family.

The family unit of production was normally led by the male head of the family, either the father or a mature son, except in the case of widows with only young children. The head of the family decided on the means of employing the available family resources, decided what crops to plant in a certain year and with what investments, and commanded assistance from family members available for work. He was the main laborer who did the heaviest work. Women participated in almost all types of farm work except the heaviest, such as plowing; and the children's part in production was determined by their ability in varying stages of their maturity. The work of the women and children received no separate remuneration; and women's household activities were never regarded as a part of production work in the family's effort to acquire an income. Women were not admitted to the professional types of handicrafts such as carpentry and masonry.

The land, tools, house, and liquid capital were regarded as collectively owned by the family, but their disposal was generally decided upon by the male head of the family; in the case of a widow's family with minor children, the female head of the house would make the decision. Deeds to the land and house generally bore the "hall name" of the family, not the name of individuals. Individuals including females might have savings and other private property apart from the family property, and the head of the family normally had no right to such individual properties. A concubine in one of the landlords' families, for example, saved enough money given her by the husband to buy a small house in the city from which she collected a modest monthly rental. The house was bought in a "hall name" that she had adopted for herself. She kept the rent thus collected, and she could sell the house with no interference from the husband. However, with the majority of the peasants, the small family property was all that was owned by the members. Upon the death of the husband, the widow became the guardian of the family property, but she could not sell it against the will of a mature son.

Family property was generally not divided as long as old parents, the heads of the family, were still living. Upon the death of the parents, inheritance was divided among all sons, with the eldest son getting a larger share as the succeeding ceremonial head of the family in officiating at the rites of ancestor worship, and the other sons receiving theoretically equal shares of the remainder, which, however, was at times adjusted on the basis of need occasioned by the number of mouths to feed. Daughters, married or unmarried, had no right to inherit family property. The Nationalist government decreed an inheritance law in 1930 permitting daughters to inherit family property equally with sons, but this law was not generally observed even in the cities, and in Nanching the villagers had not even heard of it. This system of property ownership and inheritance gave full support to the system of status based on age and sex factors, and the dividing of the inheritance among the sons contributed directly to the smallness of the farms and the scattering of the plots. It can be seen here that family organization was deeply and intricately meshed in the economic life of the family and the community.

The Clan and Its Subdivisions

Organization and Functions of the Subdivisions

The organization of the clan subdivision was rather informal. The oldest member of a subdivision was generally regarded as the head, and he managed the affairs of the subdivision together with other elders in it. Should a subdivision possess property such as land or an ancestral hall, either an administrator or a council of management was elected. Affairs of the subdivision consisted mainly of performing worship rites for the subdivision ancestor, interceding in inter-family conflicts, and keeping unruly elements within the subdivision under control. In an inter-family conflict elders of the subdivision were frequently called upon to arbitrate before the case was taken up on the clan level. Elders were frequently asked to reprimand a young deviant or a wayward son within their own subdivision in case the immediate family should prove ineffective in restraining him. The subdivision generally had no power to mete out physical punishment; this was reserved for the clan. Kinsmen in the same subdivision generally regarded their mutual relationship closer than with those in other subdivisions, and mutual help was more active within the subdivision.

Since the clans in this village were relatively small — the largest of them, the Lee clan, consisted of less than 600 persons — direct contact between members of a clan was fairly intimate and frequent, and it was facilitated by the close congregation of the houses of the members. Consequently, the function of the subdivision in integrating kinship members into an operating unit was relatively less important. The subdivision ancestral halls in Nanching were rather idle, with few activities going on as compared with the main ancestral hall of each clan. In other localities in the province where a clan in a village contained thousands of members — as for example, the Chen clan in Chen Tsun, about forty miles down the Pearl River, which had over 10,000 members all residing in one village — the functions of the subdivision became important because of the lack of frequent, intimate contact between distantly related members in the same clan. In a broad sense, it might be said that each of the clans in Nanching was a subdivision of the large clan whose Great Ancestor first settled elsewhere in the province.

Organization of the Clan

The clan was directed by the council of elders and the business manager. In principle, the council of elders was the center of authority that made all important decisions concerning the affairs of the clan, and the business manager administered its financial activities under the supervision of the elders.

The council of elders, who served without compensation, consisted of males over sixty-five years of age. When a man reached his sixty-fifth birthday, he gave a big feast to the entire clan in order to qualify for council membership. Should this celebration be beyond his means, his close relatives might contribute money for the feast. A generation ago, as related by the villagers, the subdivision to which an old man belonged would sometimes give the feast for him should he be too poor, and the money would come from the subdivision treasury and contributions from close relatives. Now that the subdivisions were generally quite impoverished, such collective aid had not been given in the past three or four decades. The requirement of giving a feast for the clan had the actual significance of making wealth as well as age a qualification for council membership. In fact, there were several poverty-stricken old men in the village whose age was well above sixty-five, but who had never sat on the council of elders.

The business manager was elected once every three years, and in the case of the two large clans, the Wongs and the Lees, an assistant was also elected to serve with him. The manager was usually a man in his forties or fifties and at least well enough educated to be able to keep accounts. Wong Yu was the manager for his clan during the period of our investigation. The election was divided into two stages, the selection of candidates and official recognition of the result. In the first, prospective candidates for the office would make their contacts with the elders and with socially active clansmen. Usually, only two or three candidates would be active in the field, and the contest was not too complicated an affair. As a rule, the issue of who should take office was all settled in pre-election consultations, and the election itself was only an official recognition of the result. One might remark at this juncture that the Communists regard this process of informal consultation as an important element of grass-roots democracy and have come to make wide use of it in the form of "consultative meetings" and "consultative conferences" as a means of settling differences previous to any formal voting or election which is only of nominal character. Such meetings and conferences have become a part of the standard procedure in the Communist "new democracy." Herein lies a certain degree of institutional continuity between the traditional system and the Communist social and political structure.

The election, usually held in the evening in the main ancestral hall, would be announced by someone beating a pair of brass gongs through the streets where the clansmen lived. Only men attended, the traditional age requirement for a male being sixteen, with no other qualifications; but usually only a part of the clan's male adults, probably one-fourth to one-third, attended. All council elders would be present, and they would suggest the candidate for the office of business manager, who might be the current incumbent ready to serve another term or a new man. There was no formal rule excluding new nominations or suggestions from the floor, but this did not usually happen since major differences in the choice of a candidate had been settled previously. Active men in the clan as well as the elders would take turns recommending the candidate, and the election would accomplish its formal purpose by having public recognition from the members of the clan. There was no procedure of balloting or showing of hands here, although balloting was practiced in some forms of Chinese organizations elsewhere, particularly in the city guilds.

For administering the clan's financial affairs the business manager was given a modest compensation on an annual basis, usually two or three hundred catties of unhusked rice, which was not enough for one person to live on. Clan business was fairly complicated. The manager had to manage the clan land and other clan properties. He had to see that the ancestral hall was kept clean and in good repair. He had to manage the business aspect of the annual ancestral sacrifice ceremonies, one in the spring and another in the autumn. He had to participate in the business management of other events of the clan such as a community opera held once a year for the local patron god when the harvests were good and when there were no economic or political disturbances. For major expenditures, it was usual for the manager to hold consultations with and obtain approval from the council elders. For all expenditures, detailed accounts had to be written down. At the end of the year, each item of account, the purpose, the date, and the amount expended had to be separately written on an oblong slip of red paper and posted on the walls of the main ancestral hall for all to inspect. At that time of year the walls of the ancestral hall would be plastered with hundreds of red slips fluttering in the wind, and one would read such items as 5,000 catties of unhusked rice for the support of the village school, 1,000 catties for the repair of a caving wall in the ancestral hall, two catties for the manager's transportation to the city to see some official on clan affairs, three catties for tea to entertain a visiting official who came to the village on a certain date. People who questioned any item of the account could bring it up with the council elders and make it an issue in the next election of a manager.

We did not hear any charges of corruption in the village during our investigation, the accounts being too exposed to public scrutiny and social contacts in the clan being too intimate to hide any major items of expenditure. In Nanching, owing to the smallness of the compensation, the lack of any appreciable side-income deriving from the office, and the considerable amount of time and energy demanded by the work involved, there were not many aspirants for the job. Usually the candidate came from a literate middle-peasant family and needed a modest supplement to his limited family income. Large landlords and most rich peasants were rarely found in this position.

Besides the council of elders and the business manager's office, other agents might be set up in the clan to administer special affairs like the village school, a community opera to celebrate a patron god, or a major event like the building of a dike. The personnel in such bodies were generally appointed by the elders after consultation with persons active in village or clan affairs. Ordinarily, however, major events like building a new dike called for a clan conference held under the guidance of the council of elders to appoint personnel and lay down policies, in much the same fashion as the election meeting where leading differences had been threshed out beforehand in informal consultations. It was in the behind-the-scene consultations that the rich and the powerful members of the clan exercised their influence.

Functions of the Clan

The most regular and visible of the clan's leading functions was the worship of ancestors. The ancestral hall, the prominent and elaborate building that towered above the village houses, was devoted primarily to this purpose. Once in the spring and again in the autumn, sacrificial ceremonies were held in the ancestral hall, attended by most of the members of the clan. Additional sacrifice was offered at the time of the Chinese New Year. Roast pigs and other foods in dishes were placed on the long, carved teakwood sacrificial table in front of the altar on which were placed the ancestors' tablets. Candles and incense were burned. The elders led the ceremony of "kneeling three times and bowing the head nine times," and the younger members followed in rows in the order of generational levels and age. On such occasions the entire ancestral hall was swept clean, strips of red cloth were draped over the altar, and paper and cloth decorations bedecked the doorways and walls. Huge lanterns, their paper covers renewed and repainted, were lighted with big candles. The golden characters on the numerous hanging wooden plaques were cleaned and polished. Some of these plaques were old imperial decorations bestowed by emperors and local officials upon worthy sons of the clan, and some were couplets carved either with moral epithets or praises of the clan. The walls and pillars were decorated with plaques which gave moral advice to members of the clan and reminded them of past accomplishments of their illustrious predecessors. When the ceremonies were performed in this massive and elaborate building amidst such an atmosphere, in contrast to the usual drabness and monotony of village life, members participating in the scene could not fail to be impressed and inspired by the glorious past and to be proud of the present unity and strength of the clan and feel sentiments of loyalty toward it. Less elaborate ceremonies were occasionally sponsored by individual families in the ancestral hall in the event of a wedding or the birth of a first son.

Participating in such a ceremony, the individual member felt that he was not alone but a part of a large group united by the unseverable tie of blood. If the clan was an abstract image and a state of collective feeling in his daily existence, now the clan was presented in concrete visibility, in full flesh and blood, demonstrating to him the numerical strength and historical pride of the organization of which he felt himself a part. The honorific decorations and the inscribed lines of moral admonitions and social ambitions from the ancestors that bedecked the ceremonial scene reminded the living congregation of clansmen of their obligation to preserve the heritage and to measure their daily conduct against it. Thus the whole ceremonial process had the effect of lifting the clansmen's feelings and thoughts above the level of individual existence and integrating them into the unity and continuity of the group.

Another vital function of the clan was the enforcement of social and moral order among the members. Conflicts between individuals or families (usually a conflict between individuals would involve the respective families) that could not be resolved independently by the parties involved were normally arbitrated by the council elders. Simple cases were first handled by the elders of the clan subdivision to which the conflicting parties belonged. Failing that, individual elders in the clan were called upon to arbitrate. In serious cases, such as those involving serious bodily injury or property damage, the council of elders would sit in session, frequently accompanied by other clansmen active in village affairs, to consider the case, attempt reconciliations, or mete out punishment to the guilty party. A generation ago corporal punishment for the unruly young was not uncommon, but such action had not been taken in the recent two or three decades — one of the signs of the weakening of clan power.

Should the parties involved reject the arbitration or decision, they could legally take the case to court, but such action required money and official connections, and only the rich could afford to follow this course. For the majority who could not afford recourse to law, the clan's decision was binding, being supported by group pressure of the clansmen in general and by strong and rich elements in the clan in particular. Consequently, formal government and law had little to do directly with the life of the majority in the village.

The same methods were employed to deal with violation of mores and law. Both the Wong and the Lee clans had special moral rules written in the genealogy book for the clansmen to observe, and the authority of the clan was used to enforce them. In recent decades, the enforcement by the clan authority of such written rules and unwritten mores of the community had fallen into increasing neglect. When Wong Mi beat his mother, he received only a reprimand from the elders in his clan subdivision; and, for all we could see in his behavior, he was still as rude to his old mother as before. The villagers insisted that such infraction of filial piety would have been severely punished a generation ago. Again, although the rules in the Wong's genealogy book specifically prohibited gambling, quite a few members of that clan were habitual gamblers, and the elders simply ignored them.

The general group pressure of the clan was still sufficiently effective to preserve good order in the village, and in recent years there had been no cases of burglary, theft, fights involving serious bodily injury or property damage, divorce, or serious infractions of the mores of the kind which filled the pages of city newspapers. During the period of our investigation we rented and furnished a house for our field workers to live in. The house was often unoccupied for days with the doors secured only by a flimsy padlock. Nothing was ever stolen from the house, poverty-stricken as the villagers were. This did not mean that there were no bad elements among the villagers, but that moral pressure from the elders and other clansmen forced them to carry on their activities elsewhere. So long as they refrained from practicing their art within the village, both the elders and the clansmen left them alone. In a neighboring village there were several notorious bandits, but their own clan left them alone since they did not bother the people in their own village. The clan was a small and tightly knit we-group, and law and order found effective enforcement through clan authority without formal government.

As a we-group, the clan performed the function of protecting kinsmen against injustice from outsiders. We have noted the prohibition of marriage with the Chen clan as an example of such protection for the female members of the Wong clan. The clan also deterred invasion by bandits and other lawless elements by its own armed defense organization. The clans in Nanching possessed some firearms, and there were many individual villagers who possessed firearms of their own and would normally respond to the call of the clan for the protection of clansmen against outside invaders. Armed villagers had fought a battle against Japanese soldiers after killing a Japanese who had raped a village woman. The leadership of the Wong clan was an important factor in organizing the villagers for the combat.

If lawless invaders were from a nearby village, the clan would approach the invaders' clan and press for a settlement. Since hostilities frequently led to bloody feuds, the clan tried to restrain its unruly members from bothering neighboring villages. Thus, while Nanching was only two or three miles from a village harboring many notorious characters, it had never suffered any trouble from them. In this situation of "armed peace," the effect of maintenance of peace and order by the clan went considerably beyond the sphere of the clan itself. Since there was no effective police force in the vicinity, and soldiers were called out only in major disturbances, the daily maintenance of peace and order depended greatly upon clan influence. In many localities in this province, particularly in the mountainous districts, the armed force of the clans was so strong that government tax collectors frequently dared not approach the villagers directly.

Economically, the clans in Nanching were not very active; but on special occasions the clan played a vital economic function for its members, such as building the dike for the "new enclosure" and organizing the distribution of the resulting benefits to the clansmen, and in case of flood, the whole clan's manpower was mobilized to repair or reinforce the dikes on the land belonging to the clansmen. When the Wongs formerly had more clan land, its low rents were of important assistance to a large number of poor clansmen. With the Lee clan, a part of its sizable income from clan land located elsewhere went into relief for the aged poor who had no earning capacity. The village school was supported mainly by contributions from the clan incomes of both the Wongs and the Lees.

Inter-clan Relationship

Since, as already noted, Nanching was a multi-clan village, with two major and three minor clans, the nature of inter-clan relationship was vital to the life of the village. To maintain co-operation between the clans, there was an inter-clan council of elders composed of representatives of each clan. The size of membership was not rigidly fixed; generally, two or three elders were sent from each of the two major clans and one from each of the three minor ones. This council met only on such occasions as the apportionment of contributions to a special levy made by the government or to undertake projects that involved the entire village. An example was the building in 1936 of the motor road that passed through the northeastern corner of the village land. It was the inter-clan council that decided upon appropriate shares to be paid on the levy made by the government, according to the amount of land that belonged to the members of each clan. Then a wide road was built from two of the village gates to the new road so that motor vehicles could come to the gates, the expense being shared among the five clans as decided by the inter-clan council. During the Japanese invasion the council met frequently to work out common measures for the protection of the village.

Private relationships between members of the various clans were generally friendly and peaceful. Occasionally, there was firm friendship and even organized relationship among individuals across clan lines. In the teahouses in Pingan Chen during noon teatime one frequently found a group of individuals from several clans all sitting around the same table. In the village there was at least one fraternity organized by members of the Wong and Lee clans which had a high degree of solidarity. On one occasion, when one of the fraternity members was arrested by the government, the others tried every means to get him out of detention in spite of the danger of being involved in the case.

On the other hand, inter-clan rivalry was keen. Asked what he thought of several Lees, a young Wong said, "All the Lees have 'heart trouble,'" meaning that their minds worked differently. There were instances of personal animosity between members of different clans. Generally, the Lees, with greater wealth, looked down upon the poorer Wongs. On the other hand, the larger size of the Wong clan was a source of strength and pride. And both the Wongs and the Lees looked down upon the three minor clans because they were poor and numerically weak.

The rivalry between the Wongs and the Lees found one form of expression in the annual community opera which each clan presented for the celebration of the birthday of its own patron god. On this occasion, there was a traditional practice of firing rocket firecrackers. Each firecracker shot out a core high into the air, and the clansmen raced for it as it dropped to the ground. The winner would have good luck, and he was given a prize. Since all the prizes were displayed in the ancestral hall and their quality and value were taken as a criteria of clan prestige, each clan pressed its members to donate as valuable prizes as they could possibly afford. In 1949 on such an occasion the Lees displayed prizes which included, in addition to varying quantities of unhusked rice, an expensive battery radio set, a modern-style chest of drawers, and several modern table and chair sets. Such expensive modern articles, rarely seen even in landlords' homes, brought the total value of the prizes to the equivalent of 5,000 to 6,000 catties of unhusked rice. The poorer Wongs could not match this sum, so they did not have any celebration for their own patron god that year, much to their humiliation; but they promised a bigger one as soon as they could afford it.

Whether as units of co-operation or rivalry, the clans so dominated the collective life of the village that an individual without clan membership was socially isolated and looked down upon; his children could not attend the village school without paying a higher rate of tuition; he and his family would be only on-lookers at the grand ceremonial events that periodically broke the monotony of village life and imparted joy and a sense of belongingness to the participants. He might eke out a living in the village as a craftsman, a farm laborer, or even a tenant farmer, but his chance of attaining distinctive economic success was slim, for he might not easily buy land and he was not deeply trusted by his fellow villagers in case he should need a loan or other forms of economic assistance.

There were about ten families in Nanching who did not belong to a clan. They had drifted in as war refugees in the 1940's and lived on the fringe of the village, although empty houses were available inside the village; they all engaged in peddling and served as occasional farm laborers for subsistence. The natives did not regard them as leading the normal social life of the village, an impossibility without clan membership; but in the traditional process such outsiders, should they stay and multiply for several generations, might gradually acquire land, develop a clan, and attain the status of other clan-affiliated villagers.

CHAPTER VII

A Decentralized Power Structure

W E HAVE seen that the tight-knit structure and the multi-functional character of the family and the clan made the kinship system a highly autonomous and self-contained unit of collective existence, and that inter-clan co-operation was an important factor in making village community life possible. But beyond the village lay the larger concentric circles of local, regional, and national communities of which the village was a part; and both in integrating the individuals and kinship organizations within the village and in linking the village to the larger communities the systems of power were the decisive factor.

Power is regarded in the present study as the ability to induce compliance from others in the making of group decisions and in conducting collective activities. Power has to be structured in order to operate in any collectivity, but the power structure may be formal or informal. A power structure assumes a formal character when it is institutionalized into formal hierarchies of regulated authority. An informal power structure, on the other hand, is not ordered into well-defined levels or exercised through formal rules but operates by a spontaneous balance between the various power individuals or groups. In both forms, the sources of power lie in physical force, wealth or social status, and prestige.

In the public life of Nanching the formal power structure was represented by the system of central government which tied the village to the national political community, while informal power was embodied in the structure of community leadership; and the two systems were interdependent.

Formal Government

The Republican formal political structure consisted of the central government, the provincial government, the county government, and the subdistrict (*ch'ü*) offices which were the operational agencies of the county government. It can be said that in practice the system of formal government stopped at the county level, a county in China having on the average about 200,000 to 300,000 population and 200 to 500 villages, and that, traditionally, the village community was not a formal unit in the central government system. To increase the effectiveness of governing such a large population with a scantily staffed county government, there had developed the system of collective responsibility, or *pao chia,* rooted far back in Chinese history, especially in the "new policy" of the Sung prime minister Wang An-shih (1021–1086). Since Wang An-shih's time, for eight centuries the system had been alternately practiced and 'abandoned in response to the demands of historical situations.

In the Republican period, political order within the county functioned mainly through the informal local community leadership, with the county government as the supervising agent; and the village stood as a highly autonomous self-governing unit. In 1932 the Nationalist government revived the collective responsibility system. The ostensible purpose was to use it to tutor the population in self-government in preparation for democratic constitutional rule, but the actual objective was to use the system to combat the spreading of the Communist movement in the countryside.

The system was based on the family as the primary unit of collective responsibility for the proper and law-abiding conduct of all its members. Ten families formed a *pao,* and ten *pao* formed a *chia.*[1] In this particular locality, several *chia* formed a *hsiang,* sometimes called an administrative village, a unit usually composed of several villages, and the *hsiang* was subordinated to the subdistrict (*ch'ü*) office of either the county or municipal government. The subdistrict office was usually a part of the county government, but since the vicinity of Nanching belonged to the Greater Canton metropolitan administrative area, the subdistrict office was under the municipal government. From the municipal government the line of political authority traced upward to the central government. It was through these levels of organization that political authority reached down from the national capital to the individual families in the village.

In Nanching there were twenty-three *pao* and two *chia,* both of which formed a part of a *hsiang* of five villages with headquarters in a village about two miles away. The subdistrict office was located in Pingan Chen. In terms of population, the *pao* unit here was composed of about 50 persons, the *chia* of slightly over 500, and the *hsiang* of about 6,000.

Organizationally, each family sent a representative to elect the head of a *pao*, and the heads of the *chia* and *hsiang* were each elected by the respective constituting representatives. The headship of these units of collective responsibility was thus set up by indirect election which became official only after the government had added its formal appointment. The chief of the subdistrict office was directly appointed by the municipal government (by the county government for territories beyond the municipal area) without even the formality of indirect election. Under this system, the line of authority was from the top down, the head of each unit being responsible not to the constituents below but to the superior chiefs above. *Pao chia* therefore took on the nature of being an extension of the centralized bureaucratic system.

Being such, its main function was to assist the government in the administration of law and the execution of policies, and it did little or nothing to develop local welfare or to foster decision-making by the people through the democratic process. Concretely speaking, the head of each unit was held responsible to the superior chiefs for the good conduct of all constituents and for transmitting government orders to them. He and the entire constituent membership were held collectively responsible for anything that went wrong, and especially for harboring any illegal elements in the locality, the crime of one individual theoretically bringing punishment to all. As a part of routine function, the head of each *pao* unit reported regularly to the superior chief on births, deaths, marriages, movements of his constituents, and any unlawful activities found among them. He helped the tax collector to collect taxes, and in wartime, with population records in hand, he aided in conscription.

Facts show that, from its revival by the Nationalist government in 1932 to its termination by the Communist conquest in 1949, the system accomplished little in the Nanching area with respect to either its ostensible or real functions. With the family as the basic collective unit responsible to the superiors for law and order, the individual member had no direct role or active interest in the operation of the system. Devised essentially for facilitating the flow of central authority down to the village and family level, there was no genuine popular participation in the functioning of the units. After seventeen years of its existence (1932–1949) in this village, the villagers had gained little knowledge of democracy and the democratic process of self-government, the declared purpose of the revival of the system.

As already suggested, the real motivation behind reviving the system was to utilize local social groups to combat the spreading of the Communist movement. In the light of historical events, the effectiveness of the system in this direction is doubtful. During the summer of 1949, for example, when the Communist armies were driving down toward Kwangtung Province, several meetings on the *hsiang* level were held among the *chia* heads to transmit the government order to the *pao* and *chia* units, instructing them to be serious about ferreting out any hidden Communist underground elements in the vicinity. So far as known, there was no Communist underground organization in this village or its immediate neighborhood. But the rapid Communist victory attested to the failure of the system in stimulating political loyalty among the people for the Nationalist government and generating popular morale to combat the Communist revolution toward which the village as a whole showed general apprehension.

During the war against the Japanese invasion, the system here was unable to perform the function of assisting the government in military conscription, Nanching being occupied by the Japanese army during the early part of the war. In the unoccupied territories, this function at times caused the system to degenerate into an organized racket of shaking down the people by selling the privilege of exemption from conscription and by drafting those unable to pay.

The system's performance in assisting the government in the collection of taxes was no more effective. In 1948 and 1949, prior to the Communist victory, when tax collectors came frequently to the village to press the peasants for generally overdue taxes, the heads of *pao* units were called upon to assist in the matter. The heads guided the tax collector to the right door but rendered no further help. Since the tax collector was a traditionally hated figure in agrarian communities, the *pao* heads did not wish to become identified with him.

The control of criminal and disorderly elements was a major traditional function of the collective responsibility system, but its usefulness in this respect was also negligible. The general prevalence of peace and law in this village and its vicinity was due to social control by the kinship system and the local informal power structure, not to the operation of any formalized system of collective responsibility. During the Republican period, open gambling and opium smoking were alternately permitted and suppressed in the big city. During the periods of suppression, gambling houses and opium dens would mushroom in the suburban villages, including Nanching. The system of collective responsibility did nothing to suppress them. Corruption of the officials was of course one factor in the situation, but since this factor operated in the city also, a further explanation must be sought to explain the fact that the favorite hiding place for bandits and illegal traffic was not the big city, where the impersonal social milieu provided an easy cover for lawless elements, but the intimate rural community where primary group pressure was strong. One explanation is that the system of collective responsibility, the only agent of formal government in the village, was not effectively integrated with the local agents of social control. Another is that the informal power structure was not averse to occasional gambling, limited illegal traffic, or even harboring bad elements among kinsmen so long as they did not disturb the local peace.

Our conclusion is that the national government failed to substantially alter the traditional decentralized pattern of local government in which the village political life operated largely by its own local power structure and was but weakly integrated into the system of central authority. One reason for the failure was the variance between formal law and local mores. Lack of interest and knowledge in formal government on the part of the responsible personnel was another; the heads of *pao* and *chia* units were generally untrained in government affairs, and they received no remuneration for their services; many heads of *pao* units were illiterate peasants, and the others barely literate, incapable of reading any elaborate government documents, the essential communication links in the operation of an extensive system of central authority. We were told by the villagers that one *chia* chief, having over 500 people under his charge, had been an illiterate — obviously the kind of man who in an uncompensated position commanded little respect from the community and could not make the power of his office felt; and during the period of our investigation, only one *chia* chief was a man of influence in the village. Generally, men of wealth and power in the community shunned such posts.

Then there was the factor of structural incompatibility in grafting the family as a basic unit to the formal system of central authority. As a part of the kinship system, the family was of a particularistic nature, while formal law and government operated on the universalistic principle in order to produce a national political order out of heterogeneous groups. Conflict between the particularistic and universalistic systems was seen in many instances of defective operation of the *pao chia* organization. On the *pao* level, the leaders representing families had not risen above family interests and identified their position with the interests of the state, a condition plainly evident in the lack of sincere interest in helping with tax collection, conscription, and other official duties. On the higher *chia* level, where the unit comprised 100-odd families often distributed across the clan boundary, inter-clan conflict made smooth operation of the organization difficult. One *chia* leader in Nanching, Lee Feng, always had trouble in getting co-operation from the member families under him because many of them belonged to the Wong clan, which had traditional conflicts with his own clan.

The particularistic nature of the village as a localistic communal structure contributed similar difficulties to the functioning of the *hsiang* unit. Nanching always had had conflicts with a neighboring village some two miles away, but the two villages were lumped together in the same *hsiang*. It was clear that co-operation between the two villages could not be expected so long as vital interests based on the village communal units remained unaltered, and that if, for instance, one village insisted upon the suppression of gambling in another village, the action might well end in a feud. (The difficulty in the operation of the collective responsibility system across family, clan, and village boundaries was common to other parts of China, Fei noting the same phenomenon in his Yunnan study.[2])

For the peasants, the village was a self-contained little world in which most of them were born, lived, and died; and only what happened in this little world aroused their intimate interest. They had a sound knowledge of such happenings and the ways in which they were handled organizationally, but since contacts between leaders and the members were close, any elaborate hierarchy of authority was unnecessary. In fact, the homogeneous nature of the agrarian community and the relatively simple and tradition-bound character of agrarian life rendered formalized laws and regulations both superfluous and uncomprehensible to the peasants.

Moreover, they had almost no knowledge of national affairs. So long as the village was keeping its peace and order, they were not deeply interested in the state's attempt at suppressing the Communist revolution. Having little notion of national political issues, they did not know the reasons for taxation beyond the vague impression that it went to feed government officials. The ability to "talk about the affairs of the state" was the distinctive mark of a few, usually the village scholars or gentry; and in Nanching, among the 1,100-odd population, such men were extremely few. They included Lee Feng, a village leader to be mentioned later, a dozen or so returned emigrants from the cities, several large landlords who had acquired wealth mainly through underworld operations, and a few businesmen who owned land in Nanching but were no longer resident members of the community and took no active part in its public life.

It should be noted that ignorance of national affairs did not necessarily mean unawareness of the existence of a higher political entity than the village and its immediate vicinity. The Nanching peasants knew concretely that there was a class of people called officials or rulers who had little contact with them and whose power was not derived from playing a role in the local community life. They knew concretely that the power of these officials was traditionally used to maintain peace, order, and justice; that when robbers plundered their homes, it was the officials' duty to apprehend the criminals; that in case of gross mistreatment by other fellowmen beyond the limit of the local mores one way to redress the wrong was to go to the subdistrict government in the neighborhood, where judicial and administrative powers were not differentiated. They knew that above the subdistrict officers were higher authorities to whom they could appeal their case — although the average individual did not know where the municipal or county government was located, and did not know the procedure of appeal. In other words, the common peasants were fully aware of the existence of officials as a ruling group, but they had very little precise knowledge of the organization and operational procedure of formal political power. In fact, the peasants' vocabulary contained the word "official" but not the term "government"; they spoke of government merely as *kuan fu*, or the house of the officials.

The common peasants were also aware that beyond the village and its vicinity lay a greater political community. They were conscious of the existence of cities, of counties and provinces, and even the nation, but they had no precise knowledge concerning their location and area; and they had no clear idea as to how large was the outside area under one political authority or how their village was related to the greater world.

It might be added that the limited and vague knowledge of government and of the greater political community contributed toward the peasants' sense of inferiority and submissiveness to the officials who ruled the wider world, a sense so characteristic of the peasant as a human type, as Robert Redfield pointed out.[3] For the power of those outside forces was visibly demonstrated in the village by the periodic pressure of the tax collectors and the subdistrict officers, and by the intrusion of armed soldiers into the local area at times of regional and national upheavals. It would seem that the *pao chia* system of collective responsibility might well have brought the greater political world nearer to the peasants, but its structure and functions were such that apparently the peasants had no more understanding of it than they had of the system of central government as a whole.

Local Power Groups and the Informal Political Order

The Nanching peasants were fully aware of the structure and operation of the political order in the local community; and although there was no formal hierarchy or set of rules governing the positions of the individuals and groups who commanded compliance from the local population, there was a traditionalized acceptance of their informal power arrangement.

The clan had a strategic position in the maintenance of peace and order in the village not only because it executed public projects such as the construction and repair of roads, the diking of the river, and the operation of the village school, but also because its possession of firearms represented physical force. The Wongs and the Lees each had about a dozen old rifles. And there was always the fundamental clan power derived from the institutionalized acceptance of the clan's authority by the kinsmen and their dependence on the clan for many of their social and economic needs.

There were also sources of power over which the clan had imperfect control at best, among them the families of wealth; for wealth in Nanching also meant physical force. Family A was an example. Rich, having 120 mow of good land and some business in the city and employing many workers in the village, Family A was a large family with two married sons living under the same household, making a large group under its direct command. It possessed many firearms, and its strongly built house resembled an armed castle. One morning we heard a burst of machine-gun shots and found that it was Family A testing a submachine gun it had just purchased. The clan elders normally consulted such families before making any important decisions about affairs of the clan, since any decision made without their approval or support would be difficult to carry out. If any wealthy and large family exercised its power so obtrusively that it aroused general objection from a majority of clansmen, including other wealthy and large families, the clan might act to counter its power with the collective strength of the clan including that of the other influential families.

The Crop Protection Association was a third power group in Nanching. It had been organized by about twenty individuals from the Wong and the Lee clans, its stated function being to guard mature crops against theft, and its members possessed arms. It levied a charge of five catties of unhusked rice on each mow of crop, with a promise to pay indemnity to the owner of the crop for any part of it stolen. Practically every farming family had been compelled to pay the fee. We did not discover any case where an indemnity had been paid, but the villagers were satisfied that there had been no major crop thefts in recent years.

For protection from bandits from the outside, members of the association made connections with the local underworld. To establish such connections, some members belonged to local gangs of racketeers. The head of the association and his brother were such men, but many members of the association, including the secretary, were respectable villagers. The head of the association was also involved in the operation of opium dens in the village and in gambling undertakings in Pingan Chen; and he had been a member of a "navigation protection corps," an armed group sailing on ships navigating the Pearl River and its tributaries through bandit-infested territories. Since in such adventures the corps usually made previous arrangements with bandits in various sections of the navigated territory, paying them a certain sum for leaving the protected ship alone but fighting any gang trying to molest the ship, the head of the Crop Protection Association was well prepared for his local job. In a situation where the subdistrict government police force was small and ineffectual, the association performed the actual function of maintaining peace and order in a limited sense; and some of the members were participants in guerrilla warfare against the Japanese during the occupation period.

These three power groups, the clan, the powerful families, and the Crop Protection Association, functioned fairly independently of each other. The authority of the clan was vested with the council of elders, and, although other groups or individuals might influence the council's decisions, they could not invade its membership. Wealthy and large families did not belong to the Crop Protection Association or participate in its racket. The association membership consisted of one rich peasant, several middle peasants, and a majority of the poor peasants. The secretary was a rich peasant, but the head of the association was a middle peasant who farmed about ten mow of land, of which he owned six mow, performing the greater part of the farm labor himself. We saw him pumping water from a pond into his field, but there was little doubt that he derived his main income from crop protection fees, as his food and clothing were those of rich peasants and he had built a new house after World War II.

Another group possessing elements of power were fraternities with a cross-clan membership, of which there were many in the village which took active part in village affairs, their decisions and action carrying weight in the community. Each fraternity was composed of men of similar age from different clans — in other words, a peer group. It did not usually initiate new members much younger or much older than its existing members, and it passed out of existence when its members died, since younger men started their own independent fraternities. Thus, the fraternity was not a self-perpetuating organization, and could not develop into extensive organizational systems such as the fraternal orders in the United States. Nevertheless, since a new member performed a religious ceremony and gave a feast for the other members so as to cement their pseudo-kinship relation with the spirits as witness, and all had usually grown up together in the village, the degree of solidarity of such a group was high.

One purpose of the fraternity organization was mutual aid; at a member's wedding the brothers would be present to make merry and to prevent jokers from unduly molesting the bride, and we found that fraternity brothers often gave each other financial help or engaged in common enterprises. Four brothers in a fraternity jointly rented a fishpond in 1949 and raised fish. Aside from such mutual-aid functions, a fraternity with its solidarity often became a power group when it had members active in village affairs, especially when it had money and guns. A fraternity did not exert its influence as an open organization but through its members' participation in village organizations. In one fraternity, for example, one member was the business manager for the Wong clan, another member occupied the same position in the Lee clan, and several others were in the Crop Protection Association.

There was an athletic club in the village called the Lion's Club, because it had a paper lion that the members used for a lion dance like the dance one sees at Chinese festivals in American Chinatowns. Its membership included teen-age boys and young men in their early twenties, with a sprinkling of middle-aged men holding the leadership. An instructor was hired to come every three or four days to teach the members to play the paper lion, to beat rhythm with the drum and gongs and cymbals as accompanying music, and to give lessons in the old military art of shadow boxing, using swords, knives, spears, and other ancient weapons. Although such military arts had no place in modern combat, they were regarded by the villagers as traditional forms of physical culture for the young, and lion's clubs were very common among workers in the cities and among peasants in the villages in this province. Of the some thirty or forty members in this club, the vast majority were sons of middle and poor peasants.

Since such an organization dealt with physical exercise that once was an ancient military art, it occupied a certain position in the local power structure. On several occasions the older leaders of the club had used the organization to fight for their own interests or to claim a share of interest for the organization. Some years previously they had meddled in the crop protection racket but failed in getting a share of the protection fees. Under ordinary circumstances, membership in the club provided some sort of protection against injustice from bullying villagers.

Lastly, although the traditional gentry no longer existed in Nanching, there were individuals who filled a similar power position in the community. The traditional gentry was clearly defined by the qualification of having passed at least the lowest grade of the imperial examinations, which gave a man the privilege to enter county and provincial government offices and to see officials and thus gave him power as an intermediary between the government and the common people. In the Republican period, imperial examinations were discontinued. Nevertheless, the traditional power of the old gentry was maintained until about 1920 in this province. Up to that time, old scholars still were the main group that had the privilege of approaching government officials directly on private or community matters. But from then on, an increasing number of officials emerged from the new educational system, and old scholars with an imperial examination degree were rapidly thinned out from the officialdom by senility and displacement by the new group. The new officials did not restrict their contact with the common people to the scholars, but their visitors included rich merchants with little formal educational background, and at times even notorious elements. Wealth and public influence, instead of formal scholastic success, became the criteria of who could approach government officials directly. Hence, merchants, large landlords, and local politicos took the place of the old-style scholars as the intermediary between the government and the people under the Republican political order which did not change the traditional dichotomy between the ruler and the ruled.

This process of change was fully visible in Nanching. The village had two persons of the old-style gentry background still living. One had moved to the city some decades ago, but one still lived in the village during our investigation. He was Lee Ying, a man in his mid-sixties, who had a *hsiu ts'ai* degree, the lowest degree granted by the imperial examinations. Up to about three decades ago, it was he and several others like him who went to the county magistrate's office to negotiate business concerning the community or individuals in the village. Traditional respect for scholarship and the accessibility to government officials gave him a position of prestige and power in the village, and few decisions on community affairs were made without consulting him. With the frequent changes of regimes in a period of revolution, he knew the officials less and less, and they spoke increasingly in new terminology about foreign ideas quite beyond his comprehension. In our conversations with him, he expressed contempt for those new officials who spoke "a mouthful of new terms," regarding this as a sign of degeneration of the age as compared with his good traditional past. But one could well imagine that the quotations from the Confucian classics which characterized his speech was just as irksome to the new officials with their modern educational background who regarded him as a representative of a dying age.

This ideological difference between the old scholar and the new official not merely cost the former the strategic intermediary position in dealings between the government and the people, but it also abolished his old function as a supporting agent of formal government. When the traditional government stopped at the county level, it was the old gentry who used their position as community leaders to help maintain peace and order in the villages and towns which were without formal government. Furthermore, while governmental power relied heavily upon physical coercion, physical force alone could not long maintain political stability without a system of moral justification. The Confucian theory of government and its supporting ethical norms provided such a justification, and old scholars like Lee Ying made this justification effective by constant teachings of Confucianism to the villagers, particularly the young. As late as 1951, Confucian concepts were still strong in the minds of the older villagers, and Lee Ying retained a measure of respect among them.

But the larger political setting had been profoundly altered by a series of revolutions, and the government that the village must deal with was dominated by a new group not inspired primarily by Confucianism nor rigidly bound by Confucian canons in their official conduct. Consequently, for some three decades, Lee Ying neither visited the county magistrate's office, nor did he earn any money writing official petitions for litigating parties, who would now rather pay a modern lawyer in the city for such services.

The new group that had risen in the old gentry's place was much less homogeneous in composition and less well-defined in status. In Nanching during the 1920's and 1930's, the one person who had rather free access to local officialdom was the head of Family A. At that time, the locality was under the rule of a military commander who had once been a bandit leader, "a hero from among the grass and thickets," who by surrendering to and joining forces with different early Republican regimes in the province had become a political and military figure of considerable importance and came to exercise unchallenged domination over this locality, his home village being only two miles away from Nanching. His influence extended to the level of the provincial and, in a limited way, the central government. The head of Family A had been one of the commander's underlings in his "grass and thickets" days and, according to the villagers, had acquired some wealth from banditry as well as from opium traffic. He had transferred his capital to legitimate import and export business in the city. With wealth and good political connections, he enjoyed a high prestige in the village; he could see the commander, his old boss, any time he wished, and through the commander, could see other officials in the government. There had been another personage in the village like him, an underling of the same commander in his dubious days and later a substantial citizen of the village, but he had moved to the city. Neither of these men had any formal education, and both were nearly illiterate; yet they came to enjoy direct official contacts like the old gentry whose channel to prominence and power was through scholastic attainment. Needless to say, these two men, "with not one drop of ink in them," had no political ideology to teach the villagers in support of the power structure of the government except the silent message that these were times when the strong man won regardless of class background or moral conduct.

Two rich merchants, neither of them residing any longer in the village, had direct contacts with officials in the subdistrict and higher governments. One of them had donated a large sum of money to set up the new elementary school and had it legally registered with the municipal government in Canton so that its graduates might go on to public middle schools with proper recognition of their academic standing. But their dealings in village affairs had become extremely infrequent, especially in recent years.

One man who approached the characteristics of the old gentry was Lee Feng. His father had been an old scholar with modest means, and he himself belonged to the rich peasant class. He had graduated from a middle school in the city, had been in Hong Kong, and therefore had breathed the air of the modern urban world. Now, in his mid-forties, he resided in the village and was very active in village affairs. He was a member of the fraternity controlling many organized activities, and a representative to the council of the *hsiang* government. He had once been a member of the Kuomintang (Nationalist Party) and a minor officer in the local party branch. He was extremely eloquent in private conversations as well as in public speeches, and he could chair a meeting with dexterity. Looking at his peasant's clothes and his always shaggy and unshaven face, one would not suspect that he possessed abilities that fully matched those of a modern politician. He frequently visited the subdistrict and municipal government offices on village affairs. With a middle-school education and a Kuomintang membership, he had a political ideology, the Three People's Principles, to preach. He was conversant with current domestic and international politics. Motivated by modern nationalism and patriotism, he was among the leaders who had raised an armed force to fight the Japanese soldiers who had come into the village, and later he continued as a leader in the local guerilla band that harassed the Japanese occupation forces. His piercing eyes revealed a fierceness characteristic of many of the natives of this province.

Lee Feng's local position, his connection with government officials, his ideological function of providing a moral justification for the power structure of the formal government — all these brought him close to the model of the old gentry. Yet it would not be quite correct to call him a new gentry. Although an educational background was common to both cases, scholarship was no longer a restrictive qualification for the status and privileges that used to be the prerogative of the gentry in the old social order.

What had risen to take the place of the old gentry in the local political order was a group of local political bosses whose influence stemmed not merely from education but also from a variety of sources, including wealth, physical force, and political connections. Although the new group served the same function of the old gentry by acting as an intermediate link between the government and the local community, it was not an ideologically uniform group that could function as the local foundation of the national government.

Characteristics of the Local Political Order

When the operation of the power groups in the village is viewed in the over-all, it becomes clear that there was no systematic centralization of power in any single individual or group in the local power complex.

Theoretically, the clan had the power to control all groups and individuals within its kinship confine, but the powerful families and the Crop Protection Association, within limits, acted fairly independently of the theoretical central power of the clan and the inter-clan council. The crop protection group made its own decisions without going through the clan council. The rent collector of Family A would not hesitate at using duress, supported by that family's guns and influence, to force rent out of a recalcitrant tenant; and clan elders normally would not interfere in such acts. What might stay the hands of Family A would be the tenant's possible association with a powerful fraternity or an armed group which could retaliate.

The clan was, therefore, by no means all-powerful, and its control was being increasingly weakened by the rising status of the young, but it was still an accepted source of authority. It used its traditionally accepted authority to bring together two strong parties in conflict and to reconcile or arbitrate their differences; for whereas the power of individual groups was always regarded by the villagers as self-centered, the authority of the clan was still considered as representing the general interest of all the kinship members. Hence, powerful Family A had to rely frequently upon the moral position of the clan elders to smooth out its troubles with some of the villagers. In this sense, the clan organization provided a framework within which the power groups played their roles.

There was also a general concentration of power in the group of wealthier families. The power position of the large landlords' families was obvious; and although the membership of the Crop Protection Association contained a majority of the middle and poor peasants, its leadership was in the hands of a few well-to-do families. In fact, the Lion's Club, with its limited power, was probably the only group not led by wealthier elements. Nevertheless, although the wealthier families dominated the economy of the village and played a decisive part in the local power structure, they were divided into many centers of interest. Power accompanied their wealth, but that power base was not systematically organized.

In effect, then, the maintenance of peace and order in the village depended on a wholly informal balance of power among the local power groups; and no central political power could penetrate effectively into the village without either co-operating with the informal local structure, or controlling it, or replacing it with a new one. We never saw a policeman or an official in the village, except the tax collector. In 1949 there were some troops quartered in the ancestral halls in the village for a few weeks, but they had nothing to do with the local political structure. It is interesting to note that in another county in this province, when the Communist underground was becoming active in 1946, and when the system of collective responsibility was having no effect in combating them, the magistrate seized the elders from several affected villages and detained them until the names of the underground elements were handed over. Although the elders did not know who the underground elements were, others in the clan hastened to find out so as to get the elders out of detention. The kinship system succeeded where the system of collective responsibility had failed.

There appeared to be a general lack of interest in community welfare among most of the leaders in the Nanching groups, especially among those who had risen to their position through urban business adventures or through banditry and illegal traffic. Neither the head of powerful Family A nor the head of the Crop Protection Association seemed to have much interest beyond advancing their own wealth and position. The one group that still clearly identified its public position with community interest was the council of elders in the clan.

In terms of its place in the political-social order of the times as we have tried to describe it in this chapter, Nanching typified a stage in China's social development which must be briefly noted here.

As we have pointed out, village leadership had traditionally centered in the old gentry, a group deeply imbued with Confucian moral and social values which clearly defined the obligation of an educated man toward the state and the local community in return for the favored status gained.

The Confucian doctrine taught four stages of endeavor in the development of an educated man: first, try to perfect oneself; next, perfect one's own family; then, set one's kingdom in order; and finally, bring peace to the empire. In actual operation, this canon was binding only on the scholars and the gentry who constituted the extended arm of the national bureaucracy on account of their positions as community leaders and as candidates for officialdom. So the gentry were community-minded and national-minded, but the common people, especially the village peasants, were expected to observe only the first two steps of this canon, namely, to try to perfect themselves and their own families. If everyone in the community developed a sound moral character, observed his own status, lived a satisfying and contented life, died with proper burial from the kin, and thereby contributed to a peaceful and stable social order, he was considered a successful citizen and a desirable member of society. While the common man was encouraged to become educated and versed in affairs of the state, he was not expected to do so; nor did economic circumstances usually provide him with the opportunity to learn. The consequence was the development of a social order in which the scholars and the gentry constituted a national-minded minority, while the majority of the common people confined themselves largely to individual and family affairs without knowledge of the greater community and national interest and without any deep sense of moral obligation toward it.

Recent decades of social and political change had now disintegrated the old gentry as a functioning group and had elevated to power and prominence common men who did not have the educational and moral training to assume community leadership; and this situation could be plainly seen in Nanching. Although the modern educational system was producing a new group of community and national leaders whose civic knowledge was more in keeping with the requirements of the modern age than the tenets of Confucian doctrine, the recent decades of change had so widened the socio-economic gap between the urban centers and the countryside that the modern educated man almost always remained in the city and refused to return to the home village to supply it with community leadership. The few who returned were likely to be either men who were unsuccessful in the city or men with limited understanding of the modern political and social order.

Lee Feng, the only modern educated leader in the village, was typical. It has been mentioned how lavish were the prizes offered to winners in the local religious festival; and at the same time we were trying hard to locate funds for an adult education project for the village. The money that went into the prizes, not to mention the expense of hiring a theatrical troupe and building a temporary theater, certainly would have been more than needed for the project. We talked to Lee Feng about using some of the festival funds for modern adult education, but he was indifferent to the idea of curtailing traditional religious and recreational activities for a project that would help raise the peasants' ability to better their position and to meet the requirements of a new age. Lee Feng, the lone modern educated leader in the community, still lacked understanding of the social requirements of the modern age, an understanding that the old gentry had for the traditional social order.

Nanching was thus without adequate modern leadership. The community still operated in the traditional decentralized political pattern and remained largely unintegrated into the modern system of national central authority. It was poised between old and new, having lost the best of the old without having yet benefited from the dynamism of its new national setting. In this sense it represented a stage typical of the process through which every Chinese village had to go.

CHAPTER VIII

Class Stability and Mobility

Sɪɴᴄᴇ ᴇᴄᴏɴᴏᴍɪᴄ inequality between both individuals and groups was a chief characteristic of the social picture in Nanching, and the class system served to stabilize that inequality through institutionalized stratification of status, the class system was a fundamental aspect of the social order of the community. The leading criteria of class status in the village were power, education, kinship status in terms of age and generational levels, and wealth. Personal quality was a factor, but it assumed importance for the determination of class status only when it was demonstrated in the above terms. In Nanching, as elsewhere in China, the relative importance of each of these criteria had shifted considerably over the past half century.

The classical system of social stratification was a quadruple ranking of the population: the scholars, the farmers, the artisans, and the merchants. The scholars were ranked highest on the basis of their service to the people through knowledge, ethical virtue, and leadership in the affairs of the state; the farmers and the artisans occupied the next two ranks on account of their vital economic service to the people through honest labor. The merchants were placed at the bottom of society on the theory that they acquired their wealth unethically and so did not deserve the social and political importance it brought them. The system was thus founded on ethico-political grounds, with special reférence to a political economy organized mainly by the scholar-bureaucracy and agricultural production.

In an agrarian community where there was no economic ground for the breeding of wealthy merchants, the classical class system seemed to have functioned effectively to the extent that it successfully maintained the scholar gentry in the upper-class position so that the latter could lead the community in conformity to the Confucian pattern of social and political order. It was in the cities where this system was persistently challenged by the wealthy merchant class, but even there, wealthy merchants would eventually join ranks with the scholars and officials by sending their sons to schools and into the examination halls, the portals to gentry status and officialdom.

After the 1920's, with the discontinuation of the imperial examinations and the discarding of Confucianism as the orthodoxy of the state, the Confucian value system gradually lost its hold, and the class status of Confucian scholars declined. There was a collapse of the ethico-political foundation of the classical system of social stratification, and the class system which rose in its wake was based largely on wealth or the social and political benefits which wealth brought. Education remained an important determinant of class status, but it was modern education and not Confucian learning that mattered; and only a family of wealth could give a son a middle-school or college education. Although under the kinship system age and generational seniority were still countervailing factors to wealth in the determination of class status, it now was the wealth of the individual and his immediate family and not the collective wealth of the wider kinship circle that determined the class status of an individual; and even power, if it was acquired through banditry and racketeering, could not give an individual high class status until it was combined with stabilized wealth in a morally acceptable form.

Such had been the story in Nanching. Wealth had become the basic determinant of class status in the village; and upper, middle, and lower classes corresponded closely to the division of the villagers into landlords and rich peasants, middle peasants and poor peasants. As noted in Chapter IV, of the 230 families in the village, 13.0 per cent were landlords and rich peasants, 30.5 per cent middle peasants, and 43.5 poor peasants, with 13.0 per cent belonging to nonagricultural occupations. There were thirty nonagricultural families, of which nine had the equivalent of middle peasant status, while the rest belonged to the poor peasant group in terms of wealth. On this basis, 13.0 per cent of the population belonged to the upper class, 34.4 per cent to the middle class, and 52.6 per cent to the lower class. (The percentage for the upper class, which was rather high due to the ready accessibility to urban opportunities, would probably not have been typical for interior agrarian communities.)

In traditional Chinese society there had always been a great distance between the upper and lower classes. The scholar gentry regarded the peasants as such an inferior breed of men that there was little friendly sociability between the two groups. Fei's presentation of class distance between the gentry and the peasants in a Kiangsu village [1] finds valid application here. Since in the recent decades, as wealth had become the chief demarcation for class status, the social distance between the rich and the poor had been as unbridgeable as that between the traditional gentry and the peasants, the question arises here as to the stability of the class system and its acceptance by the underprivileged.

In Nanching, as in the broad national setting, the privileged had always had to defend the status quo against attacks by the malcontent, and there had always been conflict between the superior and the inferior, the rich and the poor; but here such animosity took the form of individual friction rather than organized conflict between the classes. The head of Family A, for example, had earned general hatred from the poor in the village for his harsh collection of rents from recalcitrant tenants, but the rich family who had donated land to the school was the object of warm regard by the community, and there was no mass resentment against the rich in general. Above all, the superior or the rich elements as a class had not been consciously identified as the source of misery of the inferior and the poor.

According to the clan histories, for the past two centuries Nanching had escaped the peasant uprisings that occurred sporadically in Chinese history, including the great Taiping Rebellion which affected so much of China in the nineteenth century. Consequently, since such uprisings usually succeeded only in local redistribution of class status along the old pattern, and a reversion to the traditional system generally followed the quelling of the insurrection, the class system of the village had not been even indirectly affected by the peasant revolts which had occurred elsewhere in China. In Nanching, class distinction between individuals and groups was a well accepted fact of social life, and the class system had exhibited a high degree of stability.

One factor which contributed to stability was the highly integrative character of the kinship system, which helped to restrain and resolve conflicts between members of the same clan who had different class status. It would have been inconceivable to think of the clan as formally subdivided into the rich and the poor, each organized to carry on conflict with the other; aside from the value of clan solidarity, the intricate and comprehensive interdependence of social and economic interests within the clan membership precluded such a division. In fact the clan was proud of having rich or gentry members. Moreover, although factors of class status such as wealth, education, and power were based on broad social relations beyond the confines of the kinship structure, and thus they were theoretically not subject to kinship control, in a village like Nanching, where a large proportion of the village population belonged to a single clan, kinship relations tended to moderate the isolating effect of these factors.

A perhaps even more powerful and persuasive factor in village class stability was the traditional conservatism of the peasants, a characteristic trait which historically had always underlain the submissiveness of the poor peasants to an exploitative class system. The peasants' conservative outlook toward life was rooted in many aspects of the socioeconomic order, including their lack of power and education, their highly restrictive agrarian economy which allowed little margin for risk with novel ideas, and their stress on family lineage as a foundation of life. It was rooted also, of course, in a long acceptance of Confucian orthodoxy as the basic doctrine of social order, a doctrine which gave prominent recognition to the inequality of men, imposed a regulated system of status as a means of institutionalizing such inequality, and taught that to advance peace, order, and happiness in the community, each member should observe his own status and be content with his lot. For the ambitious and capable, it encouraged advancement of status through proper channels, not through class struggle and conflict. Harmony in diversity was a central theme in the Confucian view of the social as well as the natural world.

A third fundamental reason for the popular acceptance and stability of the class system was that the social classes of this community did not have the rigidity of a caste system. Both the myth and the facts of class mobility operated in Nanching not only as they operated in any Chinese village but also in the somewhat special context of Nanching's proximity to a big city.

There were long historical beliefs, such as the old examinations as a reliable channel of class advancement open even to the poorest, the faith in thrift and industry as an assured formula of success that would elevate a person up the class scale. The traditional lore offered astounding examples of phenomenal success by men of humble origin, and such exploits of unusual men were classical lessons for the young in Nanching as in other parts of the country. As practical and concrete proof, there was the graduated scale of upper, middle, and lower classes and the further subdivisions which were like rungs on a ladder allowing step-by-step ascendance. If it seemed far-fetched to the poor to become rich, there was still realistic appeal in the possibility of first becoming a middle peasant, then a rich peasant, and finally a landlord — if not in one's own lifetime, then during the coming two or three generations. Thus the middle peasants as a class, accounting for about one-third of all families in the village, served as evidence of the improvability of one's class status; and the graduated class structure held forth hope for the poor and helped to induce faith in the system.

In reality, the extent of mobility differed with the individual class. As observed in this village, mobility had been high in the upper class, moderate in the middle class, and quite limited for the lower class, all in terms of proportion to the number of each class. The relatively mobile upper class seemed to suggest a high mobility of the entire system, but this was not the actual case. The upper class contained a rather small number of people, while the number at the base of the social pyramid was great. The elevation of a few families into the higher classes now and then gave a highly mobile character to the narrow top of the pyramid, but this produced only a small degree of mobility among the large number of people occupying lower-class status.

The mobile character of the upper class may be seen from the fact that, of the thirty-odd families occupying this status in Nanching, only one was an old family successfully maintaining its high class position for four generations, while the rest were families who had entered into this status within one to two generations. The one old family had developed business interests in the city and had sent sons into the gentry, and now lived mainly in the city, leaving only a few women in the large house in the village. Prominent among the newcomers was Family A, whose rise in one generation has been mentioned before. Wong Hung the merchant similarly rose to the upper class status in his own lifetime. Wong Yung started as a poor peasant and became a rich peasant during the war. The rest were mainly families of emigrants who had saved enough money from their urban occupations to buy land in the village within the past two generations.

The downward mobility of the upper class was considerable. We have mentioned one scholar-official family that traversed the whole cycle of rise and decline within three generations, bearing witness to the proverb, "no family retains wealth beyond three generations." The heaviest leveling hand in this situation was the absence of primogeniture and the likelihood of degeneration of the descendants of a wealthy man. The creator of a family fortune was usually a man who had won the struggle through frugality and self-discipline, and he would raise his children after his own image. Under the traditional kinship system, the children of a wealthy family remained in the same household under his authority, but the third generation would grow up in luxury and ease. When the grandfather died, the main integrating

force of the family organization waned, and dissipation more than aug-
mentation would characterize the course of development of the family.
Increasing conflict over what was the rightful share of a member
finally would bring about the break-up of the family into several independent units and the subdivision of the once sizable family property
into small parcels. Considering the usually large size of a rich family,
frequently brought about by polygamy in the form of concubinage,
few family properties could yield sizable subdivided units at the end
of the third generation.

If a wealthy family remained in the rural village, the general pressure
from the kinship system might help in preserving its solidarity and
delay the process of disintegration. Great upper-class families of three
or four generations' standing were often found in many rural villages.
But Nanching was too close to the city. As soon as a family acquired
wealth, it moved to the city and remained beyond the effective influence
of the village kinship system, in spite of the tenuous relationship still
maintained with the clan and the village by leaving behind a few
women and by occasional visits to the home soil. As a result, old upper-
class families were few here.

Our knowledge about the upper-class families was fairly clear because
there were not many of them, but information on the some eighty
middle class families was limited. The general impression was that
about thirty of these families had acquired middle-class status within
two adult generations. The middle class theoretically drew its membership both from descending and ascending families, but in Nanching
any families descending from upper-class status generally left the village
for an urban livelihood, which was easier than tilling the soil. Consequently, the newcomers were recruited from the poor peasants who
had scored moderate success either by emigrating to the cities or by
efficient farming during the war. There was little information about
the background of the status of the remaining fifty-odd middle-class
families except that they were regarded as having been in that class
position for more than two adult generations.

Our information on the mobility of the lower class was even scantier.
We knew of several families that had descended from a middle-class
position to the status of poor peasants. Many middle-class families of
the Lee clan who had relied upon remittances from emigrants sank
into poverty during the war because of the disruption of the urban
economy. We did not know the approximate degree of upward mobility
among the 120-odd families occupying the lower-class status at the
time of our investigation, but our general impression was that the

percentage of cases of ascendancy among the whole class appeared to be rather small. Those who had gone into the middle class and a few into the upper class originated from the lower class. Although we could approximate the number of such cases, since we did not know the size of the lower class at the time when such change of status occurred, we are not able to make any comparison.

One thing was fairly obvious. For the poor peasants, the road to improvement of their class status was long and hard. The exceedingly restrictive nature of a poor peasant's farm was almost an insurmountable obstacle. Working a small farm of less than two acres of mostly rented land with a negligible amount of capital, even the blessing of continuous good harvests for two or three years would give him and his family only a minimum of economic security, leaving him with little margin of savings.

The important normal step towards economic betterment for a poor peasant was ownership of his land, which was exceedingly difficult in a locality of high land value due to the rich soil, a long growing season, and proximity to the great city. At the time of our investigation, one mow of medium-grade irrigated land in Nanching was worth about 4,000 catties of unhusked rice, or the equivalent of about six years of average production of the land. This was about 20 per cent higher than the national average of land price estimated by the Chinese Land Administration Investigation Society.[2] It is difficult to imagine how a poor peasant who could hardly escape sinking into debt from year to year could accumulate 16,000 to 20,000 catties of unhusked rice to buy four or five mow of land fertile enough to maintain subsistence for an average family. At the wage level of 1948, it would have taken a landless farm laborer four years' pay to buy one mow of land, or sixteen to twenty years to buy himself a small farm of four to five mow of medium-grade irrigated land if he did not spend any part of his pay during all that period of time — hardly possible considering his personal needs and family obligations. Conditions here certainly bore out Fei's assertion that it took more than one generation of industry, frugality, and luck for a peasant to rise about poverty.

What Fei did not point out was that this situation applied largely to times of normal social and economic order but not to times of unusual conditions under which agricultural production became profitable enough so that the factor of paying rent to landlords failed to stop the financial growth of shrewd and industrious peasants. Such a situation occurred during the Japanese invasion and the inflation-cursed postwar years, when the disruption of transportation and market operations caused a steep rise in food prices in the urban areas which normally relied on supplies from great distances; and the effects of it were visible in Nanching, which profited, of course, from its proximity to the city. It was in this period that the Wongs, with a large proportion of tenant farmers among them, bought much land from the Lees, who had previously prided themselves as having many landowners, and the relative economic status of the two clans began to reverse. Many poor tenant farmers became financially secure, and a few even prospered into rich peasants. Wong Yung, for example, who was in his early forties in 1938 and had two teen-aged sons who helped him work a farm of nine mow (1.5 acres) of mostly rented land, took good advantage of the rising price of rice and fully utilized the labor of his young sons to expand his farm. By 1948 his was a large farm of about 70 mow (approximately 12 acres), of which he had come to own 30 mow.

The experience in Nanching adds weight to the hypothesis that class mobility in an agrarian economy was high at times of economic and political crises but very limited under stable circumstances. In this sense, historical periods of disturbances which had caused the downfall of many great families were fine hours for the hard-pressed poor. However, since Nanching had been until recently isolated from the outside world, the lifetimes of most of the individuals there had been spent in relatively peaceful and uneventful settings where the restrictive influence of the agrarian economy operated almost continuously; and the war experience was an exception.

The restrictive effect of the agrarian economy was not limited to farming alone but also applied to village commercial and handicraft undertakings. The grocery store and the carpentry and masonry shops were examples. Since their business operations were restricted to the confines of the local community, even a monopoly of all the business in the small area could not carry the owner far toward any sizable fortune; and all three concerns were exceedingly small, their owners relying on land for a supplementary income.

In general, then, there was available within the actual confines of Nanching local life one channel to wealth and prominence, namely, banditry, racketeering, or illegal traffic such as opium and gambling. But this channel was open only to a daring and lucky few, and only in times of disturbance when the revolutionary process had weakened the forces of government and law. For the majority of Nanching villagers any opportunity for class advancement lay outside of the agrarian community, that is, in emigration to the big city or to foreign lands. In fact, save for the head of Family A and a few other similarly doubtful characters, all the upper-class members in Nanching had made their modest fortunes outside of the village confines in the urban world, and even the majority of the less fortunate emigrants had helped improve the economic conditions of their families.

The situation in Nanching was in one sense a special one since there was close at hand the greater urban world which acted as a safety valve for the poor and the discontented in the village. But it also was a situation typical of the Chinese farm village everywhere since its people were traditionally conservative peasants. Thus, in spite of the village's accessibility to the big city and to the bigger yonder world, there were still 100-odd poor peasant families who had remained with their tiny plots of mostly rented land, reluctant to take a chance in the distant territories from whence came stories of misery as well as success, a contrast already too familiar to them in their home village. And thus, despite the increasing pace and degree of social change in the surrounding world, a process now nearly fifty years old, Nanching up to the very eve of the victory of Chinese Communism remained essentially fixed in its traditional stable social pattern.

PART II

Early Impact from the
Communist Revolution

CHAPTER IX

Class Struggle as the First Step of Land Reform

THE FOREGOING chapters have pictured a village peasant community in which the basic factor was an agrarian economy that failed to provide minimum security for about one half of the village's population, the poor peasants, whose labor yielded such a small margin of savings that normal family events such as marriage, sickness, or death sank the family in debt, and calamities such as floods, droughts, and war put them at the brink of financial ruin and starvation. At the heart of the difficulty was the smallness of their farms and the crippling burden of paying rent, a condition which existed in varying degrees in other parts of China and which for over a century had been a brewing agent for periodic peasant riots and rebellions. It had motivated Sun Yat-sen's policy of giving "land to the tillers." It had given rise to the 25 per cent agricultural rent reduction program of the Nationalist-Communist coalition regime in the mid-1920's. It had provided the rationale for Mao Tse-tung's policy of making the peasant movement the heart of the Communist revolution. But until the Communists entered the scene, peasant riots and rebellions had been temporary episodes that had left the national institution of land ownership and farm organization unchanged.

When the victorious Communist revolution reached Canton in October 1949, Nanching was engulfed by the revolutionary forces that had so far spared it, and the village became one of roughly 1,000,000 rural villages in China marked for drastic revolutionary operations.

The first ten months under Communist rule were rather uneventful. Life went on in Nanching much as before save for occasional incidents when Communist soldiers forcibly bought vegetables, pigs, and chickens from the villagers at only about one-half the market price of the goods.

This was not new to the villagers; in fact, the Communist soldiers were somewhat better than previous civil war soldiers, who had frequently expropriated produce and livestock without any compensation. But the surface serenity did not allay the anxiety of those villagers who had heard of the policy of Communist land reform.

The Chinese Communist Party was explicitly pledged to land reform as the first step in its program to transform the social, economic, and political order of the entire nation. The official organ of the Chinese Communist Party, the *Jen-min Jih-pao* (*People's Daily*), declared:

> The general situation is this. Landlords and rich peasants, who account for less than 10 per cent of the rural population, own 70 to 80 per cent of all the land, while poor peasants, agricultural laborers and middle peasants, who account for about 90 per cent of the rural population, own only 20 to 30 per cent of the land . . . The peasants in various places have to pay to the landlord . . . the greater part of the yield from the land. Consequently, the peasants toil all year around without getting enough to eat, while the landlords live a parasitic life. This situation clearly indicates that the system of land ownership based on feudalistic exploitation is at the very root of our poverty, backwardness and foreign invasion and oppression of our country; it is the fundamental obstacle against our nation's democratization, industrialization, independence, unity, prosperity and being strong.[1]

Noting that "land reform in the past twenty years has mobilized the peasants to support actively the revolutionary wars and the revolutionary government,"[2] and giving due credit to Sun Yat-sen for initiating the slogan of giving "land to the tillers," the Communists asserted that no correct line had been found to realize that slogan until the Communist Party came upon the scene under Mao's leadership.

Communist policy was promptly set forth in the "Law of Land Reform of the People's Republic of China" promulgated in 1950, and in the explanation of the basic points in this law by Liu Shao-ch'i's *A Report on the Problem of Land Reform* given before the National Committee of the People's Political Consultative Conference in June of the same year. These two basic documents set forth the fundamental objectives of "abolishing the system of land ownership based on feudalistic exploitation, and enacting the system of land ownership by the cultivators, so as to liberate rural production capacity, to develop agricultural production," and to create a vast market in the countryside to make possible the nation's industrialization.[3] Not so explicitly stated in these two documents was the intention to gain the peasants' support for the new Communist national political power by giving them land, a formula that had proven successful in the Communists' earlier struggle for power.

The basic measure in this policy was "to confiscate the land of the landlord class and to redistribute it to peasants having insufficient or no land," [4] a traditional revolutionary ideal; but it was to be carried out now by confiscating only the part of the rich peasants' land which was rented to other peasants, and that only under specified conditions, so as to make possible the "preservation of the rich peasants' economy" since it was considered beneficial to the development of the national economy at the early stage of transition toward socialism.[5] Another point of departure from previous revolutionary policies was the emphasis on orderliness in carrying out the liquidation of the class status of landlords, taking care "not to eliminate the physical existence of the landlords," the responsibility for the "historical crimes committed by the landlord class" being now laid on the old social system, and not on the individual landlords.[6] Consequently, official caution was given to land reform cadres to follow "legal procedures" in treating landlords and to avoid "indiscriminate beating and killing." The general strategy was to unite the poor peasants, agricultural laborers, and middle peasants and to neutralize the stand of the rich peasants so as to isolate the landlords.

The central land reform law was supplemented by special regulations of land reform for individual regions. Land reform in Nanching, for example, was governed by three sets of laws: the central law of land reform just mentioned, "Some Regulations by the Military and Political Commission of the Central-South Region on the Enactment of the Law of Land Reform," and the "Land Reform Regulations for Suburban Areas," all promulgated in 1950.

To continue, then, with the story of our village, within a week after the Communist troops occupied the territory, Nanching was ordered to surrender all firearms to the detachments of Communist officers and men who circulated in the area to collect them. The villagers handed over about a dozen old rusty rifles that belonged to the clans. The Communists were not satisfied and pressed for hidden arms, but private owners of arms did not yield, adopting a "wait and see" attitude. The Communists did not immediately pursue the question any further.

About June (or July) of 1950 Nanching was designated as part of a small area for a "pilot experiment" in the suburban territory of Canton. Land reform was to start here earlier than in the rest of the province so as to "absorb the necessary experiences" for application to the large-scale task of remaking the land system in the whole province. Land reform cadres appeared in the village with increasing frequency. They belonged to the subdistrict government of Pingan Chen and took orders from the Land Reform Commitee of the Canton municipal authorities, who in turn were under the Land Reform Committee of Kwangtung Province.

The land reform cadres in Nanching, three men and one woman in their late teens or early twenties, were high-school graduates and one seemed from the way he talked to have had one or two years of college. Their manners and conversation revealed an urban bourgeois background, which they carefully disguised under dirty gray uniforms and conscious attempts to imitate the peasants' mode of life, occasionally even living in the poor peasants' houses, eating their food, and helping with light farm chores in order to strike up a conversation with them for information about the village.

Their first task was to "set the masses in motion" in order to develop a situation of "class struggle," the basic step being to select "active elements" among the peasants to serve as a core for the organization of the peasants' association and the new "people's militia." Wong Ping, a middle peasant, was selected as an activist, to be the chairman of the peasants' association which was to serve as the center of the new village political power and to administer the land reform guided by the cadres. Lee Sheh-an was selected as another activist, to be the head of the new people's militia for the village.

These two were selected primarily because they had been active in village affairs. Wong Ping had once been business manager of the Wong clan, and he had acted for his old father as chairman of the village school board. He had spent considerable time in Hong Kong as a peddler, and his wife was from the urban laboring class. His wife said of him, "He is literate and never did much heavy physical labor. He can't compete favorably against others in the village in farming, which requires heavy physical exertion. I have told him time and again to find something else to do." Lee Sheh-an's father was a rich peasant and an emigrant, and Sheh-an had some years of middle-school education. But the father had died some years ago, and when the family land was divided between the boys, Sheh-an descended to the status of a middle peasant, with about eight mow of land. He rented out four mow, and farmed four mow, and he also rented seven mow from others. When he first returned to the village from school in Canton after his father's death, he had no established status in village affairs; but he was now considered an active young member who had taken part in village activities such as helping to manage the community opera and expressing opinions on public matters in group discussions held in the spacious yards of the ancestral halls during evening hours.

The selection of these two men to lead the vital new peasants' association primarily on the basis of their active part in village affairs appeared to deviate from the official Communist policy of using only elements from the poor peasants and agricultural laborers as the core of the new village leadership. Official directives repeatedly called upon the cadres to go first into a village to seek out activists from poor peasant and agricultural laborers and to get them to tell stories about conditions in the village and about their own sufferings. Poor peasants and agricultural laborers were to be coaxed to tell of their own financial plight and the harsh treatment or beatings they had received from the landlords and rich people in the village. They were to be encouraged to contrast the living conditions of the poor peasants like themselves with those of rich landowners and to see the "true root" of their own suffering by arguing the typical question of "who has supported whom?" Had the landlords supported the poor peasants by renting land to them, and the agricultural laborers by giving them jobs? Or had the tenants and agricultural laborers supported the landlords by the fruit of production from their own physical labor? Who had impoverished whom, and who had made whom rich? These were typical questions asked around the central issue of "who has supported whom?" as the initial means to arouse class enmity against the landlords and to generate a fighting spirit among the poor peasants and agricultural laborers.

After one individual was convinced of the cause and of the power of the Communist Party to support the cause, he was encouraged to contact other peasants and to have them tell similar stories of suffering in the light of the same arguments. When a sizable group of the poor peasants and agricultural laborers had come to see the "light," a militant group was considered to have been established, ready to serve as a core for the class struggle against the landlords.

This process of building the core of the peasants' association and the people's militia, as explained in the numerous land reform directives and pamphlets, was designed to achieve "purity of class composition" of the core so that it could carry out an uncompromising struggle against the landlords. To admit members from other classes into the core at this time was considered a danger which might dampen the militancy and confuse the ranks of the poor peasants and agricultural laborers. The middle peasants were allowed to join the peasants' association, but not normally to be made leaders at this stage of development. Anyone with firm connections with landlords, rich peasants, or members of the old ruling group in a village was, as a matter of official policy, to be excluded from sharing in or controlling the new leadership.

The selection of Wong Ping and Lee Sheh-an at the very outset by the land reform cadres was obviously not following the official line closely. The cadres simply came and inquired who were active in village affairs besides those formerly in control of village power, and in this way made contact with the two. The new leadership core was not a product of the process of *t'u k'u* (spitting out stories of bitterness) and *ch'uan lien* (getting others to do likewise). Rather, it was a product of the cadres' taking the least troublesome way of creating a few new leaders who were not a part of the existing formal village leadership.

This did not mean that the work of "spitting out bitterness" and "getting others to do likewise" was entirely forgotten in Nanching. The cadres did move a few peasants into pouring out their woes and their hatred for the rich and the powerful in the village. One old peasant, for example, told the story of how he had mortgaged his six mow of good land to the head of Family A when he had gone to work as a coolie on a dock in Hong Kong when he was young. He remained a poor laborer in that British colony, and in 1942, after the Japanese occupied Hong Kong and turned it into a city haunted by mass starvation, he returned to the village, wanting to redeem his land with the meager savings he had accumulated from the long hard years. But Family A refused to give up the land, and he was forced to become a poor tenant farmer. After the cadres' explanation of "feudalistic exploitation" and the liberating mission of the Communist Party, he became very bitter against landlords as a class. However, the number of poor peasants in Nanching involved in such "woe pouring" was not large.

With leadership of the cadres established among the aroused portion of the poor peasants, the stage was set for the first act in the long drama of land reform, namely, the demand for refunds of rent deposits and the excessive portions of rent. In accordance with land reform laws and regulations, before the redistribution of land, rent on agricultural land was to be reduced by 25 per cent, retroactive to the year of "liberation," which was 1949 in this territory. Rent deposit, where charged, was also to be refunded to the tenant, and charging rent deposit was prohibited by the new law. In demanding refunds of the reduced portion of the rent, tenants were not allowed by the law to go back beyond the year of "liberation" or to charge the landlord interest on the reduced portion of the rent owed to the tenant.

One September night in 1950 a group of about twenty noisy, angry peasants appeared at the door of Lee Sheh-an's house, demanding refund of the reduced portion of the rent. Lee, although already appointed by the cadres as the head of the new people's militia, became frightened. He looked out into the darkness and saw one man who was the tenant renting his four mow of land, but he did not recognize the others, who might have been from neighboring villages, and his own tenant did not speak up. It was a stranger's voice that said that Lee owed his tenant 1,000 catties of unhusked rice in reduced rent and demanded that this be paid immediately. Lee tried to argue with them, but everyone in the crowd began shouting angry, indistinct words. Several peasants pushed Lee aside, and the whole crowd rushed into the house. They searched the storage room and cleaned out every kernel of unhusked rice stored there — about 1,600 catties altogether — and carried the loot off into the darkness.

There was another similar occurrence in the village during this period, but most of the refunding of rent and rent deposits was settled peacefully. The tenant named the figure; the landlord haggled with him. With a certain amount of mediation from newly elevated men like Wong Ping, a compromise sum was agreed upon, and the issue was considered resolved. One reason for the relative peacefulness was that the large landlords had by this time fled not merely from the village but also from Communist rule by going to Hong Kong. The entire Family A, for example, had gone to Hong Kong, and the concubine of Wong Hung had also taken her two children and the servant to her Hong Kong home. Toward the end of 1950 there was no one on hand to collect rent from the land for these large landlords, and the tenants found that they were farming the land free of charge. Another reason was the large number of small owners in the village whose relationship with the tenants had been generally friendly.

The reduction of rent and the refund of reduced rent and rent deposit were the initial material enticements for further development of the class struggle aimed at the eventual liquidation of the class status of landlords. The official policy intended that the tenants should use the refunded grain for improvement of production on their farms. When refunded grain was handed over by the landlords, it was to be received by the peasants' association for distribution on the basis of need to the poor peasants, including the tenants themselves. In Nanching the grain was not handed over to the peasants' association but

was usually received by and divided among the group which had accompanied the tenant to the landlord's house to present the demand.
Many individual tenants settled the matter of refund individually with
the landlords and kept the entire refund to themselves.

According to the official Communist line, the organization of the
peasants' association as the new center of village power, the mobilization of the peasants for class struggle, and the initial step of demanding
refunds of rent and rent deposits faced one serious obstacle — the
armed force of the landlord class and of the "local bullies" who were
allied with the landlords if they were not landlords themselves. Official
Communist literature produced no clear definition of a local bully,
but in general it identified him as the head of an armed gang that ter-
rorized a village or a group of villagers by armed extortion; more often
than not, he was connected with the underworld or banditry, although
he himself did not usually engage in open, lawless acts; he was a
"swashbuckler in his native village"; he frequently beat or even killed
people who were in his way or who refused to be fleeced; he was often
engaged in the gambling and opium traffic with armed protection and
acted in league with corrupt local officials. In Communist parlance,
the bullies often "owed the people a debt of blood."

It was therefore Communist instruction that it was necessary to
eliminate such elements as the local bullies before the peasants could
feel free to take an active part in the development of class struggle
against the landlord class; and, as part of the process of land reform,
there was normally an "anti – local-bully" campaign which sometimes
preceded the reduction and refund of rent and rent deposits, and
sometimes took place concurrently with the latter. The standard technique was to arrest the local bully and put him on public trial in a
"people's court," which often pronounced a death sentence on the
victim, thus eliminating the head of the gang and terrorizing the lesser
bullies into dissolution and submission. Such mass trials were among
the most dramatic and violent mob scenes in the process of land reform.
It is disputable whether there was in Nanching any character who
would fit completely into the above description of a local bully, save
possibly the head of Family A, who had already fled the scene.

While no mass public trial was staged for anyone in the village, this
did not mean that mild cases of local bullying did not exist in the
Communist view. One example was Lee Feng. About two months after
Communist occupation of the village, a small detachment of soldiers
of the local garrison knocked at Lee Feng's door in the middle of the
night. He was so terrified that he was rather slow in opening the door.

The soldiers were angry, accusing him of taking time to hide arms and illegal documents. They made a thorough search of the house but found no illegal objects. However, they pointed to some fine things, such as a pair of porcelain vases and a set of silver-plated spoons, and said that Lee Feng was a robber since, as these fine things did not match a peasant's home, he must have obtained them illegally. Despite his arguments, and amidst the wailing of his wife and children, the soldiers tied him up and dragged him off. He was repeatedly beaten while being pushed along the village street. He was taken first to Pingan Chen and then to a prison in Canton. He was not permitted visitors. The villagers said that the police wanted to know in detail his connections with local Nationalist political circles. He was required to surrender a revolver which the police said he was seen wearing during the community opera in the summer of 1949, before the Communists came. He said that he had borrowed the revolver, and that he did not possess any firearms. He stuck to this story in spite of torture. Finally, he was accused of being a local bully and was sentenced to three months of "labor education." When released, he had yellow jaundice, his face was swollen, he appeared subdued in spirit, and he became a so-called "controlled element," with his activities and movements under strict surveillance by the peasants' association and by the Communist police force in nearby Pingan Chen. Whereas formerly he had been very popular and had many friends, now few people dared to talk to him or enter his home for social visits. He was isolated in public life, and his past political influence became a curse upon him.

The head of the Crop Protection Association, Wong Hua-ying, was another case in point. Since he was the man who had collected clan rifles in the village and handed them over to the Communist soldiers, he was viewed favorably as a collaborator with the new regime. Later, some cadres visited him in his house and saw a photograph on the wall showing a group of peasants, each holding a rifle or a sidearm. Questioned about it, he explained that the group was a "navigation protection corps" that he had once belonged to but which was no longer in existence. The cadres asked lengthy questions about the location of the men and the arms and particularly about his own rifle, shown in the picture. He pleaded ignorance about the other members of the corps and said that he had sold his own rifle some time ago. The cadres were dissatisfied. Wong Hua-ying, sensing danger, escaped from the village immediately and went into hiding, in Hong Kong, according to the villagers. That night a group of soldiers searched the house, but found nothing incriminating. They arrested his wife and her two children.

The oldest child, about six years old, was sent to a relative, and the mother took her few-months-old infant with her to prison. We learned that severe physical torture was repeatedly applied to force her to divulge where her husband was and where the firearms were hidden. Wong Hua-ying sent word back to the village that he would be willing to return to the village to stand trial if his wife and baby were released. The Communist police refused the request, applying further physical torture to the wife. Finally, she admitted that the arms were buried under the front yard of the house. The soldiers went to dig for them and found over ten pieces of firearms, including one machine gun. After several months, the wife and baby were released, but Wong Hua-ying never returned.

According to the Communist timetable, with the landlord class and their associated groups disarmed, and with the local bullies deposed from power, thus removing the physical threat against changing the economic system, the process of land reform advanced to another stage, namely the identification of land ownership and class status of the individuals in the village.

The identification of land ownership was a necessary step because of two traditional situations. One was the custom of using a "hall name" as the owner of land, and the other the fact that a person's land was frequently registered in more than one hall name, thus giving the impression of more than single ownership. This was done for many reasons, one of them being the prevention of possible foreclosure of the entire family property by creditors should the landowner contract a loan and become unable to repay it. The result was that government records of legal registration of land deeds did not reveal the total land possession of a person or a family, particularly those with extensive possessions. A third situation arose after the Communist take-over. To avoid identification as a landlord, there was a scramble among the larger landlords to hide the ownership of their land by various means, such as having a friendly poor peasant, usually a relative, take temporary ownership of a part of the land. Uncertain as to the purpose and durability of the new Communist regime, many poor peasants did this for the landlords, particularly if the parties involved were cemented by long friendship or family relations. Family A, for example, decentralized part of its land to several tenants who were kinsmen in the same clan.

When the cadres were ready to draw the demarcation of class status among the villagers, it became necessary for them to identify the real owners of the land. They used a number of poor peasants in the village as informers, to identify hall names with individuals and families. Since we were not able to see the Communist official record on this matter, it is hard to say to what extent they succeeded. From what we were able to learn, it seemed they successfully identified most of the hall names that belonged to the leading families; but later Communist press information indicated that a large number of cases of disguised temporary ownership remained hidden through 1952, leading to the re-examination of the real ownership of land in 1953.

With the ownership of land identified by about January of 1951, to whatever degree of accuracy, the stage was set for the identification of the class status of every family and the delineation of class lines among the villagers. The identification of class status was done by applying the land reform regulations governing this point to each family. Technically, each individual should be assigned his own class status, but the economic unity of the family made the family the actual unit of class status which all the members shared except when some individual member had followed another occupation and thus acquired a different economic status.

For a rural village, the essential classes established in the official regulations were landlords, rich peasants, middle peasants, poor peasants, agricultural laborers, and vagrants. While details of the definition for each of these classes can be examined in the "Decisions on the Identification of Rural Class Status" by the Administrative Council of the Central People's Government, promulgated in August 1950, it would be useful here to point out a few characteristics.

The major criteria in the determination of class status were the amount of land owned and the degree to which the land had been used as a means of "exploiting others." In addition, the standard of living was considered together with these two factors. A family dependent entirely upon renting out land for a living but having about the same standard of living as the majority of the villagers because of the large number of members in the family and because of the shortage of labor in the family were considered as small land rentiers and not as landlords. If a peasant farmed a part of his own land with the help of some hired day labor, rented out part of it, and loaned money for interest, and the total amount of "exploitation" by hired labor, renting out land, and lending money to others did not exceed 15 per cent of the total income of the family, he was considered not a rich peasant but a well-to-do middle peasant even though his standard of living might be well above that of the average family in the village.

These examples serve to illustrate the range of possible disputes over the definition of class status of a family in accordance with the official line. Since in a highly diffused situation such as the farm economy of a family it was frequently difficult to determine even the accurate amount of total income a family received in a year, the percentage of this income which represented the proceeds from exploitation was a highly controversial matter. The relative difference in the standard of living between a well-to-do middle-peasant family and a rich-peasant family or even a poor landlord's family was not always clearly marked, and the placement of a family in any one of these three categories would make a great deal of difference in the economic, political, and social treatment the family received under the new order. Frequently it meant the difference between security and bankruptcy, at times between life and death.

Deliberation on these difficult problems and the decision on the class status of each family were legally the duty of the peasants' association, on the theory that people in a village knew one another's status best. But here in Nanching the cadres from Pingan Chen did most of the deliberating and making of decisions, with several persons from the peasants' association advising them. The young cadres examined the book containing the record of each family's land ownership, asked the persons from the peasants' association for an estimate of "exploitation" income relative to the family's total income, the possible amount of surplus grain or income the family had in a year, and the general standard of living it enjoyed in comparison with that of an average family. A tentative class status was then determined for each family in the village.

By the end of January 1951 the walls of the ancestral hall of a subdivision of the Wong clan were plastered with over 200 slips of oblong red paper; on each was written the name of the head of a family and the amount of land it had, and they were grouped into landlords, rich peasants, middle peasants, poor peasants, and farm laborers. They were posted so that the villagers could come to look at them and protest cases of injustice in the identification of class status. Fourteen were listed as landlords, about four or five as rich peasants, a large number as middle peasants, an even larger group as poor peasants, and a comparatively small group as agricultural laborers. Wong Ping, the head of the peasants' association, was listed as a middle peasant, although some peasants thought he should belong to the class of rich peasants. Lee Feng was listed as a rich peasant. One Wong Wu Shih, a widow with twenty mow of land (about 3.3 acres), was listed as a landlord.

Her son had died some years ago, and since she could not farm the land, she had rented out all of it. This put her into the category of those who lived entirely by exploitation. A senior officer from the Ministry of Agriculture in Peking came to visit the village. Looking at the paper slips bearing the class status of the villagers, he thought that this woman with only twenty mow of land and no ability to farm it should be listed as a small land rentier and not as a landlord. However, he expressed a desire not to interfere with the work of the junior cadres in the village. The woman presented vigorous verbal protests to the peasants' association, but to no avail, and she was kept in the same class with Family A and other large landowners.

There were quite a few cases of change from middle- to poor-peasant status as a consequence of individual protest in the general effort to get oneself listed in as low a class status as possible. Whatever the manner in which the status of each family was decided upon, the villagers were now fully differentiated into distinctly marked classes.

The general proportion of the classes corresponded roughly to what we had learned about the class composition of the village previous to the Communist rule.* A great anxiety and tenseness pervaded the village, for now every family was assigned a status fraught with social, economic, and political consequences. Those families listed as landlords waited for the axe to fall. Those listed as rich peasants were extremely

* This picture might be compared with the pre-land reform distribution of economic status among the villagers. It would be useful to compare Nanching's distribution of class status with the combined figures of several villages that comprised another locality, Kuan Chia Tsui in Ch'i-yang county of Hunan Province, a major rice-producing area about 200 miles north of Nanching. There was a general similarity between the two communities. Nanching's larger proportion of landlords and rich peasants and nonagricultural elements was due to its considerable number of emigrants who worked in the cities, whereas Kuan Chia Tsui was an inland community rather inaccessible to urban occupational opportunities. The distribution of economic status in Nanching and Kuan Chia Tsui in 1950, prior to land reform, was as follows:

| | Number of Households | | Per cent | |
	Kuan Chia Tsui	Nanching	Kuan Chia Tsui	Nanching
Landlords and rich peasants	84	30	5.3	13.0
Middle peasants (including small rentiers)	482	70	30.4	30.5
Poor peasants and farm laborers	931	100	59.0	43.5
Nonagricultural and others	84	30	5.3	13.0
Total	1,581	230	100.0	100.0

(*Sources*: Figures for Kuan Chia Tsui, *Ch'angchiang jih-pao*, Hankow, February, 1952, p. 2; figures for Nanching, see above, Chapter IV.)

uneasy, for they knew their fate was undecided, in spite of the temporary policy of "preservation of the rich peasants' economy." They felt lucky, for the time being, for they saw rich peasants in other villages being listed as landlords because of having rented out some of their land. The middle peasants experienced considerable suspense. Whatever amount of land they owned and the degree of economic security they had built up, they considered it the result of their own hard labor, and they clung to it desperately, for they did not know of any other workable and reliable system which would protect them and their families from hunger. Now that land could be taken away wholesale by order and force, they were uncertain how long their land and property could be preserved. Furthermore, many of the relatively well-to-do were in juxtaposition to the rich peasants, and they did not know whether they would some day be "promoted" to that rank.

Here in Nanching, while all these feelings troubled the middle peasants, they probably fared better than those in other places, for several were in important positions in the peasants' association where they had a voice in the making of policies for the village. In many other villages where the peasants' associations were controlled by the poor peasants and farm laborers, the position of middle peasants was more insecure. Poor peasants and agricultural laborers were generally the more satisfied ones, since their lot could not be worse under any circumstances; a share of free land was a boon regardless of the degree of uncertainty of the future. But when Lee Ch'un, a poor peasant, and Wong Ping, both important figures in the peasants' association, talked about the forthcoming redistribution of land and how much each qualified person would get, we observed little natural expression of enthusiasm on their faces.

The Communist official strategy in this process was to "neutralize the rich peasants, unite the middle peasants with the poor peasants and agricultural laborers, and attack the landlords." Facts in Nanching suggest that this policy was only partly successful because of the uneasy feeling among the rich peasants and a large number of the middle peasants. But it was successful in generating hatred against large landlords.

Now that the landlord class was definitely identified, however the composition of this class might have been determined, the next act was to force the landlords to surrender all surplus grain, leaving them enough for subsistence until the harvest of the next crop and enough for investment in the next crop. This procedure was designed to obtain production capital from the landlords for the poor peasants and to make sure that the landlords were shorn of their economic power. As it actually worked out in Nanching, and in many other villages in this locality, few rational criteria were used in determining the amount of surplus grain to be surrendered by the landlords. An arbitrary amount was named by the cadres in conjunction with the members of the peasants' association for each landlord according to his estimated ability to pay.

One absentee landlord who owned about sixty mow of land was assigned a figure of 40,000 catties of unhusked rice to be surrendered as surplus grain. The family had moved to the city and on to Hong Kong after 1950, its house in the village having been occupied by relatives for many years; and there was no grain belonging to that family for confiscation. As a result, their residential house in the city was sealed by the government and sold, and the proceeds went to the peasants' association as surrendered "surplus grain." Family A escaped all this by having sold their property in the city and moved to Hong Kong. The woman Wong Wu Shih, who owned twenty mow, was assigned 10,000 catties of unhusked rice as "surplus grain" to be surrendered. This was beyond her ability to pay as she had less than 1,000 catties of grain in storage and only small cash savings. It was Wong Ping and several others who finally had the levy reduced to 3,000 catties, which she paid by borrowing from relatives in the city.

Nanching probably suffered less violence in the class struggle than many other villages. Nevertheless, in about one and a half years the Communist mass campaign to arouse hatred among the poor against the rich broke down the stability of an ancient social order which had kept the conflict of class interests under control. Although formerly there had been suppressed hatred between the two extremities, such as between Family A and its tenants, there had been generally peaceful co-existence among the large middle section and between the middle groups and the two extremes; but now, under the organized campaign of class struggle, the entire village population was methodically partitioned into class compartments, each set against the other.

CHAPTER X

Confiscation and Redistribution of Land

ANTICIPATING A crisis, a landlord and his family had moved out of the village in 1950. We rented his vacated house for our investigators to live in while we were collecting data. In February of 1951 one of our field workers was told by the land reform cadres to move his belongings out of the house or the belongings would be regarded as part of the property of the landlord and taken out for redistribution. We knew then that the final step of land reform, the confiscation of landlords' land and property for redistribution, was at hand. According to the Communist official policy, after identification of class status of the villagers and surrender of surplus grain by the landlords, the situation was ripe for the confiscation of landlords' land and property and subsequent redistribution to peasants who had "insufficient or no land." Like other steps in land reform, this step was governed by both central and local regulations which set forth the principles on what land and property to confiscate, who was eligible for a share of them, and how they should be divided.

Land to be confiscated for redistribution included both that owned by public organizations and that owned by individuals under certain conditions. In Nanching all land owned by organizations was subject to confiscation, and the procedure was carried out without any obvious deviation from official policy, resulting in the seizure of the following:

School land	20 mow
Clan land (Wong)	30 mow
Clan land (Lee, subdivision land)	20 mow
Temple land	10 mow
Total	80 mow

Official regulations permitted the retaining of school land for educational purposes; but Nanching school land was confiscated along with other public land on the theory that much of the income from it had in the past been manipulated by powerful families, an ill-founded accusation. The official purpose, of course, was to reduce local autonomy over education and put the school under central government control. Official regulations for the Central-South region also permitted the retaining of a certain amount of clan land for defraying the cost of ancestral sacrifice should this be desired by the peasants, and there was some talk of retaining one or two mow of the Wong clan land for this purpose, a measure which Wong Ping, head of the peasants' association, supported; but the cadres maintained that those who wanted the "superstitious" ancestral sacrifice continued could get together and pay for it. The ten mow of temple land was confiscated on the ground that the priest should live by labor and not by exploitation of others through superstition, but three mow of land was returned to the priest for sustenance.

A total of about 460 mow of private land was confiscated for redistribution. A part of this land belonged to families classified as landlords, and a part belonged to lesser landowners who rented out land amounting to twice the norm owned by the average peasant family in this village. What constituted the norm, the amount of land owned by the average peasant family, was a subject of considerable controversy. The percentage of rented land was high in Nanching, and even the middle peasants owned only two or three mow of land. If this amount was considered as the average, a large number of small landowners who rented out land would see part of their land reduced. The norm was, therefore, arbitrarily established as six mow, and any amount of land rented out in excess of twelve mow was declared subject to confiscation provided the standard of living of the family was well above the average in the village. This provision also constituted a disputed issue. The official principle of sparing the rich peasants was generally observed in Nanching, provided the rich peasant performed "main labor" on his farm aside from hiring labor to work for him; but Lee Feng had part of his land confiscated on the ground that he did not perform enough "main labor" on his land. Thus, aside from the fourteen landlords whose land was completely confiscated, a sizable number of smaller landowners who rented out land were also affected by the program. In the latter category were a number of emigrants who had invested their urban earnings in land.

The 460 mow of private land and 80 mow of public land confiscated yielded a total of 540 mow for redistribution. Official regulations prescribed that the confiscated land of several villages, which constituted a *hsiang* or administrative village, should be pooled together for re-distribution in order to equalize the situation between villages having a surplus of land and those short of it in the general effort to give each poor peasant enough land for subsistence. In a neighboring *hsiang*, where two villages owned very little land and the villagers mainly farmed the next village's land, this pooling policy was followed. But Nanching, fairly self-sufficient in land, was treated as a self-contained unit where only resident villagers could obtain a share of the confiscated land in the village.

The first question in the redistribution of confiscated land was who qualified to receive a share of it. The official principle prescribed redistribution to peasants with "insufficient or no land"; and, although it was easy to identify those without land, it was not so obvious whether a landless person was earning enough to live on from nonagricultural occupations, such as handicrafts and small businesses, and therefore deserved no share. Even more difficult was the definition of those having "insufficient land," for this involved the dual problem of the amount of land a family owned and the number of mouths it had to feed; but this problem was met by establishing a per capita norm. Figuring on a per capita norm of slightly less than one mow, coupled with the consideration of the number of persons in a household, about 130 families were to receive land. A number of controversies and protests arose against this selection made by the land reform cadres and the officers of the peasants' association. The Lees were dissatisfied because more Wongs than Lees were included in the list, and the traditional hostility between the two clans was aroused; but the cadres threatened punishment to anyone who led or plotted factional fights between the peasants on the basis of traditional clannish feelings. Since villagers by this time had learned to appreciate the violent character of the new power, the controversies and protests rested on an individual basis and did not develop into organized conflict.

Among the some 130 families, we recognized many categories of people. Outstanding in number were the 100-odd poor-peasant families who generally farmed less than six mow of land of which they owned only a small fraction. They included peddlers whose livelihood depended on selling herbs and miscellaneous items in the city, dispossessed landlords who received back their share of confiscated land on the same basis as other peasants qualified to receive land, those few emigrants who had recently returned to the village because of unemployment in the city after the Communists' take-over, and the village seeress who was no longer allowed to practice her superstitious art. One class of people whose demands for land were denied were the migratory farm laborers, the "boat people" who lived on floating homes and worked up and down the Pearl River. Since some of them had worked in Nanching regularly every year at planting and harvesting seasons, they sent several representatives to the village to talk to the cadres about sharing in the confiscated land; but the villagers raised stiff opposition on the ground that land was already short in the village, and the boat people were not established members of the village.

The formula for redistribution of land was to take the confiscated land plus all the land owned by those who were to receive land and thereby arrive at a total of land which was then divided by the number of *all* persons in every family eligible to receive land. The quotient constituted the share of land to be redistributed on a per capita basis. In Nanching the 540 mow of land confiscated from collective and private owners plus approximately 80 mow owned by families eligible to receive land made a total of 620 mow (slightly less than 100 acres) for about 650 people, a per capita share of slightly less than one mow. A family whose land amounted to less than this per capita received enough land to bring it up to this figure. For instance, Wong Mi had one mow of land and three persons (father, mother, and himself) in his family. In accordance with the formula, he received two mow of land, giving his family a total possession of three mow. A returned emigrant with two mow of land and a family of five (wife, three young children, and himself) received three mow, making a total family possession of five mow.

In the apportioning of land, the official principle was to equate the quality so that every family would get a farm of approximately equal fertility. A family owning fertile land would be given a lower grade of land, and a family already in possession of poor land would be given better plots. In the process of redistribution, the official emphasis was upon preserving the integrity of the original farm as far as possible, even to the extent of giving the original farmer somewhat more land than the average if this should be necessary to preserve the integrity of the original farm. Thus, a family of five farming six mow of land, all rented from others, would receive all of the six mow if they were marked out for confiscation and redistribution, even though this would be one mow in excess of the quota.

In Nanching the policy of balancing the quality of land was carried out through bargaining between the individual recipient and the peasants' association officials, who were thoroughly acquainted with the land quality in various parts of the village. Although apparently at least an attempt to be fair was made in the majority of cases, there was grumbling that several officers of the peasants' association received the best land and the land nearest the village site. Wong Tan, a poor peasant generally known as an unscrupulous character, who was a committee member of the peasants' association, was accused of having obtained four mow of all good irrigated land at the very edge of the village site.

In suburban areas such as Nanching all confiscated land was nationalized, being redistributed to peasants for their use but not for their ownership. Each family was issued a certificate containing the names and ages of all family members and stipulating their right to use the land distributed to them, but the land could not be sold. Although there was no stipulation concerning the inheritance of the right to use the land, the whole procedure created an uneasy feeling among the peasants in the village, even among those who were given a share of the confiscated land. They said that they were quite puzzled as to whether to call the land their own and as to how long it would remain in their hands.

In addition to land, landlords' properties subject to confiscation in accordance with official policy included surplus grain, houses, farm tools and implements, and draft animals. In the process of redistribution the landlord's family was given back a house to live in and a share of farm tools on the same basis as other recipients. In Nanching about twenty houses were confiscated for redistribution, some 10 per cent of all the houses in the village. Since all the large landlords who owned more than one house in the village had already escaped, all of their houses were confiscated and redistributed with no question of reserving a house for their own use. Small landlords generally had only one house in which they lived, and these houses were not touched.

The furniture of both large and small landlords was subject to confiscation and redistribution, and we saw all the furniture moved out of the house of one small landowner and displayed on the street. The articles included such things as old benches and wooden chairs, three tables, large earthen jugs for holding rice and water, pots, pans, some old chinaware, chopsticks, a couple of old mosquito nets, and several worn-out cotton quilts. A woman standing behind this pile was crying. A group of peasants gathered around to look over the articles. We did not see the actual process of redistribution of these things.

There were not many farm tools for redistribution, since most of the large landlords did not operate their own farms but rented out their land and therefore had not invested much in farm tools. Expensive tools and implements, like winnowers and water pumps, which poor peasants lacked were uncommon among confiscated articles. One item of considerable importance was the water buffalo, the only draft animal used for farming in the Nanching area. Several buffaloes owned by landlords for renting out were confiscated for redistribution. Since none of the 130-odd eligible families possessed any water buffaloes and since there were so few of them to go around, it was decided that several families should receive and care for one buffalo collectively — a co-operative arrangement of caring for and feeding the animal which did not work out well, and a few of the buffaloes died as a consequence.

Personal belongings like gold and silver jewelry and ornaments of landlords and their families did not appear in the process of confiscation. Presumably, many of these were squeezed out in the process of surrendering surplus grain and the rest were well hidden.

Confiscation of landlords' belongings was designed to give poor peasants the means of production and to alleviate their economic difficulties. The one category of landlords' property that the law exempted from confiscation was poultry and other animals, such as pigs; but in Nanching, as a result of mob action, all these were taken away for redistribution by selling them and dividing up the money.

The over-all policy of land reform was to "leave the middle alone while equalizing the two extremities." By equalizing the wealth between the rich and poor, it was expected that everyone in the agrarian community would possess an economic status of the middle peasants. As it worked out in Nanching, land reform appeared to have given the majority the economic status of lower-middle or upper-lower class, a situation representing a certain improvement for the poor peasants over their pre-Communist economic conditions.

In historical perspective, from the Hsin Dynasty (9–23 A.D.) on, redistribution of land had been repeatedly attempted as a solution to political and economic crises caused partly by concentration of land ownership in the hands of a minority group; but the equalized situation had never endured for long, as the forces making for concentration of land ownership soon reasserted themselves. Thus the Communist land reform, despite its Marxist twist, was not historically unique in its essential features. What we saw with vivid detail in Nanching might be regarded as a re-enactment of a historical scene in an agrarian economy which had in the past been governed by cycles of concentration and dispersion of land ownership. What made the Communist policy different from its historical precedents was its treatment of equalization of land ownership as a transitional step toward reorganization of the agrarian economy on a collectivized basis. Such economic transformation, if successful, might theoretically end the recurrence of the cycle of dispersion and concentration of land ownership as a source of agrarian crises besides contributing to the construction of an industrialized socialist state.

CHAPTER XI

Post–Land-Reform Village Economy

Now THAT the village of Nanching had been put through the convulsive process of land reform, what was the state of its economy in 1951? Were the peasants getting a larger income than before? While known facts about the village may provide an estimate, it should be kept in mind that we are trying to assess a temporary transitional situation. The reorganization of the individual farms into larger organized units was soon to begin, and land reform was but one stage in the general process of reorganization toward collectivistic agriculture. Nevertheless, an evaluation of the transitional economy after land reform and before collectivization will contribute toward an understanding of the process of transformation of the economic life in this village.

Productivity of the Soil

A primary question in assessing the village's post–land-reform economy is whether there was any increase of yield from the soil. An examination of the major factors affecting agricultural productivity warrants no positive answer to this question.

Up till 1951 no general technical improvements were visible in this territory. The campaign to adopt improved strains of rice was just starting in that year, and there were isolated instances of trial adoption in some villages in this area, but Nanching was not among them. Irrigational and water-control projects, which could raise agricultural production substantially, had not begun as a general movement in this area at this time. The repair and maintenance of a nearby dike served to keep up Nanching's production but not to increase it. In spite of the strenuous campaign to urge the peasants to collect more fertilizer, we saw in Nanching no sign of increased use of fertilizer applied to the land. Both capital and credit were extremely short in the village after land reform, and there seemed little likelihood of increased investment in fertilizer or other phases of agricultural production. The labor exertion campaign could have stimulated productive efforts among some lower-middle and poor peasants who had received free land from the land reform, but the limitation of capital investment prevented any rise of productivity of their farms above those of the middle peasants.

On the other hand, there were many situations obviously unfavorable to any increase in productivity. There was admittedly low morale among the rich peasants and a large number of middle peasants, thus reducing the productivity of the groups who had been the most efficient producers in the past, partly owing to their greater capital investment. A Communist leader who had conducted land reform in the North and now was sent to this area admitted that the first one or two years following land reform generally saw a drop in morale and productivity among most peasants, and that what was happening in Nanching was better than in a number of other places he had seen, the decline in production here not being generally noticeable. The feeling of uncertainty about the future of their property and interests haunted the rich and middle peasants and discouraged them from investing maximum capital and labor on their farms. (In many villages in this province, where the land reform process had been more violent and treatment of the richer peasants rougher than in Nanching, many peasants refused to raise more crops than absolutely needed for their own subsistence.)[1]

Therefore, in estimating productivity from the soil, we assume there was no change in this period and use the old norm of annual yield per mow as the standard. This means 700 catties of unhusked rice per mow of rice crop, and 1,400 catties per mow of vegetable gardening.

Savings on Rent

It has been pointed out that about 70 per cent of all the land in this village was rented land before land reform, and that rent constituted by far the heaviest item in the cost of agricultural production for the majority of the villagers who had insufficient or no land. The Communists had called agricultural rent the foundation of the "feudalistic system of exploitation," and it was the main target for destruction in the process of land reform. Now that land reform had been accomplished, the savings on rent were undoubtedly the most important benefit accruing to the favored poor and landless peasants.

Of the former total of about 840 mow of rented land in the village, 540 mow had been taken out of this category for redistribution. At the average rate of 300 catties per mow, this saved the tenants a total rent of 162,000 catties of unhusked rice for the entire village, about 22 per cent of the total gross yield of 740,000 catties from all the village land.

Formerly, four large landlord families owned 280 mow and used the rent of 84,000 catties of unhusked rice, somewhat over one half of the now abolished rent, to support their families in the village at a high standard of living, and a part of this rent was taken out of the village to the cities. Now those families had fled, and all this rent was retained in the village.

But land reform did not wipe out tenancy entirely, and the law still permitted renting land to others. About 300 of the original 840 mow remained in the private hands of a legally recognized group, the so-called "small land rentiers." Some of these were peasant families without enough labor to operate a farm who rented out a part of their land, usually from a fraction of one mow to two or three mow. The majority were families with adult male members working in the cities who bought small plots of land and rented them out so that their families in the village could have a subsidiary income to the periodic remittances they sent home. After land reform, some of the women in these families went into partnership with close relatives to farm the land instead of renting it out for fear of being identified as landlords. Some such families continued to rent out land because of their advanced age, unwillingness to do farm work, or inability to make joint farming arrangements. Thus, since the poor peasants who acquired free land and most of the middle peasants still urgently needed additional land because the land each family owned remained too small, tenancy still existed, even though vastly reduced. It should be noted, however, that the net proceeds from renting out agricultural land was now so drastically reduced that it was not economical for owners to rent out their land unless they could circumvent the Communist rent ceiling.

Taxes under the New Order

If the abolition of rent from the greater part of the formerly rented land lightened the heaviest burden for the majority of the peasants, this benefit was partly nullified by the fact that taxes levied by the Communists were much heavier than those imposed by previous governments. In the pre-Communist period, medium-grade irrigated land paid a tax of about 13 per cent of the gross yield, and all grades of land in the village paid an average of about 10 per cent of the total gross yield. But the average tax rate in this area during 1949 to 1951 was about 30 per cent of the gross yield, a tax which included agricultural tax (formerly called land tax), a local levy of five catties of unhusked rice per mow to help support the village school, and a levy of varying amounts for helping to defray the cost of the subdistrict police force. The last two levies were imposed not by formal tax regulations, but by local cadres independently.

The peasants' burden of taxation under the Communist government is a controversial subject, partly because of the variations in the manner of collection by local cadres in various areas and partly because of the lack of factual information aside from published government regulations and generalized formal reports. Government regulations in 1951 expected the average peasants to pay from 11 to 15 per cent of the gross yield, with a higher rate for rich peasants who worked their land with a substantial amount of hired labor. These rates continued to prevail in the regulations of 1952.[2] A rate between 11 and 15 per cent was assigned to a peasant on the basis of the estimate made partly from the quality of the land and partly from what the cadres judged as the appropriate labor capacity of the peasant.

As these regulations were carried out in Nanching, the average tax burden actually exceeded the limit of 11 to 15 per cent. Rural cadres, eager to fulfill their quota of tax collection, often assigned a higher yield for a piece of land than the occupying family could normally make it produce, with the result that a large number of peasants were paying more than the regulations intended. Raising the production quota was a common means employed by the cadres to induce the peasants to increase the yield in order to execute the policy of increasing production. One report stated that in Ch'ao-an county, about 100 miles east of Nanching, where an agricultural tax of 33 per cent was levied on a production quota of 540 catties of unhusked rice per mow, the local cadres in 1953 raised the quota to 800 catties with an additional 18 per cent of tax on a progressive basis, making a rate of 51 per cent of the yield for one mow.[3] Compared to such cases, the average of 30 per cent of the gross yield in Nanching was relatively light.

Aside from agricultural taxes paid directly by the peasants, there were other types of levies that affected the peasants directly or indirectly. There were, for example, levies for education and the police force in Nanching. Although in another county in this province there were levies on pigs raised at home, water buffaloes, and houses, and a variety of police protection fees,[4] we did not hear of any of these being collected in Nanching. There were also other collections by the government that amounted to taxation in the sense that they were financial burdens imposed by a political power. In the last months of 1949 there was the "government loan to support the battle front." Several merchant-landlord families in Nanching had to subscribe heavily, but the peasants were not bothered. In the spring and summer of 1950 there was a victory bond campaign. Again, the merchant-landlord families were the heaviest subscribers, with the village as a whole given a quota of only 50 units (about $15.00). The clans used school funds to pay for this. In 1951 and 1952 there were "Resist America and Aid Korea" donations.

Village Production and Consumption

With the foregoing information in view, we can make a rough estimate of the balance of production and consumption for the village as a whole.

In the first place, production was affected by a reduction of about seventy mow of vegetable gardens, the reason for which was twofold. When the Communist soldiers came to Canton and its suburbs in the latter part of 1949, they sent parties to Nanching to buy vegetables and meats. They would offer only a half of the current market price, and when the peasants refused to sell, the soldiers descended upon the vegetable patches, picked all that they wanted, paid the peasants the half price, and left. They did the same with pigs and chickens. As a consequence, by the time of spring planting in 1950 many peasants turned their vegetable patches into paddy fields, and many paddy fields that had gone through the three years of rotation and were ready to be turned into vegetable patches remained as paddy fields. After the summer of 1950, when a large part of the troops in the vicinity moved on to other places, forced buying at low prices no longer occurred; but by then the restriction of foreign trade with Hong Kong began to affect the marketing of vegetables grown here, particularly the leeks in which the village specialized. Local vegetable prices also saw a small decline in this period.

With this change, the gross production of the village in 1951 is estimated as follows: 670 mow of rice produced 469,000 catties of unhusked rice, 130 mow of vegetable produced 182,000 catties of unhusked rice, 400 mow of dry land produced 40,000 catties of unhusked rice, and the total gross yield for 1,200 mow was 691,000 catties of unhusked rice. Since the total gross yield of the entire village in the pre-Communist period was 740,000 catties, there was a decline of 49,000 catties, or 6.6 per cent, due to the shrinkage of vegetable acreage.

There was now no absentee rent to be taken out of the village after land reform, but there was an average of 30 per cent of the gross yield for taxes, or 207,300 catties, to be deducted, leaving a rough net yield of 483,700 catties of unhusked rice or 314,400 catties of husked rice for consumption within the village. This represented a reduction of 131,300 catties of unhusked rice from the pre-Communist net yield of 615,000 catties, a reduction of about 20 per cent.

Up until 1951 we discerned no sign of increased consumption among the villagers in general. The Communist press reported cases of poor peasants who, having acquired land, were able to eat better or buy new clothes, but there did not seem to be many such cases from our observations. The high living standard of the landlords was gone, and the rich peasants and the upper portion of the middle peasants now had a much lower standard of living. Any possible increase of consumption among some poor peasants might be balanced by the decrease of consumption among the richer portion of the village population. Therefore, it may be assumed that the entire village's minimum requirement for subsistence remained the same as in the pre-Communist period, that is, approximately 391,000 catties of husked rice a year. But the village was now producing only 314,000 catties of husked rice a year; and there was therefore a deficit of about 77,400 catties or 19.4 per cent. As in the case of the pre-Communist figure of net yield, we have not deducted the 7.0 per cent cost of fertilizer and seeds from this figure. Should we deduct 7.0 per cent from the yield, the deficit would be raised to 26.4 per cent.

In the pre-Communist period the net yield of the village was about equal to the village's total needs, but that seemingly self-sufficient picture obscured the fact that a small number of rich families consumed much more than the average peasants, a large number of whom were not able to meet their own needs. Now, land reform having abolished the high-living minority, there was a relatively uniform standard of living among the majority of the families; the over-all figure of net yield for the whole village reflected more closely the economic conditions of all the individual families. The most important factor in the new deficit was that the proportion of the yield removed from the village by Communist taxes was greater than the combined total of pre-Communist taxes and the part of absentee rent taken to the cities, the new taxes being a total of 30.0 per cent of the gross yield of the whole village.

Family Income and Consumption and Size of Farm

In estimating family consumption, the pre-Communist annual requirement of 2,141 catties of husked rice for a family of five is retained as the norm for the post–land-reform period, on the assumption that no significant general rise in consumption had yet occurred by 1951.

In estimating the gross income of the average family, we retain the pre-Communist yield of 700 catties of unhusked rice per mow of rice crop as the norm for reasons already stated. For estimating the net income, the following figures of costs were used. Taxes took 30 per cent of the gross yield, the heaviest item. Fertilizer and seeds remained the same as in the pre-Communist period, i.e., 7 per cent of the gross yield, as no general increase in this item appeared possible in this area at this stage of development of the new economic order. If the land was rented, the general rate of rent was 35 per cent of the gross yield instead of the former 43 per cent, owing to the imposition of a rent ceiling by the Communist government.

On these bases, the cost of production for one mow of land owned by the peasant and planted in rice crop was 37 per cent of the gross yield, which included 30 per cent for taxes and 7 per cent for fertilizer and seeds. In both cases, the cost of labor has not been included because of the wide differences in the amount of hired help used on different farms during the pre-Communist period and the general prevalence of self-labor, making the two situations noncomparable.

In the pre-Communist period a peasant tilling his own land would receive about 80 per cent of the gross yield, whereas now he received 63 per cent, or 17 per cent less than before. From one mow of rented land, the peasant used to get 40 per cent of the gross yield, whereas he now got 58 per cent, or 9 per cent more than in the pre-Communist days. For a person who rented out one mow of land, the normal rate of rent used to be 43 per cent and the tax rate 13 per cent for average irrigated land; he received about 30 per cent of the gross yield from his tenant. But now, while the rate of rent was only 35 per cent of the gross yield, the tax rate had hiked to 30 per cent, so he obtained a net income of about 5 per cent of the gross yield. Previously, evasion of a part of the land tax was a common practice with large landowners; but now large landowners were gone, and under rigid Communist surveillance with the help of the peasants' association leaders who had intimate knowledge of village affairs, evasion of taxes became difficult. There was no longer shifting of the tax burden by the big fellows to the average peasants, but the now more equalized burden was heavier for everybody. This tax factor accounted for the main difference in net income between the Communist and the pre-Communist periods.

From these norms of net income per mow in different types of operations, it is possible to estimate the new level of family income of the peasants in Nanching. Of the some 130 families that acquired a share of land from land reform, about 100 families were former poor peasants and farm laborers, and these 100-odd families now became the political-ly and economically decisive group. They furnished the larger propor-tion of the peasants' association leaders, owned an aggregate of 620 mow which comprised slightly over half of all the village land, and remained the numerically predominant group among the village peas-ants as before. Since in the redistribution of land each person in this group got slightly less than one mow regardless of sex and age, and the average size of the family in this village was 4.8 persons, a family of five received somewhat less than five mow of land. This acreage ap-proached the size of a farm of the upper portion of the poor peasants and the lower portion of the middle peasants in the pre–land-reform days, but the difference was that, while the farm was formerly mostly rented land, it was now rent-free.

From five mow of land for which the peasant paid no rent he reaped a gross yield of about 3,500 catties of unhusked rice if the land was all planted in rice crop. From this figure, 37 per cent or 1,295 catties should be deducted for taxes and for the cost of fertilizer and seeds. This would leave a net yield of 2,245 catties of unhusked or about 1,457 cat-ties of husked rice for the family's consumption. Since the average family of five needed about 2,141 catties of husked rice to meet the minimum annual need, there was a deficit of 684 catties or almost 32 per cent of the annual yield. To make up for this deficit by farming, the peasant would have either to rent about 1.7 mow of land if he planted only rice or devote a part of his five rent-free mow to vegetable gardening. But most of the formerly rented land being no longer for rent, the peasant had difficulty in finding land to rent.

By far the more common way to meet the deficit was to devote a part of the farm to vegetable gardening. The post–land-reform economy of one mow of vegetable garden was as follows:

Gross yield: equivalent of 1,400 c.u.r. (catties of unhusked rice)
Costs: taxes, 30 per cent of gross yield, or 420 c.u.r.; fertilizer and seeds, 15 per cent of gross, or 210 c.u.r.; total cost, 45 per cent of gross, or 630 c.u.r.
Net yield: 55 per cent of gross, or 770 c.u.r. or 500 catties of husked rice

At this estimated rate of net yield from one mow of vegetables, the peasant had to devote three mow of his land to rice and two mow to vegetables in order to get a net income of 2,128 catties of husked rice to meet approximately his family's annual need of 2,141 catties. Actual-ly, this proportion of devoting 40 per cent of the farm to vegetables and the rest to rice had been a common practice among the poor peasants and most of the middle peasants in this village. This observation was substantiated by the result of a survey made by the combined efforts of the Canton Municipal Agricultural Bureau, the South China Agricultural College and the Central-South Institute of Scientific Research which stated: ". . . Over 50 per cent of the Canton suburban peasants depend upon vegetable gardening as a vital source of income . . . vegetable crops supply about 40 per cent of the family's annual income for the average suburban peasant." [5] Although made in 1953, the report reflected Nanching's situation in 1951 as we observed it.

In this proportion between rice and vegetable acreage, the peasant family now with five mow of rent-free land could meet their minimum needs during the year. The existence was still precarious and savings remained negligible, but this was better than the pre–land-reform poor peasant who farmed six mow of land, of which 1.2 mow was self-owned and 4.8 mow were rented, giving him a net yield of 1,507 catties of husked rice and a deficit of 30 per cent of his family's annual need. This was also better than the pre–land-reform example of poor peasant Wong Mi, who worked a farm of six mow, of which one was his own and five were rented, and on which three mow were in rice and three in vegetables. This operation netted him only 1,950 catties of husked rice.

In the period before land reform, a family which could meet their average annual need without deficit was considered a member of the middle-peasant class. On this basis rested the Communist claim that land reform had elevated the poor peasants and farm laborers to the status of middle peasants. The difficulty here, however, was the shrinkage of the vegetable acreage. This seemed to be a difficulty not only for Nanching. That it applied also to other villages in the suburban area was reflected in the fact that the Communist survey just cited was made partly for the purpose of developing a domestic and foreign market for vegetables to counteract the decline in vegetable acreage.

After land reform, the middle peasants in the village generally appeared able to maintain a self-sufficient status without incurring a deficit. But middle peasants farming ten mow and over were fewer than before, and the majority of them now farmed only seven or eight mow. The reduction in size of the middle peasant's farm was a significant fact in the new economic order, due partly to the shortage of land for rent. In cases where some rental land could be had, even a farm of eight mow, with four mow hypothetically self-owned and four mow rented from others, would still bring the operator an annual net yield of 3,363 catties of unhusked or 2,186 catties of husked rice if all of the farm were devoted to rice crop. This net yield would meet the family's annual consumption requirement of 2,141 catties of husked rice, and the family budget could be balanced. Actually, the net income would be somewhat above this figure, for a part of the farm was normally given to the high-yielding vegetable crop. But should the peasant fail to find land to rent, his economic status would be reduced to that of the poorer peasants who had received land from the land reform.

Rich peasants as a group were sharply reduced in number in this area after land reform, although some new ones seemed to have appeared and some former ones became re-established after 1951, as suggested in the Communist press. The major factor here was the same as in the reduction of the size of the middle peasants' farm, namely the redistribution of land they formerly rented from landlords. The rich peasants of Nanching differed from those in some other types of rural communities in that a large part of their farms consisted of rented land. Confiscation of land owned by some rich peasants also played a part. Most of the land of two rich peasants, the former head and the secretary of the Crop Protection Association, was confiscated for redistribution, leaving their families with only a portion determined by the number of family members on the same basis as peasants who acquired redistributed land. The only outstanding rich peasant left in the village was Wong Yung, who used to farm 70 mow. In 1951 he farmed only the 30 mow of his own land which had not been touched by land reform. As a whole, the former rich peasants became middle peasants operating farms of 10 mow or less. Their living was still comfortable as compared to the average standard of the village, and they faced no financial deficit. But there was not enough rentable land, and they did not have much enthusiasm for investing capital and labor for expansion of the farm in the period immediately following land reform.

The general reduction in the size of the farm among the former upper portion of the villagers meant at least a temporary setback in the total production of the village, for this group had the capital, equipment, and enterprising management for high productivity. The Communist policy was to develop mutual-aid teams and agricultural producers' co-operatives in order to enlarge the general unit of farm operation; but up till 1951 one saw only the leveling tendency in the size of farms at the expense of the former upper minority of the village peasants. Eliminated was the situation where five large families, or about 2 per cent of all the families in the village, owned 310 mow of the best land, almost 26 per cent of the village's crop area. Now the 100-odd families of poor and landless peasants, about 43.5 per cent of the village's families, who used to own about 80 mow, or about 6.6 per cent of the village's land, owned 620 mow, or about 51.7 per cent of the village land, a percentage commensurate with their numerical proportion to the village population and in theory at least enough to enable them to make ends meet.

Shortage of Agricultural Credit

The new system of land ownership did not mean all smooth sailing for the newly favored families that acquired rent-free land. One outstanding problem was the lack of agricultural capital and rural credit. These families had always been short of agricultural capital and found it difficult to obtain credit; and even after acquiring land from land reform they faced the customary lack of tools and fertilizer and other items requiring investment, a typical situation in villages which had gone through land reform.

After the establishment of Communist rule in Nanching, and especially after land reform, credit became extremely short. While there were many calls for loans, few people were willing to lend money even to relatives and close friends, and no new credit society, a traditional device, was organized in the village in 1951. The shop in Pingan Chen that used to do a limited amount of business in lending money to peasants no longer continued the practice, and another pawnship in a neighboring village to which the desperate peasants used to turn for a loan was now closed and the manager detained by the government on the charge of usury. It was nearly impossible to obtain a loan for either production or consumption purposes. Obviously, those in the village who used to have money to lend had either fled or now belonged to the dispossessed class and had sunk into the position where they themselves could well use a loan; but the major factor in the shortage of credit was the Communist campaign against usury and Communist orders permitting peasants to nullify certain types of indebtedness.

Early in the spring of 1950 three men in Pingan Chen were arrested, tortured, and imprisoned on the accusation of lending money to peasants at usurious rates. Several peasants in Nanching who had lent money to others in the village were frightened, for they did not know whether the rates they charged — about 40 per cent per annum — would be considered usurious by the new rulers. Wong Ping, later the chairman of the peasants' association, said of the arrests: "How can you arrest and torture a man for lending money to others? Even if the rate of interest is high, the loan is contracted on the free will of the debtor." His opinion was changed after Communist indoctrination.

Although no arrests for usury were made in Nanching, the villagers were all aware of Communist policies and that the violation of Communist law could cost a man his life.

Communist regulations on the payment of debts were not alarming except to landlords — whatever credits they had granted, in whatever form, and in whatever stage of repayment were completely nullified. Loans granted by rich peasants were only partially affected. A debtor who had paid a rich peasant an amount of interest equal to the principal might stop paying interest but had to repay the principal; should the interest paid be twice the amount of the principal or over, no further payment needed to be made on either the interest or the principal. This stipulation appeared essentially fair to the peasants. Indebtedness contracted between other classes of peasants remained effective and binding.

But the details of these regulations were not carefully explained to the peasants; and some poor peasants, after hearing that it was no longer necessary to pay one's debts, simply refused to honor any of their contracted obligations regardless of their nature. The creditors, even though they might not be landlords or rich peasants, were now thoroughly frightened by the insufficiently understood government policy and did not dare to argue with the debtors. Even though there were not many such incidents in Nanching, because of the strength of the traditional sense of moral obligation and the kinship bond among the villagers, people with a little money to lend became wary. Nanching peasants were a people who knew much about customs but little or nothing about laws, and after all, there were the three examples of usurers in Pingan Chen to serve as warning.

The shortage of rural credit was so acute that in 1951 it was difficult for some poor peasants to get enough to eat in the late spring period, the time of the year traditionally known as the time of "spring famine" because the previous autumn crop had been largely consumed and the new crop was not yet harvested. Although the Communist government, aware of the critical situation, issued orders to the peasants who might have savings to lend them to those facing acute need and placed no restrictions on the rate of interest,[6] it was doubtful whether this action had any substantial effect on easing the minds of those peasants who might have had some savings to lend.

Beginning in 1951, therefore, the People's Bank was ordered to make agricultural loans to the peasants twice a year, in the spring and again in the fall. However, such loans appeared to be limited in size when compared with the needs. In addition, since about half of the funds earmarked for agricultural loans was granted for basic improvements such as water control and irrigation projects and to buy machine water pumps to start the process of mechanization of agriculture, less than one-half of the funds was intended to meet the immediate needs of agricultural production such as the purchase of fertilizer and seeds and farm tools.

No statistical figures on agricultural credit are available for 1951, but figures for 1953 seem to show a continuation of the credit shortage which we observed in 1951. Early in 1953, the Canton branch of the People's Bank made available to the suburban peasants an agricultural credit totaling 2.5 billion dollars of the inflated People's Currency (about $125,000 United States currency at the official exchange rate). Out of this sum, 1.2 billion was earmarked for loans for buying fertilizer, seeds, tools, and farm animals. The suburban area to which the loans applied was inhabited by some 200,000 peasants.[7] Assuming that one-fourth of the farm population needed to borrow money for production purposes, the average size of a loan for a family of five would be about 12,000 dollars People's Currency (approximately 60 cents United States currency). This amount was equivalent to the value of about 20 catties of unhusked rice, and would buy only 40 per cent of the fertilizer needed for one mow of rice crop. Although we do not know how Nanching as a part of the suburban area benefited by this loan, this calculation serves as an indication of the limited character of the agricultural loans made at that time by the Communist government to alleviate the acute shortage of rural credit.

Opportunities for Supplementary Income

As indicated, livelihood for the newly elevated poor peasants remained precarious, and some form of supplementary income was still necessary to the economy of the peasant family. In Nanching there were some changes in the channels of supplementary income, especially in the handicraft of embroidery and the customary seasonal work in Canton, both of which relied upon the city's economic conditions.

General business conditions in the city of Canton in the early years of Communist rule were not bright. Especially hard hit were the luxury trades, which included embroidery, a prominent item in Nanching's home industry. Domestic buying power for such products was drastically cut by the repeated heavy levies imposed upon the business class in the city. Export trade was also severely curtailed by government monopoly in leading fields of imports and exports. Consequently, beginning from the latter part of 1950, less than a dozen families in Nanching were still able to obtain some embroidery work from the city shops, and even these families sometimes failed to get any work.

Much more important than embroidery had been the opportunity for seasonal work in Canton and in Hong Kong. In the first two months of 1951 many poor and landless peasants failed to obtain the usual seasonal jobs such as stevedoring on the water front and digging and carrying dirt and crushing rocks for municipal and private construction projects. Water-front shipping declined sharply. Unemployment in the city was high, and the Communist government reserved unskilled construction jobs such as repairing and surfacing streets for registered unemployed urban residents as a means of public work relief. With the "five anti" movement against corruption in the city business class causing widespread business failures in 1952, thus adding discharged workers to the ranks of the unemployed, the volume of unemployment showed no sign of diminishing in that year. In the first part of 1953, Canton's unemployed were reported to number in the neighborhood of 130,000, who, together with their dependents, accounted for a sizable percentage of the city's population of somewhat over a million.[8] Thus the prospect was poor for seasonal job seekers from Nanching and other nearby villages. As for opportunities in Hong Kong, they were limited by political restrictions against emigration to foreign lands and vastly reduced by the over-congested situation in that city, where refugees from China's mainland were taking up every available occupation for bare subsistence.

Eight or ten peasants in Nanching still continued to depend on peddling for a supplementary income, and peddling remained a source for balancing the family budget for a limited number of families. But this trade was becoming more difficult. Whereas formerly anyone could peddle freely, now it was necessary to obtain a peddler's license from the municipal government and pay a fee before one was allowed to peddle and such licenses were not always granted because of the overcrowding of this traditionally open field. The urban economy in the early years after land reform no longer could perform the traditional function of cushioning the shock of economic difficulties in the countryside.

In sum, the acquisition of rent-free land by the poor and landless peasants was a major factor in alleviating the economic difficulties of the largest group in the village; but, with the acute shortage of credit, with many supplementary occupational activities curtailed, and with the traditional safety valve of emigration severely reduced by urban unemployment, the economic situation of even this favored group remained precarious.

CHAPTER XII

Establishing the New Power Structure

THE INTERLOCKING nature of economic and political power in the Communist system of rule made alterations of the economic and political structures inseparable parts of the revolutionary process aimed at changing the basic pattern of Chinese society. In Nanching, as elsewhere in China, the economic changes which we have just reviewed were accompanied, therefore, by an equally sweeping political transformation. In the context of the national scene, Nanching represents a southern suburban type of village in which the changes can be viewed at the basic, grass-roots level.

In Canton, on a cool clear mid-October day in 1949, when Nationalist soldiers planted explosives and set off the shattering blast which destroyed the steel bridge spanning the Pearl River, the struggle for power was over both for Canton and for its suburban area of which Nanching was a part. That terrific explosion, shaking the windows in the village, announced to the villagers that the old government which had ruled them and had collected taxes from them was now vanquished; a new power which they had long heard about with mixed feelings had finally arrived.

In a few days, small well-armed detachments of Communist soldiers came to Pingan Chen and then to Nanching, where they posted notices announcing the annulment of the previous political organization and commanding the former government personnel to remain in their old posts until their duties and official documents were transferred to the new personnel. In about a week, that transfer was accomplished. The entire *pao chia* system was abolished as being oppressive to the people, but the subdistrict government in Pingan Chen and its relationship with Nanching was essentially preserved. With the *pao* and *chia* heads removed from their duties, the abolition of the old formal government was completed so far as the village was concerned.

Since, as we have seen, formal government had never played a major role in public affairs and in maintaining peace and order here, the abolition of the old government merely scratched the surface of the local power structure. The crucial step in the destruction of the old political order was the removal of elements of local power and authority, initiated by the disarming of all groups and individuals possessing firearms. Pingan Chen and Nanching were notified that any organization or individual with firearms must surrender them to the subdistrict office, and detachments of soldiers came into the village to look up the local leaders and demand their guns.

Informed that the outstanding armed group in Nanching was the Crop Protection Association, the Communist cadres moved to disarm and destroy this organization. Each member was questioned closely, some were tortured, and hidden guns were squeezed out. Communist efforts were thorough and relentless. One member of the association, a poor peasant whom someone accused of possessing a gun, was arrested and tortured in order to force him to surrender the alleged gun and to inform on others who possessed arms. After months in prison he was released when a group of close relatives pooled their resources to buy a locally made revolver which they handed over to the soldiers. The association as an organization ceased to exist.

Since the dozen-odd rifles belonging to the clans were the first arms handed over to the new authority, the clans ceased to function as coercive organizations supported by armed might. Their informal authority was simultaneously weakened by the disintegration of their formal organization, the destruction of their economic foundation, and the weakening of their internal status system.

The power of individual wealthy families such as Family A simply disappeared when such families fled to Hong Kong beyond the reach of the Communist law, and when their houses and land, the economic foundation of their power, were confiscated during land reform.

The Lion's Club was disbanded by the Communist cadres, the Communists holding that such clubs were "martial organizations" and that their leaders, many of whom were associated with rebellious secret societies, were potential reactionary agents of the Kuomintang and imperialists. Thus, another power group in the village was destroyed.

Of all the former local centers of power, only the old gentry group, which had been losing its traditional position in the local power structure during the past two or three decades, continued to live out their last days of physical existence in an ignored corner of community life. In this suburban village, where Confucian conceptions of life had already been relegated to a secondary position and where the gentry possessed no firearms and did not command a following of those who did, the Communists did not regard gentry elements as dangerous. We saw Lee Ying several times after the Communist take-over and asked him what he thought of the new situation. He was hesitant and cautious in his replies, being careful not to criticize the existing situation.

In an amazingly short time the Communists abolished the old system of formal government in Nanching and completely disintegrated the informal local structure of power and authority which had been the traditional foundation of the village life.

The agents of the new government who entered Nanching and its vicinity in October of 1949 were not civilian officials or unarmed cadres but fully armed military officers and soldiers whose guns were symbolic of the coercive nature of the new power. Mao Tse-tung truly had said, "A revolution is no invitation to a feast." On October 1, 1950, some three or four thousand people in the general vicinity, including a group of representatives from Nanching, gathered to celebrate the anniversary of the establishment of the Chinese People's Republic by the Communists. As the crowd marched column by column through a narrow entrance into the open field, everyone could plainly see rows of formidable machine guns manned by soldiers deployed on the high grounds on either side.

One morning in the early part of 1951 peasants in the vicinity were horrified to see sixteen dead bodies lying in a pool of blood on a military drilling ground less than a mile from Nanching. The village people recognized only one of the bodies, that of a middle-aged man from a nearby village, a poor peasant of shady character who gambled habitually and was known to be connected with local gangsters. Another was that of an old man with a long beard, and the villagers wondered who he was. No crimes of the dead were ever announced, and no public trial had been held for them. Nobody knew why these victims had met their tragic end; and a nameless fear spread among the spectators and those who heard about it.

Communist pronouncements emphasized that the show of arms, the prisons and detention houses, and the examples of punishment by death were not intended for the vast majority of the common people but only for the minority who chose to be "enemies of the people." But the definition of "enemy" was not clear to the common people; and it changed from time to time. In the first months following the Communist take-over, thieves were left alone, but after that they were treated severely. Staff members in an American missionary school near the village did not become "enemies of the people" until the "Resist America and Aid Korea" movement was fully developed. They were then treated as enemies and several Chinese faculty members were imprisoned. Even some landlords were safe until the "struggle" by the masses against them was launched, and then they were transferred to the category of "enemies."

People naturally began to wonder whether they themselves might not someday be regarded as enemies and become objects of violence. The several arrests and imprisonments of persons in the village, the bloody bodies on the drilling field, the frightening stories of imprisonment and death on a variety of political charges unfamiliar to the villagers — all these made fear an integral part of the new political reality under which they now lived, and whether the stories which circulated were true did not affect the tense situation. To be sure, there was still laughter in the village, but less often than before, and certainly not while discussing public matters, especially political situations.

Sheer coercion was not the only means by which the Communist government asserted its power and authority. It also sought to win the voluntary support of the people. After land reform, a large number of benefited families came to feel that the Communist government served their interests; and Communist cadres sent to the village became welcome guests among many peasant families, where they tried to instill the idea that the Communist Party worked for the poor, as demonstrated by land reform, and to encourage the peasants to thank the Communist Party for its "favors and affection."

"Favors and affection" (*en ch'ing*) is a term for describing intimate personal relations. Under the imperial government there had been a familiar saying, "Imperial favors are as great as the sea is deep"; for in the traditional paternalistic political ideology the sentiment of "favors and affection" was often employed in reference to the relationship between the people and the imperial power — but only among the officials and the literati who were the direct beneficiaries of the "favors and affection" bestowed by the emperor, not among the common people. In the Republican period, since government benefits for the people were considered a matter of the government's rightful duty, the term was not heard. Now it was revived by the Communists in a bid for popular support, a technique of positive inducement which, in terms of "favors and affection" through land reform, reached an immeasurably larger proportion of people than the officials and literati of the imperial days.

We wondered if the resurrection of this traditional paternalistic political sentiment could offset the fear in the hearts of the peasants. We sensed that in Nanching it appeared to be increasingly accepted by the families which benefited by land reform.

The Communist local power structure was composed of three major branches: the formal government, the local groups of power and authority, and the Communist Party, which performed the unifying function between the first two branches. The new structure of government in the Nanching area was not very different from the past, except for the abolition of the *pao chia* system. The new administrative chiefs of this village were the village head and vice-head. They were part of the personnel composing the next larger political unit, the *hsiang* or administrative village, which was composed of several villages in the same neighborhood. The administrative village was in turn under the authority of the *ch'ü* or subdistrict government, located as before in Pingan Chen for this subdistrict. The subdistrict government was subordinated to the municipal government of Canton. From Canton, the line of authority reached up to the provincial and central governments. Level by level, the system of formal government linked the village with the central governing body in Peking. The major difference between this system of local government and the previous one was in the replacement of the former *pao chia* organization with the offices of village head and vice-head, which was reinstatement of an old practice that existed before the Nationalist reactivation of the *pao chia*.

Like its predecessor, the system of local government was primarily an organization for the enforcement of laws and the execution of orders imposed from above; as such, it did not implement local initiative. But it differed from the previous local government, in a very significant sense. Whereas the former system handled only a minimum amount of business, chiefly the collection of taxes and sometimes the maintenance of general peace and order, the interests of the new subdistrict and village governments extended far beyond taxation and public security to cover matters most intimate to the individual peasant's life, such as the handling of a loan for his farm and even the orientation of his thought. The new formal government drove deep into a realm of local life that used to be the autonomous concern of the individual, the family, and at times the authority of the village community.

Both the village head and vice-head were appointed by the subdistrict government. One of the major functions of the local Communist cadres working in the village was to discover "activists" among peasants outside of the previous ruling circle and to use them as the core of a new village leadership; both the head and the vice-head of the village were selected from such activists to be the leaders of the new order. The village head thus selected was a young peasant in his late twenties from the Lee clan. He had had a few years of middle-school education in the city and was a mild-mannered intelligent young man whose father, an emigrant to Hong Kong, had died some years before. When his family had become poor he had gone to work in the rice mill in Pingan Chen to supplement the rent from his three or four mow of land.

The vice-head of the village was a controversial figure. The younger brother of Wong Hua-ying, head of the former Crop Protection Association, he was known to the villagers for meddling in the gambling racket, opium traffic, and other gangster activities. He was forced to hide beyond the village for quite a few months while Communist soldiers from Pingan Chen sought to retrieve a gun said to be in his possession, but after the discovery of Wong Hua-ying's connections with former navigation protection activities he became important in the eyes of the local cadres. Because he had always harbored hostility against his elder brother, he told the cadres details of the latter's associations and activities. For this contribution to the cadres' knowledge of the local community and its personalities, he was selected as an activist and recommended for and appointed as the vice-head of the village. Such a man was locally referred to as a "bad element."

For some months after the elimination of the armed groups in the village Nanching was in effect unarmed, but early in the spring of 1950 the government organized a "people's militia" in the village, the fifteen-odd members being selected mainly from the poor peasants, and they were issued six guns. Organizationally the Nanching Militia was under the control of the municipal Bureau of Public Security, which issued arms, sent officers to train the members, and assigned duties, and was a part of the larger organizations of militia of the administrative village and the subdistrict. As such it was wholly subject to the tight chain of command which reached from the national public security (police) authorities through the provincial and municipal levels to the subdistrict, the administrative village, and the natural village units. Local autonomy became a thing of the past.

So far as political action was concerned, the peasants' association was in effect the new center of village power. At its core was a committee of seven members and its chairman. Its membership in 1951 was

about 150, representing a majority of the 230 village families, including mostly the former poor and landless peasants and a fair number of
middle peasants. Excluded were rich peasants and former landlords,
who could join only after their class status had been changed by five
years of physical labor on a farm without exploiting others and without
engaging in counterrevolutionary activities. The core committee was
selected from the activists by the cadres and formally approved in a
nominal election by the membership, a process of election not substantially different in procedure from the traditional election of clan
officers such as the clan business manager. Although the customary pre-
election consultations were widely publicized in Communist propaganda, the Communist cadres apparently made their selection of candidates with little consideration for the villagers' opinions in many cases.

There was one committee member whom the villagers had always
regarded as an undesirable character. He had been in the gambling
racket, and in the summer of 1949 shortly before the arrival of the
Communists, in an attempt to borrow some money from the seeress
in the village, he had obtained a revolver and tried to gain admission
into her home by shooting off the lock; but the cadres were impressed
by his poverty and by his comments on village personalities and affairs.
On the other hand, the chairman, Wong Ping, obviously enjoyed
popular support. He was literate, always enthusiastic about public
activities in the village, and knew a great deal about the economic
status of individual families because he had been an accountant for
different families on ceremonial occasions such as weddings or funerals.
The last qualification strengthened his position in the association
which, as its first major assignment, had to deal with classifying the
economic status of each family for land reform. Moreover, he was a
mild tempered man and knew the basic Confucian classics, which made
him acceptable to the older generation.

The composition of the native leadership, in both the new village
government and in village organizations such as the peasants' association, presented a difference from the pre-Communist picture in the
sense that the new men were elevated from the middle and poor
peasants, while the old leadership stemmed mainly from the rich
peasants and landlords, especially the latter. To this extent, the class
basis of the local power structure had definitely shifted.

Official regulations stipulated that the chief functions of the peasants'
association were to protect and develop the peasants' welfare and interests; and the villagers now turned to it in public matters formerly
handled by the clan authorities and other old power groups — the

maintenance of dikes, the repair of roads, the settlement of inter-family disputes, the general overseeing of social and political order in the village, and the financing of the village school. In the association's early stage the party cadres sent into the village supplied the initiative, made the decisions, and helped organize the members for action.

The New Democratic Youth League and the Women's Association in Pingan Chen had branches in Nanching; and, although they were popular organizations, both had considerable influence on the local political order. Two of the committee members of the peasants' association were also League members. In carrying out political campaigns like the "suppression of counterrevolutionists" campaign in early 1951, both the League and the Women's Association co-operated by sending members to spread propaganda and to ferret out the hidden enemy. Although no hidden enemy was found in Nanching, the campaign and its propaganda barrage caused tenseness in the village atmosphere. The villagers talked with care in the presence of the League members, for such individuals were ready informants for the cadres.

The striking fact that emerges from a comparison of the foregoing picture with the pre-Communist village scene is the much closer integration of the village into the national system of political power. Our observations in Nanching provided first-hand evidence of Communist success in establishing a generally stronger tie between the one million-odd villages in the country and the nation, a development which moved China perceptibly closer to the structural reality of a modern state and immensely increased the collective strength of the nation's central political power. Our data on Nanching, even though limited to the early transitional stage, clearly revealed the basic factors in that development: the all-powerful systematic control of the Communist Party, its tremendous propaganda efforts, and the multifunctional penetration of the Communist influence into the village life.

The systematic Communist control brought about a change in the basic pattern of power structure — from an informal balance of power among local influential groups to a formalized mono-center system subjecting all organized groups under a single central direction. This change facilitated the integration of the village into the national political order.

This integration resulted not only from instituting an organizational system of centralized control, but also from altering the attitudes of the peasants through intensive propaganda campaigns. Even in the rural setting of Nanching, there were the mass meetings, the small-group discussions, the operation of the "propaganda network," the newspaper reading groups where an educated leader read to the illiterate peasants, the "wall newspapers" (hand-written news bulletins pasted on walls at public places) to remedy the lack of a printing press, the countless posters bearing political slogans, and the indoctrination classes. If previously the vast majority of the peasants had never seen a map showing the village's position in the province and in the nation, they now saw such maps on wall newspapers or on posters which were explained to them by the cadres or the literate activists. If previously it was the unique qualification of the educated man to talk about the affairs of the world, the peasants were now required to listen to such talk and to learn to parrot such talk themselves. Regardless of whether the peasants' thoughts and attitudes underwent genuine transformation, there was little doubt that a whole range of new social and political concepts on the national level were being pressed into their consciousness, thus broadening the peasant mind from the narrow confine of the village world to the national political order.

Finally, integration of the village community to the national political order was effected through functional control of village life by the centralized organizational system. To every Nanching peasant the national political power had become a concrete reality. It had brought land reform. It now decided the social and economic status of each individual, the orientation of his thought, his happiness or misery, even his life or death. It decreed the way in which marriage should take place and directed the manner in which children should be raised by organizing nurseries, by taking over the village school and by organizing the young for guided group activities and political discipline. It had, indeed, penetrated the peasant's whole life.

We had seen in Nanching a microcosm of one of the most sweeping political revolutions in Chinese history, transforming a nation from a decentralized pattern of political structure composed of a loose conglomeration of innumerable semi-autonomous villages to a highly centralized pattern in which the village community was integrated into the national system of political power.

CHAPTER XIII

Alterations in the Kinship System

ALTERATION OF the traditional Chinese kinship system was one of the significant objectives of the "family revolution" which had been gathering force for some fifty years before the Communists came to power; but in the pre-Communist period it was confined to the upper and middle classes in the urban centers. The national success of the Communist revolution was followed by official action which not only quickened the tempo of change of the kinship system but also caused a rapid extension of that change from the upper and middle classes to the urban working class and from the urban centers to the countryside.

The first concrete evidence of such action in the neighborhood of Nanching was the introduction of the new marriage law. Toward the end of 1950 a notice was posted in front of the subdistrict government office in Pingan Chen announcing that henceforth marriages dictated by parents would be illegal, that a marriage must be based on the free will and free choice of the marriage partners, and that all new marriages must now be registered with the subdistrict government in order to be legally recognized. Later a young woman officer came to Nanching, held a meeting with a group of the villagers, and explained these same points. The principles of the government notice and the young woman's speech were not entirely new to the villagers, who lived too close to the big city not to have heard of marriage as a result of free choice of partners; but they had regarded such a marriage as another strange fashion in the strange modern urban living, especially among the "foreignized" rich city folks, without any thought that it could one day apply to their own intimate life.

We observed two marriages in Nanching in 1951 which, in compliance with the new law, were registered at the subdistrict government. In each case, a young cadre member asked the engaged young man and woman whether they had been forced into the marriage by parents or other parties, or were being married of their own free will and choice. Each said it was by free will. The man paid the small registration fee and received a printed marriage certificate, a totally strange object to the villagers, who had never heard of the government taking a hand in the private marital affairs of the people. But appearances were deceiving. In each case the parents in the families concerned had arranged the marriage and prompted the young couple in what to say in going through the registration. Before the marriage, the traditional practice of the boy's family offering the girl's family a ceremonial price was followed — although the new law prohibited paying a "body price" for the bride; and after the registration the full traditional wedding ceremony was enacted in the village, including the clan feast in the ancestral hall.

It was obvious that these Nanching marriages typified the conservative peasants' desire to stick to the old system, a deep-rooted conviction that could not be changed merely by the passage of a new law. In Nanching the individual still depended upon the family for economic security and development, and the parents' will and authority over the children's marriage carried the weight of economic power. A village girl's predominant notion about marriage was still that it provided her a home where she could eat and have children to support her in her old age. Arranged marriage as a means of carrying on family production had been a proven formula of economic security; and until a new system of economic security became equally proven of its worth, it was not easy to induce the peasants to give up economic security for romance. Furthermore, the village clung to the strong tradition of sex segregation, and opportunity for normal social life between the sexes was still too limited for the development of romantic associations. Lee Ying, the old Confucian scholar, at first refused to be interviewed by our girl student investigator. After we convinced him that it was perfectly normal to talk to a young girl, he consented to answering questions, but he talked to her with his face averted, stealing frequent sidelong glances at her.

After the Communists were established in the village, they insisted that both men and women should come to the increasing number of political meetings, and an amateur theatrical group was organized in which boys and girls worked together. The New Democratic Youth League established a branch in the village, and among the small membership in 1951 three or four were girls. These were the small beginnings of a social life between the sexes.

Whereas the effect of Communism on the kinship system as measured by its impact on the traditional marriage procedure was bound to be a gradual one, its destructive influence on the internal kinship status system was immediate. We have already noted the diminishing value of age as a serious factor in the growing difficulty of the older generation in trying to continue the subordination of the young and maintain the social order built on age and generational level. The Communist accession to power greatly accelerated this development. The peasants' association, the new center of power in the village, was mostly staffed by young men under thirty, and Wong Ping, the head of the association, was only in his mid-forties. The New Democratic Youth League branch was a political organization of considerable importance in the public affairs of the village. Older villagers were frightened of its members because of the new power they wielded and fear that they would betray family secrets to the police or cadres. One of the notable features of Communism was that the young, who as a group had never been taken seriously by traditional society or given responsible duties, now came to the fore in social prestige and political importance.

Communist policy aimed explicitly at changing women's status. The new marriage law granted women a higher status in the family and in society than before; and the new legal freedom of divorce gave them an outlet from extreme mistreatment from their husbands and mothers-in-law. At least one woman in Nanching learned about and use this new right in our time there. Women began to emerge from family confinement to attend meetings and take part in public activities sponsored by the cadres and the peasants' association. The new amateur theatrical group in the village included women, something previously unheard of; and there was a Women's Association in Pingan Chen to which the village sent several women representatives. This association was doing little more than participate in political campaigns under the guidance of local cadres, but the very presence of an independent organization of women dealing with public affairs was in itself a new phenomenon of considerable importance, something entirely out of context with the traditional social order based on sex segregation and the exclusion of women from public affairs.

Land reform had a direct effect on the internal structure of the family. Since land was redistributed not to the family as a whole but to each member on an equal-share basis regardless of age and sex, land reform gave the young and the women an unprecedented sense of importance in contrast to the traditional system of family property ownership, in which the head of the family had sole right to dispose of the family property and female descendants enjoyed no inheritance rights. Moreover, the land reform regulations stipulated that each member of the family might take his or her share of the family land out of the family, for instance in case of a divorce, an egalitarian arrangement of roles of the members and the economic leverage that clearly strengthened the position of the young and the women.

The drastic alterations in the traditional kinship system were most dramatically symbolized by the disintegration of the formal structure of clan authority, the inevitable result not of specific Communist government orders but of the operation of the whole devastating revolutionary process of remaking the village's political and economic life.

Local public affairs were now so much more intimately related to regional politics and formal government than in the pre-Communist period that the elders' council of the clan, ignorant of the new political situation and faced by the rising importance of the modern educated younger generation in this field, were helpless. After the fall of 1950, we did not hear of a single meeting of the elders' council, although more problems involving the whole village had occurred since then than in any previous year that we knew of. The position of business manager as an agency of the clan's formal organization was practically abolished, there being now no clan property to manage as the clan land and other income-yielding properties were redistributed during land reform. Moreover, the Communists arrested many clan managers in other villages on the accusation of embezzlement of clan funds; and official directives on land reform pointed to the office of managing clan finance as a system of "feudalistic exploitation" of the clansmen, a system ridden with corruption and embezzlement.

The "class struggle," especially during the land reform, seriously weakened the solidarity of the clan by introducing a non-kinship criterion of group interest. The peasants' struggle against the landlords, the disclosing of hidden ownership of land to the Communist cadres, the tenants' accusation of cruelty and exploitation against rent collectors, the victims' charges of injustice and oppression by "local bullies," the activists' efforts in ferreting out counterrevolutionaries — all these turned many close kin against each other. The process of struggle had difficulty in getting started, especially when the case involved the young bringing charges against the old, but after the inhibition of kinship was broken down, the struggle became bitter.

We noted that during the Chinese New Year in early 1951 the ancestral halls were no longer cleaned and decorated as before; and no community operas were staged by the clans after land reform. Instead, there were the new recreational groups such as the village theatrical group which were not organized on a clan basis. Ceremonial occasions such as spring and autumn sacrifices to the ancestors were reduced to simple affairs performed only by a small number of older clansmen who also privately contributed toward the sacrificial expense which was formerly financed by the income from the now confiscated clan property. To the Communist cadres, ancestor worship was a superstition like other forms of supernatural worship, and they would do nothing to remedy the situation. Most of the ancestral halls in the village were transformed into classrooms for literacy and political training and offices for the new organizations; they no longer served as places of religious inspiration for the perpetuation and development of the clan.

Our observations in Nanching confirmed the impression that the clan was unlikely ever to recover its traditional importance in the operation of village life, and that the whole kinship framework of collective action, supported by its traditional status system, would diminish in strength while the universalistic type of political and social order would increase its influence.

CHAPTER XIV

Other Social Institutions and Their Initial Change

Literacy and Formal Education

DEFINING EDUCATION broadly as a system of transmission of knowledge and skills from one generation to another, any modern minded observer in Nanching would probably have been struck by the widespread illiteracy and the limited position of formal institutional education in the life of the community. A survey in 1950 showed an over-all literacy rate of about 38 per cent for the village population ten years of age and over, with differential rates of approximately 65 per cent for men and 8 per cent for women.

Two aspects of the traditional peasant situation should be noted here. In the first place, it was obvious that the majority of the peasants were able neither to pay tuition for their children nor to spare them from help in the fields even at an early age. Second, less obvious but just as deeply rooted was the fact that, from a functional viewpoint, literacy and traditional book knowledge had very limited practical significance in the personal life of the majority of the peasants. Since the average peasant acquired the necessary practical knowledge and skill from his family, his kinsmen, and his neighbors or fellow villagers, the process of learning for him lay in his participation in the community life, and not in an independent routine carried on by a separate social institution devoted exclusively to learning. His process of learning was verbal transmission and the observation of examples, which required neither written language nor any instruction apart from actual life; it was "learning through living."

Literacy, the main result from institutional education, served the peasant on very few occasions. Simple, small-scale family farming needed no written accounts or bookkeeping. The peasant usually kept a written account of the expenses of a wedding or a funeral, and he possessed a written deed for his property; but he hired a literate fellow villager to keep such accounts or to read the deeds to him as the occasion arose. He might receive a letter or wish to write one, an infrequent event even for families having emigrants abroad, and for this he similarly enlisted the help of a literate kinsman or friend; or for all purposes requiring literacy he could go to Pingan Chen on a market day and pay the scribe for such service. On street corners in a big city or in the less busy section of a rural market there were the make-shift desks behind which sat the scribes who, unsuccessful in scholarship and pressed by poverty, offered literacy for sale at a low price, reading or writing a letter for a few cents.

Even if a peasant acquired elementary literacy, he was likely to forget most of it through disuse; there was no mechanical press, and the mass communication system such as the daily paper and periodicals and the traditional books were out of touch with the practical reality of peasant life. Popular story books were the only important category of written material that interested the peasant. These were important reading material in the leisure hours for literate peasants, and those who were able to read such materials enjoyed retelling the stories to neighbors and kinsmen, a practice we observed among the small knots of people gathered in the courtyards of the many ancestral halls in the evening hours. Popular stories and folklore which were essential for the operation of an agrarian folk society did not require universal literacy for their transmission. For this and other traditional literacy needs in the village community, a small percentage of literates in a population served adequately.

The only serious need for literacy on the part of the peasants was in the operation of groups larger than the family. Although ancestor worship in the peasant family operated by memory about the departed members, it functioned by written records, the genealogy, in the clan. The elders' council could pass on its own decisions verbally, but the orders and directives of the national government must be disseminated by written documents; and the national cultural tradition, including the complex moral precepts and philosophical doctrines, could be preserved over the centuries only through books. Hence the men who administered the clan and guided the national political structure and social order were literate products of formal institutional education. Since those who occupied such positions, especially in the operation of the national political and social order, possessed enviable prestige and privilege, literacy had become a symbol of identification of their class status; and the common peasants valued formal education not as a necessity for their simple personal life but solely as a channel of social advancement. The traditional status of formal education which we have just described had been subjected to new influences during the Republican period, when the general trend of readapting Chinese social institutions to the requirements of modern life was strongly oriented toward mass organization and technological development. Situated close to a major urban center, the emanating point of modern influences, Nanching had been affected to a certain degree.

The first major change had occurred in the formal institutional education. The philosophy and content of Confucian classical education was largely discarded as unsuitable for modern requirements of inculcating a different concept of social and political order and teaching a different kind of technical knowledge about the physical and human world. In contrast to the exclusive teaching of the Confucian social and political creed and Chinese history, the new schools added modern arithmetic, geography, and elementary ideas of modern science; they broadened history courses to include the whole world and instituted modern citizenship training — and all these subjects were to be covered in six grades.

By 1948 there remained in Nanching only mute evidence of the once dominant position of classical education. There were only the Chinese characters "Community School," executed in graceful calligraphy and carved into the stone arch above the doorway identifying the spacious and dignified building in the middle of the village as a former institution of classical learning. That building was now used as a storage place for public property such as ceremonial furniture, and some peasants used it for storing grain, for it had been over two decades since Lee Ying as the last teacher and his some two dozen pupils had vacated the structure. Confucian ideology still held a central place in the minds of the older villagers, but even they saw no future for Confucian learning for their children in a rapidly changing modern world. The entire process of educational transformation was symbolized in the dismantling of a stone memorial arch honoring a successful village scholar of the last century, the stones being used for paving a path leading to the new elementary school in 1936, and the unmindful young pupils hardly noticed that on their way to school they daily trampled over a stone piece bearing the still discernible carvings of the name of the honored scholar and his imposing imperial titles.

The new curriculum which was imposed by the Ministry of Education of the Nationalist government was developed by officials of urban intellectual background. Although it helped to broaden the peasants' mental outlook toward the world and to integrate village life with the emerging modern state, it woefully neglected the practical, intimate needs of local peasant life. Moreover, since it was a liberal education stressing knowledge of society and government on a broadened and modernized basis and in this respect resembled the traditional Confucian education, it appeared to the peasants as the kind of knowledge destined for membership of the ruling class, and they viewed the function of the new elementary school in this light. In other words, despite the changes in formal education in the Republican period, the peasants still regarded it as a channel for social and political advancement and not as a means for improving the community and the practical aspects of peasant life.

One feature of the modern changes in education which had made some inroad in Nanching was the national campaign for universal literacy, which originated with the urban intellectuals who wished to transplant modern Western society to China. Urban enthusiasm for universal literacy overflowed to the village communities in various parts of China in the late 1920's and early 1930's. In those years in Nanching students from a neighboring college and high school held several free evening classes for the villagers, attracting a fair attendance.

The process was interrupted by the war, but in 1948 students in the same college once again held free evening classes for the village, to which came about a hundred villagers, a large majority being between eight and twelve, some between twelve and sixteen, and the rest including about a dozen adults and two spirited old men in their sixties. Both sexes were represented, although boys predominated at a ratio of about two to one. It was impressive to witness the eagerness to learn among the adult students and the energy with which they urged on the younger ones. At the close of a hard working day, they would wash the field mud off their feet, eat a hurried supper and start off to the school in a long line, often with parents toting young children, both going to the same class. Literacy and education as a special privilege was nowhere demonstrated more vividly than in this scene. It was still the traditional value of education as a channel of social advancement and not as a new tool of everyday life that was the motivating force for such high enthusiasm.

To return, then, to the status of literacy in 1950, we could see that, although education had not yet taken on a practical functional value for Nanching peasants, the modern urban movement of universal education had scored some stable gains in the village. The 1950 figure of literacy, some 38 per cent of the village population, was probably two or three times higher than it had been a generation ago; and the fact that about 75 per cent of the literates were between the ages of ten to fifteen clearly represented a new development among the younger generation in recent years. In 1950 about 50 per cent of all school-age children (from eight to fifteen years old) attended the new elementary school, and villagers said that this was a much higher rate of school attendance than among the youngsters of the previous generation. The ratio between boys and girls in the village school was about four to one, which suggested an improvement over the traditional situation in light of the fact that almost all the adult women in the village were illiterate. In reviewing these developments, it should be borne in mind that Nanching was a suburban village close to a great city, and that such progress might not be typical of interior villages.

What was the initial impact of Communism on education in this village?

Although educational renovation was a major Communist objective, it appeared that in 1951 the Nanching elementary school still operated basically as before in terms of curriculum, although the ideological content in history, citizenship, and associated subjects was now re-oriented according to the party line. However, confiscation of the school's income land for redistribution to the peasants caused serious financial difficulties. Additional levy had to be made on the village's land for school expenditures, and the staff was reduced from the original two teachers to only one in 1951. To this extent, there was a certain amount of deterioration of formal education in the village during the transitional period, although the Communist press reported substantial government support for schools in some villages in this locality, resulting in expanding teaching staff and increased scholarships.

One significant new phase of formal education introduced by the Communists to achieve rapid transition of Chinese society was the large number of short-term training courses set up for peasant leaders in various types of political and economic projects. Even in the early year of 1951, a few of the young activists in Nanching were taken to some of the training classes devoted mainly to indoctrination of the Communist ideology and instruction of organizational skills in setting up the new power structure. Since then, in the province of Kwangtung as in other parts of China, there had been established training courses for new agricultural techniques, for organizing mutual-aid teams, and for establishing agricultural producers' co-operatives, developments which would presumably involve the participation of many promising young peasants from the village.

More important in terms of the village as a whole, the movement for universal literacy received acceleration in Communist hands. Here the Communists were building on the foundations laid in the Republican period, and there was already public recognition of the importance of the movement. Workers in this field had already produced a number of simplified texts for teaching illiterate adults; and now the Communists conducted the movement as a sustained nation-wide drive on a well organized basis. From big cities to remote hamlets, literacy classes mushroomed through the national network of the Communist Party and popular organizations such as the Youth League and peasants' association. As early as 1950 the cadres in Nanching had started to organize "winter classes" through the peasants' association, the purpose being to use the relatively slack winter months for the peasants to learn to read and write; and evening classes were also organized. Although the peasants' association had to provide the books and other materials, a burden which the peasants were reluctant to assume, in the winter of 1950 about 20 per cent of the illiterate adult peasants attended such classes in Nanching.

The fundamental and revolutionary fact underlying the visible early changes in education and literacy in the village under Communism was the emergence of a practical function for education in the lives of the peasants. Looking ahead, the closer integration of village life into the broad national political and economic system was bound to compel the employment of the literacy medium as an indispensable means of communication; and as the peasant became involved in this integration movement, literacy would increasingly become a practical instrument of this life. At the local level of the new political system, since acquisition of literacy through short courses and other forms of special training was required of the activists and those elevated from among the poor peasants to share the new local political leadership with the Communists, literacy was now the operating tool for the new elite as it had been for the old gentry. Most sweeping in effect was the fact that even the common peasant was now subjected to a growing pressure to use literacy to get along in the new social and political order. Coming into the village in increasing quantities were government notices, directives, slogans, bulletins, propaganda, and educational materials in a variety of forms. Each of the many mass campaigns, from the subscription of bonds to land reform, was accompanied by the distribution of quantities of literature related to the subject. As such written materials concerned the intimate interest of everyone in the village, there was an increasingly compelling influence on the average peasant to become able to read such literature in order to know how to conduct himself in a social situation which had extended far beyond the range of personal contact and verbal communication in a small community. The mass literacy movement had indeed come to serve a new need for the common peasants.

The Reorientation of Recreation

The peasant, chained to the mechanical repetition of the organic cycle and to the unending demand of heavy physical exertion, traditionally relied on periodical recreation to combat fatigue and pessimism and to regenerate his interest and confidence in a life characterized by its meager material rewards. Anyone observing an agrarian community like Nanching in its varied recreational activities could sense in them the attempt to symbolize the intrinsic value of life as a balance against the hard and almost futile struggle for subsistence.

The most basic form of community recreation was the traditional system of festivals, based largely on the agricultural calendar and on the operation of the natural forces. The three to fifteen days of the Chinese New Year celebration, which led all traditional festivals in importance, fell at the most leisurely season of the farm routine. To insure its recreative function of releasing tension from worry and toil, there was a firm taboo against collecting debts during this period of jubilation. The Dragon Boat Festival on the fifth day of the fifth moon was related to the summer solstice, and its celebration provided a brief respite between the heavy spring planting chore and the coming summer farm work. Women's interests were taken care of by the Seventh Evening Festival on the seventh day of the seventh moon, when girls gazed at the Milky Way to watch for the imagined romantic meeting between two stars as a sign of their marital future. The time corresponded to the eve of the busy season when the women would be required to help gather the harvest and process the grain. The Moon Festival on the fifteenth day of the eighth moon was the celebration of the harvest, and it was the customary time to pay one's debts since everyone's purse was theoretically replenished at this time. The annual routine of work and burden was thus regularly punctuated with occasions of diversion and relief.

Everyone in the community took part in the festivals, the basic unit of celebration being the family; and in major festivals such as the New Year, the clan held a celebration in addition to the family celebration.

A festival celebration consisted of two central acts: the feast and the sacrifice to the gods of the occasion.

Since the most eager yearning among the majority of the peasants was for more food, one of the greatest enjoyments that life could bring was good food in abundance. Hence on festival days the family strained its purse to serve the best possible food: for the well-to-do the table was laden with delicacies; for the poor, some slivers of meat amidst the green vegetables and a sufficient quantity of staple items furnished welcome relief from the daily meager vegetable diet. Even their hard life seemed to be worth living as the members of the family sat down for the festival meal. On the other hand, the absence of a festival meal was the epitome of failure and misfortune and a cause for sadness and pessimism.

Besides giving relief from the toil and monotony of a hard life, the festival feast also was a symbol of providence. Hence the sacrifice to the gods by displaying the food in front of the family altar before consuming it. The almost insurmountable hardships in their struggle of life, the ever-threatening fear of failure and starvation, and the many sobering cases of misfortune in the community all impressed upon the peasants the limitations of human ability in achieving abundance, and suggested that in addition to man's industry and frugality, the gods' blessing was needed to avert misery and to attain success.

When the family gathered for the sacrifice and the feast, there was a reunion of its members which served to strengthen the solidarity of the family, and the major festivals traditionally required homecoming for emigrants if at all possible. This function was especially important for the solidarity of the clan, whose large membership reduced contact between individuals. When the clan gathered to offer sacrifice to the ancestors at a major festival such as at the New Year and later sat down together for the grand feast and to watch a community opera, the celebration provided an occasion for the periodic reconvening of the whole clan, demonstrating the concrete existence of the large group and renewing the kinship relations among the members in a joyous and optimistic atmosphere. The system of traditional festivals, with the major ones held once every one or two months throughout the year, thus served not only as an uplifting of the spirit among hard-working and hard-living peasants but also as a binding agent for the kinship-centered structure of the village community.

In addition to the community-wide periodic recreation, the traditional village life included small-group recreational activities. There were many different children's games which trained the young ones in the playing of social roles or prepared them for their future work through imitative acts. Among adolescents and adults, there were the familiar chess, checker, card, and tile games. There were the story-telling sessions either by a talkative fellow villager or by a professional storyteller. Going to the teahouse in small groups of from two to six men to talk and chat at noon was a favorite recreation for the financial-ly better-off peasants. Among adolescents and adults all games were sex-segregated; and excepting the Lion's Club, which was devoted to physical culture, they did not stress physical exercise and there were almost no group contests.

Singing or playing a musical instrument like a bamboo flute was fairly common among the peasants; but playing the instruments to-gether as an orchestra was uncommon among amateurs, and group sing-ing was totally undeveloped in traditional life. Art and literature were an important form of recreation only for the very small minority of the educated and well-to-do.

We observed the traditional recreational life of the Nanching vil-lagers continuing almost without change up to the time of the Com-munists' arrival in 1949. The only alteration in the system of festivals had been the dropping of the celebration of Confucius' birthday in the 1940's, marking the end of the long Confucian era in the village; and of all the new system of national holidays inaugurated during the Re-publican period only the Double Ten, celebrating the outbreak of the successful revolution on October 10, 1911, was marked at all — and that only by the holiday declared in the new elementary school.

In general, the Communist cadres did not forcibly interfere with the traditional recreational activities except in two cases. One was the disbanding of the Lion's Club as a political danger to the Commu-nist power, and the other was discouraging the holding of celebrations for the birthdays of certain gods, a result of the Communist policy to "wipe out superstition." Although the celebration of the birthday of the God of Fire, an important festive occasion in Nanching, was discontinued in 1950, the village continued to celebrate the major traditional festivals such as the Chinese New Year, the Ch'ing Ming festival on the third day of the third moon designated for "sweeping the ancestral graves," the Dragon Boat Festival, and the Moon Festival.

But Communism created a new atmosphere. The richer families had all either fled or become impoverished through the land reform process; and they had been the households whose elaborate celebrations had created the sense of prosperity and abundance during festival occasions. They had been the heavy donors in financing community celebration programs such as an opera for major festivals. With their general dis-appearance from the scene went much of the gaiety of such occasions. The new public organizations having financial resources, such as the peasants' association, were under the direction of the cadres who would not devote money to such traditional undertakings.

So far as the common peasants were concerned, land reform had not brought sufficient economic improvement to enable them to afford much celebration. In fact, the rapid succession of political and eco-nomic crises affecting the intimate life of every individual and creating a sense of uncertainty and instability caused family celebrations of tra-ditional festivals to become rather perfunctory; and clan celebrations were discontinued because of the confiscation of the clan income land. Even some of the financially better-off families refrained from putting on any elaborate celebration for fear of being classified as rich peasants, thereby inviting political reprisal.

The traditional forms of small-group and individual recreation met little forcible interference from the cadres, except the tile (mahjong) game, which was regarded as gambling. But many of these activities also were reduced by the impoverishment of the richer portion of the population. The three teahouses in Pingan Chen which had enjoyed long prosperity were now on the point of collapse. Customers were much fewer than before, and only cheap items were sold to meet the demand of those having a lower income level.

Regardless of possible economic improvement, it seemed doubtful even at that early period of Communist power that the traditional recreational life of the Nanching peasants would ever be fully restored. Recreation had now taken on a new and official meaning derived from the Marxist view that recreation belongs to the cultural superstructure founded on the needs of the forces of economic production; and the Communists were already systematically working to tie recreation directly to the requirements of building the socialist economic order.

Actors and actresses of old theatrical troupes were put through an indoctrination process to enable them to revise the old operas as vehi-cles for Communist political themes. Cadres from the Literary Work Corps and indoctrinated members of theatrical companies were or-ganized into "rural opera troupes" and sent to the countryside to present the revised and new operas to the peasants, including those in the locality of which Nanching was a part. Under the direction of the cadres, the peasants' association in Nanching started an amateur theat-rical troupe in 1951, presenting propaganda plays and operas to the villagers. Motion pictures were introduced into the countryside with regularity, and those shown in this locality included: "Conservancy of Water and Soil," "Eradicating Larvae of Insects," "Exercise and Health," "How to Raise Children," "Depth Plowing for Greater Production," "Wiping Out Flies," "Rural Sanitation," and "Short Courses on Literacy."

The novelty of the Communist entertainment attracted a good audience at first, but fatigue from the monotony of the political propaganda lines soon set in, and the utilitarian nature of the new recreational items nullified their entertainment value. They obviously did little to relieve the tension of the work routine; and there was a gradual decrease in attendance.

Besides the spectator type of entertainment, the Communists were vigorously introducing the participation type of organized group recreation. Western-style group games and, above all, group singing were conducted by the cadres, especially among the young peasants. Although the initial reception was not enthusiastic, members of the Youth League and the Young Pioneers were getting used to them, being especially attracted by the mixing of the sexes in the group games and singing. It was apparent that Communism had set in motion a new force which could be exploited to change the life of the community.

The Religious Aspect of Community Life

The traditional worship of the supernatural in the Chinese peasants' life arose from the need for confidence and strength in the face of humanly insurmountable circumstances in man's struggle with nature and his adjustment to the social order.* The predominance of direct struggle with the overpowering elemental forces in an agrarian community was embodied in the pantheistic system presided over by Heaven and staffed mainly by deities representing forces of nature. Heaven, with its sun, moon, stars, and the meteorological elements, was the symbol of the most powerful forces directly affecting the peasants' life. Next to Heaven were the many deities directly related to agriculture such as the God of Flood, the God of Dragon (controller of water and rain), the God of Earth and Grain, and the God of Oxen — all represented in the temples in Nanching and the surrounding villages. Because the kinship system was a basic unit in agricultural production and agrarian life, ancestor worship was developed to strengthen and perpetuate the system. Thus the worship of Heaven, agricultural deities, and ancestors became the basic religious system of

* A fuller study of the functions and structure of religion in Chinese society is the subject of my work, *Religion in Chinese Society*, University of California Press, 1961.

the agrarian community because of their close relation to the economic foundation of peasant life.

The formal system was augmented by a host of supernatural beliefs. To the struggling peasant, success appeared to be not the achievement of man's efforts alone but the result of a combination of human endeavor and good fortune bestowed by the gods. Under such circumstances, there were countless occasions when man had to appeal to the supernatural as the limit of human resources was reached. Just outside the West Gate of Nanching stood the Temple of the God of Fire, and we were told by the priest there that the vast majority of the worshipers came to pray either for the return of health or for a son. When we interviewed some of the villagers who went to the temple to pray for the return of health, we found that most of them would have preferred a doctor had they been able to afford one. Unable to pay for medical attention, the cheapest alternative was to hope for favorable supernatural intervention through prayer to the appropriate god.

It is worth noting in this context that, although superstitions were numerous, they did not vitiate the peasants' realistic view of their struggle with the natural and social environment. There was strong traditional insistence upon the injunction: "Do the utmost within human power, but accept the ordinance of Heaven," and there was general social pressure against and popular contempt for those who did nothing but appeal to the spirits and gods for help.

In considering the social functions of religion in a peasant village like Nanching it is essential to do so in terms of its two structural types: institutional religion and diffused religion. In institutional religion the theology, the organization of the personnel, and the cultic symbols and practices are separate from the secular social institutions, thus making religion an independent social institution. In diffused religion these factors have no separate institutional existence but are diffused into the concept and structure of several different institutions. In Nanching, and in Chinese society as a whole, diffused religion represented the structurally stronger and more pervasive force in the lives of the common people.

The outstanding symbol of institutional religion in this village was the Temple of the God of Fire. This temple had an independent theology, Taoism; a separate organization, the lone Taoist priest; and its cultic symbols and practices all belonged to a system of religious life conducted outside the context of the secular social institutions. Besides the temple, the only other sign of institutional religion was the village seeress, who had a private altar in her home and a professionalized practice which was not a part of the secular institutions. The temple priest and the seeress together comprised a total personnel of two persons representing institutional religion in Nanching — less than 0.2 per cent of the village population. They operated independently, with only loose association with other priests in the vicinity; there was no hierarchical structure which might give them financial or organizational assistance, and under them was no organized congregation among the followers.

The situation in Nanching was thus characteristic of the polytheistic tradition, the worshipers had no permanent or exclusive connection with any single temple or priest, but visited temples or priests of different faiths as personal occasions demanded. Villagers worshiped in other temples in the surrounding villages and nearby towns in addition to the one in this village. With the priesthood so weak in terms of number, organization, and relation to the followers, it is apparent that such a system of institutional religion was in no position to offer resistance against Communist pressure. The only strong institutional religion in the vicinity of Nanching was the Christian church, and that had only about a half-dozen followers from the village.

In contrast was the position of diffused religion in Nanching. The most imposing religious structures in the village were the ancestral halls or temples. The theology of ancestor worship was an integral feature of the basic concept of the kinship system; its priesthood were the elders, who were members of the kinship organization; and its well integrated congregation was represented by the members of the family and the clan. It was an all-pervasive influence in the peasants' life.

Moreover, there were other peasant cults similarly diffused into various institutionalized aspects of the agrarian community life. At the center of the village stood a small altar of the God of Earth and Grain, one of the most universal deities in agricultural China, its theodicy being elaborately woven into the general concept of well-being of the agrarian community. There was no specialized priest connected with the cult. Villagers worshiped this god individually on private occasions, offering a variety of prayers concerning personal affairs; and on his birthday the community leaders officiated at the grand community celebration. Prior to the arrival of the Communists, there was a secular organization called the *sheh*, meaning the God of Earth (and Grain), which managed the garbage disposal of the entire village, thus diffusing the cult into one aspect of community organization under elected secular leadership. In surrounding villages the gods of many typically peasant cults such as the God of Dragon, which controlled water, were

worshiped as patron deities for their respective community, the annual
celebrations of their birthdays being organized by local secular leaders
and serving to unite the agrarian community as a functioning group.

For at least a half-century before the coming of Communism to
Nanching, the traditional system of religion in both its institutional
and diffused forms had shown signs of progressive weakening owing to
the spreading influence of modern science and materialism from the
urban centers. In the Republican period the development of modern
education yielded, among other things, a strong "anti-superstition"
movement among the younger generation in the cities, and there was a
distinct drift toward secularization in the general trend of social change
in modern China. In the cities some of the major religious events
which had formerly played an important part in community life were
quietly discontinued because of lack of leadership and interest from
the younger generation. The Yü Lan Chieh, once a most popular and
colorful religious festival held for homeless spirits as recently as the
early 1920's, passed into history in most localities. But such drastic
changes had been mainly urban phenomena, and rural communities
like Nanching, even though close to the big city, remained largely un-
affected up to the time of the Communist victory.

The Communists, being not only a product of the urban secularization trend but also ardent supporters of the atheist tradition of Marxist
materialism, set as an explicit objective the extension of the urban
secularization trend to the countryside. The path of Communist advance was marked at the beginning by many smashed temples and
sporadic antireligious violence, but as they moved to consolidate the
social and political order of the newly conquered land their policy
was to suppress only those organized religious activities which held
a real or suspected political threat to them, and to take milder and
gradual measures against general religious influences. In criticism
against the young Communist officers for their harsh suppression of
superstition among the peasants, Mao Tse-tung declared that one could
not dig the superstitious ideas out of the peasants' mind but the peasants
would automatically shed their superstitions when their material
life became substantially improved and secure. To this extent, the
Communists were sincere in their declared policy of permitting religious freedom, so long as it did not interfere with the Communist
political program. This policy had a familiar traditional ring in the
sense that the old imperial government rigidly suppressed organized
religion that had any political significance but generally left alone
nonpolitical religious worship and activities.

Most summarily affected by this Communist policy was Christianity, which was regarded as closely allied with Western political influence, and a series of purges were aimed at divorcing the Christian church from any foreign connections. Since there were only a few Christian converts in Nanching, the effect of such purges was relatively slight in the total picture of the community's religious life. Suppressive action against Western missionaries and many Chinese Christian leaders elsewhere in the vicinity began vigorously with the Korean War in 1950 and lasted until 1954. After that, many imprisoned Chinese ministers were released, and there was a gradual and limited restoration of Christian religious activities. But the disorganizing effect from the persecution of Christianity as an organized religion clearly remained.[1]

With regard to traditional institutional religion, the Temple of the God of Fire in Nanching remained unmolested, and villagers continued to pray there. But most of its ten mow of land was redistributed to the peasants, with a share retained for the priest who now had to farm the land for a living instead of relying on the rent, the meager donations from the worshipers being insufficient for his existence and maintenance of the temple. The seeress received a share of land from the land reform, and the Communist officers pressed her to give up the practice of superstition. It appeared that her open religious activities were greatly reduced. One officer charged that she was making a living by fraud when she practiced magic to heal illnesses, since as he pointed out, she patronized a medical doctor instead of relying on her own magic when she became sick, but the seeress was not put up for public trial or made to face any other forms of mob violence.

Ancestor worship was still carried on in the families, but the sacrificial ceremonies of the clan were curtailed because of the confiscation of the clan income land; and the celebration of religious festivals in honor of the gods was so consistently discouraged by the Communist authorities that after 1950 no community religious festivals were held in the village.

In general it could be said that the early impact of Communism on religion in Nanching probably pretty well typified official Communist policy. Without violence, but by the impoverishment of the rich families and the clans, religion was, so to speak, driven from public view back into the homes, where the unchangeable older generation of peasants could cherish their traditional customs and beliefs undisturbed. But the power of religion to strengthen community spirit and to evoke a sense of community sharing was already nearly destroyed. Most important of all, the Communists had embarked on a long-term program the effects of which could not yet be calculated but which was aimed at the eradication of traditional religious influence in Chinese life. At the heart of that program was the education of the younger generation. It was not on the compulsive remaking of the minds of those who were beyond the age of thirty that the Communists pinned their main hope for the final triumph of atheism, but on the youth who were now universally subjected to Communist education. The outcome of this vastly ambitious plan was a question for the future.

Ideology and Its Change

A social system, even in a relatively simple agrarian community like Nanching, needs an ideology to provide the structural principles and the operational values for the integration of the various institutional aspects of life and to develop functional consistency and unity in the variegated pattern of social action. It is beyond the scope of this study to render a full analysis of the complex problem of ideology in Nanching; but it is necessary to point out the salient features of the traditional ideological system and its recent change in order not to lose sight of the fact that ideological change was a vital aspect of the social transformation we are recording.

We have noted that Confucianism provided the traditional ideology that guided the functioning of the institutional framework of this community, and that the scholar-gentry traditionally acted as the custodians of the Confucian orthodoxy and served as its interpreters to the illiterate common people. Through centuries of conscious and unconscious effort, the basic features of that doctrine were intricately woven into every major aspect of the common people's life and became internalized values, a development aided by the adaptability of its social structural principles and its value system to the agrarian society dominated by the kinship organization and primary group existence, as evidenced by its emphasis on familial ties and on moral values most applicable to direct personal relations. We have also noted that in the Republican period Confucianism as an institutionalized orthodoxy lost irretrievable ground among the younger generation.

In 1948, the year before the Communists came, we made an attitude survey among the villagers in an attempt to discover their understanding of current ideologies. We asked the respondents to explain a list of terms concerning the basic principles of social organization and the social values of Confucianism, democracy, and Communism. For Confucianism we listed structural terms such as the Five Cardinal Relations (between emperor and subjects, father and son, elder and younger brothers, husband and wife, and friends), and value terms such as the Eight Virtues (filial piety, fraternal submission, loyalty, fidelity, propriety, righteousness, incorruptibility, and sense of shame). The structural terms for democracy included election, presidency of the Republic, and status of citizens, and the value terms included the freedoms of speech, assembly, and worship. The two sets of terms for Communism included dictatorship by the proletariat, democratic centralism, "exploitative life," and "supremacy of physical labor."

Analyzing the results, we found that villagers over forty years of age had a fairly complete comprehension of the Confucian terms; they were hazy about all democratic terms except that they knew there was no emperor in a Republic; and they were totally ignorant of the Communist terms. Among villagers between the ages of fifteen and forty, the generation which grew up under the Republic, there was moderate understanding of the Confucian values but a low degree of comprehension of the Confucian structural terms. Their understanding of the democratic terms was slightly better than that of the older generation, most of them having, for instance, a general idea of modern elections. But they were as ignorant of Communism as the older generation. The age-old absolute dominance of a single ideology, Confucianism, was broken. The predominance of Confucianism in the minds of the older generation was in conflict with the realism of an emerging democratic social and political order under the Republic which exerted increasing influence on the life of the village. There was apparent ideological chaos in the minds of the younger generation. Both their understanding and their acceptance of the Confucian orthodoxy had been much weakened, but they had no sound knowledge or visible interest in democratic ideas which were supposed to be the orthodoxy of the Republic. Most of the younger generation, for instance, equated the president with the emperor.

These facts had significant implications. The lack of a consistent system of well-understood and well-accepted ideology implied progressive social disorganization. It suggested that what helped maintain the social order of the community was the dominance of the ideologically consistent older generation in the operation of the major social institutions in the village life. But this local condition was in contrast to the growing dominance of the younger generation in strategic political, economic, and social positions in the rapidly modernizing urban world, and it was doubtful that it could be sustained. Lastly, it was evident that, up to 1948, Communist ideology had been suddenly superimposed upon the village from the outside with no gradual process of incipient introduction among the villagers young or old. This was the ideological situation which confronted the Communists when they came to Nanching in 1949.

Communist strategy in the transition period was to concentrate intensive indoctrination upon the elite, both old and new. This meant ideological remolding of the former leadership portion of the population in pre-Communist society and intensive indoctrination for the young activists marked for leading the new social order.

We have mentioned the arrest of Lee Feng, the middle-aged leader in pre-Communist village affairs. During his months of detention in the labor re-education camp, he had to attend ideological lectures and discussions every morning, and the afternoons were devoted to physical labor in repairing a highway in the vicinity of Canton, a procedure designed to acquaint political prisoners with the importance and hardship of production labor and to purge thoughts of exploitation from their minds. The silence of subdued Lee Feng after his release from the labor camp clearly indicated covert hatred for his new masters instead of any genuine ideological transformation.

The two teachers in the village elementary school had to attend indoctrination classes in Pingan Chen along with teachers from other village schools in the vicinity. The classes were held in the evening during the summer months of 1950. The teachers' indoctrination, aimed ultimately at molding the thoughts of the young generation, showed signs of considerable success. If the adult villagers were still quite ignorant of and distinterested in Communism, pupils from the elementary schools in 1951 were already enthusiastically singing Communist songs and parroting Communist slogans, and many of them acted as informants for the Communists on affairs of the village and even of their own families.

Indoctrination sessions and general propaganda carried on within the new organizations such as the peasants' association and the Youth League were already producing a crop of young leaders who could follow the Communist directives with at least superficial understanding of the new terminology. Nanching provided visible evidence that the generation under twenty years of age were most receptive to ideological remolding.

The remolding of the thoughts of the common peasants was left largely to the general propaganda process; and group pressure, psychological suggestions, and coercive threats from propaganda movements undoubtedly served to impress upon their minds some of the basic themes of the Communist ideology. But the degree of acceptance of such themes by the hard-headed peasants depended largely upon actual benefits they derived from the new social and economic order. If the young activists showed considerable genuine conviction in the new ideological line, it was partly due to the concrete benefits they reaped from the change, including prestige and material gain from being elevated to the new status of leadership. But the common peasants generally did not share these benefits, and they were still pressed by the problem of eking out a bare subsistence for themselves and their families.

It was our observation, then, that the early impact of Communism on the ideology of the great majority of the Nanching peasants left them apathetic, skeptical, and submissive rather than showing any genuine enthusiasm and conviction toward Communism. The destruction of the Confucian orthodoxy created, especially for the older generation, an ideological vacuum, a situation which had significance for the development of the new social and political order.

PART III

National Changes in the Village Community under Collectivization

Chapter XV

From Mutual-Aid Teams to
Full Collectivization

LAND REFORM was one of the most momentous events in the history of China. When the entire process had been concluded for the nation as a whole, some 700 million mow of land (about 43 per cent of all cultivated land) had been distributed to 300 million landless or land-short peasants (approximately 60 per cent of the peasant population).[1] But this was only the first step in the Communist program of trying to raise China's agricultural productivity and drastically remaking the agrarian economy. Beyond land reform lay the even more momentous and drastic event of agricultural collectivization, which, since it uprooted the institutions of private ownership of land and the family farm, had the most intimate effect on the life of almost the entire agrarian population.

Since our field observations of Nanching ended with the land-reform stage, the collectivization process as it occurred in this particular village lay beyond the range of our investigation. Nevertheless, with collectivization now nationally realized, it is necessary to give some thought to this aspect of transformation of the rural community so as to keep the study of Nanching in realistic perspective. If our field data on Nanching serve as a microcosmic reflection of the macrocosm, the macrocosmic picture of the nation and the region may similarly show the general nature of the political and economic force to which the village was subjected. Hence the subsequent chapters present a brief analysis of the national collectivization movement as a generalized account. Whenever available, we employ regional data from Kwantung Province and local data from districts around the city of Canton to bring the picture close to the village of Nanching. Meanwhile, our acquaintance with the pre-collectivized conditions of this village aids our interpretation of the general collectivization process.

Land reform performed the vital functions of removing the most uncompromising opposition to socialism from rural power groups and enlisting the support of one part of the agrarian population. However, since it retained the small family farm economy, with all its political and economic limitations, land reform by itself could not substantially raise agricultural productivity and usher in the socialistic rural economy envisaged in Communist ideology, and the reorganization of the family farm along the collectivist line became an inevitable development.

In our observation of Nanching, we have noted the excessively small scale of the farm unit, the wide scattering of its plots, and the limited manpower and financial resources of the microscopic family farm. This small-farm economy, which was common to the vast majority of China's village communities and had long posed the basic problem for any effort to modernize Chinese agriculture, stood as the chief obstacle to the Communist socialization program, which was based on the Leninist theory that the only way to lift the peasantry out of its age-old economic plight was to transform the farm into an agricultural factory where modern principles of division of labor and mechanical techniques could be applied. Moreover, since the small-farm economy was the result of a complexity of traditional practices rooted in the system of property ownership and family economy and deeply connected with the vested interests of the land-owning peasants, it was obvious that any sudden enlargement of the farm unit through reconsolidation would be a tremendous shock to the peasants and cause at least a transitional chaos in the agrarian economy. The Communists therefore devised a three-stage national agricultural program intended to make the collectivization process a gradual one that would be acceptable to the peasants.

The first step was to be the organization of mutual-aid teams in order to bring the peasants out of their family farm as a working unit. The mutual-aid team would begin as a seasonal organization and later be transformed into a year-round team after the working arrangement had become stabilized. The second step was to be the consolidation of groups of successful year-round teams into a lower or elementary agricultural producers' co-operative in which the land would be pooled and farmed as a collective unit, but with each member retaining the ownership of his land and being remunerated partly according to his labor and partly according to his proportionate share of that part of the yield set aside for the recognition of land ownership. Members would also transfer to collective ownership their heavy farm equipment and draft animals, and receive appropriate compensation from the co-operative. The third and final stage was to be the transformation of this organization into a higher or advanced agricultural producers' co-operative, in which private ownership of land would be abolished and a member's reward would be measured only by the quality and quantity of his labor. In all major organizational aspects, the advanced type of co-operatives would be full-fledged collective farms like those in the Soviet Union, the two differing only in name, as officially interpreted by the Communist authorities.[2] An additional form of agricultural collectivism would be the large state farms to be set up in different regions partly to demonstrate how large farm units should operate.

There were some traditional roots for mutual-aid teams. It has been mentioned previously that the poor and middle peasants in Nanching often exchanged labor among themselves because of their inability to afford hired help at peak seasons, a practice also common in other parts of China.[3] Such traditional mutual aid normally involved only two families and lasted only for the duration of the task requiring such mutual help; and in Nanching kinship tie was usually a factor in such arrangements. The Communist-designed seasonal mutual-aid team was generally made up of a half dozen to about twenty peasant families whose labor, tools, and farm animals were pooled to work on the land belonging to the member families. It might disband when the farming season was over. When it continued in operation the whole year round, doing not only farm work but also collective supplementary activities such as handicraft or fishing in the streams during slack seasons, it became a year-round team.

In the Northeast and North China, where the Communists took hold earlier than in the South, land reform had a head start, and over 70 per cent of all the peasant families were said to belong to mutual-aid teams by 1952, with about 20 per cent of the teams reported as the year-round type.[4] In Kwangtung Province, where Nanching is located, since land reform was not generally completed until the end of 1952, the organization of mutual-aid teams came later. Even for the suburban area of Canton, where land reform took place relatively early, the organizing campaign for mutual-aid teams did not become an extensive movement until early 1953.

Immediately before the spring planting of 1953, the Agricultural Bureau for the Canton Suburban Area, an agency under the Canton Municipal Government, issued a call for the rural cadres to intensify their efforts in organizing mutual-aid teams and agricultural producers' co-operatives. The Bureau conducted a short course to train peasant leaders in the organization and operation of mutual-aid teams before the spring planting of 1953, hoping to develop a large number of seasonal teams for the spring planting, and to gradually transform them into permanent teams at a later date.[5] By the time spring planting was completed, it was reported that 247 mutual-aid teams had been established in the northern and western suburban areas.[6] In one village near Nanching, 90 per cent of the peasant families were said to have joined mutual-aid teams. One team leader in that village described his team:

> Our team comprises seven families, all poor peasants and former farm laborers. We faced a shortage of labor during busy seasons, and we were too poor to afford hired help. We were also short of farm tools and too poor to buy fertilizer. In the past, we were not able to finish our farm chores in the proper time, and it was hopeless to think of increasing production.
>
> But we organized our mutual-aid team in the fall of last year [1952]. We pooled our labor and farm tools for systematic use and thus overcame the shortage of labor and tools. We also mobilized every family to collect and accumulate fertilizer, and solved our fertilizer problem. The autumn crop was a bumper crop, and we had surplus grain to buy tools and fertilizer . . . Our objective for this year is to produce 1,300 catties of unhusked rice per mow, representing more than 20 per cent increase over the yield of last year. We also plan to develop auxiliary industries such as raising pigs and poultry, and to reclaim some waste land to increase our crop area . . .[7]

In another neighboring village several mutual-aid teams were organized just before the spring planting of 1953. One team was composed of eight families, with 45 mow (7.5 acres) of land altogether, and four water buffaloes. It pooled all its labor, tools, and animals, and claimed to have completed plowing and planting in a shorter time than was formerly required. It took eight days to transplant the rice seedlings for all of the 45 mow, whereas it would have taken about fifteen days to plant the same area if the families had worked independently.[8]

Although such Communist reports did not offer conclusive evidence concerning the over-all superiority of the mutual-aid team as a production organization over the traditional family farm, they provide some facts for analysis of the economic advantages or disadvantages of the mutual-aid team.

There was apparently a real advantage in the mutual-aid pooling of farm tools and equipment. This applied especially to the poor and lower-middle peasants who were hindered by a shortage of such items. Since different families might possess different tools, pooling them was a practical way to at least temporarily overcome the shortage. In addition, equipment such as the winnowers were in use only for a short time for each farming season. In the past, peasants in Nanching usually borrowed such equipment from more prosperous kin or friends and at times paid a small rental in cash, grain, or labor. There was therefore apparent economic value in the joint use of such items by a mutual-aid team through pooling tools and equipment. Theoretically, there was a similar advantage in the mutual-aid teams' joint use of draft animals such as the water buffalo. But when a buffalo was transferred to a team, it was often overworked, under-fed, and poorly cared for, as attested to by the high mortality rate among draft animals belonging to mutual-aid teams. This difficulty of poor collective care and high mortality rate remained a problem under the agricultural producers' co-operatives of both the lower and higher forms, posing a serious difficulty in the development of collectivism in agricultural production.

The problem of labor efficiency under the mutual-aid organization was more complex and the picture is less clear. Working in collectivity, the mutual-aid team seemed able to alleviate to a certain extent the shortage of labor during peak seasons which had handicapped the poor and lower-middle peasants who had been unable to afford much hired help. Published reports from different parts of the country were fairly consistent in showing that well-organized teams were able to complete their work faster than if the families had worked independently. In the traditional practice of exchanging labor there was the uncertainty of finding someone to exchange labor with, and the exchange arrangement was limited to one task at a time. The mutual-aid team, if successfully organized and operated, stabilized the labor-exchange relationship among a group of families and put it on a comprehensive basis to include not only one task at a time but all tasks involved in the production of a crop or in auxiliary industries.

Related to labor efficiency was the complicated problem of remuneration according to quantity and quality of labor. Although Communist authorities issued general guiding principles for classifying skilled and unskilled labor and the proper ways of remuneration, each local team had to work out its own detailed rules, with the resulting difficulty of producing an arrangement pleasing to every participating family. For most types of farm work, remuneration was based on the labor unit, representing one man performing an average day of labor, with little differentiation between skilled and unskilled labor. The labor-unit system also frequently failed to distinguish the industrious from the lazy within the same class of work, thus causing dissatisfaction and conflict among members. This was often the reason for which the efficient middle peasants refrained from joining mutual-aid teams or withdrew from them, as indicated in many Communist press reports. In addition, the Chinese had traditionally relied upon family and friendship relations in carrying out economic activities. It would take considerable readjustment of this traditional pattern to new economic relations on a business basis such as required in the operation of a well-adjusted mutual-aid team. It is doubtful whether such readjustment was successfully made in a majority of the teams.

Whatever the merits and failings of the mutual-aid team, it was set up as the initial organization for increasing direct state planning and control of agricultural production. Its basic function of effecting the transfer of agriculture from private operation to an economy under state planning and control was made clear in the following excerpts from a directive issued by the Suburban Agricultural Bureau of the Canton Municipal Government in 1953, which was typical of similar directives issued in the same period:

> The government's production plan for the suburban area this year lays main emphasis upon the production of food and the increase of its productivity. The goal is 810 catties of unhusked rice per mow, an increase of 12.3 per cent over last year. The suburban villages are now busy completing preparations for spring planting, such as the examination and repair of water control works, the killing of pests, the collection of fertilizer, and the development and consolidation of mutual-aid organizations. Besides, the villages are actively initiating the patriotic bountiful production emulation campaign, getting an early start on spring planting so as to complete spring farming according to schedule.
>
> . . . The earth work for the Pachow dike, Yunkuei dike and Tangchi dike must be completed by the end of March, and the dams and culverts must be completed by April 10 of this year [1953]. Besides, the local district organization must add thickness and height to existing dikes as needed. Where droughts are frequent, more reservoirs must be deepened by one to two feet, with the goal of supplying water for irrigation for thirty rainless days . . .
>
> The peasants must be mobilized to collect more fertilizer, with the goal of applying 20 per cent more fertilizer to each mow over that of last year . . . Pest control committees must be established in the subdistricts and villages . . .

. . . In all subdistricts, the patriotic bountiful production emulation campaign must be developed among the masses. At least 75 per cent of the year-round mutual-aid teams must join this campaign, but special effort must be made to induce the independent peasants (who have not joined any mutual-aid team) to participate in the emulation and to lead them toward the organization of mutual-aid teams and co-operatives. Regulations of rewards should be worked out for this year's emulation campaign. Stories of model laborers in the bountiful production emulation campaign should be introduced to the people, and the experience of the model laborers should be popularized so as to break through the peasants' conservatism and awaken them to participate in the emulation voluntarily.

For this year's spring planting, all subdistricts have held peasants' representatives conferences which have developed production plans for the year and concrete measures to carry out production for the spring crop, including the development of the production emulation campaign. Each of these conferences has also issued calls for the peasants to carry out intensive farming and to start early on their spring crop.[9]

Such directives pointed to drastic change, indeed. In planning his farming operation, the individual peasant traditionally followed his own considerations of land, water, capital investment, and methods of cultivation; and the amount of labor to be exerted was determined by the age and health of the peasant and his family members, his economic needs, moral pressure and discipline from his kinship group and the village community, his own ambition, and encouragement from the chance of success which varied generally in proportion to the peasant's economic status. The plan and goal of production was a matter for the individual peasant family to decide. Now the state was to impose a uniform target of production: 810 catties per mow, or an increase of 12.3 per cent over the pre-Communist level. In the past, a peasant would start preparing his field for spring planting by consulting the old almanac, looking at the weather, and following the lead of experienced neighbors. Now cadres held meetings in front of the ancestral temple to exhort them to start spring planting early. Posters on the walls carried the same injunction. In some villages, peasants' association leaders even beat a pair of brass gongs through the streets, shouting the same slogans. In the past, gongs were used to warn villages of approaching danger or to call them to emergency meetings. Now the routine matter of starting the spring crop was elevated to the emergency level.

It was clear that such changes, violating all traditional practice, could not be successfully carried out among a conservative peasantry by relying on the sporadic spontaneous response from individual peasants. Hence the importance of the mutual-aid team as an instrument for obtaining guided collective response to government calls and for getting individual peasants into line with the directives.

One of the major techniques used to raise agricultural production was the production emulation campaign to stimulate greater labor exertion. Although Communist propaganda encouraged independent peasants to join in such emulation, it was apparent that the main burden of the campaigns rested on the collective participation of the mutual-aid teams, with one team setting up a quota of production per mow as a challenge to other teams. In some villages near Nanching such group emulation seemed to have raised production enthusiasm, and there were Communist press reports of increased production of as much as 20 per cent per mow over the level of the previous year. But also commonly reported in the Communist press were cases of falsification of accomplishment, at times involving the Communist cadres responsible for the direction of the emulating teams, an indication of the difficulty in arousing genuine enthusiasm among conservative peasants for new activities unintelligible to them. Although there was no systematic official report on the general success or failure of planned targets in the suburban area as a whole, we might note in passing that in pre-Communist Nanching a 12 per cent increase in yield of rice was often achieved by some peasants through adequate application of fertilizer and water without altering the form of farm organization.

Mutual-aid teams were instrumental in the selection of "model laborers" in agricultural production, individuals who were propagandized as local heroes for their personal achievements at farm work. The "model laborer" rose as a new figure on the Communist social scene, signifying a new glorified role for the manual laborer which was in dramatic contrast to the traditional emphasis on the prestige of the brain-worker and the scholar and the low esteem for manual achievement. The mutual-aid teams were similarly instrumental in the technical aspects of increasing agricultural production. It was mainly through the organized action of the teams that the Communist leaders spurred the peasants to collect more fertilizer, improve water control and irrigation works, and adopt new methods of cultivation such as using better strains and close-planting of rice seedlings.

In attempting a general evaluation of the mutual-aid teams, one would say that their most significant accomplishments were the pooling of tools and labor and the collective attempt to stimulate enthusiasm for increased production. Since they had no permanent common property assets, their ability to undertake technical improvements was limited to those requiring collective labor but little or no capital investment, such as certain types of hydraulic projects and adoption of the close-planting method. How far the mutual-aid teams in the period 1952–1955 fulfilled hopes in helping to raise agricultural production and ease the transition toward full collectivism is a question to which Communist reports offered no conclusive answer. It might be inferred from the sudden acceleration of the collectivization program after 1955, a move which indicated a decisive change in official policy, that the mutual-aid teams had failed to come up to the expectations of the Communist planners.

At any rate, after 1955 the Communist regime undertook to speed up the transition toward full collectivism almost to the point of discarding the original program of gradual transformation by stages.

The slow growth in the number of co-operatives of both the lower and the higher types during the first years of the agricultural program had been consciously designed to allow the mutual-aid teams to become stabilized organizations so as to provide a firm foundation for full collectivization. For the whole country, there were only 300 agricultural producers' co-operatives of both types in 1951, 4,000 in 1952, and 14,000 in 1953, the year when the mutual-aid teams first emerged as an established nation-wide movement. The rise in the number of co-operatives to 650,000 by the end of June in 1954, with a membership of 16,900,000 farm households or about 15 per cent of the nation's total, was impressive, but after 1955 was practically explosive. Chou En-lai, the Communist premier, reported: "By the end of June 1956 a total of 992,000 agricultural producers' co-operatives have been organized throughout the country. Their members make up 91.7 per cent of the country's peasant households; those joining co-operatives of the higher type constitute 62.6 per cent of all peasant households." [10] This significant development led Liao Lu-yen, Minister of Agriculture, to declare that "the small peasant economy has been transformed throughout the country." [11] By the spring of 1957, although consolidation of smaller units reduced the total to 752,113 co-operatives, with 93.3 per cent of all farm households in the nation belonging to the higher type and only 3.7 per cent belonging to the lower type, these co-operatives comprised 118,908,965 peasant households or 97 per cent of the nation's total.[12] In harmony with this national trend, the Communist leadership in Kwangtung Province hastened to achieve "complete cooperativization" in 1956.[13]

Thus almost complete national collectivization was effected mainly in the three-year period of 1955–1957, especially the year 1956. In view of the magnitude of the peasant population involved, it is highly doubtful whether such rapid development could have followed the original policy of gradual transition through the seasonal mutual-aid team, the year-round mutual-aid team, and lower type, and finally the higher type of agricultural producers' co-operatives.

A vital turning point in the acceleration of collectivization was Mao's announcement to the Communist Party leadership in July 1955 of the decision to speed up the collectivization process. When the secret decision finally appeared in the Communist press some three months later, it revealed a goal of collectivizing one-half of the 120,000,000 farm households in China by 1958 and complete collectivization by 1960.[14] As shown in the above figures, the speed of actual development exceeded that in Mao's decision.

Mao's policy of sudden acceleration was based both on the Communist unshaken belief in collectivism as the ultimate means of raising agricultural production and on the pressing need to resolve the growing number of problems besetting the current situation of drastic social and economic transition.

It was admitted at last that equalization of land ownership through land reform alone had not greatly improved the situation of mass poverty caused in a large measure by excessive population pressure on the land. Mao said:

> China's situation is this: there is a large population with insufficient cultivated land (a per capita average of three mow for the nation, and one mow or fractions of one mow in many places in the South). Natural calamities and famine occur frequently, and there are backward methods of farm management. As a result, although land reform has brought certain improvements or great improvements to the life of the broad peasantry, many people still face difficulties, still are not well-off: Well-off peasants constitute only a minority. Hence the majority of the peasants have the positive tendency to pursue the course of socialism.[15]

Elaborating on this statement, Mao pointed out that in the post–land-reform period "60 to 70 per cent of the peasants are still poverty stricken or not well-off, and only 20 to 30 per cent are well-off or relatively so."

Moreover, there was a "spontaneous regeneration of capitalism" in the post–land-reform countryside. Said Mao:

> In the past few years, there has been a tendency for capitalistic influences to grow in the countryside. Many peasants have become rich. On the other hand, we see the aggravation from the conditions of poverty of many peasants who are compelled to sell their land and to hire out their own labor. If such conditions are given no immediate improvement, the poor peasants will complain to us, and criticize us for not providing any help.

. . . To attain the ideal goal of agricultural reform, there is the need for speedy promotion of the cooperative organization.[16]

In addition to these urgent economic and political problems stemming directly from conditions in the countryside, the pressing needs of the industrialization program for increased agricultural production played an important part in the acceleration of collectivization. There was the need for feeding a growing urban population which had increased from 71,000,000 in 1952 to 92,000,000 in 1957, a gain of 29.6 per cent.[17] There was the need to provide food for peasants in an expanding area devoted to industrial crops such as cotton. Agricultural products were the main exports available to exchange for foreign machinery and capital goods for the five-year plans. And there were the yearning mouths from the annual increment of 12,000,000 new population now growing at the rate of 2 per cent a year. Lu Chih-heng, a Communist writer, concluded from this situation:

> The growth of small peasant farming could not catch up with the growth of consumption, and this contradiction could be traced to the productive relations of small private ownership which could not provide a broad field for development of the productive forces. Although after liberation small private ownership replaced feudal ownership, making it possible to restore and develop agricultural production, the insurmountable limitation of small peasant economy made it impossible to increase agricultural production to a considerable extent or to free itself completely from backwardness and poverty. Further, it shows the contradiction between small peasant economy and socialist industrialization. Small peasant economy could not meet the rapid growth of demand for marketable grain arising from the development of industry. When the peasants keep more grain for self-consumption, marketable grain is reduced with its effect produced on the supply of marketable grain. This is a serious problem which, if not solved, will cause tremendous difficulty to socialist construction and socialist transformation.[18]

This statement, typical of others made by Communist leaders including Mao Tse-tung, clearly implied that collectivization would serve not only to raise agricultural productivity but also to facilitate the extraction of agricultural products from the peasants in order to meet growing needs. Whereas with private ownership the government would have great difficulty in buying products from the peasants at a price low enough to enable the government to finance an extensive industrial program without incurring inflation, political control of the co-operatives would make it possible to insure delivery of agricultural products to the government at low prices; and, while it would be almost impossible to exert direct control over some 120,000,000 peasant farms, it would be feasible to do so with about three-quarters of a million co-operatives.

It is not difficult to see that the Communist motives for speeding up collectivization in agriculture reflected conditions as we knew them in the village of Nanching.

CHAPTER XVI

Economic Problems of the Agricultural Producers' Co-operatives

Productive Function

ACCEPTING THE Communist claim that by 1957 collectivization had been achieved in some form in the entire country, the question arises as to the stability and soundness of the innumerable hastily
organized co-operatives. Enjoying no support whatever from institutionalized traditions, the co-operatives were created by law on the
theory that they could increase agricultural production and income;
and only successful performance of this primary function could justify
their coming into existence. Mao Tse-tung stated that it would serve no
purpose to organize co-operatives if they did not result in increased
production from the land and more income for the peasants,[1] and the
Communist Ministry of Agriculture issued elaborate guiding principles
for increasing production among the co-operatives and improving income for 90 per cent of the members.[2] A first question, then, is whether
the co-operatives actually increased production.

Generally speaking, the Communist reports offered three categories
of information to vindicate the superiority of the co-operatives as a
productive organization: increase of national agricultural production,
increase of production per unit of land area, and samples of individual
co-operatives having increased production. In using Communist information, one is confronted with a mass of statistics often lacking in
consistency and giving little opportunity for verification or checking of
errors. The total food grains output for 1956, for example, was vari-
ously stated as 365 and 385.5 billion catties in different sources. In the
absence of reliable means of verification, we have used the latest figures
on the presumption that the required information had been made
increasingly available to the Communist government.

One set of figures compared national agricultural production under Communist leadership with that in the 1930's before the Japanese invasion, when Chinese farm production was at a prewar peak, in order to demonstrate the over-all superiority of the Communist system over the small family farm economy at a period of its best performance. The

	1932–1936	1952–1956	Change in percentage
Food grains (in billion catties)	1,300	1,658	+ 9.0
Cotton (in million tan)	60.5	103	+ 54.0

data presented in the accompanying tabulation are from "The Policy of Unified Purchase and Sale of Grain Shall Not Be Frustrated," by Chou Po-ping, in *Liang Shih* (Grain), no. 7, July 1957. It should be noted that one ton equals 1,814 catties or 18.14 tan, the tan being the equivalent of 100 catties.

Another group of figures presented a continuous annual growth of national production of major agricultural products from the Communist assumption of power in 1949 to 1957, in order to prove specifically the correctness and effectiveness of the collectivistic program. The following table is a sample showing the total annual production of food grains (including potatoes) which represented the backbone of China's agricultural production. The figures from 1950 through 1957

Year	Food grains (billion catties)	Annual increase (billion catties)	Annual increase (per cent)
1949	216.0	—	—
1950	264.3	48.3	22.3
1951	287.4	23.1	8.7
1952	327.8	40.4	14.0
1953	333.7	5.9	1.8
1954	339.0	5.3	1.6
1955	367.9	28.9	8.5
1956	385.5	17.6	4.8
1957	402.7 (estimate)	17.2	4.5

are from "Outlines of Propaganda on the Policy of Unified Purchase and Unified Sale of Grain," by the Editorial Department of *Shih Shih Shou Ts'e* (Current Events), no. 17, September 6, 1957. The figure for 1949 is from "Is the People's Life Not Bettered?" by Ching Chi, in the same publication, no. 15, August 6, 1957.

While the total national output of agricultural production was the result of a combination of many factors of which collectivization was but one, the second category of information on the output per unit area (mow) reflected more specifically the performance of the collectivist system. In this respect, available information was given not in the form of concrete figures on a year-to-year basis, but in percentage comparison between two years, each representing a different situation. An example was the percentage increase of production per unit area in 1956, when collectivization became a national fact, as compared with 1949, when the Communists first came into power. Thus, with 1949 as 100, the 1956 production of rice was 131, wheat 142, miscellaneous grain 134, potatoes 142, and the average for these food crops was 138.[3] In other words, 1956 as the year of national collectivization showed an increase in per unit area output ranging from 31 per cent for rice to 42 per cent for potatoes. A range of increase from 28 to 43 per cent was registered for the industrial crops of cotton, jute and hemp, tobacco, sugar cane, and peanuts; and only sweet beet and rapeseeds showed a slight decrease per unit area.

The third category of information contained a large number of cases of individual co-operatives showing for the most part an increase in productivity as further support for the general theme that collectivization had brought an increase in national agricultural production and in the national average of production per unit area. Such information covered the early 1950's, when co-operatives began to appear sporadically in different parts of the country, to 1957, when national collectivization was considered achieved. Thus a co-operative in the northern part of Shansi Province reported in 1951 an increase of 32.7 per cent per mow of wheat compared to 1950, when the co-operative was not yet organized.[4] A co-operative in the southern part of Chekiang Province claimed a 25 per cent increase of yield of rice per mow in 1953,[5] and another in Chieh-yang county of Kwangtung Province reported an increase of 33 per cent per mow of rice in the same year,[6] as compared with 1952 before the co-operatives came into existence in either locality. In Linfen county of Shansi Province the "model" Red Star Co-operative reported in 1957 a yield of 332 catties of wheat per mow on the average, showing an increase of 42 catties or 14.5 per cent over 1956.[7] All co-operatives in Lungki county of Fukien Province averaged 470 catties of rice per mow for the early crop in 1957, making a 6 per cent increase over that in 1956.[8]

As in the case of national figures, there is no means of checking the accuracy of these and other local figures. In the case of the average figure for the co-operatives in Lungki county of Fukien Province, however, the locality is within 250 miles of Nanching, and because of re-

gional proximity and environmental similarity, the experience of Nanching may serve as a measurement. In pre-Communist Nanching certain
above-average farms did yield 450 catties of rice per mow a crop in a
traditional double-crop system. Given certain organizational and technical improvements, the reported 470 catties of yield per mow appears
feasible. No evaluation of accuracy can be rendered for the other
figures quoted.

Communist sources occasionally admitted decreased production with
poorly organized co-operatives, without giving factual details. For instance, in the midst of the "great debate" on socialism in 1957 the
Nanfang Jih-pao in Canton printed on September 14 a generalized
statement from many Communist leaders assigned to co-operatives in
Kwangtung Province: "In my co-operative, production has actually
decreased, and the members have many opinions. How can I talk about
the superiority of co-operativization?" This and other similiar statements printed in Communist sources pointed out the obvious, namely,
the presence of co-operatives having decreased production along with
those showing increased production. Despite the Communist claim
that the vast majority of all co-operatives in the country had raised
their production in 1957 over the previous year, so long as the claim
was a vague one unsupported by convincing statistics and relevant
factual information, the question remained as to the proportion of such
co-operatives among the nation's 750,000 co-operatives.

A common Communist argument for the over-all success of the nation's co-operatives in raising production was the steady annual increase
in national agricultural output since 1949, despite losses from serious
natural calamities in some years. Without the increase in productivity
by the co-operatives as a counterbalancing factor, so went the argument, the years of serious natural calamities would have shown a
decrease instead of an increase in national farm output. Thus damages
from typhoons, floods, and droughts in 1956 were considered the most
serious in recent decades, but national output in food grains forged
ahead 4.8 per cent over that in 1955. This argument was not borne out
by an examination of the damage figures resulting from natural calamities as made public by the Communists; these figures appear in the
accompanying tabulation and are computed from "The Policy of
Unified Purchase and Sale of Grain Shall Not Be Frustrated," by Chou
Po-ping, *Liang Shih* (Grain), no. 7, July 1957.

It is obvious that even in 1956, when damage from natural calamities
was the greatest in the years listed, the actual loss in output amounted to
only 0.063 per cent of the nation's total, an amount too negligible to

Year	Loss in output of food grains (million catties)	Total national output of food grains (billion catties)	Percentage of loss to national output
1953	150	333.7	.045
1954	177	339.0	.052
1955	127	367.9	.035
1956	244	385.5	.063

affect substantially the annual increase or decrease in national output. On the other hand, 1953 suffered the least damage in absolute figures, and yet that year's national output of food grains had an annual gain of only 1.8 per cent, among the lowest since 1949. It is thus evident that neither losses from natural calamities nor collectivization can entirely explain the annual fluctuations in national grain output since 1949 unless the statistical figures, especially those with regard to damage, are grossly inaccurate.

Surveying the above categories of figures together, there is the strong possibility that national output experienced a general increase. Even if one should discount the small increases in some of the years as a margin of error, the cumulative increases over a period of several years seemed too sizable to be discounted the same way. The food grains output of 1957 represented an increase of 82 per cent from that of 1949 and 18.8 per cent from that of 1954, the year when co-operatives began to mutiply rapidly. This assumption of a certain amount of increase in output found support in many agricultural measures undertaken during these years which should result in growth of production. While it is still difficult to isolate the factor of collectivization in such measures, we can attempt some tentative analysis of it.

A leading measure was the expansion of cultivated land through reclamation. Statistics in this respect varied in different Communist sources. The total cultivated land of the country, according to one version, stood at 1,670 million mow in 1957, representing an increase of 14 per cent over 1949, the year the Communists came into power, and an increase of 5.2 per cent over 1953, the beginning of the first five-year plan and the year before collectivization picked up momentum.[9] Reclamation of waste land was emphasized in the Communist agricultural policy. An expansion of the area under cultivation would naturally add to the nation's agricultural production, but the contribution of collectivization to the extensive reclamation of land is hard to determine. Concerted action from a large team had apparent advantages over an individual peasant and his family in reclaiming new land which required collective labor in leveling the land, in irrigation, or in draining waterlogged areas. Reclamation was a frequent item in the reports of accomplishments by the mutual-aid teams in the early 1950's and the co-operatives.

Of paramount importance to Chinese agricultural production are water control and irrigation. In this respect, there is little doubt that the Communist government had achieved prominent tangible results, with collective labor from the co-operatives a noticeable contributing force. Large-scale hydraulic projects now in progress, such as the control of the Huai River and the Yellow River, are undertakings by provincial and central governments, as traditionally practiced, with little direct relation to collective labor provided by the co-operatives. But numerous small local projects were accomplished with collectivization as an apparent contributing factor. From 1949 to 1956, irrigation ditches and ponds constructed numbered over fourteen million and in 1956 alone over four million. In the same years over five million irrigation wells were dug, with over three million dug in 1956. During these seven years, the Ministry of Water Conservancy lent the peasants (presumably mainly to the co-operatives) over one million water wheels, 500,000 of which were loaned in 1956.[10]

The result of these undertakings was the expansion of high-yielding irrigated acreage. In 1956 there were 515 million mow of irrigated land, accounting for about 31 per cent of the country's total area under cultivation in the same year. This irrigated area represented an increase of 41.6 per cent over the some 300 million mow in 1949, and about 100 million or 46.5 per cent of the 215 million mow of new expansion were brought under irrigation in 1956.[11]

This process of expansion went on vigorously in most of the provinces. In Honan Province there were seven million mow of irrigated land before the Communists came; between 1949 and 1955 this was expanded to 14 million mow, doubling the area. But an additional 36 million mow was brought under irrigation in 1956 by utilizing the collective labor of the co-operatives to open ditches, sink wells, and build ponds and reservoirs.[12] Co-operatives in Yüsi special administrative district of Yunnan Province were reported to have turned 1,180,000 mow of the total of 2,020,000 mow of arable land into irrigated fields in 1956.[13]

In Kwangtung Province, where Nanching is located, hydraulic projects also developed speedily. Between 1950 and 1956 dams were built across more than 300 streams,[14] and 208 water control and irrigation projects were completed costing over 20,000 yuan each (about $8,000 United States currency at the official rate) and 75,000 projects were completed, each of which cost less than 20,000 yuan. These projects brought irrigation to 7,730,000 mow of land, or about 14 per cent of the province's crop area.[15] The co-operatives were instrumental to these developments. In San-shui county of this province, for example, a co-operative mobilized 1,300 men and women to complete a 300-foot dam to control spring floods and to relieve autumn droughts.[16] In a country of irrigational agriculture like China extensive development of hydraulic projects alone is likely to bring about appreciable increase in agricultural output. In pre-Communist Nanching agricultural experts had long proposed the construction of two reservoirs on the high points on the northern side of the village so that water could be collected and stored from the surrounding higher slopes; this water could be gravity-fed through ditches to the village's dry land on the low hill sides, turning the land into paddy fields. It was estimated that completion of this project would raise the rice output of the village by at least one-third. The heavy financial requirement for labor and land site had discouraged clan leaders from seriously considering such a project. Assuming collectivization of the village's farms, both collective labor and land site could be provided by the co-operative without great difficulty.

Closely related to hydraulic projects and vital to increased agricultural production is the expansion of double-crop areas. Published Communist information indicated a steady expansion of double-crop acreage. It was claimed that from 1953 to 1956 double-crop land increased by 8.7 per cent (no concrete figures given).[17] In 1956 alone there was an increase of 100 million mow of new double-crop land, or slightly less than 6.0 per cent of the nation's total cultivated land.[18] In Kwangtung Province 14 million mow or about 25 per cent of the total of 56 million mow of cultivated land were double-crop acreage in 1956. A survey showed that an additional 16 million mow of the province's cultivated land could be planted with a winter crop in addition to the spring crop, thus increasing the double-crop area from 25 to 53.5 per cent of all land under cultivation in the province. The Communist authorities were setting this as a target.[19] Even partial success would obviously bring substantial increase in the province's total agricultural output.

Other measures in improving agricultural production which the Communists undertook with varying degrees of success included the popularization of superior strains of plants and certain methods of cultivation. As early as 1951 strenuous propaganda was directed toward popularization of superior strains tested for higher yields and suitability to different localities. By 1956, 36 per cent of the country's total crop area was said to be planted in superior strains, and 90 per cent of all the cotton acreage was reported to be in superior strains.[20] In Kwang-tung Province the Communist authorities were trying to popularize a strain of rice called "Golden Bamboo" with the claim that it was able to yield up to one-third more per mow than the current varieties. There is no information about the success of this effort. In the rice region Communist sources of information claimed widespread success in intro-ducing to vast areas the method of close planting of rice seedlings as a means of raising production. The traditional method was to plant rice seedlings in large clumps and to space the clumps rather far apart. The new method is to plant the seedlings in small clumps closer together. By 1955, 27 million mow or 46.2 per cent of the province's crop land was said to have been planted by the new method.[21]

In other aspects of farm improvement the Communists seemed to have been less successful. Increasing fertilizer is vital to the effort of raising production. The Communists, faced with a shortage of capital and facilities for manufacturing chemical fertilizer, have stressed labor exertion in collecting human and animal excreta, garbage, compost, and dirt from bottoms of streams and ponds. This "fertilizer collection movement," while requiring no capital investment aside from labor, faced the obstacles of a shortage of fertilizer that could be economically collected in comparison to the vast needs, and of initial organizational difficulties of the co-operatives. With reference to the latter, while many co-operatives reported overfulfillment of the quota of fertilizer to be collected,[22] many others lagged far behind the target and resorted to falsifying information to cover up their failure. Thus in Jung-an county in Kwangsi Province the People's Council reported in early 1956 that the amount of fertilizer accumulated exceeded the need of spring farming by 50 per cent and amounted to 90 per cent of the year's total requirement. Later investigation by higher Communist authorities disclosed that even the best co-operatives in that district had collected only 15 per cent of the fertilizer required for the year, and that the poorly organized co-operatives had collected but 5 per cent of the annual need.[23] A start has been made in enlarging the chemical fer-tilizer industry, but its national output was only 747,000 tons in 1956. It has been estimated that not until 1962, the end of the second five-year plan, can the output reach six million tons a year,[24] a quantity commensurate with the nation's requirements.

Another aspect of farm improvement in which the Communists have failed to score significant advancement up to 1958 is the matter of tools and implements. Certain simple improvements were introduced into traditional tools such as the plough, but their unstandardized quality, their short supply, and their unsuitability to local conditions in some regions remained unresolved problems.[25] General use of mechanized implements such as the tractor, the symbol of modern agriculture, is admitted to be some years away.[26] Although such equipment is suited to the large collectivized farm on flat terrains, limited production from the infant agricultural implement industry and the difficulty of operating mechanized equipment on hilly terrains in many parts of the country preclude extensive mechanization as an immediate means of raising the nation's agricultural production.

Thus the different aspects of farm improvement presented varying degrees of success and failure. In view of the several vital areas in which the Communists had obviously made advancement, it is probable that the nation's total agricultural output had increased partly because of the collectivization program. The advantage of collective labor in reclamation and hydraulic projects has been pointed out. In other forms of farm improvement such as double-cropping, popularization of superior strains, and better planting methods, the contribution of the co-operative lay in the centralized direction and control of farming operation by the cadres who followed directives with little regard for the inertia of traditional methods. While control of the co-operatives by agriculturally uninitiated cadres damaged certain aspects of production, as admitted in Communist documents, the collective system facilitated extensive adoption of certain standardized measures helpful to the growth of production.

Intimately related to the improvement of farming and increase of production was the supply of capital. A part of the rationale for liquidating the economic status of the landlords was to transfer their land and wealth to the poor peasants for use in production. However, as previously pointed out, peasants after land reform were still in critical need of capital. This situation hampered the operation of the mutual-aid teams and later the co-operatives. T'ao Chu, Governor of Kwangtung Province, stated: "Many co-operatives have neither a single buffalo with which to plow the land nor a single cent as working capital." [27] Before the spring planting of 1956, co-operatives in Ying-teh county in the same province faced a shortage of 500 buffaloes and a large quantity of seed.[28]

Now that the landlords' wealth had been transferred to the peasants, where could fresh capital come from? One source was of course the income from the co-operatives, which was emphasized in Communist documents. Liu Jui-lung, Vice-Minister of Agriculture, suggested setting aside 15 to 20 per cent of the co-operative's gross receipts for capital accumulation,[29] but there were serious difficulties in putting this procedure into practice due to its depressing effect on the income of the co-operative's members, the majority of whom had trouble in making ends meet. Another source of capital could be the peasants' savings. There were reports of individual co-operatives which had succeeded in raising their needed capital mainly from its members,[30] but it is doubtful whether such cases can be regarded as at all typical. However, credit co-operatives, drawing savings from individuals, were reported growing rapidly in the countryside, totaling 116,000 throughout the nation in 1956, during which every rural district was said to have one or more.[31] If successfully developed, such organizations could be of financial assistance to the co-operatives, but there was no information on the size of their capital or details of their operations.

Thus government loans were the major source of capital supply about which there is some general information. For instance, in 1956, the state made agricultural loans amounting to 2.2 billion yuan, in addition to 1.2 billion yuan paid in advance by the state for purchase of agricultural products from the co-operatives.[32] But there was little information on the nature of such state loans and the extent to which the country's vast needs were adequately met. Perhaps some inference could be made from the figures in Kwangtung Province. In 1956 the government banks extended rural credit to the total of 40,000,000 yuan for the entire province. Of this total, 14,000,000 yuan was for helping poor peasants pay admission costs to the co-operatives and the rest was to assist the co-operatives in buying buffaloes and defraying other costs of production.[33] On the assumption of complete collectivization of the province's farms, we may measure the adequacy of the loans by distributing all of the 40,000,000 yuan over the province's 56,000,000 mow of crop land. This yields an average of about 0.70 yuan (27 cents United States currency) per mow, insufficient for the annual cost of fertilizer alone.

In the long run, the co-operatives would, if successfully developed, provide their own capital; but in the initial stage of development the shortage of capital and the apparently small assistance from the state might handicap the co-operatives from performing their primary function of increasing production.

Income Distribution

It is income, not production, that offers incentive for the members and functions as an integrating goal for the cohesion of the collective organization. For the peasants the basic function of any economic institution, whether in the form of the family farm or a co-operative, is to provide an organized means for making a living, and if possible, achieving abundance; and for a peasantry whose majority constantly struggled between subsistence and starvation this function was to be realized *now* and not in the near or distant future. Hence, upon the amount of income depended the loyalty of the membership toward the newly enacted organization of the co-operatives.

It has been pointed out that income represented only a part of the production from the land. As a national average for 1956, the most consistent among many Communist versions assigned 68.5 per cent of the gross production of the co-operatives to be the income distributed to the members, after deducting 6.5 per cent for taxes and 25.0 per cent for collective expenditures including production costs, management expenses, and funds for capital accumulation and membership welfare. This 68.5 per cent of the total output was equivalent to a per capita income of 580 catties of food grains in 1956, as compared with 521 catties in 1952, thus showing an increase in per capita income of 11.3 per cent since land reform.[34]

Another set of Communist figures, comparing the income of 1956 to that of 1949, allowed only 60 per cent of the national total agricultural output as the peasants' net income. In monetary terms, the per capita net income of the peasants was 42 yuan in 1949 and 66 yuan in 1956, registering an increase of 24 yuan or 57.4 per cent.[35] While this set of figures gave no explanation for allowing 60 per cent of the ouput as net income, its monetary figures are useful for studying the regional and group variations of income.

What did the 66 yuan per capita peasant income mean in terms of the actual standard of living? A general picture can be obtained from one of the few factual cases given in Communist publications, the expense record of a Li family in a co-operative in the central-south province of Hunan in 1955.[36] This family of six members spent a total of 301 yuan (about $92 United States currency) or 50 yuan a person in that year for the following items: husked rice, 2,310 catties at a total cost of 174.9 yuan; melon, 800 catties at 10.6 yuan; cooking oil, 24 catties at 13.44 yuan; salt, 60 catties at 9 yuan; pork, 40 catties at 18.4 yuan; bean curd and salted beans, 3.6 yuan; sugar, 2 catties at .96 yuan; soy bean and vermicelli, 5.3 yuan; gourmet powder, 1.5 yuan; cloth, 72 Chinese feet (or 12 Chinese feet per person) at 28.8 yuan; stockings, 6 pairs at 3 yuan; rubber shoes, 1 pair at 4.5 yuan; expense for production, 12 yuan (private sideline production); and medical expenses, 12 yuan.

This listing of expenses represented a comfortable standard of peasant living which could be bought at the cost of 50 yuan per capita in Hunan and adjacent central-southern provinces and would be similar to the middle peasant's standard in pre-Communist Nanching. Considering the differences in prices and local standard of living, a similar standard of living could be had for about 10 yuan more per capita in South China and the Northeast and for 10 yuan less in North China.[37] If the average peasant throughout the country made about 60 yuan per person in 1956, his standard of living would be comparable to that of the well-to-do middle peasant, and he would definitely fare better than before collectivization.

However, since the figures for national average per capita income were not accompanied by any standard deviation or other associated statistical information, and therefore could represent a wide range of individual variations which would seriously affect its representative character, we should examine the regional differences.

In Lungchi county of Fukien Province, one of the high-output and high-income localities in South China, the average per capita income in 1956 was 99.3 yuan, and the per capita cost for an average comfortable peasant living was 80 yuan. There was a surplus of some 20 yuan per head or 100 yuan per family of five. In the eastern coastal province of Kiangsu, the per capita income for 1956 varied greatly among its 83 counties: over 100 yuan in two counties, 70 to 99 yuan in 23 counties, 50 to 69 yuan in 16 counties, 20 to 49 yuan in 14 counties, and only 19.5 yuan in one county. In view of the fact that in order to have a living comparable to that of the Li family it would take between 50 to 79 yuan per head, depending on the locality, a good number of the counties had an insufficient per capita income. In the northern province of Shensi the average per capita income also differed widely: 125.7 yuan in the industrial crop (mainly cotton) region containing 15.3 per cent of the province's rural population, 42.8 yuan in the hilly region containing 34.6 per cent of the province's rural population, and 15.6 yuan in the poor mountain region containing 8.7 per cent of the province's rural population. Since it would cost about 40 to 50 yuan per person to have a tolerable life in this province, it is apparent that a substantial portion of the rural population were unable to meet their minimum economic needs.[38]

These regional figures of income, like the national averages, embodied a range of individual cases varying from the well-to-do to the destitute poor. The Yenpei district of Shensi Province, where the minimum cost of living was around 40 yuan per capita, furnishes an example. Here in 1956, according to a Communist investigation of 2,926 co-operatives with over 1.5 million members, about 550,000 peasants or 37.0 per cent of the membership had an average per capita income of more than 40 yuan, about 370,000 or 25.3 per cent had an average income of less than 17 yuan, and 40,000 or 2.7 per cent, an income below 10 yuan.[39] In other words, in this region roughly a third of the co-operative members received an income adequate to meet the minimum needs of life.

A very interesting case study is a Communist report on nineteen co-operatives in Anyang county of Honan Province in 1956. The locality was free of natural calamities in that year, and the nineteen co-operatives were picked from grain-producing areas, industrial crop areas, and poor mountain areas. The accompanying table is a stratified comparison between average per capita income and average per capita expenditure in the years of 1955 and 1956.[40] The table shows that in 1955 all groups from the poor peasants to the upper-middle peasants had a financial deficit, and that in 1956, while the poor peasants were still unable to make ends meet, all the other groups seemed to have received an income slightly in excess of their expenditure. Expenditure figures

TABLE 1

	1955		1956		Per cent change between 1955 and 1956	
Status	Per capita income (yuan)	Per capita expenditure (yuan)	Per capita income (yuan)	Per capita expenditure (yuan)	Per capita income	Per capita expenditure
Poor peasants	39.52	44.65	51.84	55.60	+31.17	+24.60
New lower-middle peasants	48.82	54.40	61.38	58.80	+25.72	+ 8.10
New upper-middle peasants	53.73	57.46	63.41	61.50	+18.01	+ 7.04
Former lower-middle peasants	54.59	56.64	62.07	60.40	+14.85	+ 6.65
Former upper-middle peasants	51.00	57.20	59.08	61.45	+15.85	+ 7.45
Former rich peasants	41.19	—	56.45	—	+37.04	—
Former landlords	37.39	—	52.12	—	+39.39	—
General average	49.53	—	59.63	—	+20.30	—

were not given for former rich peasants and landlords, but judging from their income figures, their average expenditures could only be in the range of the poor peasants. It is interesting to note that these two groups received the largest percentage increase in their income in 1956, the year of wholesale collectivization.

Since the income figures were averages for entire classes, the fact that an entire class showed an increase does not preclude the possibility that some members suffered a decrease. For instance, in this area the average per capita income in 1956 as compared with that in 1955 showed an increase for 74.74 per cent of the poor peasants, no change for 20.08 per cent, and a decrease for 5.17 per cent. The corresponding percentages for former upper-middle peasants were 62.13, 19.73, and 18.14.[41] For the nation as a whole, comparing the per capita incomes in 1956 with those of 1955, the Communists claimed that 75.50 per cent of all peasants enjoyed an increase, 14.72 saw no change, and 9.87 suffered a decrease.[42]

To sum up, if we accept the Communist figures at their face value, the co-operatives brought improvement in income to the peasants in certain regions and at certain economic levels, but a large portion of the peasants in general still had difficulty meeting their minimum economic requirements. Thus, about 25 to 30 per cent of the nation's peasants were said to be leading a well-to-do middle peasant's life, 15 per cent were poor peasants still suffering from cold and hunger, and the remaining 55 to 60 per cent ranged between the two extremes.[43]

Granting that extensive agricultural improvements such as water conservancy and increase of double-crop areas brought certain gains to the national farm output under collectivization, it still remains to estimate how much of those gains went to increase the income of the peasants. If it can be assumed that in 1957 somewhat less than one-third of the peasantry in the nation received a satisfactory income, and that the income for the rest was still too small to offer a satisfactory or even tolerable living, it is then necessary to examine the factors that have claimed part of the agricultural output against the peasants' income.

A major claim on the peasants' production has always been taxes paid to the government. Communist sources of information have disclosed no consistent figures or any clear picture as to how much taxes the peasants as members of co-operatives have paid to the state. Communist sources have stated that the principal agricultural tax amounted to 10.7 per cent of the nation's total agricultural output in 1956, as against 13.2 per cent in 1952, showing a lightening of taxes under collectivization.[44] The computation of another Communist source put the agricultural tax in 1956 at only 8.3 per cent of the nation's grain output.[45] But these figures did not include the local surtax, which varied from 15 to 20 per cent of the principal tax according to localities and in certain places was even higher. These figures of both principal tax and surtax were percentages of agricultural output and not of the peasants' total income, which included agricultural and subsidiary production. As a national average in 1956, the taxes took 6.5 to 7.0 per cent of the nation's total agricultural and subsidiary production, but this national average, even if accepted at its face value, contained wide local variations. In 1956 the percentage of the total income from agricultural and subsidiary production going into taxes was 12.7 for 121 higher co-operatives in Chiahsing Special District of Chekiang Province, but it was from 7.0 to 9.0 per cent in Haining, Yühang, and Wukang in the same province.[46] These and similar sample figures from different localities suggest that 10 per cent of the co-operatives' income might be a more representative figure for taxes.

A heavier share taken away from income was the cost of production, which included production costs and management expenses such as salaries for the administrative personnel. A survey of 26,935 co-operatives in different parts of the country in 1956 showed that the average cost of production was 25.3 per cent of the co-operatives' total income, with local variations ranging from 14.5 per cent in the efficient co-operatives, and 20.93 per cent for those with medium efficiency, to 30.1 per cent for those with low efficiency.[47] Communist sources furnished no itemized analysis of these composite figures of costs of production. While cost items such as seed, fertilizer, and tools had been traditional expenses in the old family farm, management expenses were distinctly new burdens. Management expenses could be rather heavy payments to the administrative cadres who performed no physical labor, as could be inferred from the substantial reduction of the total cost of production by several suburban co-operatives in Peking after drastically reducing the administrative personnel.

Another cost item connected with operation of the co-operative was the funds for capital accumulation and for membership welfare such as subsidies for orphans and widows and families having low labor earning power. This generally took about 5 per cent of the co-operative's total income.[48]

If it can be generally assumed that of the total agricultural and subsidiary production of a co-operative about 10 per cent went for taxes, 25 per cent for production cost, and 5 per cent for public funds, then about 60 per cent of the total output was retained as income to be distributed to the peasant members. In localities where surtaxes were high and the co-operatives were saddled with excessive management costs, only about 50 per cent of the total output went for income for the members. On the other hand, when these cost items were low, the peasants would get about 70 per cent of the output.[49]

Inadequate as these figures are, it is interesting to compare them with pre-Communist conditions. One Communist source stated that during the period 1931–1936 land rent and government taxes accounted for about 36 per cent of the peasants' income from agricultural and subsidiary production, excluding costs to the peasants in the forms of usury and commercial exploitation by grain merchants.[50] This gave the peasants an income of about 64 per cent of their total production, before deducting costs of production, an income which compared closely with what the peasants received under collectivization. Comparing these national averages with pre-Communist Nanching as a southern suburban village, the net income under collectivization represented a gain for the tenant farmers but a setback for the owner farmer, as the tenants kept only about 50 per cent of the gross yield after deducting rent and costs of production, with the land owner paying the taxes, but the owner-farmer kept about 80 per cent of the gross income after deducting taxes and costs of production. What makes it difficult to draw a clear-cut comparison is the fact that in pre-Communist Nanching a majority of the villagers were neither pure tenants nor pure owner-farmers but a combination of the two. If we may venture a guess, for these peasants their pre-Communist net income as a percentage of their gross output compared very closely with the 60–70 per cent range under the co-operatives.

In addition to taxes and costs of production, including the newly imposed management expenses, another factor affecting the peasants' income was the compulsory delivery of agricultural products to the government at low prices, a situation common to all Communist states practicing agricultural collectivization. The basic reason for this practice was the state's vast needs for grain and agricultural commodities at a low price so that industrialization could be accomplished without disturbing the price equilibrium by inflation. Without political compulsion, peasants obviously would not part with their grain for prices lower than obtainable in a free market, which still existed to a limited extent in spite of rigid government control and nationalization of commerce. This was clearly indicated in Communist statements such as the following:

> . . . the principle and policy . . . consists, on the one hand, of stepping up agricultural production, that is, immediate introduction of socialist transformation and technical reform of agriculture to increase grain output rapidly so as to ensure the needs arising from growth of the national economy. This is a fundamental way of solving the problem, but *it would take a long time* [italics added] before it can be achieved. On the

other hand, the guiding principle and policy consists in making rational distribution of stocks of grain and regulating the circulation of marketable grain so that the existing stocks of grain can meet the needs of society before agricultural production can be stepped up rapidly. That is to say, purchase and sale of grain should be planned . . . The spontaneity of the peasants is restricted . . . Inasmuch as the state has fixed the quantity of grain to be produced by the peasants and the quantity of grain to be purchased from the peasants, production tasks and sale tasks are assigned to the peasants who are under obligation to fulfill these tasks, thereby obliging the peasants to interest themselves in the socialist construction of the country.[51]

Under this policy, the peasants were required to deliver at government prices 80 to 90 per cent of the *surplus* grains after deducting the needed amount for food consumption for the family, for seed, and for animal feed. The food quota which a family was allowed to keep for its own consumption was figured on a per capita basis, which varied with the types of staples in different regions, the individual's age, and whether his occupation involved heavy physical labor. In the rice region this per capita quota ranged from 264 to 660 catties a year, with an average of about 450 catties. In the North, where the climate is colder and the staples consist mainly of millet and *kaoliang* (giant millet), the average could be about a hundred catties above this.[52] With the quota of grain for home consumption rigidly fixed, it was clear that the government intended to extract the maximum amount of surplus from the peasants' output, and that the co-operatives were an important means of achieving, through collective control, disposition of the production from the land.

The Communist policy of "unified purchase and unified sales" was instituted in 1953, the beginning of the first five-year plan. Since then, how much grain was thus extracted from the countryside? We have the figures in the accompanying tabulation for the country as a whole (in 100 million catties of grain).[53] As widespread protests against the com-

	1954–55	*1955–56*	*1956–57*
Total output	3,390	3,679	3,855
State taxes and purchase	1,078	1,041	994
Sold back to rural areas	494	405	490
Net grain taken out of rural areas	584	636	504
Net grain taken out as percentage to total output	17.2	17.3	13.1

pulsory delivery system rose in the country, the Communists pointed to these figures as evidence that the net amount of grain removed from the countryside was not excessive, that it was decreased in 1956–57, and that the government also sold back at low prices to the countryside almost one-half of what was taxed and purchased so as to help rural families that produced insufficient grain for home consumption.[54] It was further pointed out that a sizable part of the agricultural products collected was spent for the benefit of the peasants in the form of agricultural improvements, education, health, and communications.[55]

While these arguments had merit, they did not succeed in reducing the peasants' dislike for the system of compulsory delivery and the cooperatives as an instrument of this policy. For the impoverished peasants there was realistic meaning only in their actual share after deducting taxes and state purchase, a per capita amount which was said to be 549 catties in 1954–55, 577 catties in 1955–56, and 620 catties in 1956–57 [56] and which did not leave much margin beyond the estimated minimum per capita grain consumption of about 450 catties in the rice region and 550 catties in the wheat region. Judging from Communist statistics that 18.43 per cent of some 110,000,000 farm households in 1955 were poor peasants without enough food to eat, and that about 30 per cent of them had surplus grain for hoarding and speculation, it is possible that about 50 per cent of the peasant households had little or no surplus, and that nearly one-fifth of them were in want, despite the contrary claim that 62.36 per cent of them belonged to the grain-surplus category.[57]

What had made the peasants restive, of course, was the price paid by the government for the delivered grain. Communist sources of information pictured the government prices as fair and satisfactory on three grounds. First, government prices had shown a percentage increase every year since 1952. Second, while agricultural prices had gone up 48.76 per cent in 1950–56, prices of industrial goods had come down 27.89 per cent. Third, after deducting the costs of production and taxes, the government prices in 1957 gave the producers a profit of 31.41 per cent for each catty of soy bean, 21.45 per cent for corn, 34.62 per cent for kaoliang, and 54.18 per cent for rice.[58] But no Communist source has provided information on the actual prices paid by the government for agricultural products, thus making impossible any comparison with the free market prices before 1953 or with pre-Communist prices. Despite the Communist charge that the peasants demanded speculation prices for their grain, whether the prices were satisfactory to the peasants could be inferred from popular reaction toward them.

After inauguration of the compulsory delivery system in 1953, there arose a general complaint among the peasants: "Government purchase has no limit, and it serves no purpose to increase production." [59] Hoarding of grain became a common practice. Even Chou En-lai admitted: "But we also made mistakes. In 1954, because we did not completely grasp the situation of grain production in the whole country, and purchased a little more grain from the peasants than we should have, there was discontent among a section of the peasants." [60] In spite of the overall increase in crop areas in the country as a whole since 1952, as indicated in Communist statistics, the crop area in many localities saw a decrease as a result of the peasants' discontent over compulsory delivery. In Ssu-hui county of Kwangtung Province, about 80 miles south of Nanching, the planted area of early crop was reduced from 36,000 mow in 1955 to 24,000 mow in the spring of 1956, a reduction of 38.2 per cent, owing mainly to the peasants' complaint that what they harvested did not belong to them.[61]

There is no information as to what effective steps were taken after 1956 to remedy this situation aside from an assertion from Mao Tse-tung:

> We are prepared to maintain, in several years, the quantity of food grains collected and purchased at the level of over 80 billion catties (about 21 per cent of the 1957 total output) so that agriculture will be developed, co-operatives will be consolidated, some households which are short of food grains at present will not be short of food grains, all peasant households, except those in the industrial crop areas, will be turned into self-sufficient households . . .[62]

Still another factor affecting the peasants' income was the reduction of subsidiary production under collectivization. The weight of this factor lay in the traditional importance of subsidiary occupations as a supplement to the main crop income in an agrarian economy troubled by shortage of land, a situation which continued under collectivization, as attested by the Communist statement: "In China, the income of peasants from subsidiary occupations has always reached around one-third of their income." [63] This average, of course, embodied a wide variation of local conditions. In the Northeast, where land is comparatively plentiful, subsidiary occupations did not account for as heavy a share of the peasants' total income as they did in China Proper. Again, in suburban villages such as Nanching subsidiary occupations had only limited importance because of the proximity to seasonal urban employment and sizable emigrants' remittances. But in Chiahsing Special District of Chekiang Province in 1956 side occupations accounted for 50 yuan or 14.3 per cent of 350 yuan, the total average annual income of a peasant family. A survey of fourteen co-operatives in Kiangsu

Province in 1957 revealed that side occupations contributed 50 to 60 per cent to the total income in the northern part of the province and 40 to 50 per cent in the southern part.[64]

It is therefore apparent that partial or complete removal of this source of income would result in serious economic crisis for the peasant family unless the lost income were counterbalanced by a corresponding increase of income from the main crop. It is also apparent that, even granting a certain increase in main crop production from technical improvements under collectivization, any major setback in subsidiary occupations would lead to a net reduction of the total income of the peasants. This was evidenced in actual cases occasionally mentioned in Communist sources. In the Yungming Co-operative in Tunghsiang county of Kiangsi Province in 1956, when the number of subsidiary occupations in which its members used to engage was forcibly reduced in the process of "simplification of production," 45 per cent of its members had their income reduced despite the fact that its rice crop showed an increased output of 39.4 per cent over 1955.[65] Many were the cases in various parts of the country in which interference with subsidiary occupations by the Communist leaders in the co-operatives led to a decline in the peasants' income.

Subsidiary production suffered a widespread drop in the country, particularly during 1955 and 1956, chiefly because of two reasons: the shortage of capital and forcible suppression by the cadres. After collectivization, co-operatives were under pressure to concentrate all available financial and labor resources to fulfill assigned quotas of main crop production, thus leaving little investment for subsidiary occupations. An important point in the situation was that, since subsidiary occupations were generally taken up by the family as a private enterprise, when peasants found their total income decreased under collectivization and turned to subsidiary production they diverted available labor force in the co-operative from crop production, which was the main preoccupation of the cadres directing the co-operatives. Hence the cadres gave no encouragement to subsidiary production and even forcibly suppressed such activities in certain cases. Some peasants who busied themselves with side-line enterprises to the neglect of regular production in the co-operative were harshly handled and made to recant their "mistake" in public.[66]

The consequence of such action was, of course, a drastic reduction in subsidiary production. Silk and tea, leading items of subsidiary production in the past, showed a precipitous drop. The nation's production of silk cocoons was 4,416,000 tan (1 tan equals 100 catties or 133 pounds) in 1931, but only 1,625,000 tan in 1957. The nation's tea production in 1932 was 4,500,000 tan, but the estimate for 1957 was only 2,525,000 tan.[67] An interesting example is provided by the history of a co-operative consisting of 368 households in Mach'eng county in Hupei Province. In 1948, the year before the Communists came to power, the income from subsidiary occupations among these families totaled 42,000 yuan; this amount was reduced to 28,000 yuan in 1951, 26,000 in 1953, and finally to 14,000 yuan in 1955, the year when the families were pooled into a co-operative.[68]

One of the significant effects of the reduction of the peasants' income due to serious decline in subsidiary production was the heavy exodus of peasants from the countryside in many parts of China in 1955 and 1956. A Communist official report pointed out that in Kweip'ing county of Kwangsi Province decline in subsidiary production caused a mass exodus of peasants and created such a labor shortage that the spring plowing of 1956 reached only 40 per cent of the planned crop area. A traditionally important subsidiary occupation in that county was the collection of seeds from wild camellias for the pressing of oil. In 1955, because of interference from the cadres, the seeds were allowed to rot on the ground.[69] Owing to the same cause, only 35 per cent of the labor force remained in the co-operatives in Wuch'uan county in Kwangtung Province; the rest left for other places in search of a living.[70] For China as a whole, the decrease in income, whether due specifically to decline in subsidiary occupations or to a combination of other causes, was largely responsible for the fact that, from 1953 to 1957, over 8,000,000 peasants drifted to the cities, causing Communist authorities to adopt measure after measure to disperse them back to the countryside.[71]

The unsatisfactory state of the co-operatives led not only to exodus of peasants from the countryside but also to extensive withdrawals from and disbandment of co-operatives during the last months of 1956 and the first half of 1957, a spontaneous movement that seemed to affect more southern provinces than northern ones. There are no published nationwide statistics on this issue, but local figures occasionally found in Communist sources, although inadequate for analysis, reflected the extensiveness of the peasants' dissatisfaction with collectivization in many parts of the country.

Thus in May 1957 Communist authorities in Kwangtung Province reported that since the last part of 1956, 117,916 peasant households had walked out of co-operatives in the province, and that 102,149 households later rejoined, leaving a net loss of 15,767 households.[72] The number of affected peasant households in proportion to the total

households was given in the case of Hsienchu county of Chekiang
Province. In this county, during April and May of 1957, the proportion
of collectivized farm households to all farm households dropped precipitously from 95 per cent to 16 per cent, amounting to a general
dissolution of the co-operatives. It was stated that some 30,000 households had returned to the co-operatives by the fall of 1957, raising the
proportion of collectivized households among all households to over
70 per cent, which was still some 25 per cent below the previous proportion of 95 per cent.[73] There was no available information as to how
representative this case might be in comparison with other affected
localities. The rise of collectivized farm households among all farm
households from 92 per cent in 1956 to 97 per cent in 1957 in China
as a whole seemed to suggest that the infectious movement of withdrawals and disbandment was not allowed to take its spontaneous
course, but that effective pressure herded the disaffected peasants back
into the co-operatives.

It was obvious that herding the peasants back into the co-operatives
did not guarantee the continued stability of the collective organization
unless the basic causes of its instability were removed. Communist discussions on this issue laid the blame for the withdrawals and disbandment mainly on the incitement by "unlawful landlords, rich peasants
and counterrevolutionaries," who demanded selling less surplus grain
to the government and distributing more among the co-operatives'
members, and who resented the collective system in general.[74] But the
extensive following for these arguments among middle and poor
peasants indicated a general dissatisfaction with the co-operatives beyond the confine of the minority of former landlords, rich peasants,
and counterrevolutionaries who had led in voicing it.

The base of peasant dissatisfaction was the inadequacy of income for
a large section of the co-operatives' membership. Taxes, the compulsory
delivery system, management expenses of the co-operative, and suppression of subsidiary occupations in the interest of the state's demand
for increased production of main crops all laid claims on the total
output of the co-operative against the personal income of the members.
Communist discussions recognized this situation and termed it a contradiction of interests between the state, the co-operative organization,
and the peasants.[75] Viewed in terms of organizational stability of the
co-operative, the situation involved a contradiction of goals. As the co-
operative was a newly enacted organization unsupported by the inertia
of tradition, the peasants were willing to remain in it only so long
as its goals were tangible in relation to their immediate personal in-

terests. The interests of the state and the collective organization sounded vague and distant to a peasantry whose minds were still concerned largely with the small local world and the family, and whose economic status still rested on a narrow margin between subsistence and deprivation. Even if collectivization were able to effect a certain increase in agricultural production, curtailment of personal income as a share of the output would remove the main incentive of tangible benefits which alone could successfully integrate the peasants to the co-operative organization.

The Communist leadership, fully aware of this situation, tried to resolve it by various means. By stabilizing the amount of grain to be taxed and purchased by the government to an absolute level of about 80 billion catties for the nation, they aimed at distributing a larger share of the increased production to the members so as to provide incentive for raising production in the co-operatives. The original target was to distribute 60 to 70 per cent of the total output to the members. A more liberalized policy toward subsidiary production was adopted in 1957, organizing certain subsidiary enterprises on a collective basis while leaving certain others to the peasants as private family undertakings. It was stated that, in Lin-an county of Chekiang Province, when subsidiary occupations were revived in 1956, 106 out of 146 co-operatives were able to give 90 per cent of their members an increase of income over the previous year.[76]

Political pressure and propaganda were employed along with other policies to stabilize the co-operatives. In 1957 there was the nationwide anti-rightist movement which, in the countryside, was aimed at suppressing articulate well-to-do peasants and other minority elements who led the movement of withdrawal from the co-operatives. There was the "great socialist debate," intended to convince the poor and lower middle peasants of the superiority of the co-operative organization over the small family farm, an argument supported by some cases of poor peasants who withdrew from the co-operatives only to find themselves at the mercy of usurers and "exploiters" who employed them as hired hands.[77] Whether the new policies of increasing the peasants' income, suppressing opposition, and strengthening propaganda efforts were able to stabilize the collective system remains uncertain.

CHAPTER XVII

Organizational Problems of the Agricultural Producers' Co-operatives

BASIC TO the organizational problems of collectivization was the sudden integration of the small family farm into a large operational unit totally strange to the peasants' knowledge of group life and to their traditional sense of self-interest. A wide range of problems arose from the very factor of size of the collective organization.

The 1,088,000 co-operatives in the spring of 1956 had an average of 50 farm households per unit of the elementary type and 250 households per unit of the advanced type.[1] By the spring of 1957 a vast majority of the elementary co-operatives had been consolidated into the much larger advanced types, and some of the oversized advanced co-operatives were reduced somewhat in membership, with the result that the number of co-operatives totaled 752,113, averaging 158.1 farm households per co-operative.[2] In the majority of cases, "one village– one co-operative" became a general guiding principle, although a large village might contain more than one co-operative and several small villages in close proximity might form one co-operative.[3] On the basis of five persons to the household, a co-operative of 158.1 households would contain approximately 800 persons. Although these are averages embodying a range of sizes, it seems likely that the village af Nanching, with its 230 families and about 1,100 population, was transformed into one large co-operative.

Structurally, as of 1957, the collective organization was subdivided into two levels: the family at the base was responsible for "mobilizing the labor force"; the production teams, consisting of about 20 farm households each, were the operational units for specific tasks of agricultural production. There were subdivisions of unspecified size for subsidiary production. The central administrative committee of the co-operative exercised unified management over the production teams on matters such as the use of means of production, production plans, capital construction, technical measures, raising of funds, distribution of labor power, labor point norms, distribution plans, and fiscal and accounting system.[4] In 1957, production teams were found to be hampered by excessively rigid control from the administrative committee and were granted limited authority over production plans, technical measures, work norms, and fiscal work.[5]

This structural picture more accurately reflected the policy of the Communist authorities on the co-operatives' organization than it reflected the actual situation, which differed widely with individual co-operatives and localities. In view of the many directives issued on the subject, it was probable that the functioning of the organizational system had not yet become stabilized. Since effective administrative power lay solely in the hands of the Communist cadres assigned to lead the co-operatives, administrative committees had interfered unduly and unwisely with production teams, the basic operational units. On the other hand, the Communists had been hesitant about giving the production teams too much autonomy for fear of disrupting the unity of management of the co-operative.

The relationship between the individual peasant and the co-operative was similarly beset with serious transitional problems arising from the abrupt rearrangement of economic relations from that of the small family farm to that of the large collective organization. In the close personal relationships of the small family farm, the economic organization was carefully and flexibly geared to the personal needs of a limited number of members, and the simplicity and intimate nature of the family enabled each member to clearly see family welfare as the group goal and the relation of his own interest to that goal. Furthermore, these and other less apparent relationships between the individual and family interests had been stabilized by a system of traditional values pertaining to the family as a socio-economic base of life. The family group, therefore, was a well-integrated working team in which everyone knew his production role and understood the significance of every production act, and in which all available labor and material resources were used to carry on the common undertaking of the family farm.

In the process of collectivization, the individual was suddenly wrenched from this well-knit matrix and thrown into a large organization of 800 or even a thousand people whose goal of group welfare appeared only intangibly related to the individual's interest. Moreover, whereas in the functioning of the family farm there was a low degree of personnel differentiation in matters such as production plans, use of tools, distribution of financial and labor resources, enforcement of work norms, and fiscal and accounting system, in the co-operative these tasks became operations of specialized functionaries, thus reducing the average peasants to mechanical laborers tilling the soil and decreasing their personal involvement with the total operation of the farm. It is not difficult to see why there was lack of understanding and personal concern for the proper functioning of the co-operative on the part of the family–farm-minded peasants, and why in many localities the family subsidiary production and the family vegetable plots thrived while the co-operative fields were poorly worked. In one co-operative in Tseng-ch'eng county of Kwangtung Province, Communist officials found the majority of the members preoccupied with their family vegetable plots and such side-line enterprises as sugar making, with only a small minority working on the winter crop of the co-operative and on repairing dikes, so that the co-operative lagged behind its production quota.[6]

The difficulty of adjustment by the family–farm-minded peasants to the impersonal and specialized operation of the collective organization was vividly shown in the case of a co-operative in Hsin-an village in Hun-yuan county of Shansi Province.[7] This co-operative had only 17 farm households in 1953 but grew to 127 households in 1955, accounting for 83.5 per cent of all households in the village. After 1953 the yield per mow in the co-operative decreased and the crop acreage shrank, the main causes of the set-back being general demoralization of the members, especially among the middle peasants, and the high death rate of their sheep. Since in this locality raising sheep furnished a major subsidiary income for the peasants and supplied manure as fertilizer for the village's fields, the Communist cadres had organized co-operative flocks herded into co-operative sheds. The result was loss of interest in sheep raising. When ewes were dropped, they frequently froze to death because of inadequate care. Before 1937 the village had over 600 head of sheep; there were only 241 in 1955. The number of "loads" of sheep manure per mow of crop land was 5.7 in 1953, 4.3 in 1954, and 3.6 in 1955.

An old peasant, Wu Fu, expressed his opinion on this stiuation: "When sheep were raised at home, they did not need any labor from the adults, for the children would take care of them. Under the children's loving care, the sheep grew fat and strong, with few deaths. Whatever food scraps could be spared in the family were fed to the sheep. Now a co-operative flock needs specially assigned labor, and there is a high rate of disease and death among the flocks." Subsequently, the co-operative flock was disbanded, the sheep were returned to the owners, and the peasants' morale showed improvement.

In this case, we see the contrast between personal care of the family flock and impersonal labor in a co-operative flock; we see the meticulous economy with which sheep were raised at home and the requirement of special labor and investment in the collective arrangement; we see the lack of identification of the members' personal interests with the collective goal; we see the ignorance among members about the proper procedures of operating a large organization, and we see the adverse effect of all these on the productivity of the land. This same set of factors led to the poor condition and high death rate of draft animals in localities where they were placed under centralized feeding and care,[8] a situation that reduced the farming efficiency of a large number of co-operatives.

The adjustment of the peasants to the new economic relations and operational procedures was complicated not only by the nature of the peasant himself but also by the comparative inflexibility of the co-operatives in relation to the needs of the individual members. In a family farm, labor and financial resources were arranged to meet the general as well as the particular needs of all members, and in an emergency even land or capital equipment could be sold to tide over an individual or family crisis. But the large co-operative farm was structurally adjusted to the standardized needs of the extensive membership, leaving the individual to shift for himself to satisfy his particular personal needs; the use of labor and financial resources in a co-operative was governed by uniform regulations, and could not be arranged to suit personal needs of individual members. The standardized collective system might work among a people having moderate savings to meet particular individual or family needs, but it proved difficult for a peasantry living largely from hand to mouth, as evidenced by the peasants' complaints about the inflexibility of the co-operatives and many cases of borrowing and overdrawing from the co-operative by poor peasants which impaired the financial operation of the co-operatives.[9]

At another level, the sudden establishment of some three-quarters of a million collective organizations introduced the universal problem of availability of leadership adequately trained in the new organizational concepts and operational techniques. Administrative leaders of the co-operatives fell into two categories: progressive peasants, and Communist leaders with some modern education. Leaders with peasant backgrounds had the merit of knowing the practical business of farming but suffered from the disadvantage of ignorance in operating a large organization. Those with an intellectual background generally lacked any knowledge of farming and often were plagued by bureaucratism and the old intellectual tradition of disdaining physical labor or practical work.

Indicative of technical and administrative incompetence among large numbers of co-operative leaders was the official campaign against their "waste and extravagance" in operating collective organizations during 1954–1956. Such waste and extravagance consisted mainly of unnecessary large outlays for headquarters buildings, clubhouses and expensive furnishings, nursery toys, playgrounds, investments in sports and cultural programs, electrical wiring in suburban villages, costly and not urgently needed modern farm implements. Expenditures for these items often exceeded the total liquid capital assets and available labor resources of a co-operative, and were defrayed by loans which sank many co-operatives into financial insolvency.[10] In Tz'u-hsi county of Chekiang Province 19.9 per cent of 640 co-operatives were reported to have committed serious waste.[11] Such practices seemed to have abated in 1957 after Communist official efforts to curb them.

In the highly mixed record of performance of the urban-bred cadres there was another serious shortcoming — what the Communists called bureaucratism. Although the Communists gave it no definition, we take it to mean confinement by the administrator to the formalistic activities of paper work and applying rules and regulations, thus isolating himself from the actual situation under his charge and from the membership under his command. It was well illustrated by the case of Changli county in Hainan Island in Kwangtung Province.[12] At the beginning of 1956 the co-operatives in that county set a target to increase agricultural production by 118 per cent. When higher authorities examined the actual situation before spring planting, they discovered that collected fertilizer amounted to three catties per mow, only a fraction of the needed quantity, and that only 1.2 per cent of the projected water-conservancy work had been completed. It appeared that the local officers had made production plans not by studying production data in the field but by holding meetings in the office, and then had continued to confine themselves to the office to receive false reports of operational results on which they based the "conclusions" they handed to superior authorities.

The lack of contact between leadership and members in co-operatives was vividly seen in a number of cases. To stimulate production, large numbers of co-operatives in Kwangtung Province took the label,

"Thousand-catty Co-operative," signifying their goal of raising the annual production of rice to one thousand catties per mow. In 1956 cadres gave such labels to eleven co-operatives in Tseng-ch'eng county, about 60 miles south of Nanching. An investigation revealed that on the eve of spring planting no effort had been made to collect fertilizer, and that most members were completely ignorant of the fact that their co-operative carried the "Thousand-catty" label.[13]

These two illustrations are reminiscent of the classical scholar-official personality who, disdaining physical labor and reluctant to participate in actual operations with the common people, was inclined to conduct his life and work in an office, relying solely upon subordinates and retainers; and in this context it is interesting to note that, with the rapidly expanding system of modern education turning out more graduates than could be absorbed in urban employment, an increasing number of them were being sent to the countryside. In 1957 alone, over two million graduates from middle and elementary schools were sent to rural areas,[14] a large proportion of them being assigned jobs in the three-quarters of a million co-operatives in the country. If these new graduates adjusted to the rigorous hardship of rural life, they might have proven useful to the co-operatives in performing jobs requiring modern administrative and technical skills and eventually become administrative leaders. On the other hand, if these "cultured peasants" should have become critical of the way the cadres ran the co-operatives, or come into conflict with them, or be unable to bear the hardships of rural life, they might have become the articulate core of latent restive forces and function as a disruptive influence in the co-operatives. The shortage of effective leadership was undoubtedly at the root of the problem of proper functioning and cohesion of the co-operative organization.

When we consider the day-to-day working-level performance of the co-operatives in contrast to the functioning of the farm as a family affair, where administrative decisions were the result of informal interaction in an intimate family circle, with the performance of tasks by each member of the family team guided by the traditionalized routine, and the distribution of reward based on personal needs and the status system, we find that the complex problems of an organization consisting of some 800 members required new operational facilities.

Prominent among such needs was a system of bookkeeping and accounting, a problem which troubled the operation of many mutual-aid teams, and which had become more serious in the larger organization of co-operatives. The majority of peasants were traditionally

ignorant of such skills; and apparently there were not enough educated leaders in each co-operative to perform such tasks in every subunit
of the collective organization. In a co-operative in Wu-hsiang county of
Shansi Province, many of the production team leaders were illiterate
peasants who could not write names or figures. Others who were barely
literate were extremely casual about keeping accounts as required of
them by the new regulations because they were ignorant of the practical
function of this new task. Some of them put the accounts on paper fans
they happened to be using, and others jotted them down on bits of scrap
paper. Another co-operative lent 70 yuan to the members, got back 30
yuan, but failed to find the debtors who owed the rest, because of the
absence of accounts. In still another co-operative with about one
hundred member households, even the members themselves did not
remember the exact number of man-day labor units they had each put
in.[15] As man-day labor units were the basis on which remuneration
was distributed to the members, the confusion in the co-operative can
be imagined.

With formal impersonal business relationship in the co-operative
replacing the informal personal relationship of the family farm, there
was obviously required some system of standards of work norms and
man-day labor units, a complex matter governed not only by general
principles but also by local and individual conditions. Communist
authorities had issued guiding principles on the classification of skilled
and unskilled labor, the definition of the work-day labor unit, and the
proper ways of remuneration; but local co-operatives still faced numerous difficulties in working out arrangements satisfactory to the members
and also capable of maintaining work discipline and morale. Even when
the problem of classification of skilled and unskilled labor had been
resolved, the system of labor units often failed to distinguish the industrious from the lazy in the same class of work, thus leading to dissatisfaction among the members. Communist reports indicated that this had
been a frequent complaint from efficient middle peasants and at times
their reasons for withdrawing from the co-operatives.[16]

Presumably, the influx of the millions of new graduates from the
schools into the co-operatives, the vigorous literacy campaigns in the
countryside, and the operation of many technical training classes would
solve many of the problems requiring literacy and skills such as those
required for setting up accounting systems; and such problems as the
establishment of satisfactory work norms and labor units could be
solved through the process of practical adjustment if adequate administrative leadership were available. There was bound to remain over a

considerable period, however, the problem of peasant attitudes and values deeply rooted in the traditional way of life.

It was clear that underlying the problems of effective organization and operation of the co-operatives was a conflict between the new value system and the old. The efficient management of a co-operative inevitably required an impersonal businesslike attitude toward obligations and reward, something lacking in the traditional system. In the old family farm, obligations and reward were defined by a status system and operated on a life-time basis. Beyond the household, the peasant's economic relationships were mainly with relatives and intimate friends, obligations and reward were similarly settled on a long-term basis, and any insistence on immediate return for whatever services performed was considered "calculating" and offensive to the "warm sentiments" that tied the parties together. When the peasant was required to accept an impersonal definition of obligation and the practice of immediate or precisely timed reward under the co-operative arrangement, his reaction was one of calculating self-protection which wholly ignored the common interest of the co-operative group. Moreover, there was the persistently lingering influence of family and clan ties. The successful functioning of the collective organization relied on the uniform application of standardized values and rules to all members regardless of family or clan affiliation, but for the peasant the interests of the co-operative were vague and distant as compared to the realities of family concerns. For him, even though the family farm had been removed, the family continued to be a deeply rooted group of economic interest. When the co-operatives failed to function smoothly and when the individual's interests were not advanced by the large organization, the peasants instinctively reverted to time-tested family ties as a means of carrying on economic activities, as attested to by their preoccupation with subsidiary occupations and family vegetable plots in poorly operated co-operatives.

In concrete form the fundamental issue of reconciling the new with the old was revealed by the efforts made by the co-operatives to satisfy the peasants in the complicated matter of adjusting their differences in economic interests. This involved both the disposition of property belonging to the upper middle and rich peasants and the differential distribution of income among the general membership.

The upper middle peasants, estimated to constitute 20 per cent of the rural population in 1957, lost much in joining the co-operatives. They used to own more land than the average peasants, and now the advantage of land ownership was abolished. Their fish ponds, mulberry patches, orchards, and timber stands were collectivized under the general policy of eliminating private production enterprises, and the compensation they received for these properties was often inadequate and unfair. At times it took the form of collective credit to be paid back over a long period of years.[17] Their feeling that they had not been treated fairly had an adverse effect on the cohesion of the co-operatives. They were essential because they were more efficient farmers than the average,[18] and their numbers were substantial; and their leadership in withdrawal from and disbandment of many co-operatives was a powerfully disruptive influence.

As to the distribution of income, the co-operatives had no previous experience to guide them. Since under the influence of the Communist doctrine there was a general egalitarian mood among the masses, particularly the poor, at first some co-operatives tried equal sharing on a per capita basis. The result was that, as the main income was in the form of food grain, equal sharing gave some households with several young children a surplus of food, while other households with working adults but few or no young children were faced with a food shortage. In the latter case, people had to buy food from the government or took odd jobs for a supplementary income. Some wandered off to other places in search of work, their departure naturally affecting the production of the co-operative and reducing the collective income. A typical case concerned a co-operative in Fangch'eng county in Honan Province. "Under equal distribution of food grain, the hard-working peasants often complained against the households with a number of children, and lost interest in production. For instance, when grain was distributed last autumn [1956], a one-month-old baby of Tso Chun-teh's household shared the same amount of food grain as Chen Chin-yu, another co-operative member. Chen was so angry over it that he refused to work for five days and had a quarrel with Tso Chen-teh." After some discussion, the co-operative members finally agreed to distribute food grain according to need instead of equal sharing.[19]

For most co-operatives the distribution of income was based neither on equal sharing nor on individual needs but on the quantity and quality of labor performed under the system of labor units or points. This system favored families with many working adults and penalized the small families and those with several small children who earned no labor units. The figures in Table 2 show the differential distribution of income in relation to family size in the First and Fourth Higher Co-operatives in Yuch'eng Hsiang, Haiyen county, Chekiang Province.[20] Except for the unspecified category of "others," which seemed

TABLE 2

	No. of house- holds	No. of per- sons	Average no. of persons per house- hold	1956 net income		Per- centage increase in income over 1955
				house- hold (yuan)	per- son (yuan)	
Total	422	1,578	3.7	353.1	94.4	25.0
Poor peasants	68	193	2.8	218.3	76.8	24.3
Lower-middle peasants						
new	59	209	3.5	291.7	82.3	30.1
old	122	412	3.4	337.0	99.8	20.2
Upper-middle peasants						
new	32	142	4.4	436.0	98.2	30.1
old	132	592	4.5	455.9	101.8	26.8
Others	9	30	3.3	184.1	55.2	3.5

to comprise destitute families, the poor peasants had the smallest family size as a correlate to their having the lowest income on both the per family and the per capita bases. The reason could be traced to the man-day labor unit system as the basis of income distribution. This was shown in the case of the First Higher Co-operative of Yuch'eng Hsiang in 1956 (see Table 3). When the number of able-bodied adult workers in a household became the determinant of income, naturally,

TABLE 3

	No. of house- holds	No. of per- sons	Average no. of persons per house- hold	Average no. of labor units per house- hold *	Average no. of work days per household in a year
Total	271	1,269	4.7	16.0	318.6
Poor peasants	32	105	3.3	7.9	166.2
Lower-middle peasants					
new	99	421	4.3	15.3	280.4
old	48	226	4.7	16.6	287.8
Upper-middle peasants					
new	56	265	4.7	20.9	371.8
old	36	252	7.0	23.9	517.8

* Every 10 labor units are considered one standard labor power, or one man-day. Thus, a household capable of performing 16 labor units has 1.6 labor power.

small families received the lowest income. Many of the poor-peasant households consisted of orphans, widows, and other nonworkers weakened by illness. For them the co-operatives were ordered to provide relief from the welfare funds under the so-called five-guarantee system (to be provided with food, clothing, fuel, an education, and a funeral).

There is no information concerning how adequate and how generally available such relief was.

It would appear that under the co-operatives' system of remuneration by labor units peasants would strive for large families. Since the poor peasants were at a disadvantage owing to their inability to support many young children and the prevalence among them of high rates of miscarriage and infant mortality, it would be the well-to-do peasant who would be successful in raising a large family and gaining the progressive advantage of economic betterment. In other words, the situation in the pre-Communist agrarian communities, as exemplified by our observation of Nanching, would seem not only to be perpetuated by the labor-unit system but also accentuated, since the mitigating influence of inheritance for some of the relatively fortunate small families had now been removed by collectivization.

Recapitulating the foregoing analysis, it appears that, through technical improvements, the co-operatives achieved a certain increase in agricultural production both in the total national output and in per unit area productivity for major crops. Much less conclusive is how substantial and how general an increase in income the co-operatives brought the peasants. If the pre-collectivization picture was one in which only 20 to 30 per cent of the peasants had a satisfactory income, while the rest ranged from destitution to bare subsistence, it is doubtful whether this situation was substantially changed up to the beginning of 1958.

Up till that time, the co-operatives had yet to resolve many vital structural problems pertaining to their large size, the supply and functioning of leadership, the establishment of operational norms and facilities, and the differential distribution of income. The disorganized state of a number of co-operatives was indicated by the exodus of peasants to the cities, mass walk-outs and even disbandment of co-operatives in many localities, and the sending of hundreds of thousands of functionaries from all levels of government to the rural areas in the spring of 1957 to correct the shortcomings of some co-operatives and to get some paralyzed ones back into operation.[21] In Fan Ning county, Hainan Island, Kwangtung Province, farm hands in the co-operatives remained idle on the eve of spring planting until the magistrate and the cadres personally went down to the fields and plowed the soil.[22]

Such an unsatisfactory state of collective organization was to be expected in the light of the rapidity of the transformation, and the hastiness with which some 750,000 co-operatives were set up. In the few years 1951 to 1956 the country had precipitously shifted from the small family farm, through the tumultuous land reform and the faltering mutual-aid teams, to sudden collectivization, which was mainly accomplished in the one year of 1956.

Even in an age of revolution, the speed in effecting such momentous change was explosive when we consider the magnitude of the task, involving 500,000,000 tradition-bound peasants and covering some 3,000,000 square miles of highly diversified areas, and the drastic and complex differences between the small family farm and the large collective organization. It is apparent that the time was too brief for properly carrying out the transitional steps such as originally entertained by the Communist leadership. It was claimed that 80 to 90 per cent of the co-operatives established in 1955 were built on the foundation of mutual-aid teams, but an examination of local conditions raises the question of how sound those teams were. In Lanli and Huangp'i counties of Hupei Province, 50 per cent of the mutual-aid teams were reported to be in a disorganized state, and 20 per cent were disbanded.[23] But there is no indication that the vast majority of the co-operatives, set up in 1956, had a firm foundation of mutual-aid teams. Neither had most of the higher types of co-operatives evolved from the lower types.

Transitional difficulties were probably not unexpected to the Communist leadership. Pressed by urgent needs, Mao Tse-tung in 1956 announced his strategy of launching the co-operatives first, regardless of expected difficulties, and correcting their shortcomings by later repeated "rectification campaigns."[24] In 1957, in the face of widespread difficulties and disorganization, he stuck to this decision by declaring that he would allow five or more years to build a good co-operative.[25] The Communist leaders who made this bold decision of sudden national collectivization were seasoned in the shuffling and reshuffling of millions of men into different political and military formations in the gigantic struggle for power which they won; and it is possible that they approached the reshuffling of some 500,000,000 peasants into the collective formation with the same determination and confidence. But men in a deadly political and military struggle are temporarily taken out of the complex context of normal social life and focused on the single objective of winning a contest, whereas men on a farm are subjected to the pressure from a multiplicity of immediate practical problems involved in normal community life. Whether successful political and military experience could be effectively applied to the development of a new form of economic organization, only unfolding events can tell.

Transitional difficulties do not necessarily lead to the conclusion that the entire collectivization movement represents but a mirage from the Marxist-Leninist ideology, a dream which will not be realized on Chinese soil. The excessively small farm unit in the pre-Communist peasant economy, the inefficiently scattered tiny plots, the backward farming methods, the further diminution of the peasants' microscopic income due to the land tenure system, the relentlessly oppressive man-land ratio — all these had long demanded some form of drastic change. In our observations of Nanching, we noted that farming under these conditions failed to provide a majority of the peasants with minimum subsistence without supplementation from urban employment. The widespread existence of this situation underlay the great agrarian crisis in modern China. The most consistently proferred solution has been the application of modern technical improvements; the knotty problem lay in the development of an organizational vehicle to implement it. The technical limitations of the small family farm and its financial stringency in this connection are obvious. The tractor and the harvest combine, the epitome of modern agricultural technology in Chinese eyes, could not even turn around in many of the scattered microscopic plots, not to mention the astronomical financial distance between the peasant's purse and the cost of the mechanical giant.

One of the organizational alternatives is the enlargement of the farm unit through some form of pooling of the land, labor, and material resources so that through collective strength the advantages of modern technology and rational use of land and labor can be brought within range of practicability. It is here that some form of collectivism would find the social foundation on which to grow. Whether this alternative would succeed in China depends on the development of a suitable form of collectivism and a workable transitional strategy to stave off un-manageable chaos and disorganization.

Among the transitional difficulties we have analyzed, two deserve added attention: the heavy agricultural taxes and the system of com-pulsory delivery of products to the government at low prices. These removed a sizable proportion of any possible benefit the new organiza-tion might give its members. They prevented effective demonstration of whatever potential merits the co-operatives might have for the vital problem of increasing production and income for the peasants. True, the policies of taxes and compulsory delivery were designed to meet urgent needs of industrialization, and, in this respect, the Communist leadership was confronted with the hard problem of capital accumula-tion for the economic modernization of a vast country. But to sacrifice heavily for the nation's industrialization, which might motivate the behavior of an intellectual or an enlightened politician, would not easily interest peasants preoccupied with immediate problems of keeping themselves and their families from starvation, and whose mentality had long been conditioned by the tangibility of the organic cycle and the small visible village world. The forcible drain of farm products for a distant cause held no appeal to them and deprived the hastily installed co-operatives of an opportunity to gain cohesion and stability.

These national events impinged upon our little suburban village of Nanching as they did other villages in the rest of the country. Much of our data on collectivization is from Kwangtung Province of which Nanching is a part. Assuming that Nanching had not remained an untouched island in the relentless current of collectivization, the analysis of the situation given in these two chapters would apply generally to conditions in this village.

CHAPTER XVIII

Changing Structure of
the Village Community

WHILE LAND reform and its accompanying political measures have wrought changes in the institutional framework of the village community, the influence from collectivization in this respect is far stronger and much more pervasive. This chapter will summarize the major changes in the structural pattern of the village community caused by collectivization.

The most pronounced structural alteration is the functional replacement of the kinship system by the co-operative farm as the core of the village structure. Previously, family ownership of the means of production and the organization of the family as a production team provided the economic foundation for the traditional system of parental authority and the gerontocratic arrangement of status, the strong family solidarity, and the pervasive importance of the family in the individual's private and public life. Now that the process of collectivization has removed land and major farm equipment from family ownership and replaced the family as the basic production team, it is obvious that the family cannot long maintain its status system, its strong solidarity, and its former position of serving a wide range of economic and social functions.

The system of arranged marriage, a vital factor in the cohesion and stability of the traditional family, was to a considerable extent founded upon economic considerations, and the movement of marriage by free choice of partners had so far failed to penetrate deeply into rural communities largely because of the continued submission of the young to parental economic control. But the abolition of the family farm has altered the parents' production role and reduced their financial authority over the young. This seriously weakens the bulwark against the movement of marriage by free choice of partners and the associated influences from the "family revolution." The enforcement of the new marriage law, highly subversive to the solidarity and stability of the traditional family, has found a powerful alliance in the collectivization of the family farm. Thus, with its functions, status arrangement, and the marriage system seriously affected by collectivization, it would be difficult for the family to continue as the core of the village community structure.

However, the development of these effects on the family system depends on the success of the co-operative farm in giving the peasants a stable and satisfactory livelihood. Up till the early part of 1958, large numbers of co-operatives were still in varying degrees of instability and disorganization, and a sizable section of the peasants lived under economic insecurity. Under such difficulties many peasants reverted partially to family production by concentrating on subsidiary occupations and family vegetable plots. It was indeed hard to divorce the tradition-bound peasantry from the time-tested dependability of family economic relationships and the family production roles. Although reduced in importance, the family still retained an extremely strategic position not only as a reliable group in a situation of transitional chaos, but also as a stable group for income management and for raising the young. The labor-unit system of income distribution under the co-operatives reinforced the traditional value of the large family. But any attempt to revive the traditional importance of the family as the center of community structure would be restricted by the insurmountable obstacle of being without land and major farm equipment on which rested the foundation of the traditional family economy.

We have noted the removal of the clan's economic and political functions and the disorganization of ancestor worship so vital to clan solidarity. The collectivization process clearly intensified this aspect of change in the village community. Irrigation and other forms of agricultural work requiring mass labor became part of the co-operative's function, no longer involving the clan organization. Factors which undermine the family system of status and authority, as just discussed, would be even more destructive to the system of status and authority of the clan and its traditional ability to maintain peace and order within the village community. If the confiscation of clan properties and the shortage of public funds during the land reform period had all but stopped the performance of sacrificial rites to the ancestors, collectivization of the village's farms would render the situation irreversible, for the cadres who controlled the distribution of the collective income of the entire village would be most unlikely to assign public funds to ancestral sacrifice which they regarded as superstition marked for eventual eradication. Thus, the clan could no longer continue as the central organization in southern villages such as Nanching.

Turning our attention to the political aspect of the village community, we discern trends of similarly drastic change which began after the Communist assumption of power but became intensified by the collectivization process which united the political and economic powers in the hands of one ruling group on a systematic basis. When the entire village became one big farm under a centralized management controlled by the party machinery which also controlled the village government, the mono-center power structure imposed a routinized systematic economic grip over the political behavior of the peasantry in addition to military and political coercion. Aside from directly determining the income of the peasants, the co-operatives controlled local hydraulic projects that concerned not only agricultural production but also the safety of the community from inundation by floods, distributed welfare funds to families with insufficient labor power to earn the minimum income, lent money to needy cases in the form of loans or overdrawals in excess of one's share of the collective output of production, and by paying surtaxes supported local schools and a variety of public undertakings. When the real power of directing such an organization rested with the same party apparatus which governed the local political order, it strongly reduced the chance for any successful organized dissension to rise from the different economic levels and interest groups. The new situation effectively destroyed the old multi-center pattern of village power structure in which there was no centralized control or formal co-ordination over the local interest groups.

During the land reform period, there was obvious instability in the emerging mono-center power structure as observed in Nanching and as indicated in events happening in villages in many parts of the country. One of the leading reasons was the lack of indigenous party members to form a stable core for the new power structure. Since then, the political order in the countryside has gained general stability resulting from, among other reasons, the vast expansion of party membership. Repeated membership drives were vigorously launched after 1953.[1] Such drives tapped two leading sources of membership among the peasants. One was the New Democratic Youth League, which was renamed the Communist Youth League in 1957 and had 23,000,000 members in that year.[2] With plastic minds and inclination toward idealism and adventure as characteristic of youth, league members were standing candidates for selection as party members. Another source of prospective members were the poor peasants, especially those who had participated in the struggle against landlords during land reform, for they were the ones most dissatisfied with past conditions and looked to the new economic order for salvation. Fed from these two sources as well as from urban workers, the Communist Party attained a national membership of 12,000,000 in 1957. This phenomenal growth was likely to have produced local party members in every village community, including Nanching, and contributed to the stabilization of the new political order.

We have previously observed the replacement of the semiautonomous village community with a functional and structural integration of the village into the national political order. The vastly expanded membership of 12,000,000 in the Communist Party and 23,000,000 in the Youth League, in addition to some 1,500,000 officials in government services,[3] further reflects an intensified change in structural relationship between the village and the national system of government.

In surveying the change in the relationship between the village and the national political order, it is relevant to consider the fact that the party and league members are functionally comparable to the traditional gentry in the sense that both Communist membership and the gentry have a national political consciousness believing in a single ideology, both are intimately related to the national bureaucracy, and both serve as the extended arm of the formal national political power. But the two differ markedly in numerical size and in organizational strength.

In the second half of the nineteenth century, there were about 1,500,000 members in the gentry group in China, giving a statistical average of 2.14 per cent of the population. This gentry group, plus the bureaucracy which filled the some 40,000 official positions in the entire empire, constituted the ruling class for the vast country.[4] Organizationally, the gentry had its local literary societies, fraternal bodies and supporting kinship systems, but as a ruling group, it had no systematic structure integrating the individual members for collective operation on either local or national levels. The small size and the lack of broad organization of the gentry were limiting factors in any effective and close integration between the national system of government and the innumerable village communities throughout the land. During the Republican period, the bureaucracy grew somewhat, but the number of educated rural leaders with national political consciousness shrank, and the integration of the village to the state was no closer than in the imperial times.

In contrast to this, the 12,000,000 members of the Communist Party and the 23,000,000 members of the Youth League add up to a total of 35,000,000. This is 5.83 per cent of 600,000,000, the 1957 Communist figure of China's total population, as compared with 2.14 per cent of gentry in the population of the last century. In addition, the 1,500,000 Communist officials represent an immeasurably larger bureaucracy than the 40,000 official positions in nineteenth-century China. The numerical growth of the Communist ruling group is apparent. Both the Communist Party and the Youth League, as well as the large number of popular organizations under their control, are rigidly structured into a formal system for collective action. It is thus easy to see the relation of the expansion and organization of the Communist political leadership to the closer integration of the village community with the state.

With closer integration of the village community to the state, the Communist political power was being felt by the villagers more intimately than under any previous national political power. With the drastic reduction of local autonomy, the individual freedom of the peasants has been visibly curtailed in many ways. But individual political freedom has not been an outstanding demand among the peasants. To them, the struggle for economic security has been more significant than a quest for political freedom in the Western sense of the term, which has been lacking in their group-minded tradition. It is the problem of adequately feeding the peasants rather than the granting of individual freedom that will determine the stability of the new political order. In this lies the strategic importance of the success or failure of agricultural collectivization.

The economic and political upheavals deeply affected the class structure in the village community through alteration of the economic levels of a sizable proportion of the peasantry. Land reform and collectivization were two forces from the Communist revolution that had the most potent impact on the village community, and both forces had a leveling influence on the old rural class structure. Under the policy of general equalization of land ownership, land reform eliminated the economic status of the whole top class, the landlords and a part of the rich peasants. Most of the landlords were reduced to the poor-peasant status, and some even lost their lives in the struggle. In the few years that followed, a small group of new rich peasants rose from the former rank of poor peasants. They were industrious efficient farmers, after the land reform gave them the principal means of production, land. Therefore, in the post–land-reform village, the rural class structure had rich, middle and poor peasants as before the land reform, but without the landlords and those rich peasants who rented out a substantial amount of land.

With collectivization, the economic status of the rich peasants was depressed through the pooling of their land and major equipment into the co-operative and the abolition of their efficient independent farm organization. As a consequence, there were only poor and middle peasants in the co-operatives that now embraced 97 per cent of the nation's peasant households. A glimpse of this new pattern of class structure may be had by re-examining the case of two co-operatives in Haiyen county of Chekiang Province, mentioned in the last chapter. Table 4 shows the class distribution of the members of these two co-operatives.

TABLE 4

Classes	Households		Persons		1956 net income (yuan)	
	Number	Percentage	Number	Percentage	Per household	Per capita
Total	422	100.0	1,578	100.0	353.1	94.4
Poor peasants	68	16.0	193	12.2	218.3	76.8
Lower-middle peasants	181	43.0	621	39.4		
new	59	14.1	209	13.2	291.7	82.3
old	122	28.9	412	26.2	337.0	99.8
Upper-middle peasants	164	39.0	734	46.5		
new	32	7.6	142	9.0	436.0	98.2
old	139	31.4	592	37.5	455.9	101.8
Others	9	2.0	30	1.9	184.1	55.2

Any attempt to analyze this sample of class structure is limited by two facts: that the locality represents one of the richest in rural China, and that no standard of income is provided in the classification of the peasants. That the locality is unusually rich may put the percentage of poor peasants lower than that which may be found in other sections of the country; there is no comparable data to check against this possible distortion. However, we can partly overcome the second limitation by taking the lower-middle peasant's annual income of roughly 300 yuan per household or 85 yuan per capita as the absolute minimum for subsistence in this locality — a minimum that leaves a very small margin for comfort or savings against sicknesses, births, deaths, or a poor crop. In the table, the small group of "others" may be merged with the "poor peasants" who were without sufficient food or clothing.

With this in mind, we may say that 46.5 per cent of the collectivized peasantry in this sample had the status of upper-middle peasants, who had an annual surplus of roughly 100 to 150 yuan per household or 10 to 15 yuan per capita for small items of comfort or for meeting crises. Life on this scale may be considered satisfactory in rural China. The rest of the peasants in this sample, 61.0 per cent of the households and 53.5 per cent of the population, were in a range from tolerable living to insecure subsistence. With the status of landlords and rich peasants eliminated, what distinguishes this class structure from the pre-Communist one is that the social distance between the well-off and the poor has been considerably reduced. The leveling influence of collectivization has produced a relatively egalitarian pattern of economic status.

This sample also provides limited data for analysing the vital problem of class mobility under the violent impact of the revolution. The figures show that the turbulent upheavals left a large proportion of the peasants, 60.3 per cent of the households and 63.7 per cent of the population, in their old middle-peasant status. The revolutionary process also brought 21.7 per cent of the households and 22.2 per cent of the population in this sample into the new status of middle peasants. For the poor and the destitute, comprising 18.0 per cent of the households and 14.1 per cent of the population, no indication is given as to whether they were old or new.

There is no information on the origin of the group of new middle peasants. Being in a middle position, they could either have risen from the poor peasants or been reduced from the status of rich peasants. Circumstantial evidence strongly suggests that this new group represented for the most part an upward mobility from the bottom. Rich peasants in pre-collectivization days usually constituted a small percentage of the total village population, and thus could not supply so many candidates for the new group of middle peasants in a downward movement. On the other hand, the pre-Communist stratum of poor peasants was large, much larger than the 16.0 per cent of the households and 12.2 per cent of the population as represented in the sample. Thus numerically they could supply candidates for the group of new middle peasants. Furthermore, the newcomers constituted 38.5 per cent of the lower but only 19.3 per cent of the upper middle peasants, suggesting the characteristic process of step-by-step rise from the bottom. On this assumption, keeping in mind that a few newcomers might have come down from the rich peasants, we may say that some 20 per cent of the village population made their way up to middle-peasant status, while 63.7 per cent successfully cushioned the revolutionary shock and held their old economic status. Many households of orphans and widows which formerly might have been among the middle peasants now sank to the status of the poor and destitute through loss of land to the co-operatives without remuneration and by lacking sufficient "labor power" to draw a middle peasant's share from the collective income. Many former landlords were also depressed into the class of poor and destitute in the downward class movement.

Class mobility of considerable proportion was thus a part of the structural change in the village community. The leading cause in the downward mobility was the abolition of property ownership as a major source of income. The factors in upward mobility were more compli-cated. A large family with an abundance of "labor power," together with other labor factors such as skill and diligence, could certainly enhance their income and class status. Government scholarships and the many free training classes opened the door of education wider than before as a channel of self-advancement for the common peasant. A new channel of status improvement were the many new organizations, including the co-operative farm, the women's association, the peasants' association, and the Youth League, which supplied a relatively free opportunity for the attainment of local leadership and power for the ambitious and capable who were willing to accept the Communist way of life. The rise in power and prestige of the new elite generally brought them improvement of economic position.

Closer integration of the village with the region and the state and operation of the large collectivized farm required literacy and many types of modern knowledge on the part of local leaders. This new re-quirement tended to place the institution of formal education in a role of increased importance in the institutional framework of the village community, for both literacy and modern knowledge are trans-mitted not informally at home and in the neighborhood but formally in the classroom. This institutional change was being effected by many Communist educational measures such as the vigorous campaign to eliminate illiteracy among peasants, increased state subsidy for local schools, granting of large numbers of scholarships to the politically loyal and socially deserving, operation of innumerable short-term training courses for political and economic purposes; all these would compel a change in the relative role of formal education which had only limited significance for the common peasant in the pre-Communist village.

The role of religion in the institutional framework of the village community was likely to continue to decline under collectivism and the increased stabilization of the Communist political order. This would be especially true with collective religious activities requiring financial outlay and political permission from the cadres for mass-organized action. Colorful mass celebrations of religious festivals that formerly were rallying occasions for community solidarity, and large-scale sacrifices to clan ancestors such as those we have observed in Nanching, would have difficulty in continuing owing to control of the village's collective income and large-scale organized activities by the atheistically inclined cadres. Individual worship appeared likely to continue, especially with the older generation and at times of momentous revolutionary crisis when the individual would continue to be troubled by anxiety and uncertainty of situations beyond his control. But the younger generation was growing up under atheistic indoctrination together with a pattern of village life in which mass religious exercises no longer played a vital role in periodically reinforcing community solidarity. The structure of the village was henceforth characterized by its exclusive reliance on secular forces as formal integrating factors, leaving religious activities in an individualized and unorganized form.

In this new structural framework of the village community, there was an apparent lack of a congruent and stabilized "moral climate" or a corresponding system of internalized values in the minds of the common people. The new pattern is imposed by a violent revolution from the urban world and not generated spontaneously from among the peasantry or evolved from a tradition. This means that the operation of the new rural social order could not rely on the spontaneity of the moral conscience, but must depend heavily on political coercion, economic pressures and propaganda devices exercised by the ruling elite. This characteristic of the new system deeply affects its stability.

This seems to be inevitable with a transitional revolutionary situation. The Communist revolution is a gigantic social experiment, sweeping the life of the people into a totally uncharted area in which the fabric of traditional society is forcibly shattered and the familiar paths of life are obliterated. As an experiment dedicated to an unconventional ideal, the revolution must devise momentary measures and expedients to harness the new forces and unfolding situations. The breathless pace of development of the revolution leaves little time for its goals, policies, and measures to develop consistent supportive values rooted in the moral conscience of the people.

The frequent radical shifting of policies as dictated by unexpected developments in a revolution adds further difficulties to the fostering of popular understanding and acceptance of an unfamiliar system of life. The tactics of secrecy and surprise are a function of the underground phase of the revolution, but the continued employment of such tactics after the attainment of formal, open political power serves to demoralize and confuse the people by offering them no dependable rule to follow. To the popular mind, there can be little consistency or stability in a value system in which what is considered a virtue today could be a crime tomorrow.

Although we left Nanching at its land reform stage in 1951, we may be able to infer what subsequently happened there as a reflection of the national process of collectivization and its influence on the institutional framework of rural life, for the broad directions of change have been universal to agrarian communities in mainland China. In this sense, as suggested by the foregoing three chapters, we have seen the traditional world of Nanching being replaced by a collectivized village with a changing community structure lacking as yet in institutional stability.

The village of Nanching as we originally knew it typified a traditional social order which derived much of its high degree of stability from successful institutionalization of group practices in various aspects of social life. The villagers followed these practices as unchanging ways of wisdom conducive to the basic interests of both the individual and the group, and the functioning of these practices relied on a consistent system of values fully internalized in the people's conscience and commanding their automatic conformity. Coercion by the formal government was limited to controlling a small deviant minority. To achieve long-term stability, the Communist system must eventually institutionalize its concepts, values, and basic devices in the operation of the new pattern of life so as to produce a supportive and voluntarily accepted moral order.

What, then, would we expect to find if we were permitted to revisit Nanching in the early part of 1958?

There would be generally the same familiar physical landscape and mostly the same familiar faces, but an entirely different form of group activities would dominate the scene. "The fields, the gardens, the houses, and the ancestral graves," would still be there, but the pattern of community life woven about them would differ significantly from that which we observed when we first entered the village in 1948. The complex lines of earth embankments which divided the village's fields into a huge jig-saw puzzle would be replaced by a continuous open field; gone would be the dirt embankments which traced out a visible geometric design of the family farms and private ownership of land. No longer would we see individual peasants and their families scattered thinly through the fields as they worked. Instead there would be large production teams concentrated in certain work locations. The same houses would still be standing, but the ownership of some would have changed hands. The ancestral graves would still occupy the same hillsides overlooking the village, but the massive ancestral halls that towered above the houses would no longer be the sites of impressive ceremonies and headquarters of an institution which less than a decade ago shaped the pattern of life for this agrarian community. Traditional Chinese regarded "the fields, gardens, houses, and ancestral graves" as the roots of life. Now these very roots of life have been altered by the relentless pressure of a violent revolution; and, although the most compelling factors in the change is the collective organization that turns the entire village into one huge farm, and the new political structure that ties the village closely to a regional and national system of communities, neither has yet become a stabilized system, and the new institutional concepts are neither well understood nor completely accepted by the villagers. We would therefore find the peasants in Nanching in a situation where a return to the old roots of life is impossible and where the road toward collectivization and socialism is fraught with uncertainties.

Notes

Chapter I. The Village of Nanching

1. George B. Cressey, *China's Geographic Foundations*, New York, 1934, p. 353.
2. *Ibid.*, p. 352.
3. J. L. Buck, *Land Utilization in China, Statistics*, Nanking, 1937, p. 27.
4. Quoted in Cressey, p. 354; see note 1.
5. *Chung-hua Jen-min Kung-ho-kuo Ti-t'u* (Map of the Chinese People's Republic), Peking, 1951, p. 28.
6. See Cressey, p. 355; see note 1.
7. See Cressey, p. 262; see note 1.
8. T. H. Shen, *Agricultural Resources of China*, New York, 1951, p. 21.
9. *Panyü Hsien Chih* (Gazetteer of Panyü County), edited by Liang Ting-fen, Canton, 1931, chuan 42.
10. Shen, p. 97; see note 8.
11. *Ibid.*
12. C. K. Yang, *A North China Market Economy*, Institute of Pacific Relations, New York, 1944, p. 38; Shen (n. 8), p. 109; J. L. Buck, *Land Utilization in China*, Nanking, 1937, p. 353.
13. *Hsin-hui Nan-men Lee-shi Tsu-pu*, re-edited by Lee Peng-chu, 1921, chuan 1, pp. 3–11.

Chapter II. Population Composition

1. G. B. Cressey, *China's Geographic Foundations*, pp. 255, 362.
2. See for example C. M. Chiao and others, *An Experiment in the Registration of Vital Statistics in China*, Oxford, Ohio, 1938, which gives the sex ratio of 111.7:100 for the rural population of Kiang Yin. Also see Ta Chen, *Population in Modern China*, Chicago, 1946, which gives the sex ratio of 103.02:100 for Kunming Lake region.
3. Ta Chen, *ibid.*, pp. 18–19.
4. *Ibid.*, Table 6, p. 84.
5. *Ibid.*, pp. 38–39.
6. *Ibid.*, pp. 28–32.
7. See for example the case of Kiang Tsun village described in Fei Hsiao-tung's *Peasant Life in China*, New York, 1939.

Chapter III. The Land and Its Exploitation

1. Fei Hsiao-tung, *Peasant Life in China*, chap. xii.
2. The catty used here is the traditional *ssu ma chin* and not the *shih chin* or market catty, the former still being the standard measure for the villagers.
3. T. H. Shen, *Agricultural Resources of China*, p. 109.
4. Fei Hsiao-tung, *Earthbound China*, Chicago, 1945, chap. i, xii, xxii, and his *Peasant Life in China*, chap. ix.
5. Chen Han-seng, *Agrarian Problems in Southernmost China*, Shanghai, 1936, Table 28, p. 135.
6. Sun Hsiao-tsun, "The Problem of Farm Management in Contemporary China," Part III, *Quarterly Review of the Sun Yat-sen Institute*, vol. III, no. 2, 1936, Nanking.
7. Liu Tuan-sheng, "A Farm Management Study of 3,412 Peasant Families in Chiahsing," *Quarterly Review of the Sun Yet-sen Institute*, vol. IV, no. 2, Summer 1937, Nanking.
8. Chen, Table 25A, p. 133; see note 5.

Chapter IV. Land Ownership and Tenancy

1. Chen Han-seng, *Agrarian Problems in Southernmost China*, Table 13, pp. 127–128.
2. *Ibid.*, p. 32.
3. *Ibid.*, Table 9, p. 126.
4. T. H. Shen, *Agricultural Resources of China*, p. 98.
5. Chen, p. 56; see note 1.

Chapter V. Production, Consumption, and Supplementary Income

1. Fei Hsiao-tung, in his study of the Yunnan villages, maintains that husking reduces the grain by 60 per cent by weight, leaving only 40 per cent of husked rice (see his *Earthbound China*, p. 51). This percentage of husked rice seems too low when compared with the local facts here. Actually, records of rice mills in this vicinity show that unhusked rice sometimes yields over 70 per cent of husked rice, and a net yield of 80 per cent is by no means uncommon. The difference may be a result of the variety of rice and conditions such as the degree of dampness of the grain at the time of milling.
2. Fei, *Earthbound China*, p. 51.
3. This compares with 0.74 in Fei's calculation (*ibid.*, pp. 51, 219).
4. This compares closely with Fei's estimate of 3.7 adults for a family of five (*ibid.*, p. 219).
5. Chen Han-seng, *Agrarian Problems in Southernmost China*, pp. 87–88, and Table 25A, p. 133.
6. Fei, *Earthbound China*, pp. 120–121.
7. Chen, pp. 89–90; see note 5.

Chapter VI. Kinship System

1. See Hu Hsien-chin, *A Study of the Common Descent Group in China,* New York, 1948, and Ch'ü T'ung-tsu, *Chung-kuo Feng-chien Sheh-hui* (Chinese Feudal Society), Shanghai, 1944, for description of the classical principles of clan organization.

2. This system of status is graphically presented in Feng Han-yi's chart; see his "The Chinese Kinship System," *Harvard Journal of Asiatic Studies,* vol. II, no. 2, July 1937, p. 160. Also cf. Marion J. Levy, Jr., *The Family Revolution in Modern China,* Cambridge, Mass., 1949, chap. iii, and C. K. Yang, *The Chinese Family in the Communist Revolution,* chap. v.

Chapter VII. A Decentralized Power Structure

1. For further details see Fei Hsiao-tung, *China's Gentry,* Chicago, 1953, pp. 75–90.

2. *Ibid.*

3. Robert Redfield, *Peasant Society and Culture,* Chicago, 1956, chap. ii.

Chapter VIII. Class Stability and Mobility

1. Fei Hsiao-tung, "Peasantry and Gentry," *American Journal of Sociology,* July 1946.

2. Yu Lin, "On Revision of the Land Law," in *Chung-kuo Nung-ts'un* (Chinese Rural Communities), vol. III, no. 6, June 1937.

Chapter IX. Class Struggle as the First Step of Land Reform

1. *Jen-min Jih-pao* (People's Daily), Peking, editorial, June 30, 1950. This editorial reflects the basic points in Liu Shao-ch'i's *"A Report on the Problem of Land Reform,"* which is the most basic document on land-reform policy after the Communist accession to national power.

2. Liu Shao-ch'i, *"A Report on the Problem of Land Reform."*

3. *Ibid.*

4. *Ibid.*

5. *Ibid.*

6. *Ibid.*

Chapter XI. Post-Land Reform Village Economy

1. *Wah Kiu Yat-po,* Hong Kong, April 19, 1953.

2. See the summary of these regulations in the *Economic Survey of Asia and the Far East,* 1952, United Nations, Department of Economic Affairs, p. 68.

3. *Wah Kiu Yat-po*, Hong Kong, April 19, 1953, p. 4.

4. *Ibid.*, April 4, 1951, p. 2.

5. *Ta Kung Pao*, Hong Kong, June 19, 1953, p. 2.

6. *Wah Kiu Yat-po*, Hong Kong, April 15, 1953, p. 4.

7. *Nanfang Jih-pao*, Canton, January 3, 1953, p. 1.

8. *Wah Kiu Yat-po*, Hong Kong, April 20, 1953, p. 4.

Chapter XIV. Other Social Institutions and Their Initial Change

1. See the report of Wu Yao-tsung, a Protestant leader, to the People's Political Consultative Conference in Peking, New China News Agency, March 8, 1957.

Chapter XV. From Mutual-Aid Teams to Full Collectivization

1. Ma Yin-ch'u, "Grain Production and Peasant's Livelihood in China," *Jen-min Jih-pao* (People's Daily), June 15, 1957.

2. "Is There Any Difference between a Higher Agricultural Producers' Co-operative and a Collective Farm?" *Cheng-chih Hsüeh-Hsi* (Political Study), no. 6, June 1956.

3. See, for example, the mutual-aid arrangement among peasants in Yunnan villages studied by Fei Hsiao-tung in his *Earthbound China*, p. 118.

4. *Nanfang Jih-pao*, August 16, p. 3.

5. *Ta Kung Pao*, Hong Kong, March 26, 1953.

6. *Ibid.*, April 26, 1953.

7. *Ibid.*, April 29, 1953.

8. *Ibid.*

9. *Nanfang Jih-pao*, Canton, March 24, 1953.

10. Chou En-lai, *Report on the Second Five Year Plan*, delivered to the Chinese Communist Party Eighth National Congress on September 16, 1956. New China News Agency, Peking, September 20, 1956.

11. Liao Lu-yen, "Explanations on Regulations Governing the Demonstration Models of the Advanced Type of Agricultural Producers' Co-operatives," *Jen-min Jih-pao*, June 17, 1956, p. 2.

12. "China's APCs Achieved Great Results in Past Six Months," New China News Agency, Peking, July 4, 1957.

13. *Jen-min Jih-pao*, February 4, 1956, p. 2.

14. Mao Tse-tung, "The Problems of Co-operativization of Agriculture," *Hsin Chung-kuo Fu-nü* (New China's Women), no. 10, October 1955, pp. 2–8.

15. *Ibid.*

16. Quoted in *Wah Kiu Yat-po*, Hong Kong, October 19, 1955, p. 4.

17. "How to Organize Agricultural Labor Power," by Wang Kuang-wei, *Chi-hua Ching-chi* (Planned Economy), no. 8, August 9, 1957.

18. Lu Chih-heng, "The Food Problem and Party Food Policy During the Transition Period," *Liang-shih Kung-tso* (Food), no. 12, June 29, 1956.

Chapter XVI. Economic Problems of the
Agricultural Producers' Co-operatives

1. Mao Tse-tung, "The Problems of Co-operativization of Agriculture," *Hsin Chung-kuo Fu-nü* (New China's Women), no. 10, October 1955, pp. 2–8.

2. *Jen-min Jih-pao*, May 20, 1956, p. 2.

3. "Peasants' Burden in 1956: Conditions and Problems," by Li Shu-teh, in *Ts'ai Cheng* (Finance), no. 8, 1957.

4. *Jen-min Jih-pao*, March 21, 1951, p. 2.

5. *Ta Kung Pao*, Hong Kong, March 10, 1953.

6. *Nanfang Jih-pao*, April 22, 1953.

7. Ts'ao Ping-chia, "The Beginning of a Good Harvest," *Shih-shih Shou-ts'e* (Current Events), no. 14, July 21, 1957.

8. *Ibid.*

9. "The Problem of Agricultural Mechanization in China," by Chao Hsüeh, in *Chi-hua Ching-chi* (Planned Economy), no. 4, April 9, 1957; "Achievements of China's First Five-year Plan Analysed," New China News Agency, September 30, 1957; "A Brief Description of China's Agricultural Production in 1949–1956," in *Tung-chi Kung-tso* (Statistical Bulletin), no. 14, July 24, 1957.

10. "A Brief Description of China's Agricultural Production in 1949–1956," in *Tung-chi Kung-tso* (Statistical Bulletin), no. 14, July 24, 1957.

11. "Development of Irrigation Works in China," by Hsu Kuai, *Ta Kung Pao*, Peking, September 27, 1957.

12. "All Is Well with Agricultural Production and Cooperation," by Chung Ch'iu, *Shih-shih Shou-ts'e* (Current Events), no. 15, September 1957.

13. Editorial, *Jen-min Jih-pao*, October 22, 1957.

14. *Ta Kung Pao*, Hong Kong, April 23, 1956, p. 1.

15. *Ibid.*, March 29, 1956, p. 3.

16. *Wah Kiu Yat-po*, Hong Kong, April 16, 1956, p. 4.

17. See note 10.

18. Editorial, *Jen-min Jih-pao*, October 27, 1957.

19. *Jen-min Jih-pao*, February 4, 1956, p. 2.

20. See note 10.

21. *Ta Kung Pao*, Hong Kong, March 17, 1956, p. 1.

22. *Jen-min Jih-pao*, February 4, 1956, p. 2.

23. *Wah Kiu Yat-po*, Hong Kong, April 21, 1956, p. 4.

24. *Ta Kung Pao*, Peking, October 9, 1957.

25. *Wah Kiu Yat-po*, Hong Kong, April 13, 1956, p. 4; April 14, 1956, p. 4.

26. Mao Tse-tung, see note 1.

27. T'ao Chu's report to the Provincial Political Consultative Conference, quoted in *Wah Kiu Yat-po*, April 16, 1956, p. 4.

28. *Wah Kiu Yat-po*, Hong Kong, April 13, 1956, p. 4.

29. *Jen-min Jih-pao*, May 20, 1956, p. 2.

30. "Are Agricultural Loans Small This Year?" Editorial in *Chung-kuo Chin-jung* (China Finance), no. 5, March 1957.

31. *Ta Kung Pao*, Tientsin, August 21, 1956.

32. "On Distribution of Income in the Higher Agricultural Producers' Co-

operatives," by Li Pai-Kuan, in *Hsin Chien-sheh* (New Construction), no. 7, July 4, 1957.

33. *Ta Kung Pao*, Hong Kong, April 2, 1956, p. 3.

34. See note 3.

35. "A Preliminary Study of the Income and Living Standard of the Peasants of China," by T'an Chen-lin, *Jen-min Jih-pao*, May 5, 1957.

36. *Ibid.*

37. *Ibid.*

38. *Ibid.*

39. *Ibid.*

40. *Ibid.*

41. *Ibid.*

42. See note 3.

43. T'an Chen-lin, see note 35.

44. See note 3.

45. "On Distribution of Income in the Higher Agricultural Producers' Co-operatives"; see note 32.

46. *Ibid.*

47. *Ibid.*

48. *Ibid.*

49. *Ibid.*

50. See note 3.

51. Lu Chih-heng, "The Food Problem and Party Food Policy During the Transition Period," *Liang-shih Kung-tso* (Food), no 12, June 29, 1956.

52. *Jen-min Jih-pao*, August 25, 1956, p. 2.

53. "The Policy of Unified Purchase and Sales of Grain Shall Not Be Frustrated," by Chou Po-p'ing, in *Liang-shih* (Grain), no. 7, July 1957.

54. *Ibid.*

55. See note 3.

56. See note 3.

57. See note 3.

58. "Food-grain Prices Fixed by the State Are Reasonable," by Liu Yuan, *Liaoning Jih-pao*, Mukden, September 20, 1957.

59. *Jen-min Jih-pao*, August 25, 1955, p. 2.

60. Chou En-lai, *Report on the Second Five-year Plan*, delivered to the Chinese Communist Party Eighth National Congress on September 16, 1956. New China News Agency, Peking, September 20, 1956.

61. Statement by the Department of Agriculture and Forestry of Kwangtung Province, quoted in *Wah Kiu Yat-po*, Hong Kong, April 21, 1956, p. 4.

62. "Is the People's Life Not Bettered?" by Ching Chi, *Shih-shih Shou-ts'e* (Current Events), no. 15, August 6, 1957.

63. "On Distribution of Income in the Higher Agricultural Producers' Co-operatives"; see note 32.

64. *Ibid.*

65. *Ibid.*

66. *Jen-min Jih-pao*, May 7, 1956, p. 2.

67. "How to Organize Agricultural Labor Power," by Wang Kuang-wei, *Chi-hua Ching-chi* (Planned Economy), no. 8, August 9, 1957.

68. *Jen-min Jih-pao*, May 24, 1956, p. 1.

69. *Ibid.* May 7, 1956, p. 2.

70. Shang Chi-ch'eng, "Why We Must Properly Develop Secondary Occupations in the Countryside," *Shih-shih Shou-ts'e* (Current Events), no. 9, May 10, 1956.

71. Wang Kuang-wei, see note 67.

72. New China News Agency, May 15, 1957.

73. "Broken-up Co-operatives in Hsienchu Hsien Rapidly Re-integrate," New China News Agency, Hangchow, September 29, 1957.

74. *Nanfang Jih-pao,* Canton, September 14, 1957.

75. "On Contradictions and Democratic Management in Agricultural Producers' Co-operatives," by Teng Tzu-Kuei, *Jen-min Jih-pao,* May 7, 1957.

76. *Ibid.*

77. "Poor Peasants Subjected to All Forms of Exploitation in Lufeng Hsien amid Clamors for Withdrawal from Co-operatives," New China News Agency, Canton, September 2, 1957.

Chapter XVII. Organizational Problems of the Agricultural Producers' Co-operatives

1. *Jen-min Jih-pao,* April 30, 1956, p. 1.

2. "China's Agricultural Producers' Co-operatives Achieved Great Results in Past Six Months," New China News Agency, Peking, July 4, 1957.

3. "CCP Central Committee's Directive to Overhaul Agricultural Co-operatives," New China News Agency, September 24, 1957.

4. *Ibid.*; and "CCP Committee's Directive to Improve Administration of Production in Agricultural Producers' Co-operatives," New China News Agency, Peking, September 15, 1957.

5. "On Contradictions and Democratic Management in Agricultural Producers' Co-operatives," by Teng Tzu-Kuei, *Jen-min Jih-pao,* May 7, 1957.

6. *Wah Kiu Yat-po,* Hong Kong, June 27, 1956, p. 4.

7. *Jen-min Jih-pao,* August 30, 1955, p. 2.

8. Teng Tzu-Kuei, see note 5.

9. *Jen-min Jih-pao,* May 21, 1956, p. 2.

10. *Ibid.,* August 19, 1955, p. 2.

11. *Ibid.,* April 10, 1956, p. 1.

12. A report made by T'ao Chu, governor of Kwangtung Province, to the Provincial Political Consultative Conference, quoted in *Wah Kiu Yat-po,* April 16, 1956, p. 4.

13. *Wah Kiu Yat-po,* Hong Kong, February 17, 1956, p. 4.

14. *Kuang-ming Jih-pao,* Peking, September 22, 1957.

15. *Jen-min Jih-pao,* June 2, 1955, p. 2.

16. *Ibid.,* May 21, 1956, p. 2.

17. "CCP Central Committee's Directive on Methods of Applying the Policy of Mutual Benefit Among Co-operative Members," New China News Agency, September 15, 1957.

18. *Ibid.*

19. "Democratic Assessment and Determination of Quota According to Needs," by Sun Teh-tseng, *Jen-min Jih-pao,* June 13, 1957.

20. "On Distribution of Income in the Higher Agricultural Producers' Co-operatives," by Li Pai-Kuan, in *Hsin Chien-sheh* (New Construction), no. 7, July 4, 1957.

21. "CCP Central Committee Calls on All Rural Work Cadres to Take Part in Production," *Jen-min Jih-pao*, April 30, 1957.

22. "Labor Participation by 70,000 Cadres in Kwangtung Changes Rural Life," New China News Agency, Canton, May 5, 1957.

23. *Jen-min Jih-pao*, May 7, 1955, p. 1.

24. Mao Tse-tung, "The Problem of Agricultural Co-operativization," *Hsin Chung-kuo Fu-nü* (New China's Women), no. 10, October 1955, pp. 2–8.

25. Editorial, *Jen-min Jih-pao*, October 9, 1957.

Chapter XVIII. Changing Structure of the Village Community

1. *Nanfang Yat-po*, Canton, January 4, 1953, p. 1.

2. New China News Agency, May 12, 1957.

3. *Ibid.*

4. Chang Chung-li, *The Chinese Gentry*, University of Washington Press, Seattle, Washington, 1955, pp. 94–164; statistical average computed from data on p. 114; also see restatement of Chang's data in Franz Michael, "State and Society in Nineteenth Century China," *World Politics*, vol. VII, no. 3, April 1955, p. 422.

5. "On Distribution of Income in the Higher Producers' Co-operatives," by Li Pai-Kuan, *Hsien Chien-sheh* (New Construction), no. 7, July 4, 1957.

Index